HEWLETT-PACKARD'S PRETEXTING SCANDAL

HEARING

BEFORE THE

SUBCOMMITTEE ON OVERSIGHT AND INVESTIGATIONS

OF THE

COMMITTEE ON ENERGY AND COMMERCE
HOUSE OF REPRESENTATIVES

ONE HUNDRED NINTH CONGRESS

SECOND SESSION

SEPTEMBER 28, 2006

Serial No. 109-146

Printed for the use of the Committee on Energy and Commerce

Available via the World Wide Web: http://www.access.gpo.gov/congress/house

U.S. GOVERNMENT PRINTING OFFICE

31-472DF WASHINGTON : 2006

For sale by the Superintendent of Documents, U.S. Government Printing Office
Internet: bookstore.gpo.gov Phone: toll free (866) 512-1800; DC area (202) 512-1800
Fax: (202) 512-2250 Mail: Stop SSOP, Washington, DC 20402-0001

COMMITTEE ON ENERGY AND COMMERCE

JOE BARTON, Texas, *Chairman*

RALPH M. HALL, Texas
MICHAEL BILIRAKIS, Florida
Vice Chairman
FRED UPTON, Michigan
CLIFF STEARNS, Florida
PAUL E. GILLMOR, Ohio
NATHAN DEAL, Georgia
ED WHITFIELD, Kentucky
CHARLIE NORWOOD, Georgia
BARBARA CUBIN, Wyoming
JOHN SHIMKUS, Illinois
HEATHER WILSON, New Mexico
JOHN B. SHADEGG, Arizona
CHARLES W. "CHIP" PICKERING, Mississippi
Vice Chairman
VITO FOSSELLA, New York
ROY BLUNT, Missouri
STEVE BUYER, Indiana
GEORGE RADANOVICH, California
CHARLES F. BASS, New Hampshire
JOSEPH R. PITTS, Pennsylvania
MARY BONO, California
GREG WALDEN, Oregon
LEE TERRY, Nebraska
MIKE FERGUSON, New Jersey
MIKE ROGERS, Michigan
C.L. "BUTCH" OTTER, Idaho
SUE MYRICK, North Carolina
JOHN SULLIVAN, Oklahoma
TIM MURPHY, Pennsylvania
MICHAEL C. BURGESS, Texas
MARSHA BLACKBURN, Tennessee

JOHN D. DINGELL, Michigan
Ranking Member
HENRY A. WAXMAN, California
EDWARD J. MARKEY, Massachusetts
RICK BOUCHER, Virginia
EDOLPHUS TOWNS, New York
FRANK PALLONE, JR., New Jersey
SHERROD BROWN, Ohio
BART GORDON, Tennessee
BOBBY L. RUSH, Illinois
ANNA G. ESHOO, California
BART STUPAK, Michigan
ELIOT L. ENGEL, New York
ALBERT R. WYNN, Maryland
GENE GREEN, Texas
TED STRICKLAND, Ohio
DIANA DEGETTE, Colorado
LOIS CAPPS, California
MIKE DOYLE, Pennsylvania
TOM ALLEN, Maine
JIM DAVIS, Florida
JAN SCHAKOWSKY, Illinois
HILDA L. SOLIS, California
CHARLES A. GONZALEZ, Texas
JAY INSLEE, Washington
TAMMY BALDWIN, Wisconsin
MIKE ROSS, Arkansas

BUD ALBRIGHT, *Staff Director*
DAVID CAVICKE, *General Counsel*
REID P. F. STUNTZ, *Minority Staff Director and Chief Counsel*

SUBCOMMITTEE ON OVERSIGHT AND INVESTIGATIONS

ED WHITFIELD, Kentucky, *Chairman*

CLIFF STEARNS, Florida
CHARLES W. "CHIP" PICKERING, Mississippi
CHARLES F. BASS, New Hampshire
GREG WALDEN, Oregon
MIKE FERGUSON, New Jersey
MICHAEL C. BURGESS, Texas
MARSHA BLACKBURN, Tennessee
JOE BARTON, Texas
(EX OFFICIO)

BART STUPAK, Michigan
Ranking Member
DIANA DEGETTE, Colorado
JAN SCHAKOWSKY, Illinois
JAY INSLEE, Washington
TAMMY BALDWIN, Wisconsin
HENRY A. WAXMAN, California
JOHN D. DINGELL, Michigan
(EX OFFICIO)

CONTENTS

HEWLETT-PACKARD'S PRETEXTING SCANDAL

THURSDAY, SEPTEMBER 28 2006

HOUSE OF REPRESENTATIVES,
COMMITTEE ON ENERGY AND COMMERCE,
SUBCOMMITTEE ON OVERSIGHT AND INVESTIGATIONS,
Washington, DC.

The subcommittee met, pursuant to notice, at 10:06 a.m., in Room 2123 of the Rayburn House Office Building, Hon. Ed Whitfield [Chairman] presiding.

Present: Representatives Whitfield, Stearns, Bass, Walden, Burgess, Blackburn, Barton (ex officio), DeGette, Schakowsky, Inslee, Baldwin, and Dingell (ex officio).

Staff Present: Mark Paoletta, Chief Counsel for Oversight and Investigations; Thomas Feddo, Counsel; Andrew Snowdon, Counsel; Krista Carpenter, Counsel; Peter Spencer, Professional Staff Member; John Halliwell, Policy Coordinator; Clayton Matheson, Analyst; Ryan Ambrose, Legislative Clerk; Matthew Johnson, Legislative Clerk; Chris Knauer, Minority Investigator; Consuela Washington, Minority Senior Counsel; and Chris Treanor, Minority Staff Assistant.

MR. WHITFIELD. Today, the Subcommittee on Oversight and Investigations will examine how and why Hewlett-Packard Company, one of America's largest technology companies, used pretexting and other nefarious practices as part of an internal corporate investigation.

This subcommittee has been examining the practice of pretexting for the past 8 months. To be clear, pretexting means using fraud, deceit and impersonation to acquire someone's personal records without his or her consent. The relative ease with which unscrupulous pretexters can obtain private information is cause for great concern.

During our hearings we heard testimony from witnesses who were unsettlingly proficient in obtaining personal information regarding phone calls, bank accounts, credit card charges and other information without the consent of the person whose information they obtained.

We also discovered that pretexting is commonly used for investigation purposes as well as for the purposes of identity theft, and we heard testimony how it was used frequently by the national news media.

Hewlett-Packard has long been one of the most admired companies in America. Consequently, people were really shocked to learn that a company of this stature would resort to such tactics in an effort to identify the source of Boardroom leaks. Pretexting for phone records, physical surveillance, monitoring of e-mail were all part of the plan. HP's investigative team even tried to plant or discuss planting electronic tracing software into a reporter's e-mail account and even considered planting undercover spies in several newsrooms.

While there is nothing objectionable on its face about Hewlett-Packard trying to determine the source of leaked confidential information, the methods used were clearly unacceptable. Obtaining private call records by pretexting is an invasion of privacy and probably is illegal.

For over a year, the most senior levels of management at the company were designing and directing the investigation. This isn't a case of some out-of-control and overzealous contractor who was hired to conduct a search for a leaker. Rather, this investigation was led by the Chairman of the Board Patricia Dunn; the company's Senior Legal Counsel Ann Baskins; and the day-to-day operations were overseen by, of all people, the company's chief ethics lawyer Kevin Hunsaker.

We hope to get a better understanding today why no one among this group of very smart and experienced people had the good sense and courage to say, stop, this may be illegal, and at the very least it is not the way we should be doing business. And how, after all was said and done, could the Board's outside counsel, Mr. Larry Sonsini, review the investigation and say that pretexting for phone records of Board members, employees and journalists was above board and legitimate?

Further, I give little credence to the argument that HP was unaware that its outside consultants were inappropriately gaining access to confidential telephone records. If there are legitimate ways to obtain someone's private records without their consent, short of a subpoena, I would be interested in knowing what they are. Our hearings this past June demonstrated that there are really none, and testimony from the FBI suggested that the Federal Wire Act may be implicated by pretexting. It is the company's responsibility to know what those operating on its behalf are doing and how they are doing it.

If you turn to the first page of the Hewlett-Packard Standards of Business Conduct, it reads, "Hewlett-Packard conducts its business with uncompromising integrity. Every member of the Hewlett-Packard community, directors, executives, managers, employees and business partners, have a duty to comply with all applicable law and adhere to the highest standards of business ethics." It appears that they fell short this time.

The committee began its oversight work of the Hewlett-Packard matter just a short time ago on September the 11th. We moved aggressively to learn as much of the facts as possible and hold this hearing and share the information with the American people. Our pace meant reviewing tens of thousands of documents in very short order, and I would like to commend Hewlett-Packard for doing everything in its power to cooperate fully and completely with the committee's investigation on our schedule to ensure that this hearing was productive and we had all the information. I want to thank you for that.

[Prepared statement of Hon. Ed Whitfield follows:]

PREPARED STATEMENT OF THE HON. ED WHITFIELD, CHAIRMAN, SUBCOMMITTEE ON OVERSIGHT AND INVESTIGATIONS

Good morning. Today the Subcommittee on Oversight and Investigations will examine how and why Hewlett-Packard Company, one of America's most famous corporations, used "pretexting" and other nefarious practices as part of an internal corporate investigation. Documents reviewed by the Committee have revealed a series of investigations that were part *Keystone Cops*, part *Mission Impossible*, and part *All the President's Men*. Sometimes the truth really is stranger than fiction.

This Subcommittee has been examining the practice of "pretexting" for the past eight months, and to date we have held two hearings on this topic. To be clear what we are talking about, pretexting, or "social engineering," means using fraud, deceit, and impersonation to acquire someone's personal records without his consent. In this high-tech age, personal information is not only valuable, but vulnerable, and the relative ease with which unscrupulous pretexters can literally con their way into our personal lives is cause for great concern.

Lest anyone think that pretexting is limited to shady collection agencies, private investigators, and bail bondsmen, the recently-emerged scandal involving Hewlett-Packard proves otherwise. But, according to an email written this past June by H-P's outside counsel, Mr. Larry Sonsini, pretexting is "[a]pparently a common investigatory method" and H-P's pretexting was "well done and within legal limits." If a corporate icon like H-P can sink to this level, then all bets are off.

Hewlett-Packard and its storied past would easily make the cut for a corporate Hall of Fame, if there were one. Consequently, I was absolutely shocked to learn a few weeks ago that a company of this stature would resort to such despicable tactics in an effort to identify the source of boardroom leaks. Pretexting for phone records, physical surveillance, monitoring of email, and background investigations were all part of the plan. H-P's investigation team tried to plant electronic tracing software into a reporter's email account, and even considered planting undercover spies in several newsrooms.

While there is nothing objectionable on its face about H-P trying to determine the source of leaked confidential information, the methods used here were clearly unacceptable. Sneaking into someone else's private calling records is a tremendous invasion of privacy. These records provide a virtual roadmap of people's daily lives – who they talk to, when, for how long, and even from where they make those calls. Calling records expose business activities and personal interactions.

What is especially puzzling to me is how nobody at H-P saw this train wreck coming, especially H-P's General Counsel. For over a year, the most senior levels of management at the company were designing and directing the investigation. This isn't a case of some out-of-control and overzealous contractor who was hired to conduct a search for a leaker. Rather, this investigation was led by the Chairman of the Board, Patricia Dunn, and the company's General Counsel, Ann Baskins, and the day-to-day operations were overseen by, of all people, the company's chief ethics lawyer, Kevin Hunsaker.

Yet, Ms. Baskins resigned her position as General Counsel just this morning. Mr. Hunsaker and another H-P security employee who participated in the internal investigation, Mr. Anthony Gentilucci, left the company just this week. Why weren't they fired a long time ago? If I were Mr. Hurd, I would have made a wholesale housecleaning months ago, when it became clear to the Board and others exactly what unsavory investigative methods were used by these H-P executives, lawyers, and employees.

The company's records show that H-P senior management – Patricia Dunn, Ann Baskins, and Mark Hurd – were aware of the pretexting and of the plot to "sting" a journalist. Exactly what did they know about the use of pretexting? What did they know about planting spyware on an email to a journalist? The records also show that even the company's CEO, Mark Hurd, was provided information about the results of the two main phases of the investigation and of the email sting operation. Exactly what did Mr. Hurd know about the methods used during the investigation, and did he know about the electronic tracer used during the email sting of the reporter?

I have to say, if I were a corporate executive, and my staff came to me with the last 300 cell phone calls of the CEO of a competitor company – say, Michael Dell's last 300 calls – I would be incredulous, and a lot of alarm bells would go off. Why should the spying on phone records here be any different? The individuals at H-P who sanctioned this are very smart, high-level managers and officers, and on many levels it is a questionable and inadequate defense to say "the lawyers said this was okay." We heard that unacceptable excuse with Enron, and other corporate investigations. And even if it were legal in some sense, is it ethical conduct?

I hope to get a better understanding today why nobody among this group of very smart and experienced people had the good sense and courage to say, "Stop. This may be illegal, and at the very least it's not the way we should be doing business." And how, after all was said and done, could the Board's outside counsel, Larry Sonsini, review the investigation and say that pretexting for phone records of Board members, employees, and journalists was above board and legitimate?

Further, I give little credence to the argument that H-P was unaware that its outside consultants were inappropriately gaining access to confidential telephone records. If there are ***legitimate*** ways to obtain someone else's private records without their consent -- short of a subpoena -- I'd be interested in knowing what they are. Our hearings this past June demonstrated that there are none, and testimony from the FBI suggested that the Wire Act may be implicated by pretexting. It is the company's responsibility to know ***what*** those operating on its behalf are doing and ***how*** they are doing it.

I intend to get to the bottom of Hewlett-Packard's widely publicized pretexting scandal today, and I thank all of the witnesses for appearing. Perhaps by shedding some light on H-P's conduct, we can discourage other companies from utilizing such unconscionable practices in the future. I also hope this provides some momentum for the Congress to pass this Committee's legislation, H.R. 4943, and make pretexting for phone records explicitly illegal.

I now recognize the Ranking Member of the Subcommittee, Mr. Stupak.

MR. WHITFIELD. At this time I would like to recognize the Ranking Minority Member, Ms. DeGette of Colorado, for her opening statement.

MS. DEGETTE. Thank you very much, Mr. Chairman. And, Mr. Chairman, I bring Mr. Stupak's apologies for not being here. He is at a funeral today.

I would also ask unanimous consent to put my full statement and the statements of Mr. Stupak and other committee members in the record.

MR. WHITFIELD. Without objection.

MS. DEGETTE. Thank you so much, Mr. Chairman.

Mr. Chairman, over the last few years this committee has looked at major corporate scandals in this country, like Enron and WorldCom. I was privileged to serve on this committee during those hearings as we helped shine a light on corporate excess and pave the way to reform.

One thing I felt at the end of the first series of hearings was that we left issues of Board accountability on the table. And I think it is important as today we continue this committee's oversight role in looking at issues of corporate accountability, and in particular board accountability.

Today, as we continue our series of hearings on pretexting, this time in the corporate context, this gives us a good opportunity to open the window for some of the practices that are going on in corporations around the country.

The corporate context of pretexting that we are talking about today, of course, involves Hewlett-Packard. It is a sad day for this proud company, and I have been sad to see all the witnesses, the fine corporate representatives who one by one have announced their intentions to exercise their Fifth Amendment rights, although I have got to say, given the facts, I don't blame them.

HP is a company of iconic status in the U.S. and around the world, and frankly, looking around this committee room, Mr. Chairman, there are many products that we are using today that bear the HP logo. This company was started in a small garage in Silicon Valley and grew to be one of the Nation's largest employers. So we know how proud so many are about what Hewlett-Packard became over the years.

But something has really gone wrong at this institution, and one of the questions I want to ask today is is it just with this institution, or is it endemic through corporate America that the kinds of excesses that we will hear about and that we have seen in the voluminous documents and interviews are going on throughout corporate America?

Mr. Chairman, this hearing really is about more than sorting through the mess that has sullied Hewlett-Packard. It is more than about how the Hewlett-Packard way became synonymous with digging through people's trash, setting up bogus e-mails which were approved at the highest levels of the company, and stinging unsuspecting reporters. And it is more than about how a computer company suddenly found itself in the business of trailing and photographing board members across the globe, or surveilling journalists using ex-FBI agents who sat in cars and watched as if their subjects were busy making truck bombs.

As I reviewed all of the documents for this hearing today, I felt like I was looking at a proposal for a made-for-TV movie. And maybe this will be a made-for-TV movie, but I think it is awfully, awfully sad.

What this hearing is really about is sorting through a dark chapter of corporate governance so that shareholders and the employees themselves can look and see is this the kind of corporate practice that we believe in in this country?

Understanding what happened here hasn't been easy. As you said, Mr. Chairman, our staffs have reviewed thousands of documents and interviewed many witnesses in a short period of time. But we have been able to formulate some key questions. Why were such marginal methods used in this investigation? Who approved them? And who knew about them, and when? Have these tactics been used before, and, if so, where? And will they ever be used again at Hewlett-Packard? I think I know the answer to that already. What assurances can the company give that protections are in place so they will not be used? And for those that did approve them, what was the justification? And did they believe that that approval showed good judgment? And finally, where were the legal and ethical guardians of HP's corporate interests when all of this was happening, and whose job was it to steer this ship clear of the icebergs?

For example, was it not a red flag when discussions were occurring about fraud and deception to obtain third-party phone records from journalists? Was it not a red flag when discussions were broached about even the possibility of placing janitors or fake employees in news organizations like the Wall Street Journal or CNET to engage in spying? Was it not a red flag when covert photographers were photographing board members or tracking their wives to Bingo parlors or reporters to their children's schools?

I am very concerned, Mr. Chairman, about the judgment that went into these decisions, and I am concerned more about whether this is just an accepted practice throughout corporate America.

Finally, I am just as concerned about who made--about other people who may have known about these things and didn't say no. I don't understand how the entire Board of Directors, all of them potential targets of this spy ring, the CEO or the general counsel saw or knew so little when so much was going on.

Finally, Mr. Chairman--and I will finish. We passed a bill on pretexting out of this committee last spring. We passed this bill on a unanimous bipartisan basis and sent it to the floor. It was scheduled for a vote on May 2nd of this year, where it apparently fell into a black hole. I think that these practices, which we now all agree--the pretexting which were illegal need to be stopped, and Congress needs to send a clear message. That message is we need to pass our pretexting legislation.

Thank you very much, Mr. Chairman.

MR. WHITFIELD. Thank you, Ms. DeGette.

[The prepared statement of Hon. Diana DeGette follows:]

PREPARED STATEMENT OF THE HON. DIANA DEGETTE, A REPRESENTATIVE IN CONGRESS FROM THE STATE OF COLORADO

Opening Statement

Thank you, Mr. Chairman and thank you for having this hearing.

Over the past few years we have experienced major corporate scandals in this country. At companies like Enron and WorldCom, Americans witnessed corporate executives break the law to enrich themselves at the expense of their customers and shareholders.

This Committee held multiple hearings on these corporate abuses. I was proud to be a Member during that time, as we helped shine a light on corporate excess and pave the way for reform. And, while the specific issues before us are different, I expect that we can play that same role again as we continue our series of hearings on "pretexting," this time in the corporate context.

The corporate context of pretexting we will be talking about today involves Hewlett-Packard, or H-P. It is indeed a very sad day for this very proud company. H-P is a company of iconic stature both here in the U.S., and frankly around the world. In fact, as I look around this room, there are many products – from the computers to PDA's to monitors to printers – all bearing the H-P name.

This company -- as we all know -- was started in a small garage in the Silicon Valley and grew to one of the nation's largest employers. We all know the story. We all know about how proud many should be about what H-P became over the years.

But Mr. Chairman, something has gone wrong -- terribly wrong -- at this once venerated institution.

I begin my statement by talking about the positive aspects of H-P because what we say here and what we do here will affect the lives of tens of thousands of the company's workers, and it is my opinion that they frankly do not deserve the wrath --- or taint -- that has been brought on them or this company's name by the actions of a few.

Unfortunately, though, what we will hear about today is one of the darker chapters of corporate chicanery this committee has seen in quite some time. And sadly, it is unavoidable, but the H-P name is at the center of it.

Let me be clear, Mr. Chairman, this is no Enron. I believe that at the heart of H-P's operations you will find a good product and a good workforce. You will also find some of the best traits of American business, namely entrepreneurship and competitive innovation. It is precisely because this company's now sullied reputation is reversible, that explains why we need to have this hearing. Indeed, it is because H-P is not Enron, that we need to find out what happened and who's accountable.

-- Mr. Chairman, this hearing is about more than sorting through the mess that has sullied the HP name;

-- It is about more than how the "H-P Way" became synonymous with digging through people's trash, setting up bogus emails (approved at the highest levels of the company) and stinging unsuspecting reporters;

-- It is about more than how a computer company suddenly found itself in the business of trailing and photographing board Members across the globe or surveilling journalists using ex-FBI agents who sat in cars and watched as if their subjects were busy making truck bombs;

-- It is about more than how a company that purportedly respects electronic privacy found itself using deception and subterfuge to procure -- and then rummage through -- the private phone records of Americans (in some cases, their Social Security numbers given out to the world as well).

Mr. Chairman, what this hearing is about is this Committee's attempt to sort through a dark chapter of corporate governance so that <u>shareholders and the existing employees</u> themselves can judge and determine who should be entrusted to continue making key decisions which may affect H-P's survival.

Understanding what happened here has not been easy. We have reviewed thousands of documents and countless reports. We have spent endless amounts of time working with the many lawyers who now represent

the key players in this scandal. But unfortunately, many who we would have liked to have spoken to about this matter before this hearing, have not made themselves available for interviews. Nonetheless, we have formulated a number of key questions that, again, I believe shareholders, current H-P employees -- and victims of certain tactics -- deserve answers to. These include the following:

-- **Why were such marginal methods used in this investigation and who approved them and who knew about them (and when)?**

-- **Have such tactics been used before (if so where) and will they ever be used again by H-P? What assurances will the company give us that they will not?**

-- **For those that did approve them, what was their justification and did such approval show good judgment?**

-- **Where was the legal and ethical guardians of HP's corporate interest when all of this was happening and whose job was it to steer the ship clear of the icebergs? For example, was it not a red flag when discussions were occurring about using fraud and deception to obtain third-party phone records from journalists? Was it not a red-flag when discussions were broached about even the possibility of placing janitors -- or fake employees -- in news organizations such as the Wall Street Journal or CNET to engage in spying? Was it not a red flag when covert teams began**

photographing board members or tracking their wives to bingo parlors or reporters to their children's schools?

I am very concerned about the judgment that went into these decisions and why with a company of H-P's sophistication, nobody -- neither the board, nor its CEO, nor its General Counsel, nor its outside counsel had the common sense to say "NO, this is not the 'H-P Way.'"

Finally, Mr. Chairman, as concerned as I am about who MAY have known about these things, and didn't say "NO," I am perhaps even more concerned about those who apparently now claim they DIDN'T know about these things. I frankly, can't understand how the entire board of directors -- all of them potential targets of a renegade HP spy ring – the CEO, or the General Counsel saw or knew little when it came to perhaps the most sensitive investigations ever conducted at the company. In sum, Mr. Chairman, who was on the bridge -- or at the helm -- when the HP hit the iceberg? Apparently nobody.

Mr. Chairman, I will conclude by saying that I look forward to obtaining answers at today's hearing and allowing the witnesses to hopefully set the record straight. But it is my prediction, that much of what we will hear today will be a "see no evil, hear no evil, speak no evil" set of answers. If that occurs, it really will be in the hands of shareholders and victimized employees to take the helm and put this once proud and distinctive ship back on course.

With that, I yield back.

MR. WHITFIELD. The Chair recognizes Mr. Walden for his opening statement.

MR. WALDEN. Thank you very much, Mr. Chairman. I appreciate the work that you have put into this and that our committee staff has put into this as well.

This is a most troubling day, as you can tell, for all of us in this room, certainly for you at Hewlett-Packard, in terms of what went on and what we now know and what we may learn today. It is troubling for, I think, all of us as Americans to know that this practice goes on all across this country.

And if this practice were so simply described as legal, then I ask you why are so many witnesses today either going to take the Fifth Amendment or have quit their jobs?

Clearly when the spotlight of public scrutiny is put to bear on this practice, it is obvious that nobody believes this is right, and I think that is the fundamental question here. For those who said conveniently, well, we are told it is legal, so it must be okay, where was somebody to say this just isn't right? Somewhere some adult should have stepped forward and said, stop this, this isn't right.

Planting spies in newsrooms? I have a journalism degree. I can't imagine in a newsroom having spies planted there to find out who might be leaking. Setting up e-mail spyware, tracking down who calls whom from their private cell phone or their home phone?

This is not about law, this is about ethics and, I think, morality. I just find it horribly offensive and outrageous conduct, I really do. I spent 5 years on a community bank board, 5 years on a hospital board, I have been a small business owner for 20 years. I understand the importance of keeping proprietary information proprietary, but to go to this level to try and find out who might be leaking something, there is no excuse for it. There just isn't.

I agree with my colleagues on this committee. We have a fine piece of legislation that will draw a bright line about what is legal and not. You know, Congress passed a law that says you can't find out what videos we rent. We need to pass a law, for anybody who questions this practice, that it is clear that this is illegal to go find out who I call, when I call them and divulge that information. Of course, pretexting goes much beyond phone records, as we have, unfortunately, learned in this committee, so we need to pass that legislation into law, and we need to do it soon.

I also want to know, are these practices used on other boards in America? And some of our witnesses today probably serve on multiple boards. I want to know whether these practices of pretexting are thought to be okay to go after competitors to find out what they may know or who they are talking to. And I am not alleging that HP engages in that, but clearly this is a practice that, frankly, 6 months ago I didn't even know existed. I never heard of the word "pretexting," and I doubt that I am alone in that. Because to me, the synonym of pretexting is lying, because that is what it is about; I am going to lie to somebody to get the personal and private information on somebody else so that I can use it to my advantage. And I just think that is unacceptable, it is outrageous, and people better come clean about how they have done it and how they are never doing it again, and then we need to make sure that the law is crystal clear.

Mr. Chairman, I appreciate the work you put into this, and I look forward to hearing from the witnesses who will be actually willing to testify today. Thank you.

MR. WHITFIELD. Thank you, Mr. Walden.

MR. WHITFIELD. At this time the Chairman recognizes the Ranking Member of the full committee, Mr. Dingell of Michigan.

MR. DINGELL. Mr. Chairman, thank you, and thank you for holding this hearing.

This morning we have a fine case study of deceit, dishonesty, improper behavior, probably criminal misbehavior, and we have a fine display of arrogance, coverup, and probably gross stupidity.

We have before us today witnesses from Hewlett-Packard, a respected American company, to discuss a plumbers' operation that would make Richard Nixon blush were he alive. And calling the folks who did or allowed or participated in this "Keystone Kops" is an insult of the grossest sort to the original Keystone Kops.

Hewlett-Packard, as I have mentioned, is a well-respected company in the halls of Congress and around the world, appears before us to answer for using lies and deception to obtain telephone records and other sensitive personal information in order to uncover the source of leaks to the press. Now, I have to ask our witnesses, "What were you thinking?"

Where was the management while this investigation was running amok? Why weren't you paying attention at the briefings, and why didn't you read the reports that raised red flags?

Where was the Board of Directors? I understand board leaks could undermine a company's planning and curtail frankness at board discussions, but the cure here proves to have been far worse than the disease; it now poses a severely greater threat to Hewlett-Packard. Where was the board leadership and responsibility?

One interesting thing is where were the lawyers? The red flags were waving all over the place raising questions about the legality of pretexting, but none of the lawyers stepped up to their responsibilities.

This morning we are probably going to have a very interesting exercise in which witnesses appearing at that crowded witness table amongst the lawyers will be taking the Fifth Amendment. One must ask, have we here a law which is so obscure, curious or nonexistent that lawyers couldn't tell what was the law? Or that they participated actively? Or that they were part of the exercise about which we are now having proper complaints?

Now, I note that the Congress has not stepped up either. What happened to this committee's legislation, H.R. 4943, the Prevention of

Fraudulent Access to Phone Records Act? It came out of this committee with a heavy vote, bipartisan participation, under the effective leadership of our Chairman and the senior Members on both sides of the aisle, and indeed all of the Members. That bill would permit the FTC to seek civil penalties against pretexters, and to provide expanded protections to customers' call records. The bill came out, as observed by Ms. DeGette, and on May 2, 2006, it was scheduled for consideration on the floor of the House of Representatives. In some curious fashion, it disappeared. It was pulled from the suspension calendar where it would have passed comfortably under expedited process. But without explanation of any sort, it has not been heard of or heard from since. Why did this happen? Who did it, and why?

Also, no one in the Administration is stepping up either. I submitted questions for the record of this subcommittee's June 21 hearing asking comments from the executive branch, homeland security and law enforcement agencies on how the bill could be changed to address any concerns that they might have from a national security standpoint. I have been informed that the response is being held up--I assume diligently--by the Office of Management and Budget, which appears to be another black hole.

I commend the Chairman of the subcommittee for holding 2 days of hearings on this matter, it is most important; but hearings are going to be a poor substitute if the committee's bill remains in legislative limbo. I suggest that we all should get behind the bill again and see to it that it is enacted into law so that perhaps we don't have so many distinguished Americans coming before this committee in the most profound embarrassment to take the Fifth or explain in some curious red-faced way why they or the entity of which they are a part is engaged in such shameful and shameless behavior.

Thank you very much.

[The prepared statement of Hon. John D. Dingell follows:]

PREPARED STATEMENT OF THE HON. JOHN D. DINGELL, A REPRESENTATIVE IN CONGRESS FROM THE STATE OF MICHIGAN

Mr. Chairman, thank you for holding this hearing. We have before us witnesses from Hewlett-Packard to discuss a plumbers' operation that would make Richard Nixon blush were he still alive. And calling folks who did this, or allowed this, "Keystone Kops" is an insult to the original Keystone Kops.

Hewlett-Packard, a company well respected in the Halls of Congress and around the globe, appears before us today to answer for using lies and deceptions to obtain telephone records and other sensitive personal information in order to uncover the source of leaks to the press. I have to ask our witnesses, "What were you thinking?"

-- Where was management while this investigation was running amok? Why weren't you paying attention at briefings and why didn't you read the reports that raised red flags?

-- Where was the board of directors? I understand board leaks can undermine a company's planning and curtail the frankness of board discussions. But the cure, in this case, was far worse than the disease, and now poses a far greater threat to Hewlett-Packard. Where was board leadership and responsibility?
-- Where were the lawyers? There were red flags waving all over the place, raising questions about the illegality of pretexting. But none of the lawyers stepped up to their responsibilities.

Unfortunately, Congress has not stepped up either. What happened to the Committee's legislation, H.R. 4943, the "Prevention of Fraudulent Access to Phone Records Act"? That bill would allow the FTC to seek civil penalties against pretexters, and provide expanded protections to customer call records. On May 2, 2006, this bill was scheduled for consideration on the Floor of the House of Representatives. It was pulled from the Suspension Calendar, without explanation, and has not been seen or heard from since. Who did it, and why?

Also, no one in the Administration is stepping up either. I submitted questions for the record of this Subcommittee's June 21, 2006, hearing, seeking comments from Executive Branch homeland security and law enforcement agencies on how the bill could be changed to meet any concerns they might have. I have been informed that the response is being held up by the Office of Management and Budget. Why can't I get answers?

I commend the Chairman of the Subcommittee for holding two days of hearings on this important issue. But hearings will be a poor substitute if the Committee's bill remains in legislative limbo.

MR. WHITFIELD. Thank you, Mr. Dingell.

MR. WHITFIELD. At this time I recognize Mrs. Blackburn of Tennessee for her opening statement.

MRS. BLACKBURN. Thank you, Mr. Chairman. I do want to thank you for holding the hearing today.

The Energy and Commerce Committee has focused on the pretexting issue this year, as you have heard my colleagues mention in their statements, and it appears we were correct to recognize that this subject was a problem.

Today's inquiry, I believe, will reaffirm our previous work, which showed a need for legal clarity regarding pretexting, and we thank our witnesses for coming before us today.

We are not here to serve as judge and jury of HP and their actions; their shareholders, the stakeholders and the legal system have that responsibility. Our job today is to focus our attention on the action and the practice of pretexting.

Currently, the law regarding pretexting is ambiguous. As Mr. Dingell just said, this case does illustrate how some have taken advantage of that ambiguity. Ethical behavior is not always something that we can regulate. We certainly cannot mandate it, but we certainly can punish actions that are both unethical and a violation of others' rights.

Our committee is correct to be concerned with corporate governance and the American corporate culture. The trust and integrity of the

American people toward the American corporate culture and our free enterprise system depends on ethical behavior and an element of trust. It is with deep regret that we see that there is a violation of that trust.

I think we ought to be clarifying the concept of pretexting. The term sounds innocuous, but the reality is that it is theft, and the act of pretexting is purposeful. It is an action meant to deceive, defraud and obtain information one is not entitled to have. It is a more modern problem, but one this committee has recognized and is working to address.

In January, my colleague Representative Inslee and I introduced the Consumer Telephone Records Protection Act of 2006. The bill dispenses with the ambiguity in laws governing the action prohibiting individuals or entities from fraudulently obtaining another person's telephone records under false pretext, soliciting someone to obtain phone records under false pretext, selling phone records or fraudulently obtaining under false pretext. Violations would be criminal offenses punishable by up to 5 years in prison, and $250,000 in fines for individuals and $5,000 in fines for companies, which is a Class D felony. These penalties are doubled for an aggravated offense.

We have passed a similar bill with civil penalties; these bills would clearly have penalized those who engage in the sort of behavior we will hear testimony about this morning.

We are already receiving information that numerous companies are profiting by using suspect and irresponsible methods to gain access to consumers' telecommunications records. When a Fortune 15 company contracts with one of these companies, yes, it gets our attention, and rightfully so.

We want to know who in the company or in the private investigation firms came up with the proposal to pretext. Who created and ran the Jacob Project, which used suspect methods to gain information from media sources? We hope companies aren't using these methods to engage in corporate espionage to gain a competitive advantage over other companies or over innovators or other creators, but we do want to know how pervasive is this practice in America's corporate boardrooms. Are there other companies that are using pretexting for other reasons?

I look forward to the testimony today. I hope we learn that HP is no longer using the services of the companies to monitor their Board members or the employees, or, just as concerning, using these tactics to monitor or spy on other companies.

Thank you, Mr. Chairman, I yield back.

MR. WHITFIELD. Ms. Schakowsky of Illinois is recognized for her opening statement.

MS. SCHAKOWSKY. Thank you, Mr. Chairman and Ranking Member, for holding today's hearing on Hewlett-Packard's pretexting scandal. I am glad that we have the opportunity to further examine what is undoubtedly the most notorious case of pretexting for personal phone records to date.

In July 2005, I circulated a letter to my congressional colleagues drawing attention to the burgeoning practice of pretexting of phone records. I urged them to join me as cosponsors of the SAFECALL Act, which is a somewhat tortured acronym for Stop Attempted Fraud Against Everyone's Cell and Land Lines Act, a bill that would expressly prohibit pretexting for phone records. I am proud that my bill was used as the basis for title 1 of H.R. 4943, the Prevention of Fraudulent Access to Phone Records Act, which passed our committee unanimously. We drafted the bipartisan H.R. 4943 because questions were raised about whether pretexting for phone records was legal, not to mention the safety and privacy concerns that it raises.

The FTC had successfully brought pretexting cases under its Section 5 authority which prohibits unfair or deceptive acts and practices. You would have thought that that would have set the stage for understanding that this is not a legal act. A number of States, including my home State of Illinois, under our Attorney General Lisa Madigan, used their general consumer protection and consumer fraud statutes to file suits against the practice, and now, along with 11 other States, Illinois has passed a law. But obviously there are still those who missed the point and choose to dabble in what they claim is a grey area of the law.

We need to pass H.R. 4943, and maybe instead of naming post offices for the rest of--most of today, we can do it before we recess.

Hewlett-Packard is a perfect example. When Kevin Hunsaker, HP Senior Counsel and Director of Ethics, asked whether pretexting for board members' and reporters' phone records was, quote, "above board," unquote, Tony Gentilucci, HP's Investigations Manager, replied, quote, "I think it is on the edge, but above Board," unquote. Hunsaker, instead of demanding an explanation or ringing the alarm bells, responded, quote, "I shouldn't have asked," unquote.

Additionally, HP's September filing with the FCC revealed that the Board was advised by its outside General Counsel Larry Sonsini that pretexting for phone records was, quote, "not generally unlawful," unquote. The filing went on to say, "but such counsel could not confirm that the techniques employed by the outside consulting firm and the party retained by that firm complied in all respects with the applicable law," unquote.

Hewlett-Packard's action and hedging about pretexting's legality demonstrates just how pressing it is to pass our bill to put an end to all questions.

As I said, Congress and at least 12 States that have passed antipretexting laws agree that pretexting is unacceptable, and that the ends, in HP's case it was squelching Board leaks, do not justify the means.

What makes the HP story more disheartening was HP was believed to be a corporation that set business standards that others should follow. In January 2005, HP was named the most trusted company in America for privacy. In July 2006, the Commerce, Trade, Consumer Protection Subcommittee, of which I am the Ranking Member, invited HP to testify about what it does to raise the bar on consumer privacy protections. Little did we know that when we were trying to learn about its best practices, HP had just been engaging in the worst practices out there. If corporations that are supposed to be so reputable are employing such legally and ethically questionable behavior--I would argue actually that the case is settled--we have to ask what other corporations are doing.

So I very much look forward to hearing from today's witnesses. I wish all of those that were called today would fully testify. And I truly hope that we can get to the bottom of this scandal. Thank you.

MR. WHITFIELD. The Chair recognizes Mr. Barton of Texas, who is Chairman of the full Energy and Commerce Committee.

CHAIRMAN BARTON. Thank you, Chairman Whitfield. Thank you, Ranking Member Stupak, for continuing this investigation.

We are convened here to examine the facts of the Hewlett-Packard pretexting scandal. Pretexting is the use of deception to discover who you have been on the phone with, and maybe even where you were. In plain language, it is pretending to be somebody you are not to get something you probably shouldn't have to use in a way that is probably wrong.

We have been investigating it because most Americans believe that their phone records are theirs, that their private property should only be accessed with their permission.

Pretexting first came to this subcommittee's attention when it was reported that the Chicago Police Department, of all people, had warned undercover police officers that suspicious drug dealers could expose them just by poking through their phone records. Months of investigations and hearings produced plenty of troubling facts and even some news. Now today at this hearing it is global news, as you can see all the cameras and reporters that are in the room, because nobody would have guessed that such a great company as Hewlett-Packard, one of the first high-tech companies in the United States, would employ the methods of pretexting that are sometimes used to chase after cheating spouses in order to stalk its own Board members, and believe it or not, even tail journalists.

But against what standard should Hewlett-Packard's conduct be measured? I guess the best place would be a quote from an e-mail written by a Hewlett-Packard security employee on August the 23rd of this year. The subject line of that e-mail reads, "Standards of Business Conduct," and the author writes, and I quote, "This investigation will be a defining case which will test the company's claim of having uncompromising integrity," end quote. I should say so.

This hearing is going to examine a year-long course of questionable conduct led by Hewlett-Packard's Chairman of the Board and reviewed by Hewlett-Packard's General Counsel, who I am told has resigned this morning, or has announced that she is going to resign. That conduct included, among other things, obtaining personal phone records through pretext, physical surveillance, monitoring of employees' instant messaging over the Internet, planting spyware or attempting to plant spyware on a journalist's computer, and even planning to put spies in newsrooms.

I think it will be some time before the American corporate icon of Hewlett-Packard can reclaim its mantle, self-imposed, but again, "uncompromising integrity," end quote. The public, Hewlett-Packard shareholders, and this committee are all very concerned that such a great company has strayed off course. And I have to say that as alarming as these details that have been disclosed are, I wonder if Hewlett-Packard would have and could have done more to right the ship. The company seems paralyzed.

On September the 6th of this year, HP publicly disclosed to the Securities and Exchange Commission that the company had obtained personal phone records procured through pretext as part of an effort to find an individual who was leaking confidential information. Records provided to this committee show that phone records were being pulled by HP's internal investigation team for more than a year, with the approval and knowledge of both then-Chairman Dunn and General Counsel Baskins.

It is my understanding that the day-to-day operations were controlled by the company's lead ethics attorney Kevin Hunsaker so that the investigation could be protected by the attorney/client privilege. Mr. Hunsaker would frequently report to Ms. Dunn and to Ms. Baskins about the developments in the next steps in the investigation. Yet not until last Friday, September the 22nd, did HP force Patricia Dunn's resignation.

I also have to say that I am troubled to find that the Board's outside counsel Larry Sonsini learned last April that the investigation included information from fraudulently obtained phone records. Why didn't he immediately recommend putting the brakes on the investigation? Did he ask any questions about the investigative methods employed by Ms. Dunn, Ms. Baskins or Mr. Hunsaker?

On June 28th of this year, instigated by concerns of former Board member Tom Perkins, Mr. Sonsini reported to Mr. Perkins that pretexting for phone records was, I quote, "a common investigatory method," end quote, and that the, quote, "process was well done and within legal limits," end quote. I hope that Mr. Sonsini will explain to us exactly what due diligence he undertook before providing his assessment of the legality of pretexting for phone records. And again, pretexting is pretending to be somebody you are not to get something you probably shouldn't have to use in a way that is probably wrong.

By coincidence, just a week before Mr. Sonsini's e-mail, the Federal Bureau of Investigation testified before this same subcommittee about its position on the legality of procuring records through pretexting. The FBI testified that there are compelling reasons to believe such operations violate Federal law, including the Wire Act. In fact, over the next 2 days of hearings, we actually expect several other individuals--and several is actually--I should say numerous individuals to invoke their Fifth Amendment right against self-incrimination, which they are obviously entitled to do, and to decline to answer our questions about their involvement with pretexting for phone records. It is funny to me that if you have to invoke your Fifth Amendment right, you are doing something that is illegal.

I am still waiting for someone to describe a legitimate way, short of a subpoena issued by a judge or Congress, to obtain another person's phone records without their permission.

I would like to close on this note. Whether such activities are already illegal or not, this committee has done its part to pass a bill that makes it abundantly clear where the Federal government stands regarding pretexting for personal records.

On March the 8th, the Prevention of Fraudulent Access to Phone Records Act, H.R. 4943, was unanimously, unanimously reported out of this committee. H.R. 4943 would make it illegal to obtain cell phone records fraudulently, as well as to solicit or sell such records. I am, of course, disappointed by the delays that this bill has experienced since it left this committee. It has not yet come to the floor for a vote, but I have asked early this week that it be put on the floor as soon as possible. And I am going to continue to request that the House of Representatives vote on this bill on the floor before the Congress adjourns this year.

We must make pretexting clearly illegal. There is no room in our society for pretexters getting your phone records. If it can happen to a member of the Board of directors of a Fortune 500 company like Hewlett-Packard, it can happen to any of us.

With that, Mr. Chairman, I yield back.

[The prepared statement of Hon. Joe Barton follows:]

PREPARED STATEMENT OF THE HON. JOE BARTON, CHAIRMAN, COMMITTEE ON ENERGY AND COMMERCE

Thank you, Chairman Whitfield. We are convened here to examine the facts of the Hewlett-Packard pretexting scandal. Pretexting is the use of deception to discover who you've been on the phone with, and maybe even where you were. We've been investigating it because the fact that this can be done and that it somehow seems legal is obnoxious to most and downright dangerous to some.

It first came to our attention when it was news that the Chicago Police Department had warned undercover police that suspicious drug dealers could expose them just by poking through their phone records. Months of investigation and hearings produced plenty of troubling facts, but even some news. Now it's suddenly global news, because nobody could have guessed that a great enterprise like Hewlett-Packard would employ the methods of hired gumshoes chasing after cheating spouses, in order to stalk its own Board members and tail journalists.

But against what standard should H-P's conduct be measured?

I guess the best place would be with a quote from an email, written by a Hewlett-Packard security employee on August 23rd of this year. The Subject line of that email reads: "Standards of Business Conduct," and the author writes: "This investigation will be a defining case which will test the company's claim of having uncompromising integrity."

I should say so. This hearing will examine a year-long course of questionable conduct led by the company's Chairman of the Board and reviewed by H-P's General Counsel. That conduct included, among other things, obtaining personal phone records through pretext, physical surveillance, monitoring of employees' instant messaging, planting spyware on a journalist's computer, and even planning to put spies in newsrooms. Mr. Chairman, I think it will be some time before this American corporate icon can reclaim the mantle of "uncompromising integrity" again.

The public, H-P's shareholders, and this Committee are all very concerned that the company has strayed far off course. And I have to say that, as these alarming details have been disclosed, I wonder if H-P could have done more to right the ship. Until recently, a company known for innovation and agility seemed paralyzed.

On September 6, 2006, H-P publicly disclosed to the Securities and Exchange Commission that the company had obtained personal phone records procured through pretext, as part of an effort to find an individual who was leaking confidential business information. Records provided to this Committee show that phone records were being pulled by H-P's internal investigation team for more than a year, with the approval and knowledge of both then Chairman Dunn and General Counsel Baskins. It is my understanding that the day-to-day operations were controlled by the company's lead ethics attorney, Kevin Hunsaker, so that the investigation could be protected by the attorney-client privilege. Mr. Hunsaker would frequently report to Ms. Dunn and Ms. Baskins about the developments and the next steps in the investigation. Yet not until last Friday, the 22nd of September, did H-P force Patricia Dunn's resignation.

I also have to say that I am troubled to find out that the Board's outside counsel, Larry Sonsini, learned last April that the investigation included information from fraudulently obtained phone records. Why didn't he immediately put the brakes on H-P's investigation? Did he ask any questions about the investigative methods employed by Ms. Dunn, Ms. Baskins, or Mr. Hunsaker?

On June 28th of this year, instigated by the concerns of former Board member Tom Perkins, Mr. Sonsini reported to Mr. Perkins that pretexting for phone records was "a common investigatory method" and that the "process was well done and within legal limits." I hope that Mr. Sonsini will explain to us exactly what due diligence he undertook before providing his assessment of the legality of pretexting for phone records.

By coincidence, just a week before Mr. Sonsini's email, the Federal Bureau of Investigation testified before our Subcommittee about its position on the legality of procuring records through pretext. The FBI testified that there are "compelling reasons" to believe such operations violate federal law, including the Wire Act. In fact, over the next two days of hearings, we actually expect several individuals to invoke their Fifth Amendment right against self incrimination – as they are obviously entitled to do – and decline to answer our questions about their involvement with pretexting for phone records. I am still waiting for someone to describe a legitimate way – short of a subpoena – to obtain another individual's personal phone records.

I would like to close on this note, Mr. Chairman. Whether such activities are already illegal or not, this Committee has done its part to pass a bill that makes it abundantly clear where the Federal government stands regarding pretexting for personal phone records. On March 8th, the "Prevention of Fraudulent Access to Phone Records Act," (H.R. 4943) was unanimously reported out of this Committee. H.R. 4943 would make it illegal to obtain cell phone records fraudulently, as well as to solicit or sell such records. I am of course disappointed by the delays, but will continue to push the House leadership to get our bill to the floor for a vote this Fall. We must make pretexting clearly illegal. There is no room in our society for pretexters getting your phone records. If it can happen to a member of the board of directors of a Fortune 500 company, it can happen to any of us.

I yield back.

MR. WHITFIELD. The gentlelady from Wisconsin, Ms. Baldwin, is recognized for 5 minutes.

MS. BALDWIN. Thank you, Mr. Chairman.

Unfortunately, it has taken this Hewlett-Packard boardroom spying scandal to make pretexting a household word.

Pretexting is simply a fancy term for lying and deceiving. Regrettably, this type of private invasion will now be associated with the HP way, a once proud reputation of the highest integrity and ethical standards now tainted.

The committee's investigation so far has turned up a textbook case of exactly how not to operate as a corporate board. Bickering and division between HP's Board members created an atmosphere of antagonism and mistrust.

Investigation into the source of boardroom leaks concerning what appears to be rather benign, albeit confidential company information were authorized against at least seven Board members, nine journalists and two HP employees, as well as some of their relatives. Unsavory techniques, including pretexting phone records, trafficking of Social Security numbers, a sting operation through a fictitious person, tracer spyware, physical surveillance, the planting of undercover operatives, even the search of individuals' trash at home may have been employed during this investigation.

Despite the involvement of teams of lawyers specializing in corporate ethics, events of the investigation code-named Kona 1 and Kona 2 unfolded like the plot of a third-rate detective novel. The laundry list of inappropriate investigative conduct, lax oversight and poor legal advice will be further explored today. But even when the dust settles, when we get to the bottom of who knows what when, an impression of corporate America turned rogue spying operation will persist in the minds of the public. It is one of the highly unfortunate consequences of HP's conduct. People will wonder how many companies hire third-party investigators to spy on their own employees, Board members or outside contacts. They will wonder how their own phone records could be obtained by their employers under false pretenses, or how their Social Security numbers could be unscrupulously shared with strangers, and how their e-mails could be embedded with spyware, secretly mining personal information.

HP, known for durable high-tech products, has now given us another lasting artifact, the perception of corporate America as our next Big Brother. Still, one silver lining of this scandal is that the public is now much more aware of the concept of pretexting.

I believe pretexting in the wireless industry is only the tip of the iceberg; therefore, a comprehensive legislative approach is necessary to cover all sectors where pretexting is a possible method to breach personal data security.

Our committee has worked diligently and in a bipartisan manner to pass legislation that would outlaw the specific tactics involved in the HP scandal. And I would further urge criminalization of pretexting to encompass the full spectrum of telecommunications and communication services, including records obtainable from calling cards and Internet websites. The protection of consumers' fundamental rights to privacy simply cannot rely on patchwork policymaking.

Now, make no mistake, I believe that existing law covering unfair and deceptive business practices already prohibits pretexting, but if corporate America desires further guidance on whether highly unethical behaviors are indeed legal or illegal, as demanded by some of the witnesses testifying before us today, our committee should provide assistance by enacting clear and overarching bright line rules to outlaw such behavior once and for all.

When Dr. George Keyworth, one of the subjects of the leak investigation, was confronted with the results of the probe during a

Board meeting, he reportedly exclaimed, and I quote, "I would have told you all about this. Why didn't you just ask?"

It seems that HP could have easily avoided this whole mess by applying the most basic principles of transparency and common sense. For working Americans in 2001, the scandal surrounding Enron challenged their trust in the markets. Today the HP scandal is shattering their expectations of telecommunications privacy. HP has led the Nation on an expedition into corporate intrigue. As they were trying to contain the damage, the public deserves to know what steps will be taken not only to restore confidence in this company, but also to shore up the boundaries of privacy breached by the scandal.

Thank you, Mr. Chairman.

MR. WHITFIELD. Thank you.

The Chair recognizes the gentlemen from Texas, Dr. Burgess.

MR. BURGESS. Thank you, Mr. Chairman. And thank you for continuing your leadership in investigating this important issue.

Today's hearing is, unfortunately, additional evidence of the deceptive practice of pretexting. I am confident that our committee will continue to work diligently to protect the American public and their private records. The war on privacy is fully engaged, and we need to provide consumers with additional protections.

Pretexting, as Chairman Barton told us, is the impersonation of others to gain access to others' personal information, probably crossing some legal line, but we all learned from an early age that prying is wrong, and I don't understand how an intelligent board from a venerable old company in this country could not know that these deceptive actions were wrong. Even if you somehow believed that what you were doing wasn't completely illegal, the questions you asked shows that reasonable minds would still view these actions as completely out of bounds. Others on this panel have already asked, "What in the world were you thinking?"

The past 2 years your company even won awards such as the most trusted company for privacy award, and that is--you are supposed to be celebrating your respect for people's privacy and encourage a safer digital marketplace. Your business model depends upon the public's trust in a digital marketplace.

While Hewlett-Packard's headlines have brought the issue of pretexting in the public eye, this committee has been working on the matter for much of this year. In fact, this past spring the Energy and Commerce full committee marked up comprehensive legislation--you have heard others reference it, H.R. 4943--that will make pretexting for telephone records illegal and will strengthen security measures taken by telecommunications carriers to protect such records. Perhaps a silver lining to this cloud is that the questionable actions will be a call to action to get this important legislation passed.

You have heard plenty of questions from, in fact, both sides of the dais. You know, a lot of people in this country, myself included, worry about outsourcing, worry about sending American jobs and manufacturing overseas. But at the same time, these types of actions--and you have heard people reference it this morning--we may be forced to add additional regulatory layers trying to legislate the corporate board to simply behave responsibly, a Sarbanes-Oxley for ethics, if you will. I shudder to think what that will look like. But it begs the question, how widespread is this practice; how entrenched is this practice in corporate boardrooms in this country?

And you have to worry about the collateral damage. You have 140,000 employees worldwide, 57,000 in this country, almost 10,000 in my home State in Texas, 200 in my home district in north Texas. What about the responsibility to those employees? What about the responsibility to the shareholders, not just direct shareholders, but all those people hold mutual funds, 401(k)s, exchange trading funds, Thrift Savings Plan programs? Hewlett-Packard is a big player in all of those.

And then finally, you heard it referenced already, the violation of the public trust. Again, the war on privacy is fully engaged from several sectors in our society. And, Mr. Chairman, I hope that we can encourage others in the Congress to get our bill to the House floor and give consumers at least one more tool to fight back.

And I yield back the balance of my time.

MR. WHITFIELD. The reason we are hesitating for a moment, we have some Members here today who are not members of this subcommittee, and there are members of the full committee. We are going to ask unanimous consent for them to be able to make a brief statement, but we want to get through the subcommittee first.

And the Chair recognizes Mr. Stearns of Florida.

MR. STEARNS. Thank you, Mr. Chairman. And of course we all appreciate this hearing.

We are holding the hearing obviously to investigate the disclosure that investigators hired by Chairwoman Patricia Dunn used pretexting to obtain the phone records of directors and journalists during the investigation into company media leaks.

Having been through the Enron oversight hearing, Mr. Chairman, there are some similarities here, but this is unique, I thought. Truth is stranger than fiction in this case. The evidence we have seen shows that this investigation is part *Keystone Kops*, it is part *Mission Impossible*, and perhaps part of *All the President's Men*, all tied together.

I think, Mr. Chairman, if we ask Ms. Dunn if she thought she was guilty, she would probably say, I was not. She would make the case that she went to the lawyers, and the lawyers told her what she is doing is acceptable, is legal; and that she continued to do that, so she hired the investigators, and they went ahead and used pretexting.

But I would remind her and others that I remember when Ken Lay was here; and Jeff Skilling, of course, testified how he used the cloak of cover, Vinson and Elkins. And they all, during the Enron hearing, used the same kind of argument, that we have a cloak of cover because we talked to legal people.

Now, when you look at the California Penal Code, which is 538.5, it says specifically, prohibits fraudulently obtaining information from a public utility. This statute makes it unlawful for any person to transmit or cause to be transmitted by means of wire, radio or television communication any words, sounds, writings, signs, signals or pictures for the purpose of furthering or executing a scheme or artifice to obtain from a public utility confidential, privileged or proprietary information, customer records, billing records, customer credit data or accounting data by means of false or fraudulent pretenses. So I think the law is that you can't use fraudulent means.

Obviously if you went ahead and did pretexting on Michael Dell of Dell Computers, and you got his last 500 calls, would you say that you had the right to do that, Ms. Dunn? I don't think you would, and I don't think Michael Dell would appreciate that. So in many ways I don't think you can hide behind the cloak of cover of your legal team, and you must take personal responsibility.

But the impetus for this hearing perhaps has much larger impact here in this country. I believe pretexting should be illegal in any context, financial or otherwise. The action by the Hewlett-Packard officials were unconscionable, but make no mistake, the recent events surrounding it are just symptoms of, I say, a much bigger problem.

Obviously the question would come, what did she know and when did she know it? But another question is for Michael Hurd. Can he say he knew nothing about this? He was advised, I think, by e-mail. Can he also say, "Gee whiz, I am just out of the picture here?" He is a Chief Executive Officer and now Chairman, and certainly when Ms. Dunn notified him either by e-mail or by voice or whatever, he did nothing; he just sat there and said, go ahead. Because he could have said to her, "What are you going to do, who are the investigators, and are they going to do something that is fraudulent here?" So I think he has a certain amount of responsibility and culpability here, and shares it with Patricia Dunn.

The growing market for personal information is enormous, and many of us have seen this, and that is why we need to pass legislation to stop this. I chair a subcommittee called Commerce, Trade and Consumer Protection. We have amassed extensive records on these issues. I have introduced H.R. 4727, the Data Accountability and Trust Act, which is designed to improve data security and attack the scourge of privacy-infringing practices like pretexting, that continue to be exploited on the Internet. The Data Act will go a long ways to protecting the privacy of all Americans, and I urge its passage. Our committee, you know, has also been involved with other hearings dealing with privacy.

So in a larger sense, Mr. Chairman, we in Congress have to step up to the plate, pass not only the Data Act, which came out of my subcommittee and passed the full committee by a unanimous vote almost, but we also must go to the heart of this unprecedented assault on personal data and, more specifically, on our private lives. And thank you, Mr. Chairman.

MR. WHITFIELD. The Chair recognizes the gentleman from Washington, Mr. Inslee, for his opening statement.

MR. INSLEE. Mr. Chairman, we are all disturbed in our unique way. I learned about this last Christmas when I was surfing the Web reading some bloggers about people who will sell your personal records on the Web for a hundred bucks, and I was astounded that this was going on. And at the time I had this sense that what was going on was there was this sort of underworld of these scoundrels and sleazes that are operating in the dark recesses of American society who are using pretexting to sell your phone records on the Internet. And the thought that a major league, respected company like HP would be involved in that just never, never crossed my mind, and that is what is so disturbing to me.

We immediately, in January of this year, Marsha Blackburn and myself, introduced a bill to make this, to close any possible ambiguity about this, to make sure these are criminal violations, and now this committee has, in fact, passed a bill that will give the Federal regulators, the FTC and the FCC, the tools they need to make sure that nobody does this, whether it is an HP or whether it is one of these lowlife scoundrels.

But I have to say there is another sort of, if not scandal, at least great disappointment here. We have now known about this since last Christmas, and Americans today at this late date do not have protections against pretexting. Neither has the loophole or any ambiguity been closed, nor has the bill that this committee basis--on a bipartisan--passed to give the regulators the tools and a tool box to put a hammer to it and stop it.

Now, I want to commend Chairman Barton for his work on this and some of my Republican colleagues, but I have to tell you, it isn't just the leadership failure in HP, there has been a leadership failure in the GOP in getting this job done. And I would like to know who in the GOP leadership has their foot on this bill that has put it on ice? We passed it, it was scheduled to be on the floor in May under Chairman Barton's leadership, we passed it in this committee in March, and nothing happens. That is a story here, too, that I would like to get to the bottom of. And while we are rightfully dumping every outrage we can on HP leadership, HP leadership may look back up here at the GOP leadership and say, how come you are not moving this bill? I have talked to the Intelligence Committee to see if they have got some hold on it. No problems there. So who is the little secret force here that has got control of this Congress that is stopping us from passing a bill to stop pretexting? I would like to know who that is, and I would like an answer from GOP leadership why they are not moving this bill.

And I also hope today that we learn some more about how deep this is. I join my colleagues in wanting to know whether or not HP, if they did this to their own, what are they doing to their business competitors? I would like to know if this is a deeper situation that is going on, because this is clearly not the act of just one rogue employee. It does appear to be a widespread, concerted effort on multiple fronts to violate people's personal privacy, and we would like to know where it is so that we can get the job done.

I will tell you one thing I hope comes out of this hearing. I hope the message is delivered to the leadership of the House of Representatives to pass this bill in the next 24 hours. We can have this on the suspension calendar tomorrow night so we can pass this bill and not have to wait until some lame-duck session. And I hope that that is one thing that comes out of this committee hearing. Thank you.

MR. WHITFIELD. The Chair recognizes the gentleman from New Hampshire for his opening statement, Mr. Bass.

MR. BASS. Thank you, Mr. Chairman. And I appreciate you holding this hearing.

A couple of observations. First of all, I think we agree on both sides of the aisle here that H.R. 4943 should be brought to the floor of the House and passed. I hope that what we have gathered from the information that we receive in this hearing is not so much who did what, where, when, how and to who, but rather whether agreeing that the process that--or the events that unfolded at Hewlett-Packard were not good, were not right, and probably not lawful, but how we can apply this issue to the legislative measure before us today, and whether or not the witnesses that are testifying today feel that the bill that we wish to have voted upon on the floor of the House is adequate to address the problem and prevent future occurrences like this from happening; or whether or not we need to address the issue in a broader fashion.

I think this is a helpful hearing to the subject at hand, and I look forward to hearing the testimony of the witnesses.

Thank you, I yield back.

MR. WHITFIELD. I believe all members of the subcommittee now have given their opening statements, and last night we were approached by two members of the full committee who wanted to make an opening statement. So I am going to ask unanimous consent that those two, Ms. Eshoo, who represents Palo Alto, be recognized for 3 minutes for her opening statement. And unless there is objection--and Mr. Otter, do you want--do you want to make an opening statement, as well? Okay, so Mr. Otter and Ms. Eshoo and Mr. Markey for 3 minutes and without objection, I will recognize Ms. Eshoo for her opening statement.

MS. ESHOO. Thank you, Mr. Chairman for allowing me to be a guest of the subcommittee this morning, as a member of the full Energy and Commerce Committee. This is obviously for the people of my Congressional district, including thousands of HP employees, a sad day for us.

HP is headquartered, as you all know, in Palo Alto. The meaning of the words, Palo Alto is tall tree. And that is what HP has been from its earliest days to this new part of a new century. It is headquartered in Palo Alto, employs thousands of my constituents, decent people who have helped to lift up this company that has made enormous contributions to the American economy.

HP is really the seminal company in Silicon Valley. It is the progenitor of so much that has followed. The two gentlemen that founded the company, Bill Hewlett and David Packard, changed our region. Silicon Valley--and those that come from the area are privileged to live there--know that we would not be what we are were it not for the billions of dollars that they have placed in trust funds that have improved health care for Lucille Packard Children's Hospital to countless, countless efforts that have made our region really the envy of so many places in the United States, and in the world.

So we are here on a troubled day, and deeply troubling, things have taken place.

There is an irony, in my view, about all of this concern about surveillance. I am not here to defend anything that isn't defensible. But the irony today is--I think it is an irony--that on the floor of the House, we are going to be considering the Administration's domestic surveillance bill, where FISA is essentially being overthrown, removed. And a whole new set of issues, and the American people better get set for surveillance.

I would like to point out something that I think the Congress, in addition to passing this bill, is going to have to address, and that is, where does a publicly held company go when they have a member of their board of directors that doesn't stop talking and damages and walks away from not only the credibility of the company, but also their fiduciary responsibility?

I think it is something that needs to be addressed. And I have some questions about it--

MR. WHITFIELD. The gentlelady's time has expired.

MS. ESHOO. I welcome everyone here and thank you, Mr. Chairman, for allowing me to be a guest of the subcommittee.

MR. WHITFIELD. The gentleman from Idaho is recognized for 3 minutes.

MR. OTTER. Thank you very much, Mr. Chairman, and I appreciate very much the unanimous consent waiver that you have given to us nonmembers of this subcommittee. But I am here more today, I suspect, out of curiosity than the seeking, the actually seeking of information. And my curiosity runs in a couple of veins, and I think it was just mentioned by the lady from California--whether or not we can really establish in this Congress in this government, the moral high ground in order to sit in judgment, write rules and regulations about activities in the private sector that we don't enjoy the same control over in the public sector.

And, so, whether it is, and I fully understand the gravity in the difference in the situations. However, the process is no different. People have an expectation of privacy. They should enjoy their privacy. Yet we find out a very strong urgent message coming from our own Justice Department about how perhaps that privacy is not so dear as when the security of our government is being threatened.

So I am looking forward with some curiosity as to how we are going to maintain in light of some of the activities of the National Security Agency and other agencies of our government, that have been questioned in the recent past and how easily we are going to sit on the bench in judgment of another who is simply trying to protect the security, and bear in mind, Mr. Chairman, I am not condoning any of this activity. I condemn it just as bad in the private sector as I do in the government. So my curiosity is going to keep me in this seat for as long as I can stay with you, Mr. Chairman and thank you for the time.

MR. WHITFIELD. Thank you, Mr. Otter. The gentleman from Massachusetts, Mr. Markey, is recognized for 3 minutes.

MR. MARKEY. Thank you, Mr. Chairman. The upshot of the HP snooping and spying program is the compromise of personal privacy for two HP employees, nine reporters, seven members of the HP Board, and various family members of the same.

It involved illegal pretexting of phone numbers, Social Security numbers, sifting through garbage, and electronic enticements to at least one reporter to download malicious software willingly.

What has happened to our corporate culture? You used to ask a company chieftain who does your PR? Who does your advertising? Now, do we have to add the question, so who does your spying? That is what the whole area has opened up. All of this from a company on its website that says HP and its subsidiaries respect your privacy and are committed to protecting it.

Today, the subcommittee will be exploring the responsibility of Hewlett-Packard's management for this illegal spying operation. Who authorized the spying operation? Who oversaw it? What were they thinking?

I am very concerned that HP may be suffering from Sergeant Schultz syndrome, some in a position of authority are now saying, I heard nothing, I saw nothing, I knew nothing. That is their defense.

It is not believable.

Where were the lawyers when all this was happening? HP has an experienced in-house legal staff as well as access to experienced outside legal counsel. Where were these legal professionals when this spying program was put into place?

Mr. Chairman, some are suggesting that there are ambiguities in existing law which made it difficult for HP and its attorneys to determine what the applicable law in this area really was. This is absolutely absurd. What happened is already illegal.

Section 5 of the Federal Trade Commission Act has long prohibited pretexting. In May of this year, the Federal Trade Commission brought five court complaints charging Internet information brokers with illegal trafficking and consumers telephone number. It is already illegal.

The Telecommunications Act of 1996 added a new Section, 222 to the Communications Act; Section 222 clearly states that customers' phone records can only be disclosed to the customer or to someone else with the permission of the customer. I know that because I was co-author of that legislation. And the wire fraud statute also prohibits that kind of a practice--

MR. WHITFIELD. The gentleman's time has expired.

MR. MARKEY. I thank the Chairman. Either this is the tip of the iceberg or it is the iceberg. If it is the iceberg, then Congress must act to ensure that we never again see this as part of corporate culture.

I thank the Chairman.

MR. WHITFIELD. At this time, the Chair will call forward the following witnesses on the first panel and I would ask the staff because we have seating assignments there, and I am not sure, it is available to everyone, to make sure they are sitting in the right seats.

But the first witness is Mrs. Ann Baskins, General Counsel for Hewlett-Packard; Mr. Kevin Hunsaker, Ethics Counsel for Hewlett-Packard; Mr. Anthony Gentilucci, Manager, Global Investigations; Mr. Anthony DeLia, Managing Director for Security Outsourcing Solutions; Mr. Joe Depante, Owner, Action Research Group; Ms. Cassandra Selvage, Owner, Eye in the Sky Investigations; Mr. Darren Brost, subcontractor to Action Research; Ms. Valerie Preston, subcontractor to Action Research; Mr. Bryan Wagner, subcontractor to Action Research; and Mr. Charles Kelly, subcontractor to Action Research. If you all would please come forward and have a seat at the table, we would appreciate it.

Just the people whose name I called will be sitting at the table. If there are legal counsel involved we will be introducing them as we move forward but just the witnesses that I called will be sitting at the table.

I apologize about the lack of space. I would say to those participants on the first panel, this is an investigative hearing. It is the tradition of the subcommittee to always take testimony under oath, and I would ask all of you, do any of you have any difficulty or do you object to testifying under oath this morning?

So if you all would please stand and raise your right hand I would like to swear you in at this time.

[Witnesses sworn.]

Thank you very much. All of you are now under oath. Under the rules of the House and the committee, each of you do have the right to be advised by legal counsel as to your constitutional rights, and I would ask each of you, do you have legal counsel here today? If you do, if you would please raise your right hand.

Okay. Now, Ms. Baskins, would you please give us the name of your legal counsel?

MS. BASKINS. I am represented by Cristina Arguedas.

MR. WHITFIELD. And Mr. Hunsaker, who is your legal counsel?

MR. HUNSAKER. Michael Pancer.

MR. WHITFIELD. And Mr. DeLia, who is your legal counsel?

MR. DELIA. Mr. Kiernan.

MR. WHITFIELD. Mr. Depante, who is your legal counsel?

MR. DEPANTE. Richard Preira.

MS. SELVAGE. Ms. Van Gelder.

MR. WHITFIELD. And who is your legal counsel?

MR. GENTILUCCI. Miles Ehrlich.

MR. BROST. Susie Rebera Ariel.

MR. WHITFIELD. All right. Thank you for introducing legal counsel. Now, Ms. Preston, do you have legal counsel?

MS. PRESTON. No.

MR. WHITFIELD. Mr. Kelly? And Mr. Wagner?

MR. WAGNER. No sir.

MR. WHITFIELD. At this time, the Chair would recognize Ms. Baskins for purposes of making an opening statement, if she so desires.

MS. BASKINS. Mr. Chairman, I have no opening statement.

MR. WHITFIELD. Turn your microphone on, I am sorry.

MS. BASKINS. I have no opening statement, Mr. Chairman.

MR. WHITFIELD. The Chair would then recognize Mr. Hunsaker for purposes of making an opening statement.

MR. HUNSAKER. I have no opening statement, Mr. Chairman.

MR. WHITFIELD. The Chair would recognize Mr. Gentilucci for purposes of making an opening statement.

MR. GENTILUCCI. Mr. Chairman, I have no opening statement.

MR. WHITFIELD. The Chair would recognize Mr. DeLia for purposes of make an opening statement.

MR. DELIA. Mr. Chairman, I do not have an opening statement.

MR. WHITFIELD. The Chair would recognize Mr. Depante for purposes of making an opening statement.

MR. DEPANTE. Mr. Chairman, I do not have an opening statement.

MR. WHITFIELD. The Chair would recognize Ms. Selvage for purposes of making an opening statement.

MS. SELVAGE. Mr. Chairman, I do not wish to make an opening statement.

MR. WHITFIELD. Chair would recognize Mr. Brost for purposes of making an opening statement.

MR. BROST. Mr. Chairman, I have no opening statement.

MR. WHITFIELD. Chair would recognize Ms. Preston for the purpose of making an opening statement.

MS. PRESTON. Mr. Chairman, I have no opening statement.

MR. WHITFIELD. Chair would recognize Mr. Wagner for purposes of making an opening statement.

MR. WAGNER. Mr. Chairman, I have no opening statement.

MR. WHITFIELD. Chair would recognize Mr. Kelly for purposes of making an opening statement.

MR. KELLY. Mr. Chairman, I have no opening statement.

MR. WHITFIELD. Chair then, since there are no opening statements, would recognize himself for 10 minutes for the purposes of questioning the witnesses.

And Ms. Baskins, does she have the exhibit book before her? Would someone give Ms. Baskins our exhibit book, please.

MR. WHITFIELD. I would ask Ms. Baskins to turn to Exhibit 124. I think they are numbered there. It is my understanding, Ms. Baskins, from Hewlett-Packard's counsel, that these handwritten notes are yours, and the notes dated June 15, 2005 have the heading "Project Kona." The first notes on the page say, "Obtaining phone numbers is a time consuming process. Call carriers Nextel, Sprint and use pretext to extract info, i.e., I didn't make the call." Now this document and others show that you were aware that HP was engaging in pretexting, that is obtaining personal telephone records through impersonation fraud, and deceit as a means of identifying the source of corporate leaks.

Ms. Baskins, did you honestly believe at the time and do you believe today that such conduct is legal, ethical and consistent with the Hewlett-Packard way?

MS. BASKINS. Mr. Chairman I respectfully decline to answer based on the rights and protections guaranteed to me by the Fifth Amendment of the Constitution of the United States.

MR. WHITFIELD. So Ms. Baskins, you are refusing to answer all of our questions today based on the right against self incrimination afforded to you under the Fifth Amendment of the U.S. Constitution?

MS. BASKINS. Yes, Mr. Chairman.

MR. WHITFIELD. And it is your intention to assert that right for any and all questions that would be asked today.

MS. BASKINS. Yes, Mr. Chairman.

MR. WHITFIELD. If there are no further questions from the members of the committee, then I would dismiss you at this time?

CHAIRMAN BARTON. Mr. Chairman, may I be recognized for a question?

MR. WHITFIELD. Yes, sir.

CHAIRMAN BARTON. Ms. Baskins, is it true that you have resigned your position from Hewlett-Packard?

MS. BASKINS. Yes, Congressman.

CHAIRMAN BARTON. Thank you.

MR. WHITFIELD. Then Ms. Baskins, you are dismissed at this time subject to the right of the subcommittee to recall you if necessary, and at this time, you are excused.

Mr. Hunsaker, if you would please turn to exhibit in the exhibit book there, Exhibit 25. This exhibit shows a January 30, 2006 e-mail exchange between you and Anthony Gentilucci. And in his e-mail to you, Mr. Gentilucci explains how Ron DeLia procured phone records for Hewlett-Packard's investigation.

"The methodology utilized is social engineering. He has investigators call operators under some ruse to obtain the call records over the phone." Mr. Gentilucci later writes, "In essence, the operator should not give it out, and that person is liable. I think it is on the edge but above board." And your response was, "I shouldn't have asked."

Mr. Hunsaker if you knew that the phone records being obtained for Hewlett-Packard's investigations were being procured through the use of a ruse or deceit, and that the legality and ethics of pretexting might be in doubt, why did you permit the use of this practice in the Kona 2 investigations?

MR. HUNSAKER. Mr. Chairman on the advice of my counsel I am asserting my rights under the U.S. Constitution and will not testify here today.

MR. WHITFIELD. So it is your intent then to assert that right in response to any further questions that may be asked today?

MR. HUNSAKER. That is correct, Mr. Chairman.

MR. WHITFIELD. If other members of the committee do not have a question, then I would dismiss you at this time subject to the right of the subcommittee to recall you if necessary, and at this time you are excused.

MR. HUNSAKER. Thank you, Mr. Chairman.

MR. WHITFIELD. Mr. Gentilucci, I would ask you in the exhibit book to please turn to Exhibit 39. If you all could pass that down to him. You will notice that this is an e-mail dated February the 7th, 2006, addressed to you from Mr. Vince Nye, who I understand worked for you at Hewlett-Packard.

In this e-mail, Mr. Nye states, "I have serious reservations about what we are doing. As I understand Ron's methodology in obtaining this phone record information, it leaves me with the opinion that it is unethical at the least, and probably illegal. If it is not totally illegal, then it is leaving HP in a position that could damage our reputation, or worse. I am requesting that we cease this phone number gathering method immediately, discount any of its information. I think we need to refocus our strategy and proceed on the high ground."

Mr. Gentilucci, despite the ethical and legal concerns expressed to you by Mr. Nye, isn't it true that you continued to utilize pretexting and other suspect tactics to obtain confidential information about HP's employees, Board members and journalists?

MR. GENTILUCCI. Mr. Chairman and other committee members, I understand the Constitution of the United States gives me the right not to be forced to be a witness against myself. And due to other ongoing investigations, I must assert that constitutional right. And I respectfully decline to answer the committee's questions today.

MR. WHITFIELD. So you are asserting yourself Fifth Amendment protection against self-incrimination, and it is your intention to assert that right in any other questions that may be asked of you today?

MR. GENTILUCCI. Yes, Mr. Chairman.

MR. WHITFIELD. If there are no further questions from other members of the committee, then I will dismiss you at this time, subject to the right of the subcommittee to recall you if necessary, and at this time, you are excused.

MR. GENTILUCCI. Thank you.

MR. WHITFIELD. At this time, Mr. DeLia, I would ask for you to please turn to Exhibit 4.

In Exhibit 4, in July of 2005, you e-mailed the report to Patricia Dunn summarizing your findings in the Kona 1 leak investigation.

In this report, you state that telephone subscriber and call registers are obtained verbally from the various telephone carriers and that the investigation into the review of telephone records and the backgrounds of BusinessWeek reporters and HP Board members is continuing.

Mr. DeLia, did you or anyone working for you on behalf of Security Outsourcing Solutions engage in pretexting, namely obtaining access to someone's personal telephone records without their consent through fraud, deceit or misrepresentation, as part of an investigation by the Hewlett-Packard Company into leaks of corporate information during 2005 and 2006?

MR. DELIA. Mr. Chairman, I must respectfully decline to answer your questions based upon the rights afforded to me by the Fifth Amendment of the Constitution of the United States.

MR. WHITFIELD. And is it your intention to assert your Fifth Amendment rights to any further questions to be asked of you today?

MR. DELIA. Yes, Mr. Chairman.

MR. WHITFIELD. If there are no further questions from other members of the committee, then I dismiss you at this time subject to the right of the subcommittee to recall you if necessary, and at this time you are excused.

MR. DELIA. Thank you, Mr. Chairman.

MR. WHITFIELD. Mr. Depante, if you would please turn to Exhibit 109 in the document book. It is the small book, not the large book. There is a small book on the table somewhere. Exhibit 109 is a request for the private phone records of Mr. Robert Knowling submitted to Action Research Group by Security Outsourcing Solutions on July 6, 2005. It appears that you procured Mr. Knowling's detailed calling record through Eye in the Sky Investigations.

Mr. Depante, did you and your company, Action Research Group, obtain and sell to Mr. DeLia, consumers' personal phone records that were obtained through pretexting, lies, deceit or impersonation?

MR. DELIA. Mr. Chairman, on the advice of counsel, I would invoke my Fifth Amendment privilege to decline comment at this time.

MR. WHITFIELD. And it is your intention to assert that right to any additional questions we may have for you?

MR. DELIA. Yes, sir.

MR. WHITFIELD. If there are no further questions from members of the committee, we will dismiss you at this time subject to the right of the committee to recall you if necessary, and at this time, you are excused.

MR. DELIA. Thank you, Mr. Chairman.

MR. WHITFIELD. Ms. Selvage if you also would look at Exhibit 109, this is a request for the private phone records of Mr. Robert Knowling submitted to Action Research Group by Security Outsourcing Solutions on July 6, 2005. The second page of this exhibit is an e-mail you sent from your Eye in the Sky Yahoo e-mail account. In it, you provided Action Research with Mr. Knowling's detailed calling records, which Action Research then passed on to Mr. DeLia.

Ms. Selvage, did you and your company, Eye in the Sky Investigations, obtain and sell to Mr. Depante consumers' personal phone records that you obtained through pretext, lies, deceit or impersonation?

MS. SELVAGE. Mr. Chairman, and members of the committee, I am joined here today by my attorney, Ms. Barbara Van Gelder. I am aware of several ongoing criminal investigations relating to Hewlett-Packard and its security contractors. I am still not aware if I am connected to these investigations, or if so, how.

Given these circumstances and considering the fact that the Fifth Amendment protects innocents who might be ensnared by ambiguous circumstances as this committee's subpoena infers I may be, I accept the advice of my counsel and respectfully decline to answer any questions posed to me today on the basis of the rights guaranteed to me by my Fifth Amendment rights.

MR. WHITFIELD. It is your intention to assert your Fifth Amendment rights for any other questions we may have?

MS. SELVAGE. Yes, sir.

MR. WHITFIELD. If there are no further questions from committee members, then we will dismiss you at this time subject to the right of recall if necessary. And at this time you are excused.

MS. SELVAGE. Thank you, sir.

MR. WHITFIELD. Mr. Brost, if you would turn to Exhibit 107, this is a document from Action Research Group, showing requests made by

Security Outsourcing Solutions to Action Research Group for phone-related records as well as the corresponding completed order.

On page 11 of this exhibit is a handwritten note from you to an Action Research employee providing subscriber information requested by Security Outsourcing Solutions.

Mr. Brost, did you obtain and sell to Mr. Depante consumers' personal phone records that you obtained through pretext, lies, deceit or impersonation?

MR. BROST. Most respectfully, on advice of counsel, I wish to invoke my Fifth Amendment rights.

MR. WHITFIELD. And is it your intention to assert your Fifth Amendment right on any additional questions we may have?

MR. BROST. Yes, Mr. Chairman.

MR. WHITFIELD. If there are no further questions from members of the committee I will dismiss you at this time subject to the right of the Chair to recall you if necessary, and at this time you are excused.

MR. BROST. Thank you.

MR. WHITFIELD. Ms. Preston, if you have the exhibit book and document book, on page 3 of Exhibit 107, this is an e-mail from you to Action Research Group which provides telephone subscriber information requested by Security Outsourcing Solutions. Pages 4 through 7 of that document also contain e-mails in which you provided personal phone records to Action Research.

Ms. Preston, did you and your company, In Search Of, Inc., obtain and sell to Mr. Depante consumers' personal phone records and other phone-related information that you obtained through pretext, lies, deceit or impersonation?

MS. PRESTON. Mr. Chairman, I respectfully invoke my Fifth Amendment right at this time.

MR. WHITFIELD. And is it your intention to assert that right for any additional questions we may have for you?

MS. PRESTON. Yes, sir, at this time.

MR. WHITFIELD. Given that, if there are no further questions from members of the committee, I will dismiss you at this time subject to recall of the Chair if necessary, and at this time, you are excused.

MS. PRESTON. Thank you.

MR. WHITFIELD. Mr. Wagner, if you would please turn to Exhibit 112, this exhibit contains three e-mails that you sent to Action Research Group in February, 2006. The first e-mail includes two pages of Marian Keyworth's detailed personal phone records. The second e-mail includes two pages of detailed phone records for the landline phone at George and Marian Keyworth's home. The third e-mail includes two pages of detailed phone records for the Keyworths' fax machine.

Mr. Wagner, did you obtain and sell to Mr. Depante consumers' personal cell phone records that you obtained through pretext, lies, deceit or impersonation?

MR. WAGNER. Mr. Chairman, I respectfully invoke my Fifth Amendment right.

MR. WHITFIELD. And is it your intention to assert that right for any additional questions we may have for you?

MR. WAGNER. Mr. Chairman, I feel I have information that could help the subcommittee in their quest to make this illegal, but there are certain questions that I would not want to answer of course.

MR. WHITFIELD. But you are asserting your legal right, your Fifth Amendment right, for all the questions we may ask today?

MR. WAGNER. Yes, Mr. Chairman.

MR. WHITFIELD. If there are no further questions from Members of the Committee we will dismiss you.

CHAIRMAN BARTON. Mr. Chairman, before we let this witness go, would you inform the subcommittee of who the Keyworths are, since you asked the question.

MR. WHITFIELD. Yes, well, Mr. Keyworth was a member of the Board of Directors of Hewlett-Packard.

CHAIRMAN BARTON. And he is the one I understand who is alleged to have leaked the information?

MR. WHITFIELD. That's true.

And so are you asserting your Fifth Amendment right?

MR. WAGNER. Yes, Mr. Chairman.

MR. WHITFIELD. If there are no additional questions from Members of the Committee then we will dismiss you at this time subject to the right of the subcommittee to recall you if necessary. And at this time you are excused.

MR. WAGNER. Thank you, Mr. Chairman.

MR. WHITFIELD. Mr. Kelly. If you would please turn to Exhibit 111. This is an e-mail that you sent to Action Research Group in January 2006. The e-mail includes 3 pages of Dawn Kawamoto's detailed phone records for the entire month of January. And I believe that Dawn is a reporter for CNET News.

Now, Mr. Kelly, did you and your company, CAS Agency, obtain and sell to Mr. Depante consumers' personal phone records that you obtained through pretexting, lies, deceit or impersonation?

MR. KELLY. Mr. Chairman, I respectfully invoke my Fifth Amendment privilege to decline comment at this time.

MR. WHITFIELD. And is it your intention to assert your Fifth Amendment rights for any additional questions we may have today?

MR. KELLY. Yes, sir.

MR. WHITFIELD. If there are no further questions from members of the committee, I will dismiss you at this time subject to the right of the subcommittee to recall you if necessary, and at this time you are excused.

MR. KELLY. Thank you.

CHAIRMAN BARTON. Mr. Chairman?

MR. WHITFIELD. Yes, Mr. Chairman.

CHAIRMAN BARTON. I have been on the committee for 20 years, and I have been on this subcommittee for over half that time. I have never had a hearing where no witness gave an opening statement, where every witness took the Fifth. It is odd to me that a practice, that every one of the individuals just before us has in various forms indicated was totally legal, has invoked their Fifth Amendment right against self-incrimination.

MS. DEGETTE. Will the Chairman yield?

CHAIRMAN BARTON. I would.

MS. DEGETTE. I agree with the Chairman and as a former lawyer myself, I cherish the right of witnesses to invoke their Fifth Amendment right against self-incrimination. It is one of our important constitutional provisions.

But it is very difficult for us in Congress to have an investigation where all the witnesses come in, and at the very last minute, inform the committee that they are invoking their Fifth Amendment rights. It becomes almost the routine rather than the exception.

And while I, in the corporate responsibility hearings, for example, I felt that there were many, many witnesses, some of whom are now in Federal prison, who should have invoked their constitutional rights; in this case, I would have to agree with the Chairman.

And furthermore I would say, I know it is not our staff's faults, but when you haul in a whole panel of people like this just to have them take the Fifth Amendment, I think it is a waste of the committee's time and resources, and I think it is a waste of the witnesses' time and resources and legal fees. I would hope we would work with witnesses in the future to prevent this kind of action.

CHAIRMAN BARTON. Reclaiming my time, until this morning indications were that only two individuals were going to take the Fifth Amendment.

MS. DEGETTE. That is exactly what I am saying, Mr. Chairman.

CHAIRMAN BARTON. Which they have the right to do, and Mr. Chairman, I would encourage you to work with the Ranking Member of this subcommittee, the information that has been put together in preparation for this hearing is very important. And I would encourage you to work with the Minority to make it available, the proper format to the general public and to law enforcement authorities that are pursuing this case in other venues, because both staffs have worked very hard to prepare for this hearing.

We have got voluminous information that I think is accurate and true information. And if we are going to put a stake through the heart of pretexting, we need to inform the public and make available the information that we have obtained, about just how prevalent it is and how obnoxious it is.

MR. WHITFIELD. Thank you, Mr. Chairman. It is certainly our intent to do that, and it has been stated before by many of our members of the subcommittee and the full committee that it is our desire to move this pretexting legislation we reported out, and hopefully, we can do that.

At this time, I would like to call to the witness table the second panel and on the second panel, we have Ms. Patricia Dunn, who is the former Chairman of the Board of Hewlett-Packard Company, Palo Alto, California. We have Mr. Larry Sonsini, who is the Chairman of Wilson Sonsini Goodrich & Rosati from Palo Alto, California. And we have Mr. Fred Adler, who is with IT Security Investigations at Hewlett-Packard in Palo Alto, California.

I want to welcome you all to the witness table.

TESTIMONY OF PATRICIA DUNN, FORMER CHAIRMAN, OF THE BOARD, HEWLETT-PACKARD COMPANY; LARRY SONSINI, CHAIRMAN, WILSON SONSINI GOODRICH & ROSATI; AND FRED ADLER, IT SECURITY INVESTIGATIONS, HEWLETT-PACKARD COMPANY

MR. WHITFIELD. We appreciate very much you all being with us this morning, and as you heard in my remarks to the earlier panel, Oversight and Investigations, our subcommittee, does take testimony under oath and, I am assuming that none of you have any difficulty or objection to testifying under oath.

MR. SONSINI. No objection.

MS. DUNN. No, sir.

[Witnesses sworn.]

MR. WHITFIELD. Thank you very much. You are now under oath, and you also understand that it is the rules of the committee and the House that you are entitled to legal counsel. And Ms. Dunn, I would ask you, do you have legal counsel with you this morning.

MS. DUNN. Yes, I do, Mr. Jim Brosnahan. He is here this morning.

MR. WHITFIELD. Thank you. And Mr. Sonsini, I know you are an attorney, but do you have legal counsel with you this morning?

MR. SONSINI. Yes, I do. My counsel is Mr. Evan Chesler.

MR. WHITFIELD. And Mr. Adler, do you have legal counsel request with you this morning?

MR. ALDER. Yes, I do. It is Mr. Malcolm Segal seated directly behind me.

MR. WHITFIELD. Well, thank you very much for, as I said, being with us and introducing your counsel, and at this time, Ms. Dunn, we will recognize you for 5 minutes for your opening statement.

MS. DUNN. Thank you, Mr. Chairman and other distinguished members of this committee, I do appreciate the opportunity to appear before you today.

All corporate directors have a solemn duty of confidentiality to their fellow directors and to the shareholders they serve. Boardroom leaks create unfair advantages for some shareholders over others because stock prices can move on the unauthorized disclosure of information.

Leaks corrode the trust that is fundamental to Board functioning and expose companies to regulatory sanction under the fair disclosure rules of the SEC. When the HP Board asked me to accept the position of Nonexecutive Chairman early last year, I expected challenges. But I never anticipated that the circumstances currently surrounding HP could ever occur.

One of the first challenges I faced came from requests made by directors to continue efforts to identify the source, or sources of leaks that were undermining the Board's functioning.

I took this mandate seriously, because the leaks touched the very heart of the company's most sensitive issues.

As detailed in my written testimony, I sought the advice of Bob Wayman, the company's CFO and then acting CEO, whom I respect greatly. He was the logical person to consult because all of HP's control functions, including its legal and security groups, reported to him.

He referred me to Kevin Huska, who had responsibility for global security who, in turn, referred me to Mr. Ron DeLia, about which I have explained in detail in my written testimony.

In my two or three conversations with Mr. DeLia over the ensuing weeks and months, I learned that checking telephone records was a standard investigative technique at HP, and that they were drawn from publicly available sources.

The first leak investigation from April to August 2005 failed to identify those responsible, but major new leaks occurred in January, 2006. These involved another publicly traded company, CSC, whose stock price may have been impacted by as much as 8 percent.

This raised the possibility of securities law violations. Mr. Hurd and I concurred that a renewed investigation was in order. Ms. Baskins advised on this matter from the start. I recommended that the company use an outside firm such as Kroll Associates to perform the investigation. However, Ms. Baskins felt strongly that the investigation should be performed by Kevin Hunsaker, who reported to her and who had responsibility for business conduct and ethics investigations.

Mr. Hunsaker brought in the same underlying investigative team, including Mr. DeLia, in the second investigation as had been used in the first when Mr. Huska was involved.

His final draft report was distributed to me and Mr. Hurd in mid-March.

Throughout the process, as detailed in my written testimony, I requested and received assurance that the investigation was being performed in the HP standard way, legally, and properly. That this was the case was reiterated in Mr. Hunsaker's final report.

In April, the report was reviewed by Mr. Sonsini and the Chairman of the Board's Audit Committee, who presented a summary of the report, which identified the director responsible for the leaks to the Board in May.

In late June, I became aware from Mr. Sonsini that former director Tom Perkins had raised concerns with him about the investigation a month or so after he had resigned from the HP Board. Mr. Sonsini attempted to allay Mr. Perkins' concerns after consultation with Ms. Baskins, concluding, in a January 28th e-mail that "the process was well done and within legal limits."

In late August, 2006, Mr. Sonsini advised the Board that its techniques were "not generally unlawful."

I am neither a lawyer nor an investigator, and in this matter, I relied on the expertise of people in whom I had full confidence based upon their positions with the company and my years of experience in working with them.

I deeply regret that so many people, including me, were badly let down by this reliance.

I would like you to know that I was a full subject of this investigation and I too was pretexted.

Based on my experience, I hope that Congress will help companies like HP and people who find themselves in my position, as well as the targets of investigations, by establishing bright line laws in this area.

In addition to protecting privacy, I hope that Congress enacts legislation to help companies protect themselves from threats arising from serious or repeated breaches of confidentiality through sanctioned legal means perhaps through investigations that can be conducted by the SEC.

I appreciate the opportunity to appear before you and I look forward to your questions.

[The prepared statement of Patricia Dunn follows:]

PREPARED STATEMENT OF PATRICIA DUNN, FORMER CHAIRMAN OF THE BOARD, HEWLETT-PACKARD COMPANY

Submission to Sub-Committee on Investigations
House Energy and Commerce Committee

My Role in the Hewlett-Packard Leak Investigation

Patricia C. Dunn

I. Why a Leak Investigation Was Necessary

When I was asked by Hewlett-Packard Company's Board to accept the newly-created position of Non-Executive Chairman in the wake of Carly Fiorina's resignation as Chairman and CEO, I was surprised and honored. Becoming Chairman was a position I neither sought nor expected, but I respected the Board's decision to split the roles of Chairman and CEO, and I agreed with their assessment that someone needed to step forward and represent the Board during a critical time. Certainly I expected there would be challenges in carrying out the important new responsibilities I was asked to undertake, but never in my worst nightmare did I anticipate that the circumstances currently surrounding HP could ever occur.

It is now well reported that the HP Board, particularly as it was constituted in the first year or so of my chairmanship, was beset by considerable conflict among directors. I was cognizant of those conflicts because I heard about them from nearly all sides. Among the most corrosive issues dividing directors was fundamental distrust driven by the fact that the Board's most sensitive discussions kept ending up in the newspapers. These concerns were brought to a head when directors read, on January 24, 2005, on page one of the Wall Street Journal, the most sensitive details of discussions from its off-site strategy meeting the prior week—including aspects of those discussions that were known only to the Board.

Not surprisingly, given this breakdown of boardroom sanctity and continued disclosures of Board-level information making their way into print over the ensuing weeks, many directors expressed to me their strong opinion that something had to be done to determine their source and bring them to an end. In fact, the majority of directors told me during my first few weeks as Chairman that, next to leading the Board's CEO search, coming to grips with HP's famously leaky Board should be my top priority. They were particularly disturbed because Carly Fiorina's attempt to do this in January, 2005, through interviews conducted by outside counsel, had come to naught. Thus, directors knew that whoever was talking to the press was unwilling to come forward to make a clean breast of the matter. This served only to deepen mutual distrust. Identifying the source of leaks on the HP Board was seen by many directors as "unfinished business" from Ms. Fiorina's tenure as Chairman.

Before explaining what I did in response to this priority as set by my fellow directors, it is important to point out that many supposedly sophisticated business commentators are astonishingly insensitive to the seriousness of the problem the Board faced. Comments ranging from, "Isn't it okay for directors to leak if they think it's for the benefit of the company?", to "What's the big deal? Did any of the leaks actually harm the company?", to "You can't stop leaking and what happened at HP shows why you shouldn't even try," reflect profound ignorance of board functioning and fiduciary responsibility.

The most fundamental duties of a director—the duties of deliberation and candor—rely entirely upon the absolute trust that each director must have in one another's confidentiality. This is true for trivial as well as important matters, because even trivial information that finds its way from the boardroom to the press corrodes trust among directors. It is even more critical when discussions can affect stock prices, as did with one of the leaks that HP suffered in January, 2006. While I wish fervently that none of this had ever happened, had undisciplined communications with the press continued and a major violation of securities regulations ensued, HP's Chairman would have been justifiably criticized by the Board and beyond for not having taken their concerns seriously enough.

The most sensitive aspects of a company's business come before its board: strategy; executive succession; acquisitions; business plans; product development; and key supplier relations. This is exactly the type of information a company's competitors and those who trade in its stock would love to have before that information becomes public. Boards have an unquestionable obligation to take appropriate steps to prevent this happening. That certain steps taken during the investigation went well beyond what was appropriate does not undermine the importance of the Board's mission in this matter.

For those still questioning the seriousness of HP's leaks, bear in mind that these disclosures touched the very heart of the Company's most sensitive issues. What could be more private than a Board's discussion of its varied opinions about its CEO, the company's performance, how the company should be organized and who should hold what responsibilities? Those subjects and more were the focus of the January 24, 2005 Wall Street Journal article.

Or consider how damaging it was that one or more directors almost certainly spoke to Business Week during the most sensitive phase of the Company's efforts to recruit a new CEO, disclosing opinions about various candidates and revealing details about the timing and conduct of the search process. If you were a top CEO candidate, would you want to work for a Company whose Board could not be trusted to keep such information confidential? In my view, HP is very lucky that it was able to recruit a candidate of Mark Hurd's caliber under such circumstances.

Furthermore, how does a Board function when management has to worry that directors may purposely or indiscreetly reveal important information inappropriately? This happened at Hewlett-Packard, and management's concerns could easily have compromised the necessary flow of information to the Board as a result.

It does not matter whether one believes that the information one discloses to the press, as a director, was intended to benefit the Company. Leaking "good" information is as unacceptable as leaking "bad" information—no one can foretell how such information may advantage or disadvantage one investor relative to another. This is why companies have such elaborate rules around confidentiality and disclosure, and why regulators have made fair disclosure such a focus of their efforts over the last years.

At Hewlett-Packard, all directors, officers and employees are bound by the same Standards of Business Conduct, to which each individual attests compliance annually. There are several sections of the code applying to confidentiality, including one that says, "You may not grant interviews or provide comments to the press without prior approval from HP Corporate Communications. Unless you receive other guidance from HP Corporate Communications, you are expected to decline the opportunity to respond to any inquiries for news or information about HP and refer the request to the appropriate HP spokesperson."

Anyone serving as an HP director who operated beyond this boundary violated the Company's Standards of Business Conduct. Repeated reminders to directors about confidentiality did not stop the behavior. Informing directors, as I did on multiple occasions, that a leak investigation was underway did not stop the behavior. Expecting the responsible party to come forward to spare the Company the expense and potential disruption of a leak investigation did not stop the behavior. Even an attempt by HP's CEO to encourage a confession during a one-on-one conversation with the responsible party in mid-March, just before the investigative report was issued, was unsuccessful.

II. The Leak Investigation

I believed that Hewlett-Packard directors were justifiably concerned about the risks posed by leaks from the Board, and knew they had delegated to me the responsibility to do something more than expect the leaker or leakers to come forward to stop the problem. I look forward to my appearance before Congress to tell you as best I can what happened. The following provides the basics.

A. I Was Referred to the Investigator Who Was Under Contract to Hewlett-Packard's Global Security Group

There was no guidebook or policy to assist the Board or its Chairman in dealing with the problem of unauthorized disclosure of confidential information. However, there was one director on the Board who had overall responsibility for the ways in which HP handled such matters on an ongoing basis. A company like HP frequently suffers unauthorized disclosures of confidential information and, to protect shareholders, must seek to identify their sources and deal with them appropriately. I therefore asked HP's then acting CEO, CFO and Director of

Administration, Bob Wayman, for his advice in responding to requests by Board members that I take affirmative action on the problem of leaks. It is worth noting that he himself, as a director and top executive, was as concerned as anyone about the problem of leaks.

Mr. Wayman is one of the longest-serving and most trusted executives at Hewlett-Packard, and one of the most respected CFOs in Corporate America. He had also served as a director of HP for many years, and was re-appointed to the Board in February, 2005. At HP, his span of authority included, at the time I consulted him in February and March of 2005, the Internal Audit function, the General Counsel's Office, Real Estate/Workplace Services & Security, and Risk Management, as well as all the typical functions reporting to the CFO, such as Treasury, Tax and Global Controllership.

I knew from working directly with a number of Mr. Wayman's top executives over many years, individuals such as the Company's General Counsel, Global Controller, and Head of Internal Audit, that people in Mr. Wayman's areas of responsibility were unquestionable for their commitment to "doing the right thing." I was impressed time and again with the integrity and high ethics of all those on his staff. As a member and Chairman of the Audit Committee for several years, I had ample opportunity to observe Mr. Wayman and key members of his staff very closely, and I knew of their unwavering commitment to strong controls, good disclosure, and thoroughness in all their undertakings.

I was also continually impressed with the level of teamwork among Mr. Wayman's key reports. It was a source of general comfort to me, as a director, that, regardless of whether key issues arose through the Global Controller, the General Counsel or the Head of Internal Audit, all were remarkably familiar with one another's priorities and issues. I found this to be a signal of a healthy, risk-management oriented culture, which was all the more impressive given the size and scope of the responsibilities carried by these individuals in a huge global company like HP. Based on this experience, I had every reason to rely upon Mr. Wayman's recommendations as to how the security issues at the Board level—which is how the leaks were defined during the first phase of the ensuing investigation—could best be handled given that all of the control functions of the Company were under his oversight.

Mr. Wayman referred me to an individual within his organization, Kevin Huska, who was introduced to me as having responsibility for Global Security at HP. I had a brief meeting with Mr. Huska around February or March 2005. We met near the CFO's office at HP's headquarters. Mr. Huska explained to me that the Company dealt day-in and day-out with violations of its Standards of Business Conduct related to unauthorized disclosure of confidential information, and that it had experienced resources at hand to deal with the problem. He seemed to understand the sensitivity and seriousness of the problem, and I had the clear impression that Mr. Huska had been briefed about why I had been referred to him. Mr. Huska told me that, if I wanted to pursue an investigation following the normal processes used by the Company, I should talk with Mr. Ron Delia, who was responsible for designing and implementing investigations involving breaches of confidential information on behalf of Hewlett-Packard. By late March (for reasons explained below), it seemed to me that Mr. Delia operated what was in effect a "captive subsidiary." By that time, I had come to understand that he worked almost exclusively for HP, which only served to increase my confidence that he would be a reliable and trustworthy agent to undertake its sensitive investigative work.

B. Mr. Delia Was Under Contract to HP When the Leak Investigation Was Undertaken

I did not "hire" the private investigators who were involved in the Kona 1 (or Kona 2) investigations. They were already under contract to HP when the leak investigation was initiated. I initiated the investigation, in response to directors who urged me to take more serious action in response to leaks. I turned to resources that HP normally used to do this type of work. The fact that these resources included an outside supplier was, in my mind, simply an artifact of the way in which the company had chosen to arrange its activities in this area. I later learned that Mr. Delia had worked in this fashion for HP for eight or nine years, so I continued to have no reason to doubt the quality of his work.

I was a director of the company, not an officer or employee, and had no authority to enter into contracts, approve invoices, or handle any similar matters. It was my assumption that Mr. Wayman, having ultimate authority over all the resources involved in security and investigations, as well as having been one of the directors who felt the most strongly about the importance of controlling leaks from the Board, had provided authorization for whatever work was undertaken. I learned in late August 2006 that the work done by Mr. Delia in "Kona 1" was authorized—by whom I do not know specifically—as an extension to a pre-existing work order under which he was performing various investigative assignments for Hewlett-Packard.

In addition to the comfort I took from being referred to Mr. Delia from within Mr. Wayman's organization, I learned in late March 2005 that he also performed sensitive work for HP's Human Resources Department. As the search for HP's new CEO was heading toward completion, both the executive search consultant engaged by HP, Andrea Redmond of Russell Reynolds, and HP's Global Head of Human Resources, Marcela Perez de Alonso, pointed out to me that every company conducts background checks on top executives before extending final offers. Ms. Redmond explained that this was not work that search consultants do on behalf of their clients, but that companies themselves undertake. Ms. Perez de Alonso confirmed this was a routine step that the Company took responsibility for performing before committing to hire executives above a certain level.

Ms. Perez de Alonso therefore put the background check in motion in the middle of March 2005 for Mark Hurd, knowing from me that he was emerging as the Board's top candidate. I contacted Ms. Perez de Alonso in the third week of March to find out if the background check was complete because I needed to report to the Board urgently on any concerns that arose. The Board unofficially decided to make an offer to Mr. Hurd on March 23 or March 24. On March 23, Ms. Perez de Alonso referred me to Mr. Delia for a verbal report in advance of his written report, which she explained to me would not be complete for several more days. I therefore spoke to Mr. Delia on March 23.

In the March 23 conversation, my notes indicate that Mr. Delia made it clear that all of the information upon which his background check was based was drawn from publicly available sources, and that one area in which I expressed interest, which was whether there were any medical issues that could interfere with Mr. Hurd's ability to carry out his responsibilities, could only be obtained upon the issuance of a court order. This seemed reasonable and right to me, and served to give me the impression that Mr. Delia conducted his business in the fully above-board manner that I would expect of any long-time employee or contractor to HP.

C. The "Kona 1" Investigation: Supervision and Conduct

When the work that eventually was termed "Project Kona" got under way, I did not at any point consider myself its "supervisor." I assumed that, given how all the control elements of HP's global functions came together under Mr. Wayman, an appropriate person such as Mr. Huska was directing the work as necessary. I expected to be kept abreast of the progress of the investigations and to respond to inquiry by those in charge of the investigation as necessary for them to conduct the work. I recall that Mr. Huska had told me that it was standard practice in company investigations that the individual who was trying to solve the problem on behalf of the business—in this case on behalf of the Board—had to provide input to the investigators and answer their questions along the way. This was consistent with my experience as an executive.

I had intermittent contact with Mr. Delia via telephone and email in the spring and early summer of 2005 during Kona 1. My attitude and approach was to try to be helpful to the smooth conduct of the investigation. As a matter of course, I asked Mr. Delia at every point of contact for his representation that everything being done was proper, legal and fully in compliance with HP's normal practices. I did this because it is the role of directors to ask questions and seek such representations from the right people. Indeed, reliance on representations from trusted sources is a bedrock concept in board governance for the express reason that directors cannot directly supervise management's actions.

At some point during the late spring of 2005, I became aware from Mr. Delia that phone records were accessed as a standard component of such investigations by HP. The clear impression I had from Mr. Delia was that such records could be obtained from publicly available sources in a legal and appropriate manner, and that this was just one of several methods that would be pursued in the investigation. I now believe that not only I, but all of the executives upon whom I relied at HP, whose integrity I have never questioned to this day, were similarly confident that these records were accessed under fully legal circumstances.

I informed the Board at its March 2005 meeting that a leak investigation in response to their concerns had been initiated. I explained, as had been explained to me that, due to its very nature, those being investigated—including me—could not know the details of how the investigation was being conducted. It had been explained to me that to do so would compromise the effectiveness of the investigation, which made sense to me.

I updated the Board at its normal July 2005 meeting that the leak investigation was still underway and had yielded no results. I also assured them that I was a full subject of the investigation. I recall informing the Board at its normal September 2005 meeting that the investigation was slowing down.

No director questioned me in Board session or privately about concerns regarding how the investigation was being conducted. I had the clear impression that they were satisfied that I had taken their priority seriously and that they fully expected whatever was being done would be done properly.

As Kona 1 progressed, I wanted to obtain greater comfort that the best people at HP were overseeing the investigation. My notes indicate that, in addition to some conversation with Ann Baskins and/or Mark Hurd on April 19, 2005, I noted on June 20, 2005, "Ann—Ron Delia follow-up." This indicates to me that by the mid-point of the project, I had reached out to Ann Baskins regarding the investigation. My notes also indicate that on the same day, June 20, 2005, I discussed the investigation with Mark Hurd, informing him I had been told that results from the investigation were "a week to ten days away/some gaps remain." I also noted "Confidentiality/Kroll," which refers to a question I had about whether the people doing the investigation were top-notch, particularly given that the investigation was inconclusive at that point. I never doubted, however, that what they were doing was legal.

I would like to note that, among all the executives with whom I have come in contact at HP, no one rates higher in my estimation than Ann Baskins for her commitment to ethics, integrity and doing the right thing for Hewlett-Packard every step of the way. I began to seek her involvement in the early summer of 2005. Similarly, Mark Hurd knew that boardroom leaks were a problem at HP, and he made it clear he was a "hawk" on the matter within his own executive team. He also made it clear to me that he found the idea of directors talking out of turn to the press to be reprehensible. At some point, apparently at least by April 20, 2005, I informed him there was an investigation underway that pre-dated his arrival on March 30. (I have found Mark Hurd to be among the most straightforward, clear-thinking and honorable executives with whom I have ever come in contact. Time and again I have heard him refer to his conscience and his ethics as driving his priorities, and I have seen him behave accordingly.)

By some time in August 2005, I was informed that the investigation had come to a stopping point. I do not recall a point where anyone informed me that Project Kona was ended, but I do recall knowing at some point that it had failed to produce results. By this time, no significant leaks from the boardroom had occurred for several months, and I hoped that simply the knowledge of an investigation had brought them to a halt. I did not take any steps to encourage the investigation to continue at that time.[1]

---

[1] I hope the Committee will bear in mind that, through this period, as important as this work was, it was far from being a major focus of my attention. For example, focusing on my work with HP alone, I was much more occupied with initiating and carrying out a

The Board advised me on August 31, 2006, after hearing the results of its outside counsel's (Wilson Sonsini Goodrich & Rosati) review of the entire investigation, that during Kona 1 I did not have sufficient support from internal or external counsel. It was explained to me by Mr. Sonsini that the Board felt that perhaps not one chairman in ten would have had the insight under the circumstances to bring in outside counsel. (I note, however, that the same individuals who were involved with Kona 1, in the chain from me to Mr. Wayman to Mr. Huska, were involved when the chain went from me to Ms. Baskins to Kevin Hunsaker in "Kona 2," as further explained below.)

D. The "Kona 2" Investigation: Supervision and Conduct

From January 19 to 21, 2006, the HP Board held its annual Strategy Board meeting in Palm Springs, California. Soon after, on or about January 24, 2006, I was informed via email from Bob Sherbin, head of HP's Public Relations Department, that there had been a major leak emanating from the off-site strategy meeting, which appeared on CNET, a widely read online technology-oriented publication, the prior day. I informed the Board immediately and received several emails expressing concern and outrage from various directors. I was asked by

---

project to overhaul the Board's governance processes, including all the documentation supporting its policies, corporate governance guidelines, and committee charters, for which I retained a governance expert (again with Board encouragement). As important as it was, Kona 1 occupied a very small proportion of my time between March and August 2005.

several if the leak investigation was still ongoing and I said I would see to it that it was re-initiated.

The CNET leaks of January 23, 2006, were serious. They referred to the most sensitive commercial relationships of the Company and its plans for those relationships (i.e., Intel and AMD, HP's micro-processor suppliers); they referred to potential acquisitions in a very concentrated part of the public markets for infrastructure software companies; they confirmed the Company's plans to target a key competitor by name in the printing business (Heidelberg Press); and they discussed the Company's plans for branding its key new offering in the enterprise computing business. A separate article on the same day referred to discussions that the Company was having with a potential acquisition target, CSC Corporation.

These are the kinds of leaks that not only exposed the Company's most intimate discussions and corroded trust in the boardroom, but exposed HP to potential violations of securities laws. I realized that the investigation needed to be re-initiated, and I had the full support of the CEO—who, unlike during Kona 1, was by then on board and well-established in his role—and the General Counsel in making this decision.

At the inception of Kona 2, I again suggested, this time to Ann Baskins, that Kroll Associates be considered to conduct the investigation. I knew of them only by reputation and thought a highly regarded outside organization might be more successful in this matter. Ms. Baskins said that, rather than go outside HP, she recommended turning the investigation over to Kevin Hunsaker, whom she described as having responsibility in the legal department for overseeing investigation into standards of business conduct. He reported directly to her. I had never heard of Mr. Hunsaker, but his title and her strong positive opinion of his work were very reassuring to me; thus I concurred with her recommendation.

The Kona 2 investigation lasted from late January 2006 to March 2006. Mr. Hunsaker supervised the project, reporting to General Counsel Ann Baskins. I thought this was an excellent arrangement and a stronger process was being employed relative to Kona 1. Mr. Hunsaker's ultimate report on the investigation specifies who was on the investigation team. I was not named as among them.

Mr. Hunsaker contacted me directly several times for guidance in the investigation, but I believe that almost all these contacts included Ann Baskins. A weekly project conference call was set up on Friday afternoons so that Ann and I could be brought up on any progress and I could answer questions as appropriate on the Board's concerns, motivations, etc. I participated in perhaps two-thirds of those calls. It was not surprising to me that the same individuals who had been brought in to do the actual investigation—Messrs. Delia and Tony Gentilucci, the latter of whose involvement I had been made aware of some time during Kona 1—were doing the underlying work once again.

Once again I was told that phone records were one of the key techniques being used in the investigation, along with "relationship mapping" and what struck me as old-fashioned detective work. I did not find it objectionable that suspected leakers might be followed to see if they were meeting with reporters.

My views of the phone-record access were the same in early 2006 as in mid-2005: I was fully convinced that HP would never engage in anything illegal, and the privacy issues related to our directors were balanced in my mind against their eagerness to get to the bottom of the problem. Indeed, given that attorneys were unambiguously overseeing the investigation in Kona 2 and were following similar practices as in Kona 1 reinforced my understanding that the investigations had been and were being handled appropriately. (It may be interesting to note that, after the HP leak scandal broke, the Associated Press polled 226 public company directors about their attitudes concerning personal privacy versus confidentiality in the boardroom. According to press reports, 85% of responding directors said they "placed a higher priority on corporate confidentiality than shielding their personal information from prying eyes." The pollster involved commented that it appears company directors have a different view from the general public on this matter.)

By the time Kona 2 was in full swing, Mr. Hurd was more aware than in Kona 1 of its activities. He was included in perhaps two or three meetings, to my knowledge, to review key milestones and provide his own input on the priority and motivations behind the investigation. Neither Mr. Hurd nor I designed or implemented the investigative techniques. However, we both were made aware of a "sting" operation that the investigators proposed in early February for the purpose of determining whether the CNET reporter to whom Mr. Keyworth was suspected of talking—and by then the investigative team had narrowed its hypothesis about the identity of the leaker to him—was in contact with Mr. Keyworth. I was contacted by Mr. Hunsaker, with Ms. Baskins in the loop on the communication, about this. Having asked for and received all needed assurances that this was a legal and common investigative technique, I referred them to Mr. Hurd for the final decision.

On March 11, Mr. Hunsaker's draft report on the leak investigation was issued to Mr. Hurd, Ms. Baskins, and me. A meeting was arranged by Mr. Hunsaker for the three of us to meet with the investigative team, including Mr. Delia and Mr. Hunsaker, on or about March 15 in Los Angeles, where the Company was holding a Board meeting in conjunction with its Annual Shareholder's Meeting. The report emphasized the lawful nature of the procedures, which was unsurprising to me, given that Mr. Hunsaker and Ms. Baskins had provided assurances for their own purposes as well as for my own and Mr. Hurd's that this was the case. The meeting in Los Angeles focused almost entirely on the conclusions of the investigations and not on its tactics.

Mr. Hurd met with Mr. Keyworth on the evening of the day that the above meeting with the investigative team took place. He has related many times to me and to others that he tried in every way he could to get Mr. Keyworth to come forward and admit his culpability. Ms. Baskins and I were sitting near them during this meeting, which occurred over cocktails in the hotel lobby, and I could see that Mr. Hurd was intensely engaged with Mr. Keyworth. Mr. Hurd subsequently described to me, to Ms. Baskins and to others that, though he gave Mr. Keyworth several chances to come forward, Mr. Keyworth declined to acknowledge his culpability.

III. The Leak Matter Comes Before the HP Board

Mr. Hurd, Ms. Baskins and I had several telephone, email and in-person exchanges in the following month to determine the best way to take the matter forward. I informed them that Mr. Perkins—whom I had informed more closely than any other director about the leak investigation given his role as Chairman of the Nominating & Governance Committee—had begun pressuring me during Kona 1 that we should not bring the identity of the leaker, if found, to the full Board. This was seen by all of us as very sensitive because Mr. Keyworth and Mr. Perkins described themselves as best friends, and were close allies on the HP Board. I explained to Mr. Hurd and Ms. Baskins that it was Mr. Perkins' strong view that the two of us should privately seek a confession from the leaker, and a promise never to do so again, at which point we would simply inform the Board that the investigation was closed, the leaker had confessed, and the matter was therefore permanently behind us without ever disclosing his or her identity.

Mr. Hurd and Ms. Baskins were as uncomfortable with Mr. Perkins' proposed process as was I. We met with HP's outside counsel, Larry Sonsini, on April 19 to discuss the matter. Having defined the matter at its essence from the beginning as a Standards of Business Conduct violation, we decided it was appropriate to involve Bob Ryan, the Chairman of the Audit Committee, in determining the right way forward. Ms. Baskins thus sent Mr. Ryan a copy of Mr. Hunsaker's draft report on April 24 at my request.

On April 27, Messrs. Hurd, Ryan, Sonsini, Ms. Baskins and I met in person at HP to discuss the best way to take the matter forward. I explained again the strength of Mr. Perkins' view that the Board should never know the identity of the leaker. Mr. Sonsini and Ms. Baskins advised us that such a "behind the scenes" process was improper, and that the full Board should be given the opportunity to deliberate on the investigation's findings and determine the right course of action to take concerning Mr. Keyworth.

In preparation for a regular HP Board meeting on May 18, 2006, Mr. Ryan worked directly with Ms. Baskins in preparing a summary of the Hunsaker report for the Board. His summary was aimed at focusing on the results of the report and helping the Board decide any appropriate actions to be taken as a result. At this point, I was relieved to have this matter completed and in the hands of the right individual for any further action.

In order to finalize the report, it was determined through consultation among Messrs. Hurd, Sonsini, Ryan and Ms. Baskins and me, that Mr. Ryan should interview Mr. Keyworth the evening before the Board meeting scheduled for May 18. It was further determined among us that I would inform Mr. Perkins on the morning of that meeting that the investigation was complete, that Mr. Keyworth had been identified, and that the matter was being brought to the full Board.

Mr. Ryan reported to the above-named group after his interview with Mr. Keyworth that Mr. Keyworth's immediate response to hearing the investigation's results was to admit he was the leaker, followed by the question, "Why didn't you just ask me?" All of us were flummoxed by this response, as it was clear to us all that for the prior 15 months Mr. Keyworth could have come forward at any time to acknowledge his culpability.

On the morning of May 18, I informed Mr. Perkins that the investigation was complete and that Mr. Keyworth had admitted his culpability. His reaction comforted me because he said, "Pattie, you had to do this investigation. It's too bad Jay has created this problem." He did not seem surprised that Mr. Keyworth had been identified. I told him that the full Board needed to hear the results, and he said he understood. Thus, I entered the Board meeting on May 18 thinking that we could get through this painful matter with a minimum of disruption.

The matter was taken up by the Board as its first item. I introduced the subject, reminded the Board that leak investigations had been underway for over a year, and said that Mr. Ryan would present its findings to them. Mr. Ryan presented his summary of the Hunsaker report without identifying the leaker, as had been requested by another director (not Mr. Perkins) at the start of his presentation in order for the Board to deliberate based on the facts and not upon personalities or relationships. Mr. Ryan ultimately identified Mr. Keyworth after a significant amount of deliberation had taken place.

Mr. Keyworth was asked by the Board to explain himself. He did not apologize in a way that convinced the Board that he understood the gravity of the matter, and he was asked to recuse himself while the Board deliberated. Mr. Ryan conducted this part of the meeting; I did not take an active part in the deliberations except to offer my own views, as a director and not as Chairman, just as every director was asked to do. My views were among the last to be heard.

Mr. Perkins became very agitated when it became clear that a majority of the Board did not think Mr. Keyworth had handled his response to the Board appropriately and thus were leaning strongly toward asking for his resignation. A secret ballot, suggested by another director, was taken, in which a strong majority of the Board voted to ask Mr. Keyworth to resign, which later in the meeting he refused to do. At that point Mr. Perkins erupted in great anger.

Mr. Perkins' anger was directed entirely at me, and centered on the "betrayal" he alleged at my not having abided by an agreement that he said we had to cover-up the name of the leaker. I had little opportunity to respond to his outburst except to say, "Tom, we had no such agreement." He discussed how a talented HP executive a few years earlier had been asked to resign because of an ethics violation, and how he thought it was wrong for Ms. Fiorina to bring such a matter to the Board because they had no choice but to advise her that he leave the company.

At no time during Mr. Perkins' outburst did he make any statements whatsoever about the leak investigation—including its justification or its methods.

Mr. Perkins told the Board he resigned and he left the room, at which point a director put a motion on the table to accept his resignation, which was then seconded and carried unanimously.

Mr. Sonsini then was asked to talk to Mr. Perkins about the reasons for his resignation. He reported back to the Board on May 18 that Mr. Perkins told him he had no disagreement with Hewlett-Packard as a company or its Board, but he had a disagreement with me personally because I "betrayed" him. The Board was not in the habit of reviewing the details of the Company's 8-K filings before the fact, as these are statements by management, not the Board. However, given the sensitivity of the matter, we did spend ten or fifteen minutes discussing this filing.

The Board was comfortable with the Company's filing the 8-K without disclosing that Mr. Perkins had a "disagreement with the Company."

IV. HP and My Role in the Leak Investigation Comes Under Fire

Mr. Perkins resigned from the Board on May 18, 2006. He made no complaint regarding the nature of the investigation into the Board leaks until about May 29, 2006, when he complained of my role in the leak investigation in an email to the NewsCorp Board and others. Mr. Perkins' memo contained false statements about my having organized and conducted an elaborate spying campaign on HP directors for no good reason except, to paraphrase, a delusion of paranoia about leaks coming from the Board. Thus, I knew that Mr. Perkins had, about ten days after his resignation, not yet calmed down.

I remember an e-mail exchange between Mr. Sonsini and Mr. Perkins that has become public. In that exchange, Mr. Perkins expressed frustration and concern about how the leak investigation had been conducted. Mr. Sonsini responded to Mr. Perkins that he had consulted with Ms. Baskins and believed that the investigation was conducted lawfully and properly. I remember that

Mr. Sonsini's e-mail used the word "pretext" in connection with the investigation. That was the first time I began to comprehend what that word meant. I still do not understand whether it is or is not legal, as opinions vary.

Mr. Perkins later demanded that the Board conduct an "investigation of the investigation" to determine whether anything illegal happened. The Nominating & Governance Committee retained Wilson Sonsini (WSGR) to review the details of the investigation. A summary of the investigation results was described by HP in its September 6, 2006, Form 8-K report to the SEC.

By early September, the Board became concerned that Mr. Perkins' changed reasons for his resignation might cast doubt on the veracity of the Company's 8-K filing of mid-May. Accordingly, HP filed a revised 8-K, filed on September 6, accurately describing Mr. Perkins' resignation in more detail.

A. From "The Investigation of the Investigation" to My Resignation

The HP Board met to hear WSGR's review of the "Investigation of the Investigation" in early September. I was informed by Mr. Sonsini that, aside from the recommendation the Board had for me as detailed at the end of the section entitled "Kona 1," above, they expressed unanimous support for my continuing as Chairman and as a director.

However, in the first week of September, intense press attention became focused on the leak investigation and my role in it. Many misleading comments were written and heard in the ensuing days—for example: that I made the decision to spy on the Board and management unilaterally; that I unilaterally retained private investigators to perform nefarious deeds in pursuit of the leaker; that Mr. Perkins resigned out of outrage over the investigation; and that I had proposed, approved and/or endorsed "pretexting," particularly of reporters themselves, which was a clear invasion of privacy, unethical, and possibly illegal.

On Friday, September 8 I was asked to comment on the record to the press and did so before I had any opportunity to review documents. This submission to Congress is a clearer presentation of what happened.

On September 11, at a special telephonic meeting, I agreed with the Board that I would step down as Chairman in January, 2007. Board members continued to assure me that they had no concern that I was involved in anything improper or illegal, but I had become a lightening rod for criticism of the Company and the Board. I was urged to remain as a director by the CEO and by several members of the Board.

However, by the Board's regularly scheduled meeting on September 21, the furor over my perceived role in the leak investigation had reached new heights. The Board did not express any new concerns with my role in the leak investigation but had become unanimous in its view that the Company could not move beyond the controversy if I remained as a director. They asked me to resign and suggested that it would be best for me if it were announced that I had come to this decision on my own. I let them know that I would only do so if it were clear they had asked me to do so, and we agreed. I left the Board with good feelings, embraces and clear messages from each director that they regretted that this had happened to me.

V. The HP Scandal as a Post-Sarbanes-Oxley Phenomenon

When the final story is written on what happened at HP, I believe that its roots will be understood as emanating from a clash between the old and the new cultures in the Boardroom, driven importantly by Sarbanes-Oxley and related regulatory changes. The clash is perhaps particularly poignant in Silicon Valley, where the culture of innovation, freedom of maneuver and creativity are seen as essential to value creation. The machinery required to implement SOX in the boardroom can be seen as cumbersome, time-wasting and a drag on directors' desires to focus on the truly interesting and valuable parts of their roles—for example, business and product strategy. I saw my role as Non-Executive Chairman as helping the Board transition from its roots as a "founder's board" to a modern, fully professional board that was driven by appropriate process as opposed to by personalities. The fact that the rules applied to everyone was not accepted by everyone on the HP Board. The fact that, in a modern board, every director is as important as every other director, was not accepted by everyone on the HP Board. I am proud of the work that I have done to improve the corporate governance at HP, including helping to bring in strong new directors who meet the test of independence in every sense. I do not agree with those who contend that a company cannot receive high marks for governance and still be innovative and successful.

I have spent my entire career as a fiduciary, entrusted for many years with the responsibility to manage billions of dollars of other people's money as carefully as though it were my own. I have been overwhelmed by the support I have received during this difficult period from people with whom I have worked who have offered their attestation to the high standards of ethics and integrity to which I dedicated myself during my career. The saying that "a reputation made over a lifetime can be ruined in minutes" has a sickening level of resonance for me. As a stickler for the sanctity of the boardroom, it pains me to be in a position where I have little choice but to go on the record with details about the HP Board's inner workings.

HP remains a great company. I am honored to have had the opportunity to be a part of bringing elements of its governance forward. It is my hope that the Board continues its process of transformation while management focuses as successfully in the future as it has in the past on creating value for HP shareholders. The stakeholders in this great company expect and deserve nothing less.

VI. What Congress Can Do to Help Make Sure the HP Scandal Does Not Recur

I am not a lawyer and I am not an investigator, but I had a responsibility to respond to HP directors' desires to stop leaks from the Board. I relied on trusted people who were lawyers and investigators to perform this work on their behalf. Along the way I requested for and received assurances that the investigation was both legal and compliant with HP's Standards of Business Conduct.

Nonetheless, serious questions have been raised about the ethics and legality of the investigation. The fact that so many lawyers who were involved in the HP matter could turn out to be either so misled or so uncertain as to the legality of "pretexting" speaks volumes as to the need for unambiguous legislation to protect individual privacy.

At the same time, every company has a duty and a responsibility to shareholders to protect the property of the corporation, which more than ever includes its intellectual property. At the board level, shareholders have a right to insist that the confidential plans and deliberations of directors be protected as, in effect, property of the company.

Let me state clearly that it would be another in the string of tragedies here if it were to be concluded that companies do not have the right to protect themselves against disclosure violations. We have all learned that companies turn to investigators to do this important work.

I would hate to think that any chairman or director of a public company would ever face the problem I faced with the result that has ensued. I therefore urge Congress to consider legislation that would provide not only clear-cut rules on "pretexting" or any other threat to individual privacy, but will give companies like HP legitimate and sanctioned ways of pursuing their responsibilities to protect their intellectual property and confidentiality.

As an example, had there been an agency of law enforcement to which HP could turn to pursue a fully lawful, sanctioned and protected investigation, based on a set of demonstrable threats to its governance arising from the unauthorized disclosure of boardroom confidences, this series of events would not have occurred.

Every company of consequence has codes of conduct, security departments and compliance officers to deal with violations. At HP, it is management's responsibility to see to it that the work done by individuals charged with these sensitive responsibilities never again expose the Company to public outrage and reputational harm.

Beyond this, I eagerly encourage Congress to consider legislation that would be of greater assistance to companies seeking to protect shareholder interests in situations when privacy and those interests may conflict. I would hope that such legislation is overarching and clear, so that teams of lawyers are not required for interpretation. If such a "bright line" can be created, then my undertakings in this matter will not have been in vain.

Ms. Dunn served as a director of the Hewlett-Packard Company from July 1998 to September 22, 2006, and as Non-Executive Chairman of Hewlett-Packard Company from February 7, 2005 until September 22, 2006.

MR. WHITFIELD. Thank you, very much, Ms. Dunn.

At this time, Mr. Sonsini, you are recognized for 5 minutes for your opening statement.

MR. SONSINI. Thank you, Mr. Chairman, members of the committee. It is an honor to be asked to appear before you today. I want to thank my client, Hewlett-Packard, for authorizing me to answer your questions. I, therefore, believe that I can address the issues presented by these hearings without violating any confidentiality obligations that I have to them.

First, let me explain my law firm's role in these matters. We were not involved in the design. We were not involved in the conduct of the so-called Kona 1 or Kona 2 investigations. Indeed, I was not even aware of them when the investigations were being conducted.

Hewlett-Packard asked my law firm to provide legal advice to the Board of Directors after the investigations had occurred.

With respect to the subject of your hearing, in my opinion, the use of pretexting and similar intrusive investigative methods in these circumstances is plainly wrong. They should not be used by businesses or others no matter what the purpose. I know this as well as anyone since public reports have indicated that my own records may have been obtained using pretexting in this investigation.

When we were asked by the Hewlett-Packard Board of Directors to investigate the matter, we told the Board that although generally pretexting except in the instances of financial institutions was not specifically unlawful, we could not confirm that the methodologies used in the investigations were legal.

It seems to me that a positive outgrowth of the recent troubles at Hewlett-Packard would be passage of legislation governing such conduct. Although pretexting is clearly wrong, unethical and improper, the law is not as clear as it needs to be. As Mr. Chairman said in his opening statement, it is probably illegal. We need to make it clearly illegal.

Having said that, the importance of preserving confidentiality within the Boardroom should not be minimized. The dominant trend in corporate governance in recent years has been to enhance the role of boards of directors, the role of not only oversight, but also the obligation to monitor management. Boards across the Nation have risen to this challenge. But a board cannot function effectively to safeguard the shareholders' interests if its most sensitive deliberations are leaked to outsiders. A board's duty of deliberation, a board's duty of care, a board's duty of candor is greatly weakened without confidentiality.

Finally, in all the recent coverage about the disputes within Hewlett-Packard, I feel that some have lost sight of the underlying greatness of the company involved. The mistakes made in handling the investigation--and there were mistakes--do not alter the fact that HP remains a company that we can all be proud of. I look forward to answering your questions to the best of my ability, and thank you again for this opportunity to make this statement.

MR. WHITFIELD. Thank you, Mr. Sonsini.

[The prepared statement of Larry Sonsini follows:]

PREPARED STATEMENT OF LARRY W. SONSINI, CHAIRMAN, WILSON SONSINI GOODRICH & ROSATI

Mr. Chairman, Members of the Committee:

It is an honor to be asked to appear before the Committee today. I want to thank my client, HP, for authorizing me to answer your questions today. I therefore believe that I can address the issues presented by these hearings without violating any confidentiality obligations.

First, let me explain my law firm's role in these matters. We were not involved in the design or conduct of the Kona 1 or Kona 2 investigations. Indeed, I was not even aware of them when the investigations were being conducted. HP asked my law firm to provide legal advice to the board of directors after the investigations had occurred.

With respect to the subject of your hearing, in my opinion, the use of "pretexting" and similar intrusive investigative methods in these circumstances is wrong. They should not be used by businesses or others, no matter what the purpose. I know this as well as anyone, since public reports have indicated that my own records may have been obtained using pretexting in this investigation. It seems to me that a positive outgrowth of the recent troubles at HP would be passage of legislation governing such conduct.

Having said that, the importance of preserving confidentiality within the board room should not be minimized. The dominant trend in corporate law in recent years has been to enhance the role of boards in oversight of management. Boards across the nation have risen to the challenge. But a board cannot function effectively to safeguard the shareholders' interests if its most sensitive deliberations are leaked to outsiders. A board's duty of deliberation and candor is greatly weakened without confidentiality.

Finally, in all the recent coverage about the disputes within the HP Board, I fear that some have lost sight of the underlying greatness of the Company involved. The mistakes made in handling the investigation do not alter the fact that Hewlett-Packard remains a company that we can all be proud of.

I look forward to answering your questions to the best of my ability. Thank you for this opportunity to make a statement to the Committee.

MR. WHITFIELD. And Mr. Adler, you are recognized for 5 minutes.

MR. ALDER. Good morning. Good morning, Mr. Chairman and members of the committee. My name is Fred Adler. I am with HP IT Security Investigations, and I am here at the invitation of the committee. No subpoena was required to compel my attendance. My fellow employees and colleagues at Hewlett-Packard have encouraged me to attend this hearing as have my employers. I believe, as do my friends at Hewlett-Packard, that the company has a tradition of being an outstanding and ethical member of the community. With the recent public disclosure of possible inappropriate conduct, I am sure that Hewlett-Packard will become a stronger company. I will be proud to continue to work there.

In order to assist the committee in evaluating my testimony, I would like you to know my background.

I spent 28 years working for the California Attorney General's office, Department of Justice, and retired before joining Hewlett-Packard.

The last 13 years at the Department of Justice, I served as a law enforcement officer. The last 7 years of my service, I was assigned to the Sacramento high technology crimes task force responsible for investigating computer-based criminal activity.

I joined HP after my retirement knowing that many of the people I would be working with at HP were former colleagues who had outstanding careers in law enforcement investigating technology-related issues.

In the time that I have worked for the company, we successfully protected the company, its customers, and vendors from criminal activity.

When requested, we have also assisted law enforcement in investigating crimes when our particular expertise was needed.

I am proud of our record and of our relationship with law enforcement. I am proud of the ethical standards that the company has set and my maintaining those standards.

Because of the pride I take in our company, earlier this year I became uncomfortable when I learned of investigative techniques being used by certain members of the unauthorized disclosure investigation team with whom I worked during the investigation of leaks to the press. Those leaks had divulged important corporate information.

In order to appreciate concerns that arose during the investigation, one must understand the legal issues surrounding the collection of relevant information.

People who work at Hewlett-Packard, as at other corporations, sign a user agreement which permits the company access to data which resides on the company network.

This includes data on desktop computers, laptop computers, e-mail accounts, servers and also includes corporate telephone records.

If so, tasked and specifically authorized, I have access to those accounts and can track the pertinent calls, e-mails and contacts for investigative purposes.

In that process, it may be helpful to know the phone numbers or e-mail identity of the employee or corporate officer or other key persons.

The information we use to make our inquiries must comply with legal standards. If we wish to obtain third party data, we must, and do, comply with the law. As a result of our law enforcement experience, we usually know what standards apply.

In this instance, when we grew concerned that legal standards may not have been met in obtaining personal phone records, a coworker and I brought the matter to the attention of our managers. My manager, a former law enforcement officer, appreciated our concerns and raised them with counsel. We were all subsequently assured by counsel everything being done met both Federal and State legal standards.

We were advised that this opinion was a result of a review by at least two attorneys.

I understand those opinions have since been questioned. I am not an attorney, and I can't pass judgment on that issue. I do believe as a former law enforcement officer, that it is important that the law be as clear--be clear, so everyone knows it has its limits.

If the problem that brought us here today starts the process of clarifying the law, some good will have will occurred. HP and its exceptional employees will get past this difficult period. It is a strong company with loyal customers and clients.

In the meantime, I am pleased to assist the committee by answering questions and providing information, particularly if it helps in passing legislation which will clarify the law. Thank you.

[The prepared statement of Fred Adler follows:]

PREPARED STATEMENT OF FRED ADLER, IT SECURITY INVESTIGATIONS, HEWLETT-PACKARD COMPANY

Mr. Chairman and Members of the Committee, my name is Fred Adler, HP IT Security Investigations, and I am here at the invitation of the Committee. No subpoena was required to compel my attendance. My fellow employees and colleagues at Hewlett Packard have encouraged me to attend this hearing, as have my employers. I believe, as do my friends at Hewlett Packard, that the company has a tradition of being an outstanding and ethical member of the community. From the recent public disclosure of possible inappropriate conduct, I am sure that Hewlett Packard will become a stronger company. I will be proud to continue to work there.

In order to assist the committee in evaluating my testimony, I would like you to know my background. I spent twenty-eight (28) years working for the California Attorney General's Office, Department of Justice, and retired before joining Hewlett Packard. The last thirteen (13) years at the Department of Justice I served as a law enforcement officer. The last seven years of my service I was assigned to the Sacramento High Tech Crimes Task Force, responsible for investigating computer based criminal activity. I joined HP after my retirement knowing that many of the people I would be working with were former colleagues who had outstanding careers in law enforcement investigating technology related crimes.

In the time I have worked for the company, we have successfully protected the company, its customers and vendors from criminal activity. When requested, we have also assisted law enforcement in investigating crimes when our particular expertise was needed. I am proud of our record and of our relationship with law enforcement. I am proud of the ethical standards our company has set and my maintaining those standards. Because of the pride I take in our company, earlier this year I became uncomfortable when I learned of investigative techniques being used by certain members of the Unauthorized Disclosure Investigative Team with whom I worked during the investigation of leaks to the press. Those leaks had divulged important corporate information.

In order to appreciate concerns that arose during the investigation, one must understand the legal issues surrounding the collection of relevant information. People who work at Hewlett Packard, as at other corporations, sign a user agreement which permits the company access to data which resides on the company network. This includes data on desk top computers, lap top computers, email accounts, servers and also includes telephone records. If so tasked and specifically authorized, I have access to those accounts and can track the pertinent calls, e-mails and contacts for investigative purposes. In that process it may be helpful to know the phone numbers or e-mail identity for the employee or corporate officer and other key persons.

The information we use to make our inquiries must comply with legal standards. If we wish to obtain third party data, we must and do comply with the law. As a result of our law enforcement experience, we usually know what standards apply. In this instance, when we grew concerned that legal standards may not have been met in obtaining personal phone records, a co-worker and I brought the matter to the attention of our managers. My manager, a former law enforcement officer, appreciated our concerns and raised them with counsel. We were all subsequently assured by counsel everything being done met both federal and state legal standards. We were advised that this opinion was the result of a review by at least two attorneys.

I understand those opinions have since been questioned. I am not an attorney and can't pass judgment on that issue. I do believe as a former law enforcement officer that it is important that the law be clear so that everyone knows its limits. If the problem that brought us here today starts the process of clarifying the law, some good will have occurred. HP and its exceptional employees will get past this difficult period, it is a strong company with loyal customers and clients. In the meantime, I am pleased to assist the Committee by answering questions and providing information, particularly if it helps in passing legislation which will clarify the law.

MR. WHITFIELD. Thank you, Mr. Adler, and we appreciate all the testimony of all the witnesses. Ms. Dunn, I think all the evidence and documents and even your testimony show that as Chairman of the Board of Hewlett-Packard, that you were certainly involved in this investigative process.

And you had mentioned in your opening statement that you thought these phone records were publicly available, that they were just available to the public.

I was just curious, I know you have had a broad range of experiences and have been quite successful in your corporate life and--but, what, where did you feel like, that people could obtain phone records and private information like that publicly?

MS. DUNN. Mr. Chairman, I did not know where this information could be found publicly. But, I was aware that the kinds of investigations done by Mr. DeLia had previously been based on solely publicly available information.

In the context of my understandings from all of those whose representations I trusted, I took the understanding without any question, and I understand why that might seem strange today, knowing what I know now, but that was my state of mind at the time.

MR. WHITFIELD. Now, Mr. DeLia, in some of his documents, which I won't ask you to turn to right now, but he stated that back in 2005, in discussions with you and others, that he discussed the methodology of pretexting and what that was all about. Do you recall a discussion with him back in 2005 about the subject of pretexting?

MS. DUNN. I have no recollection of a conversation with Mr. DeLia that included the word "pretexting" or anything about the misrepresentation of identity to obtain phone records. In fact, the first time the word "pretexting" entered my consciousness was at the time when Mr. Sonsini began responding to Mr. Perkins' concerns in late June of 2006. The word, as some members of this committee have already said in their statements, is not one that was commonly understood as to its meaning, or certainly its potential illegality.

MR. WHITFIELD. Now, when Mrs. Baskins was on the panel, I asked her about some notes that she made on June the 15th of 2005. And in her notes--and this is in Exhibit 124 of the exhibit book--these are notes of Mrs. Baskins, and the very first note says, "Obtaining phone numbers is a time-consuming process. Call carriers, Nextel, Sprint, and use pretexting to extract the information." And then they have your initials down here of questions that you asked.

Do you recall being at the meeting reflected in the notes of Ms. Baskins back in June of 2005 about pretexting?

MS. DUNN. I do not recall being in that meeting. I assume it was a telephone meeting, but I do not know. She may have been passing along questions from me, but I don't have a recollection to report to you.

MR. WHITFIELD. So your comment to this committee, then, is that the first time you really heard the word "pretexting" or understood what it meant was in Mr. Larry Sonsini's e-mail in June of 2006?

MS. DUNN. That was the first time that the word jumped out at me. And it was within days or certainly weeks that I began to understand that pretexting could involve the fraudulent misrepresentation of identity. That was not something that I had understood until that point.

MR. WHITFIELD. Because as I mentioned to you earlier in Exhibit 115, Mr. DeLia, in an interview conducted by the law firm of Wilson Sonsini on August 21, 2006, he said himself that he had no doubt that he had discussed the methodology of pretexting, including impersonation, with you; but your testimony is you simply don't recall that or are not familiar with it; is that correct?

MS. DUNN. Well, at minimum I don't recall it. I don't agree with Mr. DeLia's testimony.

MR. WHITFIELD. Okay. Now, Mr. Sonsini, I know that you're one of the most respected attorneys in the Silicon Valley. And I know that your expertise is not criminal law, and I know that some of these documents, as we went through this process of Kona 1 and Kona 2 and why your firm was not really involved in it, here say you had sent some e-mails or made some comments that it appeared to be proper what was going on, is that correct?

MR. SONSINI. Yes, it is, Mr. Chairman. I believe you're referring to an e-mail exchange with Mr. Perkins, and you--if you would like, I'd like to elaborate on that.

MR. WHITFIELD. Go ahead.

MR. SONSINI. Well, at the time Mr. Perkins inquired of me through the e-mail what was going on. I think it's important to note that I, too, at that particular point in time did not understand pretexting, it's not an area of my expertise. I immediately turned to Ms. Baskins and Mr. Hunsaker. I said, we should tell Mr. Perkins what was going on; he was the director at the time of the investigation. And I said, what can you tell me to respond to him?

I got a detailed written response from Mr. Hunsaker telling me what was done and what was lawful. I got a confirming response from Ms. Baskins. And as my e-mail indicated, I then took that information and immediately went to Mr. Perkins and I said to him, here is what I've been told. And I said: it appears based upon the repeated assurances that I was given, that what was done was within legal limits. And that was the extent of my communication with him.

MR. WHITFIELD. Now, did either one of you--are you aware of any document prepared by legal counsel within Hewlett-Packard about the legality or illegality of pretexting? And, Ms. Dunn, did you receive a legal document explaining that pretexting was legal?

MS. DUNN. I never received a formal legal opinion, but in Mr. Hunsaker's final draft report of March 14th on the investigation, as was also contained in the final report in May, he made it very clear, after laying out all of the investigative methods, that each of them were legal and proper and in conformance with the standard investigative techniques that the company had been using for years.

MR. WHITFIELD. Because I tell you, from our review of the documents--and there have been a lot of documents--we've determined that the only legal opinion ever given was by the attorney for the private investigator in Boston, what was his name? Ron DeLia. He--John Kiernan was the attorney's name, and that he wrote an opinion saying that pretexting was legal. And in further analysis, we've determined that actually a law clerk wrote that opinion. So it would appear that Hewlett-Packard, at the very highest levels, relied upon a document prepared by a law clerk hired by the private investigator saying that pretexting was legal; that's what it looks like.

MS. DUNN. I think you'll also find in the documentary evidence that there was a memo to the effect that pretexting, indeed, all the investigative techniques used in this matter, were legal. I was not familiar with the second opinion, if they may be termed--

MR. WHITFIELD. Which e-mail is that that said it was legal?

MS. DUNN. It has not been produced by the company.

MR. WHITFIELD. Oh, it has not been produced by the company? Oh, okay. Well, did you have it at the time; or when did you receive that?

MS. DUNN. I need to refresh my memory on the date of that, and I would be happy to come back to you with that answer.

MR. WHITFIELD. If you would turn to document 83. And if you would look at that and tell me, is that the document that you're referring to?

MS. DUNN. In which section, sir?

MR. WHITFIELD. The large book, document 83.

MS. DUNN. May I have a moment to review this?

MR. WHITFIELD. Sure. You don't recognize it right off?

MS. DUNN. This was a memorandum from Mr. Hunsaker to Mr. Gentilucci and Mr. DeLia. It says it's prepared at the direction of counsel--

MR. WHITFIELD. The only question I was asking is, is this the document that you relied upon that showed that pretexting was legal? That's all I want to know.

MS. DUNN. I do not recall seeing this e-mail before this moment.

MR. WHITFIELD. Okay. Just one other brief question, and then we'll move on.

Mr. Sonsini, I want to ask you this: California Penal Code 538.5 reads as follows, that it prohibits fraudulently obtaining information from a public utility--and as I understand it, that in California a public utility is considered a phone company, among other things--that this statute makes it unlawful for any person to transmit or cause to be transmitted by means of wire, radio, or telephone communication any words, sounds, writings, signs, signals or pictures for the purpose of furthering or executing a scheme or artifice to obtain from a public utility confidential, privileged or proprietary information, customer records, billing records, customer credit data or accounting data by means of false or fraudulent pretenses, representations, impersonations or promises. That almost seems like it definitely is right on line with what we're talking about.

MR. SONSINI. No doubt, Mr. Chairman. Although I'm not an expert or familiar with that statute, we did do, when we investigated the legality of the investigation, conclude that methods may very well have been used which implicated that statute.

MR. WHITFIELD. Okay. My time is expired.

I recognize the gentlelady from Colorado for 10 minutes.

MS. DEGETTE. Thank you, Mr. Chairman.

Ms. Dunn, you have been involved in the corporate world for over 30 years, as near as I can see, is that correct?

MS. DUNN. That is correct.

MS. DEGETTE. Have you ever had occasion to request or direct this type of investigation into corporate officers or employees before?

MS. DUNN. Nothing of this kind. And if I may, I would like to correct the record, as is contained in my written testimony, that I was not the person who hired Mr. DeLia--

MS. DEGETTE. Okay, I understand that. But you were the one who requested the investigation, correct?

MS. DUNN. At the--I was operating as a Nonexecutive Chairman--

MS. DEGETTE. Yes, I know that.

Now, I want to ask you, Mr. Sonsini--and I apologize, I don't mean to be short, but I only have 10 minutes.

Mr. Sonsini, I want to ask you because you are one of the most prominent Silicon Valley lawyers. We've even heard of you in Colorado. My question to you is as outside counsel for many of these corporations, is this standard business practice in the industry where leaks or other kinds of breaches are suspected to have investigations of this type? Is this something you have dealt with?

MR. SONSINI. I have never dealt with an investigation of this kind of a board of directors with respect to a leak of confidential information.

MS. DEGETTE. Have you ever seen any kind of investigation of confidentiality leaks, whether board of directors or other types of employees of a corporation, where you have pretexting, have you ever seen that?

MR. SONSINI. I have not, to my knowledge.

MS. DEGETTE. Have you ever seen investigations that involved going through trash of corporate officers, directors or employees?

MR. SONSINI. Not to my knowledge.

MS. DEGETTE. Have you ever seen investigations come up with fake employees in order to get information from reporters?

MR. SONSINI. Not that I have knowledge of.

MS. DEGETTE. So this is news to you as well.

MR. SONSINI. Yes, ma'am.

MS. DEGETTE. Now, Mr. Sonsini, as outside counsel to HP, were you briefed or were you consulted about the scope of this investigation and the methods used?

MR. SONSINI. No.

MS. DEGETTE. Were you provided with the draft of the investigation report, which is dated on March 10, 2006? It's in Tab 72 of our notebook.

MR. SONSINI. I think you're referring to a report I'm familiar with; yes, it was provided to me on or about April 6 of 2006.

MS. DEGETTE. Okay. On page 3 of that report it says, they're talking about the procedures that they used, and they talk about obtaining--obtained, reviewed and analyzed HP and third-party phone records to identify calls made to or from reporters or other individuals of interest. And then there is a footnote that says the investigation team utilized a lawful investigative methodology commonly utilized by entities such as law firms.

Did that raise any red flags to you?

MR. SONSINI. Well, I remember it, and I certainly did focus on that footnote.

At the time I had the report, of course, I was asked to deal with the issue in the Boardroom, what do we do with Mr. Keyworth? I wasn't asked at that time to investigate the investigation, and I'm certainly not an expert in such matters, so it wouldn't have been sent to me.

MS. DEGETTE. But you said you focused on the footnote. Were you concerned about what those techniques were to obtain the phone records?

MR. SONSINI. I was concerned by the scope of the investigation as evidenced by the report, and I did focus on that footnote.

MS. DEGETTE. And what did you do about your concern?

MR. SONSINI. At that point in time I did nothing further. I had discussions with Ms. Baskins. I asked her about the performance of the investigation and its legality. I asked her, did you rely upon experts, did you get legal advice, did you research it, and I was assured that they did.

MS. DEGETTE. It sort of seems to us up here like it was kind of circular reasoning, because Ms. Dunn says, look, I was just asked to stop the leak, but I wasn't in charge of the actual conduct of the investigation, right, Ms. Dunn? Is that correct?

MS. DUNN. I did not supervise this investigation. I initiated it at the request of the Board.

MS. DEGETTE. So then General Counsel Ms. Baskins, who unfortunately is not testifying, she talks to her experts, and they say, well, this is all okay. Then she asks you, and then you're relying back on Ms. Baskins; is that right, Mr. Sonsini?

MR. SONSINI. No, she never asked me. At the time I got the report, I was not asked about it whatsoever.

The fact is this investigation was conducted by the Hewlett-Packard legal department. They took the responsibility on. I learned of it after the fact, after it occurred. And it wasn't until the Board of Directors asked me to investigate it that I was able to get into the legality of the conduct.

MS. DEGETTE. Okay. Let me move on a little bit.

And I want to ask you, Ms. Dunn, about something else that happened which I think is just almost as bad as the pretexting, and that's the creation of this fictitious character named Jacob. Jacob was a fictitious employee of HP who was designed principally to find out about the potential sources of an outside reporter named Dawn Kawamoto. Now, you're familiar at least now with this operation, correct?

MS. DUNN. Yes, I am.

MS. DEGETTE. Do you know, is it common practice for HP to create fake disgruntled employees to sting outside reporters?

MS. DUNN. I do not know what normally goes on except what I have been told.

MS. DEGETTE. Did you ever hear about that type of operation?

MS. DUNN. It would not come to my attention if it were the case. As a nonemployee, nonmanager, outside director, I really can't answer your question in the way I think you need it to be answered.

MS. DEGETTE. Well, except for you're the one that ordered the investigation, right?

MS. DUNN. I initiated it at the request of the Board as Nonexecutive Chairman. And I would like to just add, this is an unusual position in corporate America. Less than 9 percent of companies have a position like this. I had no staff, no office, and I reported only to the Board. The CEO doesn't report to me, nor do any other people at HP.

MS. DEGETTE. I understand that. But if you take a look at Tab 60 in your notebook--actually, take a look first at Tab 21 in your notebook, where Mr. Hunsaker says to Mr. Gentilucci, "We DEFINITELY need to get the approval of Ann, Mark, and Pattie before doing it"--and this would be the Jacob operation. You have seen that e-mail, right?

MS. DUNN. I have.

MS. DEGETTE. And then you--if you will take a look at Tab 60, on February 22, 2006, Mr. Hunsaker sent you and Ms. Baskins an e-mail that says, "Hi, Ann and Pattie, below please find the e-mail we propose sending Dawn Kawamoto with the hope she would forward it to George Keyworth.... I made up everything in the side, trying to make it at least somewhat feasible...," and it goes on, correct?

MS. DUNN. I recall the e-mail.

MS. DEGETTE. And you saw that at the time, too. So you knew this operation was going on at the time.

MS. DUNN. I knew what--yes, I did. And--

MS. DEGETTE. And did you think there was any problem with that, someone pretending to be someone named Jacob sending e-mails to a reporter to try to get information from a reporter as to a leak within the Board?

MS. DUNN. At no time in any part of this investigation was I responsible for designing its methods.

MS. DEGETTE. Right. But you knew about--

MS. DUNN. I asked for this to be done in the HP standard way. This did raise a concern to me. I did not want to be at any point the person to whom the team turned for approval of specifics. The way I responded was to say this is a management thing.

MS. DEGETTE. Okay. I understand that. But you ordered the investigation, you knew these techniques were being used, you developed a concern. What did you do about it?

MS. DUNN. I sent the team to management to get approval for their techniques.

MS. DEGETTE. Who was that in management?

MS. DUNN. Mr. Hurd.

MS. DEGETTE. So do we have an e-mail or--

MS. DUNN. I think there is some evidence that he was aware of this and--

MS. DEGETTE. Okay. What did you say to Mr. Hurd about this Jacob situation?

MS. DUNN. I don't remember a conversation. I remember telling the team that basically they had come to the wrong person for approval, that was not my role in this matter.

MS. DEGETTE. So you knew this was going on, you're the one that ordered the investigation, you had concerns, so your response was to send them over to talk to Mr. Hurd, but you yourself didn't mention it to anyone?

MS. DUNN. If I were going to have concern, it would have been expressed to Mr. Hurd.

MS. DEGETTE. So did you express it to Mr. Hurd?

MS. DUNN. I asked him to look into it and to give his opinion.

MS. DEGETTE. And did you ever get an opinion from him?

MS. DUNN. I understand that he did give a--I don't know whether it was verbal, an e-mail or by an in-person meeting, but that they gained the approval they were seeking.

MS. DEGETTE. Okay. Mr. Sonsini, in this draft investigation report, which you had said that you saw, Tab 72, a minute ago, they talk about this Jacob situation on page 4 of that report, which you saw. They said they engineered and executed a covert intelligence-gathering operation. Were you familiar with that?

MR. SONSINI. No, ma'am.

MS. DEGETTE. So you didn't read that part--

MR. SONSINI. I read it, but I wasn't familiar with it. Other than what was--

MS. DEGETTE. Did you have any concerns that HP might be using a fake person to get information from a reporter?

MR. SONSINI. Congresswoman, at that time that was not my focus that I was retained to do.

MS. DEGETTE. Thank you.

MR. WHITFIELD. The gentlelady's time is expired.

At this time I recognize Chairman Barton.

CHAIRMAN BARTON. Thank you, Mr. Chairman.

I'm going to take my full 10 minutes, and I assume we will go to recess to go have the votes on the floor?

MR. WHITFIELD. That's correct.

CHAIRMAN BARTON. As soon as the bells stop, I'll start.

Well, first of all, I want to thank you three for not taking the Fifth Amendment; it's good to have some people willing to answer questions.

I want to start with you, Mrs. Dunn--or Ms. Dunn. You claim that your position is one that is somewhat unique and that you don't have direct staff. Who does report to you?

MS. DUNN. No one.

CHAIRMAN BARTON. No one?

MS. DUNN. No one.

CHAIRMAN BARTON. So you're purely an administrative adjunct of the Board.

MS. DUNN. As part of my written testimony, I submitted the job description for the Nonexecutive Chairman that was approved by our Board. And it is very clear it's a coordinator role, it's a facilitator role, it's a conduit--

CHAIRMAN BARTON. You had no direct management--

MS. DUNN. No.

CHAIRMAN BARTON. --responsibility? You are purely a functionary of the Board?

MS. DUNN. I served at the pleasure of the Board.

CHAIRMAN BARTON. Did you sit in on the Board meetings?

MS. DUNN. I chair the Board meetings--I did chair the Board meetings until my resignation last week.

CHAIRMAN BARTON. All right. Now, this whole investigation got started because there were leaks from materials presented in Board meetings, and perhaps leaks of discussions at Board meetings; is that correct?

MS. DUNN. That is correct, sir. And in the submission, there is a detailed chart of some of the leaks that were the most serious and undermining to our company.

CHAIRMAN BARTON. I appreciate that, but I don't have too much time.

The Board was divided, or was the Board unified? Was the Hewlett-Packard Board that you chaired a team that worked together, or were there schisms on the Board and quite a bit of controversy?

MS. DUNN. After I became Chairman, I became highly cognizant of deep schisms between various individuals on the Board.

CHAIRMAN BARTON. So some of the Board members, or member or members apparently took materials that were requested to be confidential and disseminated without permission. What steps did the Board take before you resorted to all of this sordid detail to try to get the Board members to 'fess up'? Did you all discuss it in the Board, and if so, did everybody put their hand on a Bible and swear they weren't the leaks and--

MS. DUNN. Yes. The first inquiry into leaks actually began under the administration of Carly Fiorina, who was Chairman and CEO until February of 2005. She asked Mr. Sonsini to talk with every director one-on-one about the functioning of the Board, and to seek the confession of whoever the person or persons were that were leaking this confidential information, as well as to reassert their commitment to confidentiality going forward.

The reason why the Board, by the time I got involved, was so deeply concerned was because they knew that no one had come forward to admit their culpability.

CHAIRMAN BARTON. How many Board members were there?

MS. DUNN. I believe there were nine independent directors at that time, including myself, and two members of management--one member until Mark Hurd arrived in April.

CHAIRMAN BARTON. And did the Board take a vote to initiate the investigation? How were you directed to start this investigation?

MS. DUNN. I was directed in one-on-one conversations, about which I have submitted my notes to this committee, by seven of the nine directors that next to hiring or helping the Board to identify its next CEO, my top priority was to help the Board come to grips with these leaks. And I reported to the Board in my first meeting as Chairman in March that I took that responsibility seriously.

CHAIRMAN BARTON. So 7 of the 11 Board members told you--

MS. DUNN. Seven of nine.

CHAIRMAN BARTON. Told you individually, but there was never a vote collectively to start this investigation.

MS. DUNN. There was never a vote collectively.

CHAIRMAN BARTON. Was Mr. Keyworth one of the ones who told you to start the investigation?

MS. DUNN. He was not.

CHAIRMAN BARTON. He was not. So the first investigation was Kona 1, was inconclusive; is that correct?

MS. DUNN. It was.

CHAIRMAN BARTON. And Kona 1 did not use pretexting.

MS. DUNN. I believe it did use pretexting.

CHAIRMAN BARTON. Did it use pretexting? Okay.

MS. DUNN. I'm sorry, I've just been corrected. I don't know.

CHAIRMAN BARTON. All right. Well, that's a fair answer. I don't know a lot of stuff either, and that's okay every now and then to not know.

But when did it arise to your attention that pretexting was being used? At what point, in which investigation?

MS. DUNN. Mr. Chairman, in the sense of the word that we're all using pretexting today, which is the fraudulent misrepresentation of identity, a form of identity theft, this was not something I understood until early July of 2006 as a possible component of either investigation.

CHAIRMAN BARTON. Okay. Now, I just want to make sure that we understand. We have a divided Board. Somebody on the Board is leaking information that the people that are not leaking it think is inflammatory. So there is kind of a general investigation to get people to confess and stop their bad behavior. That doesn't work, so a majority of the Board individually says: I want this stopped, I want to find out who is doing this, and by golly you're the Chairman of the Board, you start this investigation.

MS. DUNN. You work for us, we need this work done.

CHAIRMAN BARTON. You go, apparently--do you clear this with Mr. Hurd, the Chief Executive Officer, who is going to testify next?

MS. DUNN. He was not with Hewlett-Packard in the period when I was first named Chairman.

CHAIRMAN BARTON. All right. Do you go to Mr. Adler down there and say, I want you to do it? I mean, did you go to Mr. Sonsini and say, I want you to do it--

MS. DUNN. No.

CHAIRMAN BARTON. Who did you call to do it?

MS. DUNN. I went to Mr. Bob Wayman, who is the long-serving CFO of Hewlett-Packard, arguably the CFOs' CFO.

CHAIRMAN BARTON. Even though you had no direct management responsibility, you went to the Chief Financial Officer of the company.

MS. DUNN. He was a fellow director of the company, who, in his role as a director and a fiduciary, was as concerned about these leaks as any other director.

CHAIRMAN BARTON. Is the director the same as a Board member?

MS. DUNN. Yes, it is, sir.

CHAIRMAN BARTON. So he was one of the Board members who wanted to do the investigation.

MS. DUNN. He was one of the seven, yes, sir.

CHAIRMAN BARTON. Okay. And is he the one responsible who hired these outside investigators to do the investigation?

MS. DUNN. Not directly, but as noted in the reporting relationships chart, he had control over all of the functions that are involved in security investigations. He directed me to someone in his organization who directed me to someone that does this work.

CHAIRMAN BARTON. When these Board members asked you to do this or told you to do the investigation, and when you went to Mr. Wayman, who is also a member of the Board, was there any discussion about--I mean, was this personal? Was this, we want to get him whatever it takes, do what it takes? Or was it, we'd like to know, but we don't really want to cross any boundaries?

MS. DUNN. There was never any question in my mind that the Board expected this investigation to be done not only legally, but ethically.

CHAIRMAN BARTON. Well, if seven of the nine members wanted the investigation, I would start with the premise that the two that didn't were the primary suspects. Was any extra consideration given to the two Board members who didn't want the--I mean, it would seem to be they were the ones most likely to be leaking information.

MS. DUNN. I did provide background to the investigators, as I was told was the normal process in these matters, about who wished and who did not wish to have an investigation. I, as I mentioned before, was one of those six or so directors whom the investigators decided was among the Board of Directors' likely suspect. I saw myself as needing to be as independent of the investigation as possible so that they could do their work without the implication that I would not be considered.

CHAIRMAN BARTON. Mr. Adler, what is your role in this? What is IT Security Investigations? Is it a direct arm of Hewlett-Packard, or is it on retainer by Hewlett-Packard?

MR. ALDER. Mr. Congressman, I am under a completely separate entity within the Hewlett-Packard organization, and with no common point of management until Mr. Hurd. My role was to participate with regard to obtaining internal HP records, and to participate in the investigation as required or as directed by HP counsel, specifically Mr. Hunsaker. That may have included interviews or any other technical assistance, computer forensics, things of that nature.

CHAIRMAN BARTON. So you're an internal investigatory arm of Hewlett-Packard?

MR. ALDER. Yes, sir. In this particular time I was; sometimes I functioned as the sole investigator, depending on the circumstances and where jurisdiction of the investigation falls under.

CHAIRMAN BARTON. Mr. Chairman, my time is expired, and we have to go vote. I just have one final question.

If I called you up, Ms. Dunn, and said, I'd like your phone records for the last 6 months, I'm Chairman Barton of the Energy and Commerce Committee, but I'd like to look at your phone log, would you give me that?

MS. DUNN. If I understood why you wanted it--

CHAIRMAN BARTON. No. I call you up; would you give me it, your phone records?

MS. DUNN. In your position? I would give you my phone records.

CHAIRMAN BARTON. Praise the Lord. I wouldn't give you mine.

MS. DUNN. I hope that doesn't mean you have something to hide.

CHAIRMAN BARTON. I wouldn't give them.

Now, if I get with former Chairman Dingell, and he and I say we have reason to believe that we have an official right for the public to know your records, I can sign a subpoena as Chairman of this committee, with Mr. Dingell's acquiescence, and I can get your phone records, but I have to sign an official document. And I'm doing that in an official capacity. And I don't do that very often, I take that very seriously. I don't issue many subpoenas. But if I just want to peruse your background, I can't do that as an individual citizen, and I shouldn't be allowed to without your permission. And in this investigation, at some point in time people very high up in your company either didn't ask the right question or ignored it, because there was such a motivation to find out who was leaking.

Nobody condones the leaks. We have leaks in this committee, but the--

MS. DUNN. Mr. Chairman, may I make a comment on Mr. Barton's--

CHAIRMAN BARTON. And I'm going to have to go. But this whole issue of pretexting is--we understand the right of confidentiality in a boardroom and the right to conduct a private investigation. This committee is concerned because the use of the pretexting ignores what most people think is right and wrong--

MS. DUNN. I understand that, sir.

CHAIRMAN BARTON. That's our problem.

MR. WHITFIELD. Ms. Dunn, if you would hold your remarks. The reason I say that is we have 1 minute and 20 seconds to go vote on the House floor, and then we're going to have this floor, and then three more votes at a maximum of about 5 minutes each. So we're going to recess this hearing until about 1 o'clock, and then we will all come back, and then you can make whatever comment you would like to make at that time in response to Chairman Barton. So we will recess until 1 o'clock.

[Recess.]

MR. WHITFIELD. The hearing will come to order.

I said we would be back at 1:00; it's 5 after, so we were 5 minutes late.

At this time, I recognize Ms. Schakowsky for 10 minutes.

MS. SCHAKOWSKY. I want to also thank the witnesses for coming here today and being willing to testify; it really means a lot to us.

And one other preliminary remark. I want to associate myself with what Mr. Otter and Ms. Eshoo both referred to, because I want to get at the culture that is taking place in boardrooms. But I think that we as Members of Congress have to look at our own culture here, too, and the issue of the processes that we have worked in terms of NSA eavesdropping and getting phone records, and the assertion of this administration that the ends in a sense do justify the means, in this case terrorism, in your case a leak within the Board of Directors. And I am concerned about both, that we have ethical and legal processes that allow us to achieve very laudable--or sensibly laudable goals anyway.

But I think it is significant for us to talk about this issue of corporate culture. And I wanted to--Ms. DeGette was talking about the e-mails on February 22, 2006, from Mr.--is it Mr. Hunsaker--sent to you, Ms. Dunn, and Ms. Baskins about Jacob and about Dawn Kawamoto, the reporter, et cetera. And when he says, I made up everything on the sly, trying to make it at least somewhat feasible, I won't quit my day job--he is being light-hearted. While your response did say that you said as a matter of course anything that is going to be potentially outside of HP should have Mark's approval as well, et cetera. But you also said, "Kevin, I think this is very clever." And I just wondered if you would comment on that.

MS. DUNN. I will comment on that. I regret that comment; it doesn't characterize my state of mind. I may have been trying in some kind of, in retrospect, inappropriate way to tell the team that I thought they were doing a good job. In reading that comment today, it embarrasses me.

MS. SCHAKOWSKY. Thank you.

I also wanted to know--and it is Tab 29 in the book, a PowerPoint that says that it was an initial briefing--

MR. WHITFIELD. Excuse me, Ms. Schakowsky. Do you have the document book on the table?

MS. DUNN. It seems to not be here any longer.

MR. WHITFIELD. Could you bring the document book over, please? Did you say document 29?

MS. SCHAKOWSKY. Tab 29, correct. And on page 10 of that report, there are lists of either potential or ongoing investigative methods that are being proposed in this investigation. And I just wanted to walk through those a little bit and ask you if you had approved them or heard about them, or if they went forward.

Under the title "Surveillance Intelligence Operations" it reads, "Pre-trash inspection survey is in process for key subjects for the investigation." And I wondered if you knew that HP investigators were about to or were actually rummaging through the trash of certain individuals?

MS. DUNN. The direct answer is no. The context is this was a PowerPoint presentation that was given in a meeting room--

MS. SCHAKOWSKY. You did see that presentation?

MS. DUNN. I don't know that every page was actually shown. I was interested in pages 12 and 13, which focused on the work that had been done to try and legitimately hypothesize who within our Board could be responsible for these confidentiality breeches.

So to answer the question, did I focus on, did I know? It's not even clear to me that this was put up on the screen, and I do not recall getting a hard copy of it.

MS. SCHAKOWSKY. And did you know if Mr. Hurd--do you have any knowledge that Mr. Hurd knew about these activities?

MS. DUNN. I have no knowledge--I have no direct knowledge.

MS. SCHAKOWSKY. Okay. In this same document, and that is Tab--I guess in this one, it says, "Surveillance activity was conducted for G.K."--I guess that's George Keyworth--"speech in Colorado on January 31, 2006."

Did you know that HP investigators were using HP money to assemble surveillance teams for this Board member and possibly press reporters at this point? And when did you know this, and who approved of this expenditure?

MS. DUNN. I learned after this document, and I can't pinpoint the date, but probably sometime after the release of Mr. Hunsaker's report, that a security detail from Hewlett-Packard--which normally attended company events, so not specifically for the purpose of surveilling Dr. Keyworth--had reported nonetheless back to their chain that he had, on a number of occasions, disclosed confidential information orally to groups of employees who did not have authority to hear that information.

So it's not clear to me now that there were, for example, details of surveyors, surveillers to cover him specifically, but I am aware now--have come to be aware that actually for several years there were concerns among the security staff about his public comments, and that they had reported some of them through the security chain.

In terms of who approved the--if you would still like me to answer that.

MS. SCHAKOWSKY. Well, I just wanted--it included photographs of his home in Italy. Obviously trips were taken. We know that Mrs. Keyworth was observed in Breeze Restaurant. The family was also followed.

MS. DUNN. I was unaware of all of those activities until I read about them in the press within the last week or two as these documents started to find their way into the media.

MS. SCHAKOWSKY. And for reporters as well, you weren't aware? Did you see the photograph of the reporter, Ms. Dawn Kawamoto?

MS. DUNN. No. I would like to specify that I became aware that reporters had been pretexted by Ms. Baskins on--I believe it was September 6, it was a Wednesday evening of this year. That was the first awareness that I had that reporters had been pretexted as a part of this investigation.

MS. SCHAKOWSKY. Now, this PowerPoint--and I understand that you're saying that you're not sure that all the pages were being shown, but there is--on page 15 it talks about other investigative options under review. We've got misinformation/sting scenario, covert undercover operations, placement of agent in close proximity of persons of interest, most likely location news agencies.

And I guess what I'm trying to get at in this line of questioning, is all of this really the HP way? I mean, it's pretty well detailed out that whether or not--I'm not even talking about the legality issues so much as kind of the sleaze factor here, and I'm just wondering if none of this really came through to you over the period.

MS. DUNN. Well, first I have to say that I never remember seeing this piece of paper; it may or may not have been presented. My view is that it wasn't--

MS. SCHAKOWSKY. Who failed you?

MS. DUNN. May I finish answering your first question?

MS. SCHAKOWSKY. Sure.

MS. DUNN. Thank you, Madam Congresswoman--I never knew if I was Chairman or Chairwoman.

The fact is that I believe that these methods may, in fact, be quite common not just at Hewlett-Packard, but at companies around the country. Every company has a security department. Every company of consequence has people who do detective-type work in order to ferret out the sources of nefarious activities.

An example might be that at Hewlett-Packard one of the great problems that it faces worldwide is called gray marketing, where unauthorized agents for the company's products basically serve as a conduit between the company and channels of distribution. It's a huge problem. And I've heard about, in the Audit Committee of Hewlett-Packard, how there are people in the investigations team who actually pose as customers or pose as suppliers or pose--

MS. SCHAKOWSKY. As clerical workers in newsrooms, too?

MS. DUNN. That I never heard, but my point is--and I'll wind up. But companies do a lot of this type of work to protect the interests of our shareholders, and maybe we're all just coming to be aware of how common it is.

MR. WHITFIELD. The gentlelady's time is expired.

At this time I recognize Mr. Walden for 10 minutes.

MR. WALDEN. Thank you very much, Mr. Chairman.

Ms. Dunn, I'm just having some trouble here tracking all this based on what I'm reading in your document binders and what I'm hearing today, and I want to go back to make sure I understood.

When we referenced the document that was in Tab number 24, the handwritten minutes or notes of Ann Baskins from a meeting of June 15th, as I recall your testimony earlier today under oath, you said you didn't recall being in that meeting.

MS. DUNN. I have no recollection--

MR. WALDEN. No recollection.

MS. DUNN. I've seen this for the first time now.

MR. WALDEN. I'm not wondering whether you have seen this for the first time. Do you remember being part of this discussion?

MS. DUNN. I do not.

MR. WALDEN. Then I would direct your attention to Tab number 2. Tab number 2 is a copy of an e-mail message from you to Ron DeLia in which you reference Kona. It is dated June 14th of 2005, the day before this meeting. In that--I'll read it. It says, "Ron I would like to reschedule our call to include Ms. Baskins, General Counsel at HP, in the next couple of days. Ann is now involved in the confidentiality review, and it would be timely to compare notes and discuss where to go from here. Can you do it at 2 p.m. Eastern Daylight Time tomorrow, Wednesday? And can we use your conference line? Regards, Pattie."

June 14th, do you remember that e-mail?

MS. DUNN. I remember that e-mail, but without Ann's June 15th notes, which have just been put in front of me, my recollection was incomplete. I haven't seen all the evidence here.

MR. WALDEN. I understand you may not have seen her notes. My question was, do you have any recollection of having any discussion with any of these people that you set the meeting up for the next day?

MS. DUNN. I will say one more time, I do not recall the June 15th discussion. If I connect these dots, it took place, but as I--

MR. WALDEN. The importance of that is because there was a discussion about pretexting that obviously went on in the meeting, if Ann Baskins' notes are to be believed, I think you understand the relevance of that to our discussion here.

MS. DUNN. I do.

MR. WALDEN. Let me move you to Tab 116, because this is a document that includes interviews with you from August 21st, interview with you conducted by Wilson Sonsini, who apparently you are not willing to contradict Mr. DeLia's statement that he shared with you the concept of impersonation to get records. And I would note it says, and I quote, "Dunn thinks it was probable that she was told in some circumstances that they may need to use false pretenses, but that she was always assured that the methods used were lawful and consistent with HP's practices." And if you go to paragraph 26--

MS. DUNN. Could you point me to the number of the paragraph?

MR. WALDEN. The top of the page is paragraph 25, but the first notation is paragraph 26. It says, Schatz explained that Mr. DeLia believed that he shared with Dunn the concept of impersonation to get records. Dunn said she is not willing to contradict Mr. DeLia on this. And then it goes on to say, "Dunn thinks it is probable that she was told that in some circumstances they may need to use false pretenses, but she was always assured the methods used were lawful and consistent with HP practices."

Do you disagree with those findings?

MS. DUNN. I disagree with the transcription by Wilson Sonsini's lawyer of our interview, and I was never given an opportunity to review their notes.

MR. WALDEN. Do you disagree with the notion that you were not willing to contradict Mr. DeLia's view of this?

MS. DUNN. I remember what I said to Mr. Schatz was that I--if Mr. DeLia said this, I had no recollection of it. I don't recall saying I am not willing to contradict him. That seems a paraphrase.

MR. WALDEN. Mr. Sonsini, are you comfortable with what's reported here?

MR. SONSINI. Yes, I am, sir.

MR. WALDEN. And do you believe that Ms. Dunn was made aware of pretexting as a part of the investigation?

MR. SONSINI. I believe that the notes taken by Mr. Schatz, a senior partner in our firm, a former U.S. assistant attorney and Federal prosecutor, accurately reflects his recollection of that interview.

MR. WALDEN. What does probable mean? Where he writes, Dunn thinks it's probable that she was told that in some circumstances they may need to use false pretenses?

MR. SONSINI. Well, I wasn't in the interview, of course, Congressman, but I think--I shouldn't speculate on what that exchange was.

MS. DUNN. I would like to try and interpret, if I may. I believe I told Mr. Schatz that it was possible that I had seen the word "pretext," not that there were false pretenses that I was aware of and the fraudulent misidentification of identity as part of this investigation. The word "pretext" does show up in documents that I have been shown that I saw--

MR. WALDEN. So sitting here today under oath, you're going to tell us you never knew that they were going to use these techniques to spy on Board members and impersonation of others; you just never knew?

MS. DUNN. It is my sworn testimony that until July of 2006, I was unaware that the fraudulent misrepresentation of identity was a part of the standard arsenal of HP tactics or used in this investigation.

MR. WALDEN. In the document that we have here, the interview of Ron DeLia, draft from Wilson Sonsini Goodrich & Rosati--I believe it's document number 115--talking about Kona 1, 2005 investigation, and in number 4 on page 1, it says, "DeLia has no doubt that he discussed methodology of pretexting, i.e., impersonation, with Dunn at some point during the 2005 investigation."

Mr. Sonsini, this is on your corporate--your law firm's letterhead. Are you familiar with this document?

MR. SONSINI. I am, sir.

MR. WALDEN. And how should we understand that to be?

MR. SONSINI. That document reflects, sir, the investigation we made and the information we received from the parties we interviewed.

MR. WALDEN. Ms. Dunn, do you see why we're troubled by this?

MS. DUNN. I do. I think there are also references in this document to my request and ongoing, both seeking and receiving of assurances that everything being done in this investigation was legal and part of HP's normal investigative process--

MR. WALDEN. So if they told you it was legal to impersonate someone to get documents, you didn't see a problem with that?

MS. DUNN. I never understood that to be the case, sir.

MR. WALDEN. Well, Mr. DeLia said he had no doubt he discussed the methodology with you. And so what you're saying is you don't believe him.

MS. DUNN. I wish he were here so we can talk about it.

MR. WALDEN. Ann Baskins' notes discuss that as well. Do you dispute those?

MS. DUNN. I dispute having ever understood or being told that the fraudulent use of identity was a part of this investigation. And I would add that I had no reason to think that anything illegal was going on. There were batteries of experts telling me that that was not the case.

MR. WALDEN. And I understand that you were advised that way, and some of those batteries of experts are now looking for work, and I understand that. I guess my question--

MS. DUNN. I'm one of them.

MR. WALDEN. I understand that as well, and there may be more after you leave here today.

My question is, you indicated earlier, and some of these e-mails would indicate, that you signed off at--somebody--I don't know if I got that e-mail where it says you--"Pattie and Ann gave the thumbs up. Now we need to hear from Mark Hurd."

I guess my question is, you referenced earlier that you're sort of there on the Board as an outside director. You're the one that's sort of been tasked by seven Board members, without a vote of the Board, to secretly put together Kona 1, Kona 2. There is a lot of e-mail traffic back and forth.

You know, this April 19th memo to Ron DeLia from you says, "Ron, let's call this Project Kona. Attached is the information we discussed, the phone numbers of all those present at the meeting referred to in the article." I mean, these would lead me to believe that you were very involved in this. Even without a staff you were pretty active. And my question is that the e-mail from Mr. Hunsaker, which is under Tab 51, to team, from Kevin, Mr. Hunsaker says, "This is a tentative go. I've attached a document that purports to be an e-mail sent to Jacob about an announcement taking place next week. Let's talk about the content on our call. After that, Fred, can you begin to prepare the document for Cindy? We cannot put this completely in motion until they clear it with Mark, but Ann and Pattie have both given the thumbs up, so we should be prepared to send it if Mark approves. Kevin."

Do you remember that e-mail?

MS. DUNN. I have read that e-mail. I don't agree with its characterization of my giving it the thumbs up. I said it needed to be approved by management.

MR. WALDEN. In another part of this interview on August 25th, DeLia thought, page 3, "in all probability," quote, unquote, that he used the word "pretexting" with Dunn and explained the term to her, but did not have a specific recollection of using the word. DeLia said he knows he would have described the processes with Dunn, but he did not tell Dunn that he was using a subcontractor.

MS. DUNN. Sir, I am testifying here under oath; Mr. DeLia is not. I think I will leave it at that.

MR. WALDEN. Well, I'm not sure we can leave it at that. Answer my question about Mark Hurd's role about this. What was his role? You have indicated--you kind of deferred to him--can I at least finish asking the question, Mr. Chairman?

MS. DUNN. May I answer, sir?

MR. WALDEN. Yes.

MS. DUNN. The question was, what was his role?

MR. WALDEN. What was your understanding of his role in this process?

MS. DUNN. That this particular element of the investigation could not go forward without his approval.

MR. WHITFIELD. And I might add that more than likely we will have a second round as well, so--Mr. Inslee, you're recognized for 10 minutes.

MR. INSLEE. Thank you.

I want to ask about Tab 29, Ms. Dunn, about this document. I think there has been some discussion about it already. It's identified as Project Kona 2 HP. It says "Initial briefing, Pattie Dunn" on it, on the title page. It's dated February 2, 2006. It's a rather extensive document.

It's interesting in time. I introduced the first bill in Congress in this session to make it clear and to have tools against pretexting on January 31st. Two days later HP's involved in a very significant effort that I think as we go through this will show substantial willingness to defraud other people about the sources and how you were obtaining information. The timing is pretty amazing to me.

But I want to ask you about this document. It has your name on it. It is entitled "Project Kona 2," and on page 10, I believe--excuse me, page--page 10 of the document, I'll give you just a moment to get to page 10 there.

MS. DUNN. I was just asked to look at this page, so I'm familiar with it right now.

MR. INSLEE. Now, this document, as I understand, was something like a PowerPoint or a slide projection to use; is that correct?

MS. DUNN. Yes, that's how I believe it was used. It was projected during a meeting.

MR. INSLEE. And on the title page it says it's for you, you were the subject, you were the audience of this document, this presentation, I assume; is that correct?

MS. DUNN. I remember that the meeting took place, and Ms. Baskins was with me. And, yes, I was the person who on behalf of the Board was tasked with this investigation.

MR. INSLEE. So on page 10--are you with me there? Do you have that in front of you?

MS. DUNN. I'm with you.

MR. INSLEE. It's entitled "Investigation Activity Update." Now, I have to tell you, I was impressed with this document, with its extensive list of activities. Surveillance, intelligence operations, intelligence-gathering effort to document communications for all pertinent subjects. Pretrash inspection survey is in progress for key subjects. Presurveillance reconnaissance is in progress. Surveillance activity was conducted--and there is a list.

Now, I want to ask you about this last one. It says, Feasibility studies are in progress for undercover operations, clerical, in CNET and WSJ offices in SF California. Now, I would understand that to say that you were considering--undercover to me is another way of saying that someone would be lying about their status, that HP was considering a method of having a person lie about their identity or their responsibility or their presence in some fashion, and in this case it was to CNET and to the Wall Street Journal.

And so if my interpretation is correct, it appears to me that you had already stepped up over the line of being willing to falsify the identity or the role or the responsibility of a person in order to obtain this information; is that a fair statement?

MS. DUNN. I don't think that is a correct inference. I am not in the mind or was not in the minds of the investigation team. What they considered and what I saw are in many cases two different things. I think you can probably appreciate what happens when you go into a meeting and someone's got a 30-page PowerPoint deck, and you've got limited time, and you say, let's get to the meat of the matter here. I want to know who do you think did this. Let's go to the analysis, what we know about who did this.

I remember focusing on pages 12 and 13--

MR. INSLEE. Today if any CEO in the land, if they see a document that says we are considering undercover operations against major media outlets in this country, don't you think that should be a red flag to say, should we be doing undercover operations to major media outlets? And undercover, to me that means that someone is falsifying their identity or falsifying their responsibilities. Are you telling us today had you been aware of that, you would have stopped it? Or are you telling us that you weren't aware of that? Or are you telling us that you missed that? Or are you telling us that you thought it was okay to think about undercover operations, and you would think about it later? Which of those scenarios happened here?

MS. DUNN. What I'm telling you is that I don't believe I saw this. I was not responsible for designing the techniques that Hewlett-Packard uses in investigations. And I will strongly affirm your statement that I advise--and I think that is what you just asked--other CEOs--I was not the CEO, but I would advise CEOs that if anyone in their organization came to them with this proposal, that they take appropriate action to prevent it.

MR. INSLEE. So if anyone actually--what you're telling me is if anyone in the chain of command saw this proposal, they should have shut it down right there; is that a fair statement?

MS. DUNN. I think that this would have--this would have been and should have been a trigger to review the investigative methods at Hewlett-Packard from the standpoint of, say, an internal audit review to look for, on a risk basis, what was going on there that could put the company in jeopardy.

MR. INSLEE. So while I was introducing a bill on January 31st to give us tools to stop pretext calling, which is an undercover device to obtain our personal cell phone information, what was HP telling Congress about whether or not we should have these tools to stop pretexting? What were your lobbyists telling Congress?

MS. DUNN. I don't know, sir. I'm not involved in HP's lobbying efforts; I have no role in approving or even being informed about them.

MR. INSLEE. And what is HP telling Congress now? Should we pass this bill that this committee passed back in March? What is your advice to us now?

MS. DUNN. Sir, I think the right person to address that question to is Mark Hurd, who is an executive of the company. I am not, was never, and I have never been consulted about what HP does in its lobbying efforts with Congress.

MR. INSLEE. Well, what is your personal opinion, if you have one? Do you think Congress should give the tools to agencies to stop pretexting Americans?

MS. DUNN. Absolutely. I think as a--here's what I think, and this is in my testimony and my opening statement. I think that the privacy of individuals needs to be protected with crystal-clear laws. I also believe that companies like Hewlett-Packard need to have a place where they can go to have investigations that are necessary to protect shareholder interest, accomplished within sanctioned safe harbors. Just like law enforcement carves itself out from pretexting laws, there needs to be a way for companies to do the kind of investigations they need to protect intellectual property and, in this case, repeated, unconfessed serious disclosure of confidential company information.

MR. INSLEE. And do you have any information as to why the United States House of Representatives, having had a bill passed to solve this problem, introduced the same time that this was going on at HP, why the leadership of this House, do you have any information, won't schedule a vote on this bill? Do you have any information why that is? Because, frankly, it is a mystery to me. I have checked with the Intelligence Committee. They said we don't have a hold on this bill. I asked my friends across the aisle. No one admits to having a hold on this bill. And I have to tell you, my constituents are tired of a Congress with backroom holds put on bills by secret--I don't know who they are--trying to stop this scandalous behavior that's going on. So I wonder if you have any advice about what is stopping Americans from getting this protection?

MS. DUNN. Sir, if there's anything I know less about than the details on the law on pretexting or the methods that are permissible in investigations, it's how the U.S. Congress passes bills.

MR. INSLEE. Well, in this case, how they don't pass bills.

MS. DUNN. Or how they don't pass bills.

MR. INSLEE. That's the situation.

MS. DUNN. But I would be happy to talk off line about what I can do, if anything, to help you in that matter.

MR. INSLEE. Well, I hope corporate America, responsible corporations, of which there are millions and millions, thankfully, in this country, will call Republican leadership in the House of Representatives and tell them to get this bill up on the suspension calendar and pass it. I have some suspicion that maybe those calls aren't being made. Maybe they are calls with a different message to GOP leadership.

I don't know what's going on here, but I hope that responsible corporate leadership will help us pass this bill. And I hope the pain that HP is going through today helps that message to get delivered. Thank you.

MS. DUNN. Thank you.

MR. WHITFIELD. The gentlelady from Tennessee is recognized for 10 minutes.

MRS. BLACKBURN. Thank you, Mr. Chairman. And thank you to all of you for your patience today.

Ms. Dunn, to you first, please, ma'am. The document that you submitted to us with your testimony on your duties of the independent chair, it's under Tab 3, I want to go, if we can, to that document for a couple of questions for clarification for the record.

First of all, you have said that you were the--your duties as the Chairman, and you've defined how unusual those duties were. But for the record, you were compensated for those duties. You were compensated for your Board membership and then compensated for your duties, and most of that you took in HP stock, correct?

MS. DUNN. That is correct. If you would like, I'll give you some details on that.

MRS. BLACKBURN. Yes, I would.

MS. DUNN. I began as a director at Hewlett-Packard in 1998. I was required by the company I worked for to renet I think 25 percent of my director's fees in cash. So I took 75 percent in stock and 25 percent in cash.

By 2002, I was able to take 100 percent of my director's fees in stock. I have received small cash stipends for chairing committee meetings along the way; I would say in 8 years, probably a total of $50,000 or less as a committee chairman and committee fees, which are extra.

MS. DUNN. And in September, I believe in 2006, for 6 months the compensation committee at HP basically forced me to accept an additional $100,000 of compensation which I take in stock which are for my duties as Chairman. The reason I turned it down was because I thought this was a responsibility that ought to rotate among the directors and that ought to be done on the basis of the needs of the company.

MRS. BLACKBURN. I want to go down on this, duties of the independent chair, and the first cell in this chart is flow of information to the Board. And in this, you state that you oversee the flow of information, including the quality, quantity and timeliness from management to the Board, and I will have to tell you, it is a--when you read the Kona report that is under Tab 29 that we have, and I think several of us are going back to page 10 in that report, it does lead me to ask, did you make decisions of holding back information about the pretexting, or did you decide to leave things off the agenda? Were there portions of the report that you chose to share and portions that you did not? Would you like to clarify that?

MS. DUNN. Thank you for giving me the chance to do that. One of the pieces of advice that I received earliest in this process from the investigative team was that if those who are being investigated, including myself, know all of the details about how they are being investigated, you no longer have a valid investigation.

So my approach to balancing my responsibilities to inform the Board and not compromise the investigation was to report to the Board at every regular meeting between the time that the first investigation began and ended that an investigation was underway, so--

MRS. BLACKBURN. So you basically distilled the information and then brought forward what you felt was appropriate?

MS. DUNN. Especially that they had to know I had responded to their request and I was taking steps.

MRS. BLACKBURN. Okay, the last cell in your duties of the independent chair, the CEO evaluation, was the Kona project included in Mr. Hurd's evaluation?

MS. DUNN. It was not.

MRS. BLACKBURN. So it was never referenced--

MS. DUNN. Never.

MRS. BLACKBURN. In the evaluation. What about for his predecessor?

MS. DUNN. Never.

MRS. BLACKBURN. Never. So it was never mentioned, it was totally off the record, off the book?

MS. DUNN. Well, let me say that with respect to Ms. Fiorina's reviews, I don't know that they were ever written. If they were I was never privy to them. But I have no reason to think that anything related to investigating Board leaks was ever a part of the review process with her. And the same is true for Mr. Hurd. And as important as this matter is to us now, I will tell you that this never rose to the level of significance to focus on as a matter of performance by our Board the last time he received a review.

I suspect it will the next time.

MRS. BLACKBURN. You had mentioned and testified earlier in response to Chairman Barton's question that it was your intention that the investigation be carried out ethically or legally and in the Kona report on page 10, you--in talking about this, the report that was given to you, contact established covertly with DK, a nontraceable Hotmail e-mail account, a dialogue has been established further planning of this operation is in progress.

Does that sound like it is ethical? Do you believe that to be an action item that would be ethical?

MS. DUNN. That rang a bell with me, which is why just as in every other case, I did not see myself as the right person to approve methods. I am not in charge of investigations at Hewlett-Packard. I referred the matter to management.

MRS. BLACKBURN. Mr. Sonsini, when was the first time that you heard anything about this investigation?

MR. SONSINI. The first time I heard about the Kona 1 and Kona 2 investigations, I believe was a note I received from Pattie Dunn on or about March 15th of this year.

MRS. BLACKBURN. So it would have been prior to the June 19th e-mails that are in here?

MR. SONSINI. Yes.

MRS. BLACKBURN. All right, and your e-mail, which is Tab 91, I think the square, I have got a couple of questions about this, point Number 5 in this e-mail where you are talking about the investigating team did obtain information regarding cell phone calls that were made. You say in here on that point the legal team also checked with outside counsel as to the legality of this methodology.

Other than you, sir, who was that outside counsel?

MR. SONSINI. Well, I subsequently learned that the outside counsel referred to was counsel--made by John Kiernan. I believe that he was counsel specifically to the investigating, lead investigator, Mr. DeLia.

MRS. BLACKBURN. So that was a separate outside counsel, it was not you, and you have represented yourself as being outside counsel to the Board.

MR. SONSINI. I am one of many outside counsels that Hewlett-Packard uses, yes, but this reference is clearly not to Wilson Sonsini.

MRS. BLACKBURN. And then point number 6 you--point number 4 and point number 6 in that e-mail, where you have the investigating team did not attempt to obtain the phone records of nonemployee directors in point number 6, there was no secret spying example, no electronic gear.

Do you now agree that those were false assumptions?

MR. SONSINI. I think our subsequent investigation clearly is at odds with these conclusions at that time, yes.

MRS. BLACKBURN. Okay.

MR. SONSINI. And these conclusions at the time, as my e-mail points out, are based upon two separate reports I received from the HP legal department in response to my questions: What was going on?

MRS. BLACKBURN. Did you know those were false before the 8/21 memo, the Number 115 went out, this item Number 115 in our book? Did you know that those were false at that time?

MR. SONSINI. Well, this all came to light during my investigation, which took place between August 9th, I believe, and August 23rd, so that is the period of time that this came to light to us. That is when we conducted an independent investigation as to the methods employed and when we began to learn, and I began to learn exactly what the methodology was.

MRS. BLACKBURN. Okay. You know, it is so interesting to me to listen to your testimony and how you came to the awareness of what pretexting was, had you ever heard of it before this took place?

MR. SONSINI. No ma'am, I did not. Not at all. I wasn't familiar, quite frankly, with sub-rosa investigations. In 40 years of practicing law I have never been involved in one.

MRS. BLACKBURN. I find it so interesting because in your e-mail, you seem to chastise Mr. Perkins for questioning, and while at the same time, you seem to give a confidence that there is no legal issue that would surround this, that the company's Board Chairman really didn't understand or know the details of the program either, but that everything seemed to be legal, even though you give yourself some cover in saying that you weren't involved in the formulation of plan.

So it leads--as we are trying to work through this pretexting issue, you know, you seem to contradict yourself several times within the e-mail as to your level of understanding of what this is. And maybe even your doubts, and I think that is one of the reasons that we are here.

MR. SONSINI. With all due respect--

MR. WHITFIELD. Gentlelady's time has expired, but I would like you to answer the question.

MR. SONSINI. With all due respect, I am not chastising Mr. Perkins. Quite the contrary. I am being forthright as I can be to lay out to him everything that is going on. I am the first person to surface to him and to anyone that pretexting was taking place based upon the information I got from HP. That is first.

Secondly at this point in time, I had conducted no inquiry. I wasn't asked to conduct any inquiry. I was not knowledge--had no knowledge of the methodologies used. I was relying upon the HP legal department. And I required not just a telephone call--I required two separate reports confirming what they did so I could pass it on.

I was, as my e-mail points out, being transparent with Mr. Perkins in response to his questions. There is no inconsistency whatsoever in my conduct at this time. If we look at the investigation that I did do, which has been referred to and turned over to the staff, you will see it was then that we were quite clear as our views on the situation.

MR. WHITFIELD. At this time, I recognize the gentlelady from Wisconsin for 10 minutes.

MS. BALDWIN. Thank you, Mr. Chairman.

Ms. Dunn, I wanted to ask this question to Ms. Baskins, but earlier today, she pled the Fifth, so I am going to ask you. There was a press conference last week conducted by Mr. Hurd and an attorney from the law firm of Morgan Lewis.

At that press conference, there was an indication that a draft of the Kona 2 investigation was prepared in early 2006. Is that correct?

MS. DUNN. I think the first--sorry, the first report which was titled "Final Draft" was dated either March 14th or March 12, 2006.

MS. BALDWIN. Could you turn to page--I'm sorry, Tab 72 of the document book. And this appears to be something labeled draft, not final draft. And it is dated March 10th directed to Pattie Dunn, Mark Hurd and Ann Baskins. Is that the document--

MS. DUNN. Yes, I stand corrected on the date.

MS. BALDWIN. And do you believe you possibly received it around March 10th or on March 10th?

MS. DUNN. Yes, I do.

MS. BALDWIN. Ms. Dunn, can you tell me whether you met with Mr. Hurd to discuss this draft report at this stage of the investigation?

MS. DUNN. Yes. After this report was issued, I am sorry I am not remembering the date, but it is in my written testimony, there was a meeting between myself, Ms. Baskins, the investigative team. It took place in Los Angeles. It was around March 15th or 16th.

MS. BALDWIN. And can you share with the committee the nature of that discussion?

MS. DUNN. Once again, it focused on the results. We were upset about this matter. We were upset that we were going to have to ask a long-standing Board member to come forward and acknowledge after having allowed this investigation to go on with his knowledge for a year.

MS. BALDWIN. Ms. Dunn, at the time this draft was presented to you and to Mr. Hurd and to Ms. Baskins, who specifically was doing the legal analysis to ensure that the investigative methods detailed in this report were legal? Whose job was that?

MS. DUNN. From my perspective, I was relying on Ann Baskins. I believe she was relying on Mr. Hunsaker.

MS. BALDWIN. According to the same Morgan Lewis pronouncement last Friday, in April of 2006, this report was also provided to an outside corporate counsel. Is that correct?

MS. DUNN. It was provided to Mr. Sonsini as well as to the chairman of HP's Audit Committee.

MS. BALDWIN. And can you tell me who and what was the role that they were to play having been provided this report?

MS. DUNN. We, the group I will name, Mr. Sonsini, Mr. Ryan, myself, Mr. Hurd and Ms. Baskins, met at HP some time in late April, I believe, to discuss the way forward, given the results of this report.

MS. BALDWIN. Mr. Sonsini, when you received this draft--you should look at the document book also. And do you recognize that document and recall having received it?

MR. SONSINI. I do.

MS. BALDWIN. Okay. When you reviewed that, what did you think when you saw on page 3, a bullet point at the bottom of that page: "obtained, reviewed and analyzed HP and third-party phone records to identify calls made to or from reporters or other individuals of interest during the relevant time frames." And then on page 4: "obtained reviewed and analyzed--oops, I am sorry--engineered and executed a covert intelligence-gathering operation pursuant to which an undercover investigator established e-mail contact with Kawamoto, the CNET reporter using an untraceable Hotmail account." The operation included placing a legally permissible software tracing device in an e-mail attachment sent to Kawamoto?

MR. SONSINI. Yes. When I got the report, I got the report, as Pattie Dunn has indicated, with a view of what do we do with the result that we now have discovered the person who leaked the information, what do we the with the result in terms of a corporate governance point of view going forward?

And I did not focus--other than on the words and the footnotes saying that it was lawfully done--on this sub-rosa investigation. It certainly seemed to me to be somewhat over the top. But my focus at the time because I am not an expert in such matters, and they would not send this report to me to comment upon those kinds of issues, my focus was I was dealing now with a serious corporate governance issue. I've got a problem.

MS. BALDWIN. I, of course, am focusing on what you didn't focus on. So I guess I want to explore that a little bit further, because this document was now available to you and to a number of others. Who was in charge of making sure that--making sure that this--the tactics used were legal and once this was disclosed back in March, who pursued questioning the legality of the techniques?

MR. SONSINI. I think the record has become quite clear that who was in charge was the Hewlett-Packard internal legal department. They took the responsibility on rightly, wrongly, that's what happened. I came in after the fact and learned that.

So that is who is in charge.

MS. BALDWIN. Ms. Dunn, on May 24, 2006, Mr. Kevin Hunsaker produced a final report of the Kona investigation, isn't that correct?

MS. DUNN. Yes. There was nothing to the best of my knowledge that went on from an investigation standpoint from March 10th to the final report. I believe the only thing that was left to finalize it were the results of Mr. Ryan, the Chairman of the Audit Committee, interview with Mr. Keyworth.

MS. BALDWIN. And if you could turn to Document 89, I just would like to make sure that we are referring to the same document.

MS. DUNN. Yes, we are.

MS. BALDWIN. So that is the final report.

And on page 4 of that document, we see obviously the final language here, but it indicates that HP obtained, reviewed and analyzed HP phone records and third-party phone information to identify calls made to or from reporters or other individuals of interest during the relevant timeframes.

Ms. Dunn, when was the earliest that you knew that HP employees either directly or through outside investigators were obtaining third-party phone records?

MS. DUNN. As I have testified and in my written testimony as well, I became aware that phone records were a part of this investigation in circa June 2005.

MS. BALDWIN. When you read this bullet point in the final report, were you troubled by that?

MS. DUNN. I need to find the exact bullet point, but I was certainly not surprised that phone records were involved. I had known that for 9 months.

MS. BALDWIN. On that same report, page 4, third bullet point down, again, I will read it for the record, "engineered and executed a covert intelligence-gathering operation pursuant to which an undercover investigator established e-mail contact with Kawamoto, the CNET reporter using an untraceable Hotmail account, the operation included placing a legally permissible software-based tracing device in an e-mail attachment sent to Kawamoto."

Were you troubled by this bullet point in the report?

MS. DUNN. I saw that. Remember the first time I became aware of that technique was back in February. And that is when I referred it on. I did not see myself at any point as having a role in approving methods. I wanted the HP standard ways of doing these investigations to be used to investigate a standard of business conduct violation at the Board level. The Board is--the Board signs up to the same standards of business conduct as every other employee. And my view was what HP does normally to investigate these matters is the appropriate thing to use in this matter concerning our Board. That judgment may be seriously questionable in retrospect but it was my judgment at the time.

MS. BALDWIN. One closing question. How did you come by the name Kona 1 and Kona 2?

MS. DUNN. The first time I spoke with Mr. DeLia, which I believe was some time in possibly April of 2005, I was on vacation in Kona. The name Kona will never mean the same thing to me again. But he said you know when we do this work we always assign a project name to it. Do you have any preferences? And I looked down at the piece of paper in front of me and it had something about Kona and I said Kona.

MR. WHITFIELD. Chair recognizes Mr. Burgess for 10 minutes.

MR. BURGESS. Thank you, Mr. Chairman. Thank you all for being here and your forbearance; we do appreciate you providing answers to our questions.

Mr. Adler, I don't want you to feel left out, so let's talk for a minute. Can I ask you for a minute do you have the big book in front of you?

MR. ALDER. No, I do not.

MR. BURGESS. Can I ask you to get a copy of the big book and turn to Tab 20?

MR. ALDER. Did you say page 20, sir?

MR. BURGESS. Tab 20 in the great big book in front of you. Not printed on the Heidelberg press. 20. 20. Two zero.

And in this e-mail, Mr. Hunsaker asked whether there is any way to lawfully get text message content or is it the same as cell phone records, did that suggest to you that he believed accessing cell phone records was illegal?

MR. ALDER. Sir, could you please restate your question? I want to make sure I perfectly understand you.

MR. BURGESS. Well, you say here, Mr. Hunsaker says in the message or the message to Mr. Hunsaker says: "Even if we could legally obtain the records," did you have a reason to suspect that the obtaining of the records would be other than legal?

MR. ALDER. I am sorry. I am not trying to be smart about this. I do have a slight hearing deficit and I am having difficulty.

MR. BURGESS. Let me speak slowly in simple declarative sentences. When Mr. Hunsaker asked whether "Is there any way to lawfully get text message content or is it the same as cell phone records?" Did that suggest to you that he believed accessing cell phone records was, in itself, illegal?

MR. ALDER. I don't fully understand the question.

MR. BURGESS. Okay, we are not going to get an answer. Let's go to Tab 40, if you don't mind. Can I ask you to turn to Tab 40 in your book?

MR. ALDER. Thank you.

MR. BURGESS. Right in the middle of the page, under--there is a heavy line there and it says from Adler, Frederick P, which I assume is you, right, just below the middle of the page it says: "agreed I am very concerned about the legality of this information."

MR. ALDER. Yes, sir. I see it.

MR. BURGESS. Can you tell us what you were concerned about?

MR. ALDER. This message occurred between myself and my co-investigator, Vincent Nye. This message went back and forth between us after a meeting on February 7th between the investigative, the leak, undisclosed leak investigation team consisting of myself, Mr. Nye, Mr. Hunsaker, Mr. Gentilucci and Mr. DeLia.

It was at that meeting that we had, that both myself and Mr. Nye had started questioning Mr. Gentilucci and Mr. DeLia and Mr. Hunsaker about the pretext calling and how the information was being obtained and whether it was in compliance with law.

MR. BURGESS. What did you do to ensure yourself that it indeed was in compliance with the law?

MR. ALDER. This issue had already been broached the previous day with a statement by, I believe it was Mr. DeLia, that they had obtained call information from the personal call information belonging to Mr. Keyworth. That was the first time that I had been aware of any such activity.

MR. BURGESS. Mr. Adler I want to interrupt you because of the interest of time, and I do have a follow-up question that I am going to submit in written form, and ask if you would--if you wouldn't mind providing us an answer, but I am going to ask you a series of questions and it should go fairly quickly.

At any point during the Kona 2 investigation, did anyone say, what we are doing is just crazy?

MR. ALDER. Essentially, myself and Mr. Nye did. We went to--we went to--Mr. Nye went to Mr. Gentilucci, as we have already seen testimony up here today in evidence of. I went to my manager late on the 6th or early on the morning of 7 February, 2006, and told them I was deeply troubled and concerned about what happened. Shortly thereafter, Mr. Nye also contacted my manager after not receiving satisfaction through his manager, Mr. Gentilucci. My manager, Timothy O'Neill, a former law enforcement officer, also became very concerned with what was occurring. And he said that he would go forward with our concerns. He made contact with both Mr. Gentilucci and with counsel, which was Mr. Hunsaker, and expressed his concerns.

MR. BURGESS. What was Ms. Dunn's level of involvement in the Kona 2 investigation, to the best of your recollection?

MS. DUNN. The suspense level?

MR. BURGESS. No, her level of involvement in the Kona 2 investigation?

MR. ALDER. The level of whose involvement?

MR. BURGESS. Patricia Dunn.

MR. ALDER. I have only hearsay to offer to Mr. Hunsaker's statements, and that was she was being reported to during the course of the investigation as to our progress, and at the end of the investigation, she was given a report as to our findings.

MR. BURGESS. Did you attend any of the meetings with Ms. Dunn about the investigation?

MR. ALDER. No, I did not.

MR. BURGESS. During the course of the Kona 2 investigation, was Ms. Dunn aware that pretexting was being utilized to access personal telephone records?

MR. ALDER. I have no knowledge of that.

MR. BURGESS. Would that be included in that report that you just referenced?

MR. ALDER. The pretexting?

MR. BURGESS. Yes.

MR. ALDER. It could be.

MR. BURGESS. Do we have a copy of that report?

MR. ALDER. I believe--well, I don't know. It was in my e-mail, but I know the committee has received quite a bit of it, so I don't know.

MR. BURGESS. Well, did Ms. Dunn have to approve certain aspects of the investigation before you could proceed?

MR. ALDER. I don't know. That was between Mr. Hunsaker and Ann Baskins and Ms. Dunn. I have no knowledge.

MR. BURGESS. Two of those individuals took the Fifth Amendment, so I didn't have a chance to question them, so that is why I am asking you to help with that.

MR. ALDER. I understand.

MR. BURGESS. Who came up with the idea of the embedded tracking device?

MR. ALDER. That was my idea.

MR. BURGESS. And we have heard this referred to previously as a legally permissible--

MR. ALDER. Yes, at the time I understood it to be a legally permissible way to obtain information. And I still believe it to be as such. It is--it was and still is sanctioned by my management as an investigative tool. We have used it in the past for investigations for determining locations of stolen product and what not. We have also assisted law enforcement. We have recently recovered an at-risk child with the same technology.

MR. BURGESS. But who has to approve the use of that--who has to approve the use of the tracking device; it is almost like putting a wiretap on your phone Mr. Alder.

MR. ALDER. I beg your pardon, sir.

MR. BURGESS. To me, to a lay consumer, that is akin to someone putting a wiretap on my phone.

MR. ALDER. A wiretap is normally considered a real-time interception. This is not a real-time interception. It is also the interception of personal data. We did not intercept any personal data.

MR. BURGESS. Mr. Adler, it is equivalent to going through the mail in my mailbox.

MR. ALDER. I didn't go through your mail.

MR. BURGESS. Let me ask you this. Can you turn to Tab 50 for a moment. So there will be no question in anyone's mind what we have in front of us, this looks to be a how-to kit on how to put this tracking device in a zip file and attach it to an e-mail. Is that correct?

MR. ALDER. That is correct.

MR. BURGESS. And these are instructions that were sent by you to Mr. Hunsaker and Mr. Gentilucci and Mr. Nye and other people who took the Fifth Amendment earlier?

MR. ALDER. Correct.

MR. BURGESS. Does Patricia Dunn know that this recipe was being forwarded and utilized?

MR. ALDER. I have no idea.

MR. BURGESS. Ms. Dunn, do you know? Do you have Tab 50 in front of you? Do you have Mr. Adler's e-mail?

MS. DUNN. I was not copied on this e-mail and I am seeing it for the first time here.

MR. BURGESS. So this was not something you had been aware of before today?

MS. DUNN. No, sir.

MR. BURGESS. Does this strike you as being a permissible tactic to use, attaching a tracking device onto an e-mail? It is going to give me the creeps to think someone would do that. Does it bother you?

MS. DUNN. It is kind of surprising that it is legal, isn't it?

MR. BURGESS. Ms. Dunn, Hewlett-Packard has acknowledged that the personal telephone records of several directors and employees were accessed during the Kona investigations.

I would like to read to you written testimony provided by Scott Taylor the chief privacy officer of Hewlett-Packard, during a hearing of this committee's Subcommittee on Commerce, Trade, and Consumer Protection. This occurred back in June, and I quote. "As a company, Hewlett-Packard is 100 percent committed to excellence in consumer and employee privacy for two fundamental reasons: First, because it is the right thing to do. We have an obligation to fulfill the trust that Hewlett-Packard employees have given us in handling their information."

I would ask you, would you agree that accessing personal phone records of your employees and directors is a major breach of trust?

MS. DUNN. It should never have happened. I would like to add that 99.999 percent of Hewlett-Packard's employees live up to the statement you just read every day.

MR. BURGESS. I thank you. Mr. Chairman, if I can make one observation, this is a day I guess that the stock market is going to crest at a historic high that it hasn't seen since the year 2000. And we all recall it was in part the lack of corporate self-governance that brought the stock market low after its all time high of 11,700, whatever it was back in March of 2000. We have recovered from that corporate problem. We have recovered from 9/11. We have recovered from the dot com bubble. Please don't take us down that path again. I yield back.

MS. DEGETTE. Mr. Chairman, I would ask unanimous consent for 1 minute to follow up on Mr. Burgess' question, to ask Mr. Adler a question.

MR. STEARNS. I object.

MR. WHITFIELD. You object? Ms. Eshoo, I said I was going to go to you next, but it is our procedure to allow the members of the Oversight Committee to finish first, so at this time I recognize Mr. Stearns for 10 minutes.

MR. STEARNS. Mr. Chairman, I am going to give unanimous consent to the gentlelady to ask her question.

MR. WHITFIELD. Ms. DeGette is recognized for 1 minute.

MS. DEGETTE. Mr. Adler, I heard you testify in response to Mr. Burgess that this embedded technology is a technique used quite frequently. Is that correct?

MR. ALDER. I believe it to be so. There is a site called readnotify.com.

MS. DEGETTE. How long have you worked at Hewlett-Packard, Mr. Adler?

MR. ALDER. A little bit over 3 years now.

MS. DEGETTE. And how often have you used this technique of embedded technology to trace e-mails during your employment at Hewlett-Packard?

MR. ALDER. Personally?

MS. DEGETTE. Personally or your--that you know of.

MR. ALDER. I would have to venture a guess at maybe a dozen, 2 dozen times.

MS. DEGETTE. And in what circumstances?

MR. ALDER. In investigating corporate issues such as theft, as I said. Also we assisted law enforcement, just recently in locating an at-risk child with the technology. It is--

MS. DEGETTE. Have you used it to investigate internal leaks before this particular situation?

MR. ALDER. No, we have not, not to my knowledge.

MS. DEGETTE. Thank you.

MR. WHITFIELD. Mr. Stearns.

MR. STEARNS. Thank you Mr. Chairman.

Mr. Sonsini, let me just ask this question. In your written testimony, you say that the use of pretexting and similar intrusive investigative methods in these circumstances is wrong. Is that correct?

MR. SONSINI. Yes.

MR. STEARNS. In Exhibit 91, however, you conclude that "the process was well done and within legal limits." So I guess the question is what has changed between then and now? Do you want to see that Exhibit 91?

MR. SONSINI. No, I am familiar with it, Congressman. At the time of that communication, I think you are referring to my June e-mail to Mr. Perkins, I was relying upon the HP legal department in responding to me when I asked how should we respond to Mr. Perkin's concerns? Tell me what you have done?

I received a written report from Mr. Hunsaker who oversaw the investigation. I received a written report from Ann Baskins of the General Counsel. I spoke to Ms. Baskins and I asked for repeated assurances: do you believe that this was all done properly? I then took that information without any independent investigation, and sent the e-mail to Mr. Perkins and it says "it appears." "It appears."

MR. STEARNS. Can I safely say that at that point you felt you were within your legal limits to do this?

MR. SONSINI. Yes. I was asked to do this by Ann Baskins. I was asked to respond to Mr. Perkins.

MR. STEARNS. So what--knowing what you know today and what you said in your testimony, you stand by the position now that it is wrong, right?

MR. SONSINI. Absolutely. After we did conduct an investigation and I had the opportunity to look into the matter and had the opportunity to research the law, and do our investigation, we concluded quite the contrary.

MR. STEARNS. At the time of these investigations were you aware that several States including Florida, California and Georgia were considering legislation that would specifically ban pretexting for telephone records?

MR. SONSINI. I subsequently learned that. When we did our investigation in August, we looked at those statutes and we saw that the law was rapidly changing in the country regarding pretexting. That's correct.

MR. STEARNS. Perhaps you heard my opening statement. I mentioned a California statute that said it was wrong to do this. And that was in play when you were previously involved, in fact, when you said that you thought it was legally acceptable. Did you know about that statute back then?

MR. SONSINI. No, I didn't, sir. As I indicated, I didn't know about the methodologies going on then and I am no expert. I didn't even know the law of pretexting at that point in time. It wasn't until we did our investigation in August that I became cognizant of it.

MR. STEARNS. Ms. Dunn, knowing what you know today, is it your position that pretexting is wrong today?

MS. DUNN. Yes, sir, it is.

MR. STEARNS. So you are categorically saying it is wrong?

MS. DUNN. It is fraud. It is the fraudulent misrepresentation of identity. It is wrong.

MR. STEARNS. And knowing what you do today you would not have let these investigators do this?

MS. DUNN. I would have gone through the management chain. I did not supervise the investigators, but I would have either brought it to the attention of the Chairman of the Audit Committee or to the CEO if I thought fraud was involved.

MR. STEARNS. I would think that since you--and you authorized it--they would report to you regularly. Didn't they do that with progress reports?

MS. DUNN. They did provide me progress reports, but I was not the supervisor of this investigation. I had no role in management. Other people were involved in managing the investigation, choosing the techniques.

MR. STEARNS. But you got progress reports, didn't you?

MS. DUNN. I got just updates, and I was focused on the results.

MR. STEARNS. Were briefings given to you?

MS. DUNN. I had--I think there were three meetings over the course of--

MR. STEARNS. So you had three briefings by--

MS. DUNN. The course of 13 months.

MR. STEARNS. Okay. And the 3 briefings, did they ever tell you how they got the information?

MS. DUNN. I was told in I think it was April or May, I have testified earlier, April 2005, that phone records were involved and I was informed of that by Mr. DeLia.

MR. STEARNS. I think honestly, if you were notified that they were even doing pretexting, I am not sure you or many people would even know that that was wrong at that point, because you know when pretexting came up on our committee, a lot of us didn't know what it was. And when we heard it and we had a chance to think about it, we understood it was wrong, but I mean it is such a serious way that investigators do this that it has probably become widespread.

MS. DUNN. If I may offer, I think, the word "pretexting" is a pretext. It is meant to confuse.

MR. STEARNS. Yes, I understand that.

Ms. Dunn, your written testimony is 33 pages long. You go into great detail explaining why the investigation was necessary and how you were assured that these aggressive tactics were legal. You even advocate congressional action to produce clear-cut rules on pretexting, a suggestion that this committee has endorsed. However, conspicuous by its absence in your testimony is any degree of contrition or acceptance of responsibility.

And I have listened to this testimony in my office, and you have just indicated it is wrong. You indicated you had been briefed three times, and yet, there is no suggestion that you are going to accept any responsibility and no sense that what you did was wrong. So I get the sense after reading your testimony that you still do not really believe that you did anything wrong here. And I guess that is a question.

Do you feel that you are totally innocent here and with no culpability?

MS. DUNN. My understanding is that my opening statement is a part of my full submission.

MR. STEARNS. Ms. Dunn, if I--

MS. DUNN. May I answer your question, sir?

MR. STEARNS. I am asking the questions. The question I want is yes or no, do you think that your--have any culpability in this whole fiasco? Just yes or no.

MS. DUNN. I will repeat what I said in my opening statement. I deeply regret that so many people were badly affected.

MR. STEARNS. We are not talking about other people. We are talking about you personally.

MS. DUNN. Including me, that was said in my opening statement. And I would like to tell you what I would do differently--

MR. STEARNS. But regret is one thing, but culpability that you accept blame is another, and I am just trying to think--and I know, I mean, you could say you are not blamable. You can say that, but I am just trying to put on the record whether you think you are at fault for anything, other than regrets and you are sorry and things like that.

Is it just possible you could say yes or no, that you feel you have some culpability?

MS. DUNN. If I knew then what I know now, I would have done things very differently and there are some specific things I would have done very differently.

MR. STEARNS. I am interpreting that--

MS. DUNN. It is a foundational component of corporate governance that directors must rely on the reasonable representations of management.

MR. STEARNS. But--

MS. DUNN. And those I did have.

MR. STEARNS. I am interpreting what you say is that knowing what you know today it was wrong?

MS. DUNN. Absolutely.

MR. STEARNS. And knowing what you do today that you have to accept responsibility, you have to accept personal responsibility for what happened. That is my interpretation of what you are telling me. Is that a correct interpretation?

MS. DUNN. Sir, I do not accept personal responsibility for what happened.

MR. STEARNS. Okay, okay. Mr. Chairman, I think she is basically saying she is not culpable here, and she accepts no responsibilities for what occurred. I understand.

Now, under the circumstances, considering how you feel, wouldn't it, at this point, occur to you that you might want to resign because of all these problems?

MS. DUNN. I have done so, sir.

MR. STEARNS. Okay. Okay. Okay.

MS. DUNN. I will do so again, if you like.

MR. STEARNS. I guess, in your opinion, now you can tell me why you resigned.

MS. DUNN. I resigned because the Board of Hewlett-Packard asked me to resign a week ago Friday. Last Friday.

MR. STEARNS. And why do you think they asked you to resign?

MS. DUNN. Because they had voted twice in the prior 2 weeks. I am not sure if it was a vote, but I had heard that they unanimously supported me to remain as Chairman and Director until about 10 days ago, in which case, by which time the press reaction to all of this had become so intense that we agreed I should step down as Chairman in January. But I was asked to remain as a director by many directors.

The press reaction became more and more and more intense. And I think that finally, the Board decided I was a major distraction to the company getting over this problem. They asked me to resign and I accepted their decision.

MR. STEARNS. Let me ask one more question. Let me just say that, somehow in my personal opinion, that I have great empathy for you, because I have seen, I have been in these oversight committees enough to know that very competent innocent people get caught up in things they don't understand, but let me, Mr. Chairman, get my one last question in here.

Ms. Dunn, your written testimony says repeatedly that you received assurance that the tactics used in the investigation were both common and legal, but I would like you to turn to Exhibit 39. Exhibit 39, in this e-mail, one of the investigators, Vince Nye, expressed serious reservations about what was being done to gather phone records.

He says "it is very unethical at the least, and probably illegal. If it is not totally illegal, then it is leading Hewlett-Packard in a position that could damage our reputation or worse."

So my question is, even if you had been told that these tactics were legal, why was Mr. Nye apparently the only one to consider the negative publicity that might be generated and how that might harm the company? Wasn't that your job there to act and do something based upon that Exhibit 39?

MS. DUNN. The first time I heard that any member of this investigative team had concerns about its legality was from my lawyer this morning, who read it in The Washington Post, and maybe less than a week ago, I read a report that Mr. Adler had expressed concerns. There was never any hint that anyone at Hewlett-Packard had concerns. Quite to the contrary.

MR. WHITFIELD. The gentleman's time has expired. Since all members of the Oversight Subcommittee have asked questions, I recognize Ms. Eshoo for 10 minutes.

MS. ESHOO. Thank you, Mr. Chairman, very much. Thank you to the witnesses.

Ms. Dunn, I want you to know that I have a great deal of respect for what you have done with your life.

MS. DUNN. Thank you.

MS. ESHOO. You have I think been absolutely remarkable from where you began, very humble beginnings and culminating with the chairmanship of the Board of Directors of one of the most prestigious companies in the world. I want you to know I respect that.

And again, I have this heaviness about me because I think this is enormously sad. I just want to make a couple of observations.

There are teams and teams and teams of lawyers around every company, corporation, publicly held entity, and I guess that is the way it needs to be. But I think that when you drill down in this, that there is some lawyer from some shoe box outfit in Massachusetts that people ended up relying upon for legal advice.

And I think that that should send a huge message to the company--and to all companies--that, as one of my colleagues said, none of these things should be circular. People are relying from one memo to another. But there is that whole the human interaction of taking time to be thoughtful and say, besides being legal, is this right? Is this right?

That is why there is so much regret about this. Someone said to me many, many years ago, whatever you do, Anna, always remember, picture it above the fold on the front page of the newspaper, what you say, what you write, what you think and what you act on. And I think that is a lesson for all of us, there isn't anyone in this hearing room that is perfect. This is a manifestation of how less than perfect human beings are, even those that are in the highest reaches of corporations and law firms.

So with that, Mr. Adler, can you hear me?

MR. ALDER. Yes, ma'am.

MS. ESHOO. I would like to ask you a couple of questions about this whole investigative arm of HP. How long has HP had a retainer contract with either SOS, ARG or Eye in the Sky?

MR. ALDER. I am afraid I can't answer the question because I don't have the information. That was all done through, I believe, Mr. Gentilucci.

MS. ESHOO. Well, maybe we can find out from Mr. Hurd. Do you know if these companies have been on retainer with HP and if so, for how long?

MR. ALDER. I am sorry, I don't have that information either.

MS. ESHOO. How long have you worked for HP? Have you worked for HP?

MR. ALDER. I am sorry. I worked for HP over 3 years.

MS. ESHOO. And prior to this explosion of this scandal, as an employee in your position had you ever heard of any of these people that were on retainer?

MR. ALDER. Yes, I had previously been on an investigation where it was a group, more or less of a better word, task force.

MS. ESHOO. How did you use them?

MR. ALDER. Mr. DeLia SOS, a/k/a SOS, was responsible for providing background information during the course of the investigation.

MS. ESHOO. Are you aware of any pretexting ever going on through contracting with these outfits, outside of Kona 1 and Kona 2?

MR. ALDER. No, not until February 6th of this year.

MS. ESHOO. When you say you were concerned, what did you do about your concern?

MR. ALDER. I went to my manager and--

MS. ESHOO. And he was or she was?

MR. ALDER. He is.

MS. ESHOO. He is --

MR. ALDER. Timothy O'Neill, and Mr. O'Neill recognized my concerns. Mr. Nye also went to Mr. O'Neill, as I stated earlier, since Mr. Gentilucci wouldn't listen to us.

MS. ESHOO. Was it ever kicked upstairs? This is another circle, see, where people are concerned but something is not happening with it. Was it ever kicked upstairs?

MR. ALDER. This is a rather unique circumstance.

MS. ESHOO. It sure is.

MR. ALDER. It was very confidential. There were a limited amount of people who knew about it. Mr. Hunsaker was counsel and so we knew, we, meaning Mr. O'Neill and myself and Mr. Nye, that if we had gone directly to Mr. Hurd or Ms. Dunn or Ms. Baskins with our concerns, they would have immediately gone back--

MS. ESHOO. I can tell something didn't happen with it.

Let me go to Mr. Sonsini. It is good to see you.

MR. SONSINI. Thank you.

MS. ESHOO. It is a long way from Palo Alto to this hearing, but at least the weather is beautiful. It is like Palo Alto here today.

MR. SONSINI. Wonderful.

MS. ESHOO. There is a quote that is attributed to you over and over again in the press. I think that it was, I know that it was referred to today. I don't have the big briefing book in front of me with the different sections in it. But essentially it has been attributed to you that pretexting was legal.

Can you speak to that just briefly? I have some follow-up questions I would like to ask you.

MR. SONSINI. Yes. The press is absolutely wrong on that. I never took a position that pretexting is legal. Quite frankly once we investigated the matter and we got into it, we came out with a report on legality. The press took the e-mail to Mr. Perkins and turned it into a legal opinion of Mr. Sonsini. That was not it. My e-mail was very clear. Mr. Perkins made an inquiry of me. I promptly went to Ms. Baskins, and I said give me the information to respond to him. I want to be open to him, what was going on.

I just didn't receive a flippant answer. I got a written report from Mr. Hunsaker. I got a written report from Ms. Baskins. I talked to her about it, and I took that information, I conveyed it to Mr. Perkins and then I said, based upon what they told me, that it appears--that it appears--that this was within legal limits. It was not an opinion. It was conveying the truth, what I was told.

At that point in time, I was not asked to give any legal opinion. That came later. At that point in time.

MS. ESHOO. What about the form 8-K, where there is a reference to it? Can you speak to that?

MR. SONSINI. The form 8-K--that must be the 8-K filed at the end of August, and that 8-K, I think, refers now to outside counsel's view on legality. Yes, that came after we conducted the investigation which began August 9th, well after the June exchange.

MS. ESHOO. Let me ask you this. You have been the outside counsel for HP for years, and--

MR. SONSINI. One of the outside counsel.

MS. ESHOO. Yes, and I think everyone in the hearing room, if they don't know, should know that you represent a good part of companies in Silicon Valley.

When there is a director such as the one that--really I can't believe that he is not here today. This is Dr. Keyworth. How do you advise a Board when--let me ask you this. Did the Board ever come to you and say, outside of pretexting and investigations, there is a problem with this Board. I mean, it really sounds like it is somewhat dysfunctional to me. People say the parties scrap, the political parties, but boy you really had a whopper there. But, at any rate, a member of the Board of Directors of a publicly held company has a fiduciary responsibility--it is a huge responsibility, because very average people's money is placed in investment funds that are invested in premium companies: firemen, policemen, nurses, teachers, so this is, a very serious thing.

Were you ever made aware that there was someone there who couldn't keep his mouth shut and that it was damaging, that it was not only inappropriate, but proprietary information that goes right to the heart of damaging what shareholders hold?

MR. SONSINI. As a matter of fact, I was aware. I was aware back in January of 2005. The Board did come to me. Actually it was the Nominating and Governance Committee along with Carly Fiorina that came to me and said we believe we have leaks in the boardroom. What should we do?

I said there are three things we have to do. One, I should make an inquiry of each director; two, we should remind them of their confidential obligations; and three, we should conduct an evaluation of the Board. They said, you have the assignment.

So what I did do, is I talked to each director. I was unsuccessful in finding the leak.

I reminded them of their confidentiality and then--

MS. ESHOO. Did you talk to Dr. Keyworth?

MR. SONSINI. I certainly did.

MS. ESHOO. And he denied it?

MR. SONSINI. And he denied it. And then I presented a report of my evaluation of the Board--a very candid report of what I thought the problem was. You are correct, Congresswoman, that the leak is a symptom of a greater problem.

The way I dealt with it was to deal with it in the boardroom.

MR. WHITFIELD. Gentlelady's time is expired.

MS. ESHOO. Thank you, Mr. Chairman. Are we going to have another round?

MR. WHITFIELD. We are going to have another round.

The gentleman from Massachusetts is recognized for 10 minutes.

MR. MARKEY. Thank you, Mr. Chairman. Ms. Dunn, did any of the previous investigations by Mr. DeLia for HP involve the use of pretexting in order to obtain telephone records, Social Security numbers or other confidential personal information for the company?

MS. DUNN. I have no knowledge about any previous investigations done by Mr. DeLia. All I knew, and know, is that he had done work, this kind of work for the company almost exclusively for 8 or 9 years.

MR. MARKEY. Do you know, Mr. Adler, if Mr. DeLia had ever used pretexting in other investigations?

MR. ALDER. Congressman Markey, I only can offer hearsay from Mr. Nye that he had complained to his manager, Mr. Gentilucci, on previous occasions about the practice.

MR. MARKEY. Mr. Sonsini, do you know if Mr. DeLia had used pretexting in other investigations?

MR. SONSINI. I don't know. I think our investigation, when we interrogated him, there may have been an answer to that. I don't recall.

MR. MARKEY. Ms. Dunn, did any of the previous investigations by Mr. DeLia or any other person at HP or employed by HP involve spying on corporate competitors to HP? In other words, if HP was willing to spy on yourselves, did HP engage in corporate espionage of other companies?

MS. DUNN. Congressman Markey, the only investigation that HP has ever done with which I have any familiarity are the ones known as Kona 1 and Kona 2.

MR. MARKEY. Mr. Adler, do you know if there was corporate spying on other corporations?

MR. ALDER. I have no such knowledge.

MR. MARKEY. Mr. Sonsini, do you know?

MR. SONSINI. No, sir, I don't.

MR. MARKEY. Ms. Dunn, in a January 2006 e-mail to Kevin Hunsaker, Mr. Gentilucci states, quote, "We use pretext interviews on a number of investigations to extract information and/or make covert purchases of stolen property, in a sense, all undercover operations."

What do you know about this use of pretext interviews by HP which Mr. Gentilucci was referring to?

MS. DUNN. I know nothing about HP's investigations outside of Kona 1 and Kona 2, but I have testified that the methods used in those two investigations were standard at HP.

MR. MARKEY. Ms. Dunn, an amended 8-K was filed last night with the Securities and Exchange Commission. Will you please comment on the accuracy of that filing?

MS. DUNN. Congressman Markey, I have asked my attorney, Mr. Brosnahan, to communicate directly with Morgan Lewis, a copy of which letter was sent this morning. There are inaccuracies in the 8-K. I have to point out that I was certainly no longer a part of the company when that was filed, but it was based on information that could have been obtained while I was part of the directors of HP. And I'm afraid that because no one ever asked me, and they certainly haven't looked at my sworn testimony, that filing was made with a couple of mistakes.

MR. MARKEY. Okay. An 8-K filing was made by HP today which reports that HP's Board has, quote, "reviewed and approved certain benefits to Ms. Baskins," HP's General Counsel, who resigned from HP last night and took the Fifth Amendment here today and refused to testify.

Do you think that giving a more than $3.6 million golden parachute is an appropriate action by HP at this time?

MS. DUNN. Congressman, I'd like to point out that I'm no longer on the Board of HP. I did not participate in the deliberations--

MR. MARKEY. Do you think it's appropriate for her to receive a $3.6 million golden parachute last night?

MS. DUNN. The way these decisions are made are based upon deliberation. I would want to hear the other views of the directors if it were me still sitting on this Board. She was a 26-year employee of Hewlett-Packard, she bled HP blue ink. This woman, I'm sorry to say, her career is ruined. She made some errors in judgment; I relied upon her, as did many others. I'm not going to comment right now what the appropriate compensation to her is to leave HP.

MR. MARKEY. The results of HP's leaked investigation were presented to HP's Board at its May 18, 2006, meeting; is that correct?

MS. DUNN. May 18th?

MR. MARKEY. May 18th.

MS. DUNN. Yes.

MR. MARKEY. You participated in the Board's discussions of the results of the investigation. During that discussion did anyone raise any concern about how this investigation had been conducted?

MS. DUNN. No one did.

MR. MARKEY. During a meeting a majority of the Board asked Mr. Keyworth to resign, which he declined to do; is that right?

MS. DUNN. That is correct.

MR. MARKEY. During that same Board meeting Mr. Perkins announced his resignation; is that correct?

MS. DUNN. That is correct.

MR. MARKEY. Did Mr. Perkins indicate the reason for his resignation?

MS. DUNN. He did.

MR. MARKEY. Did he indicate that it was related to the leak investigation?

MS. DUNN. No. He related that it was due to what he perceived to be a betrayal by me, that we had an agreement to cover up the identity of the leaker from the Board, which I broke. And I explained to him that we never had such an agreement, but that was the reason for his resignation.

MR. MARKEY. So he did not raise at that time any concern about the methods used in the investigation?

MS. DUNN. He did not in the company's filing of the 8-K.

MR. MARKEY. No. In the meeting did he?

MS. DUNN. In the meeting he did not.

MR. MARKEY. On May 22nd did HP file a Form 8-K with the Securities and Exchange Commission which is used to report material events or corporate changes?

MS. DUNN. The company did, sir.

MR. MARKEY. Who was responsible for that filing?

MS. DUNN. That's a statement by management to the SEC; and it's the responsibility of the Legal Department, with the approval of the CEO.

MR. MARKEY. Did you review or approve this filing?

MS. DUNN. No, I did not, nor did any member of the Board. We were provided copies of 8-Ks in the normal course of events after they were filed.

MR. MARKEY. All right. On May 18th Thomas Perkins announced-- the 8-K stated on May 18th Thomas Perkins announced his resignation as a director of HP effective immediately. The text of HP's press release related to Mr. Perkins' resignation is filed with this report as Exhibit 92. That press release in turn merely states "HP announced today that Thomas J. Perkins resigned from its Board of directors on May 18, 2006 with immediate effect," and then goes on to quote Mr. Hurd as thanking Mr. Perkins for his service to the company.

Would you say that this May 22nd, 2006, SEC filing and accompanying press release gave a complete picture of the facts and circumstances surrounding Mr. Perkins' departure?

MS. DUNN. Certainly not with respect to his opinion of me, but Mr. Sonsini has much more insight as to how that filing was made than I.

MR. MARKEY. Mr. Sonsini would?

MS. DUNN. Yes, sir.

MR. MARKEY. So before this filing was made, was there any consideration given to fully disclosing HP's leak investigation, its findings, the Board request to Mr. Keyworth that he resign, his refusal to do so, and Mr. Perkins' subsequent resignation from the Board?

MS. DUNN. May I turn to Mr. Sonsini, our counsel?

MR. MARKEY. Yes. Whoever is the appropriate person to ask to answer the question.

MR. SONSINI. Yes, consideration was given to that, Congressman. We filed the 8-K report at that time--I did receive a copy and did review it--based upon the information we had of why Mr. Perkins was resigning. I specifically, before that report was filed, talked to him, and I articulated almost verbatim the requirement of the 8-K, was there any disagreement, do you have any disagreement with the company or the Board over any operation, over any policy, or any practice? He said no.

MR. MARKEY. So why did HP wait until September 6, 2006, to issue a new 8-K filing with the SEC describing the facts surrounding Mr. Perkins' resignation if the Board knew in May what his concerns were, and if HP knew even more by July, why did it take until early September to issue a more accurate disclosure?

MR. SONSINI. The 8-K was filed at the end of August. It was not filed with respect to the item about director resignation. It was filed to provide other information in the market, and it was provided then because by then we had completed the investigation that the Board requested we do about pretexting.

Mr. Perkins' disagreement was not over a company policy practice or operation. As a matter of fact, I subsequently confirmed that to him in a June e-mail, reminding him of that, and he had no--

MR. MARKEY. Well, the September 6 HP filing reports that after the May Board meeting and in response to the concerns raised by Mr. Perkins, the Board, quote, "engaged the outside counsel to conduct an inquiry into the conduct and processes employed with respect to HP's investigation of leaks, and that this outside counsel was not involved in the investigation of the leaks initiated by the chairman or the internal HP group."

Isn't it true that all of that information could have been made public much earlier in the 8-K filing?

MR. SONSINI. I don't think so. I mean, it could have been, but it really wasn't material at that point in time because our investigation wasn't completed. I am the outside counsel. So it was a judgment on materiality, when to get the information to the market, and that judgment was made.

MR. WHITFIELD. The gentleman's time is expired.

We're going to do a second round here.

And Ms. Dunn, Mr. Markey raised the issue of the May 18th Board meeting at HP headquarters in Palo Alto, California in which you informed the Board that George Keyworth was the director that was leaking information. And it was told in this article here that you laid out the surveillance and pointed out the offending director.

Now, could you describe to the committee what the surveillance data was that you laid out that at meeting?

MS. DUNN. Mr. Chairman, I'm not sure what reports you're referring to; if I may, I assume they're press reports?

MR. WHITFIELD. That is correct.

MS. DUNN. The press reports on this matter have been wrong from the beginning. My sworn testimony, as written and submitted, has the details of what happened, which I will be very happy to review with you quickly.

MR. WHITFIELD. Okay.

MS. DUNN. The Chairman of the Audit Committee, Mr. Ryan, based on a meeting that I have refreshed my memory took place on April 27th, took away the responsibility for reviewing the report and informing the Board of its findings. At the May 18th meeting, he was the person that outlined a summary of the report's findings to the Board.

MR. WHITFIELD. And could you outline a summary of that report for us?

MS. DUNN. There is a set of talking points that I believe have been produced that Mr. Ryan gave to the Board, although he presented them verbally.

MR. WHITFIELD. What was the evidence against Mr. Keyworth?

MS. DUNN. That is contained in Mr. Hunsaker's report, and it is--

MR. WHITFIELD. Could you summarize it for us?

MS. DUNN. There were 10 unauthorized media disclosures that took place over the course of a couple of years, seven of which were attributable to Mr. Keyworth and to which he later confessed.

The Board meeting, if I may continue with its conduct, Mr. Ryan presented, without naming the leaker, the evidence. Another director had suggested that the identity of the leaker not be disclosed during deliberations so that the Board could have an objective discussion about what the right move, if any, was.

MR. WHITFIELD. And who made the decision to disclose it to the Board?

MS. DUNN. Mr. Ryan disclosed the name, I did not disclose the name.

MR. WHITFIELD. So you didn't have any say-so in the disclosure whatsoever?

MS. DUNN. I had turned the matter over to Mr. Ryan on advice of counsel. There was agreement between myself, Mr. Hurd, Mr. Ryan, Mr. Sonsini and Ms. Baskins that that was the best way to take--

MR. WHITFIELD. And what was Mr. Ryan's position?

MS. DUNN. His position was that he--I'm sorry. He was the Chairman, and remains Chairman of the Audit Committee at Hewlett-Packard.

MR. WHITFIELD. Okay. And from your perspective, did that end the investigation? The May 18th Board meeting, was that the end of the investigation?

MS. DUNN. I believe the investigation ended for all intents and purposes in mid-March, except for the interview notes that came from a discussion between Mr. Ryan and Mr. Keyworth on May 17th.

MR. WHITFIELD. And from the surveillance and the investigations, Mr. Keyworth was the only one identified as leaking Board information?

MS. DUNN. That is correct.

MR. WHITFIELD. Okay. And let me just say that I understand perfectly well that the news media does not always get everything correct. I think all of us have experienced that. But in this article it also says, and I think you maybe made reference to this in your testimony, that you and Mr. Perkins really did have some personality conflicts or--would that be accurate? Or were you all the best of friends or did you all have personality conflicts?

MS. DUNN. Mr. Perkins disagreed with many of the governance moves that I made on the Board. He always told me that he had nothing personal against me, and in fact we had cordial relations--a cordial relationship until some time in early 2006, when it became clear that this report was moving in the direction of identifying his friend and ally, Mr. Keyworth.

MR. WHITFIELD. Well, the reason I was asking, because in this news article--which may or may not be true--it quotes you as saying that all of this, this investigation, all of this grew out of a personal dispute between you and Mr. Perkins.

MS. DUNN. I never said that; I have never seen a news story to that effect.

MR. WHITFIELD. So you would disagree with that?

MS. DUNN. I have never seen that news story, and it would be just one among many, many, many that are completely misleading--

MR. WHITFIELD. Who is the first Board member that came to you and said you know what, we need to investigate these leaks?

MS. DUNN. I have tried--I'm under oath here. I have tried, believe it or not, throughout this to maintain some shred of the sanctity of the boardroom. If you force me to say, I will, but I do not think that it is relevant to the public interest that I disclose my confidential discussions with directors.

MR. WHITFIELD. Was there more than one Board member that came to you?

MS. DUNN. There were seven of nine.

MR. WHITFIELD. Seven of nine said we need to investigate?

MS. DUNN. Yes, sir.

MR. WHITFIELD. Now, reading from this news report again--which may or may not be true--it says that--they characterize Mr. Perkins as sort of a person who had a broad view of things, as more of a--looked at things in a broad perspective, and they talk about you as being sort of a nuts and bolts person who crossed the Ts and dotted the Is. And it was quoted in here that Mr. Perkins was particularly, in illustrating your attention to detail, how you became upset about a discrepancy between the corporate Board of Directors handbook and the HP bylaws, and that that subject matter took up hours of Board meeting time.

Now I'm just asking this question. Would you say that is an accurate characterization or not?

MS. DUNN. I'm sure it's Mr. Perkins' view. My view was what happened was, having been asked to take the job of Nonexecutive Chairman to bring HP's governance practices up to best practice, there were a lot of things that needed to be addressed in the foundations of the Board's governance. It was in the province of the Nominating and Governance Committee to address those. I asked Mr. Perkins to serve as chairman of that committee, and it was in that committee that his impatience with dealing with those matters showed itself most clearly. He felt that that committee should be talking about strategy. I felt that the Board should be talking about strategy, not the Nominating and Governance Committee.

MR. WHITFIELD. Who gave to the agencies that did the pretexting the names of the people that you wanted surveillance on or you wanted the phone records on? Who gave the list to the--

MS. DUNN. They came up with their own list. I continue to be surprised by revelations of who was on it.

MR. WHITFIELD. So they came back--did they come back--to you and gave you the list and said, what do you think about this? Or did you just wash your hands of it and say--

MS. DUNN. Well, they asked me for--I had to provide them input, context, I was the person who had the problem on behalf of the Board that had asked me to do something about this. So in any investigation, whoever it is that has got the problem has to explain the problem to the investigators.

MR. WHITFIELD. Did you give them any names?

MS. DUNN. No. I wanted them--that was part of having a professional investigative team--to be able to do whatever they do. And as I mentioned, ultimately they concluded I was one of the suspects.

MR. WHITFIELD. And you said that they used the standards of HP, and yet this was a particularly unusual event because I'm quite confident that there has never been a surveillance or investigation of the entire Board before.

MS. DUNN. I'm sure you're right. And I believe that the surveillance was limited to their efforts to find out more evidence about whether Mr. Keyworth was in fact talking to a reporter after they had come to the strong thesis that he was the person responsible.

MR. WHITFIELD. And you have had an opportunity, I guess--have you had an opportunity to see the list of everyone that they investigated?

MS. DUNN. No, I have not seen that list.

MR. WHITFIELD. So you do not know who was investigated then?

MS. DUNN. I know some by--well, if the press reports are correct, I know some.

MR. WHITFIELD. Was Mrs. Fiorina investigated from your personal--

MS. DUNN. Yeah, that one I read about recently.

MR. WHITFIELD. Okay. Now, did you receive a severance package at the termination of your tenure on the Board or when you resigned?

MS. DUNN. I was never an employee of Hewlett-Packard. I have not had one nickel of cash flow from Hewlett-Packard in 6 years, except for committee fees. So I'm kind of out of pocket for dealing with HP right now.

MR. WHITFIELD. Let me ask one other question, and my time is expired. Were you the Chairman of the search committee that brought Mr. Hurd to HP?

MS. DUNN. I was the Nonexecutive Chairman of the Board. Our whole Board was the search committee, but I did lead the search administratively.

MR. WHITFIELD. Okay. Thank you.

I recognize Ms. DeGette.

MS. DEGETTE. Thank you, Mr. Chairman.

Mr. Adler, you told Ms. Eshoo that pretexting is--you told me that the embedded technology, the tracers is a standard technique used by Hewlett-Packard, correct?

MR. ALDER. You also used the word "pretexting" when you started. Could you clarify that?

MS. DEGETTE. You said the embedded technology, the tracers is standard practice, right?

MR. ALDER. Yes.

MS. DEGETTE. What about pretexting? I think you told Ms. Eshoo that pretexting is also a standard practice.

MR. ALDER. Within HP?

MS. DEGETTE. Yes.

MR. ALDER. I have no further knowledge of pretexting, direct knowledge. All I can offer you is what I offered Congressman Markey, and that was there was a complaint by Mr. Nye that it had been utilized prior.

MS. DEGETTE. You had never personally seen pretexting prior to this situation?

MR. ALDER. I'm sorry. Could you repeat that?

MS. DEGETTE. You had never seen pretexting prior to that situation?

MR. ALDER. No, I had not.

MS. DEGETTE. Had you heard of it?

MR. ALDER. No, I had not even heard of it.

MS. DEGETTE. Okay. Mr. Sonsini, as outside counsel to the corporation, what is your view of the use of tracer technology to track messages? Do you think that's an appropriate--I'm not asking for a legal opinion. Do you think that's an appropriate technique in these situations?

MR. SONSINI. Given what I've learned, I think any technique that invades privacy is not appropriate.

MS. DEGETTE. Including tracer technology?

MR. SONSINI. Including tracer technology.

MS. DEGETTE. Were you aware tracer technology was at least attempted to be used in this situation of the Board investigation?

MR. SONSINI. I was not aware of any methodology that was being used in this investigation.

MS. DEGETTE. Now, it seemed to me when I looked at some of the voluminous documents here, after Mr. Perkins made his allegations and you were asked to look into that, the allegations you were asked to look into were the specific allegations that Mr. Perkins made, correct?

MR. SONSINI. Correct.

MS. DEGETTE. Did anybody ever tell you that these investigators were using the tracer technology to try to trace messages?

MR. SONSINI. No.

MS. DEGETTE. Did anybody ever tell you that they were coming up with a fake individual to try to have communications with newspaper reporters?

MR. SONSINI. No, none of that. I assume you're talking about prior to our investigation of this investigation?

MS. DEGETTE. That is correct.

MR. SONSINI. No.

MS. DEGETTE. Did anybody ever tell you that they were going through the trash of the Board members or tracking their family members?

MR. SONSINI. No.

MS. DEGETTE. And what advice would you have given if somebody had said this is what we're going to do to try to find the leaks from the HP Board?

MR. SONSINI. It would be totally improper.

MS. DEGETTE. Why would that be?

MR. SONSINI. Because I think it implicates in many respects the invasion of privacy. And although I'm not an expert on legality, it certainly doesn't seem to meet the standards of ethics and integrity that we ought to have at the corporate level.

MS. DEGETTE. Right. We're all focused here on whether or not the pretexting is illegal, but in truth the rest of these techniques are just kind of sleazy and I would say not appropriate in a corporate context; would you agree with that?

MR. SONSINI. I absolutely agree. I think in today's world, particularly after what Congress has done with Sarbanes-Oxley, we have emphasized that tone at the top is very critical in the role of corporate governance, and that means ethics, that means veracity and that means integrity, and those types of tactics don't have any place.

MS. DEGETTE. Mr. Sonsini, I think you also would agree with me that the tone at the top that you refer to should also refer to corporate boards and officers and not just employees of the corporation, right?

MR. SONSINI. It should begin with the boards.

MS. DEGETTE. Exactly. This is what I've been saying for 5 years ever since we started these investigations.

Ms. Dunn, I just want to turn to just a couple more issues about this fake person that you folks were coming up with to try to get information out of reporters. And I'd like you to take a look at Tab 60, if you will, in your notebook. It's an e-mail dated--or some kind of memo dated February 22, 2006, from Mark Hurd--from Kevin Hunsaker to Mark Hurd, with a copy to you. Now have you seen this top e-mail?

MS. DUNN. I am seeing it now.

MS. DEGETTE. Okay. And underneath it there is an original message from you, Pattie, to these various people. Do you see that?

MS. DUNN. Yes, I do.

MS. DEGETTE. Do you recall sending that e-mail?

MS. DUNN. I must have sent it.

MS. DEGETTE. And that's in response to an e-mail from Kevin Hunsaker to you and to Ann Baskins. And what that original e-mail says is they're going to propose sending this e-mail to the reporter, with the hope that she would forward it to your target, the person who you thought was the leaker, and then what would happen? And the person--and Kevin says "I made up everything in the side, trying to make it...feasible." So was it your understanding this was the fake individual, Jacob, who was going to send this out to the reporter? Was that your understanding?

MS. DUNN. That is my understanding.

MS. DEGETTE. And then you said in response to that, "Kevin, I think this is very clever. As a matter of course, anything that is going to potentially be seen outside HP should have Mark's approval as well." Is that right? That's what you said to Kevin?

MS. DUNN. Yes. And what I testified earlier to is I regret the use of the word "clever" because it--

MS. DEGETTE. Right, I'm sure--

MS. DUNN. Because it does not convey what I was--

MS. DEGETTE. Right. And I'm not--I'm not trying to excoriate you for saying the word "clever," but my point is, you knew that this--you had said before, you just said go do the investigation and then they did it, you didn't know; but, in fact, you knew as it was going along that Kevin Hunsaker was doing this Jacob to try to get a reporter to respond, right? So you knew that was going on, right?

MS. DUNN. I did not see myself, nor--

MS. DEGETTE. I'm just asking yes or no, did you know that was going on?

MS. DUNN. I knew, and I did not see myself as the person who was appropriate to approve investigative methods.

MS. DEGETTE. Right. And this is what I'm saying. And Mr. Chairman, I guess I'll just say this, concluding this panel. At first I did not think this HP issue really rose to the level of the corporate responsibility issues that we looked at several years ago, but I'm becoming less convinced of that because this is exactly what we saw when we brought the executives from some of the other companies in. Of course these were situations of fraud where people have gone to jail. That's not what we're talking about here. But it could happen with another corporation. If boards don't start to realize that this is a very serious problem, that you can't just say to somebody, well, I'm only a board member or I'm not a compensated employee, and so I can put something into--I can put something into process. I can be the general counsel, I can be on the investigative team, but I'm not responsible for things that happen because it's not in my chain of command. We can't have that anymore. There is a fiduciary duty that every board member of every corporation has to that corporation.

And Ms. Dunn and Mr. Sonsini, you're both nodding, I think you would both agree with me. And that's why we really need to look and see if there is any broader public policy implications to this. Because Ms. Dunn, you knew a lot of techniques were going on, you just didn't think it was your job to do anything about it. Mr. Sonsini, you were outside counsel, and no one bothered to tell you about a lot of this.

I think it is very disturbing, and I think it is a good case study. Anyway, that is all I would have to say, Mr. Chairman.

MR. WHITFIELD. Thank you, Ms. DeGette.

I recognize Mr. Walden for 10 minutes.

MR. WALDEN. Thank you very much, Mr. Chairman, I appreciate the opportunity for another round of questions.

Ms. Dunn, I remain concerned obviously about what I've heard today based on what also is contained in some of these reports. I would refer you again to Tab 119 in that huge book you were just about to slide past you. And in it, item number 14, it says--this is again from Tony Gentilucci, it stated, DeLia told him sometime during the week of July 4th that pretexting was fully discussed with Dunn and Baskins in Kona 1. Do you dispute that that occurred?

MS. DUNN. I'm just going to have to go back to my earlier statement, sir. I had no understanding or knowledge of the fraudulent representation of identity as a standard investigative tactic at Hewlett-Packard. The word "pretext" and pretexting means a lot to us now, it meant nothing to me in June 2005.

MR. WALDEN. On August 21st, a report from Kevin Hunsaker, number 118, it's the interview of Mr. Hunsaker, who unfortunately took the Fifth and has left the company. Number 42 says, "One month into the investigation the issue of pretexting came up again, and Dunn and Baskins asked him to confirm the legality of the investigative method during a Friday phone call before the March Board meeting in Los Angeles. Dunn and Baskins wanted him to confirm the method's legality in case Hurd had any concerns during the presentation in Los Angeles."

MS. DUNN. Well, I think this is very close to true. I did ask for confirmation that the use of phone records in these investigations was permissible.

MR. WALDEN. So the issue of--but it says here the issue of pretexting came up.

MS. DUNN. Well, I think the word now has entered our lexicon as a substitute for the word "phone records."

MR. WALDEN. But why would you ask about the legality of it then?

MS. DUNN. That's what a Board member does, you look for representations--

MR. WALDEN. So they never described the process to you that they were using? I mean, he says they did. The issue of pretexting came up, they talk about investigative method.

MS. DUNN. No one ever described to me that the fraudulent use of identity was the HP way of conducting internal investigations.

MR. WALDEN. Right. DeLia, though, I'm told, mentioned impersonation during the June meeting, did that trouble you?

MS. DUNN. If I heard the word "impersonation," it probably would. I don't recall it.

MR. WALDEN. How did you think they were getting these phone records?

MS. DUNN. My understanding was that these records were publicly available.

MR. WALDEN. But I thought I read somewhere here--oh, that's right. Number 116, page five. And it says, "Dunn said that DeLia told her such information was basically publicly available," right, do you remember that?

MS. DUNN. That's my testimony here today, yes.

MR. WALDEN. That DeLia told you that "such information was basically publicly available," that is in quotes. Then it goes on down, number 30 says, "Dunn was not aware that one method for retrieving records entails the callers pretending they're someone else. Dunn thought that the investigators were able to get the information just because of the administrative sloppiness of the phone carriers." What did you mean by that?

MS. DUNN. What I meant was that I understood that you could call up and get phone records, that it was a common investigative technique.

MR. WALDEN. So you think I can call up and say anybody in the public can get your phone records?

MS. DUNN. I thought a year ago, I thought 6 months ago that indeed you could.

MR. WALDEN. You really believed this? Really? I'm sorry here, but you believe that I could call whoever your carrier is and say, I'm Congressman Greg Walden, I'd like Mrs. Dunn's phone records, cell, home, office--

MS. DUNN. It really wouldn't surprise me.

MR. WALDEN. You're serious? I'm not being funny here, I mean this. You honestly believed that it was that simple that your phone records, anybody in the world can just call up and get them? I mean, is that how you describe publicly available?

MS. DUNN. We have to make a distinction between my knowledge now and my knowledge during this investigation.

MR. WALDEN. That's what I'm trying to get.

MS. DUNN. During this investigation it was my understanding that these records were available through permitted mechanisms, and that it was the common practice within Hewlett-Packard to use phone records to perform investigations.

MR. WALDEN. But you said you thought they were publicly available, which means going to the Internet, putting in somebody's name and up pops my phone record.

MS. DUNN. That would be one idea.

MR. WALDEN. What would be others?

MS. DUNN. I don't know, I didn't give it thought.

MR. WALDEN. Then you go on to say through administrative sloppiness. That, to me, would say somebody is making a mistake at Ma Bell.

MS. DUNN. That's a transcription. I don't recall using those words.

MR. WALDEN. Mr. Sonsini, do you have any reason to doubt the summary of this?

MR. SONSINI. No, I don't.

MR. WALDEN. Do you have a transcript?

MR. SONSINI. I have no reason to doubt the transcript.

MS. DUNN. This is not a transcript like this woman is recording our comments. It is an interpretation of what I said.

MR. WALDEN. You're right. So tell me what you meant--did you use the term "administrative sloppiness"?

MS. DUNN. I don't think so. If I did, I don't understand the way that it's appearing here, administrative sloppiness. My understanding was that these--sir, my understanding was that these records were available generally to investigations such as the ones that were being conducted at Hewlett-Packard.

MR. WALDEN. Do you have any problem with us getting the transcript so we know exactly--

MS. DUNN. If one was produced.

MR. WALDEN. Mr. Sonsini, was one produced?

MR. SONSINI. I would have to ask my team, Congressman.

MR. WALDEN. Were these interviews recorded?

MR. SONSINI. Yes. These were just the interview reports, they were not recorded. There is no recording of the conversation other than the notes of those who made the inquiry.

MR. WALDEN. But you believe these notes to be accurate?

MR. SONSINI. I do.

MR. WALDEN. And Ms. Dunn believes they're not.

MS. DUNN. This is the first time that these notes have been produced for me, so I haven't had a chance to go through those notes.

MR. WALDEN. But you read the part--

MS. DUNN. No one has given me an opportunity to review, either now or previously, what I said. My understanding is, for example, that if you give a deposition under oath, you get a chance to review those deposition notes to make sure that is your sworn testimony.

MR. WALDEN. Well, this is all I have to work off of. And there are lots of issues here where lots of people have reported in the course of the investigation that Mr. Sonsini's firm did, that they believe you were told about pretexting, and that the methods were described.

MS. DUNN. I understand the problem. I understand the chain of communication and why it is confusing.

MR. WALDEN. The part of the chain of communication that I'm confused about is, you sat as an outside director, charged by a Board of seven without an official Board position, as I understand it was seven Board members, basically said please go do this, you didn't vote on it as a Board, right?

MS. DUNN. We did not. In fact, it was not a matter that could be brought to our full Board.

MR. WALDEN. And you told me you don't have a staff.

MS. DUNN. No.

MR. WALDEN. You interact with the investigative folks, you name the investigation, you provide phone numbers for investigators for certain people you would like them to look at, you're in interactions with your legal team and the investigators from time to time, you get briefed on draft findings of the investigative report, but you don't sign off on any of this yourself, you defer to senior management, correct?

MS. DUNN. With the addition that I did not hire these investigators--

MR. WALDEN. I understand, I'm trying to get to a different point, and that is who in senior management then is responsible for this investigation since you're not?

MS. DUNN. Well, the last investigation was clearly under the auspices of Mr. Hunsaker.

MR. WALDEN. Well, he's your counsel. I thought I read here where more like Mr. Hurd had to sign off on things, is that not the case?

MS. DUNN. Well, Mr. Hunsaker's title, by the time this investigation was partway through, and before, is--his title was Director of Standards of Business Conduct and Ethics Compliance--

MR. WALDEN. So he was the final decision maker on this?

MS. DUNN. No.

MR. WALDEN. Who was the final decision maker?

MS. DUNN. I would have said Ann Baskins.

MR. WALDEN. So nobody else on the Board, not Mr. Hurd--so she could overrule every other decision; is that what you're telling me?

MS. DUNN. She was responsible for the oversight of the person carrying out the investigation.

MR. WALDEN. So she reported to nobody?

MS. DUNN. Well, she reported administratively to Mark Hurd in '06 and to Bob Wayman in '05.

MR. WALDEN. Because at some point the buck stops somewhere.

MS. DUNN. I'm trying to be responsive to your question about her reporting relationship.

MR. WALDEN. That's what I was asking. I appreciate that. My time is expired.

MR. WHITFIELD. Thank you very much.

Ms. Schakowsky, you are recognized for 10 minutes.

MS. SCHAKOWSKY. Thank you, Mr. Chairman. I'm actually going to have to leave in 5, so--

Mr. Sonsini, I wanted to ask you some questions. And maybe we're going over some other turf that's already been gone over, and I hope you will bear with me, I want to explore it a little bit further.

I'm looking now at this Tab 91 in the big book, and this is the communications, the e-mails that you have in June, the last one being your June 28th e-mail to Tom Perkins regarding your--he had asked you, it was very wordy, he was asking you, you should check into the sub rosa investigation of director's communication at HP in the view of Viet Dinh, I guess that lawyer's--unqualified opinion that it was illegal, I think the Board needs to know the potential risks.

And then you respond that, quote, "The process was well done and within legal limits," unquote. And you continue that the phone records were obtained by the pretexting, and that it is, quote, "a common investigatory method which was confirmed with experts." The legal team also checked with outside counsel as to the legality of this methodology. So I'm wondering who the experts were whom you consulted?

MR. SONSINI. As the e-mail indicates, I went directly to the HP Legal Department. I went to Ms. Baskins, and she went to Mr. Hunsaker. I requested that they give me a response to these concerns and Mr. Perkins'.

Please understand that I was not conducting any investigation at that time, was not asked to and was not rendering any legal opinion. But I believe that he needed to have a response. I asked for a detailed response. I got two written responses plus oral assurances, and I reported it to Mr. Perkins. Based on those responses only, without any independent judgment, I made the statements that I made here.

MS. SCHAKOWSKY. So your legal team or--an outside counsel didn't check to determine whether pretexting was legal?

MR. SONSINI. Not at that time, not at that time at all. When we got the report, we were asked to focus, as Ms. Dunn has testified, on what do we do with the results? We have a crisis. The Board was looking to me, we need corporate governance here, what are we going to do with this. And I laid out a plan that we had to have full disclosure to the Board, this be vetted out, et cetera.

It was afterwards that the Board, through the Nominating and Governance Committee, came to me and said we need you to look into the legality of this, and it was then that my team conducted the investigation and came to the findings that we came to.

MS. SCHAKOWSKY. So you didn't check, but you conveyed to Mr. Perkins essentially that you had--

MR. SONSINI. No, I was--

MS. SCHAKOWSKY. The investigation--

MR. SONSINI. With all due respect, my e-mail was very careful. I told them this is where I went and this is what I learned. Mr. Perkins was not a director at the time. The question is whether Mr. Perkins had any standing to even request me to do anything. But because I believed it was important to get this fully reported and because I believed that he was entitled to know what legal counsel would say because he was a director at the time, I asked him, what do you want me to say, give me a thorough response. I got it and I conveyed it.

MS. SCHAKOWSKY. Well, I mean, he was clearly very worried at that time about the sub rosa investigation, and so you're saying the team did not check the Federal Trade Commission.

MR. SONSINI. I don't know what the team did, other than what they gave me. I was not involved in this investigation. When they said that they conducted this legally, when they issued a report that I received in April, well after the investigation was done, that it was done in lawful limits, you know, they were relying on their own experts. They said that they reviewed it, they said they researched it. You know, the HP Legal Department is a big department, it has over a hundred lawyers; I've worked with them for years. Not all matters are farmed out to outside counsel. And when they are farmed out, they are not all farmed out to Wilson Sonsini, they have multiple lawyers.

I was given a specific task, and it was a crisis. There was a crisis in this Boardroom because, as I said, I believe a leak is a symptom of a bigger problem, and that's what I focused on.

And I want to make that very clear that the press has it all wrong, that I was passing upon legality at that time. I passed upon it when I was required to do it, and I passed upon it thoroughly and strongly and made very difficult findings that were conveyed to the Board.

MS. SCHAKOWSKY. So then you don't stand behind the fact that appears--well, except the fact that you say it appears--that you say that the process was all "well done and within legal limits, the concerns raised in your e-mail did not occur." That's a declarative sentence.

MR. SONSINI. At that time, as I repeated, I was passing on information; I demanded that the information be thorough. And it is correct, "it appears." I was very careful with this e-mail. "Mr. Perkins, this is where I went, this is what I was told on the basis of that, it appears." I was not saying it was legal at that time. I did not understand the methodologies that were involved. There was a lot more that we needed to find out and we did find out, and that's when we started passing on legality.

Mr. Perkins took my e-mail, he thanked me for it, it gave him the information he wanted, and we were on our way.

MS. SCHAKOWSKY. Well, the information that he got was reassurances, quote, "the concerns raised in your e-mail did not occur." I would have felt--I would have liked it, too, and thanked you for that.

MR. SONSINI. I don't think Mr. Perkins was asking me for reassurances. Mr. Perkins had counsel at the time, Mr. Dinh, he had the opinion of Mr. Dinh's concern about legality; that's what he told me, and I was giving him the information.

MS. SCHAKOWSKY. Thank you.

MR. WALDEN. Ms. Schakowsky, would it be possible for you to yield to me for a question?

MS. SCHAKOWSKY. I would be happy to.

MR. WALDEN. Ms. Dunn, I have one more question for you on this topic. It's Tab 66. And this is an e-mail from Kevin Hunsaker to Vince Nye, Mr. Adler, Mr. Gentilucci, Mr. Anthony, Mr. DeLia. It says, "I just got off the phone with Pattie. She would like to put a comprehensive summary of what we've done, what resources and techniques we've used, et cetera. It should include everything we've done on the EC folks, the Board members and other employees. It should also include things like our, and in parens, unsuccessful attempts to obtain the EC members' cell phone members," et cetera. It's dated February 24, 2006.

Did you indeed have a conversation with Mr. Hunsaker on the phone on that date where you ask about resources and techniques?

MS. DUNN. I have no reason to think that he would write this e-mail without our having had that conversation. I do not remember this specific conversation. It's quite logical it took place. I believe what was going on here was that we were preparing for the issuance of the report that he--final draft or early draft of the report that came out on May 10th--sorry, March 10th, and I wanted to convey to him--I'm not sure I conveyed all the details that he says I conveyed. He may have been using the fact of a conversation with me, as sometimes happens in big companies, to put his own momentum behind something that--

MR. WALDEN. Oh, so you think this isn't what you said?

MS. DUNN. I don't know that I said all of these things, but it would be very logical that I would have said "Kevin, when that report is written, it needs to be complete, it needs to have everything in it that you've done."

MR. WALDEN. I guess I'm questioning, if you weren't in charge of the investigation and you only focused on the last couple of pages, why were you giving him that much direction?

MS. DUNN. Because I had the responsibility and was thinking ahead about what our Board was going to receive as a basis for making a very important, very sensitive decision about a fellow director--

MR. WALDEN. But this is really pretty specific about resources and techniques, it doesn't really get much beyond that.

MS. DUNN. That's his interpretation of our conversation.

MR. WALDEN. Okay, thank you.

Every one of these e-mails we have, Mr. Chairman, seems to have a different interpretation, depending upon who is reading it. Thank you.

MR. WHITFIELD. The gentlelady from Tennessee is recognized for 10 minutes.

MRS. BLACKBURN. Thank you, Mr. Chairman. And thank you to all of you for your patience.

Mr. Adler, I had a couple of questions for you. In going back to your testimony--which with all of my papers now I have misplaced. But you talked--I think it was on page 2 of your testimony where you talk about the standards, and having standards that apply. And you mention in your testimony several different times standards, legal standards, and then my assumption is HP standards that would be applicable to a corporate investigation. Would I be right in that assumption, sir?

MR. ALDER. No. The standards I referred to were the HP Standards of Business Conduct, which would be applicable to all employees. And also, as you said, the legal standards, which are all, again, applicable to everyone.

MRS. BLACKBURN. Okay. And is that a criteria, a set criteria that exists in writing, or was that just something that in your department with Mr. O'Neil as your supervisor you all had devised kind of a best operating practices?

MR. ALDER. HP practices of conduct are in writing. Every year employees are required to review those standards and are given training in them.

MRS. BLACKBURN. So these were standards that were widely known?

MR. ALDER. I'm sorry, one more time?

MRS. BLACKBURN. They were widely known?

MR. ALDER. The standards of business conduct were widely known, yes.

MRS. BLACKBURN. Another question. In reference to using the Spyware, as we call it, the tracer, you mentioned that attorneys had reviewed the information. Which attorneys reviewed that for you?

MR. ALDER. I think we're getting this confused perhaps slightly. Attorneys review with regard to--I know I did say that, with regard to the pretexting?

MRS. BLACKBURN. Yes, sir.

MR. ALDER. That was in my statement. I was making reference to the pretexting issue, that we were told that at least the attorneys had reviewed the pretexting.

MRS. BLACKBURN. But it did not apply to the investigation as a whole?

MR. ALDER. Well, Kevin Hunsaker, our chief of ethics, is an attorney, and we worked at his direction, and he was our counsel. And so everything was reviewed by him for legal compliance.

MRS. BLACKBURN. Okay. All right. Thank you.

MR. ALDER. You're welcome.

MRS. BLACKBURN. Ms. Hurd, I want to stay with this tracer.

MS. DUNN. I think the real Mrs. Hurd would be surprised by that.

MRS. BLACKBURN. Ms. Dunn, and the relationship between you and Mr. Hurd. And I'll tell you where I'm going with this. I'm going to read from your testimony again that you supplied to us yesterday, and I'm on page 20 in the first paragraph, where you say "neither Mr. Hurd nor I designed or implemented the investigative techniques; however, we both were made aware of the sting operation that the investigators proposed in early February for the purpose of determining whether the CNET reporter whom Mr. Keyworth was suspected of talking, and by then the investigative team had narrowed its hypothesis about the identity of the leaker to him, was in contact with Mr. Keyworth. I was contacted by Mr. Hunsaker, with Ms. Baskins in the loop on the communication about this. Having asked for and received all immediate assurances that this was a legal and common investigative technique, I referred them to Mr. Hurd for the final decision."

Now, did he indeed make the final decision about moving forward with all forms of the investigation?

MS. DUNN. With all forms of the investigation? No. I don't think that is true. I think that the methods were delegated to Mr. Hunsaker, with oversight from Ms. Baskins.

MRS. BLACKBURN. So he made the final decision on the sting operation?

MS. DUNN. I believe he needed to be aware of it. I don't know the way in which he communicated his views back to the investigative team.

MRS. BLACKBURN. I just have such a difficult time trying to figure out who--where did the buck stop? In HP, where did the buck stop with making the decision to conduct the sting? Where did the buck stop with making the decision to use a tracer technology? Because Mr. Hurd is going to come and tell us on page 7 of his testimony that they--let's see, "In February 2006 I was informed by the investigation team that they intended to send an e-mail to a reporter containing false information in an effort to identify the source of the leaks. I was asked and did approve the content of the e-mail. I do not recall seeing, nor do I recall approving, the use of tracer technology."

Well, we've got two different things going here. One is the Spyware, if you will, and that is attached to the e-mail, and another is the content, the text that is in the e-mail. And it is of tremendous concern that we don't seem to have anybody that wants to say yes, indeed, I was in charge, I was expected to be in charge, and I made the decisions accordingly. So I'm trying to get to that--

MS. DUNN. Well, I think some of those people have just declined to testify, and that's frustrating for us all.

MRS. BLACKBURN. Okay, let's go to Exhibit 52.

MS. DUNN. Would that be Tab 52?

MRS. BLACKBURN. Yes, ma'am.

MS. DUNN. I'm there.

MRS. BLACKBURN. Okay, great. Okay. This is an e-mail from you, starting with the original message. "I spoke with Mark. He is on board with the plan to use the info on new hand-held leader. He also agrees that we should consider doing something with the adaptive enterprise branding issue, given there is some chance D.K. will seek clarification on this from her CNET source." And then his response, the response coming back to you, "Understood, thanks. We will put this in motion in the next few hours."

So this e-mail seems to indicate that Mr. Hurd was not only aware of the operation, but he was making suggestions to you or somebody as how to implement it. Is that accurate?

MS. DUNN. That doesn't feel like what happened to me.

MRS. BLACKBURN. Well, what--

MS. DUNN. What happened was that this team was devising methods to finalize the investigation to be very confident that they have identified the correct person after nearly 2 years of problematic leaks, and that they were enthusiastically sharing their ideas with the most senior people that they could find. And I don't know how Mark responded per se. I would respectfully say that that's a question for him to answer because it would be hearsay on my part.

MRS. BLACKBURN. Okay. All right. Thank you.

Mr. Chairman, I yield back.

MR. WHITFIELD. Thank you very much.

At this time I recognize Mr. Inslee for 10 minutes.

MR. INSLEE. Thank you.

Mr. Adler, I wanted to ask you about the tracer technology, and I want to make sure that I understand how it worked. As I understand, HP would essentially send an e-mail with an attachment, with this attached to Mr. Smith, and when Mr. Smith sent an e-mail to Mr. Jones, somehow that would report back to HP indicating that Smith had sent Jones this document; is that how it works?

MR. ALDER. No, sir.

MR. INSLEE. Okay. Tell me how it works then.

MR. ALDER. It's dependent upon--well, the document itself, not the e-mail, the document is within the e-mail, the document itself must be opened.

MR. INSLEE. Correct.

MR. ALDER. Is that what you said?

MR. INSLEE. Well, you corrected me, I'm sorry. You were accurate, I misstated. It is the documents--the delivery of the document that is reported back to HP. Thank you for correcting me.

MR. ALDER. It does not report back to HP. It reports back to the company that provides the service, readnotify.com, and it's through the auspice of your personal account. You may then open the account and see if a return receipt has been provided for that particular document.

MR. INSLEE. And when does that information come back? Is it essentially contemporaneous with Jones, the recipient of the second e-mail, opening the document? Does it happen right away?

MR. ALDER. Any time the document is open, there is a report that is generated.

MR. INSLEE. So you attempted to distinguish this from a trap and trace system or an eavesdropping system or a tap by saying it's not contemporaneous; it pretty much is contemporaneous, isn't it?

MR. ALDER. No, not really.

MR. INSLEE. I mean, because as soon as Smith gets it and opens up the attachment, boom, that goes immediately back to this company; is that right?

MR. ALDER. But Smith had already received this attachment, and therein I believe lies the difference.

MR. INSLEE. I just want to make sure I understood this. When Smith sends an e-mail to Jones, as soon as Jones opens that attachment, immediately that information goes back to the reporting agency; is that right?

MR. ALDER. That is my understanding, as soon as the document is open.

MR. INSLEE. Now, is it my understanding that HP's corporate policy is that that is an acceptable corporate strategy to use trace technology like this when HP decides to use it? Is that HP's decision now, or was it during the scope of this investigation?

MR. ALDER. That was and still is current policy.

MR. INSLEE. So let's say that you have a customer of HP, you do business with them, you sell their products, they are your trusted, treasured customer to whom you expect to have a relationship of great integrity. You believe, and it is currently HP's policy, as I understand it, that you can send an e-mail to them with this tracing system. Let's say you sent it to ACME Electronics, your good customer, and when ACME Electronics then sends an e-mail to Smith, let's say their attorneys, they send an e-mail to their attorney or to their priest or to their doctor, and what they may consider to be a confidential communication, free from the prying eyes of HP, as soon as their priest or their doctor or their accountant or their neighbor or friend opens that attachment, HP will then get back a report immediately that this e-mail has been sent to that location, even though your customer has never been informed you're going to do that. Is that pretty much HP's operating procedure?

MR. ALDER. No. Number one, we don't send this type of--we don't use this type of technology with our customers. Number two, in the sense that there is no information from the recipient that is derived, other than the IP address; that is, the Internet Protocol address, that is all we get. That address may only tell us that it is in the United States, that it is in the world or in a specific region. As in the case of what we attempted to do is we've suspected it would be Mr. Keyworth that would be the recipient. The best that we would have found out from his IP address reporting back to this "read notify" was that it would have been in the Oakland area or in northern California for an AOL customer. That is what it would have discerned.

MR. INSLEE. Let me make sure I understand. You used that IP address and eventually found out where the e-mail was being sent to. That is the reason you did this. You didn't do this for a statistical sort of information purpose. You were going to use this to find out where those e-mails were being sent. That is obvious to everybody in this room. So that is pretty clear.

Now, you said you don't do it to your customers. I can see a situation where HP would want to know if your customers are having communication with your competitor, for instance, a potential contractor who is a competitor of yours. Is there an internal policy that prevents any of your thousands of employees from doing that?

MR. ALDER. I would consider it in violation of our Standards of Business Conduct, yes.

MR. INSLEE. And what standard would it violate?

MR. ALDER. Since I don't have them in front of me, I can't specifically recall which one would be the specific one that would apply in this case. I am sorry.

MR. INSLEE. Well, Mr. Sonsini, is the use of that trace technology legal, in your opinion, under Federal and/or State law?

MR. SONSINI. That is a great question. I think that the law regarding that is not as clear as it should be. Depending on how it is used and the methodologies, it could very well implicate Federal or State statutes.

I think the whole area is an area that we probably need more clarity.

MR. INSLEE. I agree with that assessment, and we--many of us have been trying to get more clarity regarding privacy laws, including the Chairman and Mr. Barton have been involved in some efforts in that regard. We have been stymied. We have this simple bill, just so you will know what is going on here in Congress--we have this--you know, a bill that we all voted for unanimously we can't even get House GOP leadership to schedule for a vote now.

But let me ask you this: Do you think, knowing what you consider to be a grayness in this area, would you suggest that there should be statutory codification clarifying this situation regarding trace technology in these e-mails?

MR. SONSINI. I think so. We do have computer statutes that make invasion of computer hardware illegal. And I am not an expert on how tracers are used in invasion, but if there is invasion of computers, we probably have good coverage.

But in the whole area of pretexting and the various methodologies used, I agree with the statements of many members of your Committee that we should have more clarity in that area. That does not mean that methodologies that are employed cannot be in violation of law, existing law.

MR. INSLEE. I want to get a clarification of something that I just did not understand. I understood you in earlier testimony you said something to the effect that this pretexting and similar type of efforts were a violation of privacy and should not be common, something to that effect. And what I didn't understand about that is that you receive this draft--I understand it was a copy sent to you from Mr. Hunsaker--which described the pretexting that had gone on in considerable detail. Then you wrote--that was on June 21st, 2006.

Seven days later on June 28, 2006, you wrote an e-mail to Mr. Perkins basically saying everything is hunky dory, there is nothing illegal. And I am reading this document, this e-mail from you, that doesn't--a fair reading of it, I think, is raising no red flags or a concern from you as counsel.

Now, given your testimony to us today that you consider pretexting to be--sinful is the wrong word, but unacceptable, a violation of people's privacy, how do you juxtapose this when you're a lawyer--you have been told this is going on with one of your treasured clients, somebody asks you for a report, you send them an e-mail, and you don't raise any red flags whatsoever. I have trouble reconciling that.

MR. SONSINI. Let me explain it. As I have testified to several times today, and I would like to elaborate on again, that e-mail to Mr. Perkins was not a legal opinion because, A, I had not conducted any research; B, I was not aware at that time of the methodologies used, I was conveying the opinion of the HP legal department.

MR. INSLEE. What do you mean you didn't know the methodology? That is where I had trouble. You were told in this that they were doing pretexting.

MR. SONSINI. Yes, and pretexting generally, other than the Gramm-Leach-Bliley Act relating to financial institutions, is not illegal.

It depends upon the methodologies in pretexting. For example, if Social Security numbers are used, then it is very likely that there is a violation of a Social Security statute. There are other laws; the Federal Trade Commission takes a viewpoint it could be an unfair trade practice.

The point is that as members of the Committee have said, we need more clarity. You have a bill in the House now that is designed to clear things up.

MR. INSLEE. Let me ask just a simple question. Pretexting to anybody here means you call up and you lie about your identity in order to get information. To any lawyer or layperson, that is what it means.

You were told that people in HP were calling up to get phone records, lying about their identity, and getting that phone record. And then you sent an e-mail that didn't raise any concerns suggesting that it stop, suggesting that the method be investigated. You didn't suggest whether Social Security numbers were involved. You did not suggest that you clarify as to whether or not you were violative of these. You didn't suggest anything suggesting that this thing was unacceptable. And I just find that unacceptable. I don't understand it.

MR. SONSINI. I want you to understand it. It is a fair question. I didn't know what pretexting was.

There was--I had no knowledge of the methodologies. I did not know Social Security were used. That is the problem. At the time that I sent that e-mail, I was being as open and transparent as I could. I was not an expert in these matters. I did not know what pretexting meant at that time. I was not asked to investigate it at that time. I was trying to do my job, reporting to him what the HP Legal Department gave me the assurances that they did.

MR. INSLEE. One more question if I can, sir. Do I understand you didn't know pretexting involved lying about the identity?

MR. SONSINI. I didn't know what pretexting was.

MR. WHITFIELD. The gentleman's time has expired.

Ms. Eshoo, you are recognized for 10 minutes.

MS. ESHOO. Thank you, Mr. Chairman.

I think that there is an awful lot that has been set down for the record, and I think that Members have really asked excellent questions from both sides of the aisle.

I have a few questions. I don't know whether I will use the 10 minutes or not, but I want to go to Mr. Adler first, again.

Are you aware of any rusing that has been used in anything at HP? Is it something employed by HP? Did you hear me?

MR. ALDER. No, not really. This is an unusual circumstance as far as my knowledge is concerned. You said rusing, correct?

MS. ESHOO. Uh-huh.

MR. ALDER. No. This is pretty much--this is unusual. It is not something that--are you maybe--

MS. ESHOO. I don't want your opinion about what you think of it. I want to know if it is something that is practiced or used. Is it a tactic that is used or has been used at HP?

MR. ALDER. What do you consider to be a ruse so I can better answer my question?

MS. ESHOO. You were just describing it to me. If you don't know, I will describe it to you.

MR. ALDER. If you want to talk about the use of the e-mail by the name of Jacob, that is the first time we have ever employed that, to my knowledge. If you want to talk about the tracer technologies in that context, then we have used it probably, as I said, a dozen times that I am aware of.

MS. ESHOO. It is a few shades off from the pretexting for sure, but it is still a deceptive method that is used to secure information. It could be used by an employee, used by a relation to impart or to convince the third party that it is the authentic party requesting the information. If you are saying no, then I will accept your answer. But--

MR. ALDER. Okay.

MS. ESHOO. You said no?

MR. ALDER. No in regard to what?

MS. ESHOO. Well, you know what, you have to be smart to play dumb. So I think I have been pretty direct about my question. I asked you if rusing has been used. Then you asked me to define it. I give it to you, and then you are confused?

MR. ALDER. Yes. Rusing, it has been used.

MS. ESHOO. It has been used?

MR. ALDER. Yes, ma'am.

MS. ESHOO. And for how long?

MR. ALDER. I don't know. I would probably say probably for the last 3 years or so that I am aware of since I have been there.

MS. ESHOO. Mr. Sonsini, what is there today in terms of our laws that direct themselves to the situation that the HP Board found itself in? And that is, a director that lied consistently that he had not leaked, when it was determined—by pretty bad ways, but it was still determined--that he was the guilty party, damaging information, damaging, I think, in terms of shareholders, and certainly, in my view, violated his fiduciary responsibility.

In advising the Board or if you were to advise the Board, what are the options that are available for a publicly held company when they have a director that they can't fire? I mean, I don't know what the directors' terms are at HP. They are probably going to go back and look at this. There is a lot of talk in politics about term limits. They are going to have to look at term limits there or shorten the term limits.

Is it simply the manual of the ethics of the company, or are there other instruments that can be used to be brought to bear in this kind of a situation? Because, I don't think, with all due respect to HP, that this is totally unique to them. Human beings make up boards. Human beings are less than perfect. God knows, there is leaking. We know sitting up here that there are leaks. And this is something that people are tempted to do, I am sure, in the private sector as well. So--

MR. SONSINI. Well, what we do, and it is a very good question, and it is very consistent with what we did back in January 2005 or February, first of all, it is very important that boards continually evaluate themselves, peer-to-peer evaluations, board evaluations where you have candid review of what you are doing and what people are doing.

Secondly, it is very important that boards adopt guidelines that deal with fiduciary duty issues, confidentiality and the like.

MS. ESHOO. But are there Federal or State laws or agencies, to go to, for example, the SEC, and say, our hands are tied, we believe there is something wrong here?

MR. SONSINI. No. It is corporate law. It requires directors to exercise due care and duty of loyalty and duty of candor. And if they step over the bounds, then they are in breach of that fiduciary obligation. They lose the protections of the business judgment rules that shield them from liability. So they have personal liability exposure, and that is the tone at the top that you have to--

MS. ESHOO. Can the corporation sue them for this if they determine--

MR. SONSINI. Yes. If a director breaches a fiduciary duty and harms a corporation, the corporation that has been harmed can bring legal action, yes.

MS. ESHOO. Well, there is an area where the law really comes into play, and that is in terms of tipping, but that is a whole other standard. That is a whole other standard.

Ms. Dunn, thank you.

Ms. Dunn, you have testified today more than once that you didn't direct the investigation; it was, in other words, this was an internal unit within HP management, that they executed and contracted out or had someone on retainer that did this.

Now, you also said that you found out what other members asked, others that were investigated. And how did you find out that you were pretexted? Is it through the press, or you were told that you were going to be?

MS. DUNN. No, I was not told I was going to be, but in all candor, there has been such a torrent of information that has come to me in the last 3 to 4 weeks about this matter, I can't tell you how I found out, but it was within the last 3 or 4 weeks that it came, someone told me that I had been pretexted, which I didn't--I hadn't realized previously. And I am sorry, I just can't remember who told me. If I could consult with my attorney, he may remember, but I don't.

MS. ESHOO. I just thought it was interesting in terms of your testimony that you were as well.

So was the whole Board investigated by--

MS. DUNN. My understanding--

MS. ESHOO. Maybe Mr. Adler knows. Mr. Adler was the entire Board investigated?

MR. ALDER. Yes, ma'am.

MS. ESHOO. Everyone?

MR. ALDER. Yes, ma'am.

MS. ESHOO. All nine?

MR. ALDER. Yes.

MS. DUNN. That is the first I am knowing this fact, so that is an interesting fact.

I would like to throw in that, you know, the attitudes by directors toward their privacy versus the confidentiality of the company they serve seems to be very different from the general public. I will draw your attention to an Associated Press survey that was done in the last week to 10 days--

MS. ESHOO. I saw that. I read that in your extended testimony. I thought that was very interesting.

MS. DUNN. And it turned out that 85 percent of directors surveyed believe that their personal privacy was secondary as director to the needs of a company to uphold confidentiality. And I have had directors say to me since this matter broke, many directors from well outside of HP, that when they join a public company board, they assume away a lot of privacy rights. It comes with the territory.

Now, I am not condoning the misrepresentation of identity through pretexting. I have said and would like to repeat that. I think there needs to be a much clearer legal backdrop for that activity.

MS. ESHOO. I want to get back to--I have my needle stuck on something.

From what I am hearing is that regardless of what a member of a board, a director, does, there really are not tools or instruments to remove that member other than kind of appealing to the director and saying, "We don't think you have lived up to your fiduciary responsibility," or whatever the case may be.

Is there something, or is there not? I mean, what is there to prevent this in the future? And are there any instruments to indeed punish someone if they don't live up to that? Is it simply--I shouldn't say simply--I know that the standard of business conduct is very important, but is there anything else?

I think Mr. Sonsini probably wants to answer that.

Thank you, Mr. Chairman.

MR. SONSINI. Directors serve at the pleasure of the shareholders. The shareholders are the ones that can appoint and remove directors. Boards can't remove directors.

What boards do is they have to evaluate themselves and decide who should stand as director. If a director takes action that harms the corporation, that director can be sued and has liability. That is basically the state of the law.

MS. ESHOO. Thank you.

MR. WHITFIELD. Mr. Markey is recognized, 10 minutes.

MR. MARKEY. Thank you, Mr. Chairman.

Ms. Dunn, on page 20 of your testimony, you say that in early February of this year, both you and Mr. Hurd were briefed about a sting operation proposed to send a fake e-mail to a CNET reporter; is that correct?

MS. DUNN. That is my testimony, yes, sir.

MR. MARKEY. Were you both told that this e-mail would include an attachment that had a tracer or spyware in it?

MS. DUNN. I never heard the word "spyware" in connection with this investigation.

MR. MARKEY. But did you hear the word "tracer"?

MS. DUNN. I did hear the word "tracer."

MR. MARKEY. What did you understand that to be?

MS. DUNN. I understood it to be a way of confirming the receipt of an e-mail by someone who was under investigation.

MR. MARKEY. So you did not understand it to mean that it would perhaps open up then this reporter's file; that would make it possible then to trace where that reporter would be going in terms of phone calls or other communications to other people?

MS. DUNN. No. That is not my understanding of how it works, and perhaps Mr. Adler could clarify how it works--

MR. MARKEY. What did you understand the word "tracer" to mean?

MS. DUNN. That it would simply confirm whether a certain e-mail had been received and not necessarily by the person, but by someone in, let's say, the area the size of the Bay area.

MR. MARKEY. So in order to catch a leaker on the Board, an investigation was launched. The concern was that these leaks are hurting HP. The Board members have a fiduciary responsibility not to hurt the company, but to grow it. And so investigating HP directors was deemed fair game given their role at HP.

But what thought was given to whether it was appropriate to spy on reporters who have no relationship, fiduciary or otherwise, with HP?

MS. DUNN. The spying on reporters was not something that was brought in any clear way to the attention of certainly me. I don't know about Ms. Baskins, but I did learn on September 6th that reporters had been pretexted.

MR. MARKEY. Can I just say this, Ms. Dunn? I understand that you are the Chair of HP.

MS. DUNN. I was the Chairman.

MR. MARKEY. You were the Chairman of HP, and it is one of the leading technology companies in the world, and you are testifying here to a decided lack of knowledge of technology and its uses, which to a committee with jurisdiction over the telecommunications industry, is a little bit disconcerting, to be quite frank with you.

MS. DUNN. May I respond to that?

MR. MARKEY. You may. But we are only congressional experts, but that means we are only experts compared to other Congressmen.

MS. DUNN. I am not an expert in technology, and that was not my role on the HP Board. A board is composed of individuals who have different skills--

MR. MARKEY. I understand what you are saying.

MS. DUNN. My particular skills were not in technology, and that was not the role I fulfilled on the HP Board. I was considered a financial expert. And ironic as it may seem to you now, I was also an expert in corporate governance.

MR. MARKEY. So who believed it was appropriate to spy on non-Hewlett-Packard individuals in this investigation, Ms. Dunn?

MS. DUNN. I don't know who at my level or Mark Hurd's level considered it was appropriate to spy on reporters.

MR. MARKEY. Are you saying that you didn't understand that the attachment with the spyware was an intrinsic part of the sting? You didn't understand that?

MS. DUNN. The word "spyware" was never a part of what I understood to be the case.

MR. MARKEY. Or some similar type of term to describe what was going to be--what the plot was with regard to this report, not necessarily spyware.

MS. DUNN. Well, as Mr. Adler has testified, this is a common investigative technique that has been used, and I am just quoting his testimony, one to two dozen times at Hewlett-Packard in sensitive investigations. It is still the policy of HP that this technique is a standard and acceptable part of its arsenal in investigative methods.

MR. MARKEY. Did you receive any substantive reports as to the subsequent success or failure of this sting?

MS. DUNN. I heard, by the by, that it didn't work.

MR. MARKEY. That it didn't work. And can you give a name to the vine? Does the vine have a name?

MS. DUNN. No. No. I was saying by the by. I heard somewhere within the chatter, if you will, that it hadn't worked. I don't recall a specific communication.

MR. MARKEY. And how often is this technique used on non-HP--

MS. DUNN. I don't know. The only knowledge I have of it firsthand is in this matter, and I was quoting Mr. Adler's previous testimony as to its use at HP otherwise.

MR. MARKEY. Mr. Adler, how often is this technique used on non-HP individuals?

MR. ALDER. I can only speak from my own personal experience, and I would venture a guess as to the rest, sir. I know that I have used it at least on two occasions on non-HP persons.

MR. MARKEY. And who were those persons?

MR. ALDER. Excuse me?

MR. MARKEY. Who were those persons?

MR. ALDER. One was the reporter, Ms. Kawamoto, and also on a suspected theft suspect in Houston. I don't recall his name.

MR. MARKEY. And to the best of your knowledge, those are the only two occasions where HP used this technique on non-HP individuals?

MR. ALDER. The only 2 occasions that I used it. I know that my coworkers have also used it. I know that law enforcement uses it.

MR. MARKEY. I am talking about just HP itself, not law enforcement. You are saying that at HP it has been used by other individuals as well on non-HP individuals?

MR. ALDER. Yes, sir.

MR. MARKEY. How prevalent? Are you talking about a handful of times, or is it a prevalent practice?

MR. ALDER. I think I offered earlier, one to two dozen times I estimate in totality.

MR. MARKEY. Mr. Sonsini, you are one of HP's outside legal counsels. Were you at all involved in the company's 8K filing made earlier today, disclosing the fact that HP had concluded an agreement with Ms. Baskins that provides her with a multi-million-dollar golden parachute?

MR. SONSINI. No, I was not.

MR. MARKEY. Thank you.

Mr. Adler, you say that you were advised that this opinion was the result of a review by at least two attorneys. Were you told who the two attorneys were who provided the legal opinion that you relied upon?

MR. ALDER. The two attorneys that I referenced were Mr. Hunsaker and an outside attorney whose name I don't know.

MR. MARKEY. Now, Mr. Adler, did you ever read any legal memos or e-mails from these two attorneys that explained their basis for their opinion?

MR. ALDER. No, I did not.

MR. MARKEY. I would like to turn to a Saturday, January 28, 2006, e-mail that HP senior counsel Mr. Hunsaker sent, and also a copy to HP's Global Security Manager Mr. Gentilucci and your colleague Mr. Nye. This e-mail says this: "Hi Fred, apparently Perkins almost never uses his cell phone and instead does just about everything by way of text message. Is there any way to lawfully get text message content, or is it the same as his cell phone records?"

Now, when Mr. Hunsaker writes to you, "Is there any way to lawfully get text messages content, or is it the same as cell phone records," doesn't that suggest that as of January 28, 2006, that Mr. Hunsaker already was aware that getting phone records was illegal?

MR. ALDER. Illegal--possibly, yes.

MR. MARKEY. I think it is clear it is yes. Is the law the same as cell phone records that you can't get them? So he knows in January of this year that it is illegal.

Now, Mr. Adler, just 13 minutes after this e-mail was sent to you, you replied back to Mr. Hunsaker, "Even if we could legally obtain the records, which we can't, unless we either pay the bill or get consent, I would highly suspect text messaging records are not kept due to volume and expense. The only other means is through real-time interception, an avenue not open to us."

MR. ALDER. Correct.

MR. MARKEY. Doesn't your reply to Mr. Hunsaker indicate that you, too, were aware of the fact that it was already illegal to obtain phone records unless you are the person paying the bill or you obtained the consumer's consent?

MR. ALDER. Correct, sir.

MR. MARKEY. So you believed it was illegal as well in January?

MR. ALDER. In January, yes, sir. Yes, sir, I had. In January, yes, I did.

MR. MARKEY. So you believed it was illegal in January.

MR. ALDER. Yes.

MR. MARKEY. And so this is something as a result that had a long fuse inside of HP, this knowledge that this was illegal activity. In other words, we don't have to pass any new laws to make this illegal, it is illegal right now.

And you knew, others knew, and it is clear that, from my perspective, Mr. Perkins at least came to know that and appreciate that fact, and it disturbed him greatly.

So I know that we are just at the tip of the iceberg here, Mr. Chairman, but this is very disturbing testimony that we are receiving, and, again, I want to congratulate you for conducting the hearing.

MR. WHITFIELD. Mr. Markey, I would like to comment that there has been a lot of discussion today about the importance of passing this pretexting bill that was reported out of this committee, I guess almost unanimously, but I think the record also does reflect that existing California law and the Wire Act, the Federal Wire Act, and the FTC's civil penalties, that it already is illegal. I think we can make a strong argument--which is the point you were making.

And I would also just reiterate, as we close up with this panel, that we hear--we heard a lot of discussion about the Board members being the subject of this investigation, but I don't think any of us want to forget that there were nine other people who were not Board members. They were members of the news media and other employees of the company that were also investigated.

And, Ms. Dunn, in closing, you have made it pretty clear today in your testimony that as the Chairman of the Board, the Board members came to you and urged that you conduct this investigation. And you turned it over to the management team, the investigative team. And we have heard a lot about the investigative team doing the daily work and making the decisions and setting the techniques and whatever. I understand that team to be--and I am not trying to put words in your mouth, and you can correct me if I'm wrong--but the team, in your mind, it was Ann Baskins, Mr. Hunsaker, Mr. Gentilucci, and who else?

MS. DUNN. For the investigation that was conducted in 2006, the team, the investigative team, was headed by Mr. Hunsaker reporting to Ms. Baskins. The only other names that I knew before today or recently were Mr. Gentilucci and Mr. DeLia. I don't know who else was on the team.

MR. WHITFIELD. So from your perspective, when you talk about the team, the investigative team, it is those four people.

MS. DUNN. To my knowledge, yes. There may have been others.

MR. WHITFIELD. Okay. Now, just one final point here. And we have gone over this a couple of times, but on Wednesday, February 22, 2006, Kevin--it is in Tab 62 if you want to look at it. I think you have already looked at it. There was an e-mail from Kevin Hunsaker to you, and he talks about this electronic tracer in this e-mail that they wanted to send to the reporter for CNET. And I think her name is Dawn, Dawn Kawamoto. And it simply said, "HP has come up with a name for its next-generation data centers. Mark is meeting with the WSJ and maybe others on the 27th. Pulled this from the presentation slides. Jacob."

So this is the Jacob that is the fictitious character and person who did not exist, and you have already said that the words you used in replying were not particularly good. And if you had to do it over again, you wouldn't say it, but you said--"I think this is very clever--but as a matter of course, anything going outside HP I hope that Mark--we should have Mark's approval." And then Kevin wrote back to you on the 23rd, the next day, saying, "For your information, I spoke to Mark a few minutes ago, and he is fine with both the concept and the content. We will either send out this afternoon or tomorrow morning, and I will keep you posted."

Is that your understanding of what happened?

MS. DUNN. I think that reflects what happened, yes.

MR. WHITFIELD. And do you know if Mark Hurd knew about the tracer technology?

MS. DUNN. I don't know firsthand. I think that is a question you will have to ask him. I am sorry, I am not trying to be unresponsive, but it would be hearsay.

MR. WHITFIELD. You said you have heard about hearsay on it? What hearsay?

MS. DUNN. I have heard a lot of legal terms in the last--

MR. WHITFIELD. But on this issue have you heard--

MS. DUNN. It would be a communication--my understanding, it was a communication from Mark to the team as reported by me would be hearsay. So I am simply suggesting that he would be the better person to respond to your question.

MR. WHITFIELD. But you don't have any other knowledge on this particular issue except for what is in this e-mail, you said, other than hearsay, which would indicate to me that you have heard additional information about whether or not Mr. Hurd knew about the tracer.

MS. DUNN. What I know is reflected by what is in the e-mail, and in response to your question about how or what Mr. Hurd did, I am simply saying it would be speculation on my part as to how he responded to the team.

MR. WHITFIELD. Can you tell us what this hearsay is?

MS. DUNN. I assume that since they did it, he gave his approval.

MR. WHITFIELD. You assume. Okay.

MS. DEGETTE. Would you yield, Mr. Chairman?

Did you ever talk to Mr. Hurd about this?

MS. DUNN. No, I did not.

MS. DEGETTE. So you just heard secondhand he had approved it?

MS. DUNN. That is what I was just trying to say.

MS. DEGETTE. You know, this is not a court of law even though it might feel like one, sometimes. So you can testify to hearsay you may have heard.

MS. DUNN. I am trying to be responsive. I just don't want to put words in someone's mouth that I didn't hear.

MS. DEGETTE. Sure.

With that caveat, what did you hear?

MS. DUNN. What I understood was that since this action went forward, my assumption is that it was based on what the e-mails say, which is that he gave his approval.

MS. DEGETTE. Thank you.

MR. WHITFIELD. Well, that concludes questions for this panel, and I want to thank you all for your patience. And this panel is now dismissed.

And I do want to--if there is not any objection, I am going to enter into the record at this point the document books, the two document books.

And in addition to that, I would like to enter into the record the report by Larry Sonsini's firm regarding this presentation made before the Board about this investigation dated August 30, 2006.

So without objection, we will enter that into the record.

[The information follows:]

Ex. #	Description	Date	Bates
1	Minutes from HP Board of Directors meeting	02/07/05	HP 00512, 15
2	Email chain between Patricia Dunn and Ron DeLia; subject: setting up "Project Kona"	4//19/05	SOS 0001-2,4, 8, 14, 18
3	Investigative report draft findings prepared by Security Outsourcing Solutions, Inc. in Kona I	06/14/05	HP 03559-65
4	Email chain between Jim Fairbaugh, Anthony Gentilucci, and Kevin Huska; subject: Security Outsourcing Solutions, Inc. investigative report	07/07/05	HP 01200-08
5	Investigative report preliminary draft prepared by Security Ourtsourcing Solutions, Inc. in Kona I	07/12/05	HP0019203-27
6	Investigative report supplemental draft findings prepared by Security Outsourcing Solutions, Inc. in Kona I	07/19/05	HP 04052-59
7	Power Point presentation by HP Global Security department in re: "Operation Kona"	07/22/05	HP 01187-99
8	Email from Anthony Gentilucci to Patricia Dunn; subject: update memo	08/06/05	SOS 0026-28
9	Update Memorandum from Anthony Gentilucci to Patricia Dunn; subject: Project Kona	08/06/05	HP 01131-34
10	Email from Dennis J. Lynch to Kevin Huska and Jim Fairbaugh; subject: Board Member Jay Keyworth's stolen laptop computer	10/09/05	HP 00729
11	Email chain between Robert Sherbin, Kevin Hunsaker, and Anthony Gentilucci; subject: name and contact information of the reporter involved in the information leak	01/20/06	HP 00473
12	Email from Anthony Gentilucci to Kevin Hunsaker; subject: Operation Kona	01/23/06	HP 03592
13	Email from Kevin Hunsaker to team members; subject: instructions regarding information leak analysis	01/23/06	HP 03273
14	Email from Kevin Hunsaker to Jim Fairbaugh; subject: potential information leak	01/23/06	HP 03282
15	Invoices from Action Research Group	01/25/06-03/08/06	HP 5822-29
16	Email from Kevin Hunsaker to Frederick Adler; subject: Board member's phone records	01/26/06	HP 00385
17	Email between Fred Adler and Ron DeLia; subject: CNET reporters phone records	01/27/06	HP 00384
18	Email from Kevin Hunsaker; subject: meeting with Patricia Dunn	01/27/06	HP 00575
19	Investigative Report; subject: IT Investigations progress to date	01/27/06	HP0008545-82
20	Email from Kevin Hunsaker; subject: obtaining text message records	01/28/06	HP 00379
21	Email from Kevin Hunsaker to Anthony Gentilucci; subject: draft email from "Jacob" to Dawn Kawamoto	01/28/06	HP 03364
22	Email between Kevin Hunsaker and Anthony Gentilucci; subject: draft message from Kevin Hunsaker as "Jacob" to Dawn Kawamoto	01/28/06	HP 03375
23	Email chain between Kevin Hunsaker and Anthony Gentilucci; subject: obtaining information from Dawn Kawamoto through "Jacob"	01/28/06	HP 03378-79
24	Email chain between Kevin Hunsaker and Anthony Gentilucci; subject: developing "Jacob" and draft message to Dawn Kawamoto	01/28/06-01/29/2006	HP 03383-86
25	Email chain between Kevin Hunsaker and Anthony Gentilucci; subject: using social engineering to obtain information	01/30/06	HP 00054

26	Email from Kevin Hunsaker to Anthony Gentilucci; subject: list of action taken and future steps to take in the internal investigation	01/30/06	HP 03404
27	Email chain between Kevin Hunsaker, Vince Nye, and Ron Delia; subject: Reuters article exposing HP non-public information	01/31/06	HP 00583-84
28	Email from Kevin Hunsaker to Anthony Gentilucci; subject: initiating contact between "Jacob" and reporter Dawn Kawamoto	02/01/06	HP 00725-26
29	Power Point presentation in re: initial briefing on Project Kona II to Patricia Dunn	02/02/06	HP 03752-76
30	Power Point presentation in re: briefing on Project Kona II to senior management	02/02/06	HP 03685-97
31	Email between Kevin Hunsaker and all investigation team members; subject: investigation update from senior management and Board members	02/02/06	HP 00589
32	Email from Ron DeLia to Kevin Hunsaker, Anthony Gentilucci, Vince Nye, and Frederick Adler; subject: Dr. George Keyworth's stolen laptop	02/03/06	HP0008651
33	Email between Kevin Hunsaker and Patricia Dunn; subject: Patricia Dunn's response to Project Kona II briefing	02/03/06	HP 00590-91
34	Email between Frederick Adler and Kevin Hunsaker; subject: installing email tracers	02/03/06	HP0017149-51
35	Email chain between Kevin Hunsaker and Ron DeLia; subject: identifying members as potential leaks and obtaining cell phone records	02/03/06	HP 00734
36	Email between Ron DeLia and Kevin Hunsaker; subject: identifying Dr. George	02/05/06	HP 000336-37
37	Email from Patricia Dunn to Kevin Hunsaker; subject: including Mark Hurd in the approval process for investigation tactics	02/05/06	HP 03415
38	Email from Ron DeLia to Kevin Hunsaker, Anthony Gentilucci, Vince Nye, and Frederick Adler; subject: discussing tactics to use against reporter Dawn Kawamoto	02/06/06	HP 00747-48
39	Email from Vince Nye to Anthony Gentilucci and Kevin Hunsaker; subject: legality and ethics of obtaining George Keyworth's phone records	02/07/06	HP0016866-75
40	Email chain between Vince Nye, Frederick Adler, and Ron DeLia; subject: call time and duration from Dawn Kawamoto's cell phone to Keyworth's home	02/07/06	HP0008987-89
41	Email from Ron DeLia to Kevin Hunsaker; subject: lack of Federal laws prohibiting pretexting, noting FTC jurisdiction	02/07/06	HP 00058
42	Email from Jose Gurgel-Neto to Ron DeLia; subject: national licensing for Private Investigators	02/07/06	HP 4215
43	Email chain between Arthur Molineaux and Frederick Adler; subject: bending the rules to obtain cell phone records	02/08/06	HP0009001-03
44	Email from Kevin Hunsaker; subject: step-by-step instructions for Phase #1 of covert operation for Kona II	02/08/06	HP 00759-60
45	Email chain between Anthony Gentilucci, Fred Adler, and Kevin Hunsaker; subject: new investigative techniques	02/09/06	HP0007184-86
46	Email from Vince Nye to Fred Adler; subject: initiating activity of two surveillance teams	02/09/06	HP0007189
47	Email from Frederick Adler to Arthur Molineaux; subject: records provided	02/09/06	HP0007190
48	Email chain between Patricia Dunn, Ann Baskins, and Kevin Husaker; subject: leaking HP handheld device media advisory as a technique to gain credibility for "Jacob"	02/09/06	HP 03445-46
49	Email chain between John McLean and Anthony Gentilucci; subject: tracking devices	02/09/06	HP0019021-25

50	Frederick Adler emails re. launching of tracking software	02/9/2006-02/10/06	HP0007245-46, 50-52, 54, 56-57, 66, HP0007319
51	Email from Kevin Hunsaker; subject: draft version of HP handheld device credibility leak and seeking approval for leak from Mark Hurd	02/09/06	HP 03451-52
52	Email between Kevin Hunsaker and Patricia Dunn; subject: verifying Mark Hurd's approval for providing HP handheld device credibility lead to Dawn Kawamoto	02/09/06	HP 03454
53	Revised investigation summary prepared by Security Outsourcing Solutions, Inc.	02/10/06	HP 00302-09
54	Email from Ron DeLia to Kevin Hunsaker, Anthony Gentilucci, Vince Nye, and Frederick Adler; subject: surveillance results from February 10, 2006	02/11/06	HP0007094-95
55	Email chain between Kevin Hunsaker and Fred Adler; subject: message from "Jacob" to Dawn Kawamoto leaking information on HP handheld device	02/13/06	HP 00612-13
56	AOL Instant Messaging chain between Mike Moeller and Pui Wing Tam	02/16/06	HP 0007496-98
57	Email between Kevin Hunsaker and Ron DeLia; subject: phone records used to brief Patricia Dunn and Ann Baskins	02/17/06	HP0008048-49
58	Email between Kevin Hunsaker and investigation team; subject: Phase II draft message	02/21/06	HP 00624
59	Email from Kevin Hunsaker to Anthony Gentilucci; subject: Patricia Dunn's approval of Phase II name	02/22/06	HP 03813
60	Email chain between Kevin Hunsaker and Mark Hurd, Ann Baskins, and Patricia Dunn; subject: Phase II	02/22/06	HP0007539-41
61	Email from Jose Gurgel-Neto to Ron DeLia; subject: cell phone records	02/23/06	HP 4402
62	Email chain between Kevin Hunsaker and Patricia Dunn; subject: Mark Hurd's approval of information leak to reporter Dawn Kawamoto	02/23/06	HP 03531-32
63	Email from Ron DeLia to Kevin Hunsaker; subject: setting up surveillance and pretexting information for Dawn Kawamoto	02/23/06	HP 00067
64	Email between Ron DeLia and Kevin Hunsaker; subject: surveillance photos of Dawn Kawamoto	02/23/06	HP 00916-17
65	Email between Ron DeLia and Kevin Hunsaker; subject: using pretext calls in surveillance of Dawn Kawamoto	02/23/06	HP 00064-66
66	Email between Ron DeLia and Kevin Hunsaker; subject: providing Patricia Dunn with a comprehensive summary of the techniques and resources used in the investigation	02/24/06	HP 00927-28
67	Email from Ron DeLia to Kevin Hunsaker, Anthony Gentilucci, Vince Nye, and Frederick Adler; subject: surveillance activity update	02/26/06	HP 00931
68	Statement from Action Research Group to Security Outsourcing Solutions	02/27/06	HP 5850
69	Email from Kevin Hunsaker to Vince Nye, Ron DeLia, and Anthony Gentilucci; subject: monitoring telephone calls and IM traffic	03/02/06	HP 00635
70	Email between Ron DeLia and Action Research Group; subject: cell phone records	03/02/06	HP 4207
71	Email from Jose Gurgel-Neto of Action Research Group to Ron DeLia; subject: cell phone records	03/03/06	HP 4200
72	(SBC) Draft Investigation Report from Kevin Hunsaker to Patricia Dunn, Mark Hurd, and Ann Baskins	03/10/06	HP 03909-26
73	Email from Kevin Hunsaker; subject: Ron DeLia and Anthony Gentilucci to brief Mark Hurd on Operation Kona	03/13/06	HP 00655

74	Email from Vince Nye to Ted Crawford; subject: obtaining cell phone records	03/17/06	HP0014011
75	Email chain between Kevin Hunsaker and Anthony Gentilucci; subject: using pretexting to obtain information in the investigation	03/21/06	HP0007646-47
76	Email from anon. to Anthony Gentilucci re: Clemons v. Waller	03/24/06	HP0007629-34
77	Email from Kevin Hunsaker to Anthony Gentilucci and Ron DeLia; subject: including a conversations between Mark Hurd and Thomas Perkins into the investigation report	03/29/06	HP 03958
78	Kona II - LA Surveillance Report	04/06/06	HP0007465-67
79	Email between Patricia Dunn, Ann Baskins, and Kevin Hunsaker; subject: updating Ann Baskins and Patricia Dunn on the status of the investigation	04/14/06	HP 00468-69
80	Email from Ron DeLia to Kevin Hunsaker, Anthony Gentilucci, Vince Nye, and Frederick Adler; subject: surveillance photos	04/18/06	HP 00985-86
81	Email chain between Jose Gurgel-Neto, Ron DeLia, and Kevin Hunsaker; subject: Dr. George Keyworth's laptop	04/22/06	HP0018733-36
82	Email between Ann Baskins, Robert Ryan, and Kevin Hunsaker; subject: Kona II draft report	04/24/06	PD 00045
83	Email from Kevin Hunsaker to Anthony Gentilucci and Ron DeLia; subject: investigation techniques used in the Kona II investigation to obtain phone records	04/28/06	HP 00056
84	Email from Ron DeLia to Tony Gentilucci; subject: Kona II cost breakdown	05/02/06	HP0007129-31
85	Minutes from HP Board of Directors meeting	05/18/06	HP 04060-71
86	Email from Patricia Dunn to Ann Baskins and Larry Sonsini; subject: PR strategies	05/19/06	HP0018525
87	United States Securities and Exchange Commission Form 8-K filed 5/19/06	05/19/06	-
88	Email from Ann Baskins to Patricia Dunn; subject: Robert Ryan's talking	05/22/06	PD 00070-78
89	Final Investigation Report from Kevin Hunsaker to Mark Hurd, Ann Baskins, and Members of the Board	05/24/06	HP 03984-4001
90	Email from Thomas Perkins to media contacts; subject: Mr. Perkins resignation from the Board of Directors	05/31/06	PD 00027-28
91	Email chain between Larry Sonsini and Thomas Perkins; subject: the conduct of the Operation Kona investigation	6/19/06-6/28/2006	-
92	Letter from Thomas J. Perkins to the Directors of the Hewlett-Packard Company	undated	-
93	Email chain between Ann Baskins and Tom Perkins; subject: May 18th Board of Directors' meeting	07/17/06-07/28/06	-
94	Email from Thomas Perkins to Ann Bakins and Members of the Board; subject: Thomas Perkins statement to the Board	07/28/06	PD 00023-24
95	Memorandum from Pattie Dunn; subject: Thoughts on the TJP Situation	08/17/06	PD 00079-81
96	Email from Vince Nye to Michael Katalinic; subject: HP Standards of Business Conduct	08/23/06	HP0007180
97	Email from Jose Gurgel-Neto to Ron DeLia; subject: AT&T filing lawsuits against data brokers	08/26/06	HP 4085-86
98	Memorandum from Pattie Dunn; subject: "Wrapping up on the Last Board Meeting"	09/02/06	PD 00083
99	Email from Patricia Dunn to Robert Sherbin; subject: Pretexting	09/05/06	PD 00013
100	Email from Timothy O'Neill to John Craparo and Ryan Sherry; subject: media reports and articles from the Board of Directors' investigation	09/06/06	HP0008089-90
101	Email from Peter Hunt to Anthony Gentilucci; subject: reaction to Newsweek article	09/06/06	HP0006684-87

102	Email from Paul Taaffe to Robert Sherbin; subject: Board awareness of the investigation	09/07/06	PD 00008-09
103	United States Securities and Exchange Commission Form 8-K filed 9/6/06	09/06/06	-
104	Email chain between Kevin Huska and Anthony Gentilucci	09/07/06	HP0006153-54
105	Statement from Ann Baskins regarding Board meeting minutes	-	PD 00107
106	Email from Patricia Dunn to Rober Sherbin; subject: BusinessWeek article inaccuracies	09/18/06	PD 00032-35
Ex. #	Pretexting Records	[illegible]	Bates
107	Phone records procured for ARG by Valerie Preston and Darren Brost	03/7/05-03/11/05	-
108	Ben Elgin's phone records provided to SOS by ARG	04/22/05	-
109	Robert Knowling's phone records, procured for ARG by Cassandra Salvage	07/06/05-07/08/05	-
110	Carly Foirina's phone records, requested by SOS from Action Research	07/08/05	-
111	Dawn Kawamoto's phone records, procured by Charles Kelly for ARG	01/30/06	-
112	George & Marion Keyworth's phone records, procured by Bryan Wagner for ARG	02/06/06, 02/08/06	-
113	Tom Perkins' phone records, obtained by ARG	January-06	-
Ex. #	WSGR Interviews	Date	Bates
114	Interviews with Ann Baskins	08/21/06, 08/25/06, 08/28/06	-
115	Interviews with Ron DeLia	08/21/06, 08/25/06	-
116	Interviews with Patricia Dunn	08/21/2006, 08/28/06	-
117	Interview with Jim Fairbaugh	08/25/06	-
118	Interviews with Kevin Hunsaker	08/21/06, 08/22/06, 08/25/06	-
119	Interviews with Anthony Gentilucci	08/14/06, 8/30/06,	
120	Interview with Mark Hurd	08/25/06	-
121	Interview with Kevin Huska	08/25/06	-
122	Interview with John Kiernan	08/21/06	-
123	Conversation with Bob Ryan	08/21/06	-
Ex. #	[illegible]	[illegible]	[illegible]
124	Handwritten document by Ann Baskins - Project Kona	06/15/05	HP0019620
125	E-mail communication between Hunsaker and Baskins re: EC Cellphones	01/28/06	HP00378
126	E-mail chain between DeLia and Hunsaker re: number lookups	02/06/06	HP00319
127	E-mail from DeLia to Hunsaker, etc. with list of calls	02/08/06	HP00311
128	E-mail from DeLia to Hunsaker, etc. re: DK calls from Disneyland	02/16/06	HP00909

129	E-mail from DeLia to Hunsaker, etc. re: Jan 31 phone calls	03/05/06	HP00143
130	Hunsaker E-mail chain re: GK cell calls	03/05/06	HP00436
131	E-mail from DeLia to Hunsaker, etc. re: Feb 3rd call from GK ro DK	03/06/06	HP00134
132	E-mails between DeLia and Hunsaker with KONA Markoff chart	03/10/06	HP00108
133	PDJ 1099 Summary, April 2000 through April 2005		

TAB 1

MINUTES OF A MEETING OF THE BOARD OF DIRECTORS OF HEWLETT-PACKARD COMPANY

February 7, 2005

Pursuant to notice duly given, the Board of Directors of Hewlett-Packard Company, a Delaware corporation ("HP"), duly held a meeting on February 7, 2005 at The Hyatt Regency O'Hare, Chicago, Illinois. The meeting commenced at 9:30 a.m. All Directors were present and in attendance at the meeting. In addition, Tom Perkins, a Nominee to the Board of Directors, and Larry W. Sonsini, of Wilson Sonsini Goodrich & Rosati attended the meeting.

Bob Knowling, as Chairman of the Governance Committee of the Board, opened the meeting and set forth the initial agenda.

The first order of business was to accept the resignation of Sandy Litvack as a Member of the Board of Directors. Mr. Sonsini reported on Mr. Litvack's resignation and the requirement to file a Form 8-K Report with the Securities and Exchange Commission to report the resignation. Mr. Sonsini gave a report on his phone conversation with Mr. Litvack and in that call Mr. Litvack stated that he was resigning for personal reasons and had no disagreement with the Company, management or the Board of Directors. Following a motion duly made, seconded and carried, the resignation was unanimously accepted.

Mr. Knowling then opened for discussion the appointment of a presiding independent Director for the purposes of presiding at executive sessions of the Board. After discussion and upon motion made, seconded and unanimously carried, Pattie Dunn was appointed the presiding Director for executive sessions.

determination of Management bonuses. He commented upon these two reviews which reflected the CEO's performance at her "peer" group and that she was compensated accordingly. Further discussion took place among the Directors regarding the March 2004 evaluation as well as the bonus award and option grants that took place in December. It was noted that there was no written evaluation of the CEO and the Board recommended that going forward a written record of performance of the CEO be kept either at the Committee or Board level records;

3. The Board then discussed the evaluation and performance of the CEO in light of the Company's performance. Through this discussion a number of issues were raised including, among others, (i) the differences the Board has with the CEO as to execution of the Company's strategy, (ii) the accomplishments of the CEO during her tenure (which were well received by the Board) as well as the skill set of a CEO that the Board feels will be required to execute the Company strategy going forward and to compete with the Company's major competitors, and (iii) an assessment of the CEO's performance with respect to execution of the Company's strategic plan, and (iv) the CEO's development of the management team and the performance, depth and quality of that management team, including a discussion of the weaknesses and strengths of the CEO and management.

The Board then discussed the pros and cons of considering making a change of the CEO at this time and various views were discussed. A particular note, was a discussion as to whether or not this was the appropriate time to make a change and whether or not the CEO should be given further time for execution of the Company's

TAB 2

----- Message from "Patricia Dunn-Jahnke" [redacted] on Tue, 19 Apr 2005 19:26:52 -0400 -----
To: "Ron DeLia" <rrd@security-outsourcing.com>
Subject: Project Kona
Ron, let's call this Project Kona.
Attached is the information we discussed:
- the outline of Ben Elgin's article
- the phone numbers of all those present at meetings referred to in the article
I am not sure how to defiine the "three insiders" referred to in your message. Let me know and we'll go from there.
Regards,
Pattie

Ron.doc HP.BUSWEEK.doc

----- Message from "Ron DeLia" <rrd@security-outsourcing.com> on Tue, 19 Apr 2005 22:40:57 -0400 -----
To: "Patricia Dunn-Jahnke" [redacted]
Subject: RE: Project Kona
Pattie,
Received information and for the time being we will refer to the insiders as Internal 1NY, 2NM and 3CA.
Ron
The content of this email transmission is intended only for the use of the individual or entity named above and may contain legally privileged or confidential information. If you are not the intended recipient, you are hereby notified that any disclosure, copying, dissemination, distribution, or use of this email transmission, or information contained herein, is strictly prohibited. If you have received this email transmission in error, please destroy all copies of this email and its attachments and notify the person whose name appears above.
Security Outsourcing Solutions, Inc.
Tel: ( ) or (

-----Original Message-----
From: Patricia Dunn-Jahnke [mailto:[redacted]]
Sent: Tuesday, April 19, 2005 7:27 PM
To: Ron DeLia
Subject: Project Kona
Ron, let's call this Project Kona.
Attached is the information we discussed:
- the outline of Ben Elgin's article
- the phone numbers of all those present at meetings referred to in the article
I am not sure how to defiine the "three insiders" referred to in your message. Let me know and we'll go from there.
Regards,
Pattie
----- Message from "Patricia Dunn-Jahnke" [redacted]> on Wed, 20 Apr 2005 19:58:32 -0400 -----
To: "Ron DeLia" <rrd@security-outsourcing.com>
Subject: RE: Project Kona
Ron, sorry to be dense, but I'm not remembering how these three individuals were selected (did I point them out in our first conversation?) Also not

sure which NY director is referred to.

Tx
PCD

From: "Ron DeLia" <rrd@security-outsourcing.com>
To: "Patricia Dunn-Jahnke" [redacted]
Subject: RE: Project Kona
Date: Tue, 19 Apr 2005 22:40:57 -0400

Pattie,

Received information and for the time being we will refer to the insiders as
Internal 1NY, 2NM and 3CA.

Ron

The content of this email transmission is intended only for the use of the individual or entity named above and may contain legally privileged or confidential information. If you are not the intended recipient, you are hereby notified that any disclosure, copying, dissemination, distribution, or use of this email transmission, or information contained herein, is strictly prohibited. If you have received this email transmission in error, please destroy all copies of this email and its attachments and notify the person whose name appears above.
Security Outsourcing Solutions, Inc.
Tel: (or (

-----Original Message-----
From: Patricia Dunn-Jahnke [mailto:[redacted]
Sent: Tuesday, April 19, 2005 7:27 PM
To: Ron DeLia
Subject: Project Kona

Ron, let's call this Project Kona.

Attached is the information we discussed:
- the outline of Ben Elgin's article
- the phone numbers of all those present at meetings referred to in the article

I am not sure how to defiine the "three insiders" referred to in your message. Let me know and we'll go from there.

Regards,
Pattie

----- Message from "Patricia Dunn-Jahnke" [redacted]> on Wed, 20 Apr 2005 23:30:03 -0400 -----
To: "Ron DeLia" <rrd@security-outsourcing.com>
Subject: Fw: Important on HP
Ron, the reporter below is the person BK has known for 8 years. BK says he is a fairly junior African American (as is Bob) reporter; that in the

---

Roger Crockett

Chicago Deputy Mgr.

BusinessWeek

roger_crockett@businessweek.com

----- Message from "Ron DeLia" <rrd@security-outsourcing.com> on Thu, 21 Apr 2005 00:21:51 -0400 -----
To: "Patricia Dunn-Jahnke" <pcdunn1@hotmail.com>
Subject: RE: Important on HP

Pattie,
Our research located a "Michael Arndt in Chicago" who co-authored a March 21, 2005 in a Business Week Article with Ben Elgin and Peter Burrows. We will run the cell number provided and further identify Roger Crockett in Chicago. Also note, Roger Crockett lists his title as "Chicago Deputy Mgr." Not sure what the title refers to, however, we are also checking into it.
Ron
The content of this email transmission is intended only for the use of the individual or entity named above and may contain legally privileged or confidential information. If you are not the intended recipient, you are hereby notified that any disclosure, copying, dissemination, distribution, or use of this email transmission, or information contained herein, is strictly prohibited. If you have received this email transmission in error, please destroy all copies of this email and its attachments and notify the person whose name appears above.
Security Outsourcing Solutions, Inc.
Tel: or

-----Original Message-----
From: Patricia Dunn-Jahnke [redacted].com]
Sent: Wednesday, April 20, 2005 11:30 PM
To: Ron DeLia
Subject: Fw: Important on HP

Ron, the reporter below is the person BK has known for 8 years. BK says he is a fairly junior African American (as is Bob) reporter; that in the voicemail he received from Crockett he said he saw the story and as a friend wanted to make sure BK was not surprised by it. For what it's worth BK told me he has not had any contact with Crockett or anyone else at BW in over 5 months.
My current top guesses as to the sources are 3CA and Carly Fiorina. We have no control over her activities with the press, but we still need to know if there are leaks coming from "internal" sources as previously discussed.
Pattie
From: "Knowling Bob" <BKnowli@nycboe.net>
To: [redacted]
Subject: Fw: Important on HP
Date: Wed, 20 Apr 2005 22:54:49 -0400

SOS 0004

office:
home:
cell:

PB
office:
home:
cell:

Regards,
Pattie

----- Message from "Ron DeLia" <rrd@security-outsourcing.com> on Mon, 16 May 2005 21:03:52 -0400 -----
To: "Patricia Dunn-Jahnke" [redacted]
Subject: RE: Phone Numbers
Pattie,
Receive the two messages,
Ron
The content of this email transmission is intended only for the use of the individual or entity named above and may contain legally privileged or confidential information. If you are not the intended recipient, you are hereby notified that any disclosure, copying, dissemination, distribution, or use of this email transmission, or information contained herein, is strictly prohibited. If you have received this email transmission in error, please destroy all copies of this email and its attachments and notify the person whose name appears above.
Security Outsourcing Solutions, Inc.
Tel: or

-----Original Message-----
From: Patricia Dunn-Jahnke [redacted]
Sent: Monday, May 16, 2005 5:38 PM
To: Ron DeLia
Subject: Phone Numbers

Here are their numbers:
BE
office:
home:
cell:
PB
office:
home:
cell:

Regards,
Pattie

----- Message from "Ron DeLia" <rrd@security-outsourcing.com> on Mon, 16 May 2005 21:35:43 -0400 -----
To: "Patricia Dunn-Jahnke" [redacted]
Subject: RE: Phone Numbers
Pattie,
The number you provided for BE cell phone is the one we located, therefore, it appears BE utilizes his personal cell and home telephones

Advanced Search

----- Message from "Ron DeLia" <rrd@security-outsourcing.com> on Tue, 14 Jun 2005 13:31:55 -0400 -----
To:
"Patricia Dunn-Jahnke" [redacted]
Subject:
KONAPattie,

Attached is the draft report on our findings to date.

Ron

Case 05-04-423 (Project KONA) Prlim Findings June 14 05.doc

The content of this email transmission is intended only for the use of the individual or entity named above and may contain legally privileged or confidential information. If you are not the intended recipient, you are hereby notified that any disclosure, copying, dissemination, distribution, or use of this email transmission, or information contained herein, is strictly prohibited. If you have received this email transmission in error, please destroy all copies of this email and its attachments and notify the person whose name appears above.
Security Outsourcing Solutions, Inc.
Tel: (. or (

----- Message from "Patricia Dunn-Jahnke" [redacted] on Tue, 14 Jun 2005 18:00:23 -0400 -----
To:
"Ron DeLia" <rrd@security-outsourcing.com>
cc:
<ann.baskins@hp.com>
Subject:
RE: KONA
Ron, I would like to re-schedule our call to include Ann Baskins, General Counsel at HP, Cin the next couple of days. Ann is now involved in the confidentiality review and it would be timely to compare notes and discuss where to go from here.

Could you do this at 2 pm EDT tomorrow (Wednesday)? Ann, could we use your conference line?

Regards,
Pattie

From: "Ron DeLia" <rrd@security-outsourcing.com>
To: "Patricia Dunn-Jahnke" [redacted]
Subject: KONA
Date: Tue, 14 Jun 2005 13:31:55 -0400

Pattie,

SOS 0014

its attachments and notify the person whose name appears above.

Security Outsourcing Solutions, Inc.
Tel: or

<< Case05-04-423(ProjectKONA)PrilimFindingsJune14,05.doc >>

----- Message from "Ron DeLia" <rrd@security-outsourcing.com> on Tue, 26 Jul 2005 23:01:20 -0400 -----
To:
"Patricia Dunn-Jahnke" [redacted]
Subject:
KONAPattie,

Tony Gentilucci (HP Manager of Investigations) and I would like to schedule a time to talk with you regarding your insight to the personalities of BOD members and discussions at BOD meetings. Our schedules are flexible and we will meet with you at a location that is convenient for you.

Ron

The content of this email transmission is intended only for the use of the individual or entity named above and may contain legally privileged or confidential information. If you are not the intended recipient, you are hereby notified that any disclosure, copying, dissemination, distribution, or use of this email transmission, or information contained herein, is strictly prohibited. If you have received this email transmission in error, please destroy all copies of this email and its attachments and notify the person whose name appears above.
Security Outsourcing Solutions, Inc.
Tel: or

----- Message from "Ron DeLia" <rrd@security-outsourcing.com> on Fri, 29 Jul 2005 19:39:18 -0400 -----
To:
"Dunn, Pattie BGI SF" <Pattie.Dunn@barclaysglobal.com>
Subject:
Follow Up
Pattie,

Tony Gentilucci and I would like to schedule some time with you to follow up on July 22nd meeting. Will you be traveling to the East Coast anytime soon?

Ron

The content of this email transmission is intended only for the use of the individual or entity named above and may contain legally privileged or confidential information. If you are not the intended recipient, you are hereby notified that any disclosure, copying, dissemination, distribution, or use of this email transmission, or information contained herein, is strictly prohibited. If you have received this email transmission in

SOS 0018

TAB 3

PREPARED FOR HEWLETT PACKARD BY SECURITY OUTSOURCING SOLUTIONS, INC.
Investigative Report
This report is a confidential and privileged communication between the attorney and the investigator.

CLIENT # HP-99-01
CASE # 05-04-423
DATE: June 14, 2005

DRAFT

(PROJECT KONA ET AL)
Preliminary Draft Findings

EXECUTIVE SUMMARY:

Security Outsourcing Solutions was retained to conduct an investigation into the unauthorized dissemination of proprietary information to members of the Press. The focus of the investigation is to identify the individual and/or individuals responsible for providing confidential information to unauthorized sources. The investigative activity conducted to date focused on determining if members of HP's Board of Directors were involved in providing proprietary information to reporters for Business Week magazine Ben Elgin and Peter Burrows. The investigation encompassed conducting background investigations on Ben Elgin, Peter Burrows, Roger Crockett and members of HP's Board of Directors. The investigative activity conducted included analyzing intelligence gathered through telephone subscriber records, public and proprietary database sources, media, civil litigation indices and Internet content.

It should be noted, telephone subscriber and call registers are obtained verbally from the various telephone carriers and is subject to human error. Therefore, SOS is diligent in the company's attempts to verify information obtained from its sources.

The investigation to date has not identified the internal HP source and/or sources that are responsible for providing proprietary information to Business Week reporters Ben Elgin, Peter Borrows and/or Roger Crockett.

Telephone research revealed several areas of interest, which are detailed in this report.

It should be noted, this firm has expanded the investigation to include third party non HP employees, which will be discussed further in this report. It should be noted, the investigation into the review of telephone records and the backgrounds of Business Week reporters and HP board members is continuing.

It should be noted, investigations of this nature are complex, time consuming and require a redirection of investigative activity as information is received and analyzed.

PREPARED FOR HEWLETT PACKARD BY SECURITY OUTSOURCING SOLUTIONS, INC.
Investigative Report
This report is a confidential and privileged communication between the attorney and the investigator.

An analytical review of the intelligence gathered to date suggests several scenarios by which proprietary information may have been leaked to Business Week reports Ben Elgin and Peter Burrows. It should be noted, the following scenarios are assumptions based on the information developed to date.

Research revealed Robert Knowling "Knowling" relationship with former CEO, Carly Fiorina began in 1996 when Knowling was the head of operations for US West. According to published media articles Knowling asked Fiorina to fly out to Denver to discuss failed phone service at US West. During the early December meeting, Knowling "read Fiorina the riot act" in front of her boss. By January 1, the entire Lucent support team serving US West had been replaced and Knowling's problems were fixed. According to the article, since that time, the two executives have had a tremendous respect for each other.

Robert Knowling is recorded as one of former CEO Carly Fiorina strongest supporters and is the board member most likely to maintain contact with the former CEO.

It should be noted, according to a chapter 5 (pages 90 & 91) in Peter Burrow's book "BACK-FIRE," Carly Fiorina has a history of "leaking" tips to the press. The content refers to Calvin Sims a reporter for the New York Times covering the story regarding AT&T's allegations the GSA had discriminated against the company. Calvin Sims reported, Carly "at times, she seemed to good a source, making Sims check himself to make sure he wasn't being used."

Therefore, it is possible proprietary information is being forward from a board member to a third party (Carly Fiorina) and then to Ben Elgin, Peter Burrows and/or Roger Crockett. Therefore, this firm is in the process of attempting to identifying cell phone numbers listed to Carly Fiorina.

Research has also revealed Robert Knowling appears to have had a personal relationship with Roger Crockett, Deputy Bureau Manager of Business Week's Chicago's office. Media and Internet content searches revealed Knowling was quoted in an October 1999 Business Week article, which was authored by Roger Crockett and Knowling was one of four individuals named as a top entrepreneur in Business Week's January 10, 2000 issue "The Top Entrepreneurs." Crockett and Knowling are also associated with the Kellogg School of Management at Northwestern University and appear to share an interest in the furtherance of African American advancement in corporate America and the technology industry.[1]

[1] Crockett was a winner of Northwestern University's Medill School of Journalism and the Kellogg School of Management has posted an article authored by Crockett and another article is part of the Class 1 curriculum for TECH-914. Robert Knowling is a member of the

Research revealed Crockett has been a reporter primarily covering the telecommunications industry for the past ten (10) years an industry Knowling has worked in from 1977 to 2000.

The timing of Robert Knowling's disclosure of his friendship with Roger Crockett is also a concern. It is our understanding Knowling's disclosure came after a board discussion regarding the leaking of information to the media and what measures should be taken to identify the source of the leak. The disclosure may have been an attempt to front Knowling's relationship with Crockett prior to the relationship surfacing in an investigation. It should be noted, Knowling stated he had received a "Text Message" from Crockett altering him that Business Week was planning to run a story on HP.

This firm is attempting to verify if Knowling received text messages on his cell phone and on what days the messages were received.

It should be noted, research revealed Ben Elgin placed a call to Roger Crockett's cell phone on March 9, 2005 from his (Elgin) cell phone and Crockett placed two (2) calls to Elgin's cell phone on March 9, 2005.

Research revealed 321 "out going" telephone calls placed from Roger Crockett's business cell phone [redacted] from December 27, 2004 to April 25, 2005. Identification of subscriber information for the 321 telephone numbers is continuing.[2]

It should be noted, the investigation has been somewhat hindered by the inability to date, to obtain information on the telephone calls placed from Robert Knowling's cell phone [redacted] during the period January 1st to April 2005. The aforementioned cell phone is reportedly a restricted government phone account and records on this type of account are difficult to obtain. Knowling's home telephone number [redacted] was identified, however, a review of the "out going" telephone calls from January 24, 2005 to March 28, 2005 were unremarkable. Only 20 "out going" calls were made during the aforementioned time period, of which, three (3) were to Knowling's home in CO, five (5) were to a John T. Welch in Albany, NY, four (4) were to a J. Welch Jr. in IL, two (2) were to a Melissa Amerian in Woodhills, CA, one (1) call to a John Bonfiglio in San Diego, one (1) to a Robert & Geneva Reynolds in Sacramento CA and the remainder appeared to be placed to retail establishments.

Advisory Board of Kellogg School of Management and received a master's degree from Kellogg Graduate School of Business.

[2] The process of obtaining subscriber information on telephone numbers identified in this report is time consuming. Inquires are frequently hindered by unpublished land lines and there are no directories of cell phone numbers.

Our sources have also identified a cell phone [redacted] registered to a Robert E. Knowling. The aforementioned cell phone is active; however, to date our research indicates no "out going" calls have been made.[3] The activity on this cell phone continues to be monitored. Initial research indicates the subscriber billing address is recorded as [redacted], which was the former address of Robert Knowling in NYC.[4]

It should be noted, Robert Knowling was appointed to the position of CEO for Vercuity, Inc. a Telecommunications Expense Management Provider located in CO and research has indicated Robert Knowling transferred the cell phone number [redacted] to Vercuity, Inc. his current employer. Research indicates the aforementioned number was activated on June 9, 2005 and the subscriber is registered as Vercuity, Inc. and the bills are sent to Vercuity, Inc., PO Box 489, Newark, NJ 07101. The transfer of the aforementioned telephone number may allow access to calls placed as of June 9, 2005 from Knowling's cell phone. The calls made from the aforementioned cell phone would be available after the first billing cycle ends, which is July 9, 2005.

It should be noted, research is continuing in an attempt to obtain telephone records for the two (2) cell phones identified for Knowling.

To date our research has not identified an "out going" call placed from Roger Crockett, Ben Elgin or Peter Burrows cell phones to Robert Knowling's cell [redacted]r home telephone [redacted] Research also revealed no "out going" calls from Ben Elgin or Peter Burrows' home telephones to the two aforementioned cell phones for Robert Knowling.

This firm's attempts to obtain the calls made from Elgin and Burrows' office telephones were not successful. Due to the number of lines associated with the account, a pin is required to access the call register information.

Research was also conducted on the calls placed from George Keyworth's cell phone [redacted] on selective dates in January, February, March and April. The dates selected corresponded to the dates of board meetings held in January, March and February 2005.

---

[3] Repeated calls placed to the aforementioned cell phone are not answered and are greeted by a voice mail message instructing the caller to leave a message. The cell phone's owner is not identified on the recorded message.

[4] Research is continuing to verify the aforementioned subscriber information.

PREPARED FOR HEWLETT PACKARD BY SECURITY OUTSOURCING SOLUTIONS, INC.
Investigative Report
This report is a confidential and privileged communication between the attorney and the investigator.

An analyses of the telephone intelligence revealed Keyworth made no calls from his cell phone [redacted] on January 12, 13, 14, 15, 16 or 17th. Calls of interest placed in January were one (1) to Lucy Salhany [redacted] on January 22nd, one (1) to Larry Sonsini [redacted] on January 23rd and one (1) call to Bob Ryan [redacted] on January 28, 2005.

An analysis of the telephone calls placed from Keyworth's cell phone in February 2005 revealed the following calls of interest. Two (2) calls were placed to the Hyatt Regency O'Hare [redacted] in Chicago on February 6th, one (1) call was placed to Lucy Salhany [redacted] on February 7th, one (1) call was placed to the New York Times' San Francisco News Bureau [redacted] and (1) call placed to Patricia Dunn [redacted] on February 9, 2005.[5] One (1) call was placed to Dick Hackborn on February 19th, 25th, and March 2, 2005. Calls were placed to Tom Perkins [redacted] on March 9, 15, 21 and the 24th. It should be noted, 122 calls were or are in the process on being analyzed. One (1) call was placed to Australia [redacted] on March 24th. Research is in progress to identify the subscriber for the Australian telephone number.

Research into Larry Sonsini's background did not reveal a history of communications and/or an association with Ben Elgin or Peter Burrows. Extensive media searches found no evidence of Sonsini providing proprietary information to the press.

Research into the background of Larry Babbio did not reveal a history of communications and/or association with Ben Elgin or Peter Burrows. Extensive media searches found no evidence of Babbio providing proprietary information to the press. Babbio was report as a strong supporter of the former CEO, however, due to Babbio's position with Verizon no attempts to obtain calls made from his cell phone were attempted.

It should be noted, while all the following telephone calls were analyzed and the focus of the review centered on the following key dates.

- January 12, 2005 to January 16, 2005 (Board Annual Strategy Meeting, San Francisco, CA)
- February 6, 2005 to February 7, 2005 (Board Special Meeting, Chicago, IL)
- March 15, 2005 to March 17, 2005 (Regular Board & Committee Meetings)

[5] Two pretext calls were placed to the aforementioned telephone number. The first call was answered by a recorded voice mail message "Dunn (phonetic) News Bureau and the second call conducted a week later 'to leave a message for John Marcoft (phonetic). A third pretext call verified the number is listed to the New York Times, San Francisco News Bureau.

This firm analyzed 107 "out going calls" made from Ben Elgin's cell phone [redacted] between January 4, 2005 and March 28, 2005. Also analyzed were 36 "outgoing calls" made from January 6, 2005 to April 12, 2005 from a second residential number [redacted] listed to Elgin's residence. It should be noted, it appears this telephone number is utilized by Elgin for business.

A review of the "out going" calls made to the telephone number [redacted] which is also listed to Ben Elgin's [redacted] address revealed only 11 calls were made from January 10, 2005 to April 12, 2005.

The following out going calls made from Ben Elgin's cell phone were of interest.

- February 9, 2005 – two (2) calls were made to Elgin's extension at Business Weeks' office in CA [redacted] and one (1) call [redacted] to Business Weeks' NYC office (Kimberly Quinn's extension).
- March 8, 2005 – One (1) call to Business Weeks' CA office [redacted]
- March 9, 2005 – Three (3) calls to Business Weeks' CA office [redacted] and Roger Crockett's cell [redacted]
- March 10, 2005 - Three (3) calls to Business Weeks' CA office [redacted]
- March 24, 2005 – One call [redacted] to the residence of Vyomesh Joshi the head of HP's Printer Division.

PETER BURROWS:

This firm analyzed 408 "out going" telephone calls made from Peter Burrows cell phone [redacted] from January 2, 2005 to March 23, 2005. In addition, 194 "out going" telephone calls from Peter Burrows home telephone [redacted] from January 13, 2005 to April 8, 2005 are also being analyzed. The results of the review to date have been unremarkable with the exception of the following call to an HP address in Palo Alto, CA. It should be noted, work is continuing to identify telephone subscriber information on calls placed from Crockett's cell phone.

One (1) call of interest was placed to [redacted] which our sources indicate the subscriber is [redacted]., Palo Alto, CA 94304.

PREPARED FOR HEWLETT PACKARD BY SECURITY OUTSOURCING SOLUTIONS, INC.
Investigative Report
This report is a confidential and privileged communication between the attorney and the investigator.

ROGER CROCKETT:

This firm analyzed 321 "out going" calls placed from Roger Crockett's cell phone [redacted] from December 2004 to April 25, 2005. The results of the review completed to date are unremarkable. It should be noted, Robert Knowling has indicated Roger Crockett has been a friend for eight (8) years; however, no calls were placed to Knowling's cell or home telephone numbers in a five (5) month period from Crockett's cell phone.

END OF DRAFT PRELIMINARY REPORT

TAB 4

From: Fairbaugh, Jim (Global Security)
Sent: Thursday, July 7, 2005 6:11 PM
To: Gentilucci, Anthony R. <tony.gentilucci@hp.com>; Huska, Kevin (Global Security) <kevin.huska@hp.com>
Subject: FW: KONA
Attach: Case05-04-423(ProjectKONA)PrilimFindingsJune14 05.doc

---

Privileged and confidential

Here is the SOS report we have been waiting to see.

R, Jim

Jim Fairbaugh
Global Security

Hewlett-Packard
3000 Hanover Street, ms 1004
Palo Alto, CA 94304-1112

650-857-3330 Tel
650-857-7103 Fax
jim.fairbaugh@hp.com

-----Original Message-----
From: Baskins, Ann
Sent: Thursday, July 07, 2005 1:46 PM
To: Fairbaugh, Jim (Global Security)
Cc: Baskins, Ann
Subject: FW: KONA

Privileged and confidential.

-----Original Message-----
From: Patricia Dunn-Jahnke [mailto[redacted]
Sent: Tuesday, June 14, 2005 12:31 PM
To: Baskins, Ann
Subject: FW: KONA

fyi

From: "Ron DeLia" <rrd@security-outsourcing.com>
To: "Patricia Dunn-Jahnke" [redacted]
Subject: KONA
Date: Tue, 14 Jun 2005 13:31:55 -0400

Pattie,

Attached is the draft report on our findings to date.

Ron

Security Outsourcing Solutions, Inc.
Tel: (508) 394-3390 or (781) 444-9616

PREPARED FOR HEWLETT PACKARD BY SECURITY OUTSOURCING SOLUTIONS, INC.
Investigative Report
This report is a confidential and privileged communication between the attorney and the investigator.

CLIENT # HP-99-01
CASE # 05-04-423
DATE: June 14, 2005

DRAFT

(PROJECT KONA ET AL)
Preliminary Draft Findings

EXECUTIVE SUMMARY:

Security Outsourcing Solutions was retained to conduct an investigation into the unauthorized dissemination of proprietary information to members of the Press. The focus of the investigation is to identify the individual and/or individuals responsible for providing confidential information to unauthorized sources. The investigative activity conducted to date focused on determining if members of HP's Board of Directors were involved in providing proprietary information to reporters for Business Week magazine Ben Elgin and Peter Burrows. The investigation encompassed conducting background investigations on Ben Elgin, Peter Burrows, Roger Crockett and members of HP's Board of Directors. The investigative activity conducted included analyzing intelligence gathered through telephone subscriber records, public and proprietary database sources, media, civil litigation indices and Internet content.

It should be noted, telephone subscriber and call registers are obtained verbally from the various telephone carriers and is subject to human error. Therefore, SOS is diligent in the company's attempts to verify information obtained from its sources.

The investigation to date has not identified the internal HP source and/or sources that are responsible for providing proprietary information to Business Week reporters Ben Elgin, Peter Borrows and/or Roger Crockett.

Telephone research revealed several areas of interest, which are detailed in this report.

It should be noted, this firm has expanded the investigation to include third party non HP employees, which will be discussed further in this report. It should be noted, the investigation into the review of telephone records and the backgrounds of Business Week reporters and HP board members is continuing.

It should be noted, investigations of this nature are complex, time consuming and require a redirection of investigative activity as information is received and analyzed.

PREPARED FOR HEWLETT PACKARD BY SECURITY OUTSOURCING SOLUTIONS, INC.
Investigative Report
This report is a confidential and privileged communication between the attorney and the investigator.

An analytical review of the intelligence gathered to date suggests several scenarios by which proprietary information may have been leaked to Business Week reports Ben Elgin and Peter Burrows. It should be noted, the following scenarios are assumptions based on the information developed to date.

Research revealed Robert Knowling "Knowling" relationship with former CEO, Carly Fiorina began in 1996 when Knowling was the head of operations for US West. According to published media articles Knowling asked Fiorina to fly out to Denver to discuss failed phone service at US West. During the early December meeting, Knowling "read Fiorina the riot act" in front of her boss. By January 1, the entire Lucent support team serving US West had been replaced and Knowling's problems were fixed. According to the article, since that time, the two executives have had a tremendous respect for each other.

Robert Knowling is recorded as one of former CEO Carly Fiorina strongest supporters and is the board member most likely to maintain contact with the former CEO.

It should be noted, according to a chapter 5 (pages 90 & 91) in Peter Burrow's book "BACK-FIRE," Carly Fiorina has a history of "leaking" tips to the press. The content refers to Calvin Sims a reporter for the New York Times covering the story regarding AT&T's allegations the GSA had discriminated against the company. Calvin Sims reported, Carly "at times, she seemed to good a source, making Sims check himself to make sure he wasn't being used."

Therefore, it is possible proprietary information is being forward from a board member to a third party (Carly Fiorina) and then to Ben Elgin, Peter Burrows and/or Roger Crockett. Therefore, this firm is in the process of attempting to identifying cell phone numbers listed to Carly Fiorina.

Research has also revealed Robert Knowling appears to have had a personal relationship with Roger Crockett, Deputy Bureau Manager of Business Week's Chicago's office. Media and Internet content searches revealed Knowling was quoted in an October 1999 Business Week article, which was authored by Roger Crockett and Knowling was one of four individuals named as a top entrepreneur in Business Week's January 10, 2000 issue "The Top Entrepreneurs." Crockett and Knowling are also associated with the Kellogg School of Management at Northwestern University and appear to share an interest in the furtherance of African American advancement in corporate America and the technology industry.[1]

---

[1] Crockett was a winner of Northwestern University's Medill School of Journalism and the Kellogg School of Management has posted an article authored by Crockett and another article is part of the Class 1 curriculum for TECH-914. Robert Knowling is a member of the

Research revealed Crockett has been a reporter primarily covering the telecommunications industry for the past ten (10) years an industry Knowling has worked in from 1977 to 2000.

The timing of Robert Knowling's disclosure of his friendship with Roger Crockett is also a concern. It is our understanding Knowling's disclosure came after a board discussion regarding the leaking of information to the media and what measures should be taken to identify the source of the leak. The disclosure may have been an attempt to front Knowling's relationship with Crockett prior to the relationship surfacing in an investigation. It should be noted, Knowling stated he had received a "Text Message" from Crockett altering him that Business Week was planning to run a story on HP.

This firm is attempting to verify if Knowling received text messages on his cell phone and on what days the messages were received.

<u>It should be noted, research revealed Ben Elgin placed a call to Roger Crockett's cell phone on March 9, 2005 from his (Elgin) cell phone and Crockett placed two (2) calls to Elgin's cell phone on March 9, 2005.</u>

Research revealed [redacted] "out going" telephone calls placed from Roger Crockett's business cell phone [redacted]) from December 27, 2004 to April 25, 2005. Identification of subscriber information for the 321 telephone numbers is continuing.[2]

It should be noted, the investigation has been somewhat hindered by the inability to date, to obtain information on the telephone calls placed from Robert Knowling's cell phone [redacted]) during the period January 1st to April 2005. The aforementioned cell phone is reportedly a restricted government phone account and records on this type of account are difficult to obtain. Knowling's home telephone numbe[redacted] was identified, however, a review of the "out going" telephone calls from January 24, 2005 to March 28, 2005 were unremarkable. Only [redacted] "out going" calls were made during the aforementioned time period, of which three (3) were to Knowling's hom[redacted]. five (5) were to a[redacted], [redacted]r (4) were to a[redacted] two (2) were to a[redacted] in [redacted]. one (1) call to a[redacted] one (1) to a[redacted]e remainder appeared to be placed to retail establishments.

Advisory Board of Kellogg School of Management and received a master's degree from Kellogg Graduate School of Business.

[2] The process of obtaining subscriber information on telephone numbers identified in this report is time consuming. Inquires are frequently hindered by unpublished land lines and there are no directories of cell phone numbers.

Our sources have also identified a cell phone [redacted] registered to a Robert E. Knowling. The aforementioned cell phone is active; however, to date our research indicates no "out going" calls have been made.[3] The activity on this cell phone continues to be monitored. Initial research indicates the subscriber billing address is recorded as [redacted], New York, NY 10036, which was the former address of Robert Knowling in NYC.[4]

It should be noted, Robert Knowling was appointed to the position of CEO for Vercuity, Inc. a Telecommunications Expense Management Provider located in CO and research has indicated Robert Knowling transferred the cell phone number [redacted] to Vercuity, Inc. his current employer. Research indicates the aforementioned number was activated on June 9, 2005 and the subscriber is registered as Vercuity, Inc. and the bills are sent to Vercuity, Inc., PO Box 489, Newark, NJ 07101. The transfer of the aforementioned telephone number may allow access to calls placed as of June 9, 2005 from Knowling's cell phone. The calls made from the aforementioned cell phone would be available after the first billing cycle ends, which is July 9, 2005.

It should be noted, research is continuing in an attempt to obtain telephone records for the two (2) cell phones identified for Knowling.

To date our research has not identified an "out going" call placed from Roger Crockett, Ben Elgin or Peter Burrows cell phones to Robert Knowling's cell [redacted] or home telephone [redacted]. Research also revealed no "out going" calls from Ben Elgin or Peter Burrows' home telephones to the two aforementioned cell phones for Robert Knowling.

This firm's attempts to obtain the calls made from Elgin and Burrows' office telephones were not successful. Due to the number of lines associated with the account, a pin is required to access the call register information.

Research was also conducted on the calls placed from George Keyworth's cell phone (505-690-5651) on selective dates in January, February, March and April. The dates selected corresponded to the dates of board meetings held in January, March and February 2005.

---

3 Repeated calls placed to the aforementioned cell phone are not answered and are greeted by a voice mail message instructing the caller to leave a message. The cell phone's owner is not identified on the recorded message.

4 Research is continuing to verify the aforementioned subscriber information.

An analyses of the telephone intelligence revealed Keyworth made no calls from his cell phon[redacted]) on January 12, 13, 14, 15, 16 or 17th. Calls of interest placed in January were on[redacted] on January 22nd, one (1)[redacted] on January 23rd and one (1) call t[redacted]) on January 28, 2005.

An analysis of the telephone calls placed from Keyworth's cell phone in February 2005 revealed the following calls of interest. Two (2) calls were placed to the[redacted] in Chicago on February 6th, one (1) call was placed t[redacted]) on February 7th, one (1) call was placed to the New York Times San Francisco News Bureau[redacted]) and one (1) call placed to [redacted]on February 9, 2005.[5] One (1) call was placed to Dick Hackborn on February 19th, 25th, and March 2, 2005. Calls were placed to Tom Perkins[redacted]on March 9, 15, 21 and the 24th. It should be noted, 122 calls were [redacted] process on being analyzed. One (1) call was placed to Australia [redacted]) on March 24th. Research is in progress to identify the subscriber for the Australian telephone number.

Research into Larry Sonsini's background did not reveal a history of communications and/or an association with Ben Elgin or Peter Burrows. Extensive media searches found no evidence of Sonsini providing proprietary information to the press.

Research into the background of Larry Babbio did not reveal a history of communications and/or association with Ben Elgin or Peter Burrows. Extensive media searches found no evidence of Babbio providing proprietary information to the press. Babbio was report as a strong supporter of the former CEO, however, due to Babbio's position with Verizon no attempts to obtain calls made from his cell phone were attempted.

It should be noted, while all the following telephone calls were analyzed and the focus of the review centered on the following key dates.

- January 12, 2005 to January 16, 2005 (Board Annual Strategy Meeting, San Francisco, CA)
- February 6, 2005 to February 7, 2005 (Board Special Meeting, Chicago, IL)
- March 15, 2005 to March 17, 2005 (Regular Board & Committee Meetings)

---

[5] Two pretext calls were placed to the aforementioned telephone number. The first call was answered by a recorded voice mail message "Dunn (phonetic) News Bureau and the second call conducted a week later 'to leave a message for John Marcoft (phonetic). A third pretext call verified the number is listed to the New York Times, San Francisco News Bureau.

This firm analyzed [redacted] "out going calls" made from Ben Elgin's cell phone [redacted] between January 4, 2005 and March 28, 2005. Also analyzed were [redacted] "outgoing calls" made from January 6, 2005 to April 12, 2005 from a second residential number [redacted] listed to Elgin's residence. It should be noted, it appears this telephone number is utilized by Elgin for business.

A review of the "out going" calls made to the telephone number [redacted] which is also listed to Ben Elgin's [redacted] San Francisco, CA address revealed only 11 calls were made from January 10, 2005 to April 12, 2005.

The following out going calls made from Ben Elgin's cell phone were of interest.

- February 9, 2005 – two (2) calls were made to Elgin's extension at Business Weeks' office in CA [redacted] and one (1) call [redacted] to Business Weeks' NYC office (Kimberly Quinn's extension).
- March 8, 2005 – One (1) call to Business Weeks' CA office [redacted]
- March 9, 2005 – Three (3) calls to Business Weeks' CA office [redacted] and Roger Crockett's cell [redacted]
- March 10, 2005 - Three (3) calls to Business Weeks' CA office [redacted]
- **March 24, 2005** – One call [redacted] to the residence of Vyomesh Joshi the head of HP's Printer Division.

PETER BURROWS:

This firm analyzed [redacted] "out going" telephone calls made from Peter Burrows cell phone [redacted] from January 2, 2005 to March 23, 2005. In addition [redacted] "out going" telephone calls from Peter Burrows home telephone [redacted] from January 13, 2005 to April 8, 2005 are also being analyzed. The results of the review to date have been unremarkable with the exception of the following call to an HP address in Palo Alto, CA. It should be noted, work is continuing to identify telephone subscriber information on calls placed from Crockett's cell phone.

One (1) call of interest was placed to [redacted] which our sources indicate the subscriber is [redacted]

PREPARED FOR HEWLETT PACKARD BY SECURITY OUTSOURCING SOLUTIONS, INC.
Investigative Report
This report is a confidential and privileged communication between the attorney and the investigator.

ROGER CROCKETT:

This firm analyzed [redacted] "out going" calls placed from Roger Crockett's cell phone [redacted] from December 2004 to April 25, 2005. The results of the review completed to date are unremarkable. It should be noted, Robert Knowling has indicated Roger Crockett has been a friend for eight (8) years; however, no calls were placed to Knowling's cell or home telephone numbers in a five (5) month period from Crockett's cell phone.

END OF DRAFT PRELIMINARY REPORT

TAB 5

PREPARED FOR HEWLETT PACKARD BY SECURITY OUTSOURCING SOLUTIONS, INC.
Investigative Report
This report is a confidential and privileged communication between the attorney and the investigator.

CLIENT # HP-99-01
CASE # 05-04-423
DATE: July 12, 2005

DRAFT

(OPERATION KONA)
Preliminary Draft

SECTION I – EXECUTIVE SUMMARY:

Security Outsourcing Solutions was retained to conduct a due diligence/background on several individuals privy to information being disclosed to members of the press. The focus of the investigation will be to identify the existence of any affiliations individuals who are members of the board or employees of HP may have with correspondents of BuisnessWeek, the Wall Street Journal and The New York Times. The investigation encompasses proprietary and public database research, employment information and extensive media/internet research.

The investigation has revealed some notable affiliations between Roger Crockett, Peter Burrows and Robert Knowling as well as Peter Burrows, John Markoff and George Keyworth. Peter Burrows indicated in his book "Backfire" that none of HP's top executives or members of the board of directors have spoken with him since the merger, except for George Keyworth. Review of the "Sources" and "A note about sourcing" sections of the book reveal that Mr. Keyworth provided some significant information to Peter Burrows. It is also important to note that according to Burrows, information relating to past board meetings missed by Walter Hewlett came from George Keyworth, Larry Sonsini and Marty Korman. Peter Burrows prepared a March 7, 2005 article for BuisnessWeek which identified Robert Knowling and Lawrence Babbio as members of the compensation committee who signed off on the severance package of Carly Fiorina. He also indicated they were the only two dissenters on the request for her resignation.

Investigation on George Keyworth revealed a common affiliation with John Markoff of the New York Times. John Markoff has covered the technology industry since 1977 and specifically the defense industry from 1977 to 1981. This overlaps the same period of time that Mr. Keyworth served during the Reagan presidency. After Mr. Keyworth's telephone call to John Markoff on February 7, 2005, Markoff contributed to an article on February 10th announcing the removal of Carly Fiorina at HP. Markoff in the past has prepared technology related stories which contained content or quotes from George Keyworth specifically in 1990 and 2000. John Markoff was connected to another correspondent from the New York Times, Calvin Sims. Markoff and Sims are colleagues and have a mutual friend in Japan. In 2000, Markoff traveled to Tokyo had dinner with the mutual friend and Sims, then the Tokyo Correspondent for The New York Times. It is important to note Calvin Sims is noted in Peter Burrows book "Backfire" to have had home access to Carly Fiorina and she had been always been available to him during her days at AT&T. They had even met on several occasions according to Sims.

Additional investigation regarding web content revealed a blog which indicated John Markoff has inside sources in the technology industry identified as Steve Wozniak (a former HP engineer and co-founder of Apple Computer), Paul Saffo (Director of the Institute for The Future) and Richard Doherty (Director of the Envisioneering Group). George Keyworth has been linked to Richard Doherty via an article and indirectly to Steve Wozniak through a common speaking engagement with Wozniak's colleague.

Press releases, articles and columns in both print and electronic versions issued by BusinessWeek continue to be monitored for stories related to HP by any of the interested parties such as Peter Burrows, Ben Elgin, Roger Crockett, Michael Arndt, Joe Weber or Cliff Edwards.

Investigation related to Roger Crockett revealed three articles, two for Robert Knowling and one for Lawrence Babbio. In all cases, the board members provided quotes in the articles. Roger Crockett is the Deputy Bureau Chief in Chicago for BusinessWeek which is somewhat contrary to a Knowling description of a "low level reporter." Roger Crockett and Robert Knowling, share a common affiliation with Northwestern University and Kellogg School of Management. Mr. Knowling is a graduate and serves on their advisory board, while Mr. Crockett is known to attend several functions at the university, and provides a column for the Kellogg School of Management.

Aside from common affiliations with Roger Crockett, Robert Knowling was profiled in an article by Peter Burrows in May of 2000 about his ascension to Covad Communications CEO. Interestingly, he was named a "Top 100" entrepreneur by BusinessWeek for 1999, yet resigned from Covad in November of 2000. Of note, is that prior to taking his next position at SimDesk Technologies, Knowling notified approximately 100 members of an association called Black Men of Silicon Valley via an e-mail that he'd soon be making a decision on his professional career, either in the Valley or in Texas. That e-mail made it to a press contact.

Research on Ben Elgin did not reveal any significant affiliations with the interested parties. It is interesting to note, in March of 2002 while Mr. Elgin was preparing a story on the company Moxi, someone had impersonated him using a Hotmail e-mail address and began contacting those close to the company. The individual was trying to ferret out who had been giving information to BusinessWeek.

Media research on Larry Sonsini and Marty Korman did not produce any significant or consistent patterns of affiliation with the interested parties. Aside from information contained the Burrows book that both Sonsini and Korman provided information relating to missed board meetings, neither appears to talk very much with the press. Possible employment information or affiliation for Marty Korman's spouse, Elizabeth at Cadwalader, Wickersham and Taft was uncovered. They are another highly regarded law firm.

Investigation relating to Thomas Perkins did not yield any significant affiliations. Aside from a prior address in 1996 close to that of John Markoff (NY Times Reporter), Mr. Perkins was mentioned in a January 27, 2005 article which appeared on IT Jungle.com. It mentioned that he was being asked to return to the board of directors. Of concern in that article titled "HP Board to Clip Fiorina's Wings or Force Her to Delegate?" indicated "that someone from the board of directors who knows someone, has been talking to the editors of the Wall Street Journal about what is going on inside HP's board meetings."

Cursory investigation on Richard Hackborn with the interested parties did not produce any consistent affiliations with the interested parties.

Cursory investigation on Susan Holm did not reveal any significant affiliations with the interested parties.

No significant affiliations have been identified for Michael Arndt, Terry Moya (former Covad Exec.), Carra Scott (former Covad Exec.), Charles Tribbett (RR), Andrea Redmond (RR) or Eric Dash (The New York Times). Portions of the investigation are ongoing.

Investigation may be expanded to include Cliff Edwards, a contributor to the news articles of a technology nature at BusinessWeek.

END OF SUMMARY

SECTION II - PERSONAL PARTICULARS - PETER BURROWS:

In April of 2005, Security Outsourcing Solutions searched proprietary databases containing identifying information compiled by various consumer reporting agencies, which verified Peter Burrows, the subject of this investigation, utilizes SSN [redacted] and was born on [redacted] The following (14) addresses were associated with Peter Burrows.

> [redacted]

An employment search for Peter Burrows yielded only McGraw Hill as a reporter.

The spouse of Peter Burrows was identified as [redacted] An employment search for her did not return any records. However, she is credited with the photograph of Peter Burrows in his book "Backfire."

REAL PROPERTY

A search of property records in California revealed the following property ownership for Peter Burrows:

- [redacted]

POTENTIAL AFFILIATIONS

Media and Internet research yielded the following affiliations of Peter Burrows to interested parties in this investigation.

- Covers the technology field and specifically Hewlett-Packard for BusinessWeek magazine for the last 11 years.
- Authored a May 20, 2000 article on Robert Knowling which profiled his professional accomplishments up to that date. It was favorable and detailed Mr. Knowling's ascension to Covad Communications CEO.
- Authored book "Backfire" in which he himself indicates he has numerous unnamed sources at HP.
- Contributed to a July 1999 article titled Jesse's New Target: Silicon Valley. The article was also authored by Roger Crockett and questioned the lack of presence of minorities in the Silicon Valley. Robert Knowling, then CEO of Covad Communication provided a quote for the article.

SECTION III - PERSONAL PARTICULARS - ROGER O. CROCKETT:

In April of 2005, Security Outsourcing Solutions searched proprietary databases containing identifying information compiled by various consumer reporting agencies, which verified Roger O. Crockett, the subject of this investigation, utilizes SSN [redacted] and was born on [redacted] The following (12) addresses were associated with Roger Crockett.

- [redacted]

An employment search for Roger Crockett revealed McGraw Hill since November of 1997 as a reporter and Deputy Bureau Manager. This would represent a higher position of authority than a "low level reporter" as Mr. Knowling referred to him. Prior employment included The Oregonian Newspaper, The Enquirer in Michigan and Newsweek.

The spouse of Roger O. Crockett was identified as [redacted] and employment information at Mobil Corp. was returned. No information as to the date of that employment could be located.

REAL PROPERTY

A search of property records in Illinois revealed the following property ownership for Roger Crockett:

- [redacted]

POTENTIAL AFFILIATIONS

Media and Internet research revealed the following affiliations of Roger Crockett to interested parties in this investigation.

- Authored an October 1999 BusinessWeek article titled Faster, Faster, Faster related to Internet speed and quoted Robert Knowling, then CEO of Covad Communications.

- Authored a July 1999 BusinessWeek article titled Jesse's New Target: Silicon Valley; High-Tech Land claims it's a meritocracy. So where, Jackson asks, are all the blacks and Hispanics. Robert Knowling, then CEO of Covad Communications, provided a quote for the article.

- Roger Crockett and Robert Knowling both have affiliations with the Kellogg School of Management at Northwestern University.

- Roger Crockett has been a reporter covering the Telecommunications Industry (primarily) in the Midwest for at least the last ten years. Robert Knowling was employed in same during that coverage period.

- Shares a view of furtherance of African American advancement in the corporate world and technology industry.

- Roger Crockett had a speaking engagement in May of 1999 at a telecommunications conference, which also included Covad Communications and US West executives as speakers.

- Contributed to two BusinessWeek stories dated October 7, 2002 (The Telecom Depression When Will It End?) and August 4, 2003 (Verizon's Gutsy Bet) which contained quotes from Lawrence Babbio, Jr.

SECTION IV - PERSONAL PARTICULARS - BEN ELGIN:

In April of 2005, Security Outsourcing Solutions searched proprietary databases containing identifying information compiled by various consumer reporting agencies, which verified Ben Elgin, the subject of this investigation, utilizes SSN [redacted] and was born on [redacted] The following (7) addresses were associated with Ben Elgin.

[redacted]

Employment search for Ben Elgin revealed only McGraw Hill as a reporter.

A spouse was not located for Ben Elgin. One relative, named [redacted] Elgin shared a common address at one time. [redacted] Elgin reported an address in Fort Collins during the time frame surrounding 1998. An employment search for the individual did not return any records.

REAL PROPERTY

No property records were identified for Ben Elgin.

POTENTIAL AFFILIATIONS

Aside from several articles in which Ben Elgin contributed to a story with Peter Burrows or other BusinessWeek correspondents, an obvious affiliation was not identified with an interested party.

However, the media and Internet search returned an interesting article that might have related to a source.

- An article dated March 4, 2002 in BusinessWeek titled "Curiouser and Curiouser." The article indicated that during the reporting of the story something unusual happened to Ben Elgin in that someone had impersonated him, utilizing a Hotmail e-mail address. Elgin was gathering information for a Moxi story and that person began getting in touch with people associated with Moxi, in an attempt to "ferret out who was giving information to

Business Week." Moxi is considered a media center for your television, similar to that of TIVO.

SECTION V - PERSONAL PARTICULARS - MICHAEL ARNDT:

In April of 2005, Security Outsourcing Solutions searched proprietary databases containing identifying information compiled by various consumer reporting agencies, which verified Michael Arndt, the subject of this investigation, utilizes SSN [redacted] and was born on [redacted] The following (14) addresses were associated with Michael Arndt.

- [redacted]

An employment search for Michael Arndt yielded only McGraw Hill as a Deputy Manager and correspondent.

An individual named Marjorie Arndt, believed to be a former spouse of Michael Arndt was located in Catonsville, MD. No employment information was returned.

REAL PROPERTY

A search of property records in California revealed the following property ownership for Michael Arndt:

- [redacted] 60614 – Purchased in September of

POTENTIAL AFFILIATIONS

Media and Internet research did not return any significant affiliations to the interested parties of this investigation.

SECTION VI - PERSONAL PARTICULARS - LAWRENCE BABBIO

In April of 2005, Security Outsourcing Solutions searched proprietary databases containing identifying information compiled by various consumer reporting agencies, which verified Lawrence T. Babbio, the subject of this investigation, utilizes SSN [redacted] and was born on [redacted] The following (10) addresses were associated with Lawrence Babbio.

[redacted]

An employment search for Lawrence Babbio yielded Vice Chairman and President of Verizon Communications.

The spouse of Lawrence Babbio was identified as [redacted] and did not return any employment information.

REAL PROPERTY

A search of property records revealed the following property ownership for Lawrence Babbio:

[redacted]

POTENTIAL AFFILIATIONS

Media and Internet research revealed the following affiliations of Lawrence Babbio to interested parties in this investigation.

- Lawrence Babbio was quoted in two articles in BusinessWeek dated October 7, 2002 and August 4, 2003 to which Roger Crockett contributed. The articles were titled "The Telecom Depression, When Will It End" and Verizon's Gutsy Bet; Will it's massive rollout of fiber optic cable right to customers homes and offices keep it ahead of the pack.

- Babbio is mentioned in March 7, 2005 BusinessWeek article by Peter Burrows titled Commentary: Ousting Carly Was Just The Start. The indicated that Lawrence Babbio and Robert Knowling were on the compensation committee that signed off on her severance package. He also wrote that "an insider says they were the only two board members to oppose Fiorina's ouster."

PREPARED FOR HEWLETT PACKARD BY SECURITY OUTSOURCING SOLUTIONS, INC.
Investigative Report
This report is a confidential and privileged communication between the attorney and the investigator.

SECTION VII - PERSONAL PARTICULARS - THOMAS J. PERKINS:

In June of 2005, Security Outsourcing Solutions searched proprietary databases containing identifying information compiled by various consumer reporting agencies, which verified Thomas J. Perkins, the subject of this investigation, utilizes SSN [redacted] and was born on [redacted] The following (14) addresses were associated with Thomas Perkins.

[redacted]

Mr. Perkins re-elected to the Board of Directors at HP in February of 2005 is a General Partner at Kleiner, Perkins, Caufield & Byers, a private investment partnership since 1972. Mr. Perkins is also a director of News Corporation.

REAL PROPERTY

Research was not conducted.

POTENTIAL AFFILIATIONS

Media and Internet research did not reveal any confirmed affiliations with the interested parties.

However, the following points should be noted for Thomas Perkins:

- Exhibited an address history at 4 Embaracadero Center in San Francisco, CA (believed to be an office address) as early as 1996. John Markoff, correspondent of New York Times (SF Bureau) reported a prior address at 1 Embaracadero Center in San Francisco, CA at the same time.

- Media research revealed an article that appeared on www.ITJungle.com on January 27, 2005. Mr. Perkins was part of the subject matter in the article. The article is titled "HP Board to Clip Fiorina's Wings, or Force Her to Delegate?" and was written by Timothy Prickett Morgan. The first lines of the article read in this manner "somebody who knows someone on the board of directors at HP has been talking to the editors of the Wall street Journal again about what is going on inside HP's board meetings." It alluded to a disclosure prior to a January 12, 2005 meeting and then indicated information discussed during the January 12th through 15th meetings was divulged. Mr. Perkins had not yet been re-elected to the board of directors, only is return to the board was discussed.

SECTION VIII - PERSONAL PARTICULARS - GEORGE (JAY) KEYWORTH:

In April of 2005, Security Outsourcing Solutions searched proprietary databases containing identifying information compiled by various consumer reporting agencies, which verified George Keyworth, the subject of this investigation, utilizes SSN [redacted] and was born on [redacted] The following (16) addresses were associated with George Keyworth.

[redacted]

An employment search for George Keyworth revealed he is Chairman of the Progress and Freedom Foundation and also The Keyworth Company.

Mr. Keyworth's spouse (possibly former) was identified as [redacted], yet no employment information was located.

REAL PROPERTY

Property records were not searched.

POTENTIAL AFFILIATIONS

Media and Internet research yielded the following affiliations of Peter Burrows to interested parties in this investigation.

- [redacted]

- Provided previous information to Peter Burrows in the 2003 book "Backfire."

- Mr. Keyworth served as Science Advisor to President Reagan and was the Director of the White House Office of Science and Technology Policy from 1981 to 1985. He was on the National Security council's committee on telecommunications Policy from 1981 to 1985. John Markoff (NY Times) covered "Technology" and "Defense" from 1977 to 1988.

- Three articles were published by the New York Times in February of 2005 and authored by John Markoff. Two articles were on February 14th, but more notable was the February 10th article titled "Hewlett's Board force Chief Out After Rocky stay." The article hit the newswires on February 9th (two days after Keyworth's call to Markoff).

- Two additional articles were uncovered that had been authored by John Markoff and cite George Keyworth.

  - New York Times article titled Fiber Optic network Is Urged at Conference dated October 30, 1990 by John Markoff is an article about regulatory barriers to building a fiber optic network to deliver electronic information. The article quoted Dr. George Keyworth as he was the director of research at the Hudson Institute who had sponsored the conference covered by Markoff.

  - New York Times article titled The Soul of the Ultimate Machine dated December 2000 related to an article about mobile electronic commerce and Dr. Larry Smarr. However, in the course of writing the article, Markoff noted that Dr. Smarr had in 1983, submitted an unprecedented $50 million proposal to George Keyworth who was the director of the National Science Foundation for the creation of a supercomputer.

- One other possible link between the two can be explained in this way. John Markoff covered the Technology and Defense Industries in the early 1980's. George Keyworth and RVA John Poindexter both served in the Reagan Administration, Keyworth as Science Advisor and Director of White House Office of Science and Technology Policy from 1981-1985. Poindexter as Deputy Asst. to the President for National Security Affairs from 1983-1986. Links to information on both John Poindexter and John Markoff appear on a website at http://epistolary.org/s-13686.html. The site is a blog with content relating to Poindexter and Markoff. It is believed that both John Poindexter and John Markoff may have shared some common interest/similar views on computers, technology and defense. Perhaps, this might have initiated an introduction to George Keyworth.

SECTION IX - PERSONAL PARTICULARS - ROBERT KNOWLING, JR.:

In April of 2005, Security Outsourcing Solutions searched proprietary databases containing identifying information compiled by various consumer reporting agencies, which verified Robert E. Knowing, Jr., the subject of this investigation, utilizes SSN [redacted] and was born on [redacted] The following (15) addresses were associated with Robert E. Knowling.

[redacted]

An employment search for Robert Knowling revealed he was recently named as CEO for Vercuity, Inc.

The spouse of Robert Knowling was identified as [redacted] An employment search for her returned Numar Corp. A time frame for this was not verified.

REAL PROPERTY

A property record search was not conducted for Robert Knowling.

POTENTIAL AFFILIATIONS

Media and Internet research yielded the following affiliations of Robert Knowling to interested parties in this investigation.

- October 1999 BusinessWeek article titled Faster, Faster, Faster by Roger Crockett quoted Robert Knowling, then CEO of Covad Communications.

PREPARED FOR HEWLETT PACKARD BY SECURITY OUTSOURCING SOLUTIONS, INC.
Investigative Report
This report is a confidential and privileged communication between the attorney and the investigator.

- Robert Knowling and Roger Crockett both have affiliations with Northwestern University/Kellogg School of Management.

- Roger Crockett has been a reporter covering the Telecommunications Industry for the last 10 years, particularly the Midwest. Robert Knowling has been employed in same.

- Roger Crockett had a speaking engagement in May of 1999 at a Telecommunications Conference, which also included Covad Communications & US West executives as speakers.

- If Roger Crockett was referred to as a "low level reporter" it would be to the contrary as he is Deputy Bureau Chief and Correspondent for the Chicago Bureau of BusinessWeek.

- A January 23, 2001 article by Peter Delevett titled Wiretap Column mentioned Robert Knowling. The column appears daily in the Jose Mercury News and contains "scoop" on business happening. The article explained that Knowling sent an e-mail to 100 fellow members of Black Men of Silicon Valley, a network of African American executives, that "Things are very well and I couldn't be happier" and that "he will be announcing his newest venture very soon and it will be either a firm here or one in Texas." That information was forwarded to the media, namely Peter Delevett. The article also indicated that Peter Delevett was communicating with Robert Knowling via e-mail on his plans to take a position with a new firm. We know that he ultimately made the decision to join SimDesk Technologies in Texas.

- Peter Burrows authored a favorable May 2000 article titled "Robert Knowling" which profiled Mr. Knowling and detailed his ascension to CEO of Covad Communications.

- Peter Burrows identified Mr. Knowling as a member of the compensation committee in a March 7, 2005 article in BusinessWeek. He indicated in the article that Mr. Knowling and Mr. Babbio both signed off on the severance package given to Carly Fiorina and according to an insider "were the only two members of the board who voted against her removal."

SECTION X - PERSONAL PARTICULARS – LARRY SONSINI:

In April of 2005, Security Outsourcing Solutions searched proprietary databases containing identifying information compiled by various consumer reporting agencies, which verified Larry Sonsini, the subject of this investigation, utilizes SSN [redacted] and was born on [redacted] The following (7) addresses were associated with Larry Sonsini.

[redacted]

Aside from a member of the Board of Directors for HP, Mr. Sonsini is the Chairman for Wilson, Sonsini, Goodrich & Rosati.

The spouse of Larry Sonsini was [redacted] An employment search for her did not return any records.

REAL PROPERTY

A search of property records in California revealed the following property ownership for Peter Burrows:

[redacted]

POTENTIAL AFFILIATIONS

Media and Internet research revealed several corporate affiliations for Larry Sonsini as his name is supplied as the registered agent for several entities. Although, his name is cited in several media articles, we did not find any obvious affiliations with the interested parties.

Some of the following records may be noteworthy:

- Noted as a source in Peter Burrows book "Backfire."

- September 1996 Issue of American Lawyer profiled Larry Sonsini and his career. Identified his clients as Steve Jobs, once of Apple Computer, now CEO of Pixar Animation Studios, Alan Shugart of Seagate Technology, Scott McNealy of Sun Microsystems, etc. It explained the unique relationships he has personally established several of the technology companies.

- BusinessWeek April 5, 2002 article by Peter Burrows titled However Investors Could Win the HP Battle; quotes Larry Sonsini in the context of outside counsel for HP.

- BusinessWeek December 31, 2001 article by Peter Burrows titled Walter Hewlett: Behind His Big Switcheroo cited Larry Sonsini. Burrows indicated in the article that according to a Hewlett colleague Sonsini told Hewlett he would not be able to stop the merger.

- It's important to note that in Burrows book "Backfire" he alludes to the substantial fees that Sonsini's firm received for the completing the merger with Compaq.

SECTION XI - PERSONAL PARTICULARS – MARTY KORMAN:

In July of 2005, Security Outsourcing Solutions searched proprietary databases containing identifying information compiled by various consumer reporting agencies, which verified Marty Korman, the subject of this investigation, utilizes SSN [redacted] and was born in [redacted] The following (11) addresses were associated with Marty Korman.

- [redacted]

Marty Korman is an attorney with Wilson, Sonsini, Goodrich & Rosati.

The spouse of Marty Korman was identified as [redacted] An employment search under her name returned an affiliation with [redacted], [redacted], another highly regarded law firm. This may warrant additional investigation.

REAL PROPERTY

Property records were not searched for this individual.

POTENTIAL AFFILIATIONS

Media and Internet research did not return any obvious affiliations with the interested parties in this investigation. According to media that was reviewed, Marty Korman is considered "a star" within the firm by the 2005 edition of Chambers USA: America's Leading Business Lawyers. Evidence of excessive exposure in the media for this individual was not located.

- Marty Korman is a graduate of Yale Law School. It may be important to note that George Keyworth is also a graduate of Yale.

- Noted as a source in Peter Burrows book "Backfire."

SECTION XII - PERSONAL PARTICULARS - JOHN MARKOFF:

In June of 2005, Security Outsourcing Solutions searched proprietary databases containing identifying information compiled by various consumer reporting agencies, which verified John Markoff, the subject of this investigation, utilizes SSN [redacted] and was born on [redacted] The following (14) addresses were associated with John G. Markoff.

[redacted]

An employment search for Peter Burrows yielded only McGraw Hill as a reporter.

The spouse of John Markoff was identified as [redacted] An employment search for her returned an employer as Studios Materials Librarian.

REAL PROPERTY

Property records were not searched.

POTENTIAL AFFILIATIONS

Media and Internet research revealed the following affiliations of John G. Markoff to interested parties in this investigation.

- John Markoff covers Technology for the New York Times, San Francisco Bureau and has written on HP on numerous occasions.

- Mr. Markoff has covered Technology since 1977 and the Defense Industry from 1977 to 1981. This coincided with the time served by George Keyworth in the Reagan Administration.

- Telephone call from Keyworth to Markoff on February 7th 2005, next article published by The New York Times is February 10th by John Markoff on the removal of Ms. Fiorina.

- John Markoff is mentioned on several occasions on the blog site of a friend, Joi Ito at www.joi.ito.com in several contexts. In October of 2000 Markoff visited Japan and his friend Joi Ito as outlined below in Ito's blog. It reads as follows; "**John Markoff, a good friend and my favorite technology journalist (from The New York Times) came to Japan for the first time and I took him and Calvin Sims (the Tokyo correspondent) out to eat Japanese cured beef tongue**."

  "Markoff was the first to write about me in a major newspaper, and was also the person who gave me a disk that had the first PPP Internet access utility that I ever used. I like Markoff because, even though he is a journalist, he is above all things a geek. He also loves network games, although I always kill him when we play."

  Calvin Sims was identified in the book "Backfire" (page 91) by Peter Burrows as a New York Times Reporter who was covering a story when Carly Fiorina was at AT&T. Burrows recalls that Sims described Fiorina as "always available" and that "he (Sims) could call her at home anytime" and they had even met on occasion.

- Blogs on Ito's site were reviewed and included two references to Markoff that were noteworthy.

  From Marc Canter, May 17, 2003 – "Not sure if it's more fun reading Anil quote Dvorak or cherish the priceless photo. One unknown factor here is integrity."

  "Regardless of how many times - Dvorak has played devil's advocate (and pissed off a WHOLE bunch of people), Markoff has been lambasted and attacked for insider's game playing and sucking up to special interests or Joi attacked for being a VC - the three of you together is priceless."

  - From Dave Winer, August 8, 2004 – "Why bother reading blogs when you can get all the news from Markoff and his three sources, Richard Doherty, Paul Saffo, and Steve Wozniak."

- Investigation is ongoing with regard to Paul Saffo, Richard Doherty and Steve Wozniak. Paul Saffo is the Director of the Institute for the Future in Palo Alto, CA. Richard Doherty is a writer for the Electronic Engineering Times and directs digital technology testing and market research at the Envisioneering Group in Seaford NY.

- Richard Doherty authored an article for the Electronic Engineering Times on April 22, 1991 titled "TV Answer look like first two-way system." George Keyworth was quoted in the article on the FCC allowing two-way services over public airwaves.

Steve Wozniak was a co-founder of Apple Computer and an HP engineer from 1973-1976. Wozniak, Mitch Kapor and John Barlow were co-founders of the Electronic Frontier Foundation, an organization which deals with social, political and legal implications of globally networked computing. In 1992, Barlow and George Keyworth were among the speakers at the First International Symposium: National Security & National Competitiveness: Open Source Solutions.

- John Markoff authored a November 9, 2002 article titled Intelligence; Pentagon Plans a Computer System That Would Peek at Personal Data of Americans. The article outlined an effort by the government to construct computer systems to allow intelligence analysts and law enforcement officials to access certain personal data. The director of the effort was Vice Admiral John M. Poindexter (White House military assistance 1981-1985, National Security Advisor, 1985). It is likely that Mr. Poindexter and Mr. Keyworth were familiar with one another.

- New York Times article dated December 10, 2000 titled The Soul of the Ultimate Machine by John Markoff. The article related to mobile electronic commerce and the creation of a supercomputer center. At the center of the article was a Dr. Smarr who in 1983 as a junior faculty member at University of Illinois, sent a $50 million proposal to the director of the National Science Foundation, George Keyworth.

- New York Times article dated October 30, 1990 titled Fiber-Optic Network Is Urged at Conference written by John Markoff. John Markoff quoted George Keyworth regarding a fiber optic network. Mr. Keyworth, was at the time, Director of Research at the Hudson Institute, who had sponsored the conference.

TAB 6

PREPARED FOR HEWLETT PACKARD BY SECURITY OUTSOURCING SOLUTIONS, INC.
Investigative Report
This report is a confidential and privileged communication between the attorney and the investigator.

CLIENT # HP-99-01
CASE # 05-04-423
DATE: July 19, 2005

DRAFT

(PROJECT KONA ET AL)
Supplemental Draft Findings

EXECUTIVE BRIEFING SUMMARY:

Security Outsourcing Solutions was retained to conduct an investigation into the unauthorized dissemination of proprietary information to members of the Press. The focus of the investigation is to identify the individual and/or individuals responsible for providing confidential information to unauthorized sources. The initial investigation focused on determining if members of HP's Board of Directors were involved in providing proprietary information to reporters for Business Week magazine Ben Elgin and Peter Burrows. The investigation encompassed conducting background investigations on Ben Elgin, Peter Burrows, Roger Crockett and members of HP's Board of Directors. The investigative activity conducted included analyzing intelligence gathered through telephone analysis, public and proprietary database sources, media, civil litigation indices, informed sources and Internet content. The scope of the investigation was expanded in Phase II to include Pui-Wing Tam, a reporter for the WSJ, SF Bureau and John Markoff, a reporter for the NY Times, SF Bureau, George Anders, Senior Editor, WSJ SF Bureau and other persons related through common affiliations.

The investigation to date has not identified the internal HP source and/or sources that are responsible for providing proprietary information to Business Week reporters Ben Elgin, Peter Borrows, Roger Crockett, Pui-Wing Tam, a reporter for the WSJ, SF Bureau, John Markoff, a reporter for the NY Times, SF Bureau and George Anders "Anders," a Senior Editor for the Wall Street Journal, SF Bureau and author of "Perfect Enough" a book published in February 2003, which examines the philanthropic work of the Hewlett and Packard families and devotes a significant content to the Compaq merger. George Anders appears to have had more access to HP executives and members of the board. Anders book appears to be pro HP and pro Compaq merger and comments, Fiorina's HP may have a shot at regaining its faded greatness. Peter Burrows book appears more skeptical about HP's future and indicates HP management has lost its special bond with employees.

It should be noted, George Keyworth and Robert Knowling were interviewed several times by Anders and are the only directors appearing individually in the books photo section.

Therefore, the possibility exists George Anders is the WSJ source receiving proprietary information and is feeding the information to Pui-Wing Tam. The aforementioned scenario would allow George Anders to remain anonymous and divert attention away from him and his internal HP sources (s).[1]

The investigative activity conducted to date supports the assumption there are multiple sources responsible for the dissemination of proprietary information to members of the press and other unauthorized individuals.

It should be noted, there is no evidence proprietary information was leaked to the press during the May 18th to May 20th board meeting. **Therefore, attendance records for the board meeting should be reviewed.**

Research to date, has identified the following areas, which may be of interest.

GEORGE KEYWORTH:

An association between board member George Keyworth and BusinessWeek reporter Peter Burrows and New York Times SF Bureau reporter John Markoff were noted.

There is intelligence, which indicates George Keyworth and New York Times reporter John Markoff (SF Bureau) may have communicated on **February 9, 2005**. It should be noted, Markoff authored an article "When + Adds Up to Minus" and contributed to a second article "Hewlett Board Forces Chief Out After Rocky Start" on the removal of the former CEO on **February 10, 2005**.

George Keyworth was identified by Peter Burrows (BusinessWeek reporter) as the only member of the board to speak with Burrows on the record after the HP merger with Compaq. Peter Burrows wrote a book "Back-Fire" detailing Carly Fiorina's tenure at HP and has demonstrated the ability to obtain proprietary information discussed at HP board meetings.

It should be noted, additional intelligence has been requested for the period from May 18th to the 20th and July 1st to July 31, 2005

JOHN MARKOFF:

Research revealed John Markoff is associated with **Calvin Sims** a former reporter for the NY Times. Calvin Sims is the reporter Carly Fiorina utilized to leak information to the press during a lawsuit filed by AT&T against the GSA.

---

[1] The aforementioned scenario is an assumption base on the intelligence gather to date.

Calvin Sims is quoted and describes his relationship with Carly Fiorina in Peter Burrows book Back-Fire. It should be noted, Carly Fiorina was employed at [redacted]

Calvin Sims is a former reporter and Tokyo correspondent for the NY Times. It should be noted, in 2000 John Markoff traveled to Japan and reportedly had dinner with Calvin Sims and Joi Ito a Japanese Internet entrepreneur.

Research located an Internet Blog, which indicated John Markoff's three (3) sources of information are Apple co-founder Steve Wozniak, Paul Saffo, Director of the Institute For The Future and Richard Doherty the President of the Envisioneering Group. It should be noted, in 1999 Richard Doherty authored an article in the Electronic Engineering Times on a company named TV ANSWER, which George Keyworth was quoted and identified as a board member.

It should be noted, Paul Saffo the Director of The Institute For The Future in Palo Alto, CA appears in a photograph with Bill Joy (co-founder of Sun Microsystems) in 2003 at a "Japan Dinner" in Davos, Switzerland. Bill Joy is a longtime Limited Partner and currently a "Partner" in the VC firm Kleiner, Perkins, Caufield & Byers. It should be noted, Thomas Perkins is the co-founder and "Partner Emeritus" of the aforementioned VC firm. It should be noted, Sun Microsystems is a client of Larry Sonsini's law firm "WSGR." It should be noted, Thomas Perkins bio indicates he was HP's first General Manger of the company's computer division.

Steve Wozniak is the co-founder of Apple Computer and a one time HP Engineer. It should be noted, Larry Sonsini's law firm WSGR was involved in taking Apple Computer public in the 1980's.

The aforementioned analysis was undertaken to demonstrate the probability a board member may have divulged proprietary information to a trusted colleague, who in turn passed on the information to another trusted individual and/or a reporter.

Research located a cell phone number for John Markoff [redacted]). To date, no record of the aforementioned cell phone number appears on any of telephone information reviewed to date. Additional information pertaining to calls made on specific dates from Markoff's cell phone is in progress, to include July 7, 2005 to July 31, 2005. Research identified four (4) telephone lines listed to Markoff's residence. An analysis of the four (4) aforementioned land lines is in progress.

Additional background information and intelligence is in progress to identify other personal and professional affiliations for John Markoff. The results will be forwarded in a supplemental report.

PUI-WING TAM:

Pui-Wing Tam a staff reporter with the Wall Street Journal authored an article on January 24, 2005 "Hewlett-Packard Board Considering Reorganization" utilizing the term "People familiar with the matter, people close to the situation and one person close to the situation." Pui-Wang Tam authored an article on July 14, 2005 "Hewlett-Packard Expected To Announce Restructuring" through the Dow Jones News Service at 22:32 GMT, which is 3:32 PM PST.[2] It should be noted, the information scheduled to be posted to the BOD web site on July 14, 2005 was posted on July 15, 2005. Therefore, Pui-Wing Tam had access to the information prior to it being posted on the BoD web site. A review of all the media appearing on February 10, 2005 relating to the removal of the former CEO revealed Pui-Wing Tam's article is the only one to references a board meeting on January 12 to the 16th and the location of meeting. The only other article identifying the date of January's board meeting was Markoff's February 10th article, which references January 12th.

It should be noted, ITJungle.com's Timothy Prickett Morgan's article posted on January 27th indicates, "somebody who knows someone on the board of directors at Hewlett Packard has been talking to the editors of the Wall Street Journal again about what is going on inside HP's board meetings."[3]

Pui-Wing Tam career began at Newsday in New York and she graduated from Columbia University in 1994. Research indicates Pui-Wing Tam began working for the Asian Wall Street Journal and the Wall Street Journal in January 1995. Pui-Wing Tam was engaged in New York and married Stephen Eng in San Francisco. The couple married in June 2001 and appears to have moved to San Francisco in 2001.[4] Research is continuing into the background of Pui-Wing Tam.

Research identified a business telephone number [redacted] listed to [redacted], SF, [redacted]. Call information has been requested for specific dates on the aforementioned telephone number. A business cell number [redacted] a Pui-Wing Tam listed to [redacted] A total of seventy-eight (78) [redacted] business cell phone from April 16, 2005 to June 16, 2005.

---

[2] Greenwich Meridian "GMT" marks the starting point of every time zone in the world, which is the mean "average" time that the earth takes to rotate from noon to noon. It is the place form were all time zones are measured.

[3] George Anders title at the WSJ is Senior "Editor."

[4] It should be noted, no bio was located for Pui-Wing Tam. The information contained in this report was reconstructed through media, Internet content and proprietary databases.

An analysis of the subscriber information on the seventy-eight (78) telephone numbers is in progress and the results will be forwarded in a supplemental report.

Request for additional intelligence pertaining to specific dates is also in progress and the results will be forwarded in a supplemental report.

Research is continuing into Pui-Wing Tam's background in an effort to identify additional personal and professional associations. The results will be forwarded in a supplemental report.

GEORGE ANDERS - SENIOR EDITITOR - WSJ, SF BUREAU:

George Anders "Anders" authored the book "Perfect Enough" published in February 2003.

Anders appears to have had more access to HP executives and members of the board. Anders' book appears to be more pro HP and pro merger than Peter Burrows' book Back-Fire.

In the book Perfect Enough Anders examines the philanthropic work of the Hewlett and Packard families and the HP/Compaq merger. The two authors appear to have different conclusions on Carly Fiorina's tenure and the merger. Anders indicates Fiorina's HP may have a shot at regaining its faded greatness. Burrows' book appears to be more skeptical about the HP's future and management has lost its special bond with workers.

- Perfect Enough, George Anders, 19 yrs w/ WSJ, currently Sr. Editor with WSJ, formerly with Fast Company.com
- Anders is married to Elizabeth Corcoran a 20 yr. Technology writer, Forbes, Scientific American & Washington Post
- The book appears to focus on the history and backgrounds of the HP founders
- The book has detail on the rise of Carly Fiorina at AT&T and her interest in the HP CEO position and the hiring process
- The book also focus on Carly Fiorina's agenda, employee perception, the merger, the vote and the litigation
- The book mentions Carly Fiorina handled Robert Knowling's account while he was at Illinois Bell and Carly was with AT&T

- George Keyworth and Robert Knowling were interviewed several times for Anders' book and are the only two directors appearing in individual photographs the book's photo section

- The book reports in 1998 Lawrence Babbio urged Forbes to name Carly Fiorina the most powerful woman in American business

- Anders appears to have had more access to HP executives, board members and appears to report favorably on the HP/Compaq merger

- It appears Anders book was written to offset the fall out from Peter Burrows book Back-Fire

- Anders' book credits his wife (Elizabeth "Betsy" Corcoran) a former reporter with knowing all there is about HP

Research is continuing to identify cell, office and home telephone numbers for George Anders. When telephone numbers are identified a request for call information pertaining to specific dates will be submitted and the results will be forwarded in a supplemental report.

Research is continuing into George Anders and his wife's background in an effort to identify additional information, personal and professional associations. The results will be forwarded in a supplemental report.

CARLTON (CARLY) FIORINA:

Research identified the following telephone and fax numbers associated with Carly Fiorina.

- Home telephone [redacted] (A total of 31 calls were placed from Dec. 24, 2004 to April 14, 2005. An analysis of subscriber information for the calls revealed no matches to subscriber information on file.

- Fax number [redacted] – No outgoing information

- Cell number [redacted] ser Carly Fiorina) – Our sources have indicated the account was activated in May 2005 and no prior call information is available. It appears the account was changed to a different billing contact. Our sources indicated the name on the account is Frank Fiorina and there are two (2) additional numbers on the account.

➢ The two (2) additional cell phone numbers associated with this account are [redacted]). The two (2) numbers were also activated in May 2005 and no prior information is available on either number.

It should be noted, a total of one-hundred fifteen (115) calls were placed from the aforementioned three (3) cell phones in June 2005. An analysis of the subscriber information is in progress and the results will be forwarded in a supplemental report.

Additional call information has been requested for the period from July 1, 2005 to July 15, 2005 for the three (3) aforementioned telephone numbers identified for Carly Fiorina. The results will be forwarded in a supplemental report.

ROBERT KNOWLING:

Research revealed Robert Knowling made a total of twelve (12) cell phone [redacted] calls from June 9, 2005 to June 13, 2005. An analysis of subscriber information is in progress.

Robert Knowling, Jr. indicated he had an acquaintance who was a "low level" reporter for BusinessWeek, identified as Roger Crockett. Roger Crockett is the Deputy Bureau Chief for BusinessWeek in Chicago. Robert Knowling and Roger Crockett have affiliations with Northwestern University and the Kellogg School of Management.

BusinessWeek has quoted Robert Knowling in articles authored by Crockett and Burrows. BusinessWeek named Knowling as a "Top 100 Entrepreneur" for 1999 in January of 2000. Roger Crockett has covered the Telecommunications industry in the Midwest since 1995. It should be noted, Carly Fiorina, Robert Knowling and Lawrence Babbio have extensive careers in the Telecommunications industry. It should be noted, Knowling and Babbio were the only two to vote against the removal of the former CEO (According to the March 7, 2005 Peter Burrows article)

Intelligence has verified Peter Burrows, Ben Elgin and Roger Crockett reporters for BusinessWeek communicate with each other.

LARRY SONSINI AND MARTY KORMAN:

Research revealed there is no evidence Larry Sonsini and Marty Korman are or have a history of disseminating proprietary information to the media. It should be noted, Sonsini and Korman were identified as a source "on the record" for author Peter Burrows in his book Back-Fire. It should be noted, Sonsini's law firm affiliations and/or past and present business relationships with professionals and company's in the Silicon Valley has been documented in a relationship chart, which is attached to this report.

LAWRENCE BABBIO:

Lawrence Babbio, another telecommunication executive, was quoted in two (2) articles authored by Roger Crockett in 2002 and 2003. According to Anders book "Perfect Enough," Fortune writer Patricia Sellers decided to rank the 50 most powerful women in business. Seller had called Lucent to schedule an interview with Pat Russo an Exec. VP. The press chief at Lucent also suggested Sellers might want to speak with Carly Fiorina. Sellers then contacted Lawrence Babbio for more information due to Bell Atlantic knowledge of Lucent.

LB quote, pg 52.....

"I am not going to pick between Pat and Carly." "But let me tell you this. I don't care what other forty-nine people are on your list. If CF doesn't come out on the front cover, then I 'm going to cancel every Fortune subscription at Bell Atlantic, because I've just determined that you people don't know what your talking about!"

The October 12, 1998 issue of Fortune named CF as "The Most Powerful Woman in American Business"

ANCILLARY INVESTIGATIVE ACTIVITY:

Research to date has not produced an affiliation of interest between Richard Hackborn, Susan Holm, Thomas Perkins, Eric Dash, Michael Arndt, Charles Tribett, Andrea Redmond, Carra Scott and Terry Moya. It should be noted, some media exists between interested parties, however, a consistent pattern of quotation or affiliation was absent.

END OF EXECUTIVE BRIEFING

TAB 7

Operation KONA

HP Global Security
July 22, 2005

HP 01187

Agenda

- Investigation Background
- Investigation Results - Methodology
- Investigation Results – Media Analysis
- Investigation Results – Media Time Line
- Investigation Results – Media Relationships
- Conclusions
- Recommendations
- Discussion

HP 01188

Background

- Starting in January 2005, based upon a series of articles in Business Week (BW), the New York Times (NYT) and the Wall Street Journal (WSJ), it appears reporters for the aforementioned media outlets have an inside source, or sources, on the HP Board of Directors (BoD)
- Multiple articles analyzed and reviewed appears to confirmed those suspicions
- A letter received from two reporters from Business Week, after the BoD March 2005 meeting, contained specific details of BoD discussions that re-affirmed previous observations and concerns
- On July 15, 2005, the company decision on workforce reductions and structural changes was printed four days prior to its intended release, further reconfirming suspicions

Investigation Results
"Methodology"

- **Investigation Objective:** Confirm and/or deny that a source or sources, internal to HP and/or the HP BoD, is providing proprietary HP information to media personnel or another third party(s) without authorization
- Due to the nature of the investigation, HP Global Security was not advised of the initial investigative effort
  - Outside Investigative Consulting Firm retained on April 19, 2005
- HP Global Security engaged week of July 4, 2005
- Focus of investigation is on HP interests, HP BoD, versus external parties, however, investigation involves determining if associations and relationships exist between BoD members and members of the media
- Methodology utilized to date:
  - Due diligence and intelligence review of available information in regards to the HP BoD as it pertains to the apparent unauthorized disclosure of proprietary HP information:
    - Print media
    - Internet content
    - Public and Proprietary databases
    - HP internal records and databases
    - Other intelligence gathering efforts

Investigation Results
"Media Analysis"

- **Based upon the investigation there were five media personnel of interest as it relates to possible associations with BoD members:**
  - Peter Burrows (PB); Business Week
  - Ben Elgin (BE); Business Week
  - Roger Crockett (RC); Business Week
  - John Markoff (JM); New York Times
  - Pui Wing Tam (PWT); Wall Street Journal
- **Over (3,000) articles reviewed and analyzed**
- **Business Week – Peter Burrows – Ben Elgin**
  - Prior to September 30, 2004, an analysis of BW - B/E articles revealed that in regards to "sources" there was only references to "former" HP executives and employees
  - On September 30, 2004, the BW - B/E articles (sourcing of operations exec) begin to make the following references in regards to sources:
    - "according to **sources**"
    - "this person said"
    - "insiders say"
    - "according to two sources"
    - "according to sources with knowledge of the matter"
    - "two insiders say"
    - "say two high ranking HP managers"
    - "say two HP managers"
  - References specific to BoD discussions or meetings appear to start in January 2005
- **Wall Street Journal – Pui Wing Tam**
  - References specific to BoD discussions or meetings appear to start in January 2005
    - "**people** familiar with the situation"
    - "people familiar with the matter
    - "these "people" said
    - "people close to the situation"
    - "one person close to the situation said"
    - "according to **people** familiar with the matter"
    - "said one of these "people"
- **NY Times – John Markoff**
  - References specific to BoD discussions or meetings appear to start in January 2005
- **Final Analysis of Articles:**
  - For all three media outlets, references specific to BoD discussions or meetings appear to start in January 2005
  - Review of articles suggests two BoD sources may be responsible
    - "says a source familiar with the proceedings"
    - "according to **sources** familiar with the proceedings"
  - Internal (BoD) proprietary information is reported by the press in January 2005
  - Articles on BoD proceedings appeared in press either the day before a BoD meeting and/or significant event, or several days there after

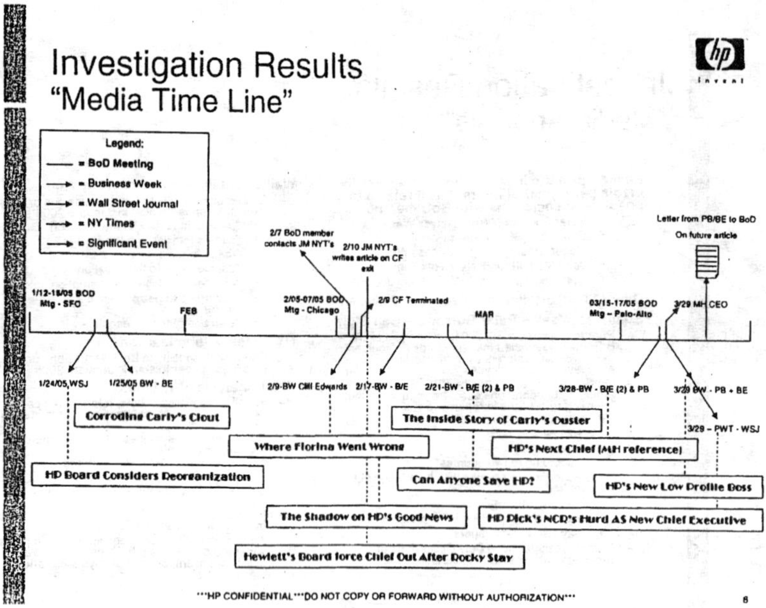

Investigation Results
"Media Time Line"
invent
Legend:
= BoD Meeting
= Business Week
= Wall Street Journal
= NY Times
= Significant Event
1/12-18/05 BOD Mtg - SFO
FEB
2/7 BoD member contacts JM NYT's
2/10 JM NYT's writes article on CF exit
2/05-07/05 BOD Mtg - Chicago
2/9 CF Terminated
MAR
03/15-17/05 BOD Mtg – Palo-Alto
3/29 MH CEO
Letter from PB/BE to BoD On future article
1/24/05 WSJ
1/25/05 BW - BE
2/9-BW Cliff Edwards
2/17-BW - B/E
2/21-BW - B/E (2) & PB
3/28-BW - B/E (2) & PB
3/29 BW - PB + BE
3/29 – PWT - WSJ
Corroding Carly's Clout
Where Fiorina Went Wrong
HP Board Considers Reorganization
The Shadow on HP's Good News
Hewlett's Board Force Chief Out After Rocky Stay
The Inside Story of Carly's Ouster
Can Anyone Save HP?
HP's Next Chief (MH reference)
HP's New Low Profile Boss
HP Picks NCR's Hurd AS New Chief Executive
HP CONFIDENTIALDO NOT COPY OR FORWARD WITHOUT AUTHORIZATION***
6

HP 01192

Investigation Results
"Media Time Line"

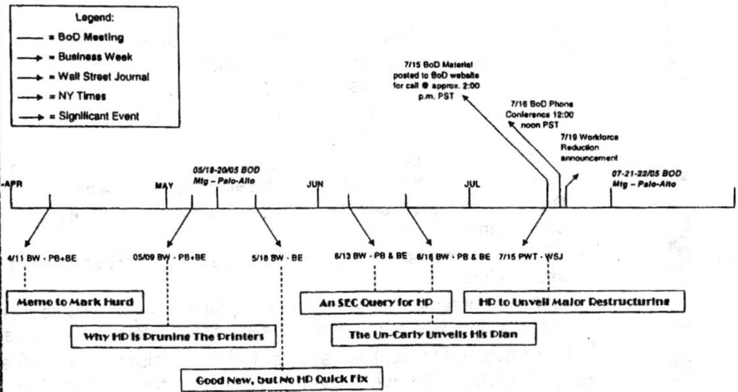

HP 01193

Investigation Results
"Media Relationships – General Overview"

- As noted, at least five reporters have been identified who have apparent access (directly and/or indirectly) to proprietary information relating to discussions from BoD meetings.
  - Several articles and one letter received by the BoD contained information from BoD discussions.
  - Articles follow a pattern of being published either the day before, the day of, or several days after BoD meetings or other significant events
  - Research suggests several of the five reporters may share the same source and/or sources
  - Of the five reporters, it appears three are the primary sources of information
  - Of these three reporters, one of the reporters may have at least two collaborators who may assist in the information collection process ?
- At least two BoD members appear to have a closer than arms length "relationship" with several of the reporters in question
- Two additional BoD members appear to have an association with two of the five reporters

HP 01194

Investigation Results
"Media Relationships" – BoD Member 1

- Based upon research and intelligence gathered to date it appears, at least one BoD member has a personal and professional "relationship" with a Deputy Bureau Chief, Chicago Business Week.
  - The BoD member informed another BoD member, "a good friend" (Business Week reporter for the past 8 years) informed the BoD member Business Week was about to publish an article on HP. The "good friend" was extending an invitation to HP to comment on the details forwarded to the BoD in the letter sent by BW reporters.
    - The BoD member indicated he had a "friend" who worked for Business Week as a "low level" reporter
    - The investigation has revealed the BoD's "friend" is BusinessWeek's Deputy Bureau Chief, Chicago, IL and not a "low level" reporter
    - The BoD member and reporter are affiliated with the Kellogg School of Management
    - The BoD member's professional career and accomplishments have been reported on by the reporter in several BuisnessWeek articles
    - This reporter is associated with the same newspaper as two other Business Week reporters who have co-authored and/or published articles containing HP proprietary information and the BoD member
    - Intelligence indicates all three reporters communicate

HP CONFIDENTIALDO NOT COPY OR FORWARD WITHOUT AUTHORIZATION*** 9

Investigation Results
"Media Relationships" BoD Member 2

- Identified a BoD member with a past and current association with a reporter from the New York Times and Business Week
  - The BoD member was covered by this NY Times reporter while serving on Presidential committee during the Reagan Administration
  - Intelligence revealed that this BoD member appears to have contacted the Chicago Hyatt Regency twice on 02/06/05
  - Intelligence revealed the BoD member appears to have contacted the NY Times reporter on 02/07/05, which was during the BoD meeting in Chicago.
  - Three days after the Chicago BoD meeting, the reporter published an article on the former CEO's departure
  - The BoD member was identified as the only BoD member who would talk to a Business Week reporter (identified as a reporter with access to the BoD) after the HP/Compaq merger
  - The business week reporter stated the BoD member provided "significant information" to the reporter in a book the reporter published
- There were at least two other BoD members had some form of affiliation with two other BoD members

HP 01196

Investigation Results
Conclusions

- Information developed to date, although not conclusive, appears to indicate two HP BoD members may have a closer than arms length relationship with at least two and possibly three of the reporters involved with publishing "internal" proprietary information discussed during recent HP BoD meetings.
- The two aforementioned BoD members, based upon the investigative results to date relationships with reporters are of interest and may require additional investigative activity.
- There are also other areas of concern relating to the possibility a BoD member is providing information to the former CEO, which in turn is being provided to the reporters in question.

Recommendations

- Continue on with current investigation effort
  - Recent leak under investigation and results may develop additional formation on the potential sources leaking BoD information.
  - Anticipated this most recent leak investigation may take another 7-14 days
- Investigation recently initiated on BoD relationships with, PWT – NYT's relationship as that subject was not on the investigation team's initial objectives
  - Results anticipated in the next 7-14 days
  - Investigation inclusive of most recent leak
- Engage Senior Manager of HP IT Security Investigations as part of the investigation team
- HP Legal to invoke the attorney-client privilege
  - Recommend assign an attorney to direct the investigation
- Recommendation that all future briefings being conducted verbally and keep written work product to a minimum
  - Given media relationships, the investigation and management team must be sensitive to "media's" right to publish information
- Moving forward post investigation:
  - Focus majority of efforts on Proactive versus Reactive initiatives
- Proactive recommendations for consideration:
  - Have BoD sign confidentiality agreement that documents "disclosure" subject to civil litigation
    - More "teeth" than verbal attestation
    - Benchmarking could be initiated by investigation team on othe "like" efforts
  - Implement IT Security tracking methodology for electronic soft copies of documents posted to the BoD web set
  - Initiate Information Security "risk assessment" of the entire BoD communications process
  - Have all BoD electronic communications conducted within the HP IT infrastructure
    - More Secure; provide BoD members with communication equipment; laptops, possible cell phones
  - Expeditious implementation of "Unauthorized Disclosure Investigation Team" for future events company wide
    - Comprehensive collection and tracking
    - Consistency in delivery
    - Same team leads to Operational Excellence
    - Lessons learned assist in solution development

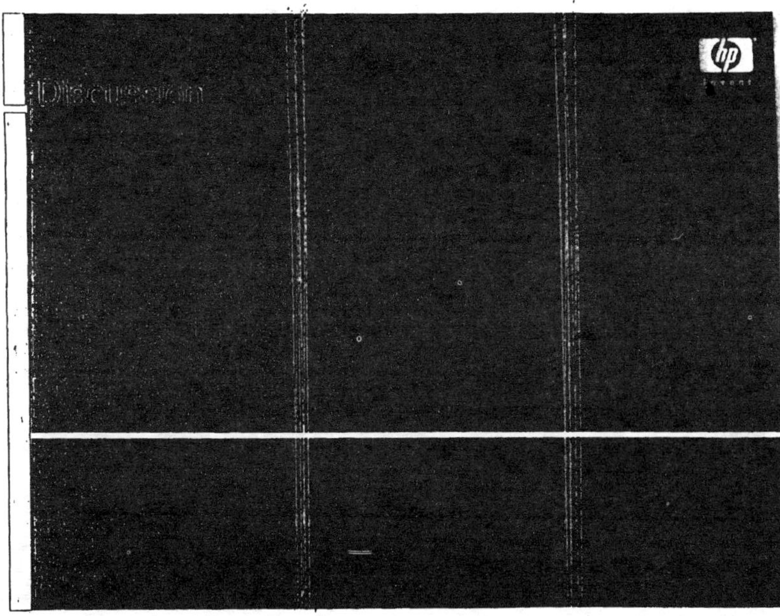
Discussion

TAB 8

From: "Gentilucci, Anthony R." <tony.gentilucci@hp.com>
To: "Patricia Dunn-Jahnke" [redacted]
CC: "Ron DeLia" <rrd@security-outsourcing.com>
Subject: Update Memo and Request for Input / Direction - Project KONA ***HP CONFIDENTIAL***
Date: Sat, 6 Aug 2005 11:53:17 -0400

Pattie,

Attached is an update memo which contains some ongoing and planned investigative activity as well as several questions and recommendations requiring your input. Understanding that you are about to go on business trip and vacation, if you are unable to address these questions prior to your departure, we will continue with ongoing investigative action items and regroup with you on upon you return. As an FYI, I will also forward a copy of this memo to Ann Baskins and Jim Fairbaugh.

If we don't have the opportunity to speak, safe travels and enjoy your time off.

Best Regards,

Tony

<< Case_ProjectKONA_UpdateMemo_05_AUG_05.doc >>

From: Ron DeLia
Sent: Tuesday, April 19, 2005 10:16 AM
To: 'Patricia Dunn-Jahnke'
Subject: Proposal
Importance: High

Patricia,

The following outlines the investigative activity recommended and estimated cost projections to provide the required services. The details contained in this document are based upon our initial assessment of the information provided to date. The focus of the investigation is to identify the person and/or persons responsible for the unauthorized dissemination of proprietary information to the press.

While the following provides a broad outline of the work to be completed and an estimate of the cost of services, it should be understood, these are only guidelines. The parameters may vary considerably once more is known about the professional and personal particulars of the subjects of the investigation.

The absence of the aforementioned information has dictated that we utilize assumptions in projecting the cost for our investigative services for the purposes of this email. The cost assumptions are based on our experience in providing these types of investigative services in similar matters.

Our recommendation is to conduct discreet limited background investigations on the three (3) internal and two (2) external subjects. The purpose of the limited backgrounds is to obtain personal particulars, life style assessments, educational institutions attended, address and employment history and personal habits, i.e., vacation spots, restaurants, bars, etc. frequented by the two (2) external sources. The limited backgrounds on the three (3) internal subjects will focus on travel habits, vacation properties, educational and employment backgrounds, family tree, etc. in an effort to identify a common denominator linking an internal subject to an external subject.

Ancillary investigative activity to include, but not limited to, discreet on site inspections/pretext interviews of places of employment, vacation properties, restaurants, bars, etc. of the two (2) external subjects.

Electronic surveillance of email and/or other communication accounts, where applicable (To be discussed verbally).

The cost of providing the aforementioned investigative services is projected to be $35,000 to $50,000, which includes expenses. Note: As discussed, projecting a generic cost for these types of investigative services is not an exact science; therefore, the actual cost may exceed the maximum dollar amount quoted.

Patricia, in an effort to maintain confidentiality, this email provides limited information on the investigative activity to be conducted, please feel free to call if you have any questions.

Ron

Security Outsourcing Solutions, Inc.
Tel: (508) 394-3390 or (781) 444-9616

TAB 9

Project KONA
Update Memo
Confidential

Hewlett-Packard Company
Global Security Investigations
617-551-7694
Security.investigation@hp.com

Subject: Investigative Plan of Action and Questions Requiring Input

From: Tony Gentilucci, Manager, Global Security Investigations

Date:

To: Patricia Dunn, Chairperson, HP Board of Directors

CC: Ann Baskins, HP OGC, Jim Fairbaugh, Dir. Corp. Security Ron Della Investigative Consultant

A. Update:

1. Based upon information obtained to date, as well as direction from a meeting with Pattie Dunn, Ann Baskins, and the Investigation team on 28-JUL-05, the following investigative activity has been undertaken.

   - Interview and limited background of Bob Sherbin
     - In progress (Note: two (2) interviews conducted to date)
   - Meeting with Rosemary Thomas
     - Completed - BoD meeting attendance records obtained
   - Ongoing intelligence gathering of interested parties
     - In progress (Internal & External Sources)
   - Update of investigation timeline based upon the above
     - Ongoing
   - Meeting with Pattie Dunn
     - Tentative management briefing scheduled for August 31, 2005

B. Next Steps:

Informational interviews have been conducted with HP employees, which has developed several investigative leads. Based on this information the following investigative activity will be conducted.

1. Bob Sherbin Interview

   - Conduct an Information gathering interview with Michael Moeller (Note: Initial contact established)
   - Note: According to Bob Sherbin, Moeller stated Tam informed him (Moeller) "She (Tam) and Burrows share the same source"
   - Moeller is a former Business Week reporter and may have some insight on BW's information gathering techniques (Note: The allegations set forth in action item 2 below)
   - Follow-up with Sherbin in regards to Sherbin attempting to identify the person who informed him they observed Jay Keyworth meeting with Pui Wing Tam in a San Francisco hotel approximately one year ago. Question, were any BoD meetings held in a SF hotel approximately one year ago? It should be noted, information has been developed, which indicates Pui Wing Tam attended the HP Annual Meeting in Chicago in March 2005.
   - Obtain original e-mail Peter Burrows sent to Bob Sherbin containing information on the pending business week story

2. Interview "informant" who approached Global Security team member and stated Michael Moeller was pre-releasing information to the media.

   - Initial indications are the Informant (Former HP Media Relations Manager - MS) is willing to talk to investigation team members

3. Based upon the above, initiate a background investigation on HP media relations employee Michael Moeller, to include internal HP e-mail/phone analysis

4. Conduct Information gathering interviews with HP Global Employee Protection team members (Dennis Lynch / Mark Denning)

   - GEPP employees may have some insight due to their job requirements and interactions with former CEO, EC and BoD

5. Have Ann Baskins write memo to release BoD meeting minutes to the investigation team

   - Review minutes in correlation to known events

6. Schedule a second information gathering meeting with Rosemary Thomas

C. Recommendations and Questions Requiring Input

1. Are BoD members aware of the current "KONA" investigation?

2. Identify the media article published shortly after the March 2005 BoD meeting, which contained detailed information pertaining to confidential BoD conversations. The aforementioned article was discussed during a conference call on August 4th with Pattie Dunn, Tony Gentilucci and Ron DeLia.

3. At the appropriate time determine if any individual in the Head Hunter firm utilized by HP for the CEO and Director searches, other than the two (2) designated contacts, who would have had access to the CEO & BoD candidates names.

   - Were the CEO finalist resumes faxed to members of HP's BoD by the Head Hunter firm, if yes, details?

4. It is recommended the investigative team interview Larry Sonsini. The interview would focus on the results of Sonsini's investigation into the unauthorized dissemination of proprietary information to the press.

   - Investigation team is looking for Pattie Dunn and Ann Baskin's input and guidance on this recommendation.

End of Memo:

From: Patricia Dunn-Jahnke <[redacted]>
Sent: Saturday, August 6, 2005 10:20 PM
To: Gentilucci, Anthony R. <tony.gentilucci@hp.com>
Cc: rrd@security-outsourcing.com
Subject: RE: Update Memo and Request for Input / Direction - Project KONA ***HP CONFIDENTIAL***

Tony, I am leaving in the morning but will give this a look on the plane and try to get some reaction to you in the next few days.

Regards,
Pattie

From: "Gentilucci, Anthony R." <tony.gentilucci@hp.com>
To: "Patricia Dunn-Jahnke"[redacted]>
CC: "Ron DeLia" <rrd@security-outsourcing.com>
Subject: Update Memo and Request for Input / Direction - Project KONA ***HP CONFIDENTIAL***
Date: Sat, 6 Aug 2005 11:53:17 -0400

Pattie,

Attached is an update memo which contains some ongoing and planned investigative activity as well as several questions and recommendations requiring your input. Understanding that you are about to go on business trip and vacation, if you are unable to address these questions prior to your departure, we will continue with ongoing investigative action items and regroup with you on upon you return. As an FYI, I will also forward a copy of this memo to Ann Baskins and Jim Fairbaugh.

If we don't have the opportunity to speak, safe travels and enjoy your time off.

Best Regards,

Tony

<< Case_ProjectKONA_UpdateMemo_05_AUG_05.doc >>

HP 01134

TAB 10

To: Huska, Kevin (Global Security); Fairbaugh, Jim (Global Security)
Subject: FW: Jay Keyworth
Importance: High

Kevin/Jim: HP Board Member Jay Keyworth was robbed recently at his home/villa outside Florence, Italy. (See the note below from Rosemarie.)

It is unknown at this time whether this was a targeted event, and that he/or his house, was under surveillance.

Jay admitted that he has never locked his door at this residence in the past.

He did file a police report; and he did contact the local US Embassy for new Visas and Passports.

Items taken from the residence were as follows:

1.) Passports (Both Jay's and Marion's - his girlfriend.)
2.) PC - Jay's HP. N410C personal computer
3.) Travelers Checks
4.) Marion's purse and ID's.
5.) Jay's HP ID

It is unknown what type of HP Company information was kept on Jay's local disk drive. Geoffrey Mo is ordering Jay another HP

computer; he is also going to be de-briefing Jay as to what HP information was kept on the local drive. It was G-Mo's opinion

that the stolen disk drive would be re-formatted and sold. (*Jay's ActivCard was NOT stolen.)

I'll ask Kelin Brown to shut off his card access to the HP site.

Denis

-----Original Message-----
From: Thomas, Rosemarie Ann
Sent: Sunday, October 09, 2005 11:35 AM
To: Huska, Kevin (Global Security); Denning, L Mark (Global Security); Lynch, Denis J (Global Security)
Subject: Jay Keyworth
Importance: High

HP Confidential

Jay was robbed in Italy and they got his pc (which Geoffrey and I are taking care of as far as Board site) and because he did not have his access card in his wallet it was also taken. Please shut down access to HP and we can then issue him a new access card later this month when he returns. He is coming back on the 30th.

Rosemarie

HP 00729

TAB 11

From: Gentilucci, Anthony R. <tony.gentilucci@hp.com>
Sent: Friday, January 20, 2006 9:23 PM
To: Hunsaker, Kevin <kevin.hunsaker@hp.com>
Subject: RE: CONFIDENTIAL

OK, I'll send you an overview of the old case, I would love to nail this one big time, major challenge, outside the HP realm, difficult to track, trace, etc.

Tony

-----Original Message-----
From: Hunsaker, Kevin
Sent: Friday, January 20, 2006 11:09 PM
To: Gentilucci, Anthony R.
Subject: RE: CONFIDENTIAL

Thanks Tony. I have forwarded it to Ann. Based on the emails, I imagine she'll want the privilege to apply.

I'll let you know what she says.

Kevin T. Hunsaker
Senior Counsel
HP Legal Department
650 857-3079 (phone)
650 857-3710 (fax)
[redacted]voicemail network number)

-----Original Message-----
From: Gentilucci, Anthony R.
Sent: Friday, January 20, 2006 6:50 PM
To: Hunsaker, Kevin
Subject: FW: CONFIDENTIAL

Here is the reporter

-----Original Message-----
From: Sherbin, Robert
Sent: Friday, January 20, 2006 6:53 PM
To: Fairbaugh, Jim (Global Security)
Cc: Gentilucci, Anthony R.
Subject: CONFIDENTIAL

Jim. The reporter who has the latest leak is Tom Krazit, an SF based reporter for CNET. His cell is: [redacted] and his desk fone is: [redacted] Mark believes the names worth looking at are Hackborn, Babbio, Salhany, Keyworth and Perkins. I'm always happy to talk if you'd feel it useful. Best, B.

TAB 12

From: Gentilucci, Anthony R. <tony.gentilucci@hp.com>
Sent: Monday, January 23, 2006 6:57 AM
To: Hunsaker, Kevin <kevin.hunsaker@hp.com>
Subject: Copy of Investigation Results Previous BoD Investigation
Attach: Case_Operation KONA_DRAFT V8_20_JUL_05_KH Copy.ppt

Privileged Communications

Kevin, attached are the results of the previous BoD investigation. You should know that Patti Dunn approached our group for a recommendation for an outside resource to do some research, we recommended Security Outsourcing Solutions. For months we were not privileged to the investigation, however, Ron Delia, asked me, to ask Jim F, to get the investigation transferred internally, sounds strange, it was, but eventually we got engaged. The key subject of our investigation, unexpectedly left the BoD I think late summer/fall, no leaks in 6 plus months. In any event, these are tough cases to prove as the BoD mostly communicates outside the HP infrastructure, a lot of time and effort went into everything we gathered on this slide set. If you need a data dump, this slide set is best discussed with Ron and myself at some point. At the time, I asked that you get engaged as Ann Baskins and Patti Dunn were our key points of contact and Ann was/is obviously very busy, Patti was actually good to work with, but I felt we needed ACP invoked and a working an attorney.

I think you mentioned this crosses the GSBCT theshold, in the past, the thought was it didn't involve an employee/SBC violation, but certainly with this new one, the potential is there that this is could be an HP employee as well as BoD member or both. Talk later today.

Tony

HP 03592

TAB 13

From: Hunsaker, Kevin <kevin.hunsaker@hp.com>
Sent: Monday, January 23, 2006 10:53 AM
To: Nye, Vince <vince.nye@hp.com>; Adler, Frederick P. <fred.adler@hp.com>; Lynch, Denis J (Global Security) <denis.j.lynch@hp.com>
Cc: Gentilucci, Anthony R. <tony.gentilucci@hp.com>; Huska, Kevin <IMCEAEX-_O=COMPAQ_OU=HPED_cn=Employees_cn=KEHUS-5@Compaq.com>
Subject: Info Leak – Privileged Communication

Team,

Per our discussion a few moments ago, we need to contact Bob Sherbin to determine whether, or to what extent, the information communicated to the journalist was an inappropriate disclosure of sensitive HP information. As such, Vince and Fred, will you please contact Bob and have a discussion with him regarding his thoughts on the disclosure, as well as any input he may have received from either Pattie Dunn or Mark Hurd. Once you have done so, please send a quick email to the group summarizing Bob's comments – be sure to mark the email "Prepared at the Direction of Counsel."

I will meet with Ann Baskins and do the same.

Thanks.

Kevin

Kevin T. Hunsaker
Senior Counsel
HP Legal Department
650 857-3079 (phone)
650 857-3710 (fax)
[redacted]voicemail network number)

TAB 14

From: Hunsaker, Kevin [kevin.hunsaker@hp.com]
Sent: Monday, January 23, 2006 3:29 PM
To: Fairbaugh, Jim (Global Security)
Subject: Potential Information Leak – Privileged Communication

ATTORNEY-CLIENT PRIVILEGED. DO NOT FORWARD.

Hi Jim,

I believe you are already aware of this matter, but I wanted to send you the link to the article that came out this morning.

Ann Baskins has asked me to oversee the investigation into this in order to protect the attorney-client privilege in the event there is litigation or a governmental inquiry of some sort.

As an FYI, we have assembled the Investigation Team and commenced looking at a number of potential sources and leads with respect to the leak. As we move forward in the investigation, I will be happy to provide you with updates on our progress.

In the interim, please don't hesitate to give me a call if you have any questions.

Kevin

TAB 15

ACTION RESEARCH GROUP

Please visit us at: www.actionresearchgroup.com
Email assignments: actionresearch1@aol.com

DATE: 01/27/06

ASSIGNMENT NO. 99377886

SENDER: BOBIEJO

S. 15

COMPANY NAME: S.O.S.

CLIENT NO. 2010

CONTACT NAME: RON

REFERENCE:

SERVICE REQUEST: 900A

PRICE $20.00

INFORMATION PROVIDED:

REDACTED

PHONE NO: (415) [redacted]

PRIVILEGED COMMUNICATION
HP CONFIDENTIAL

INFORMATION REQUESTED:

NAME: C-NET NETWORK

REDACTED

ADDRESS: [redacted]
SAN FRANCISCO, CA 94105

THANK YOU FOR USING OUR SERVICES!!

NOTICE: ALL CANCELLATION REQUESTS MUST BE IN WRITING

Terms & Conditions:

All information obtained by us, or our affiliates, is intended for legitimate and lawful use only: by proceeding forth with this information request, you (the client), agree to indemnify, hold harmless, protect and defend (in a court of law) Action Research Group and/or it's affiliates if the information is misused in anyway. While Action Research Group believes the information to be reliable, human or mechanical error remains a possibility. Therefore, Action Research Group makes no guarantee to its accuracy. Neither Action Research Group nor any of our sources of the information requested shall be responsible for any error or omissions, or for the use or results obtained from the use of this information.

A finance charge in the amount of 1.5% p month or 18% per annum will be charge on all past due accounts, in addition to a necessary costs and attorney's fees incurre to enforce collection.

HP 5822

ACTION RESEARCH GROUP

Please visit us at: www.actionresearchgroup.com
Email assignments: actionresearch1@aol.com

DATE: 01/25/06

ASSIGNMENT NO. 99377746

SENDER: BOBIEJO

S. 16

COMPANY NAME: S.O.S.

CLIENT NO: 2010

CONTACT NAME: RON

SERVICE REQUEST: 900C/V x2

PRICE $145.00 (C=$45, 2 V's=$100)

REQUESTED INFORMATION:

NAME: DAWN YOSHITAKE-KAWAMOTO
REDACTED [redacted], ALBANY, CA
SSN: [redacted]
REDACTED

PRIVILEGED COMMUNICATION
HP CONFIDENTIAL

INFORMATION REQUESTED:

NAME: DAWN & JON KAWAMOTO

HOME NO: (510) [redacted]
REDACTED

REDACTED
CELL #1: (510) [redacted]
CELL #2: (510) [redacted]
REDACTED

THANK YOU FOR USING OUR SERVICES!!

NOTICE: ALL CANCELLATION REQUESTS MUST BE IN WRITING

Terms & Conditions:

All information obtained by us, or our affiliates, is intended for legitimate and lawful use only: by proceeding forth with this information request, you (the client), agree to indemnify, hold harmless, protect and defend (in a court of law) Action Research Group and/or it's affiliates if the information is misused in anyway. While Action Research Group believes the information to be reliable, human or mechanical error remains a possibility. Therefore, Action Research Group makes no guarantee to its' accuracy. Neither Action Research Group nor any of our sources of the information requested shall be responsible for any error or omissions, or for the use or results obtained from the use of this information.

A finance charge in the amount of 1.5% pe month or 18% per annum will be charge on all past due accounts, in addition to a: necessary costs and attorney's fees incurre to enforce collection.

ACTION RESEARCH GROUP

Please visit us at: www.actionresearchgroup.com
Email assignments: actionresearch1@aol.com

DATE: 01/25/06 ASSIGNMENT NO. 99377747

SENDER: BOBIEJO S. 16

COMPANY NAME: S.O.S. CLIENT NO: 2010

CONTACT NAME: RON

SERVICE REQUEST: 900C PRICE $45.00

REQUESTED INFORMATION:

NAME: THOMAS J. KRAZIT
[redacted] MENLO PARK, CA
REDACTED

PRIVILEGED COMMUNICATION
HP CONFIDENTIAL

INFORMATION REQUESTED:

NAME: THOMAS KRAZIT & SHANNON THOKE

REDACTED
PHONE NO: (650) [redacted]

→ PLEASE NOTE: THERE ARE NO CELLULAR ACCOUNTS UNDER HIS INFORMATION, POSSIBLY UNDER SHANNON'S NAME. WOULD YOU LIKE US TO RUN HER INFORMATION FOR A CELLULAR? IF SO, PLEASE LET US KNOW!!

THANK YOU FOR USING OUR SERVICES!!

NOTICE: ALL CANCELLATION REQUESTS MUST BE IN WRITING

Terms & Conditions:

All information obtained by us, or our affiliates, is intended for legitimate and lawful use only: by proceeding forth with this information request, you (the client), agree to indemnify, hold harmless, protect and defend (in a court of law) Action Research Group and/or it's affiliates if the information is misused in anyway. While Action Research Group believes the information to be reliable, human or mechanical error remains a possibility. Therefore, Action Research Group makes no guarantee to its' accuracy. Neither Action Research Group nor any of our sources of the information requested shall be responsible for any error or omissions, or for the use or results obtained from the use of this information.

A finance charge in the amount of 1.5% pe month or 18% per annum will be charge on all past due accounts, in addition to al necessary costs and attorney's fees incurrer to enforce collection.

ACTION RESEARCH GROUP

Please visit us at: www.actionresearchgroup.com

Email assignments: actionresearch1@aol.com

INVOICE COPY

DATE: 01/26/06 ASSIGNMENT NO. 99377885

SENDER: BOBIEJO S. 66

COMPANY NAME: S.O.S. CLIENT NO. 2010

CONTACT NAME: RON

REFERENCE:

SERVICE REQUEST: 900A PRICE $20.00

INFORMATION PROVIDED:

REDACTED

PHONE NO: (415) [redacted]

PRIVILEGED COMMUNICATION
HP CONFIDENTIAL

INFORMATION REQUESTED:

NAME: SMITH - KETTLEWELL

REDACTED

ADDRESS: [redacted]
SAN FRANCISCO, CA 94115

THANK YOU FOR USING OUR SERVICES!!

NOTICE: ALL CANCELLATION REQUESTS MUST BE IN WRITING

Terms & Conditions:

All information obtained by us, or our affiliates, is intended for legitimate and lawful use only: by proceeding forth with this information request, you (the client), agree to indemnify, hold harmless, protect and defend (in a court of law) Action Research Group and/or it's affiliates if the information is misused in anyway. While Action Research Group believes the information to be reliable, human or mechanical error remains a possibility. Therefore, Action Research Group makes no guarantee to its' accuracy. Neither Action Research Group nor any of our sources of the information requested shall be responsible for any error or omissions, or for the use or results obtained from the use of this information.

A finance charge in the amount of 1.5% pe month or 18% per annum will be charge on all past due accounts, in addition to al necessary costs and attorney's fees incurre to enforce collection.

HP 5825

INVOICE COPY

ACTION RESEARCH GROUP

PLEASEVISIT US AT: WWW.ACTIONRESEARCHGROUP.COM
EMAIL ASSIGNMENTS: ACTIONRESEARCH1@AOL.COM

DATE: 3-8-06 ASSIGNMENT NO. 99380614

SENDER: IVORY S. 8

COMPANY NAME: S.O.S. CLIENT NO. 2010

CONTACT NAME: RON

SERVICE REQUEST: 900A PRICE $20.00

REFERENCE:

REQUESTED INFORMATION:

REDACTED

PHONE NUMBER: 760-[redacted]

INFORMATION REQUESTED:

NAME: YOUNG WILSON

REDACTED

ADDRESS: [redacted] ESCONDIDO, CA 92026

THANK YOU FOR USING OUR SERVICES!!

NOTICE: ALL CANCELLATION REQUESTS MUST BE IN WRITING

Terms & Conditions:
All information obtained by us, or our affiliates, is intended for legitimate and lawful use only: by proceeding forth with this information request, you (the client), agree to indemnify, hold harmless, protect and defend (in a court of law) Action Research Group and/or it's affiliates if the information is misused in anyway. While Action Research Group believes the information to be reliable, human or mechanical error remains a possibility. Therefore, Action Research Group makes no guarantee to its' accuracy. Neither Action Research Group nor any of our sources of the information requested shall be responsible for any error or omissions, or for the use or results obtained from the use of this information.

A finance charge in the amount of 1.5% p month or 18% per annum will be charge on all past due accounts, in addition to a necessary costs and attorney's fees incurre to enforce collection.

ACTION RESEARCH GROUP

Please visit us at: www.actionresearchgroup.com
Email assignments: actionresearch1@aol.com

INVOICE COPY

DATE: 03/06/06 | ASSIGNMENT NO. 99380591

SENDER: BOBIEJO | S. 66

COMPANY NAME: S.O.S. | CLIENT NO. 2010

CONTACT NAME: RON

REFERENCE: PRIVILEGED CASE

SERVICE REQUEST: 900A | PRICE $20.00

INFORMATION PROVIDED:

REDACTED
PHONE NO: (415) [redacted]

PRIVILEGED COMMUNICATION
HP CONFIDENTIAL

INFORMATION REQUESTED:

NAME: J.P. MORGAN CHASE

REDACTED
ADDRESS: [redacted]
SAN FRANCISCO, CA 94105

THANK YOU FOR USING OUR SERVICES!!

NOTICE: ALL CANCELLATION REQUESTS MUST BE IN WRITING

Terms & Conditions:

All information obtained by us, or our affiliates, is intended for legitimate and lawful use only: by proceeding forth with this information request, you (the client), agree to indemnify, hold harmless, protect and defend (in a court of law) Action Research Group and/or it's affiliates if the information is misused in anyway. While Action Research Group believes the information to be reliable, human or mechanical error remains a possibility. Therefore, Action Research Group makes no guarantee to its' accuracy. Neither Action Research Group nor any of our sources of the information requested shall be responsible for any error or omissions, or for the use or results obtained from the use of this information.

A finance charge in the amount of 1.5% per month or 18% per annum will be charged on all past due accounts, in addition to all necessary costs and attorney's fees incurred to enforce collection.

HP 5827

INVOICE COPY

ACTION RESEARCH GROUP

Please visit us at: www.actionresearchgroup.com
Email assignments: actionresearch1@aol.com

DATE: 03/02/06 **ASSIGNMENT NO. 99380266**

SENDER: BOBIEJO **S.**

COMPANY NAME: S.O.S. **CLIENT NO. 2010**

CONTACT NAME: RON

REFERENCE:

SERVICE REQUEST: 900A **PRICE $20.00**

INFORMATION PROVIDED:

REDACTED

PHONE NO: (530)[redacted]

PRIVILEGED COMMUNICATION
HP CONFIDENTIAL

INFORMATION REQUESTED:

NAME: MARION SCHWARTZ-KEYWORTH

REDACTED

ADDRESS: [redacted]
TRUCKEE, CA 96161

THANK YOU FOR USING OUR SERVICES!!

NOTICE: ALL CANCELLATION REQUESTS MUST BE IN WRITING

Terms & Conditions:

All information obtained by us, or our affiliates, is intended for legitimate and lawful use only: by proceeding forth with this information request, you (the client), agree to indemnify, hold harmless, protect and defend (in a court of law) Action Research Group and/or it's affiliates if the information is misused in anyway. While Action Research Group believes the information to be reliable, human or mechanical error remains a possibility. Therefore, Action Research Group makes no guarantee to its' accuracy. Neither Action Research Group nor any of our sources of the information requested shall be responsible for any error or omissions, or for the use or results obtained from the use of this information.

A finance charge in the amount of 1.5% p month or 18% per annum will be charge on all past due accounts, in addition to a necessary costs and attorney's fees incurre to enforce collection.

HP 5828

ACTION RESEARCH GROUP

Please visit us at: www.actionresearchgroup.com
Email assignments: actionresearch1@aol.com

DATE: 03/02/06

SENDER: BOBIEJO

COMPANY NAME: S.O.S.

CONTACT NAME: RON

REFERENCE NAME:

SERVICE REQUEST: 900C (verify)/V x2

ASSIGNMENT NO. 99380239

S. 6=C, 16=V

CLIENT NO: 2010

ACCOUNT NO:

PRICE $125.00 (V=$100,C=$25)

REQUESTED INFORMATION:
MARION SWARTZ KEYWORTH
[redacted], TRUCKEE, CA
REDACTED

INFORMATION REQUESTED:

PRIVILEGED COMMUNICATION
HP CONFIDENTIAL

NAME: MARION SWARTZ

REDACTED REDACTED
CELL NO: (510)[redacted] & 510)[redacted]

HOME #: (530)[redacted] ~ Only active line at the address listed above.
REDACTED

THANK YOU FOR USING OUR SERVICES!!

NOTICE: ALL CANCELLATION REQUESTS MUST BE IN WRITING

Terms & Conditions:

All information obtained by us, or our affiliates, is intended for legitimate and lawful use only: by proceeding forth with this information request, you (the client), agree to indemnify, hold harmless, protect and defend (in a court of law) Action Research Group and/or it's affiliates if the information is misused in anyway. While Action Research Group believes the information to be reliable, human or mechanical error remains a possibility. Therefore, Action Research Group makes no guarantee to its' accuracy. Neither Action Research Group nor any of our sources of the information requested shall be responsible for any error or omissions, or for the use or results obtained from the use of this information.

TAB 16

From: Hunsaker, Kevin <kevin.hunsaker@hp.com>
Sent: Thursday, January 26, 2006 2:08 PM
To: Adler, Frederick P. <fred.adler@hp.com>
Subject: unauthorized disclosure – privileged communication

Hi Fred,

Are you (and others working for you, I presume) pulling the email and phone records on all the EC members who were present at the Board meeting? I think you said you were, but I just wanted to make sure. Given the visibility this investigation could ultimately have, I really want to make sure we're checking into all potential subjects.

Thanks Fred -- I know you've been burning the midnight oil on this one, and I really appreciate everything you're doing.

Kevin

Kevin T. Hunsaker
Senior Counsel
HP Legal Department
650 857-3079 (phone)
650 857-3710 (fax)
[redacted]voicemail network number)

TAB 17

From: Adler, Frederick P. <fred.adler@hp.com>
Sent: Friday, January 27, 2006 2:27 PM
To: Ron DeLia <rrd@security-outsourcing.com>
Cc: Hunsaker, Kevin <kevin.hunsaker@hp.com>; Gentilucci, Anthony R. <tony.gentilucci@hp.com>; Nye, Vince <vince.nye@hp.com>; Adler, Frederick P. <fred.adler@hp.com>
Subject: RE: Privileged Communication - HP Confidential

I have a list of approximately 25-30 numbers.

I'll forward it with all my other promised info.

Fred

Fred Adler
HP IT Security Investigations
(916) 785-8025, fred.adler@hp.com

-----Original Message-----
From: Ron DeLia [mailto:rrd@security-outsourcing.com]
Sent: Friday, January 27, 2006 2:48 PM
To: Hunsaker, Kevin; Gentilucci, Anthony R.; Nye, Vince; Adler, Frederick P.
Subject: Privileged Communication - HP Confidential
Importance: High

Privileged Communication – HP CONFIDENTIAL

Kevin,

Have we obtained a list of contact numbers for CNET reporters from Bob Sherbin? As mentioned earlier, Pattie Dunn obtained similar info from Bob Sherbin during the last investigation. The information is critical to identify all contact numbers for Kawamoto, Krazit, Stephen Shankland and other CNET reporters. We want to insure we have all the phone numbers for each reporter.

Ron

The content of this email transmission is intended only for the use of the individual or entity named above and may contain legally privileged or confidential information. If you are not the intended recipient, you are hereby notified that any disclosure, copying, dissemination, distribution, or use of this email transmission, or information contained herein, is strictly prohibited. If you have received this email transmission in error, please destroy all copies of this email and its attachments and notify the person whose name appears above.

Security Outsourcing Solutions, Inc.
Tel: (617) 426-3900 or (781) 444-9616

TAB 18

From: Hunsaker, Kevin <kevin.hunsaker@hp.com>
Sent: Friday, January 27, 2006 4:28 PM
To: Nye, Vince <vince.nye@hp.com>; Adler, Frederick P. <fred.adler@hp.com>; Gentilucci, Anthony R. <tony.gentilucci@hp.com>; Ron DeLia <rrd@security-outsourcing.com>; Lynch, Denis J (Global Security) <denis.j.lynch@hp.com>
Subject: Meeting with Pattie Dunn -- privileged communication

---

When: Thursday, February 02, 2006 9:30 AM-1:00 PM (GMT-08:00) Pacific Time (US & Canada); Tijuana.
Where: Canton Room, Building 20C, Palo Alto

~~*~*~*~*~*~*~*~*

Team,

Pattie will be joining us in person at 10:00 am. The purpose of the meeting will be to both interview her to gather her insights, etc. and to give her a briefing on where things stand, what we know, what we plan to do, what the various investigative opportunities are, etc.

We really need to be prepared . . . . Let's discuss this in more detail early next week.

Kevin

TAB 19

Hewlett-Packard
Information Security Investigations
8000 Foothills Blvd / MS 5626
Roseville, Calif. 95747 - 5200

Privileged & Confidential
Attorney Work Product

invent

Investigative Report

Client: Kevin Hunsaker, Legal, SBC Investigations
From: Fred Adler, Information Security Investigator
Date: 1/27/06
Re: CITSIRT #2006000350

Summary:

Assistance was requested in determining the source of HP confidential information which appeared in an on-line journal. Examinations were made of corporate communications in an ongoing effort to determine the source. Included in this report is an accounting of IT Investigations progress to date.

Investigation:

On 1/21/06, I was contacted by Kevin Hunsaker, HP Legal, and advised an HP Standards of Business Conduct (SBC) investigation had been launched relative to the unauthorized release of confidential HP information. The information appeared in an Internet news report at CNET.com on 1/23/06, and detailed a number of HP business strategies. The article was labeled as authored by Dawn Kawamoto and Tom Krazit, with a special thanks to Stephen Shankland. Also provided by Hunsaker was information it was felt the content of the on-line article had been derived from an HP Board of Directors (BOD) meeting, held a week earlier.

I immediately initiated a series of Internet searches on information on Kawamoto, Krazit and Shankland, obtaining the following information:

[redacted]

Telephone numbers for CNET [redacted]

Telephone numbers for IDG [redacted]

All obtained numbers were run against HP telephone records for the past year, with no result. A request was made to search all incoming and outgoing HP e-mail for activity to the CNET and IDG domains, as well as any e-mail to or from "dawnk", "krazit", "shankland" and "kawamoto" for the past month. Results of the e-mail search are forthcoming.

Initials

HP0008545

Hewlett-Packard
Information Security Investigations
8000 Foothills Blvd / MS 5626
Roseville, Calif. 95747 - 5200

Privileged & Confidential
Attorney Work Product

invent

Investigative Report

A search of HP Internet proxy servers was also made on the parameters of "dawnk", "krazit", "shankland" and "kawamoto", for the period of the past several months. Results were examined and a single record of interest was noted. On the morning of 1/20/06, a search of two Internet search engines was accomplished for the name "Dawn Kawamoto" by HP employee, Brigida Bergkamp, utilizing the DHCP IP address 15.246.42.78 (Attachment-1 (times in GMT)). A later cursory direct examination of Bergkamp's computer verified the activity (Internet Explorer History) but nothing seemingly related in content to the information leaked was found as an active file in her system. Bergkamp also never appeared to conduct another search related to Kawamoto. Nothing remarkable was found in her Internet History.

A check of Bergkamp's server based e-mail determined she received a copy of the article, through automated process, early Monday morning, 1/23/06. Additionally, an e-mail referencing Kawamoto was located in Bergkamp's account (Attachment-2). Within the e-mail was a telephone number for contacting Kawamoto [redacted] Bergkamp's HP telephone activity for the past year was also accessed and is provided in Attachment-3.

A cursory search of Internet based contact information for Kawamoto, Krazit, Shankland, CNET and IDG was conducted. Results are provided in Attachment-4. A check of telephone numbers obtained in the search against HP telephone records provided no matches.

On 1/24/06, HP Investigator Vince Nye and myself interviewed HP Public Relations person Bob Sherbin (see report of Nye). Sherbin was interviewed since he had been contacted by Krazit for information to support Krazit's later ("leak") article. During the interview, Sherbin mentioned receiving a telephone call from Krazit on 1/20/06, at approximately 1430 hours. A check of Sherbin's telephone records provided a number of [redacted] for Krazit (Note: the determined number for Krazit appears to fall in the range of numbers previously determined for CNET, provided in Attachment-4). HP call records were checked for activity over the past year to Krazit's number. Only several recent calls during January 2006 were found, which are provided in Attachment-5.

On 1/24/06, information was provided by Kevin Hunsaker that four HP employees were responsible for construction of a presentation given to the BOD which included the information of concern, Marius Haas, Scott Porter, Prakash Jothee and Michael Nold. E-mail accounts for all four individuals were accessed for information indicating dissemination. Although correspondence relating to the presentation material was found, it was limited strictly to compilation and finalization. No indication of dissemination of the completed presentation was found.

On 1/26/04, Ron DeLia, Security Outsourcing Solutions, Inc., provided two telephone numbers for Wall Street Journal writer Pui-Wing Tam, [redacted] and [redacted] HP telephone records were then searched for contact with the two numbers. Results are provided in Attachments-6 and Attachment-7, respectively.

De Lia also verbally provided three phone numbers associated with Kawamoto, [redacted], [redacted] and [redacted]. All three numbers were run against HP telephone records with no results found.

Hewlett-Packard
Information Security Investigations
8000 Foothills Blvd / MS 5626
Roseville, Calif. 95747 - 5200

Privileged & Confidential
Attorney Work Product

hp invent

Investigative Report

On 1/30/06, results for the HP email portal search (all e-mail traffic in and out of HP during the month of January) were received and reviewed. No e-mail was found associated with known or common e-mail addresses for Kawamoto (dawnk, dawn.kawamoto, kawamoto, dkawamoto, etc.) E-mail associated with Krazit (Attachment-8) and Shankland (Attachment-9) was located. Also located during the search is a possible secondary e-mail address for Krazi[redacted]

A request, by Kevin Hunsaker, was also made to determine actual locations of telephones used to communicate with Tam, but not defined by location, included in Attachments-6 and 7. The findings are included in Attachment-10.

End of report.

Initials

Hewlett-Packard
Information Security Investigations
8000 Foothills Blvd / MS 5626
Roseville, Calif. 95747 - 5200

Privileged & Confidential
Attorney Work Product

invent

Investigative Report

List of Attachments

Attachment-1	Bergkamp's Proxy (Internet) History
Attachment-2	Bergkamp's E-mail Referencing Kawamoto
Attachment-3	Bergkamp's Telephone History
Attachment-4	Krazit, Kawamoto, Shankland, CNET and IDG Contact Info
Attachment-5	HP-Krazit ([redacted] Telephone Calls
Attachment-6	HP-Tam[redacted] Telephone Calls
Attachment-7	HP-Tam[redacted] Telephone Calls
Attachment-8	HP-Krazit E-mail Traffic
Attachment-9	HP-Shankland E-mail traffic
Attachment-10	Telephone Call Locations

[redacted]

Hewlett-Packard
Information Security Investigations
8000 Foothills Blvd / MS 5626
Roseville, Calif. 95747 - 5200

Privileged & Confidential
Attorney Work Product

hp invent

Investigative Report

Attachment-1

01/20/2006 19:00:06	384	15.246.42.78	30009	vocuspr.vocus.com/vocuspr30/DotNet/XR/PickListValidate.aspx?PickListDefinitionID=MediaContactPickList&ControlName=mediaContactNamePickList&ControlValue=Kawamoto%2C%20Dawn&ControlValueID=&GroupID=0&AllowMultipleSelections=true&AddEqualSign=true&ClientOnChange=&OneResultOnly=true
01/20/2006 19:00:04	183146	15.246.42.78	0	dw.com.com/clear/c.gif?ts=1137783493&edId=3&sId=1&dwpubsysid=1&ptid=6070&onId=5&part=&subj=Dawn+Kawamoto&tag=srch&xref=http://www.cnet.com/
01/20/2006 18:59:38	42	15.246.42.78	372	dw.com.com/clear/c.gif?ts=1137783575&edId=3&prtnr=CNET%20Networks,%20Inc.&oid=5208-6132-0&ptId=5208&onId=6132&sId=7&asId=0&astId=1&cval=FR|Viruses%20%26%20security%20alerts|NEWS%20-%20January%2019,%202006&ctype=forum&xref=http://cnet.search.com/search&xrq=chkpt=astg.cnet.fd.search.cnet%26q=Dawn+Kawamoto%26tag=srch
01/20/2006 18:59:35	36	15.246.42.78	430	dw.com.com/redir?edId=3&oid=6070-5_1-0&siteid=1&ontId=5&tag=ksrch_mb_1&subj=Dawn+Kawamoto&destcat=5_1-0&desturl=http%3A%2F%2Freviews%2Ecnet%2Ecom%2F5208%2D6132%2D0%2Ehtml%3FforumID%3D32%26threadID%3D151178%26messageID%3D1683719
01/20/2006 18:59:23	35	15.246.42.78	372	dw.com.com/clear/c.gif?ts=1137783563&edId=3&sId=1&dwpubsysid=1&ptid=6070&onId=5&part=&subj=Dawn+Kawamoto&tag=srch&xref=http://www.cnet.com/

Hewlett-Packard
Information Security Investigations
8000 Foothills Blvd / MS 5626
Roseville, Calif. 95747 - 5200

Privileged & Confidential
Attorney Work Product

invent

Investigative Report

01/20/2006 18:59:23	648	15.246.42.78	31691	cnet.search.com/search?chkpt=astg.cnet.fd.search.cnet&q=Dawn+Kawamoto&tag=srch
01/20/2006 18:59:22	1055	15.246.42.78	504	www.search.com/redirect?q=Dawn+Kawamoto&tag=srch&target=http%3A%2F%2Fcnet.search.com%2Fsearch%3Fchkpt%3Dastg.cnet.fd.search.cnet&x=23&y=3
01/20/2006 18:58:04	2953	15.246.42.78	32077	cnet.search.com/search?chkpt=astg.cnet.fd.search.cnet&q=Dawn+Kawamoto&tag=srch
01/20/2006 18:58:03	122	15.246.42.78	504	www.search.com/redirect?q=Dawn+Kawamoto&tag=srch&target=http%3A%2F%2Fcnet.search.com%2Fsearch%3Fchkpt%3Dastg.cnet.fd.search.cnet&x=25&y=10

Hewlett-Packard
Information Security Investigations
8000 Foothills Blvd / MS 5626
Roseville, Calif. 95747 - 5200

Privileged & Confidential
Attorney Work Product

invent

Investigative Report

Attachment-2

From: Kinley, Pat
Sent: Friday, January 06, 2006 5:58 AM
To: Bergkamp, Brigida
Subject: RE: ON DEADLINE: CNET: digital entertainment scaleback

We handled this. thanks

Pat Kinley
HP Digital Entertainment PR Manager
pat.kinley@hp.com
office: +1 760-944-7057
mobile: [redacted]

-----Original Message-----
From: Bergkamp, Brigida
Sent: Thursday, January 05, 2006 12:38 PM
To: Kinley, Pat
Subject: ON DEADLINE: CNET: digital entertainment scaleback
Importance: High

Hi Pat -- Dawn Kawamoto wants to speak with someone on HP's digital entertainment efforts. She is asking about HP scaling back on media hub efforts from Carly's days. Needs to hear back within the hour. Tel. [redacted]anks for handling, Brigida

Initials

Hewlett-Packard
Information Security Investigations
8000 Foothills Blvd / MS 5626
Roseville, Calif. 95747 - 5200

Privileged & Confidential
Attorney Work Product

invent

Investigative Report

[redacted]

Attachment-3

Date/Time	Incoming Origination	Extension	Destination	Duration
1/6/2006 08:18:06		[redacted]	[redacted] GRENSPOINT TX	1.9
1/6/2006 08:21:30		[redacted]	[redacted] SAN FRAN CA	0.5
1/6/2006 09:03:06	[redacted]	[redacted]		25.9
1/6/2006 09:04:42	[redacted]	[redacted]		1.3
1/6/2006 09:32:30		[redacted]	[redacted] VANCOUVER WA	1.5
1/6/2006 09:39:48		[redacted]	[redacted] VANCOUVER WA	1.2
1/6/2006 09:48:54	[redacted]	[redacted]		15.1
1/6/2006 10:04:54		[redacted]	[redacted] VANCOUVER WA	1.1
1/6/2006 10:57:18		[redacted]	[redacted] GRENSPOINT TX	0.7
1/6/2006 10:58:06	INCOMING	[redacted]		3.9
1/6/2006		[redacted]	[redacted]	3.2

[redacted]

Hewlett-Packard
Information Security Investigations
8000 Foothills Blvd / MS 5626
Roseville, Calif. 95747 - 5200

Privileged & Confidential
Attorney Work Product

invent

Investigative Report

11:02:48		Brigida Bergkamp	GRENSPOINT TX	
1/6/2006 11:36:48	INCOMING	E		1.2
1/6/2006 11:50:36	[redacted]	E		7.4
1/6/2006 12:43:06		E	[redacted] VANCOUVER WA	0.9
1/6/2006 12:54:36		E	[redacted] GRENSPOINT TX	2.4
1/6/2006 12:56:54		E	[redacted] PHILA PA	3.1
1/6/2006 15:05:54	[redacted]	E		1.1
1/6/2006 15:18:42		B	[redacted] VANCOUVER WA	2.3
1/6/2006 15:58:42	[redacted]	B		6.3
1/6/2006 16:49:06	[redacted]	B		3.9
1/9/2006 08:55:54		B	[redacted] GRENSPOINT TX	3.1
1/9/2006 09:21:30		B	[redacted] GRENSPOINT TX	0.5
1/9/2006 09:32:00	[redacted]	B		2.0
1/9/2006 09:34:30		B	[redacted] HYATTSVL MD	2.5
1/9/2006 09:37:54		E	[redacted] HOUSTON TX	1.1
1/9/2006 10:19:54	[redacted]	E		3.1

[redacted]

Hewlett-Packard
Information Security Investigations
8000 Foothills Blvd / MS 5626
Roseville, Calif. 95747 - 5200

Privileged & Confidential
Attorney Work Product

invent

Investigative Report

1/9/2006 10:38:18			ɔ	Redacted VANCOUVER WA	0.7
1/9/2006 10:49:24	Redacted		ɔ		1.6
1/9/2006 12:44:42	INCOMING		ɔ		0.3
1/9/2006 12:45:42	INCOMING		p		0.3
1/9/2006 13:18:06	Redacted		p		1.9
1/9/2006 13:21:30			p	Redacted PHILA PA	0.5
1/9/2006 15:06:24	Redacted		p		13.6
1/10/2006 06:22:24			p	Redacted GRENSPOINT TX	1.6
1/10/2006 06:56:30			p	(866) 639-4754 TOLL FREE	127.5
1/10/2006 09:04:24			ıp	Redacted GRENSPOINT TX	0.6
1/10/2006 09:19:42			ıp	Redacted GRENSPOINT TX	2.3
1/10/2006 10:22:06			ıp	Redacted RANCHO BERNARDO CA	2.9
1/10/2006 10:58:48			ıp	Redacted HOUSTON TX	5.2
1/10/2006 13:15:00	INCOMING		ıp		1.0
1/10/2006 13:31:24			ıp	Redacted RANCHO BERNARDO CA	21.6
1/10/2006 14:43:18			np	Redacted EULESS TX	3.7

Hewlett-Packard
Information Security Investigations
8000 Foothills Blvd / MS 5626
Roseville, Calif. 95747 - 5200

Privileged & Confidential
Attorney Work Product

invent

Investigative Report

1/10/2006 14:49:36		E		[redacted] NEW YORK NY	0.4
1/10/2006 18:06:36		E		[redacted] SAN FRAN CA	0.4
1/11/2006 09:30:36		E		[redacted] GRENSPOINT TX	3.4
1/11/2006 09:35:00		E		(866) 639-4731 TOLL FREE	28.0
1/11/2006 10:31:54		E		[redacted] GRENSPOINT TX	60.1
1/11/2006 11:59:12	INCOMING	E			6.8
1/11/2006 12:14:30		I		[redacted] GRENSPOINT TX	3.5
1/11/2006 12:22:36		I		[redacted] PHILA PA	2.4
1/11/2006 12:54:42		I		[redacted] GRENSPOINT TX	0.3
1/11/2006 15:00:42		I		[redacted] SAN DIEGO CA	2.3
1/11/2006 15:03:30				[redacted] SAN DIEGO CA	2.5
1/11/2006 15:44:00				[redacted] RANCHO BERNARDO CA	1.0
1/11/2006 15:49:24				[redacted] EULESS TX	3.6
1/11/2006 16:22:24	INCOMING				20.6
1/11/2006 16:46:30				[redacted] SAN DIEGO CA	0.5
1/11/2006 16:52:30				[redacted] SAN DIEGO CA	1.5

Initials

Hewlett-Packard
Information Security Investigations
8000 Foothills Blvd / MS 5626
Roseville, Calif. 95747 - 5200

Privileged & Confidential
Attorney Work Product

Investigative Report

1/12/2006 09:38:18	[redacted]	3.7
1/12/2006 10:02:30		1.5
1/12/2006 10:38:06		0.9
1/12/2006 11:11:12		0.8
1/12/2006 14:20:42		1.3
1/12/2006 14:31:30		1.5
1/12/2006 14:49:12		2.8
1/12/2006 15:01:36		1.4
1/12/2006 17:52:54		0.1
1/13/2006 08:50:42		1.3
1/13/2006 09:01:18		5.7
1/13/2006 09:09:30		4.5
1/13/2006 09:31:48		34.2
1/13/2006 10:33:24		36.6
1/13/2006 11:30:18		1.7
1/13/2006 11:58:36		0.4

Hewlett-Packard
Information Security Investigations
8000 Foothills Blvd / MS 5626
Roseville, Calif. 95747 - 5200

Privileged & Confidential
Attorney Work Product

invent

Investigative Report

1/13/2006 12:00:48	[redacted]	33.2
1/13/2006 12:31:54	[redacted]	1.1
1/13/2006 12:35:54	[redacted]	29.1
1/13/2006 13:05:24	[redacted]	21.6
1/13/2006 13:19:48	[redacted]	1.2
1/13/2006 13:31:48	[redacted]	1.2
1/13/2006 13:33:30	[redacted]	0.5
1/13/2006 13:38:18	[redacted]	1.7
1/13/2006 13:40:36	[redacted]	2.4
1/13/2006 15:03:48	[redacted]	12.2
1/13/2006 15:05:42	[redacted]	0.3
1/13/2006 15:16:36	[redacted]	20.4
1/13/2006 15:40:00	[redacted]	1.0
1/13/2006 15:41:30	[redacted]	14.5
1/13/2006 16:05:12	[redacted]	0.8
1/13/2006 16:15:30	[redacted]	1.5

Initials

Hewlett-Packard
Information Security Investigations
8000 Foothills Blvd / MS 5626
Roseville, Calif. 95747 - 5200

Privileged & Confidential
Attorney Work Product

hp
invent

Investigative Report

1/15/2006 17:16:42		0.3
1/17/2006 08:17:06		0.9
1/17/2006 08:56:42		0.3
1/17/2006 08:57:18		3.7
1/17/2006 09:32:42		42.3
1/17/2006 10:25:36		0.4
1/17/2006 10:26:24		1.6
1/17/2006 11:01:12		1.8
1/17/2006 11:04:06		1.9
1/17/2006 11:12:30		7.5
1/17/2006 11:30:42		10.3
1/17/2006 11:33:06		1.9
1/17/2006 11:46:00		13.0
1/17/2006 12:12:36		2.4
1/17/2006 12:15:54		3.1
1/17/2006 12:29:48		1.2

Hewlett-Packard
Information Security Investigations
8000 Foothills Blvd / MS 5626
Roseville, Calif. 95747 - 5200

Privileged & Confidential
Attorney Work Product

invent

Investigative Report

1/17/2006 12:32:00				1.0
1/17/2006 12:40:24				5.6
1/17/2006 14:12:54				1.1
1/17/2006 14:16:18				0.7
1/17/2006 14:18:42				6.3
1/17/2006 14:24:30				0.5
1/17/2006 14:41:36				0.4
1/17/2006 14:52:30				1.5
1/17/2006 14:54:06				3.9
1/17/2006 15:07:18				0.7
1/17/2006 15:19:42				4.3
1/17/2006 15:42:06				7.9
1/17/2006 16:00:36				11.4
1/18/2006 07:33:42				0.3
1/18/2006 07:52:36				15.4
1/18/2006 08:07:54				21.1

Hewlett-Packard
Information Security Investigations
8000 Foothills Blvd / MS 5626
Roseville, Calif. 95747 - 5200

Privileged & Confidential
Attorney Work Product

invent

Investigative Report

1/18/2006 08:30:42		)	0.3
1/18/2006 09:30:30		p	0.5
1/18/2006 09:49:42		ıp	0.3
1/18/2006 11:03:30		)	1.5
1/18/2006 11:05:06		)	1.9
1/18/2006 11:08:42		)	0.3
1/18/2006 11:09:30		)	0.5
1/18/2006 11:15:12		)	0.8
1/18/2006 11:19:00		)	2.0
1/18/2006 12:47:30		)	1.5
1/18/2006 12:49:54		)	2.1
1/18/2006 13:11:12		)	2.8
1/18/2006 13:44:30		)	0.5
1/18/2006 14:53:42		)	0.3
1/18/2006 14:54:00		)	2.0
1/18/2006 14:57:24		)	0.6

Hewlett-Packard
Information Security Investigations
8000 Foothills Blvd / MS 5626
Roseville, Calif. 95747 - 5200

Privileged & Confidential
Attorney Work Product

hp invent

Investigative Report

1/18/2006 14:59:36		E		16.4
1/18/2006 15:15:48		E		4.2
1/18/2006 15:22:00		E		1.0
1/18/2006 15:57:36		E		1.4
1/18/2006 16:13:18		E		17.7
1/18/2006 16:32:00		E		1.0
1/18/2006 16:51:30		E		8.5
1/18/2006 17:05:18		E	F	3.7
1/18/2006 17:23:24		E		0.6
1/18/2006 17:25:00		E		2.0
1/18/2006 17:28:36		I		0.4
1/18/2006 17:35:00		I	F	2.0
1/18/2006 18:13:54		I		0.1
1/18/2006 18:18:18		I		0.7
1/19/2006 05:14:42		I		1.3
1/19/2006 09:29:36				0.4

Initials

Hewlett-Packard
Information Security Investigations
8000 Foothills Blvd / MS 5626
Roseville, Calif. 95747 - 5200

Privileged & Confidential
Attorney Work Product

invent

Investigative Report

1/19/2006 09:52:24			0.6
1/19/2006 09:53:48			1.2
1/19/2006 10:52:00			1.0
1/19/2006 11:07:00			1.0
1/19/2006 11:28:42			1.3
1/19/2006 11:30:48			2.2
1/19/2006 11:46:30			4.5
1/19/2006 11:59:36			1.4
1/19/2006 12:01:06			46.9
1/19/2006 12:59:42			0.3
1/19/2006 13:00:18			1.7
1/19/2006 13:02:30			0.5
1/19/2006 13:03:48			19.2
1/19/2006 13:32:30			21.5
1/19/2006 13:52:30			1.5
1/19/2006 13:55:00			7.0

Hewlett-Packard
Information Security Investigations
8000 Foothills Blvd / MS 5626
Roseville, Calif. 95747 - 5200

Privileged & Confidential
Attorney Work Product

invent

Investigative Report

1/19/2006 14:53:30	[redacted]	[redacted]	12.5
1/19/2006 15:49:00			12.0
1/19/2006 18:40:36			0.4
1/19/2006 18:41:00			4.0
1/20/2006 08:55:54			4.1
1/20/2006 09:00:42			0.3
1/20/2006 09:47:36			0.4
1/20/2006 09:59:30			0.5
1/20/2006 10:00:48			1.2
1/20/2006 10:02:06			17.9
1/20/2006 10:45:36			1.4
1/20/2006 11:02:18			0.7
1/20/2006 11:44:12			0.8
1/20/2006 11:59:24			0.6
1/20/2006 12:05:30			1.5
1/20/2006 12:18:48			3.2

Hewlett-Packard
Information Security Investigations
8000 Foothills Blvd / MS 5626
Roseville, Calif. 95747 - 5200

Privileged & Confidential
Attorney Work Product

invent

Investigative Report

1/20/2006 12:35:18			1.7
1/20/2006 12:51:42			5.3
1/20/2006 12:59:18			0.7
1/20/2006 13:01:42			2.3
1/20/2006 13:23:36			2.4
1/20/2006 13:32:00			1.0
1/20/2006 14:01:12			0.8
1/20/2006 14:04:36			1.4
1/20/2006 14:17:12			0.8
1/20/2006 14:19:36			0.4
1/20/2006 14:29:06			3.9
1/20/2006 14:30:24			2.6
1/20/2006 15:02:06			0.9
1/20/2006 15:04:12			0.8
1/20/2006 15:20:30			0.5
1/20/2006 17:26:24			0.6

Hewlett-Packard
Information Security Investigations
8000 Foothills Blvd / MS 5626
Roseville, Calif. 95747 - 5200

Privileged & Confidential
Attorney Work Product

invent

Investigative Report

[redacted]	[redacted]	[redacted]	Total Call Count	Total Duration
[redacted]	[redacted]	[redacted]	202	1,114.3

Attachment-4

Internet Research on CNET, Kawamoto, Krazit and Shankland

Email:

[redacted]

CNET telephone numbers:

[redacted]

IDG telephone numbers:

[redacted]

Hewlett-Packard
Information Security Investigations
8000 Foothills Blvd / MS 5626
Roseville, Calif. 95747 - 5200

Privileged & Confidential
Attorney Work Product

Investigative Report

Attachment-5

Date/Time	Incoming Origination	Extension	Destination	Duration
1/20/2006 14:28:54				4.1
1/20/2006 15:41:00				2.0
1/25/2006 10:08:27				1.8
1/25/2006 11:02:28				2.5
1/25/2006 12:16:21				6.1
1/26/2006 16:13:00				1.0
			Total Call Count	Total Duration
			6	17.5

Hewlett-Packard
Information Security Investigations
8000 Foothills Blvd / MS 5626
Roseville, Calif. 95747 - 5200

Privileged & Confidential
Attorney Work Product

Investigative Report

Attachment-6

Date/Time	Incoming Origination	Extension	Destination	Duration
1/27/2005 16:23:06				2.9
1/31/2005 11:08:54				15.1
2/1/2005 15:52:42				6.3
2/9/2005 08:03:24				2.6
2/9/2005 09:10:51				2.5
2/9/2005 09:45:06				0.9
2/9/2005 14:01:36				0.4
2/9/2005 15:42:42				0.3
2/9/2005 16:47:30				0.5
2/10/2005 13:03:00				1.0
2/10/2005				3.7

Hewlett-Packard
Information Security Investigations
8000 Foothills Blvd / MS 5626
Roseville, Calif. 95747 - 5200

Privileged & Confidential
Attorney Work Product

invent

Investigative Report

14:07:18						
2/10/2005 17:07:24						3.6
2/14/2005 09:44:42						3.3
2/14/2005 11:50:24						4.6
2/14/2005 11:55:30						1.5
2/15/2005 10:04:42						0.3
3/1/2005 09:44:30						0.5
3/1/2005 10:46:12						15.8
3/1/2005 14:19:00						1.0
3/7/2005 09:19:12						0.8
3/10/2005 15:24:18						6.7
3/21/2005 13:37:12						0.8
3/21/2005 15:27:00						1.0
3/28/2005 14:21:06						0.9
3/29/2005 13:13:06						1.9
3/29/2005 13:31:54						2.1

Hewlett-Packard
Information Security Investigations
8000 Foothills Blvd / MS 5626
Roseville, Calif. 95747 - 5200

Privileged & Confidential
Attorney Work Product

invent

Investigative Report

3/29/2005 14:14:18						7.7
3/29/2005 16:28:54						7.1
3/29/2005 16:54:18						6.7
4/1/2005 14:14:42						0.3
4/12/2005 14:08:00						2.0
4/12/2005 14:26:42						3.3
4/12/2005 16:21:42						12.3
4/13/2005 10:07:24						0.6
4/13/2005 12:42:24						0.6
4/13/2005 16:00:12						16.8
4/14/2005 16:58:30						9.5
4/15/2005 09:31:24						3.6
4/15/2005 16:43:45						1.6
4/18/2005 14:01:48						7.2
4/26/2005 13:24:54						5.1
4/27/2005 11:52:36						0.4

Hewlett-Packard
Information Security Investigations
8000 Foothills Blvd / MS 5626
Roseville, Calif. 95747 - 5200

Privileged & Confidential
Attorney Work Product

invent

Investigative Report

4/28/2005 16:03:18						11.7
5/2/2005 13:52:30						3.5
5/2/2005 14:24:18						1.7
5/3/2005 11:18:54						1.1
5/16/2005 13:52:06						2.9
5/16/2005 13:57:12						0.8
5/17/2005 13:14:12						5.8
5/18/2005 15:46:00						5.0
5/19/2005 08:15:30						0.5
5/23/2005 12:52:18						0.7
5/23/2005 14:09:48						2.2
5/23/2005 18:15:30						0.5
5/24/2005 18:10:36						0.4
5/25/2005 08:19:42						0.3
5/26/2005 11:41:18						2.7
5/26/2005 15:43:18						2.7

Initials

Hewlett-Packard
Information Security Investigations
8000 Foothills Blvd / MS 5626
Roseville, Calif. 95747 - 5200

Privileged & Confidential
Attorney Work Product

invent

Investigative Report

5/31/2005 11:02:30						3.5
5/31/2005 13:54:12						1.8
5/31/2005 16:17:36						4.4
5/31/2005 17:25:00						39.0
5/31/2005 18:33:18						3.7
6/1/2005 12:12:42						0.3
6/3/2005 13:35:54						1.1
6/3/2005 14:38:18						0.7
6/3/2005 15:19:48						13.2
6/6/2005 14:10:36						2.4
6/7/2005 14:54:36						0.4
6/8/2005 08:07:24						0.6
6/17/2005 14:49:24						0.6
6/27/2005 09:21:00						1.0
6/27/2005 14:49:00						17.0
6/30/2005 11:49:54						9.1

Hewlett-Packard
Information Security Investigations
8000 Foothills Blvd / MS 5626
Roseville, Calif. 95747 - 5200

Privileged & Confidential
Attorney Work Product

invent

Investigative Report

7/5/2005 13:17:36				4.4
7/5/2005 13:43:00				1.0
7/5/2005 16:01:42				1.3
7/5/2005 16:53:24				13.6
7/6/2005 11:15:12				5.8
7/7/2005 14:32:36				5.4
7/8/2005 14:47:24				0.6
7/8/2005 14:55:42				1.3
7/12/2005 12:28:30				1.5
7/12/2005 14:50:42				0.3
7/13/2005 15:51:54				2.1
7/14/2005 11:47:12				5.8
7/14/2005 12:35:06				5.9
7/14/2005 15:04:06				19.9
7/14/2005 16:50:36				0.4
7/15/2005 13:07:00				20.0

Hewlett-Packard
Information Security Investigations
8000 Foothills Blvd / MS 5626
Roseville, Calif. 95747 - 5200

Privileged & Confidential
Attorney Work Product

invent

Investigative Report

7/15/2005 14:58:36					42.4
7/15/2005 16:09:06					1.9
7/18/2005 09:31:42					1.3
7/18/2005 10:58:42					0.3
7/18/2005 16:14:54					2.1
7/19/2005 08:24:30					5.5
7/19/2005 12:56:06					5.9
7/19/2005 14:32:06					9.9
7/21/2005 09:16:48					1.2
7/27/2005 17:07:30					0.5
8/4/2005 09:01:00					4.0
8/9/2005 10:49:36					0.4
8/11/2005 14:47:18					5.7
8/16/2005 13:49:42					1.3
8/25/2005 13:21:48					1.2
9/16/2005 11:45:42					0.3

Hewlett-Packard
Information Security Investigations
8000 Foothills Blvd / MS 5626
Roseville, Calif. 95747 - 5200

Privileged & Confidential
Attorney Work Product

hp invent

Investigative Report

9/16/2005 11:54:54					4.1
9/19/2005 08:29:42					0.3
9/19/2005 10:33:12					10.8
10/10/2005 15:32:37					0.7
10/11/2005 12:20:12					2.8
10/17/2005 14:53:17					1.5
10/20/2005 12:05:42					0.6
10/24/2005 09:15:57					0.8
10/27/2005 12:18:40					0.6
10/27/2005 13:02:20					3.5
10/27/2005 16:59:48					6.2
10/28/2005 11:26:00					2.6
10/31/2005 12:50:10					0.7
11/1/2005 17:48:26					1.2
11/8/2005 10:41:30					1.5
11/14/2005 09:55:54					1.1

Hewlett-Packard
Information Security Investigations
8000 Foothills Blvd / MS 5626
Roseville, Calif. 95747 - 5200

Privileged & Confidential
Attorney Work Product

invent

Investigative Report

11/23/2005 13:56:12				12.8
11/28/2005 09:02:24				16.6
11/28/2005 16:44:18				1.7
12/1/2005 16:16:54				14.1
12/7/2005 09:22:42				0.3
12/7/2005 09:30:18				0.7
12/7/2005 09:59:36				3.4
12/8/2005 08:58:24				2.6
12/8/2005 13:52:18				0.7
12/9/2005 12:26:54				11.1
1/3/2006 13:34:18				0.7
1/4/2006 11:43:06				0.9
1/4/2006 13:45:36				4.4
1/4/2006 15:07:48				4.2
1/12/2006 09:18:06				2.9
1/12/2006 11:29:54				11.1

Initials

Hewlett-Packard
Information Security Investigations
8000 Foothills Blvd / MS 5626
Roseville, Calif. 95747 - 5200

Privileged & Confidential
Attorney Work Product

invent

Investigative Report

1/17/2006 09:01:30		[redacted]	[redacted]	0.5
1/25/2006 09:56:42				13.3
			Total Call Count	Total Duration
			140	621.1

Attachment-7

Date/Time	Incoming Origination	Extension	Destination	Duration
2/1/2005 12:21:42		[redacted]	[redacted]	0.3
2/3/2005 13:26:42				0.3
2/3/2005 16:03:12				2.8
2/9/2005 05:06:12				0.8
2/9/2005 16:52:42				0.3
2/9/2005 17:11:36				2.4
2/23/2005 17:37:12				0.8
2/23/2005 18:03:42	[redacted]			6.3
3/3/2005 14:25:18				0.7
3/21/2005 13:38:12				0.8

Hewlett-Packard
Information Security Investigations
8000 Foothills Blvd / MS 5626
Roseville, Calif. 95747 - 5200

Privileged & Confidential
Attorney Work Product

invent

Investigative Report

3/30/2005 14:55:12				1.8
3/30/2005 15:57:18				4.7
4/15/2005 17:10:06				0.9
5/17/2005 17:20:42				0.3
5/24/2005 16:58:24				0.6
5/25/2005 09:30:42				1.3
5/25/2005 09:32:24				8.6
6/2/2005 17:19:42				3.3
6/5/2005 12:10:54				0.1
6/9/2005 14:45:48				1.2
6/13/2005 09:57:00				1.0
6/13/2005 10:01:00				2.0
6/13/2005 10:11:42				0.3
6/13/2005 10:29:42				3.3
6/13/2005 12:33:06				0.9
6/13/2005 13:15:54				1.1

Hewlett-Packard
Information Security Investigations
8000 Foothills Blvd / MS 5626
Roseville, Calif. 95747 - 5200

Privileged & Confidential
Attorney Work Product

hp invent

Investigative Report

6/13/2005 13:22:12	Redacted	Redacted	Redacted	1.8
6/13/2005 15:54:06				2.9
6/15/2005 17:25:24				2.6
7/6/2005 17:12:06				3.9
7/11/2005 08:04:49				1.4
7/14/2005 16:56:42				0.3
7/15/2005 11:12:48				5.2
7/15/2005 15:00:36				3.4
7/18/2005 11:00:48				5.2
7/18/2005 17:33:24				9.6
7/19/2005 06:35:42				3.3
9/15/2005 09:08:36				7.4
10/25/2005 08:25:00				1.0
12/5/2005 19:00:24				7.6
12/8/2005 17:13:24				0.6
1/23/2006 16:57:36				1.4

Initials

Hewlett-Packard
Information Security Investigations
8000 Foothills Blvd / MS 5626
Roseville, Calif. 95747 - 5200

Privileged & Confidential
Attorney Work Product

invent

Investigative Report

[redacted]	[redacted]	[redacted]	Total Call Count	Total Duration
[redacted]	[redacted]	[redacted]	42	104.5

Attachment-8

------------------------Searching for Message ID 22669344AB------------------------
Jan 8 19:51:29 tayrelbas03 postfix/smtpd[10764]: 22669344AB: client=address.hp.com[192.151.81.14]
Jan 8 19:51:29 tayrelbas03 postfix/cleanup[10755]: 22669344AB: message-id=<e378bcc4a7ea.43c16d35@optonline.net>
Jan 8 19:51:29 tayrelbas03 postfix/qmgr[10489]: 22669344AB: from=<krazit@optonline.net>, size=8087, nrcpt=1 (queue active)
Jan 8 19:51:30 tayrelbas03 postfix/smtp[10688]: 22669344AB: to=<psa67302.routing@am3.exch.hp.com>, relay=tayexg12.americas.cpqcorp.net[16.103.130.127], delay=1, status=sent (250 2.6.0 <e378bcc4a7ea.43c16d35@optonline.net> Queued mail for delivery)
Jan 8 19:51:30 tayrelbas03 postfix/qmgr[10489]: 22669344AB: removed

------------------------Searching for Message ID 33D7D37CD9------------------------
Jan 26 13:34:32 palrel10 postfix/smtpd[4445]: 33D7D37CD9: client=cacexg12.americas.cpqcorp.net[16.92.1.72]
Jan 26 13:34:32 palrel10 postfix/cleanup[4528]: 33D7D37CD9: message-id=<8A5D221431633647BC24429483A06702079EB27E@cacexc05.americas.cpqcorp.net>
Jan 26 13:34:32 palrel10 postfix/qmgr[3740]: 33D7D37CD9: from=<ann.finnie@hp.com>, size=1548, nrcpt=1 (queue active)
Jan 26 13:34:33 palrel10 postfix/smtp[4019]: 33D7D37CD9: to=<tom.krazit@cnet.com>, relay=c12-mail.cnet.com[216.239.127.176], delay=1, status=sent (250 ok: Message 44705748 accepted)
Jan 26 13:34:33 palrel10 postfix/qmgr[3740]: 33D7D37CD9: removed

------------------------Searching for Message ID 0781336371------------------------
Jan 13 15:19:41 palrel10 postfix/smtpd[10032]: 0781336371: client=cacexg11.americas.cpqcorp.net[16.92.1.67]
Jan 13 15:19:41 palrel10 postfix/cleanup[10118]: 0781336371: message-id=<E1B5ED6D9758854BBA4ADB149BD646D702F07545@cacexc06.americas.cpqcorp.net>
Jan 13 15:19:41 palrel10 postfix/qmgr[9815]: 0781336371: from=<ryan.j.donovan@hp.com>, size=2306, nrcpt=1 (queue active)

Initials

Hewlett-Packard
Information Security Investigations
8000 Foothills Blvd / MS 5626
Roseville, Calif. 95747 - 5200

Privileged & Confidential
Attorney Work Product

invent

Investigative Report

Jan 13 15:19:43 palrel10 postfix/smtp[9922]: 0781336371: to=<Tom_Krazit@idg.com>, relay=idg.com.mail5.psmtp.com[64.18.5.10], delay=2, status=sent (250 Thanks)
Jan 13 15:19:43 palrel10 postfix/qmgr[9815]: 0781336371: removed

---------------------------Searching for Message ID DBAA5346C0---------------------------
Jan 13 14:00:44 palrel10 postfix/smtpd[7652]: DBAA5346C0: client=cacexg13.americas.cpqcorp.net[16.92.1.76]
Jan 13 14:00:44 palrel10 postfix/cleanup[7402]: DBAA5346C0: message-id=<1B041AED29D9DD439A568D592ABD80E6018DDF53@cacexcsp04.americas.cpqcorp.net>
Jan 13 14:00:44 palrel10 postfix/qmgr[6028]: DBAA5346C0: from=<robert.sherbin@hp.com>, size=2301, nrcpt=1 (queue active)
Jan 13 14:00:29 palrel10 postfix/smtp[7599]: DBAA5346C0: to=<Tom_Krazit@idg.com>, relay=idg.com.mail5.psmtp.com[64.18.5.10], delay=-15, status=sent (250 Thanks)
Jan 13 14:00:29 palrel10 postfix/qmgr[6028]: DBAA5346C0: removed

---------------------------Searching for Message ID 6C83D36A5D---------------------------
Jan 13 13:56:35 palrel11 postfix/smtpd[21322]: 6C83D36A5D: client=atarelrim04.atl.hp.com[192.151.27.12]
Jan 13 13:56:35 palrel11 postfix/cleanup[20945]: 6C83D36A5D: message-id=<OFA09A0CAC.1F77FF5D-ON852570F5.0075D286-882570F5.0078601D@ipsidg.com>
Jan 13 13:56:35 palrel11 postfix/qmgr[20141]: 6C83D36A5D: from=<Tom_Krazit@idg.com>, size=2194, nrcpt=1 (queue active)
Jan 13 13:56:35 palrel11 postfix/smtp[21218]: 6C83D36A5D: to=<rsh46703.routing@am4.exch.hp.com>, relay=cacexg11.americas.cpqcorp.net[16.92.1.67], delay=0, status=sent (250 2.6.0 <OFA09A0CAC.1F77FF5D-ON852570F5.0075D286-882570F5.0078601D@ipsidg.com> Queued mail for delivery)
Jan 13 13:56:35 palrel11 postfix/qmgr[20141]: 6C83D36A5D: removed

---------------------------Searching for Message ID 3CE0D34419---------------------------
Jan 26 16:54:40 palrel12 postfix/smtpd[22055]: 3CE0D34419: client=smtp.cce.hp.com[161.114.21.24]
Jan 26 16:54:40 palrel12 postfix/cleanup[22063]: 3CE0D34419: message-id=<A4E1DBA513CA414B8C13A0B5C74436BA9DE46B@CNET6.cnet.cnwk>
Jan 26 16:54:40 palrel12 postfix/qmgr[18805]: 3CE0D34419: from=<Tom.Krazit@cnet.com>, size=2644, nrcpt=1 (queue active)
Jan 26 16:54:41 palrel12 postfix/smtp[21906]: 3CE0D34419: to=<afi1977.routing@am4.exch.hp.com>, relay=cacexg13.americas.cpqcorp.net[16.92.1.76], delay=2, status=sent (250 2.6.0 <A4E1DBA513CA414B8C13A0B5C74436BA9DE46B@CNET6.cnet.cnwk> Queued mail for delivery)
Jan 26 16:54:41 palrel12 postfix/qmgr[18805]: 3CE0D34419: removed

Hewlett-Packard
Information Security Investigations
8000 Foothills Blvd / MS 5626
Roseville, Calif. 95747 - 5200

Privileged & Confidential
Attorney Work Product

invent

Investigative Report

Attachment-9

-- Postfix id E22D234494 --

```
-
Jan 11 14:59:41 palrel10 postfix/smtpd[10822]: E22D234494:
client=cacexg11.americas.cpqcorp.net[16.92.1.67]
Jan 11 14:59:41 palrel10 postfix/cleanup[10869]: E22D234494: message-
id=<52C656C82F0D174F80D963B4C30DDE11059937F3@cacexc05.americas.cpqcorp.net>
Jan 11 14:59:42 palrel10 postfix/qmgr[9678]: E22D234494: from=<elizabeth.archibald@hp.com>,
size=1836, nrcpt=1 (queue active)
Jan 11 14:59:42 palrel10 postfix/smtp[10010]: E22D234494: to=<Stephen.Shankland@cnet.com>,
relay=c12-mail.cnet.com[216.239.127.176], delay=1, status=sent (250 ok:  Message 40634518 accepted)
Jan 11 14:59:42 palrel10 postfix/qmgr[9678]: E22D234494: removed
```

Initials

Hewlett-Packard
Information Security Investigations
8000 Foothills Blvd / MS 5626
Roseville, Calif. 95747 - 5200

Privileged & Confidential
Attorney Work Product

invent

Investigative Report

Attachment-10

	Owner	Location
(408)[redacted]	Cindy Carpenter(hotel phone)	Cup Bldg 49D U cube 3-b02-00
(408)[redacted]	Boulders Conf	Cup Bldg. 45 SU
(650)[redacted]	Shane Robinson (Poly at his desk)	20B Pillar B9F
(650)[redacted]	Commitee Room (Poly)	20B Pillar B9F
(650)[redacted]	Exec Conf Room	20B Pillar B9F
(650)[redacted]	Buffalo Conf Room(Poly)	20B Pillar B3L
(650)[redacted]	Vernal Conf Room	3 Lower Pillar J33

TAB 20

From: Hunsaker, Kevin <kevin.hunsaker@hp.com>
Sent: Saturday, January 28, 2006 11:15 AM
To: Adler, Frederick P. <fred.adler@hp.com>; Gentilucci, Anthony R. <tony.gentilucci@hp.com>; Nye, Vince <vince.nye@hp.com>
Subject: RE: perkins -- privileged communication

thanks.

Kevin T. Hunsaker
Senior Counsel
HP Legal Department
650 857-3079 (phone)
650 857-3710 (fax)
[redacted](voicemail network number)

-----Original Message-----
From: Adler, Frederick P.
Sent: Saturday, January 28, 2006 10:53 AM
To: Hunsaker, Kevin; Gentilucci, Anthony R.; Nye, Vince
Subject: RE: perkins -- privileged communication

Even if we could legally obtain the records, which we can't unless we either pay the bill or get consent, I would highly suspect text messaging records are not kept due to volume and expense. The only other means is through real time interception, an avenue not open to us.

Fred Adler
HP IT Security Investigations
(916)[redacted] fred.adler@hp.com

-----Original Message-----
From: Hunsaker, Kevin
Sent: Saturday, January 28, 2006 10:40 AM
To: Adler, Frederick P.; Gentilucci, Anthony R.; Nye, Vince
Subject: perkins -- privileged communication

Hi Fred,

Apparently, Perkins almost never uses his cell phone, and instead does just about everything via text message. Is there any way to lawfully get text message content, or is it the same as the cell phone records?

Kevin

Kevin T. Hunsaker
Senior Counsel
HP Legal Department
650 857-3079 (phone)
650 857-3710 (fax)
[redacted] (voicemail network number)

HP 00379

TAB 21

From: Hunsaker, Kevin <kevin.hunsaker@hp.com>
Sent: Saturday, January 28, 2006 5:47 PM
To: Gentilucci, Anthony R. <tony.gentilucci@hp.com>
Subject: investigation – privileged communication

Hi Tony,

So, I plunked out a very rough draft of an email we could send to Kawamoto. We would obviously need to prepare a document to send along with it, but I could easily put one together based on the Acquisition Committee slides.

We DEFINITELY need to get the approval of Ann, Mark and Pattie before doing it, but I think it's a very-creative idea that just might work.

Here's the draft:

Dawn,

As I said in my first message, I am an avid reader of your columns, and they are typically very accurate and current. However, the piece you wrote last Monday about a potential CSC deal never making the radar of HP's executives and directors was completely inaccurate. It was definitely on our radar—I know, because I was involved in the discussions. And, the directors most certainly knew about it – I know because I was involved in preparing the briefing documents.

I don't think I'm comfortable sharing many details at this point, but I can tell you it was initially called Project _______ [kth comment – I'll get the original name of the project]. In fact, I've attached a portion of one of the documents that was first used to brief the Board. Please feel free to share it with your HP "sources" to see if it jogs their memory about whether CSC was on our radar. However, please DO NOT publish the document. There is a fairly small group of people who have access to this document, so publishing the document will make it much more likely that HP will be able to find out I gave it to you.

Once you've confirmed that I know what I'm talking about (and that your other source or sources were dead wrong), maybe I can give you a few additional details about the deal.

Thanks for listening. Actually, just telling you this makes me feel like I've just lifted a huge weight off my chest.

Jacob

Kevin T. Hunsaker
Senior Counsel
HP Legal Department
650 857-3079 (phone)
650 857-3710 (fax)
[redacted] (voicemail network number)

TAB 22

From: Gentilucci, Anthony R. <tony.gentilucci@hp.com>
Sent: Saturday, January 28, 2006 9:05 PM
To: Hunsaker, Kevin <kevin.hunsaker@hp.com>
Subject: RE: investigation – privileged communication

Kevin,

I like it, but I am guessing there is an e-mail before this one, to keep her on a string while we get the green light, or red light, and gives us time to think the e-mail through a bit more. And maybe there is a second before the "document e-mail", play it out a bit. A question in my mind, do we interview Moeller Wednesday, or does the word get out (Moeller/Others) that we are "actively" investigating this? Something to talk about Monday. What if we get a cell phone with a NM exchange, we never answer it, voicemail, but it may get her brain racing, could cause her to call JK, and/or the CNET reporter it's dad. etc., etc., maybe we should do it before Keyworth's speech.......

Let's work it through, I like it.

Tonu

From: Hunsaker, Kevin
Sent: Saturday, January 28, 2006 8:47 PM
To: Gentilucci, Anthony R.
Subject: investigation -- privileged communication

Hi Tony,

So, I plunked out a very rough draft of an email we could send to Kawamoto. We would obviously need to prepare a document to send along with it, but I could easily put one together based on the Acquisition Committee slides.

We DEFINITELY need to get the approval of Ann, Mark and Pattie before doing it, but I think it's a very creative idea that just might work.

Here's the draft:

Dawn,

As I said in my first message, I am an avid reader of your columns, and they are typically very accurate and current. However, the piece you wrote last Monday about a potential CSC deal never making the radar of HP's executives and directors was completely inaccurate. It was definitely on our radar—I know, because I was involved in the discussions. And, the directors most certainly knew about it – I know because I was involved in preparing the briefing documents.

I don't think I'm comfortable sharing many details at this point, but I can tell you it was initially called Project _______ [kth comment – I'll get the original name of the project]. In fact, I've attached a portion of one of the documents that was first used to brief the Board. Please feel free to share it with your HP "sources" to see if it jogs their memory about whether CSC was on our radar. However, please DO NOT publish the document. There is a fairly small group of people who have access to this document, so publishing the document will make it much more likely that HP will be able to find out I gave it to you.

Once you've confirmed that I know what I'm talking about (and that your other source or sources were dead wrong), maybe I can give you a few additional details about the deal.

Thanks for listening. Actually, just telling you this makes me feel like I've just lifted a huge weight off my chest.

Jacob

Kevin T. Hunsaker
Senior Counsel
HP Legal Department
650 857-3079 (phone)
650 857-3710 (fax)

HP 03375

TAB 23

From: Hunsaker, Kevin <kevin.hunsaker@hp.com>
Sent: Saturday, January 28, 2006 9:13 PM
To: Gentilucci, Anthony R. <tony.gentilucci@hp.com>
Subject: RE: investigation -- privileged communication

I agree -- there's definitely an email that comes before this saying Jacob feels more comfortable interacting via email.

The Moeller question is one we should get the whole team's input on. I hadn't considered that word may get out if we start interviewing him, Bergkamp, etc.

Keyworth doesn't live in [redacted]anymore. He lives in [redacted] Heck, we could leave Kawamoto a voicemail after hours from an HP conference room in Palo Alto Wednesday or Thursday, then she'd know it was coming from an HP person. Of course, I'm not sure we want this directly traceable back to HP . . . .

In any event, I think it will make for a healthy discussion on Monday.

Kevin T. Hunsaker
Senior Counsel
HP Legal Department
650 857-3079 (phone)
650 857-3710 (fax)
[redacted](voicemail network number)

-----Original Message-----
From: Gentilucci, Anthony R.
Sent: Saturday, January 28, 2006 9:05 PM
To: Hunsaker, Kevin
Subject: RE: investigation -- privileged communication

Kevin,

I like it, but I am guessing there is an e-mail before this one, to keep her on a string while we get the green light, or red light, and gives us time to think the e-mail through a bit more. And maybe there is a second before the "document e-mail", play it out a bit. A question in my mind, do we interview Moeller Wednesday, or does the word get out (Moeller/Others) that we are "actively" investigating this? Something to talk about Monday. What if we get a cell phone with a NM exchange, we never answer it, voicemail, but it may get her brain racing, could cause her to call JK, and/or the CNET reporter II's dad. etc., etc., maybe we should do it before Keyworth's speech.......

Let's work it through, I like it.

Tonu

From: Hunsaker, Kevin
Sent: Saturday, January 28, 2006 8:47 PM
To: Gentilucci, Anthony R.
Subject: investigation -- privileged communication

Hi Tony,

So, I plunked out a very rough draft of an email we could send to Kawamoto. We would obviously need to prepare a document to send along with it, but I could easily put one together based on the Acquisition Committee slides.

We DEFINITELY need to get the approval of Ann, Mark and Pattie before doing it, but I think it's a very creative idea that just might work.

Here's the draft:

Dawn,

As I said in my first message, I am an avid reader of your columns, and they are typically very accurate and current. However, the piece you wrote last Monday about a potential [redacted]deal never making the radar of HP's executives and directors was completely inaccurate. It was definitely on our radar—I know, because I was involved in the discussions. And, the directors most certainly knew about it – I know because I was involved in preparing the briefing documents.

I don't think I'm comfortable sharing many details at this point, but I can tell you it was initially called Project _______ [kth comment – I'll get the original name of the project]. In fact, I've attached a portion of one of the documents that was first used to brief the Board. Please feel free to share it with your HP "sources" to see if it jogs their memory about whether [redacted] was on our radar. However, please DO NOT publish the document. There is a fairly small group of people who have access to this document, so publishing the document will make it much more likely that HP will be able to find out I gave it to you.

Once you've confirmed that I know what I'm talking about (and that your other source or sources were dead wrong), maybe I can give you a few additional details about the deal.

Thanks for listening. Actually, just telling you this makes me feel like I've just lifted a huge weight off my chest.

Jacob

Kevin T. Hunsaker
Senior Counsel
HP Legal Department
650 857-3079 (phone)
650 857-3710 (fax)
[redacted] (voicemail network number)

TAB 24

From: Gentilucci, Anthony R. <tony.gentilucci@hp.com>
Sent: Saturday, January 28, 2006 9:51 PM
To: Hunsaker, Kevin <kevin.hunsaker@hp.com>
Subject: RE: investigation -- privileged communication
Attach: Draft _ DK Letter_Privileged Communications.doc

Kevin,

I think we have to figure out who Jacob is, weak, strong, vindictive, a Bill and Dave fan, possibly lower level employee, (admin?), will dictate the tone of the e-mail, that kind of influenced my changes.

Tony

From: Hunsaker, Kevin
Sent: Sunday, January 29, 2006 108 AM
To: Gentilucci, Anthony R.
Subject: investigation -- privileged communication

Hi Tony,

I fiddled with the first version. Not sure either version has the right tone, but it's a start. I inserted a little blurb about Pui Wing Tam, which I thought might feed any competitive fire in Kawamoto. I also inserted the original name of the project. And, I've created the document we can use -- it's an actual slide from the Acquisitions Committee presentation, but it only contains publicly available information about CSC (except that I include the name of the project).

Dawn,

As I said in my first message, I often read your columns, and they are typically very accurate and current. In fact, I have found that you and Pui Wing Tam from the WSJ provide the most consistent, accurate accounts of what is going on at HP. However, the piece you wrote last Monday about a potential CSC deal never making the radar of HP's executives and directors was completely inaccurate. It was definitely on our radar -- I know, because I was involved in the discussions. And, the directors most certainly knew about it -- I know because I was involved in preparing the briefing documents.

I don't think I'm comfortable sharing many details at this point, but I can tell you it was initially called Project Lion. In fact, I've attached a portion of one of the documents that was first used to brief members of the BoD. While it doesn't specifically identify CSC, it could not be clearer that CSC is the target company -- just check the CSC website to confirm the accuracy of the data. Please feel free to share it with your other HP "sources" to see if it jogs their memory about whether CSC was on our radar. However, please DO NOT publish the document. There is a fairly small group of people who have access to this document, so publishing the document will make it much more likely that HP will be able to find out I gave it to you.

Once you've confirmed that the information set forth about is accurate (and that your other source or sources were dead wrong), maybe I can give you a few additional details about the deal. I'm not sure it's a BIG story, but the deal may not be completely dead....

Thanks for listening. Actually, just telling you this makes me feel like I've lifted a huge weight off my chest.

Jacob

Kevin T. Hunsaker
Senior Counsel
HP Legal Department
650 857-3079 (phone)
650 857-3710 (fax)
[redacted](voicemail network number)

Dawn,

~~As I said in my first message, I often read your~~ *(I don't think we should suck up to her too much, lets come across more executive level type, direct??)* Your columns are typically very accurate and current. *(I wouldn't front PWT's name, knowledge is power, she may think we are dealing with her too, let her think she is exclusive, and most importantly, PWT is a seasoned reporter, sharp, from what I understand, this business is incestuous, in particular in Bay Area, they may team up, figure something out – I say isolate her);* ~~In fact, I have found that you and Pui-Wing Tam from the WSJ provide the most consistent, accurate accounts of what is going on at HP.~~ The piece you wrote last Monday about a potential CSC deal never making the radar of HP's executives and directors was completely inaccurate. It was definitely on ~~our~~ HP's radar -- ~~I know, because I was involved in the discussions.~~ ~~(Again I think that is too much information, next line gives her a taste but not the whole nine yards, she may think, exec and/or admin)~~ And, the directors most certainly knew about it – I know because I was involved in preparing the briefing documents *and more.*

I need to think through a few things before I give you some additional insights, this isn't something I thought I would do, but in time, if I share what I know, my motivation will be easy to see. So at this time I don't think I'm comfortable sharing *many more details.* ~~at this point.~~ I can tell you it was initially called Project Lion. In fact, I've attached a portion of one of the documents that was first used to brief members of the BoD. While it doesn't specifically identify CSC, it could not be clearer that CSC is the target company -- just check the CSC website to confirm the accuracy of the data. ~~Please feel free to share it with your other HP "sources" to see if it jogs their memory about whether CSC was on our radar. However, please DO NOT publish the document.~~ *(Kevin, it could be the investigator in me, but that seems like a set-up, we have to assume she will do that, need to play the game a bit, I think) Obviously, keep the document close hold. (I think the document is after an e-mail like paragraph one, then paragraph II is the bulk of the content for a third e-mail/document)* ~~There is a fairly small group of people who have access to this document, so publishing the document will make it much more likely that HP will be able to find out I gave it to you.~~

Once *you learn that* ~~you've confirmed that the~~ *(again assume she will corroborate)* information set forth about is accurate, *unlike your previous sources,* (and that your other source or sources were dead wrong), maybe I can give you a few additional details about the deal, because . ~~I'm not sure it's a BIG story, but~~ that deal *and there may be others,* (*not sure about the language here, just some thoughts)* may not be completely dead . . . .

Thanks for listening. ~~Actually, just telling you this makes me feel like I've lifted a huge weight off my chest. (~~

Jacob

From: Hunsaker, Kevin <kevin.hunsaker@hp.com>
Sent: Sunday, January 29, 2006 8:01 AM
To: Gentilucci, Anthony R. <tony.gentilucci@hp.com>
Subject: RE: investigation -- privileged communication
Attach: Draft _ DK Letter_Privileged Communications.doc

He's already identified himself as a senior executive and that he was tired of broken promises, misguided initiatives and generally bad treatment. So, I think we have to stick with that as his baseline persona. He also sucked up to her in the first email ["I am an avid reader of your columns"], which is why I stuck with it in the one I wrote.

I think most of the changes you suggest look good. I fiddled with it a little more, made it shorter and more to the point, etc. Let me know what you think.

Kevin

Kevin T. Hunsaker
Senior Counsel
HP Legal Department
650 857-3079 (phone)
650 857-3710 (fax)
1220 8573079 (voicemail network number)

-----Original Message-----
From: Gentilucci, Anthony R.
Sent: Saturday, January 28, 2006 9:51 PM
To: Hunsaker, Kevin
Subject: RE: investigation -- privileged communication

Kevin,

I think we have to figure out who Jacob is, weak, strong, vindictive, a Bill and Dave fan, possibly lower level employee, (admin?), will dictate the tone of the e-mail, that kind of influenced my changes.

Tony

From: Hunsaker, Kevin
Sent: Sunday, January 29, 2006 108 AM
To: Gentilucci, Anthony R.
Subject: investigation -- privileged communication

Hi Tony,

I fiddled with the first version. Not sure either version has the right tone, but it's a start. I inserted a little blurb about Pui Wing Tam, which I thought might feed any competitive fire in Kawamoto. I also inserted the original name of the project. And, I've created the document we can use -- it's an actual slide from the Acquisitions Committee presentation, but it only contains publicly available information about CSC (except that I include the name of the project).

Dawn,

As I said in my first message, I often read your columns, and they are typically very accurate and current. In fact, I have found that you and Pui Wing Tam from the WSJ provide the most consistent, accurate accounts of what is going on at HP. However, the piece you wrote last Monday about a potential CSC deal never making the radar of HP's executives and directors was completely inaccurate. It was definitely on our radar -- I know, because I was involved in the discussions. And, the directors most certainly knew about it -- I know because I was involved in preparing the briefing documents.

I don't think I'm comfortable sharing many details at this point, but I can tell you it was initially called Project Lion. In fact, I've attached a portion of one of the documents that was first used to brief members of the BoD. While it doesn't specifically identify CSC, it could not be clearer that CSC is the target company -- just check the CSC website to confirm the accuracy of the data. Please feel free to share it with your other HP "sources" to see if it jogs their memory about whether CSC was on our radar. However, please DO NOT publish the document. There is a fairly small group of people who have access to this document; so publishing the document will make it much more likely that HP will be able to find out I gave it to you.

Once you've confirmed that the information set forth about is accurate (and that your other source or sources were dead wrong), maybe I can give you a few additional details about the deal. I'm not sure it's a BIG story, but the deal may not be completely dead . . . .

Thanks for listening. Actually, just telling you this makes me feel like I've lifted a huge weight off my chest.

Jacob

Kevin T. Hunsaker
Senior Counsel
HP Legal Department
650 857-3079 (phone)
650 857-3710 (fax)
1220 8573079 (voicemail network number)

TAB 25

From: Hunsaker, Kevin <kevin.hunsaker@hp.com>
Sent: Monday, January 30, 2006 12:33 PM
To: Gentilucci, Anthony R. <tony.gentilucci@hp.com>
Subject: RE: phone records -- privileged communication

I shouldn't have asked . . . .

Kevin T. Hunsaker
Senior Counsel
HP Legal Department
650 857-3079 (phone)
650 857-3710 (fax)
1220 8573079 (voicemail network number)

-----Original Message-----
From: Gentilucci, Anthony R.
Sent: Monday, January 30, 2006 12:00 PM
To: Hunsaker, Kevin
Subject: RE: phone records -- privileged communication

The methodology utilized is social engineering, he has investigators call operators under some ruse, to obtain the call record over the phone, its verbally communicated to the investigator, who has to write it down. In essence the Operator shouldn't give it out, and that person is liable in some sense, Ron can describe the operation obviously better, as well as the fact that this technique since he, and others, have been using it, has not been challenged. I think its on the edge, but above board. We use pretext interviews on a number of investigations to extract information and/or make covert purchases of stolen property, in a sense, all under cover operations.

Tony

From: Hunsaker, Kevin
Sent: Monday, January 30, 2006 2:32 PM
To: Gentilucci, Anthony R.
Subject: phone records -- privileged communication

Hi Tony,

How does Ron get cell and home phone records? Is it all above board?

Kevin

Kevin T. Hunsaker
Senior Counsel
HP Legal Department
650 857-3079 (phone)
650 857-3710 (fax)
1220 8573079 (voicemail network number)

HP 00054

TAB 26

From: Hunsaker, Kevin <kevin.hunsaker@hp.com>
Sent: Monday, January 30, 2006 8:39 PM
To: Gentilucci, Anthony R. <tony.gentilucci@hp.com>
Subject: Things done/to be done – privileged communication

Hi Tony,

Here's a list off the top of my head of the things I've done, the interviews we've conducted, and the interviews we will likely need to conduct at some point. I'm sure there's a ton more, but this was the stuff that immediately came to mind.

Kevin

Actions taken (by KTH):

- Obtain and review all presentations from Board and Committee meetings
- Obtain and review all Board meeting minutes from 2000 to present
- Electronic background research on Kawamoto, Krazit, Shankland and PWT
- Review articles, columns and blogs containing info from "sources" written by Kawamoto, Krazit, Shankland and PWT
- Prepare summary of articles by Kawamoto citing a "source" or "sources"
- Prepare possible electronic correspondence and document to be sent to Kawamoto by fictitious HP executive
- Review materials from previous investigation – KONA
- Compile list of all who attended the January Board meeting
- Obtain detailed contact info on BoD
- Obtain detailed contact info on HP media contacts
- Obtain detailed contact info on EC members
- Daily Team meetings to discuss progress and new developments

Interviews conducted to date:

- Ann Baskins – several background and fact finding interviews (KTH)
- Bob Sherbin – interview conducted by Nye and Adler
- Charles Charnas – background on Acquisitions Committee meeting; Project Club (KTH)
- Mark Hurd – informal discussion between Jim Fairbaugh and MH

Interviews to be conducted:

- Shane Robison – he runs/oversees the Technology and Acquisition Committees (next week?)
- Marius Haas – he prepared and finalized all the slides for the Board meeting (next week?)
- Bob Wayman – exposure to individuals, issues and dynamics involved (Thursday)
- Alan Haggard – details re: Technology Committee meeting (Tuesday or Wednesday)
- Brigida Bergkamp – unexplained searches for Kawamoto on Friday the 20th (next week?)
- Michael Moeller – lots of contacts with PWT (next week?)
- Pattie Dunn – Chairman of Board, exposure and insight into individuals, issues and dynamics (Thursday)
- Tom Perkins – one of main subjects (next few weeks)
- Jay Keyworth – one of main subjects (next few weeks)
- Dick Hackborn – next level subject (next few weeks)

Kevin T. Hunsaker
Senior Counsel
HP Legal Department
650 857-3079 (phone)
650 857-3710 (fax)
1220 8573079 (voicemail network number)

TAB 27

From: Hunsaker, Kevin <kevin.hunsaker@hp.com>
Sent: Tuesday, January 31, 2006 10:54 AM
To: Nye, Vince <vince.nye@hp.com>
Subject: RE: Privileged Communication - HP CONFIDENTIAL

It should have been attached to Ron's original message -- the article written by Tam that came out this morning. If it wasn't, let me know and I'll forward it to you.

Kevin T. Hunsaker
Senior Counsel
HP Legal Department
650 857-3079 (phone)
650 857-3710 (fax)
1220 8573079 (voicemail network number)

-----Original Message-----
From: Nye, Vince
Sent: Tuesday, January 31, 2006 10:52 AM
To: Hunsaker, Kevin
Subject: RE: Privileged Communication - HP CONFIDENTIAL

Kevin: Nothing is attached....

From: Hunsaker, Kevin
Sent: Tuesday, January 31, 2006 10:33 AM
To: 'Ron DeLia'; Gentilucci, Anthony R.; Nye, Vince; Adler, Frederick P.
Subject: RE: Privileged Communication - HP CONFIDENTIAL

Team,

Just spoke with Ann -- she and Pattie want this to be made part of the investigation. There is information in the article that is both accurate and VERY non-public. Not many sources within HP had access to this info -- the entire Board was well aware of it, though.

Fred, can you pull phone records related to Tam out of Palo Alto? Maybe we should wait until tomorrow AM to do that, so we'll have everything through yesterday afternoon.

Kevin T. Hunsaker
Senior Counsel
HP Legal Department
650 857-3079 (phone)
650 857-3710 (fax)
1220 8573079 (voicemail network number)

-----Original Message-----
From: Ron DeLia [mailto:rrd@security-outsourcing.com]
Sent: Tuesday, January 31, 2006 7:01 AM
To: Hunsaker, Kevin; Gentilucci, Anthony R.; Nye, Vince; Adler, Frederick P.
Subject: Privileged Communication - HP CONFIDENTIAL

KONA Attorney-Client Privileged Communication - HP CONFIDENTIAL

Guys,

Pick up on Reuters by Tony, this AM.

See attached article referencing by Tam.

HP 00583

Ron

Security Outsourcing Solutions, Inc.
Tel: (617) 426-3900 or (781) 444-9616

TAB 28

From: Hunsaker, Kevin <kevin.hunsaker@hp.com>
Sent: Wednesday, February 1, 2006 6:23 PM
To: Gentilucci, Anthony R. <tony.gentilucci@hp.com>
Subject: FW: Privileged Communication - HP CONFIDENTIAL

Kevin T. Hunsaker
Senior Counsel
HP Legal Department
650 857-3079 (phone)
650 857-3710 (fax)
1220 8573079 (voicemail network number)

-----Original Message-----
From: Ron DeLia [mailto:rrd@security-outsourcing.com]
Sent: Saturday, January 28, 2006 11:50 AM
To: Hunsaker, Kevin; Gentilucci, Anthony R.; Nye, Vince; Adler, Frederick P.
Subject: Privileged Communication - HP CONFIDENTIAL
Importance: High

Attorney-Client Privileged Communication - HP CONFIDENTIAL

Guys,

We have initiated contact and begun a dialogue Dawn Kawamoto, via a hotmail email account. DK's response indicates she prefers to have contact with her sources, by telephone from her office line [redacted] between 5:00 AM to 2:00 PM, Monday through Friday. We have not responded to DK's reply. I suggest a con call with the team to put together a plan to maintain a dialogue with DK.

Following is the initial email sent to DK.

Hello, I am a senior level executive with a high tech firm in the valley and an avid reader of your columns.
My real name is not used, you might understand why. Not quite sure how to approach you on this, but I'll attempt anyway.
In short, tired of broken promises, misguided initiatives and generally bad treatment.

Have some information that I would be interested in passing along.
Felt it might be appropriate to contact you.

Below is DK's response.

Attorney-Client Privileged Communication - HP CONFIDENTIAL

Hi Jacob,

The descriptions you gave below can apply to a number of high tech firm in the valley. So, yes, please give me a call. I would suggest calling is the best way to handle this.

I can be reached at the office from 5 am to 2 pm (PST), Mon.-Fri. My number is below. Just identify yourself as Jacob from the e-mail when you call.

Thanks, Dawn

Dawn Kawamoto, Senior Reporter
CNET News.com

HP 00725

415.344.2238 ofc.

Security Outsourcing Solutions, Inc.
Tel: (617) 426-3900 or (781) 444-9616

TAB 29

Project KONA II

Attorney Client Privileged
DO NOT COPY OR FORWARD
WITHOUT AUTHORIZATION

Initial Briefing – Pattie Dunn
February 2, 2006
Palo-Alto, CA

DO NOT COPY OR FORWARD WITHOUT AUTHORIZATION

hp

HP 03752

Project KONA II

- **Investigation Team:**
  - **Cross functional team of experts**
    - Kevin Hunsaker, HP Legal – Global SBC Team
    - Anthony R. Gentilucci, Manager, Global Security Investigations
    - Vince Nye, Global Security Investigations
      - Two investigative analysts, Global Security Investigations
    - Tim O'Neill, Manager, IT Security Investigations
    - Fred Adler, IT Security Investigations
    - Denis Lynch, Global Employee Protection Program
    - Ron Delia, Security Outsourcing Solutions
      - External security support
      - Multiple security investigators and analysts
    - Other security consulting firms

HP 03754

Investigation Approach:

- **Investigation Objective:**
  - Determine the identity of the individual or individuals leaking confidential, non-public HP information to media personnel, or other third parties, without authorization
    - Due to the nature of the information being leaked, the investigation is focused mainly on internal sources, such as members of the BoD, the EC and other HP employees with access to sensitive information.
    - While time is of the essence, the investigation must be comprehensive, accurate, and in compliance with all laws and accepted investigative principles.

HP 03755

Investigation Approach:

Investigative Advantages:

- As a result of relationships established during KONA I with Media Relations, the Investigation Team was aware of the issue immediately
  - Multiple investigative tasks initiated on 20-JAN-06, three days *before* the article was published
- Significant relevant information immediately available as a result of previous investigation
- New Unauthorized Disclosure Investigation Team mobilized
  - Resources from previous investigation teamed with new resources
    - No learning curves
    - No down time
- Attorney-Client Privilege quickly invoked

HP 03756

Investigation Approach:

- **Investigation Landscape:**
  - As in the past, and unlike most "Unauthorized Disclosure" investigations, the subjects of this inquiry are primarily external to the HP IT infrastructure, databases, and other company records
  - Ability to track, trace and document evidence of a leak is more difficult
  - Uncovering direct, tangible evidence will be difficult
  - Likelihood of multiple leaks impacts ability to track, trace and identify specific sources
  - Confidentiality of the investigation
    - Impacts investigative alternatives and decisions

HP 03757

Investigation Activity Update:

- **Investigation Team:**
  - Since 20-JAN-06 investigative resources have been working on investigation 24x7
  - Daily Team meetings to discuss progress and new developments
    - All investigative alternatives are being considered
  - Meeting with Brian Jenkins to consultant on options in our plan

- **Obtain BoD Meeting Information:**
  - Attendees, location, dates, times
    - Subcommittee meetings
    - After hour events
  - Hotel records
  - Presentations, minutes from all meetings
  - Review document distribution, collection and destruction
  - Interview of key personnel who coordinated and attended the meeting
    - BoD Administration
    - HP Global Security
      - Review countermeasures activity
      - Pre-BoD Security Activities
      - Post-BoD Security Activities

HP 03758

Investigation Activity Update:

Interviews – Background Information

- Ann Baskins
- Bob Sherbin
- Charles Charnas
- Mark Hurd
- Alan Hagard
- Brian Jenkins
- Industry media expert – background information

HP 03759

Investigation Activity Update:

- **Research and Analysis:**
  - Extensive review of previous materials from KONA I
  - Collect key contact information on pertinent subjects
    - HP employees (EC and others)
    - BoD
    - Media
  - Phone records
  - E-mail records
  - HP Internet proxy servers
  - Comprehensive backgrounds on 8 subjects and affiliated persons
  - Media Analysis:
    - CNET Articles
    - WSJ Articles
    - IDG Articles
  - Electronic background research on pertinent media people of interest: DK, TK, SS and PWT
    - Extensive Media and Internet Content Research to develop links to Members of the BOD, other reporters or HP employees.
    - Review articles, columns and blogs containing info from "sources" written by DK, TK, SS and PWT
    - Summary of articles by Kawamoto citing a "source" or "sources"
    - Development of link analysis between media, BoD, HP Media Relations
  - Development of time line with key events

HP 03760

Investigation Activity Update:

- Undercover Operation:
  - Contact established covertly with DK via a non-traceable hotmail email account. A dialogue has been established. Further planning of this operation is in progress.
- Surveillance/Intelligence Operations:
  - Intelligence gathering effort to document communications for all pertinent subjects of the investigation.
  - Pre-trash inspection survey is in progress for key subjects of the investigation.
    - Legal assessment of activity
  - Pre-surveillance reconnaissance is in progress for G.K., DK, PWT, SS, and TK
  - Surveillance activity was conducted for G.K. speech in CO on January 31, 2006.
  - Feasibility studies are in progress for undercover operations (clerical) in CNET and WSJ offices in SF, CA.
- Anticipated Interviews (BoD):
  - Ann Baskins 360° discussions – opportunity to construct surgical questions
  - Consult with behavioral analysis consulting firm for possible participation in interview process

HP 03761

What We Know – General Examples:

- The leaker or leakers were present in person at the various Committee and Board meetings
  - Interviews – Slide Review
- Three of the specific items from the DK article likely came directly from the Technology Committee meeting.
  - JK; TP; BR; DH; H; PD; MH; AL; SR; AH
- GH and JK were encouraged by CF during the merger to develop a relationship with DK
  - Analysis indicates that JK has most likely provided anonymous quotes to DK in the past (March 2002)
  - Previous investigation documented JK had direct relationships with other media reporters
- Both TP and JK have previously made internal statements similar to those contained in the article
  - More than one person has heard TP and JK make certain statements that appeared in the January 23rd article

HP 03762

What We Know – Link Analysis:

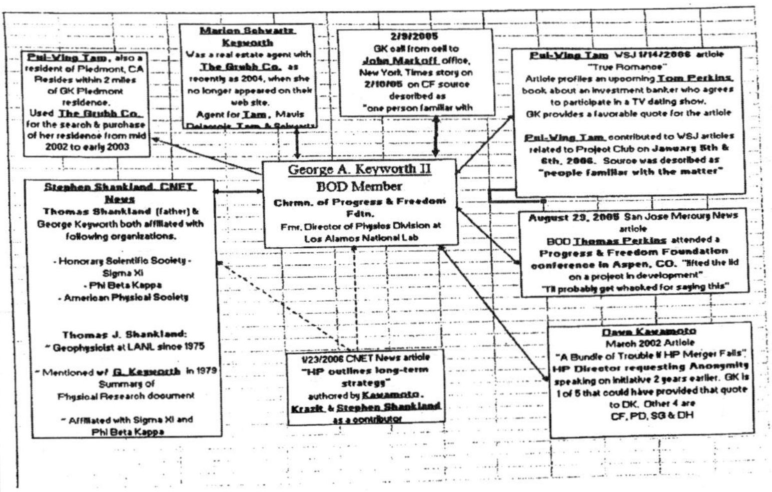

HP 03763

What We Know – Link Analysis:

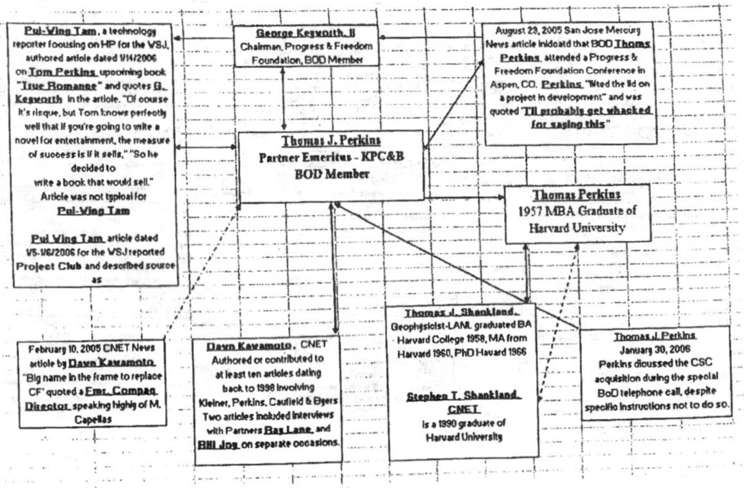

ATTORNEY CLIENT PRIVILEGED***DO NOT COPY OR FORWARD***

HP 03764

Anticipated Next Steps:

- **Actions Planned:**
- Multi-focused investigation
  - Not just BoD or EC focused
    - Multiple leaks over time
    - BoD – EC
    - Media Relations
    - Others?
- Complete all ongoing research, intelligence gathering and analysis
- Implement any surveillance activity deemed appropriate
- Make a decision on undercover operation
- Continue to conduct information gathering and subject interviews
- Assessment of information to determine next steps and possible interviews of BoD and EC members
- Scheduled updates to Pattie Dunn; Ann Baskins; Mark Hurd
- Forward Thinking: Security and investigation plan for March BoD meeting in Los Angeles
  - Countermeasures
  - Document security
    - Technical tracking
  - Undercover operation
  - Intelligence Gathering

- **Potential Interviews:**
  - Shane Robison – HP exec responsible for Technology and Acquisition Committees
  - Marius Haas -- he prepared and finalized all the slides for the Board meeting
  - Bob Wayman -- exposure to individuals, issues and dynamics involved (Friday)
  - Brigida Bergkamp -- unexplained searches for Kawamoto on Friday the 20th (next few weeks)
  - Michael Moeller -- lots of contacts with PWT (next few weeks)
  - Tom Perkins -- one of main subjects (next few weeks)
  - Jay Keyworth -- one of main subjects (next few weeks)
  - Dick Hackborn -- next level subject (next few weeks)

Other Investigative Options Under Review:

- Forensic assessment of BoD members systems for external compromise
- IT tool to capture data on the systems of HP employees, possibly BoD members
- Expand monitoring capabilities of BoD website
- BoD Interviews (multiple possible techniques)
- Covert undercover operations
  - Placement of agent in close proximity to person of interest
  - Most likely location – new agencies
- Misinformation/sting scenario(s)
- Polygraph examination of pertinent subjects
  - Not recommended
- Other

HP 03766

HP 03767

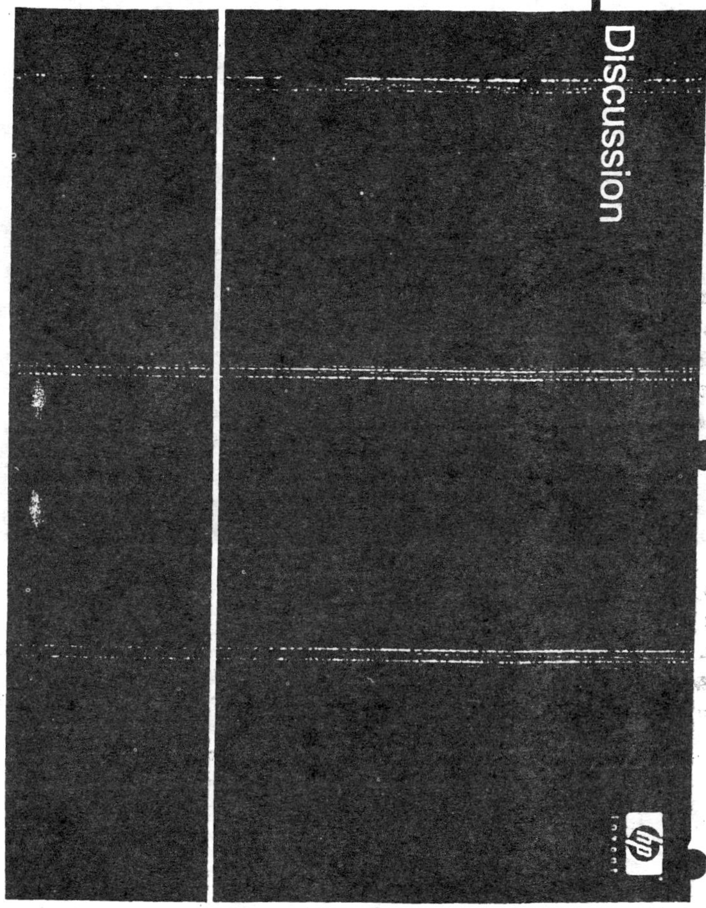

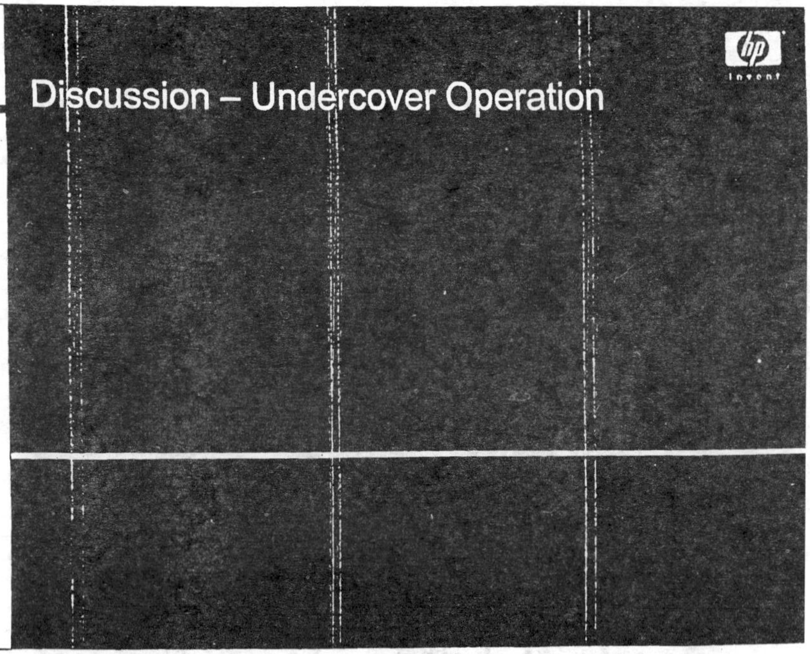

HP 03768

Responses to Covert E-mail

26-JAN-06

Hello, I am a senior level executive with a high tech firm in the valley and an avid reader of your columns. My real name is not used, you might understand why. Not quite sure how to approach you on this, but I'll attempt anyway.

In short, tired of broken promises, misguided initiatives and generally bad treatment.

Have some information that I would be interested in passing along.
Felt it might be appropriate to contact you.

28-JAN-06:
"Hi Jacob, The descriptions you gave below can apply to a number of high tech firm in the valley. So, yes, please give me a call. I would suggest calling is the best way to handle this. I can be reached at the office from 5 am to 2 pm (PST), Mon.-Fri. My number is below. Just identify yourself as Jacob from the e-mail when you call. Thanks, Dawn

Dawn Kawamoto,
Senior Reporter CNET News.com415.344.2238 ofc."

30-JAN-06:
Hi,
Back in the office if you want to give a call.
Dawn
Dawn Kawamoto, Senior Reporter
CNET News.com
415.344.2238 ofc.

HP 03769

Proposed "next step" covert e-mail

Dawn,

I've read a number of your columns, and have found that they are typically very accurate and current. However, the piece you wrote last Monday about a potential CSC deal never making the radar of HP's executives and directors was completely inaccurate. It was definitely on HP's radar, and that directors most certainly knew about it – I know because I was involved in preparing the briefing documents.

I can tell you the CSC deal was originally called Project Lion, and I've attached a slide from one of the documents that was first used to brief members of the BoD. While the slide doesn't specifically identify CSC, it couldn't be clearer that CSC is the target company.

Jacob

Project Lion Overview

Margin %	6.4%	6.5%	6.5%	6.7%

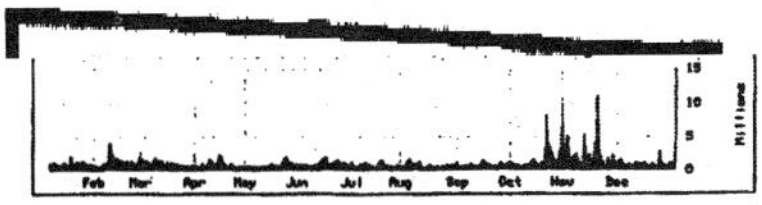

03771

Source: Capital IQ
August 14, 2006

HP outlines long-term strategy
CNET / Jan. 23, 2006
By Dawn Kawamoto

- Hewlett-Packard executives are mulling plans to improve over the next 18 months the technology the company uses to manage its direct sales, while it continues with commercial printing efforts and acquisitions of software companies.
- Two weeks ago, HP CEO Mark Hurd, the company's board of directors and senior executives gathered at the computer giant's annual management retreat to discuss long-term strategies.
- HP execs are mulling plans to improve over the next 18 months the technology the company uses to manage its direct sales, while it continues with commercial printing efforts and acquisitions of software companies.
- In marathon sessions that spanned the course of several days at the posh Esmeralda Resort & Spa in Indian Wells, Calif., HP's leadership hashed out HP's long-term strategy. **Those in attendance worked from early morning to late evening, with few breaks given beyond meals, said a source with the company.**
- **By the time the lectures were done at 10 p.m., we were pooped and went to bed," the source said.** An HP representative declined to comment on the planning sessions.
- **According to the source, HP is considering making more acquisitions in the infrastructure software arena.**
- Those acquisitions would include security software companies, storage software makers and software companies that serve the blade server market.
- The acquisitions would dovetail with HP's growth plans for its Technology Systems Group, which has already bought companies such as AppIQ for storage management.
- Hurd has previously said market trends indicate a movement away from mainframe computers and a shift to blade servers, as well as virtualized storage. HP is likely to follow those trends.
- Meanwhile, in HP's Imaging & Printing Group, the long-term plan to develop commercial printers is likely to continue.
- **"We want to develop the next Heidelberg press," the source said.** Of course, HP said basically the same thing back in 2002.
- On the chip front, although HP and Intel have had a long relationship involving their collaboration on the Itanium chip, **delays by Intel have created frustration in the HP camp, the source said.**

HP 03772

HP outlines long-term strategy
CNET / Jan. 23, 2006
By Dawn Kawamoto

- As a result, HP may use Intel's archrival Advanced Micro Devices as a cattle prod of sorts to the chip giant, the source noted.
- "We plan to use AMD's Opteron more and more," the source said.
- Opteron competes chiefly with x86 chips such as Intel's Xeon. HP sells ProLiant-brand servers with as many as four Opteron or Xeon processors. However, x86 chips have steadily gained in computing power and overlap in abilities with HP's lower-end Itanium servers.
- Intel declined to comment, other than to note that HP has been a very valuable partner, said Scott McLaughlin, an Intel spokesman. Personal Systems Group
- **One area expected to get an internal technology revamp in the coming year and a half is direct sales, the HP source said.**
- Last July, HP announced that it had hired Randy Mott, Dell's former chief information officer. Mott, who serves as HP's CIO, previously managed Dell's Internet and Web-based infrastructure and had also worked at retailing giant Wal-Mart Stores, where he devised the retail and supply chain automation systems.
- Mott will help HP implement the back-end processes that are needed to operate a top-notch direct-order Web site, said Roger Kay, president of Endpoint Technologies Associates. Information-intensive tasks like gathering and sorting reams of customer data and quickly reacting to changes in component costs are vital to improving the efficiency of a direct sales operation, and Mott's experience implementing such a system at Dell will be invaluable to HP, Kay said.
- At the same time, HP has to avoid antagonizing its retail and channel partners with a renewed push toward direct sales, he said.
- "When you go from direct to indirect, the only people who get upset are your own sales force," Kay said. "But if you've got distribution and you go direct, you're competing against the people that help you."
- Improving its direct-sales operation allows HP to get closer to its customers and learn more about the areas the company needs to improve, said Stephen Baker, director of industry analysis at NPD Techworld. This could actually help HP's retail and channel business by allowing it to understand what its channel partners go through when making a sale or dealing with support, he said everyone can understand.

HP outlines long-term strategy
CNET / Jan. 23, 2006
By Dawn Kawamoto

- HP has little choice but to improve its direct sales model to compete with Dell and to sell its products more efficiently, said Baker. Retailers are faced with the same problem, and several have resorted to carrying inexpensive private-label brands to compete against direct sales vendors, he said.
- **Though HP's direct sales technology is expected to undergo changes, one thing that's not likely to happen is a merging of the HP and Compaq PC brands, the source said.** Because the Compaq brand is still recognized in the market, it offsets the additional costs associated with maintaining two brands, the source said.
- This approach makes sense, but HP needs to do a better job of differentiating between the two brands, Baker said.
- The Compaq brand has gone through several changes since HP bought Compaq, from a leading PC brand to the low-cost position it currently occupies within HP, he said.
- Clearly, getting a better handle on what customers want is a big item on the agenda. Hurd has already talked about developing a next-generation data center architecture, which would consolidate the information it has spread across 700 different locations into a data center that would provide one, simplified view of its information.
- Through its beefed up data center, HP hopes to gain a greater understanding of its customers and markets, Hurd has said in the past.
- And from a services perspective, HP is hoping to leverage its own beefed-up data center with its services business, via running customer data through its own center.
- **And while HP has struggled with getting customers and the market to understand its "Adaptive Enterprise" concept, the same mistake will *not* happen with HP's "Next Generation Data Center Architecture," the source said.**
- **"Adaptive Enterprise. What is that? No one understood it," the source said. "But the 'Next Generation Data Center' is something that everyone can understand. The name is (cumbersome). Don't be surprised to see it changed."**

HP 03774

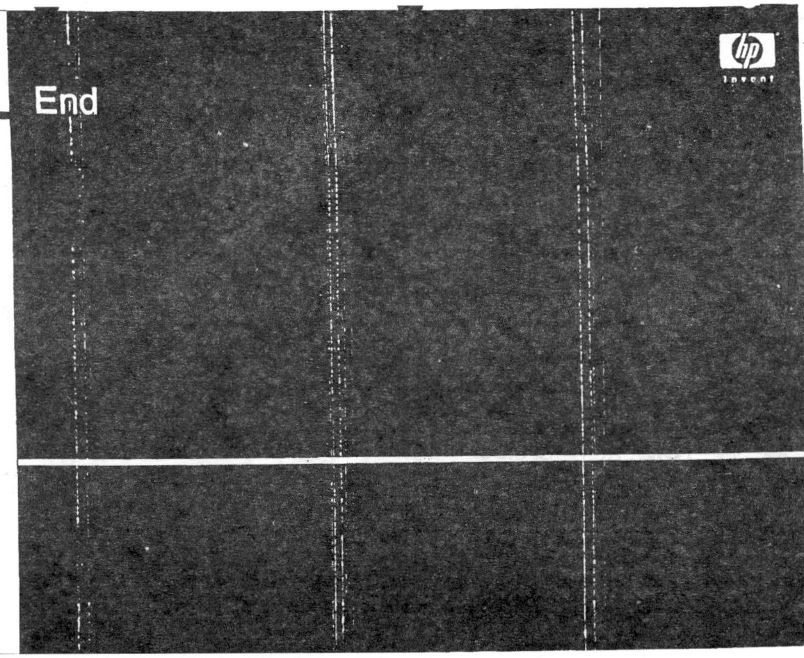

HP 03775

Proactive recommendations for consideration:

- Have BoD sign confidentiality agreement that documents "unauthorized disclosures" subject to civil litigation
  - More "teeth" than verbal attestation
  - Benchmarking could be initiated by investigation team on other "like" efforts
- Initiate Information Security "risk assessment" of the entire BoD communications process
- Implement IT Security tracking methodology for electronic soft copies of documents posted to the BoD web site
- Have all BoD electronic communications conducted within the HP IT infrastructure
  - More Secure; provide BoD members with communication equipment; laptops, possible cell phones

HP 03776

TAB 30

Project KONA II
DRAFT 1.0

Attorney Client Privilege
DO NOT COPY OR FORWARD
WITHOUT AUTHORIZATION

Senior Management Briefing
February 2, 2006
Palo-Alto, CA

DO NOT COPY OR FORWARD WITHOUT AUTHORIZATION

hp

HP 03685

Project KONA II

- Introductions
- Investigation Background and Approach
- Investigation Results and Conclusions
- Investigative Options
- Recommendations
- Discussion

Project KONA II

- **Investigation Team:**
  - Cross functional team of experts
    - Kevin Hunsaker, HP Legal – Global SBC Team Legal liaison
    - Anthony R. Gentilucci, Manager, Global Security Investigations
    - Vince Nye, Global Security Investigations
      - Two investigative analysts, Global Security Investigations
    - Fred Adler, IT Security Investigations
    - Denis Lynch, Global Employee Protection Program
    - Ron Delia, Security Outsourcing Solutions
      - External security consultancy support
      - Multiple security investigators and analyst
    - Other security consulting firms
    - Daily Team meetings to discuss progress and new developments
    - Since 20-JAN-06 investigative resources have been working on investigation 24x7

Project KONA II

- **Previous Investigation Update:**
  - After last briefing, July 22, 2005, additional investigative work into September did not produce any new significant leads
  - Once the CEO was in place for several months, the environment seemed to stabilize
  - Additionally, the key subject of the investigation, Knowling, left the BoD
  - With environment stabilized, investigation team deemed that interviews of previous leaks, months later, may in fact create turmoil with stabilized BoD.
    - Broad based interviews of the BoD appeared not to be constructive at the time
  - In the interim, per proactive recommendations, HP Unauthorized Information Disclosure Team was developed and implemented.
    - 24X7 Operation facilitated by CITSIRT
    - GSI and IT Security led initiatives
    - Analyst assigned to team scan media daily

Investigation Approach

- **Investigation Objective:**
  - Confirm and/or deny that a source or sources, internal to HP and/or the HP BoD, is providing proprietary HP information to media personnel, or other third parties, without authorization
  - Focus of investigation is on HP interests, HP BoD, versus external parties, however, investigation involves determining if associations and relationships exist between BoD members and members of the media
  - Conduct comprehensive and expeditious investigation in an effort to resolve this issue as soon as possible

Investigation KONA I: What are the differences from KONA II?
  - As a result of the communication established after KONA I with HP MR, notification to the team of an issue was immediate
    - Multiple investigative tasks immediately the evening of 20-JAN-06
  - Wealth of information that took months to develop was already in hand from past investigation
  - New Unauthorized Disclosure Investigation mobilized
    - Resources utilized and familiar with past investigation were teamed with new resources
    - No learning curves
    - No down time
  - Attorney-Client Privilege quickly invoked
- **Investigation Limitations:**
  - As in the past, unlike most "Unauthorized Disclosure" investigations, the subjects of this inquiry are primarily external to the HP IT infrastructure, databases, and other company records.
  - Ability to track, trace and document evidence of a leak is more difficult
- **Investigation Predicate:**
  - Any and all legal investigative methodologies under consideration to optimize the success of the cross functional team notified hours by HP Media Relations

HP 03689

Investigation Activity Update:

- **Chronicling of BoD Meeting:**
  - Attendees, location, dates, times
    - Subcommittee meetings
    - After hour events
  - Hotel records pull
  - Minutes of the meetings
  - Review document distribution, collection and destruction
  - Presentation collection and content review
  - Interview of key personnel who coordinated or attended the meeting
    - BoD Administration
    - HP Global Security
      - Review countermeasures activity
      - Pre-BoD Security Activities (Report Received)
      - Post-BoD Security Activities (Report Received)
- **Interviews – Background Only:**
  - Ann Baskins -- several background and fact finding interviews (KTH)
  - Bob Sherbin -- interview conducted by Nye and Adler
  - Charles Charnas -- background on Acquisitions Committee meeting; Project Club (KTH)
  - Mark Hurd -- informal discussion between Jim Fairbaugh and MH
  - Rosemary Thomas – Denis Lynch
  - Industry media expert – background information (RD)

HP 03690

Investigation Activity Update:

- **Research and Analysis:**
  - Extensive review of previous materials from KONA I
    - Review media and public records for interested parties retrieved during first investigation to assess any potential affiliations to Tom Krazit, Dawn Kawamoto, Stephen Shankland and Pui-Wing Tam.
  - Collect key contact information on pertinent subjects
    - HP employees
    - BoD
    - Media
  - Phone records
  - E-mail records
    - Analysis of the above for any links between concerned parties and salient events
  - Due diligence investigations on 8 subjects and affiliated persons
    - Background Investigation to include employment, property, civil and criminal records and other proprietary and public records to prepare a profile of occupation, employment, education, address history, personal and professional acquaintances.

- **Research and Analysis (cont.):**
  - Media Analysis:
    - CNET Article
    - WSJ Articles
    - Pull of all recent pertinent articles
  - Electronic background research on Kawamoto, Krazit, Shankland and PWT
    - Extensive Media and Internet Content Research to develop links to Members of the BOD or other reporters or HP employees.
    - Review articles, columns and blogs containing info from "sources" written by Kawamoto, Krazit, Shankland and PWT
    - Summary of articles by Kawamoto citing a "source" or "sources" Analysis of above with presentations, conversations and events at BoD meeting
  - Development of link anlysis between media, BoD, HP Media Relations
  - Development of time line with key events
  - Consult with behavioral analysis consulting firm for possible participation in interview process

Investigation Activity Update:

- **Covert Operations:**
  - Contact established covertly with Dawn Kawamoto via a non-traceable hotmail email account. A dialogue has been established. Further planning of this operation is in progress.
    - NOTE: Discussion topic, to we attempt to establish s similar contact with Pui-Wing Tam.
  - Intelligence gathering effort to document communications for all pertinent subjects of the investigation.
  - Pre-trash inspection survey is in progress for key subjects fof the investigation.
  - Pre-surveillance reconnaissance is in progress for G.K., Kawamoto, Tam, Shankland and Krazit. Note: Due to T.P.'s travel schedule, which is part, is reported on in the press, may not allow for surveillance activity. However, preliminary intelligence gathering is in progress.
- **Covert Operations (cont.):**
  - Surveillance activity is scheduled for G.K. speech in CO on January 31, 2006. Pre-surveillance intelligence gathering and plans have been prepared and the surveillance team has been assembled and will be operational January 30, 2006. Note: Intelligence gathering is continuing and briefing is schedule for 9:00 PM this evening.
  - Feasibility studies are in progress for undercover operations (clerical) in CNET and WSJ offices in SF, CA.
  - Feasibility studies are in progress for undercover operations (cleaning company employees) for the buildings were the WSJ and CNET SF Bureau offices are located.

Investigation Results to Date:

- To Be Completed on Wednesday at our meeting

Anticipated Investigation Activity

- **Next Steps: General Strategy**
  - Complete all ongoing research, intelligence gathering and analysis
  - Implement any surveillance activity deemed appropriate
  - Make a decision on undercover operation
  - Conduct probability assessment of all information
  - Conduct information gathering and subject interviews of BoD and Media Relations
  - Report back to Patti Dunn; Ann Baskins; Mark Hurd

- **Interviews:**
  - Shane Robison -- he runs/oversees the Technology and Acquisition Committees (next week?)
  - Marius Haas -- he prepared and finalized all the slides for the Board meeting (next week?)
  - Bob Wayman -- exposure to individuals, issues and dynamics involved (Thursday)
  - Alan Haggard -- details re: Technology Committee meeting (Tuesday or Wednesday)
  - Brigida Bergkamp -- unexplained searches for Kawamoto on Friday the 20th (next few week)
  - Michael Moeller -- lots of contacts with PWT (next few week)
  - Pattie Dunn -- Chairman of Board, exposure and insight into individuals, issues and dynamics (Thursday)
  - Tom Perkins -- one of main subjects (next few weeks)
  - Jay Keyworth -- one of main subjects (next few weeks)
  - Dick Hackborn -- next level subject (next few weeks)

Other Investigative Options Under Review:

- Polygraph examination of pertinent subjects
- Covert undercover operation (placement of agent in close proximity to person of interest)
  - Most likely location – new agencies
- Misinformation initiative
- Other

HP 03695

Discussion

Proactive recommendations for consideration:

- Have BoD sign confidentiality agreement that documents "unauthorized disclosures" subject to civil litigation
  - More "teeth" than verbal attestation
  - Benchmarking could be initiated by investigation team on other "like" efforts
- Initiate Information Security "risk assessment" of the entire BoD communications process
- Implement IT Security tracking methodology for electronic soft copies of documents posted to the BoD web site
- Have all BoD electronic communications conducted within the HP IT infrastructure
  - More Secure; provide BoD members with communication equipment; laptops, possible cell phones

TAB 31

From: Hunsaker, Kevin <kevin.hunsaker@hp.com>
Sent: Thursday, February 2, 2006 8:36 PM
To: Nye, Vince <vince.nye@hp.com>; Gentilucci, Anthony R. <tony.gentilucci@hp.com>; Adler, Frederick P. <fred.adler@hp.com>; Ron DeLia <rrd@security-outsourcing.com>; Lynch, Denis J (Global Security) <denis.j.lynch@hp.com>; O'Neill, Timothy (IT Security) <tim.oneill@hp.com>
Subject: Great Job! – privileged communication

Team,

Late this afternoon, I met with Ann Baskins, who had a meeting with Pattie shortly after we briefed her. According to Ann, Pattie indicated that she thought we were doing an excellent job, and that she was confident we are doing everything possible to identify the individual or individuals who are leaking information.

I just wanted to say thanks for putting in all the long hours and working so hard to gather as much relevant information as we have in such a short period of time. It is truly all of your hard work that has made us look so good. I really think we've positioned ourselves as well as possible to break this case. Great investigative teams make their own luck, and I think we're really going to get a good break on this one and identify the culprit(s).

Thanks again for everything you've done so far. Let's keep the pressure on and see what we can come up with.

Kevin

Kevin T. Hunsaker
Senior Counsel
HP Legal Department
650 857-3079 (phone)
650 857-3710 (fax)
1220 8573079 (voicemail network number)

TAB 32

From: Ron DeLia
Sent: 02/03/2006 07:53:46 AM
To: Hunsaker, Kevin; Gentilucci, Anthony R.; Nye, Vince; Adler, Frederick P.
Subject: KONA Privileged Communication - HP CONFIDENTIAL

Tony/Kevin,

Please forward the police report for the theft of Keyworth's laptop in [redacted] I have spoken to our investigators in [redacted]. Our contacts will talk with the local police and inform them we are interesting in obtaining the laptop and there is a reward for its return. We will also contact the local criminal element and inform them there is a reward (no questions asked) for the return of the laptop.

Ron

The content of this email transmission is intended only for the use of the individual or entity named above and may contain legally privileged or confidential information. If you are not the intended recipient, you are hereby notified that any disclosure, copying, dissemination, distribution, or use of this email transmission, or information contained herein, is strictly prohibited. If you have received this email transmission in error, please destroy all copies of this email and its attachments and notify the person whose name appears above.

Security Outsourcing Solutions, Inc.
Tel: (617) 426-3900 or (781) 444-9616

TAB 33

From: Hunsaker, Kevin <kevin.hunsaker@hp.com>
Sent: Friday, February 3, 2006 10:28 AM
To: Nye, Vince <vince.nye@hp.com>; Adler, Frederick P. <fred.adler@hp.com>; Gentilucci, Anthony R. <tony.gentilucci@hp.com>; Ron DeLia <rrd@security-outsourcing.com>; O'Neill, Timothy (IT Security) <tim.oneill@hp.com>; Lynch, Denis J (Global Security) <denis.j.lynch@hp.com>
Subject: FW: Investigation -- privileged communication

Team,

I wanted to share with you all the email I received from Pattie Dunn this morning. As you can see, she was impressed with what we put together for her and is confident we are on the right track.

Great job, guys. It's a pleasure to be part of such a quality team.

Kevin

Kevin T. Hunsaker
Senior Counsel
HP Legal Department
650 857-3079 (phone)
650 857-3710 (fax)
1220 8573079 (voicemail network number)

-----Original Message-----
From: Pattie [mailto:[redacted]]
Sent: Friday, February 03, 2006 9:46 AM
To: Hunsaker, Kevin
Subject: Re: Investigation -- privileged communication

Kevin, I came away with a good sense of what you and the team are doing, and encouraged that this effort is on the right track. As discussed, this is an unusually sensitive matter and we need to tap into the necessary expertise wherever it resides. I will count on you and the team to continue to do so.

Regards,
Pattie

-----Original Message-----
From: "Hunsaker, Kevin" <kevin.hunsaker@hp.com>
Date: Thu, 2 Feb 2006 19:32:22
To:"Pattie" [redacted]
Subject: Investigation -- privileged communication

Hi Pattie,

Thank you for taking such a big chunk of time out of your schedule to meet with us today. It was very helpful to get your thoughts and insights regarding the information contained in the article and the possible motivation behind the disclosures. I hope you found our overview of where things stand and where we're headed helpful.

I will have Fred Adler get in touch with you in the next day or two to discuss the transfer of the emails you mentioned during our discussion.

Thanks again for meeting with us.

HP 00590

Kevin

Kevin T. Hunsaker
Senior Counsel
HP Legal Department
650 857-3079 (phone)
650 857-3710 (fax)
1220 8573079 (voicemail network number)

Sent via BlackBerry from Cingular Wireless

TAB 34

From: Adler, Frederick P.
Sent: 02/03/2006 07:45:21 PM
To: Hunsaker, Kevin; Gentilucci, Anthony R.; Nye, Vince; O'Neill, Timothy (IT Security)
Subject: RE: tracer -- privileged communication

I took some time to ponder on this issue and came up with the following thoughts:

Any action we take should be viewed from a risk vs. reward perspective, as there is inherent risk in any action, this included.

Will this move be detected??? We have no idea as there are so many variables that exist out of our control. Adequate testing today could be inadequate as early as tomorrow. So let's view this from the worst case scenario, the possibility it is detected:

1) The document gets trashed......................No harm done

2) The document is somehow "sanitized"........No harm done

3) Human greed and curiosity wins over, the document is opened/unblocked anyway.......... We win

4) The web bug is detected and analyzed:

a. Does the recipient really want to announce their findings? They have no idea if there is one web bug or several. Media people know that announcing their discovery can jeopardize their source and offer success to those responsible. Employees receiving the document would be in the same position.

b. If a covert, non-HP addressed server is used for serving the web bug, they have no idea who is truly responsible, assuming proper protections are in place. Probing the web bug server jeopardizes the media and increases the chances of their receiving the document being discovered. They can only look to the anonymous "informant" as possibly unreliable, and possibly HP as a source, but there is nothing they can prove, unless they can link the covert server to HP.

We might also consider establishing a second contact, prior to sending the bug. We can then develop trust in the second source prior to sending the web bug. If the first is "informant" is "burned", the second "informant" can then continue. This approach is far more effective than trying to establish a second contact after the first is compromised and allows us a second chance to try another tactic, such as feeding a bogus document.

Any other thoughts anyone?????????????

Fred

Fred Adler
HP IT Security Investigations
(916)[redacted] fred.adler@hp.com

-----Original Message-----
From: Hunsaker, Kevin
Sent: Friday, February 03, 2006 4:26 PM
To: Adler, Frederick P.; O'Neill, Timothy (IT Security)
Subject: tracer -- privileged communication

Hi guys,

If/when we put the tracer in an email and/or document to the reporter, is there any chance it will be discovered? Is it something that a firewall could pick up, or anti-virus? Maybe if I ask it this way: would it make it through HP's security stuff and get to, say, my email?

This needs to be part of the risk assessment. If CNET knows something like that was sent to them, and they ultimately trace it back to us somehow, we could end up with some seriously bad publicity.

Thanks.

Kevin

Kevin T. Hunsaker
Senior Counsel
HP Legal Department

650 [redacted] (phone)
650 [redacted] (fax)
[redacted] (voicemail network number)

TAB 35

From: Hunsaker, Kevin [mailto:kevin.hunsaker@hp.com]
Sent: Friday, February 03, 2006 10:49 PM
To: Ron DeLia
Cc: Gentilucci, Anthony R.
Subject: RE: directors -- privileged communication

Thanks Ron. I now strongly believe it's Keyworth. I also think Perkins is leaking info for personal reasons, but I think BOTH January 23rd articles by Kawamoto were leaked by Keyworth. Can you please see if we can find out Marion Keyworth's cell number and pull those records? And, can we try to figure out where Keyworth was the week before and the week after the Board meeting? We should figure out who he could have been with and check their cell phone records, too.

Maybe you, me and Tony can get on the phone over the weekend and I can explain my logic.

Thanks very much.

Kevin

Kevin T. Hunsaker
Senior Counsel
HP Legal Department
650 857-3079 (phone)
650 857-3710 (fax)
1220 8573079 (voicemail network number)

-----Original Message-----
From: Ron DeLia [mailto:rrd@security-outsourcing.com]
Sent: Friday, February 03, 2006 5:53 PM
To: Hunsaker, Kevin
Subject: RE: directors -- privileged communication

Kevin,

See attached list, which was obtained from SEC filings.

Ron

The content of this email transmission is intended only for the use of the individual or entity named above and may contain legally privileged or confidential information. If you are not the intended recipient, you are hereby notified that any disclosure, copying, dissemination, distribution, or use of this email transmission, or information contained herein, is strictly prohibited. If you have received this email transmission in error, please destroy all copies of this email and its attachments and notify the person whose name appears above.

Security Outsourcing Solutions, Inc.
Tel: (617) 426-3900 or (781) 444-9616

-----Original Message-----
From: Hunsaker, Kevin [mailto:kevin.hunsaker@hp.com]
Sent: Friday, February 03, 2006 8:09 PM
To: Ron DeLia
Subject: directors -- privileged communication

Hi Ron,

Who were the HP Board members in 2000?

Kevin

Kevin T. Hunsaker
Senior Counsel
HP Legal Department
650 857-3079 (phone)
650 857-3710 (fax)

HP 00734

TAB 36

From: Ron DeLia [rrd@security-outsourcing.com]
: Sunday, February 05, 2006 10:38 AM
To: Hunsaker, Kevin; Gentilucci, Anthony R.; Nye, Vince; Adler, Frederick P.
Subject: RE: Privileged Communication - HP CONFIDENTIAL

Kevin,

It is also interesting; Rachel Konrad (Stephen Shankland's wife) authored an article "Failed HP-Compaq merger would be painful" on Nov. 12, 2001 in which she states "including HP insiders." It should be noted, Dawn Kawamoto and Stephen Shankland contributed to the aforementioned article.

Ron

Security Outsourcing Solutions, Inc.
Tel: (617) 426-3900 or (781) 444-9616

-----Original Message-----
From: Hunsaker, Kevin [mailto:kevin.hunsaker@hp.com]
Sent: Sunday, February 05, 2006 12:09 AM
To: Ron DeLia; Gentilucci, Anthony R.; Nye, Vince; Adler, Frederick P.
Subject: RE: Privileged Communication - HP CONFIDENTIAL

Thanks Ron. This is very helpful. I think the information in the articles makes it much more likely that the Kawamoto leaker is Keyworth. It also makes it more likely that the second Kawamoto article on the 23rd was an intentional plant of false information by Keyworth. I'll explain to everyone why on Monday.

In an effort to rule out Larry Sonsini as the potential leaker on the second story from the 23rd, can you pull his cell phone records – I seem to remember that you did it as part of the first investigation, so hopefully you have his cell number. If the leaker on that story was not Sonsini, then I think it was definitely Keyworth.

Kevin

Kevin T. Hunsaker
Senior Counsel
HP Legal Department
650 857-3079 (phone)
650 857-3710 (fax)
1220 8573079 (voicemail network number)

-----Original Message-----
From: Ron DeLia [mailto:rrd@security-outsourcing.com]
Sent: Saturday, February 04, 2006 6:29 PM
To: Hunsaker, Kevin; Gentilucci, Anthony R.; Nye, Vince; Adler, Frederick P.
Subject: Privileged Communication - HP CONFIDENTIAL
Importance: High

Kevin/Tony,

Our analyst completed the initial research on the 2000 potential acquisition of PWC.

Attached are reports, which represent all of the media, located to date, generated outside of the interested parties.

A select few articles may look like duplicates; however, they were retrieved under different search terms.

Also attached are the articles, which reference or where authored by Tam, Shankland, Kawamoto and Rachel Konrad (Shankland's wife). Initial review of the articles indicates none of the aforementioned reporters appear to have covered the PWC story in-depth.

NOTE: I have not had the opportunity to review all of the articles personally. However, in the interest of time I am forwarding the articles.

The report of all the articles will be placed into a three ring binders and sent FedEx early in the week.

Note: We are continuing to work on the Kawamoto articles, which we anticipate will be completed by Monday.

Ron

Security Outsourcing Solutions, Inc.
Tel: (617) 426-3900 or (781) 444-9616

TAB 37

From: Patricia Dunn-Jahnke [redacted]
Sent: Sunday, February 5, 2006 3:55 PM
To: Hunsaker, Kevin <kevin.hunsaker@hp.com>
Subject: RE: investigation -- privileged communication

Kevin, this sounds promising. I will be in contact with Mark and come back to you with an indication of joint approval as soon as we connect.

Regards,
Pattie

From: "Hunsaker, Kevin" <kevin.hunsaker@hp.com>
To: "Pattie" [redacted]
Subject: investigation -- privileged communication
Date: Fri, 3 Feb 2006 17:36:23 -0800

Hi Pattie,

We have refined the "sting" somewhat and incorporated your suggestion about adaptive enterprise. I think we might really be able to make it work. We will, however, need to give one (small) accurate piece of advance information before we can spring the false one. I talked to Bob S and asked if he could give me a small piece of information, preferably in the adaptive enterprise space, one day early. He said he would see what he could do in the next week or so. Before we pass it on, I will need to get both your and Mark's approval to do so.

Does the general plan sound acceptable? If yes, is it something you can run by Mark? I am more than happy to do it, but I know he is heading to EMEA next week, and it's unlikely I will be able to lay the entire "sting" out for him before then, so we would lose an entire week. However, I realize there is some likelihood you and he might speak in the next couple days, so if it works out it would be great if you could run it by him.

As I said in the first paragraph, however, even if you both are fine with the general plan, I WILL NOT pass anything on unless and until you both know exactly what it is I intend to pass and tell me it's okay to do so.

Please call me on my cell [redacted] or at home [redacted] anytime if you have any questions or if you want to discuss this further.

Thanks.

Kevin

Kevin T. Hunsaker
Senior Counsel
HP Legal Department
650 857-3079 (phone)
650 857-3710 (fax)
1220 8573079 (voicemail network number)

TAB 38

From: Ron DeLia [rrd@security-outsourcing.com]
: Monday, February 06, 2006 9:31 AM
To: Hunsaker, Kevin; Gentilucci, Anthony R.; Nye, Vince; Adler, Frederick P.
Subject: Privileged Communication - HP CONFIDENTIAL
Importance: High

Team,

I may be a few minutes late on the 1 PM EST call.

I had a lengthy conversation with our former reporter regarding our approach to Kawamoto. Following are Diane's comments.

Diane would recommend we do not send an email asking Kawamoto to continue our communications via email. We should not raise the issue unless Kawamoto does and continue with our current mode of contact. Note: Online reporters are more comfortable conducting business electronically. Since the reporter sent a second email back, this indicates the reporter has an interest.

Sending a story in advance would build credibility. This would establish we are a person in the know. However, the information should be sent 2 day in advance of any release. According to Diane, information provided one day in advance is already floating around and there are a number of ways to obtaining this information. PR departments, secretaries, have access to info the day before it is released to the public. Information obtained 2 days prior to its release has more of an "insider feel." Reporters always have interest in "something of substance." The reporter has to feel comfortable or have a sense the source is someone who has accurate information and is in a position to know. Note: A reporter will always attempt to verify a story with established sources.

The message should be short and to the point. Do not attempt to characterize. An example would be "**Here is something you may be interested in**." Note: Online news services are not generally restricted to time deadlines as Print Media. Therefore, Online has the ability to get a story out in hours if need be.

A ...rter will always attempt to identify the source of information. Note: Reporters and editors are very sensitive about verifying sources. An editor would want to know "who is this individual." The editor would ask for independent conformation of any story of substance coming from an anonymous source. Therefore, the likelihood of the reporter contacting and established source for conformation is high. The reporter would also let her source know, "as a favor," that somebody else is talking to the press. The reporter would tell their source "this is on my desk." Note: Reporters normally want to know who the source is. They do not want to be sandbagged. However, the reporter may write the an article stipulating the information came from a 'unconfirmed source," as long as the information is not a "smoking gun" and is only a "preview of what is coming."

A reporter may have in person meetings with a source if the source is located close to the reporter. (G.K. resides 2 miles from Tam's home). It is not uncommon for a source to utilize more than one reporter to leak information.

If 2 reporters are mentioned in a by line they are working as a team. If a reporter is acknowledged at the end of an article they provided a piece of information. If the reporter that authored the article goes out of their way to acknowledge another reporter this is due to contributing more than a little piece of information to the story.

Question, are we jumping the gun in attempting for a one shot or nothing approach? Should we coordinate a more elaborate sting? By sending 2 prerelease stories do we allow us 3 bites at the apple? This would leave three possible foot prints to follow, i.e., electronic bugs (we may learn vital info from the first bug), more of an opportunity to track a phone call to or from GK and Kawamoto, etc.

Ron

Security Outsourcing Solutions, Inc.
Tel: (617) 426-3900 or (781) 444-9616

TAB 39

From: Nye, Vince
Sent: 02/07/2006 09:32:17 AM
To: Gentilucci, Anthony R.
CC: Hunsaker, Kevin
Subject: RE: Privileged Communication - HP CONFIDENTIAL

Importance: High
Sensitivity: Confidential

Tony:

I have serious reservations about what we are doing. As I understand Ron's methodology in obtaining this phone record information it leaves me with the opinion that it is very unethical at the least and probably illegal. If is not totally illegal, then it is leaving HP in a position of that could damage our reputation or worse. I am requesting that we cease this phone number gathering method immediately and discount any of its information.

I think we need to re-focus our strategy and proceed on the high ground course.

Vince

From: Gentilucci, Anthony R.
Sent: Monday, February 06, 2006 9:33 PM
To: Hunsaker, Kevin; 'Ron DeLia'; Nye, Vince; Adler, Frederick P.
Subject: RE: Privileged Communication - HP CONFIDENTIAL

Too close for comfort, appears to be a "key" piece of the puzzle, "worth" a lot of weight in this case. Sorry, couldn't help myself. Lets keeping on moving forward with the plan. Good work team.

Tony

From: Hunsaker, Kevin
Sent: Monday, February 06, 2006 10:42 PM
To: 'Ron DeLia'; Gentilucci, Anthony R.; Nye, Vince; Adler, Frederick P.
Subject: RE: Privileged Communication - HP CONFIDENTIAL

Is the number publicly listed? I just looked them up on Yahoo People Finder and neither Keyworth nor Schwartz came up with the number. It did come up under [redacted] when I did a Google search. Sure seems odd to me that Kawamoto would know to call that number.

Kevin T. Hunsaker
Senior Counsel
HP Legal Department
650[redacted] (phone)
650[redacted] (fax)
[redacted] (voicemail network number)

-----Original Message-----
From: Ron DeLia [mailto:rrd@security-outsourcing.com]
Sent: Monday, February 06, 2006 7:52 PM
To: Hunsaker, Kevin; Gentilucci, Anthony R.; Nye, Vince; Adler, Frederick P.
Subject: RE: Privileged Communication - HP CONFIDENTIAL

The number is registered to [redacted] prior to Keyworth moving to [redacted] Keyworth placed a lot of calls to the number during and around BoD meetings in 2005.

The content of this email transmission is intended only for the use of the individual or entity named above and may contain legally privileged or confidential information. If you are not the intended recipient, you are hereby notified that any disclosure, copying, dissemination, distribution, or use of this email transmission, or information contained herein, is strictly prohibited. If you have received this email transmission in error, please destroy all copies of this email and its attachments and notify the person whose name appears above.

Security Outsourcing Solutions, Inc.
Tel: (617) 426-3900 or (781)[redacted]

-----Original Message-----
From: Hunsaker, Kevin [mailto:kevin.hunsaker@hp.com]
Sent: Monday, February 06, 2006 10:24 PM
To: Ron DeLia; Gentilucci, Anthony R.; Nye, Vince; Adler, Frederick P.
Subject: RE: Privileged Communication - HP CONFIDENTIAL

Is Keyworth's [redacted] # in the phone book? If not, how the hell did Kawamoto know the number? Keyworth's only lived there for a couple months, right? Which means he must have given it to her recently . . . .

Kevin T. Hunsaker
Senior Counsel
HP Legal Department

650 [redacted] (phone)
650 [redacted] (fax)
[redacted] (voicemail network number)

-----Original Message-----
From: Ron DeLia [mailto:rrd@security-outsourcing.com]
Sent: Monday, February 06, 2006 7:22 PM
To: Hunsaker, Kevin; Gentilucci, Anthony R.; Nye, Vince; Adler, Frederick P.
Subject: RE: Privileged Communication - HP CONFIDENTIAL

Kevin,

Checking on that know,

Ron

The content of this email transmission is intended only for the use of the individual or entity named above and may contain legally privileged or confidential information. If you are not the intended recipient, you are hereby notified that any disclosure, copying, dissemination, distribution, or use of this email transmission, or information contained herein, is strictly prohibited. If you have received this email transmission in error, please destroy all copies of this email and its attachments and notify the person whose name appears above.

Security Outsourcing Solutions, Inc.
Tel: (617) 426-3900 or (781) [redacted]

-----Original Message-----
From: Hunsaker, Kevin [mailto:kevin.hunsaker@hp.com]
Sent: Monday, February 06, 2006 9:36 PM
To: Ron DeLia; Gentilucci, Anthony R.; Nye, Vince; Adler, Frederick P.
Subject: RE: Privileged Communication - HP CONFIDENTIAL

Ron,

Do we have the outbound calls from Keyworth's home from that date, so we can confirm that he and/or his wife made calls from the house that day (indicating that they were at home)? Any other way anyone can think of that we can verify that Keyworth was at home that day? It was a Wednesday -- timing's right, 2 days before Sherbin got the call from Kawamoto about the story.

Do you know what time of day the call went from Kawamoto to the Keyworth residence?

I'll find out if Keyworth reported any attempted contact by Kawamoto or any other members of the media in the past several weeks.

I'm starting to get excited . . . .

Kevin

Kevin T. Hunsaker
Senior Counsel
HP Legal Department
650[redacted] (phone)
650[redacted] (fax)
[redacted] (voicemail network number)

-----Original Message-----
From: Hunsaker, Kevin
Sent: Monday, February 06, 2006 6:18 PM
To: 'Ron DeLia'; Gentilucci, Anthony R.; Nye, Vince; Adler, Frederick P.
Subject: RE: Privileged Communication - HP CONFIDENTIAL

Thanks.

This is definitely great news, though. May be the direct connection we've been looking for!

Kevin T. Hunsaker
Senior Counsel
HP Legal Department
650[redacted](phone)
650[redacted](fax)
[redacted](voicemail network number)

-----Original Message-----
From: Ron DeLia [mailto:rrd@security-outsourcing.com]
Sent: Monday, February 06, 2006 6:35 PM
To: Hunsaker, Kevin; Gentilucci, Anthony R.; Nye, Vince; Adler, Frederick P.
Subject: RE: Privileged Communication - HP CONFIDENTIAL

I don't believe we can determine this, however, I will ask...

The content of this email transmission is intended only for the use of the individual or entity named above and may contain legally privileged or confidential information. If you are not the intended recipient, you are hereby notified that any disclosure, copying, dissemination, distribution, or use of this email transmission, or information contained herein, is strictly prohibited. If you have received this email transmission in error, please destroy all copies of this email and its attachments and notify the person whose name appears above.

Security Outsourcing Solutions, Inc.
Tel: (617) 426-3900 or (781)[redacted]

-----Original Message-----
From: Hunsaker, Kevin [mailto:kevin.hunsaker@hp.com]
Sent: Monday, February 06, 2006 9:09 PM
To: Ron DeLia; Gentilucci, Anthony R.; Nye, Vince; Adler, Frederick P.
Subject: RE: Privileged Communication - HP CONFIDENTIAL

How long was the call?

Kevin T. Hunsaker
Senior Counsel
HP Legal Department
650 [redacted] (phone)
650 [redacted] (fax)
[redacted] (voicemail network number)

-----Original Message-----
From: Ron DeLia [mailto:rrd@security-outsourcing.com]
Sent: Monday, February 06, 2006 6:25 PM
To: Hunsaker, Kevin; Gentilucci, Anthony R.; Nye, Vince; Adler, Frederick P.
Subject: Privileged Communication - HP CONFIDENTIAL
Importance: High

Team,

I received the following from our analyst this evening. **I will personally review the call logs to verify the following information**. It should be noted, the call was placed to Keyworth's residence from Kawamoto. Therefore, it is possible Kawamoto was attempting to solicit information from Keyworth. Do we know if Keyworth reported to the BoD or PD that a reporter (Kawamoto) attempted to contact him? It would appear out of contact if Keyworth did not, since he saved Pui-Wing Tam's attempts to contact him last year. We are also checking to determine if the following number has voice mail.

Ron

ATTORNEY CLIENT WORK PRODUCT - CONFIDENTIAL

We have prepared a chart of each spreadsheet you forward to date.

Kawamoto on 1-18 called 510[redacted] (The aforementioned telephone number is registered to [redacted] at her residence in [redacted]

During our telephone analyses last year, George KEYWORTH called the aforementioned number as follows in 2005:

Date phone number

George Keyworth

1/10/2005

510[redacted]

George Keyworth

2/7/2005

510[redacted]

X3

George Keyworth

2/19/2005

510-[redacted]

George Keyworth

2/20/2005

510-[redacted]

X3

George Keyworth

2/21/2005

510-[redacted]

X3

George Keyworth

2/24/2005

510-[redacted]

George Keyworth

2/25/2005

510[redacted]

George Keyworth

2/28/2005

510[redacted]

X4

George Keyworth

3/1/2005

510[redacted]

X5

George Keyworth

3/2/2005

510-[redacted]

George Keyworth

3/6/2005

510-[redacted]

George Keyworth

3/7/2005

510-[redacted]

George Keyworth

3/9/2005

510-[redacted]

X2

George Keyworth

3/24/2005

510-[redacted]

The content of this email transmission is intended only for the use of the individual or entity named above and may contain legally privileged or confidential information. If you are not the intended recipient, you are hereby notified that any disclosure, copying, dissemination, distribution, or use of this email transmission, or information contained herein, is strictly prohibited. If you have received this email transmission in error, please destroy all copies of this email and its attachments and notify the person whose name appears above.

Security Outsourcing Solutions, Inc.
Tel: (617) 426-3900 or (781) [redacted]

TAB 40

From: Nye, Vince
Sent: 02/07/2006 01:46:44 PM
To: Adler, Frederick P.
Subject: RE: Privileged Communication - HP CONFIDENTIAL

Its clear from the earlier call, that this is "Don't ask Don't tell" with regard to Ron's Role....

Key comments this morning:

"I think Ann knows" Kevin
"Ron"

"Yes she knows" - Ron.. (Knows what--I doubt that she knows the exact mechanics of this)

Kevin Thinks.......He doesn't want to go make sure she knows... This is the guy who is suppose to keep us above the board!!!!!!!!

Ditto...I am very concerned about this myself.

From: Adler, Frederick P.
Sent: Tuesday, February 07, 2006 2:42 PM
To: Nye, Vince
Cc: O'Neill, Timothy (IT Security)
Subject: RE: Privileged Communication - HP CONFIDENTIAL

Agreed, I am VERY concerned about the legality of this information.

Fred Adler
HP IT Security Investigations
(916) 785-8025, fred.adler@hp.com

-----Original Message-----
From: Nye, Vince
Sent: Tuesday, February 07, 2006 1:30 PM
To: Adler, Frederick P.
Subject: FW: Privileged Communication - HP CONFIDENTIAL

Fred: This information is two detailed to obtain via voice over the phone by a pretense operative......

From: Ron DeLia [mailto:rrd@security-outsourcing.com]
Sent: Tuesday, February 07, 2006 2:51 PM
To: Hunsaker, Kevin; Gentilucci, Anthony R.; Nye, Vince; Adler, Frederick P.
Subject: Privileged Communication - HP CONFIDENTIAL

Following is the time and duration of the call made from Kawamoto's cell to Keyworth's home.

Ron

18-Jan

Redacted

7:37pm / 1 minute

Redacted

6:20pm / 2 minutes

Redacted

6:04pm / 3 minutes

Redacted

5:25pm / 1 minute

[redacted]

3:25pm / 2 minutes

[redacted]

3:18pm / 2 minutes

[redacted]

3:15pm / 1 minute

[redacted]

3:13pm / 2 minutes

[redacted]

1:51pm / 1 minute

Security Outsourcing Solutions, Inc.
Tel: (617) 426-3900 or (781) 444-9616

TAB 41

From: Ron DeLia [mailto:rrd@security-outsourcing.com]
ent: Tuesday, February 07, 2006 2:12 PM
To: Hunsaker, Kevin
Subject: PRIVILEGED COMMUNICATION - HP confidential

Kevin,

I sent an email to my source in FL and asked them if there were any state laws prohibiting pretexting telephone companies for call records. Following is their response. We are comfortable there are no Federal laws prohibiting the practice. Note: The Federal Trade Commission has jurisdiction. The firm has been in business for over 20 years and is properly licensed in FL and other states. I have been utilizing their services for approximately 8 to 10 years.

Ron

"As of right now there are no laws against pretexting. We are on top of everything going on regarding this issue and if any law were to pass we will be the first to let you know."

Security Outsourcing Solutions, Inc.
Tel: (617) 426-3900 or (781) 444-9616

TAB 42

Jose Gurgel-Neto

From: Actionresearch1@aol.com
Sent: Tuesday, February 07, 2006 4:56 PM
To: Ron DeLia
Subject: Re: License Privileged Communicatioin CONFIDENTIAL

There is no such thing as a national license for Private Investigators. Each state has different laws and regulations and certain states do not even require you to be licensed sadly.

Matt

In a message dated 2/7/2006 4:05:37 PM Eastern Standard Time, rrd@security-outsourcing.com writes:

> Matt,
>
> Is Action Research licensed in other states?
>
> I apologize for all the questions. Our client is the one asking them.
>
> Ron

TAB 43

From: Molineaux, Arthur
Sent: 02/08/2006 08:47:22 AM
To: Adler, Frederick P.
Subject: RE: Confidential Privileged Communication

Hi Fred -

Marks is available to me and is HP property. Sorry for the confusion, I meant they bent the rules to give me the two T-Mobile accounts.

Regards,

Arthur

-----Original Message-----
From: Adler, Frederick P.
Sent: Wednesday, February 08, 2006 11:38 AM
To: Molineaux, Arthur
Subject: RE: Confidential Privileged Communication

Hi Art,

I fully understand that all of the other phone numbers and individuals names I submitted (with the exception of Hurd's) are personal phones and that records are not legally available. My question did not reference those numbers or names in any manner.

I am strictly speaking now to the matter of Hurd's phones. I understood your comment about "bending the rules" for billings to apply to Hurd's assigned units only. Again, I don't understand why the rules have to be "bent" in order to obtain a billing HP has a legal right to request/possess????

Fred

Fred Adler
HP IT Security Investigations
(916) 785-8025, fred.adler@hp.com

-----Original Message-----
From: Molineaux, Arthur
Sent: Wednesday, February 08, 2006 8:22 AM
To: Adler, Frederick P.
Subject: RE: Confidential Privileged Communication

The only one in the name of HP was Mark Hurds'. The others are all in the name of the person owning the cell phone. They probably pay the bill with a HP AMEX card but the liability if they default on payment is with the individual. Do you want to call me so we can discuss quickly ?

Regards,

Arthur M.

-----Original Message-----

From: Adler, Frederick P.
Sent: Wednesday, February 08, 2006 10:59 AM
To: Molineaux, Arthur
Subject: RE: Confidential Privileged Communication

Hi Art,

You wrote, "I got lucky as they really should not give this to me but sometimes my contacts bend the rules."

I don't understand why we should have to "bend the rules" to obtain a company billing. I understand these accounts are in the name of HP and paid for by HP funds, thus HP has a legal entitlement to the billing information?????

Did I misunderstand? I want to make sure everything that is done here is legal.

Fred

Fred Adler
HP IT Security Investigations
(916) 785-8025, fred.adler@hp.com

-----Original Message-----
From: Molineaux, Arthur
Sent: Wednesday, February 08, 2006 7:37 AM
To: Adler, Frederick P.
Subject: RE: Confidential Privileged Communication

Hi Fred -

As soon as the T-Mobile is available for these two, which will be 2/20/06, I will try and get that info. I got lucky as they really should not give this to me but sometimes my contacts bend the rules. The Cingular and Sprint folks did not provide the info.

Regards,

Arthur M.

-----Original Message-----
From: Adler, Frederick P.
Sent: Wednesday, February 08, 2006 10:20 AM
To: Molineaux, Arthur
Subject: RE: Confidential Privileged Communication

Hi Art,

Thanks for your efforts in this matter.

I will also require billings through January 28th of this year. Is it possible to have you forward those on, as available?

Thanks,

Fred

Fred Adler
HP IT Security Investigations
(916) 785-8025, fred.adler@hp.com

-----Original Message-----
From: Molineaux, Arthur
Sent: Wednesday, February 08, 2006 6:53 AM
To: Adler, Frederick P.
Subject: Confidential Privileged Communication
Importance: High

Hello Fred -

I was able to get the T-Mobile information from 12/20 to 1/19/06 which is the most current billing info available fo[redacted] and [redacted] Hopefully this will be all that you need. The info for [redacted] will be gathered shortly.

[redacted]

Regards,

Arthur Molineaux
Hewlett-Packard Company
Global Delivery Infrastructure Services
Global Voice Communications Solutions
Global Wireless Program Manager
978-506-4200
fax 978-506-4366

TAB 44

From: Hunsaker, Kevin <kevin.hunsaker@hp.com>
Sent: Wednesday, February 8, 2006 2:10 PM
To: Nye, Vince <vince.nye@hp.com>; Adler, Frederick P. <fred.adler@hp.com>; Gentilucci, Anthony R. <tony.gentilucci@hp.com>; Ron DeLia <rrd@security-outsourcing.com>
Subject: Investigation -- privileged communication

Team,

Below please find a first draft of the step-by-step process for Phase #1 of the covert operation. Once we are all in agreement that the Phase #1 info is accurate and complete, I'll draft the Phase #2 info.

Please look at the below with a harsh eye to make sure we capture everything anyone on the team thinks is important.

Thanks.

Kevin

Step by Step – Covert Email String: DK

Phase #1 (releasing of accurate information)

- BS sends press release to KTH 2 days early
- KTH revises content as necessary; KTH confirms same with Team
- KTH obtains approval of specific content from PD and MH
- KTH sends press release info to FA
- FA does the following:
  - Creates pdf file setting forth the release information
  - Runs program to strip metadata from pdf file
  - Embeds tracer in pdf file
- FA forwards pdf to RD
- RD forwards pdf to his consultant/contractor
- Consultant/contractor sends email message and pdf to DK
  - Email message reads: "Dawn, here is something you may be interested in. Jacob"
- Entire Team needs to be available in case DK sends a response to Jacob's email – quick strategy session will be needed to determine what, if anything, Jacob says in return.
- FA to monitor and determine:
  - When DK opens pdf
  - Whether anyone else opens pdf, and if so, obtain IP information
  - [anything else? – do we intend to send an advertisement to them? If it looks like a Board member, do we have PD send a message to the person right away? Anything we haven't discussed that is a possibility?]
- After DK opens the pdf – should we have surveillance on her? Since she lives so close to JK, there's a chance they meet in person someplace close to their homes; she could simply print the pdf document, quickly ping JK and schedule an in-person meeting later that day, or the next, etc. Is it worth doing some surveillance?]
- [Anything else on Phase #1?]

Phase #2 (inaccurate information on Adaptive Enterprise) – to be completed once we all agree that the Phase #1 information above is complete and accurate.

Kevin T. Hunsaker
Senior Counsel

HP 00759

HP Legal Department
650 857-3079 (phone)
650 857-3710 (fax)
1220 8573079 (voicemail network number)

TAB 45

From: Gentilucci, Anthony R.
Sent: 02/09/2006 08:28:38 AM
To: Adler, Frederick P.; Hunsaker, Kevin; Nye, Vince
Subject: RE: investigation -- privileged communication

Excellent, thanks....

From: Adler, Frederick P.
Sent: Thursday, February 09, 2006 11:24 AM
To: Gentilucci, Anthony R.; Hunsaker, Kevin; Nye, Vince
Subject: RE: investigation -- privileged communication

It is what we are using............

Fred Adler
HP IT Security Investigations
(916) 785-8025, fred.adler@hp.com

-----Original Message-----
From: Gentilucci, Anthony R.
Sent: Thursday, February 09, 2006 8:20 AM
To: Adler, Frederick P.
Subject: RE: investigation -- privileged communication

Fred,

Check this out, http://www.readnotify.com/. Don't know if this is the same thing we are using, or risky, but looks pretty neat. What your read on this.

Tony

From: Gentilucci, Anthony R.
Sent: Thursday, February 09, 2006 11:00 AM
To: Hunsaker, Kevin; Nye, Vince; Adler, Frederick P.; 'Ron DeLia'
Cc: Gentilucci, Anthony R.
Subject: RE: investigation -- privileged communication

All,

Good to go on this, guess we can start at 1:30. Secondly, yesterday we held an HTCIA meeting in Boston, one of the speakers was a lady (Kelly Cooper) who use to work at BBN, (now a consultant) basically, the way I understand it, BBN invented the Internet. She is what I would call an expert when it comes to IP addresses and talked about tracing back IP's etc. I asked and received a copy of her presentation. Fred, this stuff will likely make sense to you, and did to me a little bit as well, but she may be a resource we can tap into, she is amenable to help (did not go into details versus generic description of what we were trying to do with the document/tracker). She did state AOL would pose some challenges. During her discussion, a Special Agent with the IRS talked about some "other" tracking device, kind of like a blemish on an HTML document, that seemed to be, (and maybe its the same thing as our tracker), but seemed to be a bit more robust than our device, kind of a guarded law enforcement "secret" but not illegal, etc. I spoke to Detective JJ McLean, assigned to the Middlesex County DA's office Computer Crimes Unit, and on the Board with me, as well as a long time friend and associate about this "other" device. (Fred, I think you might know JJ through HTCIA). JJ is a seasoned computer forensics investigator (you all may have met him at the HTCIA Christmas party when you were out here). He said its available to the public. Actually Ron and I had dinner with him last night along with several other members from my team. He is more than willing to share or help us in anyway he can. Again, like Kelly, all he knows is that we want to send out a document and have it ping us back with it's location. Also, mentioned during the above discussions at the meeting, Jack Connolly, (who everyone knows), talked about a technique he used to locate an individual in Egypt via e-mail, (and Fred, he called this a "return notification"), not read receipt, but similar, but invisible to the average computer user, unless the user is a very astute technical person like yourself. I can discuss on the call, but found the timing of all this very fortuitous. I offer this as thoughts only, but maybe we could have several layers of tracking, if not on this upcoming covert event, may be on some of the follow-up documents.

Also attached find Kelly and JJ's Bio, imbedded with the other speakers at our meeting.

Talk a little later.

Tony

From: Hunsaker, Kevin
Sent: Wednesday, February 08, 2006 9:03 PM
To: Nye, Vince; Adler, Frederick P.; 'Ron DeLia'; Gentilucci, Anthony R.
Subject: investigation -- privileged communication

We just got a doozy of a story to pass on, but it may simply be too hot. I've asked Ann B and Pattie if they think it's too hot. If they think we should do it, I'll give you guys the details.

It's going to be announced Monday, so we would have all day tomorrow to get it ready.

Kevin

Kevin T. Hunsaker
Senior Counsel
HP Legal Department
650 857-3079 (phone)
650 857-3710 (fax)
[redacted]

TAB 46

From: Nye, Vince
Sent: 02/09/2006 08:52:53 AM
To: Adler, Frederick P.
Subject: FW: Privileged Communication - HP CONFIDENTIAL

STRAP ON YOUR HELMETS FELLAS, WE'RE GOIN IN!!!

PS: Thanks Fred for the nice letter of support....you're a good man!

From: Ron DeLia [mailto:rrd@security-outsourcing.com]
Sent: Thursday, February 09, 2006 10:05 AM
To: Hunsaker, Kevin; Gentilucci, Anthony R.; Nye, Vince; Adler, Frederick P.
Subject: Privileged Communication - HP CONFIDENTIAL

Kevin,

A surveillance team (utilized in previous investigation and conducted pre surveillance recon for this investigation) is prepared to initiate surveillance activity (2 teams) Friday AM in [redacted]. Surveillance team leader (32 year Bureau) has been briefed and is waiting on green light.

Ron

The content of this email transmission is intended only for the use of the individual or entity named above and may contain legally privileged or confidential information. If you are not the intended recipient, you are hereby notified that any disclosure, copying, dissemination, distribution, or use of this email transmission, or information contained herein, is strictly prohibited. If you have received this email transmission in error, please destroy all copies of this email and its attachments and notify the person whose name appears above.

Security Outsourcing Solutions, Inc.
Tel: (617) 426-3900 or (781) 444-9616

TAB 47

From: Adler, Frederick P.
Sent: 02/09/2006 09:19:04 AM
To: Molineaux, Arthur
BCC: O'Neill, Timothy (IT Security)
Subject: RE: Confidential Privileged Communication

Hi Art,

I just wanted to touch bases with you after our phone conversation yesterday.

Again, with relation to any records you provide me, please only provide those that provided are the property of HP. As for the non-HP owned records you obtained and sent to me in an unsolicited, good faith attempt, please make absolutely sure you delete them as you stated you would. I will do the same.

Thanks for all your help,

Fred

Fred Adler
HP IT Security Investigations
(916) 785-8025,

Page: 1 of 1

HP0007190

TAB 48

From: Pattie [redacted]
Sent: Thursday, February 9, 2006 9:24 AM
To: Hunsaker, Kevin <kevin.hunsaker@hp.com>; Baskins, Ann <ann.baskins@hp.com>; Pattie Dunn-Hotmail [redacted]
Subject: Re: investigation -- privileged communication

Sounds good. I have a call in to Mark but am not sure whether he is well enough to call back. Ann, if you talk to him please run this by him. Let's touch base by email or phone by 3:30 to see where we are.

Regards,
Pattie

-----Original Message-----
From: "Hunsaker, Kevin" <kevin.hunsaker@hp.com>
Date: Thu, 9 Feb 2006 09:05:46
To:"Baskins, Ann" <ann.baskins@hp.com>, "Pattie" [redacted]
Subject: RE: investigation -- privileged communication

Ann and Pattie,

I just heard from Bob S, and apparently this info is not going to be an announcement, but will instead be a media advisory, which led Bob to classify it as "second tier news." If that is the case, then maybe this is an excellent piece to use as part of the DK operation.

We would need to send it out by end of day today for it to be effective. I will have Fred start working on the technical aspects of preparing a document, and will await your (and Mark's?) comments before putting anything in motion.

Please let me know what you think about using this.

Kevin

Kevin T. Hunsaker
Senior Counsel
HP Legal Department
650 857-3079 (phone)
650 857-3710 (fax)
1220 8573079 (voicemail network number)

-----Original Message-----
From: Hunsaker, Kevin
Sent: Wednesday, February 08, 2006 6:00 PM
To: Baskins, Ann; 'Pattie'
Subject: investigation -- privileged communication

Ann and Pattie,

Would it be too big of deal to pass on the info about the new Handheld Business Unit and the guy who will be heading it up? They are announcing it on Monday, so I could pass it to DK tomorrow sometime and gain some major credibility. However, it's a pretty big deal and Todd will likely be pissed if it gets out early, given the IPAQ stuff that's made its way out there lately.

Thoughts?

Are we better off waiting for something smaller and less of a hot button for one of the execs? Frankly, I think we should probably wait on something else, but this would really establish some major credibility, which is why I'm asking you both.

Thanks.

Kevin

Kevin T. Hunsaker
Senior Counsel
HP Legal Department
650 857-3079 (phone)
650 857-3710 (fax)
1220 8573079 (voicemail network number)

Sent via BlackBerry from Cingular Wireless

TAB 49

From: John J. McLean
Sent: 02/09/2006 09:39:40 AM
To: Gentilucci, Anthony R.
Subject: Tracking Issues

Hi Tony (and team):

I do not know what exact digital signature/tracking/reporting device or certificate validation/authentication – process you are using to account and track the asset you are interested in... I'm sure it is good.

However, what I do know is, so long as it captures the REMOTE ADDRESS VARIABLE (IP) & HOST NAME & some other stuff too (we can start to play with it) But remember, if Onion Routing, Proxy Servers or Anonymous Servers are involved – we will have a hard time tracing the IP unless we do some U/C work and/or "Legal Tricks".

Now, if your server is capturing the - IP address – and it is resolved to a Private ISP then in order to ID that party we would need a Sub. D/T or perhaps a company "Legal Compliance Letter" for Subscriber Identity to that ISP.

If the IP address comes back to a med/large company, then all you have to do is reach out to management and have them tell you the assigned IP addresses for that specific time/data from the logs and settings (sometimes this works out).

I believe, once you get the IP address, you should cross reference this IP to PAST LEGAL AND IDENTIFABLE COMMUNICATION that this guy engaged in to make a matching nexus to him. We have found this information in Network Logon/Emails and other corporate logs that grab IP's. Or be prepared to look at the time of the actual IP capture for other activity he engaged in on your services/network and match those IP's minutes/seconds (before/after). If someone sends him IM's, Email and other stuff and he responds at the same time the IP's should be consistent (after one looks at email headers & netstat's IM/DC connection - the IP's should match).

Of course, we like STATIC IP addresses and not DYNAMIC. We have had some luck with matching DYNAMIC ASSIGNED IP from the same/close range, but the ASSIGNMENT TIME for these dynamic IP's varies.

You have some great resources at your company who could easily design a technical data/capture protocol to support this and future investigation.

The only thing I would stay away from (because the box is partly owned by him and it is in his house and I don't know about your Computer Use Policies that would apply to this) is any intrusive programs like (back doors/Trojans/monitoring and illegal content/data grabbing).

Good luck! Fred/Mike/Ron can call me later today...

Detective Lieutenant John J. McLean (CISSP, EnCe, CIFI)

N.E.M.L.E.C. Computer Crime Unit *(serving 46 departments)*

Medford Police Department – Investigative Services Division

90/100 Main Street, Medford, MA 02155 USA

781-396-0893 (Voice Line)

781-393-2136 (Direct Line)

781-396-4638 (Fax)

781-395-1212 (911 Center – Emergencies)

Email: JMcLean@medfordpolice.com

WEB Site: www.medfordpolice.com/ComputerCrime.htm

NEMLEC Web Site: www.NEMLEC.com

-----Original Message-----
From: Gentilucci, Anthony R. [mailto:tony.gentilucci@hp.com]
Sent: Thursday, February 09, 2006 10:47 AM
To: John J. McLean
Subject: RE: PPT

Great, I'll let you know, hey what was the name of that tracking device, paint ball, whatever it is called.

From: John J. McLean [mailto:jmclean@medfordpolice.com]
Sent: Thursday, February 09, 2006 10:48 AM
To: Gentilucci, Anthony R.
Subject: RE: PPT

Yes, I can talk about the tracking device – perhaps after 2:00PM – if that is OK.

Detective Lieutenant John J. McLean (CISSP, EnCe, CIFI)

N.E.M.L.E.C. Computer Crime Unit *(serving 46 departments)*

Medford Police Department – Investigative Services Division

90/100 Main Street, Medford, MA 02155 USA

781-396-0893 (Voice Line)

781-393-2136 (Direct Line)

781-396-4638 (Fax)

781-395-1212 (911 Center – Emergencies)

Email: JMcLean@medfordpolice.com

WEB Site: www.medfordpolice.com/ComputerCrime.htm

NEMLEC Web Site: www.NEMLEC.com

-----Original Message-----
From: Gentilucci, Anthony R. [mailto:tony.gentilucci@hp.com]
Sent: Thursday, February 09, 2006 10:42 AM
To: John J. McLean
Subject: RE: PPT

JJ, the ladies on the team were watching the news at the hotel and called me. congratulations. Our pleasure on the dinner, hey do you have time today to talk about the tracking device and some of the ideas we talked about.

Tony

From: John J. McLean [mailto:jmclean@medfordpolice.com]
Sent: Thursday, February 09, 2006 10:42 AM
To: Gentilucci, Anthony R.
Subject: PPT

Hi Tony:

Thank you for the dinner last night. It is always good to see you and the crew. (did you see the NEWS?)

Enclosed is that PPT you wanted.

Detective Lieutenant John J. McLean (CISSP, EnCe, CIFI)

N.E.M.L.E.C. Computer Crime Unit *(serving 46 departments)*

Medford Police Department – Investigative Services Division

90/100 Main Street, Medford, MA 02155 USA

781-396-0893 (Voice Line)

781-393-2136 (Direct Line)

781-396-4638 (Fax)

781-395-1212 (911 Center – Emergencies)

Email: JMcLean@medfordpolice.com

WEB Site: www.medfordpolice.com/ComputerCrime.htm

NEMLEC Web Site: www.NEMLEC.com

[This message is for the intended receiver. If you have received this message in error please indicate so]

TAB 50

From: Adler, Frederick P.
Sent: 02/09/2006 10:25:09 AM
To: Hunsaker, Kevin; Gentilucci, Anthony R.; Nye, Vince; 'Ron DeLia'
Subject: E-mail Tracking, Privileged Communication

Role of IT Investigations for E-mail tracking:

1) Receive .pdf file to be sent
2) Modify .pdf file w/ read-notify embedded information (file is now active)
3) Clean .pdf of metafile information
4) Zip .pdf file to prevent premature activation
5) Zip .pdf file forwarded to PA operative
6) Monitor activity

Note: I will need the Hotmail account info of the operative (ex: operative @ hotmail.com)

Role of operative

1) Prepare message body
2) Unzip pdf file and attach to message
3) Address message to target with required amendment (ex: suspect @cnet.com.readnotify.com)
4) Send message

Fred Adler
HP Information Security Investigations
8000 Foothills Blvd., Bldg R-6L, MS 5626
Roseville, CA 9574
916.785.8025 Office
[redacted]
916.785.1142 Fax
fred.adler@hp.com

From: Menz, Michael James
Sent: 02/09/2006 11:08:27 AM
To: Adler, Frederick P.
Subject: RE: Email document -- privileged communication
Attachments: DK message.pdf

Here is the cleaned PDF. Once it is sent to the dawnk@cnet.com.readnotify.com address it will be active

---

From: Adler, Frederick P.
Sent: Thursday, February 09, 2006 10:49 AM
To: Menz, Michael James
Subject: RE: Email document -- privileged communication

dawnk@cnet.com

Fred Adler
HP IT Security Investigations
(916) 785-8025, fred.adler@hp.com

-----Original Message-----
From: Menz, Michael James
Sent: Thursday, February 09, 2006 10:43 AM
To: Adler, Frederick P.
Subject: RE: Email document -- privileged communication

I still need the target email address - the one we are sending it to

Michael Menz
Hewlett Packard Company
Corporate IT Security Investigations and Forensics
michael.menz@hp.com
TN 785-1641
Phone +1(916) 785-1641
Fax +1(916) 785-1142

-----Original Message-----
From: Adler, Frederick P.
Sent: Thursday, February 09, 2006 10:42 AM
To: Menz, Michael James
Subject: FW: Email document -- privileged communication

Amended doc

Fred Adler
HP IT Security Investigations
(916) 785-8025, fred.adler@hp.com

-----Original Message-----
From: Hunsaker, Kevin
Sent: Thursday, February 09, 2006 10:41 AM
To: Adler, Frederick P.
Subject: FW: Email document -- privileged communication

New version.

Kevin T. Hunsaker
Senior Counsel
HP Legal Department
650 857-3079 (phone)
650 857-3710 (fax)
1220 8573079 (voicemail network number)

-----Original Message-----
From: Hunsaker, Kevin
Sent: Thursday, February 09, 2006 9:51 AM
To: Nye, Vince; Adler, Frederick P.; 'Ron DeLia'; Gentilucci, Anthony R.
Subject: Email document -- privileged communication

Team,

This is a tentative "go". I've attached a document that purports to be an email sent to Jacob about an announcement taking place next week. Let's talk about the content on our call. After that, Fred, can you begin to prepare the document for sending? We CANNOT put this completely in motion until they clear it with Mark, but Ann and Pattie have both given the thumbs up, so we should be preparing to send it if

Mark approves.

Kevin

Kevin T. Hunsaker
Senior Counsel
HP Legal Department
650 857-3079 (phone)
650 857-3710 (fax)
1220 8573079 (voicemail network number)

From: Adler, Frederick P.
Sent: 02/09/2006 12:08:51 PM
To: 'Ron DeLia'
Subject: RE: Need to contact you, Privileged Communication
Attachments: DK message.pdf

The "payload" is attached. Once it is unzipped, attached and sent to the "dawnk@cnet.com.readnotify.com" address, it will be active.

Fred

Fred Adler
HP IT Security Investigations
(916) 785-8025, fred.adler@hp.com

-----Original Message-----
From: Ron DeLia [mailto:rrd@security-outsourcing.com]
Sent: Thursday, February 09, 2006 12:25 PM
To: Adler, Frederick P.
Subject: RE: Need to contact you

Fred,

Should be ready to go, call me if there is a problem.

Ron

The content of this email transmission is intended only for the use of the individual or entity

named above and may contain legally privileged or confidential information. If you are not the intended recipient, you are hereby notified that any disclosure, copying, dissemination, distribution, or use of this email transmission, or information contained herein, is strictly prohibited. If you have received this email transmission in error, please destroy all copies of this email and its attachments and notify the person whose name appears above.

Security Outsourcing Solutions, Inc.
Tel: (617) 426-3900 or (781) 444-9616

-----Original Message-----
From: Adler, Frederick P. [mailto:fred.adler@hp.com]
Sent: Thursday, February 09, 2006 2:28 PM
To: Ron DeLia
Subject: Need to contact you

Please give me a good contact number for you. We need to talk ASAP.

Fred

Fred Adler
HP Information Security Investigations
8000 Foothills Blvd., Bldg R-6L, MS 5626
Roseville, CA 9574
916.785.8025 Office
[redacted]
916.785.1142 Fax
fred.adler@hp.com

From: Ron DeLia
Sent: 02/09/2006 12:29:55 PM
To: Adler, Frederick P.
Subject: Hot Mail

Fred,

Our undercover hotmail password is **bluebird10**. Is this helpful.

Ron

Security Outsourcing Solutions, Inc.
Tel: (617) 426-3900 or (781) 444-9616

From: Ron DeLia
Sent: 02/09/2006 01:08:43 PM
To: Hunsaker, Kevin; Gentilucci, Anthony R.; Nye, Vince; Adler, Frederick P.
Subject: Privileged Communication - HP CONFIDENTIAL

Team,

The package has been lanuched. Fred, myself and the UC investigator coordinated the launch. One surveillance team will be operational 2:30 PST.

Ron

Security Outsourcing Solutions, Inc.
Tel: (617) 426-3900 or (781) 444-9616

From: Gentilucci, Anthony R.
Sent: 02/10/2006 09:32:07 AM
To: Ron DeLia; Hunsaker, Kevin; Nye, Vince; Adler, Frederick P.
Subject: RE: Privileged Communication - HP CONFIDENTIAL

This is like waiting for the Apollo 13 spacecraft to emerge from the dark side of the moon.....

Tony

From: Ron DeLia [mailto:rrd@security-outsourcing.com]
Sent: Friday, February 10, 2006 11:17 AM
To: Hunsaker, Kevin; Gentilucci, Anthony R.; Nye, Vince; Adler, Frederick P.
Subject: Privileged Communication - HP CONFIDENTIAL
Importance: High

Team,

Pretext call made approximately 5 minutes ago to SF Bureau verified Kawamoto is in the office.

Ron

Security Outsourcing Solutions, Inc.
Tel: (617) 426-3900 or (781) 444-9616

TAB 51

From: Hunsaker, Kevin <kevin.hunsaker@hp.com>
Sent: Thursday, February 9, 2006 10:41 AM
To: Adler, Frederick P. <fred.adler@hp.com>
Subject: FW: Email document -- privileged communication
Attach: DK message.doc

New version.

Kevin T. Hunsaker
Senior Counsel
HP Legal Department
650 857-3079 (phone)
650 857-3710 (fax)
1220 8573079 (voicemail network number)

-----Original Message-----
From: Hunsaker, Kevin
Sent: Thursday, February 09, 2006 9:51 AM
To: Nye, Vince; Adler, Frederick P.; 'Ron DeLia'; Gentilucci, Anthony R.
Subject: Email document -- privileged communication

Team,

This is a tentative "go". I've attached a document that purports to be an email sent to Jacob about an announcement taking place next week. Let's talk about the content on our call. After that, Fred, can you begin to prepare the document for sending? We CANNOT put this completely in motion until they clear it with Mark, but Ann and Pattie have both given the thumbs up, so we should be preparing to send it if Mark approves.

Kevin

Kevin T. Hunsaker
Senior Counsel
HP Legal Department
650 857-3079 (phone)
650 857-3710 (fax)
1220 8573079 (voicemail network number)

-----Original Message-----
From:
Sent: Thursday, February 09, 2006 9:40 AM
To:
Subject: PSG Announcement – Confidential

FYI, Todd is establishing a new, separate Handheld group in PSG. I think they plan to announce it next week sometime. He's bringing on a guy named Dave Rothschild, who I think was at Sun most recently. The plan is to have Rothschild oversee handhelds worldwide – he'll be a VP reporting directly to Todd.

TAB 52

From: Hunsaker, Kevin <kevin.hunsaker@hp.com>
Sent: Thursday, February 9, 2006 10:49 AM
To: Pattie[redacted]; Baskins, Ann <ann.baskins@hp.com>
Subject: RE: Kona

Understood.

Thanks. We will put this in motion in the next few hours.

Kevin T. Hunsaker
Senior Counsel
HP Legal Department
650 857-3079 (phone)
650 857-3710 (fax)
1220 8573079 (voicemail network number)

-----Original Message-----
From: Pattie[redacted]
Sent: Thursday, February 09, 2006 10:47 AM
To: Baskins, Ann; Hunsaker, Kevin
Subject: Kona

I spoke with Mark and he is on board with the plan to use the info on new handheld leader. He also agrees that we should consider doing something with the adaptive enterprise branding issue, given there is some chance DK will seek clarification on this from her CNET source.

Regards,
Pattie

Sent via BlackBerry from Cingular Wireless

TAB 53

Prepared by Security Outsourcing Solutions, Inc.
Privileged Communication – HP CONFIDENTIAL

Investigation Summary (Revised 2/10/06)

DRAFT

EXECUTIVE SUMMARY:

1. G.K. received a call on his home telephone from Dawn Kawamoto cell phone on Jan. 18, 2006. The call was placed at 5:25 PM and the duration was 1 minute. Note: The telephone at G.K. and Marion Schwartz Keyworth's home is listed under Howard Schwartz, Marion's former husband. GK and Stephen Shankland's father, Thomas J. Shankland worked at the Los Alamos National Laboratory and are both member of at least 3 of the same organizations. Stephen Shankland and a colleague have reported on announcements and events at the Aspen Summit, a conference put on annually by the Progress and Freedom Foundation. Other colleagues of GK have spoken at the Summit in which he plays an active role. Colleagues included, Carly Fiorina, Lawrence Babbio, and Shane Robison.

2. Referenced two articles authored by Dawn Kawamoto, one in which an HP Director who requested anonymity is quoted as a source. Given the timeframe of the quote, and the content discussed, GK is one of 3 BoD's that could have possibly given the quote.

The second article referenced a former Compaq director that held Michael Capellas in high regard. Several articles were located for TP in which he also held MC in high regard and was one of the BoD's for Compaq that gave former CEO E. Pfeiffer a bad evaluation.

3. GK recently married Marion Schwartz. Ms. Schwartz has three sons from her previous marriage to Howard Schwartz a judge in Alameda County. Their eldest child Michael Schwartz was a staffer at Office of Science and Technology Policy and could have quite possibly been there at same time GK was Director of the office. From May 1995 to November 2000, Michael Schwartz worked as a management consultant with CSC Healthcare Group, formerly APM. This is the same as "Project Club" Currently, Michael Schwartz is affiliated with a company named PDXRX, Inc., a pharmacy systems supplier.

4. Pui Wing Tam authored a January 14, 2006 article about an upcoming book by TP, which has nothing to do with her normal coverage of the technology beat. One week earlier, PWT reported on Project Club and referred to her sources as "people familiar with the matter."

5. Tom Perkins attended a Progress and Freedom Foundation Conference in Aspen, CO in August of 2005 and spoke of a project in development at HP labs to a reporter form the San Jose Mercury News. GK was likely in attendance at the conference as he is the Chairman of the foundation. Note: Stephen Shankland authored an article of this event in August 2005.

6. A spreadsheet was prepared showing a call log to and from Pui-Wing Tam's desk and cell phone by Michael Moeller and Robert Sherbin. It is important to note, the duration on a majority of Robert Sherbin's calls with PWT were three minutes or less. The longest was 12 minutes and the contacts were infrequent and at one time no calls were recorded between Sherbin and PWT for three month period. In contrast, Michael Moeller spoke with PWT on a more frequent basis, and the duration of the calls were longer on average, the longest being 19.9 minutes. Interestingly, the log when compared to the release of a story referencing sources quoted, would in nearly all cases show Michael Moeller spoke with PWT the day or two before the article was published. In those cases, an H-P spokesman was not always identified,

and sources were described as "people or person familiar with the situation," "person close to the situation," "people familiar with the matter," or "person familiar with the matter."

7. Brigida Bergkamp is a former PR contact for IDG Worldwide Books, a subsidiary of IDG, Inc. aka International Data Group, also owner of IDG News Service. She remained there until some time in 2000. Tom Krazit prior to joining CNET News was a journalist for IDG News Service beginning some time in 2001.

COVERT OPERATIONS:

1. An electronic mail exchange has been initiated with Dawn Kawamoto under the pretext of providing information and develop a dialogue with the reporter. To date, two (2) responses have been received from Dawn Kawamoto, requesting the source (investigator) to call Kawamoto at her desk. Further contact is in the planning process.

2. An electronic mail with an attached file with tracking capability was sent to Dawn Kawamoto on 2/9/06 at approximately 1:00 PM PST. (Investigation team waiting for a response to the communication and notification the email has been opened and/or forwarded).

Note: Consultation (advisory) with a former investigative reporter on staff has been ongoing relating to contact with Kawamoto.

SURVEILLANCE ACTIVITY COLORADO:

On Monday, January 30, 2006 SOS, Inc. conducted surveillance on the activities of Dr. George Keyworth during his stay in Boulder, Colorado. Dr. Keyworth was giving a lecture at the University of Colorado, Boulder Campus as part of a series sponsored by the Center for Science and Technology Policy Research. The surveillance was performed from January 30, 2006 through February 01, 2006. The surveillance activity was uneventful.

SURVEILLANCE ACTIVITY CA:

On Thursday, February 9, 2006 surveillance activity was initiated at G.K.'s residence in Piedmont, CA. in an effort to determine if there was any contact between Dawn Kawamoto and George Keyworth.

The surveillance was resumed AM on February 10, 2005 on Dawn Kawamoto and George Keyworth.

The surveillance is scheduled to be conducted on Saturday, February 11, 2006 of Dawn Kawamoto and George Keyworth. Note: Surveillance teams also have photograph and vehicle description of Pui-Wing Tam.

RECOVERY OF G. KEYWORTH'S LAPTOP IN ITALY:

Efforts are underway in Italy to recover (buy back) the stolen laptop from law enforcement and criminal elements in the area of the theft. If laptop is recorded it will be forwarded to HP IT for analysis.

Prepared by Security Outsourcing Solutions, Inc.
Privileged Communication – HP CONFIDENTIAL

TELEPHONE ANALYSIS:

Note: Of 300 + telephone numbers over 240 of the numbers, subscriber information has been obtained and is currently under analysis. Also, due to some billing cycles ending mid month, a full months calls for the subjects will not be available until sometime in February.

[redacted] Keyworth home (NM) Dec. 11, 2005 to Jan. 5, 2006 obtained all NM numbers dialed.
[redacted] = Keyworth fax (NM) through Jan. 18, 2006 obtained and under analysis.
[redacted] = Keyworth cell phone cancelled on 11/1/05 no calls available
[redacted] Keyworth wife home (Marion Schwartz-Keyworth) obtained from Dec. 13th to Jan. 12, 2006
[redacted] Keyworth wife home (Marion Schwartz-Keyworth) completed
[redacted] Keyworth wife cell (Marion Schwartz Keyworth) obtained to Jan. 12, 06 and under analysis
[redacted] Keyworth addl cell number we located and calls obtained and under analysis

[redacted] = Perkins home phone obtained (Jan. 4th to the 26th) only 12 US, 3 UK & 2 Inter. calls
[redacted] Perkins fax completed only 3 faxes outgoing on Jan. 4, 5 & 6 to [redacted]
[redacted] = Perkins internet access only cell phone with no calls made
[redacted] = Perkins work phone at Kleiner, Perkins Caufield & Byers still trying to obtain info
[redacted] Perkins work fax at Kleiner, Perkins Caufield & Byers still trying to obtain info
[redacted] Perkins work fax at Kleiner, Perkins Caufield & Byers still trying to obtain info

[redacted] Salhany home office line has an unlimited monthly flat rate plan with no detail of calls
[redacted] Salhany secondary mobile disconnected no info available
[redacted] Salhany main mobile obtained calls to Jan. 12th, which are under analysis

[redacted] Hackborn home phone calls obtained to Jan. 17th, which are under analysis
[redacted] Hackborn home fax obtained outgoing through Jan. 20th, only one number [redacted]

[redacted] = Kawamoto home phone on hold for Jan calls until 2/26/06 bill posts
[redacted] Kawamoto cell phone completed Jan. 5th to Jan 29, 2006 and under analysis (Jan. 18 call to [redacted] duration of call was 1 minute and call placed at 5:25 PM)
[redacted] = Kawamoto addl cell phone calls obtained thru Jan. 29, 06, believed to be Spouses cell

[redacted] = Krazit cell actually billed under 'Shannon Thoke' on hold for Jan calls until the 02/05/06 bill posts
[redacted] = Krazit home phone obtained to Jan. 20th (only 2 calls 212-[redacted] & 415-[redacted])

[redacted] = Bergkamp office line at Hewlett Packard no calls available on this large corporate acct
[redacted] = Bergkamp cell calls obtained from Dec. 26th to Jan. 25, 06 and under analysis
[redacted] = Bergkamp home on hold for Jan calls until the 02/01/06 bill posts
[redacted] = Bergkamp addl home line we located and calls obtained from Dec. 31 to Jan. 20, 06 and under analysis

[redacted] = C-Net Networks office line (from reference case [redacted] no calls available on this large corporate acct

[redacted] = Tam cell phone obtained from Dec. 16, to Jan, 14, 2006, which are under analysis
[redacted] = Tam office line at Dow Jones no calls available on this large corporate acct

[redacted] = Moeller office line at Hewlett Packard no calls available on this large corporate acct
[redacted] Moeller office line at Hewlett Packard no calls available on this large corporate acct
[redacted] Moeller cell calls obtained from Jan. 5th to the 31st under analysis
[redacted] Moeller home phone waiting for billing cycle

NOTE: Additional telephone research not recorded above is in progress.

Prepared by Security Outsourcing Solutions, Inc.
Privileged Communication – HP CONFIDENTIAL

Thomas Krazit
1. Extensive Media/Internet Content Research to develop links to Members of the BOD. (Completed)
2. Extensive Media and Internet Content Research to develop links to other reporters such as Burrows, Elgin, Crockett, Markoff, Tam. (Complete)
3. Background Investigation to include employment, property, civil and criminal records and other public records to form a timeline for the occupation, schooling and address history for Thomas Krazit. (Complete)
4. Identification of all relatives for Thomas Krazit to determine whether there is a relationship to any member of the BOD or other reporters. (Complete)
5. Retrieval of all articles authored by Tom Krazit for relationship evaluation to HP matters and technology. (Complete)
6. Cross Check/Evaluation of all reported addresses for Tom Krazit and how they may relate to HP, BOD or reporters. (Complete)
7. Attempt to identify schooling, graduation dates and locations to cross check with other relatives of BOD, alumni, etc. (Complete)

Shannon Thoke (spouse of Tom Krazit)
1. Extensive Media and Internet Content Research to develop links to Members of the BOD or other reporters. (Complete)
2. Background Investigation to include employment, property, civil and criminal records and other public records to form a timeline for the occupation, schooling and address history for Shannon Thoke and potential relationship to members of the BOD or other reporters. (Continuing)
3. History of business (WiredAlumni.com) co-founded by Thoke and how it might relate to a VC firm or interested parties on the BOD. (Complete)
4. Cross Check/Evaluation of all reported addresses for Shannon Thoke and how they may relate to HP, BOD or reporters. (Complete)

Members of the Board of Directors/Tom Krazit/Dawn Kawamoto
1. Extensive media research to identify any prior relationships or media between both Krazit or Kawamoto and current members of the BOD. (Complete)
2. Identify any relationships between members of the BOD and IDG News Service or ZDNet.com. (Complete)
3. Cross Check/Evaluation of all reported addresses for interested parties on BOD and how they may relate to Krazit/Kawamoto and relatives. (Complete)

Review of Previous Investigation Results
1. Review media and public records for interested parties retrieved during first investigation to assess any potential affiliations to Tom Krazit (In-Progress)
2. Review media and public records for interested parties retrieved during first investigation to assess any potential affiliations to Kawamoto (In-Progress)
3. Review media and public records for interested parties retrieved during first investigation to assess any potential affiliations to Shankland (In-Progress)

Prepared by Security Outsourcing Solutions, Inc.
Privileged Communication – HP CONFIDENTIAL

Dawn Kawamoto (Staff Writer for CNET)
1. Conduct DD and Extensive Media and Internet Content Research to develop links to Members of the BOD. (Complete)
2. Extensive Media and Internet Content Research to develop links to other reporters such as Burrows, Elgin, Crockett, Markoff, Tam. (Complete)
3. Background Investigation to include employment, property, civil and criminal records and other public records to form a timeline for the occupation, schooling and address history for Dawn Kawamoto. (Complete)
4. Identification of all relatives for Dawn Kawamoto to determine whether there is a relationship to any member of the BOD or other reporters. (Complete)
5. Retrieval of all articles authored by Dawn Kawamoto for relationship evaluation to HP matters and technology. (Complete)
6. Cross Check/Evaluation of all reported addresses for Dawn Kawamoto and how they may relate to HP, BOD or reporters. (Complete)
7. Attempt to identify schooling, graduation dates and locations to cross check with other relatives of BOD, alumni, etc. (Complete)

8. Conduct Internet and Media Research between Kawamoto and D. Hackborn to determine if there are any links between the two individuals. (Complete)

9. (2/3-2/10) Retrieval of non-HP articles authored by Dawn Kawamoto dating back July 2003. (Complete)

Media Research on 2 Kawamoto articles quoting an unidentified source
1. Conduct media research for similar quotations by TP or GK to another media outlet. (Complete)

2. (UPDATED) Conducted an analysis as to the makeup of the Board of Directors from 1998 to 2005, pre and post merger from year to year and how they relate to an initiative discussed with DK by an anonymous director. (Complete)

Stephen Shankland (Staff Writer for CNET)
1. Conduct DD and Extensive Media and Internet Content Research to develop links to Members of the BOD. (Complete)
2. Extensive Media and Internet Content Research to develop links to other reporters such as Burrows, Elgin, Crockett, Markoff, Tam. (Complete)
3. Background Investigation to include employment, property, civil and criminal records and other public records to form a timeline for the occupation, schooling and address history for Stephen Shankland. (Complete)
4. Identification of all relatives, schooling, and graduation dates, locations for Stephen Shankland to determine whether there is a relationship to any member of the BOD or other reporters. (Complete)
4a. Research additional information for Thomas J. Shankland and relationship to GK. (Complete)
5. Retrieval of all articles authored by Stephen Shankland for relationship evaluation to HP matters and technology. (Complete)
6. Cross Check/Evaluation of all reported addresses for Stephen Shankland and how they may relate to HP, BOD or reporters. (Complete)

Prepared by Security Outsourcing Solutions, Inc.
Privileged Communication – HP CONFIDENTIAL

Rachel Konrad - Shankland

1. Conduct Internet and Media background research to determine whether any relationships with BOD or reporters exist. Research to include Konrad's coverage on any of GK's associations. (Complete)

Michael Moeller

1. Conduct limited due diligence for Michael Moeller and Extensive Internet and Media research to identify any potential affiliations with interested parties. All conduct research to verify the collaboration on BusinessWeek articles authored with Peter Burrows. (Completed)

John Hammergren
1. Limited Due Diligence assignment (Complete)
2. Internet and Media Research to reveal any potential relationships with reporters. (50% complete - continuing)

Shane Robison

1. Conduct limited due diligence investigation, Internet and Media on SR to determine any relationship to interest parties in media and members of the BOD. (Complete)

Summary of Media Articles

1. Prepare a summary of media articles to show reader number of articles authored by Tom Krazit that relate to technology. (Complete)
2. Prepare a summary of media articles to show reader number of articles by Dawn Kawamoto that relate to HP strategy and management (Complete)
3. Prepare a summary of media articles authored by Dawn Kawamoto that relate to partners in the VC firm Kleiner, Perkins, Caufield & Byers (Complete)

George Keyworth/Marion Schwartz-Keyworth/GK III/Tiffany Rehder-Keyworth

1. Conduct Internet / Media Research on Marion Schwartz, GK III, Tiffany Rehder for any relationships to BOD (Complete)

2. Conduct employment research on Douglas, Michael and Bryan Schwartz, sons of Marion (Complete)

3. Identified employment for GK III, identify upcoming appearances by GK, monitor media surrounding his appearances (Ongoing)

4. Conduct research to determine location of GK during the first three weeks of January 2006. Research to include civic and community organizations between both GK and MS. (Complete)

5. Conduct limited due diligence on parties to identify any relationships with interested parties in media. Research to include classification of their telephone number listing in Piedmont, CA. (Complete)

6. Conduct extensive Internet and Media research to establish further affiliations between GK and Thomas J. Shankland. (90% Complete)

Brigida Bergkamp

1. Conduct DD on B. Bergkamp (Complete)

2. Conduct Media and Internet Research for any relationships to interested reporters. (Complete)

Relationship Charts/ CALL Log Charts

1. Prepare relationship charts between interested parties. (Complete)
2. Prepare membership list of BoD for HP/Compaq pre and post merger. (Complete)

3. Prepared Call Log charts for Michael Moeller and Robert Sherbin as they relate to stories authored by Pui-Wing Tam. (Complete)

Pui-Wing Tam

1. Conduct DD on Tam (Complete)
2. Evaluate media for Pui-Wing Tam and identify articles and relationships with BOD. (Complete)

3. Prepare Call Log charts for Tam phone calls and release of articles for WSJ. (Complete).

4. Evaluate Tam articles from 1/5-1/6 regarding reporting of Project Club. (Complete)

5. Conduct Internet and Media Research for Stephen Eng, spouse of Pui-Wing Tam to determine whether any relationship to interested parties exists and his occupational background. (90% Complete)

Thomas J. Perkins

1. Conduct extensive Internet and Media research as it relates to interested parties and establish a previous relationship. (Complete)

2. Monitor all media, promotional events and press releases related to book authored by Tom Perkins and the favorable media article authored by Pui-Wing Tam from January. (In-Progress)

WATCH LISTS/Monitor

1. Prepare and monitor a "Watch List" for articles as they relate to BOD members and HP by the following individuals; Pui-Wing Tam, Stephen Shankland, Dawn Kawamoto, Thomas Krazit. (On-Going)

Examples of Board Member Removal Cases

1. Conduct research and prepare summary on two companies that have had a removal of a board of director for a reason other than retirement. (Complete)

PWC Acquisition

1. Conduct media research on two levels surrounding the potential acquisition of PwC in 2000. Assemble media coverage by interested parties in this investigation as one exhibit, and then assemble media coverage by rest of media into another exhibit. (Complete)

END OF REPORT

TAB 54

From: Ron DeLia
Sent: 02/11/2006 12:47:51 PM
To: Hunsaker, Kevin; Gentilucci, Anthony R.; Nye, Vince; Adler, Frederick P.
Subject: Privileged Communication - HP CONFIDENTIAL

Team,

Following are the results of the surveillance activity on Friday, February 10, 2006.

Ron

This morning around 10:00 am an older white male arrived at [redacted] in [redacted] (Glenn M. Laursen). While there, FedEx arrived delivering a standard envelope. Laursen remained about 1.5 hrs leaving sometime after FedEx. He was followed to [redacted] where he apparently lives. This is only 1 mile from [redacted] in Albany, CA. When we run tag # all we get is the R/O and type of car; no identifying information and no address. Surveillance team was unable to run CDL without DOB.

After lunch, M. Schwartz, was followed in her [redacted] to a local community center where she played bingo. M. Schwartz was let go after watching her there for a time.

At 8:30pm, Marion Keyworth was followed to the Oakland Airport and lost in the vicinity of the private jet center. The team did not observe G. Keyworth during the surveillance. As of 9:45pm she had not returned to her residence. The surveillance team will remain on site until we see her return or 11:00pm.

At the Kawamoto residence her husband (?) arrived in the mid-morning driving [redacted] (Reg to Jon Jiro Kawamoto). Later in the day Dawn Kawamoto was followed to a Montesori School in [redacted].

Security Outsourcing Solutions, Inc.

TAB 55

From: Hunsaker, Kevin <kevin.hunsaker@hp.com>
Sent: Monday, February 13, 2006 8:53 PM
To: Adler, Frederick P. <fred.adler@hp.com>; Nye, Vince <vince.nye@hp.com>; Gentilucci, Anthony R. <tony.gentilucci@hp.com>; Ron DeLia <rrd@security-outsourcing.com>
Subject: RE: Investigation - privileged communication

I like it.

Kevin T. Hunsaker
Senior Counsel
HP Legal Department
Phone: 650 857-3079
Fax: 650 857-3710

From: Adler, Frederick P.
Sent: Monday, February 13, 2006 8:46 PM
To: Hunsaker, Kevin; Nye, Vince; Gentilucci, Anthony R.; 'Ron DeLia'
Subject: RE: Investigation - privileged communication

I suggest something more simplistic, less leading and more intriguing, "I saw the piece by Tom Krazit on the handheld news. I should have something more in a week or so."

Fred Adler
HP IT Security Investigations
(916) 785-8025, fred.adler@hp.com

-----Original Message-----
From: Hunsaker, Kevin
Sent: Monday, February 13, 2006 6:19 PM
To: Nye, Vince; Adler, Frederick P.; Gentilucci, Anthony R.; Ron DeLia
Subject: Investigation - privileged communication

Team,

Below is the first pass at a message we can send to Kawamoto on Wednesday if we haven't heard from her and we don't get any read-receipt info. We would not imbed anything in the message. Just get the dialogue going to feel her out.

We can talk about what revisions may be necessary on our call tomorrow.

Saw the piece by Tom Krazit on the handheld news, so I assume you got the info I sent. I may have something else in a week or so.

Jacob

Kevin T. Hunsaker
Senior Counsel

HP Legal Department
Phone: 650 857-3079
Fax: 650 857-3710

TAB 56

1: Adler, Frederick P.
: Thursday, February 16, 2006 3:04 PM
[redacted]unsaker, Kevin; Gentilucci, Anthony R.; Nye, Vince
[redacted]ll, Timothy (IT Security)
ject: Information Leaks, Privileged Communication
new monitoring system that captures AOL Instant Messaging is now up and running and deployed on Moeller's computer. It instantly began to pay results:

vingtam: peter burrows asking about sales and attach rates?!! hmmmm
emoeller7703: i know
emoeller7703: i know
emoeller7703: out of the blue
vingtam: hmmmmmm
vingtam: hmmmmm
emoeller7703: hey tho
emoeller7703: fyi
wingtam: that makes me VERY uncomfrotable
emoeller7703: he isn't the competitors
emoeller7703: he isn't the competitor
emoeller7703: to you
wingtam: oh, that's whwat i was thinking
emoeller7703: nope
[redacted]am: k
[redacted]ller7703: someone else
wingtam: k
wingtam: nice results
emoeller7703. real nice
emoeller7703: shit
kemoeller7703: nice guidence
iwingtam: yup
kemoeller7703: street should love us
iwingtam: 30% increase in net income for h-p?????
iwingtam: that's crazy
kemoeller7703: INCREDIBLE

kemoeller7703: uping full year guidence by 7 cents
whohoo
iwingtam: nice
kemoeller7703: two cent increase on Q2
iwingtam: yup
iwingtam: ok i should run and write
[redacted]am: ttyl
[redacted]eller7703: go say nice things
iwingtam: ;-)
iwingtam: btw, are we speaking with randy mott at 7am or 7:30am tomorrow and what dial-in?

—

emoeller7703: 7:30
vingtam: and can you send me the slide from his industry analyst presentation before then?
eller7703: yes
am: thanks. your dial-in?
emoeller7703 [redacted]
emoeller7703: sorry
emoeller7703: [redacted]
emoeller7703: [redacted]
wingtam: got it
wingtam: slide by email?
wingtam: shud i ping someone in IR for that? just let me know
emoeller7703: by pigeon
wingtam: stop stop
wingtam: gimme that slide PRONTO!!!! ;-)
emoeller7703: actually let me walk it over to you now
emoeller7703: be there ina couple hours
wingtam: but seriously
emoeller7703: yes I'll send
wingtam: surely
iwingtam is away at 3:21:49 PM.
iwingtam returned at 3:34:18 PM.
tam signed off at 5:10:39 PM.
tam signed on at 10:16:31 AM.
iwingtam: btw, randy was good
kemoeller7703: glad to hear it
kemoeller7703: you get what you need?
iwingtam: i might ask for a bit more color later on
kemoeller7703: ok
iwingtam: but the bones are all there
kemoeller7703: good
kemoeller7703: getting the deck shortly from his exec comms person
kemoeller7703: will send when I have it
iwingtam: great, thank you
kemoeller7703: sure thing
iwingtam: tomorrow's dial in the same as today?
iwingtam is away at 1:06:46 PM.
iwingtam returned at 2:06:47 PM.
kemoeller7703: yo
iwingtam: yo
kemoeller7703: jack novia on the 23rd?
tam: likely can do. what time tho?
iwingtam: morning is better
kemoeller7703: k
kemoeller7703: i'll check

emoeller7703: fyi
vingtam: ?

l Adler
IT Security Investigations
5) 785-8025, fred.adler@hp.com

TAB 57

From: Hunsaker, Kevin
Sent: 02/17/2006 08:24:32 AM
To: Ron DeLia; Gentilucci, Anthony R.; Nye, Vince; Adler, Frederick P.
Subject: RE: Privileged Communication

Thanks Ron. This is exactly what I needed for the briefing with Pattie and Ann this afternoon.

Kevin T. Hunsaker
Senior Counsel
HP Legal Department
Phone: 650 857-3079
Fax: 650 857-3710

From: Ron DeLia [mailto:rrd@security-outsourcing.com]
Sent: Friday, February 17, 2006 8:46 AM
To: Hunsaker, Kevin; Gentilucci, Anthony R.; Nye, Vince; Adler, Frederick P.
Subject: Privileged Communication

Kevin,

The following numbers we are waiting on Feb bills to post and obtain the remainder on Jan calls is as follows:

- Kawamoto home # billed one month behind waiting on 2/26 bill for Jan calls
- Keyworth (Marion's cell) waiting on 2/12 bill
- Keyworth cell waiting on 2/10 bill
- Keyworth home waiting on 2/18 bill
- Keyworth fax waiting on 2/18 bill
- Krazit home waiting on 2/20 bill
- Salhany cell waiting on 2/12 bill
- Tam cell waiting on 2/17 bill

- Hackborn fax waiting on 2/20 bill

The only two (2) bills that may possibly be available now are the Keyworth cell for the 2/10 bill and Marion's cell for the 2/12 bill. We are attempting to obtain the calls for the billing cycles. Everything else is definitely not yet available. It takes a **minimum of 2 to 5 business days**, depending on the carrier, after the billing cycle ends for the calls to post.

Ron

Security Outsourcing Solutions, Inc.
Tel: (617) 426-3900 or (781) 444-9616

TAB 58

From: Hunsaker, Kevin <kevin.hunsaker@hp.com>
Sent: Tuesday, February 21, 2006 6:19 PM
To: Nye, Vince <vince.nye@hp.com>; Adler, Frederick P. <fred.adler@hp.com>; Gentilucci, Anthony R. <tony.gentilucci@hp.com>; Ron DeLia <rrd@security-outsourcing.com>
Subject: Phase 2 -- privileged communication

Here is my 1st draft of a possible Phase 2 message -- we can say HP has come up with a name for the Next Generation Data Center concept. I made up the name myself . . . and the rest of the stuff. I won't quit my day job.

If we tell DK that this is the new concept, and that Hurd may be telling the WSJ about it on February 27th (he is meeting with PWT on the 27th), it might just get DK to call GK, and GK might start making a few calls to HP folks to see what the hell is going on.

Anyway, let me know what you think. We can discuss it on our call tomorrow.

Infinity Data Centers – advancing
the Adaptive Enterprise

Always . . .
Available
Reliable
Expandable
Secure

Their uses and value are limitless

Kevin T. Hunsaker
Senior Counsel
HP Legal Department
Phone: 650 857-3079

HP 00624

TAB 59

From: Hunsaker, Kevin <kevin.hunsaker@hp.com>
Sent: Wednesday, February 22, 2006 10:23 PM
To: Gentilucci, Anthony R. <tony.gentilucci@hp.com>
Subject: Phase 2 – privileged

By the way, Pattie D loved the slide on the new name. She asked me to send it to Hurd so he can sign o on it. I think they might actually go with my name . . . . not. I'll let you know if/when Hurd gives the okay.

Kevin T. Hunsaker
Senior Counsel
HP Legal Department
Phone: 650 857-3079
Fax: 650 857-3710

TAB 60

From: Hunsaker, Kevin
Sent: 02/22/2006 06:23:28 PM
To: Hurd, Mark
CC: 'Pattie'; Baskins, Ann
Subject: FW: Phase 2 -- privileged communication

Hi Mark,

As I believe you are aware, I am the attorney overseeing the investigation regarding the information leak following the most recent Board meeting.

As part of the investigation, we have developed an email relationship with the reporter at issue. Phase 1 of the email exchange occurred two weeks ago, and we are now ready to put Phase 2 in motion. As with the Phase 1 information (involving the announcement regarding handhelds), we do not want to send anything out unless you have seen it and are fine with the content.

Our proposed email to the reporter, as well as the purportedly substantive slide that is part of the email, are set forth below. As you can see from the most recent email in the string, Pattie has seen the content and is fine with it. However, we will not send the message unless and until you have also indicated that you are fine with the content of the message and slide.

As an FYI, you, Pattie, Ann B, and the four other individuals making up my Investigation Team are the only people who have any knowledge of the email and slide set forth below. We did not involve any business, marketing or PR folks in preparing them.

I look forward to hearing your thoughts on this. If you have any questions, feel free to contact me on my cell [redacted] or at home [redacted] anytime this evening or early tomorrow, or at my desk anytime after 8:00 am tomorrow.

Thanks.

Kevin

Kevin T. Hunsaker
Senior Counsel
HP Legal Department
Phone: 650 857-3079
Fax: 650 857-3710

```
-----Original Message-----
From: Pattie [mailto:[redacted]
Sent: Wednesday, February 22, 2006 5:18 PM
To: Hunsaker, Kevin; Baskins, Ann; Pattie Dunn-Hotmail
```

Subject: Re: Phase 2 -- privileged communication

Kevin, I think this is very clever. As a matter of course anything that is going to potentially be seen outside HP should have Mark's approval as well. I don't want to forward this to him and lose privilege, but please do so and include this message.

Regards,
Pattie

From: Hunsaker, Kevin
Sent: Wednesday, February 22, 2006 12:24 PM
To: Baskins, Ann; 'Pattie'
Subject: Phase 2 -- privileged communication

Hi Ann and Pattie,

Below please find the email we propose sending to DK, with the hope she would forward it to GK (or at least call him to tell him about it), who would (hopefully) in turn contact one of you, or Mark, or Shane, or Randy, etc. to see if it's true. It is my understanding that Mark is meeting with the WSJ on the 27th, so we are trying to take advantage of that fact with the timing of this message to DK.

I made up everything in the slide, trying to make it at least somewhat feasible. I won't quit my day job, but hopefully neither the name nor the information on the slide are terribly off-base.

Please let me know what you think. We'd like to send the email to DK either late tomorrow or first thing Friday.

Thanks.

Kevin

Kevin T. Hunsaker
Senior Counsel
HP Legal Department
Phone: 650 857-3079
Fax: 650 857-3710

Dawn,

HP has come up with the name for its next generation data centers. Mark is meeting with the WSJ and maybe others on the 27th. Pulled this from the presentation slides.

Jacob

TAB 61

REDACTED

Jose Gurgel-Neto

From: Actionresearch1@aol.com
Sent: Thursday, February 23, 2006 1:35 PM
To: Ron DeLia
Subject: Report update privileged case

Hi Ron

Here is a breakdown of everything we have done as well as everything currently pending

On these below tolls have already been obtained and subscriber info completed and emailed back on the 14 spreadsheets:

BERGKAMP CELL	1/26 BILL COMPLETED
BERGKAMP HOME	2/3 BILL COMPLETED
HACKBORN FAX	1/20 BILL COMPLETED
HACKBORN HOME	1/20 BILL COMPLETED
KAWAMOTO CELL	2/5 BILL COMPLETED
KAMAMOTO CELL	2/5 BILL COMPLETED
KEYWORTH CELL	1/10 & 2/12 BILL COMPLETED
KEYWORTH CELL	1/12 & 2/12 BILL COMPLETED
KEYWORTH HOME & FAX	1/18 BILLS COMPLETED
KRAZIT HOME	1/20 BILL COMPLETED
MOELLER CELL	2/1 BILL COMPLETED
PERKINS HOME & FAX	1/26 BILLS COMPLETED
SALHANY CELL	1/12 BILL COMPLETED
TAM CELL	1/17 BILL COMPLETED

On these below we are waiting for the February bills to become available for tolls and will then obtain subscriber info once we have them:

KAWAMOTO HOME	>> WAITING ON 2/26 BILL
KEYWORTH HOME	>> WAITING ON 2/18 BILL
KEYWORTH FAX	>> WAITING ON 2/18 BILL
KRAZIT HOME	>> WAITING ON 2/20 BILL
SALHANY CELL	-> WAITING ON 2/12 BILL
TAM CELL	> WAITING ON 2/17 BILL
HACKBORN FAX	-> WAITING ON 2/20 BILL

On these below we have already obtained the tolls and emailed them back on spreadsheets but are still working on subscriber info:

KEYWORTH CELL (MARION'S)
KEYWORTH HOME (MARION'S)
KEYWORTH FAX (MARION'S)
KEYWORTH CELL (GEORGE)
KRAZIT (THOKE) CELL
MOELLER HOME
BERGKAMP ADDL HOME#

On these below we are still working on locating active cell/home numbers OR tolls and if any are found we will obtain all the January calls:

TAM LOCATE CELL OTHER THAN
TAM ALL JANUARY CALLS FROM HOME (
SHANKLAND LOCATING ALL CELLS AND HOME NUMBERS

TAB 62

From: Hunsaker, Kevin <kevin.hunsaker@hp.com>
Sent: Thursday, February 23, 2006 2:02 PM
To: Pattie [redacted], Baskins, Ann <ann.baskins@hp.com>
Subject: RE: Phase 2 – privileged communication

FYI, I spoke to Mark a few minutes ago and he is fine with both the concept and the content. We will either send it out this afternoon or tomorrow morning. I will keep you posted.

Kevin

Kevin T. Hunsaker
Senior Counsel
HP Legal Department
Phone: 650 857-3079
Fax: 650 857-3710

-----Original Message-----
From: Pattie [mailto[redacted]
Sent: Wednesday, February 22, 2006 5:18 PM
To: Hunsaker, Kevin; Baskins, Ann; Pattie Dunn-Hotmail
Subject: Re: Phase 2 -- privileged communication

Kevin, I think this is very clever. As a matter of course anything that is going to potentially be seen outside HP should have Mark's approval as well. I don't want to forward this to him and lose privilege, but please do so and include this message.

Regards,
Pattie

-----Original Message-----
From: "Hunsaker, Kevin" <kevin.hunsaker@hp.com>
Date: Wed, 22 Feb 2006 12:24:01
To:"Baskins, Ann" <ann.baskins@hp.com>, "Pattie" [redacted]
Subject: Phase 2 -- privileged communication

Hi Ann and Pattie,

Below please find the email we propose sending to DK, with the hope she would forward it to GK (or at least call him to tell him about it), who would (hopefully) in turn contact one of you, or Mark, or Shane, or Randy, etc. to see if it's true. It is my understanding that Mark is meeting with the WSJ on the 27th, so we are trying to take advantage of that fact with the timing of this message to DK.

I made up everything in the slide, trying to make it at least somewhat feasible. I won't quit my day job, but hopefully neither the name nor the information on the slide are terribly off-base.

Please let me know what you think. We'd like to send the email to DK either late tomorrow or first thing Friday.

Thanks.

Kevin

Kevin T. Hunsaker
Senior Counsel
HP Legal Department
Phone: 650 857-3079
Fax: 650 857-3710

Dawn,

HP has come up with the name for its next generation data centers. Mark is meeting with the WSJ and maybe others on the 27th. Pulled this from the presentation slides.

Jacob

Sent via BlackBerry from Cingular Wireless

TAB 63

From: Ron DeLia [rrd@security-outsourcing.com]
Sent: Thursday, February 23, 2006 5:15 PM
To: Hunsaker, Kevin; Adler, Frederick P.; Nye, Vince; Gentilucci, Anthony R.
Subject: RE: Phase 2 -- privileged communication

Kevin,

Do we want to set up surveillance for Saturday and Sunday on DK and GK? We can call the Disney hotels on a pretext and determine when DK checked out of the hotel and coordinate the surveillance with her departure from Disney. Since she has what appears to be a slide she may need conformation to run the story.

Let me know what your thoughts are. Note: In order to set up surveillance for Sat. or Sunday we will need as much lead time as possible.

Ron

Security Outsourcing Solutions, Inc.
Tel: (617) 426-3900 or (781) 444-9616

-----Original Message-----
From: Hunsaker, Kevin [mailto:kevin.hunsaker@hp.com]
Sent: Thursday, February 23, 2006 4:59 PM
To: Adler, Frederick P.; Nye, Vince; Ron DeLia; Gentilucci, Anthony R.
Subject: FW: Phase 2 -- privileged communication

Mark has approved this. Below please find the message and attachment.

Fred, can you strip any metadata there may be, then send it to Ron to be sent to his guy, to be sent to DK? We can probably send it either late today or first thing tomorrow.

Thanks.

Kevin T. Hunsaker
Senior Counsel
HP Legal Department
Phone: 650 857-3079
Fax: 650 857-3710

TAB 64

From: Ron DeLia [rrd@security-outsourcing.com]
Sent: Thursday, February 23, 2006 5:21 PM
To: Hunsaker, Kevin
Cc: Gentilucci, Anthony R.
Subject: RE: Photo of DK -- privileged communication
Attachments: Case 06-01-490 (Kawamoto surveillance photo) Feb 06 (2).JPG; Case 06-01-490 (Kawamoto surveillance photo 2) Feb 06 .JPG

Kevin,

See attached photos, which were taken on the recent surveillance. DK is the Asian female with short black hair and wearing a black top.

Ron

Security Outsourcing Solutions, Inc.
Tel: (617) 426-3900 or (781) 444-9616

-----Original Message-----
From: Hunsaker, Kevin [mailto:kevin.hunsaker@hp.com]
Sent: Thursday, February 23, 2006 4:24 PM
To: Ron DeLia
Cc: Gentilucci, Anthony R.
Subject: Photo of DK -- privileged communication

Hi Ron,

Do you guys have a decent photo of DK? If you do, can you forward it to Denis Lynch? They're getting ready for the Board meeting, so it would be helpful if they know what she looks like and can keep an eye out for her.

Thanks.

Kevin

Kevin T. Hunsaker
Senior Counsel
HP Legal Department
Phone: 650 857-3079

HP 00919

TAB 65

From: Ron DeLia [rrd@security-outsourcing.com]
Sent: Thursday, February 23, 2006 5:28 PM
To: Hunsaker, Kevin; Adler, Frederick P.; Nye, Vince; Gentilucci, Anthony R.
Subject: RE: Phase 2 -- privileged communication

10/4, I will have an investigator make the pretext calls ASAP. My thought is GK may want to see the slide if he is that passionate about the project.

Ron

Security Outsourcing Solutions, Inc.
Tel: (617) 426-3900 or (781) 444-9616

-----Original Message-----
From: Hunsaker, Kevin [mailto:kevin.hunsaker@hp.com]
Sent: Thursday, February 23, 2006 7:58 PM
To: Ron DeLia; Adler, Frederick P.; Nye, Vince; Gentilucci, Anthony R.
Subject: RE: Phase 2 -- privileged communication

Hi Ron,

Before we make a decision on that, can you have someone find out whether she has checked out of the hotel? I think it's unlikely that they will meet, but they do only live 5 miles away, so it's possible. However, if she's still in Disneyland, there's no need to set it up.

Kevin

Kevin T. Hunsaker
Senior Counsel
HP Legal Department
Phone: 650 857-3079
Fax: 650 857-3710

From: Ron DeLia [mailto:rrd@security-outsourcing.com]
Sent: Thursday, February 23, 2006 5:15 PM

To: Hunsaker, Kevin; Adler, Frederick P.; Nye, Vince; Gentilucci, Anthony R.
Subject: RE: Phase 2 -- privileged communication

Kevin,

Do we want to set up surveillance for Saturday and Sunday on DK and GK? We can call the Disney hotels on a pretext and determine when DK checked out of the hotel and coordinate the surveillance with her departure from Disney. Since she has what appears to be a slide she may need conformation to run the story.

Let me know what your thoughts are. Note: In order to set up surveillance for Sat. or Sunday we will need as much lead time as possible.

Ron

The content of this email transmission is intended only for the use of the individual or entity named above and may contain *legally privileged or confidential* information. If you are not the intended recipient, you are hereby notified that any disclosure, copying, dissemination, distribution, or use of this email transmission, or information contained herein, is strictly prohibited. If you have *received this email transmission* in error, please destroy all copies of this email and its attachments and notify the person whose name appears above.

Security Outsourcing Solutions, Inc.
Tel: (617) 426-3900 or (781) 444-9616

-----Original Message-----
From: Hunsaker, Kevin [mailto:kevin.hunsaker@hp.com]
Sent: Thursday, February 23, 2006 4:59 PM
To: Adler, Frederick P.; Nye, Vince; Ron DeLia; Gentilucci, Anthony R.
Subject: FW: Phase 2 -- privileged communication

Mark has approved this. Below please find the message and attachment.

Fred, can you strip any metadata there may be, then send it to Ron to be sent to his guy, to be sent to DK? We can probably send it either late today or first thing tomorrow.

Thanks.

Kevin T. Hunsaker
Senior Counsel
HP Legal Department
Phone: 650 857-3079
Fax: 650 857-3710

Dawn,

HP has come up with the name for its next generation data centers. Mark is meeting with the WSJ and maybe others on the 27th. Pulled this from the presentation slides.

Jacob

TAB 66

From: Ron DeLia [rrd@security-outsourcing.com]
Sent: Friday, February 24, 2006 5:58 PM
To: Hunsaker, Kevin; Nye, Vince; Adler, Frederick P.; Gentilucci, Anthony R.
Subject: RE: Summary of Activity -- privileged communication

Kevin,

We provided interim executive summaries, which you have copies of in KONA 1. We will begin to compile a comprehensive summary of the investigative activity conducted to date. However, from our involvement, the background research, surveillance, trash inspection recon, telephone work, etc. will take some time. We have reviewed thousands of media articles between all the reporters involved. I estimate 2 weeks. Does fit the time line or are we talking sooner?

Ron

Security Outsourcing Solutions, Inc.
Tel: (617) 426-3900 or (781) 444-9616

-----Original Message-----
From: Hunsaker, Kevin [mailto:kevin.hunsaker@hp.com]
Sent: Friday, February 24, 2006 7:38 PM
To: Nye, Vince; Adler, Frederick P.; Gentilucci, Anthony R.; Ron DeLia
Subject: Summary of Activity -- privileged communication

Hi guys,

I just got off the phone with Pattie. She would like us to put a comprehensive summary of what we've done, what resources and techniques we've used, etc. It should include everything we've done on the EC folks, the Board members, and the other employees. It should also include things like our [unsuccessful] attempts to obtain the EC members' cell phone records, etc.

It is not something that we need to have done in the next several days or anything, but if each of you could put together a comprehensive summary of what you've done, how you did it, and who you utilized to get it done, I can put it all together in a document that will ultimately establish the completeness of this investigation.

Ron and Tony,

Did you guys do something similar with respect to Kona 1? If not, is it possible to do so now based on the documents that you still have?

Thanks everybody. Have a great weekend.

Kevin

Kevin T. Hunsaker
Senior Counsel
HP Legal Department
Phone: 650 857-3079
Fax: 650 857-3710

TAB 67

From: Ron DeLia [rrd@security-outsourcing.com]
Sent: Sunday, February 26, 2006 12:36 PM
To: Hunsaker, Kevin; Gentilucci, Anthony R.; Nye, Vince; Adler, Frederick P.
Subject: Privileged Communication - HP CONFIDENTIAL

Team,

Surveillance activity was shut down at 12 noon PST on Sunday, February 26, 2006. Surveillance teams were in place from 9 AM to 12 noon and no activity was observed at either residence. It appears DK had not returned from vacation. We waited in the event she came home late Saturday evening and the family was sleeping in. However, by 12 noon the newspapers were not picked up from the driveway and a pretext call to DK's residence was not answered and went into VM.

Surveillance activity at GK's residence revealed no movement as well. There were also newspapers in the driveway that had not been picked up.

As of 3 PM EST our UC had not received an email response from DK.

Ron

Security Outsourcing Solutions, Inc.
Tel: (617) 426-3900 or (781) 444-9616

TAB 68

REDACTED

ACTION RESEARCH GROUP, INC. STATEMENT

2263 W. NEW HAVEN AVE
SUITE 399

WEST MELBOURNE, FL 32904 (321) 728-3700

Statement Date: 02/27/200

Account Number: 2010

Balance Due: [redacted]

Page: 1

SECURITY OUTSOURCING SOLUTIONS
P.O. BOX 920368
NEEDHAM, MA 02492

INVOICE NO.	DATE	CODE	DEBTOR	AMOUNT	BALANCE
99375497	12/22/105	1		40.00	40.00
99377747	01/25/106	1	THOMAS KRAZIT /	45.00	85.00
99377746	01/25/106	1	DAWN KAWAMOTO /	145.00	230.00
99377885	01/26/106	1		20.00	250.00
99377886	01/27/106	1		20.00	270.00
99379917	02/23/106	1		40.00	310.00

DUE OVER 30	DUE OVER 60	DUE OVER 90	DUE OVER 120	PLEASE PAY
230.00	40.00	0.00	0.00	310.00

Statements sent for verification only, Payments due 30 days from invoice date

HP 5850

TAB 69

From: Hunsaker, Kevin <kevin.hunsaker@hp.com>
Sent: Thursday, March 2, 2006 12:17 PM
To: Adler, Frederick P. <fred.adler@hp.com>
Cc: Nye, Vince <vince.nye@hp.com>; Ron DeLia <rrd@security-outsourcing.com>; Gentilucci, Anthony R. <tony.gentilucci@hp.com>
Subject: PWT – privileged communication

Hi Fred,

Can you please do some monitoring on incoming and outgoing calls to Pui-Wing Tam, and keep a really close eye on her IM traffic with Moeller. There is going to be a special telephonic board meeting next Tuesday to discuss a very important topic, and PWT called Tom Perkins a couple days ago asking about the precise topic the board will be discussing. According to Perkins, he told PWT "I don't know."

Anyway, this is yet another major opportunity for a leak to occur.

Thanks.

Kevin

Kevin T. Hunsaker
Senior Counsel
HP Legal Department
Phone: 650 857-3079
Fax: 650 857-3710

HP 00635

TAB 70

Jose Gurgel-Neto

From: Ron DeLia
Sent: Thursday, March 02, 2006 9:47 PM
To: 'Actionresearch1@aol.com'
Subject: RE: Update-privileged case

REDACTED

Matt,

Thanks, also attempt to locate a cell for Rachel Konrad (Stephen Shankland's wife)? Also, obtain Jan. 2006 calls.

Ron

The content of this email transmission is intended only for the use of the individual or entity named above and may contain legally privileged or confidential information. If you are not the intended recipient, you are hereby notified that any disclosure, copying, dissemination, distribution, or use of this email transmission, or information contained herein, is strictly prohibited. If you have received this email transmission in error, please destroy all copies of this email and its attachments and notify the person whose name appears above.

Security Outsourcing Solutions, Inc.
Tel: (617) 426-3900 or (781) 444-9616

-----Original Message-----
From: Actionresearch1@aol.com [mailto:Actionresearch1@aol.com]
Sent: Thursday, March 02, 2006 7:22 PM
To: Ron DeLia
Subject: Update-privileged case

Hi Ron

Here is a breakdown of everything we have done as well as everything currently pending. Let me know if I am missing anything

On these below tolls have already been obtained and subscriber info completed and emailed back on the 14 spreadsheets:

BERGKAMP CELL
BERGKAMP HOME
HACKBORN FAX
HACKBORN HOME
KAWAMOTO CELL
KAMAMOTO CELL
KEYWORTH CELL
KEYWORTH CELL
KEYWORTH HOME & FAX
KRAZIT HOME
MOELLER CELL
PERKINS HOME & FAX
SALHANY CELL
TAM CELL

On these below we are waiting for the February bills to become available for tolls and will then obtain subscriber info once we have them:

KAWAMOTO HOME >> STILL WAITING ON 2/26 BILL
KRAZIT HOME >> STILL WAITING ON 2/20 BILL
HACKBORN FAX >> STILL WAITING ON 2/20 BILL

TAB 71

Jose Gurgel-Neto

From: Actionresearch1@aol.com
Sent: Friday, March 03, 2006 5:27 PM
To: Ron DeLia
Subject: Re: Special Investitgation - Privieged Communication - *CONFIDENTIAL*

Ok I will check on all of them. *I will send you over everything* we have completed before I leave here tonight. I know we're still waiting on about 5-6 numbers for subscriber info between all the spreadsheets but I will send them over minus whatever isnt finished today so you have something. We also did obtain Kawamotos feb bill which finally posted today and that will be sent over as well

Matt

In a message dated 3/3/2006 5:17:14 PM Eastern Standard Time, rrd@security-outsourcing.com writes:

> **Matt,**
>
> **Can you check to determine if we can obtain incoming calls for Tam, Kawamoto, Keyworth (Mr & Mrs.), and Stephen Shankland's cell telephones. If so please obtain for all the calls for the months we have obtained the tolls for. Also obtain subscriber information for each number.**
>
> **Ron**

TAB 72

HP Confidential For Named Individuals on the Distribution List Only

SBC Investigation Report

Hewlett-Packard Company
Global SBC Compliance Team
3000 Hanover Street
Palo Alto, CA 94304

DRAFT

Note: The investigation of this matter is still ongoing as of the date of this report and, as such, this is a DRAFT report. A final report will be prepared once the investigation is complete.

ATTORNEY-CLIENT PRIVILEGED; ATTORNEY WORK PRODUCT

Subject: Unauthorized Disclosure – **Draft Investigation Report**

From: Kevin T. Hunsaker
Senior Counsel, HP Legal Department

Date: March 10, 2006

To: Pattie Dunn
Mark Hurd
Ann Baskins

I. Background

On Friday afternoon, January 20, 2006, CNET reporter Tom Krazit contacted Bob Sherbin (HP Media Relations), advising him that CNET was going to publish an article summarizing at least four of the issues discussed during the HP Board meeting held two weeks earlier in Indian Wells, California. Sherbin promptly informed Mark Hurd and Pattie Dunn, as well as Jim Fairbaugh and Tony Gentilucci from Global Security Investigations. Gentilucci then immediately informed HP's Legal Department, and a preliminary investigation at the direction of the Legal Department was commenced over the weekend.

On Monday, January 23, 2006, CNET published the article as indicated by Krazit on the 20th. The article was written by Dawn Kawamoto[1], and it contained a detailed, accurate summary of several issues discussed during the January 2006 Board meeting. The article attributed all of the substantive information about the issues discussed during the January 2006 Board meeting to a "source with the company." Because the information contained in the article was clearly non-public, confidential HP information that was discussed in detail during the Board meeting, Pattie Dunn requested that a formal investigation into the information leak be conducted at the direction of the Legal Department. The Legal Department immediately

[1] It should be noted that Tom Krazit co-authored the article with Kawamoto, and Stephen Shankland "contributed" to the article. A copy of the article is attached hereto as Appendix 1.

assembled a cross-functional team of individuals with appropriate backgrounds and expertise to conduct a comprehensive, objective, and independent investigation of this matter.

II. Executive Summary

The Investigation Team commenced the investigation by gathering data and information with respect to any and all individuals who may have had access to the information disclosed in Kawamoto's January 23, 2006 article. During the course of the investigation, the Investigation Team (1) gathered, generated, reviewed and analyzed thousands of internal and external documents; (2) conducted interviews of individuals in possession of relevant information; (3) conducted extensive electronic searches of HP's systems and proxy servers for information pertaining in any way to the leaks; (4) conducted extensive telephone and email searches regarding dozens of individuals (including to varying degrees members of HP's Board, members of the Executive Council, as well as other HP employees including several members of HP's Media Relations group; (5) conducted detailed background searches and link analyses with respect to several reporters and numerous potential sources of the information leak; and (6) engaged in a number of other investigative activities designed to obtain additional information potentially relevant to both the information leak and the source(s) thereof.

As a result of the foregoing investigative activities, the Investigation Team successfully narrowed the list of potential sources of the leak during the course of the investigation and, as of the date of this Draft Report, the overwhelming weight of evidence reviewed by the Investigation Team indicates the source of the leak is HP Board member George Keyworth II. Specifically, the content of each of the articles citing a "source" written by Kawamoto in the past 4 years, the numerous connections made by Investigation Team tying Keyworth to the leaks, and the telephonic contact between Kawamoto and Keyworth in January and February of 2006, all clearly identify and establish Keyworth as the only feasible source of the leaks.

The remainder of this Draft Report will set forth a comprehensive overview of the actions taken by the Investigation Team, the evidence and information supporting the Investigation Team's conclusion, and the recommendations for further action based on the conclusion reached by the Investigation Team.

III. Scope

The objective of the Investigation Team was as follows:

- **Determine the identity of the individual or individuals who leaked confidential, non-public HP information to CNET reporter Dawn Kawamoto in conjunction with the January 23, 2006 article summarizing the issues discussed during the January 2006 Board meeting.**

IV. Approach

Investigation Team Members

Kevin Hunsaker (HP Legal), Fred Adler (IT Security), Tony Gentilucci and Vince Nye (Global Security Investigations) and Ron Delia (HP Investigative Consultant) were the lead investigators. Team members who also assisted in this investigation include Denis Lynch (Global Security), Tim O'Neil (IT Security) and Jim Fairbaugh (Global Security).

Procedures

As part of the investigation of this matter, the Investigation Team took the following actions:

- Obtained, reviewed and analyzed all presentations and other documentation utilized, generated, or relied upon in conjunction with the January 2006 Board of Directors meeting.
- Obtained, reviewed, and analyzed more than ten (10) thousand electronic and hard-copy articles pertaining to HP published by CNET, the Wall Street Journal and other periodicals during the past six years; obtained and analyzed all articles (on any topic) written or contributed to by Dawn Kawamoto, Tom Krazit, Stephen Shankland, Rachel Konrad and Pui-Wing Tam in the past 10 years; identified, reviewed in detail and indexed more than 1,000 electronic and hard-copy articles written by Kawamoto.
- Obtained, reviewed, and analyzed extensive internal HP documentation and information (both electronic and hard-copy), as well as external, publicly available documentation and information regarding all the members of the HP Board of Directors, HP Executive Council, HP Media Relations, and other HP employees who potentially had access to the presentations and issues discussed during the January 2006 Board meeting.
- Conducted extensive search and analysis of email and available telephone records of each member of the Executive Council, members of HP Media Relations and other HP employees who potentially had access to the presentations and issues discussed during the January [redacted] Board meeting.
- Conducted extensive search and analysis of HP's email and internet servers to locate any traffic to and from any of the reporters or news agencies of interest in this matter.
- Conducted extensive background investigation, including obtaining, reviewing and analyzing publicly available documentation and information (both electronic and hard-copy) regarding relevant members of the media, including Kawamoto, Krazit, Shankland, Konrad and Tam.
- Obtained, reviewed and analyzed HP and third party phone records to identify calls made to or from reporters or other individuals of interest during the relevant timeframes.[2]

---

[2] It should be noted that, with respect to non-HP phone records, the Investigation Team utilized a lawful investigative methodology commonly utilized by entities such as law firms and licensed security firms in the United States to obtain such records.

- Collected and reviewed several thousand pages of documents (Word, PowerPoint, Excel, etc.) relating to the information discussed during the January 2006 Board meeting, the potential sources of the leak, the relationships of HP employees and Board members to members of the media, and other areas of inquiry relevant to the investigation.
- Engineered and executed a covert intelligence gathering operation pursuant wherein an undercover investigator established email contact with Kawamoto using an untraceable hotmail account. The operation included placing a legally permissible software based tracing device in an email attachment sent to Kawamoto. The objective of the operation was to track and determine whether the email was forwarded to the source or sources (internal or external to HP) by Kawamoto.
- Conducted surveillance activity and reviewed existing video surveillance footage in an effort to determine whether specific individuals were meeting with or speaking to certain members of the media.
- Conducted an in-depth review of all materials associated with the KONA I investigation, which was conducted in relation to information leaks that occurred during 2005 involving media sources such as the Wall Street Journal, Business Week and the New York Times.

Individuals Interviewed: The following individuals were interviewed in person by members of the Investigation Team:

- Ann Baskins (General Counsel);
- Pattie Dunn (Chairman of the Board);
- Bob Wayman (Chief Financial Officer);
- Mark Hurd (Chief Executive Officer);
- Charles Charnas (Legal);
- Alan Haggard (Legal);
- Bob Sherbin (Media Relations); and
- Rosemary Thomas (Board Liaison).

V. Findings

Based upon the documents reviewed, information collected and interviews conducted during the course of the investigation, the Investigation Team finds as follows:

(1) Did the Investigation Team determine the identity of the individual or individuals who leaked confidential, non-public HP information to CNET reporter Dawn

Kawamoto in conjunction with the January 23, 2006 article summarizing the issues discussed during the January [redacted] Board meeting?

The documents and information reviewed and interviews conducted by the Investigation Team during the course of the investigation overwhelmingly indicate that George Keyworth II is the source who leaked non-public, confidential information to Kawamoto with respect to the January 23rd CNET article.[3] During the course of the investigation, the Investigation Team narrowed the list of potential sources of the leak until it became clear that Keyworth was the source of the leak. The following is a summary of the evidence and information supporting the Investigation Team's findings.

(1) Kawamoto's January 23, 2006 Article.

Because the Investigation Team's primary objective was to identify the source of the confidential information contained in Kawamoto's January 23rd CNET article, the Investigation Team commenced the investigation by conducting a detailed review of the article. The article attributes the following six comments and quotes to the source:

- Those in attendance worked from early morning to late evening, with few breaks given beyond meals. "By the time the lectures were done at 10 p.m., we were pooped and went to bed."
- HP is considering making more acquisitions in the infrastructure software arena. Those acquisitions would include security software companies, storage software makers and software companies that serve the blade server market.
- In IPG, the long-term plan to develop commercial printers is likely to continue. "We want to develop the next Heidelberg press."
- On the chip front, although HP and Intel have had a long relationship involving their collaboration on the Itanium chip, delays be Intel have created frustration in the HP camp. As a result, HP may use Intel's archrival AMD as a cattle prod of sorts to the chip giant. "We plan to use AMD's Opteron more and more."
- One area expected to get an internal technology revamp in the coming year and a half is direct sales. Though HP's direct sales technology is expected to undergo changes, one thing that's not likely to happen is a merging of the HP and Compaq PC brands. Because the Compaq brand is still recognized in the market, it offsets the additional costs associated with maintaining two brands.
- And, while HP has struggled with getting customers and the market to understanding its Adaptive Enterprise concept, the same mistake will not happen with HP's Next Generation Data Center. "Adaptive Enterprise, What is that? No one understood it. But the Next Generation Data Center is

---

[3] The evidence also overwhelmingly indicates that Keyworth was the source who leaked non-public, confidential information to Kawamoto in conjunction with at least 6 other articles since March of 2002.

something that everyone can understand. The name is (cumbersome). Don't be surprised to see it changed."

Based upon (1) the detailed nature of the foregoing comments and quotes; (2) the Investigation Team's extensive review of each of the slide sets presented during the Board meeting and various committee meetings; (3) the Investigation Team's extensive email and internet proxy server search regarding all individuals who had access to the aforementioned slide sets; and (4) the interviews of witnesses who were present during the Board and committee meetings, it is clear that the source who leaked the information to Kawamoto was physically present during the presentations given during the Board meeting. The slide sets, which were not widely circulated (this was confirmed by electronic searches conducted by the Investigation Team), simply did not contain sufficient detail to enable someone – even someone with significant knowledge of HP's business and strategy – to make *all* of the foregoing comments and quotes based solely on reviewing the slides. The Investigation Team therefore determined that the source must have been physically present to hear the presentations given during the Board meeting, which means the source is either a member of the Board of Directors or a member of the Executive Council.

In addition, the Investigation Team concluded that the source was most likely present at the Technology Committee meeting held on January 11, 2006 (the day before the Board meeting commenced). According to witnesses present at the Technology Committee meeting, three of the topics (targeted acquisitions, Intel/AMD and Adaptive Enterprise) from the January 23rd article were discussed in significant detail (using many of the exact same terms) at the meeting, and, according to witnesses interviewed during the investigation, those same topics likely were not covered in the Board meeting in sufficient detail to give the comments and quotes as they appear in the article. The individuals present during the Technology Committee are: George Keyworth (Committee Chair), Robert (Bob) Ryan, Tom Perkins, Richard (Dick) Hackborn, John Hammergren, Pattie Dunn, Mark Hurd, Ann Livermore, Shane Robison and Alan Haggard.

The foregoing conclusions based upon the content of the January 23rd article enabled the Investigation Team to begin narrowing the list of possible sources. However, other aspects of the content and language used in the January 23rd article provided the Investigation Team with its first indications that the source may be Keyworth. Specifically, the Investigation Team made the following observations about the article:[4]

- Adaptive Enterprise and the Next Generation Data Center. According to several witnesses, Keyworth has discussed these topics both frequently and passionately. [redacted] has also often commented that he believes the Next Generation Data Center name should be changed – even suggesting a name himself (Neutron Data Center) during the January 2006 Board meeting.

- Intel/AMD. According to a number of witnesses, Keyworth is familiar with the HP/Intel relationship, the recent issues with Itanium, and HP's desire to use AMD's Opteron chip more frequently. In addition, according to one witness interviewed, Keyworth is the only Board member to bring up the Itanium subject during Board meetings. It is also worth noting that Kawamoto's "source" has previously discussed HP's relationship with Intel and our use of the Itanium chip in significant, technical detail.

- Acquisitions. A number of witnesses indicated that Keyworth has shown a keen, vocal interest in making targeted acquisitions to increase HP's breadth of products and services over the past 10 years. In addition, as the Chair of the Technology Committee and a member of the Acquisitions Committee, he would be well aware of HP's strategy with respect to acquisitions.
- Use of the term "lectures." This is an academic term, rarely used in the business environment. Keyworth is the only Board member with an academic background. Keyworth frequently gives and attends lectures on a variety of topics; this is a term he may use.
- "We were pooped." This is also an unusual term. A number of witnesses interviewed indicated that, contrary to a number of members of the Board, Keyworth often uses casual, colloquial terms in conversation, so this is a term he may use.
- Heidelberg Press. A number of witnesses interviewed indicated that this is a term many of the Board members likely would not be familiar enough with to comment on. Keyworth, however, would be.
- Several witnesses interviewed indicated that Keyworth is likely the only Board member who could speak intelligently about each of the topics set forth in the article without extensive preparation. The breadth and detail of the various subjects covered requires a fairly comprehensive knowledge of several different HP business groups.
- Stephen Shankland "contributed to this report." This fact is significant because, as will be discussed in more detail below, there appears to be a fairly substantial connection between Keyworth and Shankland.

(2) Additional Articles Written by Kawamoto

After narrowing the potential sources of the leak as set forth above, the Investigation Team reviewed and analyzed all articles written by Kawamoto regarding HP since 2001. The Investigation Team found that, since March of 2002, Kawamoto has written 10 substantive articles about HP (including the January 23rd article discussed in detail above) in which she cites a "source" who has provided non-public, confidential information in the article. The Investigation Team's detailed review of each of the 10 articles made three things clear: (1) that Kawamoto likely used the same source in each of the 10 articles; (2) that the source was a pre-merger HP director; and (3) that Keyworth was most likely the source.

Kawamoto most likely used the same source in all 10 articles. One of the first things the Investigation Team noted is that Kawamoto always cites just one "source," rather than citing "sources" or "people familiar with the situation" like other reporters who cover HP (and write far more frequently about HP than Kawamoto) such as Pui-Wing Tam, Peter Burrows, Ben Elgin, and John Markoff. In addition, based upon the Investigation Team's research, Kawamoto does not appear to contact HP to confirm her stories, whereas other reporters such as Tam and Burrows essentially *always* contact HP's Media Relations group to confirm their stories and seek comment (which is an industry practice).[5] Moreover, despite the fact that Kawamoto cites only one source and never calls to confirm the stories, the information contained in the articles is highly confidential, detailed, and accurate. Finally, because Kawamoto has written just 10 substantive articles about HP in the past 4 years, it is highly unlikely that she has cultivated multiple sources from whom she can obtain the type of information that appears in her stories.

The foregoing facts indicate that Kawamoto's source is highly placed, has access to the specific information set forth in her articles, and that she trusts the source to provide accurate information. They also strongly support the conclusion that she has been using the same source since the first article citing an anonymous "source," which was written in March of 2002.

Kawamoto's source is a pre-merger HP director. In 4 of the 10 articles, the "source" references specific events that occurred at HP before the merger, and in one of the articles, Kawamoto specifically identifies the source as an "HP director." For example, on March 19, 2002, Kawamoto quoted ***"one HP director who requested anonymity"*** as follows:

- "We had looked at consulting two years ago, when it was a growing business. But now, outsourcing is growing and consulting is not. I plan to recommend (to the board) we look at parts of Compaq's business that they might be interested in selling if the merger does not go through." [The only Board members in March of 2002 who were also Board members in 2000 were Pattie Dunn, Bob Wayman, Carly Fiorina, Sam Ginn, Dick Hackborn and George Keyworth]

On July 29, 2002, in a detailed article about the formation of the Technology Committee, Kawamoto quoted a "source close to the company" as follows:

- HP developed the idea behind Itanium before entering into a 1993 partnership under which Intel handles most of the work of designing and building it. HP's work has given the company a financial edge over competitors besides just the extra years of design experience – HP gets a deeper discount on Itanium processors than HP competitors. Because Intel doesn't pay HP Itanium royalties, that discount helps to offset some of the billions of research dollars that HP spent on Itanium. [The only Board members in July of 2002 that were even affiliated with HP in 1993 were Bob Wayman, Dick Hackborn and George Keyworth]

On March 29, 2005, in an article on the day HP announced it was hiring Mark Hurd, Kawamoto cites a "source close to the board" as follows:

- During the search, Hurd emerged as a clear frontrunner within the first month of the effort. And though the search ended quickly, Hurd was not well-known to HP prior to its CEO search. He was not among the candidates reviewed when HP selected Fiorina six years ago. [The only Board members in March of 2005 that were also on the Board when HP interviewed and hired Fiorina were Pattie Dunn, Bob Wayman, Dick Hackborn and George Keyworth]

---

[5] The only exception uncovered to date was when Krazit called Bob Sherbin on Jan 20th to ask him for comment on the story published on January 23rd.

And, finally, on January 23, 2006 (Kawamoto wrote 2 of her 10 total articles about HP on January 23rd), Kawamoto cites "an HP source" as follows:

> *Five years ago, HP dropped its bid for the consulting arm of PWC . . . . The deal fell through as HP and the PWC partners wrangled over the pricing structure and the difficulty in dealing with a partnership.* **[The only Board members in January of 2006 that were also on the Board when PWC deal was contemplated were Carly Fiorina, Pattie Dunn, Bob Wayman, Dick Hackborn and George Keyworth]**

In addition to the fact that the first article referenced above specifically attributes the quote to a pre-merger HP director, the Investigation Team was able to determine that, if the source was not an HP director before the merger, it is unlikely Kawamoto or any other reporter would accept and print the statements about events that clearly took place before the merger without confirming them with at least one additional source[6]. Since Kawamoto cites only the one source, the source most likely has personal knowledge of those items, thus eliminating any need for Kawamoto to confirm them with either HP or an additional source. The article with the information about the 1993 agreement with Intel is a good example – it seems highly unlikely that Kawamoto (or any reporter) would take the word of a pre-merger Compaq director, or of a new HP director, about the pricing HP gets or the royalty arrangements between HP and Intel based on a 1993 agreement. Consequently, the source must have had personal knowledge of the agreement, and the Investigation Team concluded that Kawamoto's source must be a pre-merger HP director.

The content of the Kawamoto articles indicates that Keyworth is most likely the source. As previously stated, since March of 2002, Kawamoto has written 10 substantive articles about HP citing a source and containing non-public, confidential information. Of those 10 articles, 7 of them contain information indicating Keyworth is most likely the source.[7] For example (and as set forth in the immediately preceding section), on March 19, 2002, Kawamoto quoted "one HP director who requested anonymity" as follows:

> "We had looked at consulting two years ago, when it was a growing business. But now, outsourcing is growing and consulting is not. I plan to recommend (to the board) we look at parts of Compaq's business that they might be interested in selling if the merger does not go through."

Because of the quote about looking at consulting two years before the date of the article, Keyworth and Dick Hackborn (Hackborn) are the only two feasible sources for this article. However, a number of individuals interviewed indicated that the language used in the article "I plan to recommend . . ." is the type of language often used by Keyworth when discussing his thoughts and ideas about HP; the same individuals felt quite strongly that Hackborn does not typically speak in this manner. In addition, because Keyworth has been a strong proponent of

---

[6] The Investigation Team further substantiated this conclusion by consulting with a media expert, who was a former investigative reporter for a large metropolitan news agency.

[7] It should be noted that the three articles the Investigation Team found to be unclear as to the source were written between July 11, 2005 and July 16, 2005 (a five day period) and covered the same topic as a July 14, 2005 containing information indicating Keyworth was most likely the source. Thus, an argument can be made that all 7 articles written by Kawamoto about different subjects contain information indicating Keyworth is most likely the source.

strategic acquisitions to enhance HP's product offering and was a vocal supporter of acquiring certain aspects of Compaq, Keyworth is more likely the source of this article.

On July 29, 2002, Kawamoto cited "a source close to the company" as follows:

> The Technology Committee will oversee some of HP's most pressing technology issues, which includes greater use of direct sales and ensuring its research work is firmly aligned with corporate strategy. "The technology committee will help the board look at the enablers for the merger." Tom Perkins suggested the creation of a technology committee and received strong support from Carly Fiorina.

> "The technology committee will receive input from the board as it reviews the complexity and evolution of moving HP to an Itanium architecture. Some of the issues include how fast should the transition move and some of the technological hurdles." It isn't known how long it will take for Itanium servers to outpace those with HP's PA-RISC and 32-bit Intel chips such as Xeon or Pentium.

> HP developed the idea behind Itanium before entering into a 1993 partnership under which Intel handles most of the work of designing and building it. HP's work has given the company a financial edge over competitors besides just the extra years of design experience – HP gets a deeper discount on Itanium processors than HP competitors. Because Intel doesn't pay HP Itanium royalties, that discount helps to offset some of the billions of research dollars that HP spent on Itanium.

Because of the quote about the 1993 agreement with Intel, Keyworth and Hackborn are the only two feasible sources for this article. In addition, because this article contains detailed, technical information, including detailed information about the 1993 agreement with Intel about Itanium, several individuals interviewed indicated that Keyworth is likely the only director who could have provided the content for this article without significant preparation. According to one witness, Itanium is an issue Keyworth has focused on for some time, and Keyworth is the only director who has ever mentioned Itanium in the board room setting. And, as will be more fully explained below, it is also significant that Stephen Shankland "contributed to this report."

On February 24, 2003, Kawamoto cited "a source familiar with the company's plans" as follows:

> HP sees licensing more of its intellectual property as a way to get a greater return on its substantial research and development budget. "HP is looking at licensing technology as a business. Currently, it has over $4 billion invested in research and development annually."

> "HP used to be a lot of disparate businesses, like the printer business, enterprise business and others loosely combined at the top . . . but over the past couple of years, Carly has made it more centralized. And now there is a better grip on the patent assets as a whole. Also, our growing portfolio of patents has been increased with the Compaq merger, which also includes technology from Compaq's DEC and Tandem mergers."

> "This has been a big area for [Carly]. She has been working with the labs and increasing the number of patent applications. There was a time in the economy where growth was valued over profit. But with the current market environment,

profit is now valued over growth. And the licensing (revenue) will fall right to the bottom line since it all stems from the investments already made in R&D."

A number of individuals interviewed felt very strongly that the source for this article was Keyworth. According to the witnesses, Keyworth has often talked about the value add from the Technology Committee with respect to intellectual property generating revenue. Keyworth was very proud of this initiative, and the quote about licensing revenue falling right to the bottom line is not only an inaccurate statement, but is a statement that Keyworth has made on multiple occasions about the issue.

On March 29, 2005, Kawamoto cites "a source close to the board" as follows:

- Hewlett-Packard has selected Mark Hurd, NCR chief executive, as its next CEO. Hurd will serve as president and chief executive, with Patricia Dunn retaining the chairwoman title. "He has done as astonishing job at NCR and had inherited similar problems" to those at HP. "NCR sells into retail and enterprise markets, and has the same complexities."
- During the search, Hurd emerged as a clear frontrunner within the first month of the effort. And though the search ended quickly, Hurd was not well-known to HP prior to its CEO search. He was not among the candidates reviewed when HP selected Fiorina six years ago. "He's young, he has a fabulous record, he understands the industry, he's tough and recruits good people."

Because of the quote about Hurd not being on the list of candidates when Fiorina was hired, Keyworth and Hackborn are the only two feasible sources for this article. According to several witnesses, Keyworth is very proud of being involved in bringing Hurd on board at HP. One witness indicated Keyworth has said he "repaid Dave Packard by bringing Mark on board." A number of individuals interviewed also indicated that the specific language used during parts of the article ("fabulous", "astonishing") is language that Keyworth uses frequently.

It should also be noted that, during a presentation at a tech conference on March 20, 2005 with 750 attendees present, Keyworth informed the attendees that HP would likely announce a new CEO in the next two weeks. He was not authorized by the Board to make such a statement.

On July 14, 2005, Kawamoto cites a "source familiar with the company" as follows:

- HP executives are expected this weekend to put the final touches on a reorganization that could result in the loss of about 15,000 jobs. The job cuts would then be announced on Monday. Despite the prospect of massive layoffs, HP's workers are responding favorably to Hurd, who has been in the CEO post only a few months.
- "People feel he is a straight shooter and doesn't mince his words. People have responded to him positively; they like and respect him and view him as a leader. This response from the employees has happened in a much shorter time than was imagined."
- "What happened was, a year ago, Duane Zitzner wanted to retire by a specific date. He kept reminding Carly that the date was approaching, but she made little effort to fill his position. So when that date came and there was no replacement

for Duane, it was put under VJ. But VJ already had his hands full and the PC business needed a lot of work, so, in the end, it was best to run them separately."

- At the same time, Hurd has found areas within HP where spending has been underinvested. The part of HP's sales force that helps large corporate customers integrate their computer systems is one area that needs further investment. Hurd is working closely with Ann Livermore, a longtime HP executive who oversees the company's server and storage group and its services and software.

A number of individuals interviewed felt the paragraph about Duane Zitzner is out of place in the article. It is essentially a derogatory remark about Fiorina that is completely unrelated to the rest of the content of the article. According to witnesses, both Keyworth and Hackborn were vocal about this particular issue, and it was a source of contention for both of them. However, according to at least one witness, the language used in the article sounds like what Keyworth would say, not Hackborn.

On January 23, 2006 (the second article written by Kawamoto on the 23rd), Kawamoto cites "an HP source" as follows:

- Despite media reports that HP and Blackstone were in preliminary discussions to acquire CSC, such a deal never made it on the radar of HP executives and directors. Reports of the preliminary discussions took HP executives by surprise. "CSC has occasionally come up from time to time as a potential acquisition, but it's nothing that we ever seriously pursued and nothing we were in talks with recently.
- Five years ago, HP dropped its bid for the consulting arm of PWC . . . . The deal fell through as HP and the PWC partners wrangled over the pricing structure and the difficulty in dealing with a partnership.

This article directly contradicts itself, which indicates it is an intentional plant of false information. The language about executives and directors being surprised by talk of a possible CSC deal indicates a complete lack of inside knowledge is completely contradicted by the language about the PWC deal, and the "throw away line" about PWC is *definitely* inside information that was not made public when HP decided not to go forward with the PWC deal in 2001. At least one individual interviewed thinks Keyworth would plant information such as this to further an acquisition he believed in. Keyworth has had a keen, vocal interest in making targeted acquisitions to increase HP's breadth of products and services over the past 10 years. This article was a very good thing for HP, as it would have the tendency to reduce CSC's stock price, which enhances HP's ability to complete the acquisition. And, because of the quote about the PWC deal (which was 5 years ago), Keyworth and Hackborn are the only two feasible sources for this article if the source was a member of the Board.

The likelihood that the information in this article was an intentional plant of false information is also enhanced by the fact that Kawamoto had not written a substantive article about HP since July of 2005 (more than 6 months). Given the lengthy break since her last substantive article about HP, it seems very unlikely that she would publish two completely different stories, based on confidential information from two completely different sources, on the exact same day. It seems more likely that the same source gave her information for both articles – and any source with detailed knowledge of what occurred during the Board meeting would know about the CSC negotiations. And, as more fully set forth in the section regarding the first January 23rd article above, the language and content of that article indicates that Keyworth is most likely the source Kawamoto used for that article, [redacted]

(3) Additional Information Connecting Keyworth to the Leaks.

Based on the foregoing overview of the Kawamoto articles, the Investigation Team found that Kawamoto likely used the same source in each of the 10 articles, that the source was a pre-merger HP director, and that, based solely on the content of the articles, Keyworth was most likely the source for at least 7 of the articles. As will be set forth in significant detail below, the additional information obtained, reviewed and analyzed by the Investigation Team, when combined with the foregoing summary of the Kawamoto articles, [redacted] (replace with [redacted] or something similar) that Keyworth was Kawamoto's source.

Keyworth's Connections to Stephen Shankland. In 3 of the 10 substantive articles written about HP by Kawamoto since 2002 citing a "source," the article says "Stephen Shankland contributed to this report." Thomas Shankland (Stephen's father) worked with Keyworth in the same department at the Los Alamos Lab in New Mexico for approximately 6 years. Keyworth then left Los Alamos to join the Reagan administration. With the possible exception of when Keyworth was with the Reagan administration, Tom Shankland and his family have lived close to Keyworth's New Mexico residence for many years. In fact, for approximately two years in the 1970s, Keyworth and Shankland lived less than two miles from each other, and Stephen and Keyworth's son, George, who are just two years apart, likely attended the same elementary school. Both Thomas Shankland and Keyworth are physicists, belonging to several of the same scientific societies (Sigma Xi an Honorary Scientific Society and Phi Beta Kappa).

Stephen Shankland also authored an article in August 2005 regarding the Progress for Freedom Foundation meeting held in Aspen, Colorado. Keyworth is the Chairman of the Progress for Freedom Foundation and was likely present during the meeting.

In addition, Stephen Shankland's wife, Rachel Konrad, a former CNET reporter and currently an AP journalist, authored a CNET article entitled "Failed HP-Compaq merger would be painful" on Nov. 12, 2001. In the article, which was written the week after Walter Hewlett announced he was going to vote against the merger, Konrad quotes "a source familiar with the board as follows: "I don't think Walter has thought this through. [If the merger fails,] [n]one of the directors, except Walter, would stay, and I guarantee a lot of the senior management would leave too." Dawn Kawamoto and Stephen Shankland "contributed to this report."

The foregoing is important not just because Konrad is Shankland's wife, but also because Peter Burrows, on page 206 of his book, "Backfire," states that, following a Board meeting on November 16, 2001, Keyworth, Hackborn and Walter Hewlett walked into Hewlett's old office and one of them said, "Look, we are all friends, Walter, but have you thought this through all the way?" [According to George Anders' book, Perfect Enough, Hackborn then explained that, if the merger failed, directors would resign and executives would quit]. Given the nearly identical nature of the two quotes, it seems likely that it was either Keyworth or Hackborn that gave the quote to Konrad and then the two of them later said the same thing to Hewlett. Hackborn has no known connections to Shankland or Konrad – Keyworth does.

Information from the KONA I investigation. In mid-2005, an investigation team composed of a number of members from the Investigation Team in this matter conducted an investigation with respect to information leaks that occurred between January and July of 2005 involving media sources such as the Wall Street Journal, Business Week and the New York Times, and reporters such as Pui-Wing Tam, Peter Burrows, Ben Elgin and John Markoff. During the KONA I investigation, the investigation team documented a call from Keyworth's cell phone to John Markoff's NY Time's office on Feb 9, 2005. This call is significant because it occurred just two days after the Board meeting in Chicago, it was the same day HP terminated Fiorina and, the following day (February 10th), Markoff published an article about HP's decision. The article also purported to contain inside information about the top two internal candidates to replace Fiorina and cited "one company insider" as having provided said information. It is unclear whether Keyworth ever disclosed this phone call to Media Relations or other members of the Board.

The KONA I investigation also established that Keyworth has, or at least as of the time of the investigation had, an ongoing relationship with Peter Burrows of Business Week. Specifically, Keyworth was identified by Burrows in his book, Backfire, as the only HP Board member who would talk to him "on the record" after the merger. In addition, Burrows states in the book that Keyworth contributed "significant information" to him.

The investigation team in KONA I also established that Keyworth has a connection to George Anders, who is the San Francisco Bureau editor for the Wall Street Journal. For example, in his book, Perfect Enough, Anders cites Keyworth as a source of information, and Keyworth is one of only two HP Board members whose [redacted] appear in the book. The book portrays HP and Fiorina in a favorable light. It should also be noted that, throughout 2005 and as recently as January 31, 2006, the Wall Street Journal (via reporter Pui-Wing Tam) has repeatedly published stories containing non-public, confidential HP information attributed to "sources" and "people familiar with the company."

Based upon the foregoing, the investigation team in KONA I determined that Keyworth was one of three most likely sources of the numerous leaks to several different reporters in 2005. The other subjects of interest during that investigation were Robert Knowling (no longer a Board member) and Tom Perkins. [redacted]

Board member Tom Perkins softens and changes his position regarding the source(s) of the leaks. When the information leaks to the Wall Street Journal, Business Week and the New York Times occurred in 2005, Tom Perkins reacted very strongly to the leaks and felt strongly the source(s) of the leak should be removed from the Board, even telling Pattie Dunn in person and via email that he supported the use of Lie Detector Tests to identify the source(s). In addition, on January 23, 2006, after reading Kawamoto's article accurately summarizing the January 2006 Board meeting, Perkins contacted Ann Baskins and Pattie Dunn, stating that the leak could not have come from a Board member, and that it must have come from a member of the Executive Council. Perkins also sent Dunn an email indicating that he thought the leak came from an EC member, reading straight from the slides presented during the Board meeting.

Then, during a recent discussion with Dunn during the week of February 6th-10th, Perkins said that, if the source of the leaks is identified, perhaps they should not automatically remove the source from the Board. He further stated that, if the source "has been a major contributor to the Board," and promises not to leak any more information to the media, maybe the person should be allowed to remain a Board member.

The foregoing dramatic change in his position about the source of the leaks is significant for at least two reasons. First, immediately following the January 23rd article, Perkins insisted to Baskins and Dunn that the source could not possibly be a Board member, yet in his recent conversation with Dunn he seemed to believe it was a Board member. This tends to indicate that he now *either has reason* to believe the source is a Board member, or that he knows who the source is, and that the source is a Board member. Second, Perkins' drastic change of position is significant because it indicates that he either knows who it is, or strongly suspects he knows who it is, and that it is someone he both knows well and supports as a Board member. Keyworth fits both descriptions, as it is well known at HP and within the Board that Keyworth and Perkins have become good friends and are closely aligned as members of the Board. In addition, according to a number of individuals interviewed, Perkins and Keyworth have worked in a coordinated fashion in the past, working together to get Perkins back on the Board in early 2005 and to remove Fiorina as HP's CEO shortly thereafter.

Also supporting the significance of Perkins' discussion with Dunn during the week of February 6th is the fact that the Investigation Team has determined that Keyworth called Perkins at least [redacted] times between January 30th and February 8th, including at least 3 times on February 3rd (the same day Keyworth called Kawamoto at her office – this call will be discussed in more detail below). This is significant because of the timing of the calls with respect to Perkins communicating his change in position on the source of the leaks, and because of the volume of calls during such a short timeframe, as Keyworth does not appear to have called Perkins more than [redacted] times during the six weeks preceding January 30th, then called him at least [redacted] times in an 8-day period. Interestingly, since all the calls between Keyworth and Perkins in early February, Keyworth's call to Kawamoto on February 3rd, and Perkins call to Dunn during the week for February 6th wherein he indicated that perhaps they should not remove the source of the leaks from the Board, as long as it was someone who had been a major contributor *and* they promised not to leak any more information to the media, Kawamoto has not written a single article about HP in which she cites a "source" (despite the fact that Kawamoto has written *several* stories about HP since February 3rd).

Keyworth has a number of direct connections to Kawamoto. According to several individuals interviewed, as well comments made by Keyworth himself during the course of the KONA I investigation, Keyworth was asked by Carly Fiorina to develop a relationship with Kawamoto and another reporter (Pui-Wing Tam) sometime in 2001. The purpose of developing the relationship was to promote the HP/Compaq merger. It appears clear that Keyworth did, in fact, develop some sort of relationship with Kawamoto[8], as Kawamoto wrote an article on August 21, 2001 in which Keyworth was quoted as follows:

---

[8] It is also clear that Keyworth developed a relationship with Pui-Wing Tam. On November 17, 2005, Keyworth contacted HP investigators in Palo Alto to report that Tam called his home phone in New Mexico on two occasions in January 2005. Keyworth indicated that Tam was attempting to ask him questions about a story she was writing, but that he did not return the calls. Keyworth stated that he had given Tam his home number during the HP/Compaq merger when the Board was encouraged to work with the press to promote the merger. He also stated that he now wanted to document Tam's calls before deleting them because of the previous issues with information being leaked out of HP to the press at that time. He also stated that he had not spoken with Tam in over two years. The messages were recorded and preserved.

> "In the early summer of 1999, when we were interviewing Carly, we discussed it would take a minimum of three years to turn things around and there would be lots of ups and downs. We are absolutely behind her and know there will be challenges."

In addition to the foregoing direct connection to Kawamoto, the Investigation Team established that, ***at 5:37 pm PST on January 18, 2006*** (just two days before Krazit called Sherbin for comment on the article CNET intended to publish), ***a call was made from Kawamoto's cell phone to Keyworth's home in*** [redacted] The call lasted approximately one minute. However, it should be noted that the phone is listed in Keyworth's wife's name (Marion Schwartz Keyworth), and there is no documented 411 call from Kawamoto's cell phone prior to the call. This indicates that Kawamoto likely knew the home phone number, which is significant because it appears as though Keyworth moved permanently into his wife's home at or around the time they were married in August of 2005. This appears to indicate that Keyworth has stayed in touch with Kawamoto during the past several years.

Keyworth did not disclose the foregoing call to Bob Sherbin or Pattie Dunn, as is expected when Board members are contacted by members of the media. In addition, the Investigation Team documented no other calls to or from Kawamoto's cell or home phones by other directors prior to the January 23rd article.

In addition to the January 18th call from Kawamoto to Keyworth, the Investigation Team also established that, ***at 2:21 pm PST on February 3, 2006, a call was made from Keyworth's cell phone to Kawamoto's office*** (her direct line, not the switchboard number) at CNET. ***The call lasted approximately 10 minutes.*** No 411 call preceded 10-minute call either from Keyworth's cell phone or from his home phone at his New Mexico residence (which, based on phone records obtained by the Investigation Team, is where Keyworth was located on February 3rd). This call is also significant because of the 3 calls documented above made from Keyworth's New Mexico residence to Tom Perkins on the same day, as well as Perkins' subsequent discussion with Pattie Dunn communicating his change of position with respect to the source of the leaks.

Keyworth did not disclose this second call to Bob Sherbin or Pattie Dunn, as is expected when Board members have contact with members of the media. [redacted]

Finally, the existence of the foregoing calls is also potentially significant because, despite the fact that Keyworth was quoted in an article written by Pui Wing Tam on January 14, 2006 about Tom Perkin's new book, there does not appear to have been any phone calls to or from Pui Wing Tam to Keyworth at or around that timeframe. As such, it appears that Keyworth likely interacts with Pui Wing Tam (and Kawamoto) via email or Instant Messenger as well. It should be noted, however, that if Tam or Kawamoto called Keyworth's home phone from their respective offices, the Investigation Team would not be able to obtain a record of any such calls.

VI. Summary Conclusion

As the foregoing summary clearly indicates, the Investigation Team successfully narrowed the list of potential sources of the leak during the course of the investigation and, as of the date of this Draft Report, the overwhelming weight of evidence reviewed by the Investigation Team indicates the source of the leak is HP Board member George Keyworth. Specifically, the content of each the 7 articles discussed in detail above, the numerous connections made by Investigation Team tying Keyworth to the leaks (including without limitation Keyworth's connections to Shankland, the information obtained during the KONA I investigation, and Tom Perkins' abrupt and dramatic change in opinion as to the source of the leaks), as well as the telephonic contact between Kawamoto and Keyworth in January and February of 2006, all clearly identify and establish Keyworth as the only feasible source of the leaks.

VII. Impact to HP

The unauthorized disclosure of non-public, sensitive information at the Board level can cause enormous, and at times, irreparable harm to HP's reputation. The disclosure of information by Board members creates an environment of uneasiness and distrust within the Board, as such disclosures are clearly a breach of the fiduciary duty owed to HP by each and every Board member. Moreover, continued and repeated information leaks like those that have occurred since January of 2005 can significantly impair HP's ability to conduct its business in an appropriate fashion. If the leaks continue, HP's executives will likley be forced to limit the information provided to the Board in order to ensure that the company's plans and strategies do not appear the following day on CNET or in the Wall Street Journal. If the executives so limit the information provided to the Board, the Board members' ability to properly and efficiently carry out their duties and responsibilities on behalf of HP's shareholders will be dramatically and negatively impacted. This, of course, creates an untenable situation that will ultimately have a negative impact on HP, its employees and shareholders.

VIII. Recommendations

Based upon the information and conclusions set forth in this Draft Report, the Investigation Team hereby recommends that the Executive Team (Hurd, Dunn and Baskins) and the Investigation Team discuss the following items before closing the investigation:

- Completing the investigative activities (including, for example, outstanding telephone and background searches) currently being undertaken by the Investigation Team;
- Whether Keyworth should be interviewed in conjunction with the investigation. There are several questions with respect to this topic:
    - Who should conduct the interview? Options include Hurd and/or Dunn, appropriate members of the Investigation Team, an impartial third party, or some combination thereof;
    - What kind of interview should be conducted? Options include information gathering, adversarial, neutral;
    - What impact will an interview have on the Board and its members?

- What is there to be gained by conducting an interview?
- What harm could be caused by conducting an interview?

- Whether other Board members such as Dick Hackborn and/or Tom Perkins should be interviewed in conjunction with the investigation;
- What other options may be available to the Executive Team at this point in the investigation (such as disclosing the Investigation Team's findings to other Board members, obtaining outside legal advice regarding the sufficiency of evidence obtained to date, taking affirmative actions to remove Keyworth from the Board, etc.).

It should also be noted that, when the investigation has been completed, the Investigation Team intends to submit a set of recommendations regarding (1) proactive actions that can and should be taken in order to help prevent leaks such as those at issue in this investigation, and (2) additional follow-up investigative items such as possible information breaches currently occurring within Media Relations and other groups within HP.

End of Draft Report

TAB 73

From: Hunsaker, Kevin <kevin.hunsaker@hp.com>
Sent: Monday, March 13, 2006 12:03 PM
To: Nye, Vince <vince.nye@hp.com>; Adler, Frederick P. <fred.adler@hp.com>; Ron DeLia <rrd@security-outsourcing.com>; Gentilucci, Anthony R. <tony.gentilucci@hp.com>
Subject: Meeting on Wednesday -- privileged communication

Hi guys,

On this morning's call, I forgot to summarize my weekly briefing with Ann and Pattie, and there was one important thing they had to say. Both of them indicated they thought it would be a good idea if Ron and Tony were also present in Los Angeles for the meeting with Mark -- both because of their familiarity with what we've done in this investigation and because of their familiarity with KONA I. Given that I know very little about what was done in KONA I and that Ron is the one with the most extensive knowledge of what his folks have done in this investigation, I think it is an excellent idea. I believe this will ensure that we can answer any question Mark throws at us.

I called Rosemarie and she still has a room reserved for Tony, and it's my understanding that Ron has at least one extra room reserved because of the surveillance activity we may be conducting. I spoke to Ron and Tony over the weekend and believe they will both be able to make it. Ron and Tony, you can both make it, right?

I think this is an excellent development, as it will enable us to cover any topic Mark wants to discuss.

My apologies for forgetting to cover this on our call.

Kevin

Kevin T. Hunsaker
Senior Counsel
HP Legal Department
Phone: 650 857-3079
Fax: 650 857-3710

TAB 74

From: Nye, Vince
Sent: 03/17/2006 02:01:12 PM
To: Crawford, Ted (Security-Boise)
Subject: Cell Phone Information (Call Data)
Attachments: Call Data Article0001.JPG

Ted: Please add your thoughts..It will be going to Tony, Kevin and Fred..Thanks

Gentlemen:

First, I'd like to thank everyone for the efforts so far in this BoD Investigation, Especially to Ron and Fred for without their work there wouldn't have been a investigation. Even though we haven't concluded this case as of date, the work product is pretty much in the appropriate hands for decisions on next steps if any.

I am forwarding a newspaper article that was recently published in the Sacramento Bee. The article was sent to me by a very good friend. The article as you can see is in regard to a issue I brought up on obtaining cell call data. Although in the opinion of our legal staff the practice of obtaining cell phone call data is legal and therefore was used in the investigation we conducted, is still in my mind a inappropriate investigative tactic and unethical.

I have the greatest admiration for everyone on this investigation team and respect the professionalism we have regarding our investigative strategy and understand we all want to do the right things for HP. Speaking for myself, I have always had a pretty good weather vane for conducting investigations and working within certain perimeters, both legally and ethically.

Laws were written with some motive and/or principal in mind and therefore as a law enforcement officer for 20 plus years my emphasis has always been having a grasp and good understanding of the motive and purpose of a particular law being considered.

If one has to hold his nose and then conduct a task, then is logical to step back and consider if the task or activity is the right thing to do. In this matter, collecting cell phone call data in my opinion was a nose closer. Granted without the phone call data, we wouldn't have been able to connect certain dots and our conclusions somewhat different.

It had been mentioned during the brief discussion on this matter, that obtaining cell phone call data was no different then our plan to send out erroneous information via e-mail with a bug was no different. I believe the comparison to be null and void. There are several substantial differences.

My intention of sending this article is to allow the team to read it and re-consider there position for future cases. I suppose it may not be totally necessary that we all agree one way of the other, but certainly would lend itself to consistent investigative practices. Again, speaking for myself I won't use this particular tactic on those cases I have assigned to lead.

Thanks,

Vince

TAB 75

From: Hunsaker, Kevin
Sent: 03/21/2006 08:59:16 PM
To: Gentilucci, Anthony R.
Subject: RE: Leak case -- privileged communication

No kidding.

Kevin T. Hunsaker
Senior Counsel
HP Legal Department
Phone: 650 857-3079
Fax: 650 857-3710

From: Gentilucci, Anthony R.
Sent: Tuesday, March 21, 2006 8:52 PM
To: Hunsaker, Kevin
Subject: RE: Leak case -- privileged communication

Just don't tell Fred and Vince.........

From: Hunsaker, Kevin
Sent: Tuesday, March 21, 2006 11:51 PM
To: Gentilucci, Anthony R.
Subject: RE: Leak case -- privileged communication

It's probably too far fetched, but you never know.

Kevin T. Hunsaker
Senior Counsel
HP Legal Department
Phone: 650 857-3079
Fax: 650 857-3710

From: Gentilucci, Anthony R.
Sent: Tuesday, March 21, 2006 8:50 PM
To: Hunsaker, Kevin
Subject: RE: Leak case -- privileged communication

OK, I'll look forward to hearing it....

Tony

From: Hunsaker, Kevin
Sent: Tuesday, March 21, 2006 11:48 PM
To: Gentilucci, Anthony R.
Subject: RE: Leak case -- privileged communication

Something totally new. It involves pretexting GK or his wife at their house . . . .

Kevin T. Hunsaker
Senior Counsel

HP Legal Department
Phone: 650 857-3079
Fax: 650 857-3710

From: Gentilucci, Anthony R.
Sent: Tuesday, March 21, 2006 8:45 PM
To: Hunsaker, Kevin
Subject: RE: Leak case -- privileged communication

OK, sounds interesting, does it have to do with DK/Jacob, something new..........

From: Hunsaker, Kevin
Sent: Tuesday, March 21, 2006 11:44 PM
To: Gentilucci, Anthony R.
Subject: Leak case -- privileged communication

When you get a chance tomorrow, give me a call -- I've got a bit of a wild idea to get the clincher against GK.

Kevin T. Hunsaker
Senior Counsel
HP Legal Department
Phone: 650 857-3079
Fax: 650 857-3710

TAB 76

From: [redacted]
Sent: 03/24/2006 11:29:39 AM
To: Gentilucci, Anthony R.
Subject: Telephone call records
Attachments: Clemons.doc

Tony:

My law clerk found only one case on point:

In *Clemons v. Waller*, the plaintiff brought an action against a licensed private investigator for procuring copies of the plaintiff's cell phone records under the Electronic Communications Privacy Act, 18 U.S.C. 2510 *et seq.*, which 'criminalizes and creates civil liability for intentionally intercepting electronic communications without a warrant.'" 82 Fed.Appx. 436, 439 (6th Cir. 2003) (attached below). There were no other causes of action asserted. The private investigator phoned the plaintiff's cell phone company and pretended that he was the plaintiff in order to obtain the plaintiff's cell phone records spanning a four-month period. *Id.* at 438. The private investigator requested that the telephone company transmit the billing records for the plaintiff's cell via the private investigator's fax machine. *Id.*

Finding in favor of the private investigator, the court held that the statute does not impose liability upon "a person not acting under color of law [who] intercept[s] a wire, oral or electronic communication where such person is a party to the communication ... unless such communications is intercepted for the purpose of committing any criminal or tortuous act in violation of the Constitution or laws of the United States or of any State." *Id.* at 439-40 (*quoting* 18 U.S.C. § 2511(2)(d)). The court further held that the private investigator was in fact "a party to the communication," and therefore not subject to liability under the Act, because the private investigator had specifically requested the records himself from the telephone company and had received them the records via his own fax machine. *Id.* at 440.

Valerie

C

Briefs and Other Related Documents

This case was not selected for publication in the Federal Reporter.NOT RECOMMENDED FOR FULL--TEXT PUBLICATION Sixth Circuit Rule 28(g) limits citation to specific situations. Please see Rule 28(g) before citing in a proceeding in a court in the Sixth Circuit. If cited, a copy must be served on other parties and the Court. Please use FIND to look at the applicable circuit court rule before citing this opinion. Sixth Circuit Rule 28(g). (FIND CTA6 Rule 28.)

United States Court of Appeals,Sixth Circuit.

Roger CLEMONS, Plaintiff-Appellant,

v.

Randall WALLER, a Action Autoliner d/b/a Action Research Group, Karl Hall, and Meridian Resources & Investigations, Defendants-Appellees.

No. 02-5342.

Nov. 13, 2003.

Background: Plaintiff brought action under Electronic Communications Privacy Act (ECPA) alleging that private investigator impersonated him in phone call to telephone company, persuaded it to fax him copies of plaintiff's cellular phone records, and then shared those records with others. The United States District Court for the Middle District of Tennessee entered summary judgment in favor of investigator, and plaintiff appealed.

Holding: The Court of Appeals, Gibbons, Circuit Judge, held that investigator was party to fax transmission from telephone company.

Affirmed.

West Headnotes

Telecommunications 372 ⚷1437

372 Telecommunications

372X Interception or Disclosure of Electronic Communications; Electronic Surveillance

372X(A) In General

372k1435 Acts Constituting Interception or Disclosure

372k1437 k. Telephone Communications.

Most Cited Cases

(Formerly 372k494.1)

Private investigator was party to fax transmission from telephone company containing third party's cellular phone billing records, and thus investigator's receipt of fax did not violate Electronic Communications Privacy Act (ECPA), even though investigator had convinced company to send records by impersonating third party, where investigator was not acting under color of law, and did not intercept fax transmission for purpose of committing any crime or tort. 18 U.S.C.A. § 2511(2)(d).

*437 On Appeal from the United States District Court for the Middle District of Tennessee.

Peter T. Skeie, Attorney at Law, Nashville, TN, for Plaintiff-Appellant.

Karl Hall, pro se, Franklin, TN, for Defendant-Appellee.

Before GIBBONS and SUTTON, Circuit Judges, and TARNOW, District Judge. FN*

FN* The Honorable Arthur J. Tarnow, United States District Judge for the Eastern District of Michigan, sitting by designation.

OPINION

GIBBONS, Circuit Judge.

**1 Plaintiff-appellant Roger Clemons sued multiple defendants under the Electronic Communications Privacy Act ("ECPA"), 18 U.S.C. § § 2510 *et seq.* He alleged that an imposter impersonated him in a phone call to BellSouth Mobility, persuaded BellSouth to fax his cellular phone records to the imposter, and then shared the records with others. The district court granted summary judgment in favor of defendants. Assuming without deciding that the fax transmission constituted an electronic communication protected by the ECPA, the district court concluded that the imposter's receipt of the fax did not constitute an illegal "interception" under the statute because it was received on a fax machine the imposter uses in the ordinary course of his business. Alternatively, the district court held that even if the imposter's receipt of the records was an "interception," Clemons would still not be entitled to relief because the statute provides that it is not unlawful for a person to intercept an electronic communication "where such person is a party to the communication," unless the interception is done for the purposes of committing a criminal or tortious act. We affirm the judgment of the district court on the basis that the party receiving the intercepted communication was a party to the communication without deciding whether the interceptor received the communication on a device used by him in the ordinary course of business.

I.

Defendant Randall Waller and his wife were engaged in divorce proceedings. To assist him with the divorce, Waller retained*438 Karl Hall, a licensed private investigator and the owner of defendant Meridian Resources & Investigation (Meridian Resources). Waller directed Hall to investigate several individuals working for Waller's wife, including Clemons. FN1 Waller instructed Hall that the investigation should include securing the private billing records associated with Clemons's cellular telephone number, 601-838-4002. In response to Waller's request, Hall contacted defendant Action Research Group ("ARS") and requested that it obtain copies of Clemons's cellular phone billing records. ARS agreed to perform the service. Mike Lee, an agent of ARS, then contacted Clemons's cellular phone service provider, BellSouth Mobility, and represented that he was Clemons. While thus impersonating Clemons, Lee requested copies of Clemons's cellular phone billing records for a four-month period. BellSouth transmitted those requested records to Lee via his facsimile machine.

FN1. Plaintiff Roger Clemons is a private investigator. Carol Waller hired Fowlers Profile Links, Inc., a private investigation company, to perform several investigative tasks for her. Fowlers Profile Links in turn subcontracted with Clemons, a licensed private investigator, to examine and copy various public records in Frankfort, Kentucky. This trip to Kentucky was Clemons's only association with the divorce proceedings, according to his complaint.

After obtaining the records, ARS sold copies of Clemons's billing records to Hall and Meridian Resources for the price of $748.25. Hall and Meridian Resources, in turn, provided the records to Waller and billed him for obtaining those records. Waller paid the bill in full.

Clemons filed the instant action on February 28, 2000. He alleged that defendants violated his rights under the federal wiretap statute, as modified by the ECPA, 18 U.S.C. § § 2510 *et seq.*, by surreptitiously securing his cellular phone billing records. Clemons argued first that the impersonator's receipt of the faxed billing records constitutes an impermissible "interception" under 18 U.S.C. § 2511(a). Clemons also argued that defendants ARS, Hall and Meridian are liable under 18 U.S.C. § 2511(c) for intentionally disclosing the contents of the intercepted fax and that defendant Waller is liable under § 2511(d) for obtaining the intercepted information. Waller, in turn, filed a motion against Clemons, requesting sanctions against him and his attorney pursuant to Fed.R.Civ.P. 11, 28 U.S.C. § 1927, and the district court's equitable powers.

**2 The district court granted summary judgment in favor of defendants and declined to award sanctions against Clemons. Clemons appealed the grant of summary judgment, and Waller appealed the denial of sanctions. Clemons subsequently dismissed his appeal to the extent that it concerns Waller and ARS, and Waller dismissed his cross-appeal for sanctions. Thus, the only two remaining defendants/appellees are Hall, the private investigator who instructed ARS to secure plaintiff's phone records, and Meridian Resources, Hall's corporation. FN2

FN2. In a letter received by this Court on August 4, 2003, Hall, now proceeding *pro se*, requested sanctions against Clemons and his attorney. It is unclear from Hall's letter whether he intends to appeal the district court's denial of Waller's motion for sanctions or whether Hall intends to raise the issue of sanctions for the first time on appeal. In either case, Hall's request must be denied. First, Hall does not have standing to appeal the district court's denial of Waller's motion. To have standing to appeal a district court's order, the appellant must have been injured by that order. *Deposit Guar. Nat'l Bank v. Roper*, 445 U.S. 326, 333, 100 S.Ct. 1166, 63 L.Ed.2d 427 (1980) ("Ordinarily, only a party aggrieved by a judgment or order of a district court may exercise the statutory right to appeal therefrom."). Waller originally filed the motion for sanctions against Clemons and the denial of the motion injured him, not Hall. Therefore, Hall does not have

standing to appeal the district court's denial of Waller's motion. Moreover, as an appeal, Hall's request would be untimely since it was submitted more than thirty days after the denial of Waller's motion for sanctions. *See* 28 U.S.C. § 2107(a).
In the event Hall is asserting a claim for sanctions for the first time on appeal, we will not consider the claim because it does not warrant deviating from the general rule that issues presented for the first time on appeal are not properly before this court. *Foster v. Barilow,* 6 F.3d 405, 407 (6th Cir.1993). The Sixth Circuit will consider issues for the first time on appeal only in exceptional cases or when doing so is required to prevent a plain miscarriage of justice. *Id.* Hall's claim does not present an exceptional case, nor does refusing to consider the claim produce a plain miscarriage of justice.

***439 II.**

This court reviews a district court's order granting summary judgment *de novo*. *Nguyen v. City of Cleveland,* 229 F.3d 559, 562 (6th Cir.2000). Summary judgment is proper if "the pleadings, depositions, answers to interrogatories, and admissions on file, together with the affidavits, if any, show that there is no genuine issue as to any material fact and that the moving party is entitled to a judgment as a matter of law." Fed.R.Civ.P. 56(c). When reviewing a motion for summary judgment, the court must view all of the evidence and any inferences that may be drawn from that evidence in the light most favorable to the nonmoving party. *Nguyen,* 229 F.3d at 562.

The federal wiretap statute, the ECPA, "criminalizes and creates civil liability for intentionally intercepting electronic communications without a judicial warrant." *Adams v. City of Battle Creek,* 250 F.3d 980, 982 (6th Cir.2001). The Act provides:
Except as otherwise specifically provided in this chapter any person who-
(a) intentionally intercepts, endeavors to intercept, or procures any other person to intercept or endeavor to intercept, any wire, oral, or electronic communication; ...
(c) intentionally discloses, or endeavors to disclose, to any other person the contents of any wire, oral, or electronic communication, knowing or having reason to know that the information was obtained through the interception of a wire, oral, or electronic communication in violation of this subsection;....
shall be punished as provided in [18 U.S.C. § 2511(4)(a)] or subject to suit as provided in [18 U.S.C. § 2511(5) and 18 U.S.C. § 2520].

18 U.S.C. § 2511(1). The statute defines "intercept" as "the aural or other acquisition of the contents of any wire, electronic, or oral communication through the use of any electronic, mechanical, or other device." 18 U.S.C. § 2510(4). "Electronic, mechanical, or other device" is defined to mean "any device or apparatus which can be used to intercept a wire, oral, or electronic communication *other than*-(a) any telephone or telegraph instrument, equipment or facility, or any component thereof, (i) furnished to the subscriber or user by a provider of wire or electronic communication service in the ordinary course of its business and being used by the subscriber or user in the ordinary course of its business ..." 18 U.S.C. § 2510(5) (emphasis added). The statute further provides:**3 It shall not be unlawful under this chapter for a person not acting under color of law to intercept a wire, oral or electronic communication where such person is a party to the communication ... unless such communication is intercepted for the purpose of committing any criminal or tortious act in violation of *440 the Constitution or laws of the United States or of any State.

18 U.S.C. § 2511(2)(d).

Clemons alleges that Hall and Meridian are liable under 18 U.S.C. § 2511(a) and (c) for intercepting the fax transmission from BellSouth. FN3 The district court assumed without deciding that the fax transmission was an electronic communication protected by the statute. Appellees do not contest that assumption. The district court then granted summary judgment on two grounds: first, on the ground that Lee's fax machine was subject to the "ordinary course of business" exception provided by 18 U.S.C. § 2510(5), and second, on the ground that Lee was subject to the "party to the communication" exception provided by 18 U.S.C. § 2511(2)(d). The district court correctly analyzed the "party to the communication" exception and properly applied it to this case. We affirm the district court's judgment on this basis alone and therefore need not consider the issue of whether the receipt of the communication over Lee's fax machine met the "ordinary course of business" exception.

FN3. Clemons characterizes the question presented as "[w]hether it violates the [ECPA] for an imposter to acquire an individual's

> telephone records by using fraud and deceit to induce the transmission of these records by a telephone company, via facsimile, to the imposter by leading the telephone ... company to believe that the records were being requested by, and would be received by, the legitimate subscriber." (Appellant's Brief at 3.) This phrasing implies that the nature of the contents of the facsimile transmission (Clemons's phone records) is relevant-that is, that the fact that it was a *telephone* company sending *telephone* records makes this suit cognizable under the federal wiretap act. This fact is immaterial. The only relevant question is whether an unlawful interception occurred. The nature of the contents of the transmission has no bearing on this question whatsoever.
>
> Appellees respond to Clemons's argument by stating that "[i]t has not been alleged, nor can it be shown[,] that any of the defendants knew the contents of any communication between the plaintiff and any other person." (Appellees' Brief at 9.) They argue that "it has been held that a list of telephone numbers is only a record that contact was attempted between one phone and another. The identity of the number is not the communication itself[,] as the U.S. Supreme Court has recognized." (Appellees' Brief at 13, citing Smith v. Maryland, 442 U.S. 735, 99 S.Ct. 2577, 61 L.Ed.2d 220 (1979).) This argument also misapprehends the issue. Clemons's complaint does not allege that defendants intercepted Clemons's cell phone calls. Rather, the complaint alleges that defendants intercepted a fax transmission intended for Clemons.

Where an individual is a "party to the communication," not acting under color of law, it is not unlawful under the ECPA for the individual to intercept the communication, "unless such communication is intercepted for the purpose of committing any criminal or tortious act in violation of the Constitution or laws of the United States or of any State." 18 U.S.C. § 2511(2)(d). A "party to the communication" is a person participating in the communication. The communication at issue is the transmission of Clemons's cellular phone records. That communication involved Lee, impersonating Clemons, and BellSouth Mobility. Lee requested Clemons's records and BellSouth Mobility transmitted those records to Lee. Lee was thereby a "party to the communication" when he received the fax transmission. Thus, to demonstrate a violation of the ECPA, Clemons must show that defendants received his billing records for the purpose of committing either a crime or a tortious act.

Alleged violations of the ECPA itself cannot constitute the additional crime or tort under § 2511(2)(d). *See Thomas v. Pearl*, 998 F.2d 447, 451 (7th Cir.1993) (presuming that an allegation that defendant broke only the wiretapping law itself *441 does not destroy the § 2511(2)(d) exception). At most, Clemons alleges that the imposter committed fraud by impersonating him in communications with BellSouth. However, he does not claim that the alleged interception was undertaken *for the purpose of* committing fraud. Rather, the alleged fraud was already complete at the time the alleged interception took place. Because Lee was a party to the communication and because Clemons failed to allege that defendants intercepted the fax transmission for the purpose of committing any crime or tort (other than violating the federal wiretap act itself), 18 U.S.C. § 2511(2)(d) relieves defendants from liability under the ECPA.

**4 Clemons's argument for reversal is that "Lee's use of fraud and deceit vitiated his claim to be a party to the communication." (Appellant's Brief at 10.) Clemons, however, cites no cases involving the ECPA or any other wiretapping statute to support this argument. Rather, he points out that fraud in the inducement voids a contract, that employing fraud in obtaining sexual intercourse is a criminal act, and that a police officer who uses fraud to obtain a search warrant is not entitled to qualified immunity. We do not dispute that utilizing false pretenses to secure information is proscribed in certain areas of the law. Notably, Congress has elsewhere imposed civil and/or criminal liability on individuals who obtain information about another by false pretenses. *See, e.g.*, 5 U.S.C. § 552a(i)(3) (imposing liability for utilizing false pretenses to secure another's record from an administrative agency); 15 U.S.C. § 1681q (imposing liability for utilizing false pretenses to obtain information about another from consumer reporting agencies); *Id.* § 6821 (imposing liability for utilizing false pretenses to obtain information about another from financial institutions); 49 U.S.C. § 30307 (imposing liability for utilizing false pretenses to obtain information about another from the National Driver Register). However, Clemons fails to cite any authority for the proposition that pretending to be someone else prevents an individual from being a "party to the communication" under 18 U.S.C. § 2511(2)(d).

Other circuits, on the other hand, have determined that impersonating an intended recipient of a communication does not violate the federal wiretap act. For example, in *United States v. Pasha*, 332 F.2d 193 (7th Cir.1964), the Seventh Circuit considered a situation in which two FBI agents, while executing a search warrant, answered a ringing telephone on the premises, listened to the callers, and pretended to be the intended recipient of the calls. The Court held that no interception had occurred: "[T]here was no tampering with the established means of communication. Indeed the officer was the immediate party to the call. The bettor intended his words to reach the officer, albeit the bettor thought he was someone else. Thus the officer did not 'intercept' a message while it was en route to another; there was no other on the line." *Id.* at 198 (quoting *State v. Carbone*, 38 N.J. 19, 183 A.2d 1 (1962)). The Court also stated that impersonating the intended recipient of a communication did not give rise to liability:

Although the callers in the instant case were unaware that they were not being heard by the intended receivers and some were even misled into believing they were talking to one or other of the defendants, the conversations between the callers and the agent cannot be said to have been intercepted. Interception connotes a situation in which by surreptitious means a third party overhears a telephone conversation between two persons. ***We believe that impersonation of the intended receiver is not an interception within the meaning of the statute.***

*442 **5 *Pasha*, 332 F.2d at 198 (emphasis added). When amending the federal wiretap act in 1968 to its current state, Congress specifically mentioned *Pasha* in its discussions of the "party to the communication" provision. In discussing § 2511(2)(c), which is *in pari materia* with § 2511(2)(d) and differs from that provision only in that § 2511(2)(c) applies to persons acting under color of law, the Senate Judiciary Committee stated:Paragraph 2(c) provides that it shall not be unlawful for a party to any wire or oral communication ... to intercept such communication. It largely reflects existing law. Where one of the parties consents, it is not unlawful.... "[P]arty" would mean the person actually participating in the communication. (*United States v. Pasha*, 332 F.2d 193 (7th Cir.1964)).

S.Rep. No. 90-1097, at 93-94 (1968), *reprinted in* 1968 U.S.C.C.A.N. 2112, 2182; *see also United States v. Campagnuolo*, 592 F.2d 852, 862-63 (5th Cir.1979) (stating that "it is clear from this passage that Congress intended to reaffirm the result in *Pasha*"). By citing *Pasha*, Congress strongly intimated that one who impersonates the intended receiver of a communication may still be a party to that communication for the purposes of the federal wiretap statute and that such conduct is not proscribed by the statute. Defendants' conduct arguably may give rise to liability under other statutes or the common law, but it is not a violation of the ECPA.

III.

Because Lee was a "party to the communication" and Clemons has not alleged that any defendant was intercepting a communication for the purpose of committing a crime or tort other than those outlined in the ECPA, we affirm the district court's grant of summary judgment in favor of defendants on the basis of 18 U.S.C. § 2511(2)(d).

C.A.6 (Tenn.),2003.
Clemons v. Waller
82 Fed.Appx. 436, 2003 WL 22734829 (C.A.6 (Tenn.))

Briefs and Other Related Documents (Back to top)

• 02-5342 (Docket) (Mar. 22, 2002)

END OF DOCUMENT

TAB 77

From: Hunsaker, Kevin <kevin.hunsaker@hp.com>
Sent: Wednesday, March 29, 2006 3:51 PM
To: Gentilucci, Anthony R. <tony.gentilucci@hp.com>; Ron DeLia <rrd@security-outsourcing.com>
Subject: Unauthorized disclosure -- privileged communication

Hi guys,

I am going to add a paragraph in the Report about the conversation Hurd had with Perkins, and the arguments between Perkins and Keyworth. Here's what I've got. Please read the stuff on the Hurd conversation and let me know if you think I've captured it accurately -- it seems like I'm missing one piece, but I'm not sure. Thanks.

It is also worth noting that, a few days before the March 2006 Board meeting, Perkins called Mark Hurd and asked him, among other things about the status of the investigation into the leaks. Hurd told Perkins that the Investigation Team had assembled a significant amount of circumstantial evidence, but that he was not sure where it would ultimately lead. In addition, during the March 2006 Board meeting, Perkins and Keyworth were seen arguing during two different breaks in the meeting. The arguments were mainly one sided, with Keyworth intently speaking and even pointing his finger at Perkins' chest several times. At the very end of the second argument/heated discussion, Keyworth was overheard saying: "they don't have enough to go there."

Kevin T. Hunsaker
Senior Counsel
HP Legal Department
Phone: 650 857-3079
Fax: 650 857-3710

TAB 78

PREPARED FOR HEWLETT PACKARD BY SECURITY OUTSOURCING SOLUTIONS, INC.
HP Confidential – Privileged Communication

CLIENT # HP-99-01
CASE # 06-01-490
DATE: April 6, 2006

(KONA II – LA Surveillance Report)
Preliminary Draft

Security Outsourcing Solutions, Inc. conducted surveillance activity at the Techno Conference held at the Hyatt Regency Century Plaza Hotel in LA, CA from April 2nd to April 5, 2006. Following are areas of interest observed by the surveillance team.

<u>4/02/06</u>

9:40pm Keyworth enters lobby with wife and sits with group of men and he appears to be the center of attention.

11:15pm Keyworth departs, down escalator, out of view. Surveillance team remains in lobby until midnight.

<u>4/3/06 Received photograph of Michael Moeller.</u>

8:15am Mrs. Keyworth observed in Breeze Restaurant.

Mrs. Keyworth Departs in Limo, California [redacted], registered to [redacted].

12:15pm Mike Moeller observed at Posterboard "Dynamic Environmental Controls Data Center" and "High Performance Acoustical Noise Suppression." After which he is observed on his Blackberry and two minutes later proceeds to cyber café.

12:30-1pm ID Moeller in cyber café, overheard conversation while sitting next to him. "Cancel reservation;" observed utilizing laptop [redacted] "Left hand wall (north) second station to the right of the printer."

1pm-10pm Moeller observed in area of California level doing various activities. Moeller was overheard changing massage appointment from Wed. 8 AM to Wed. 10 AM.

715pm	Observed Mr Keyworth on CA level walking alone from LA ballroom to elevators and then out of view.
10:00pm	Surveillance terminated.

4/4/06

9:45	Observed Moeller entering spa area, 10am massage appt.
11:38	Observed in area of cyber café utilizing laptop.
11:45am	Mr Keyworth checks out of hotel.
1250pm	Overheard Moeller conversation stating be there "soon"
12:55pm	Observe Moeller meet Christina Shneder "CS" (phonetic).
1:05pm	Observed Moeller with (Christina Shneder) lunch LA ballroom
110pm	Observed Moeller retrieving dessert
1:17pm	Observe Moeller in cyber café on California level, email, phone, socializing etc. with Christina Shneder Moeller Remains in cyber café
142pm	Moeller strolls CA lobby on cell phone, returns to Cyber Cafe
2:08pm	CS coffee/bathroom break
2:39PM	Moeller walks to CA lobby on cell phone, returns to Cyber Café

2:55pm Investigator BM joins investigator SM on CA level they are attempting to overhear Moeller's cell phone conversation, which takes place between 340pm and 4pm. The investigators overhear various snippets of Moeller's cell phone conversations.

3:40pm	Moeller goes to remote section of CA level, sits facing wall, out of sight and is overheard on cell phone saying "services and earnings" and shortly thereafter "so you can write about that."
340-400pm	The investigators also overheard the following quotes:

"tactically I don't know if I can get away with it, I'm like a bull in a china shop, but from what I know of the CEO, he is also a bull in a china shop"

"but it's a good thing I'm not blind with ambition or stupidity"

"I can't have this conversation"

445pm	Moeller sitting on sofa with group that included CS, two WM, one WF.
5:05pm	Moeller observed in Cyber Cafe

6:50	Moeller observed at dinner/speech
9:20	Moeller and CS observed attending Bird-of-a-feather session "Agile IT Services", Olympic room, plaza level.
9:40	Moeller leaves Olympic room with CS, returns to CA level.
9:40-10pm	Drinks, socializing, cocktail hour.
10pm	Event ends, bars close. Surveillance terminated.

4/5/06

7am start	Breakfast
8:10am	Moeller observed in CA level peeking in, takes phone call, walks to plaza level via escalator, finds corner, faces wall. Several minutes later, ends call, returns to CA level via escalator, out of view.
	Surveillance established in lobby
8:40	Moeller checks out, departs in limo.

It should be noted, the surveillance team did not observe Tam, Kawamoto and/or other significant parties at the event.

END OF DRAFT SURVEILLANCE REPORT

TAB 79

From: Pattie [redacted]
Sent: Friday, April 14, 2006 2:30 PM
To: Baskins, Ann <ann.baskins@hp.com>; Hunsaker, Kevin <kevin.hunsaker@hp.com>; Pattie Dunn-Hotmail [redacted]
Subject: Re: Friday call

Kevin, no worries, mate, as they say around these parts. Ann, give me a call at 3 and we will catch up.
Regards,
Pattie

Sent via BlackBerry from Cingular Wireless

-----Original Message-----
From: "Baskins, Ann" <ann.baskins@hp.com>
Date: Fri, 14 Apr 2006 11:05:21
To:"Hunsaker, Kevin" <kevin.hunsaker@hp.com>, [redacted]
Subject: Re: Friday call

Pattie,
I spoke with Larry yesterday, as he had finished reviewing the report. Shall I just call your cell at 3 California time to give you that update?

Ann

Sent from my BlackBerry Wireless Handheld

-----Original Message-----
From: Hunsaker, Kevin <kevin.hunsaker@hp.com>
To: Pattie [redacted]; Baskins, Ann <ann.baskins@hp.com>
Sent: Fri Apr 14 10:49:35 2006
Subject: RE: Friday call

I am an idiot. My flight back from San Diego today is at 2:30, so I will be in the air at 3:00. I meant to propose alternative times, but in my haste to leave town, I forgot.

There isn't much from a substantive standpoint that is new -- we've gotten in a few more phone records, none of which contained anything significant. We've also continued the background investigations on a number of folks, but nothing big has been uncovered. We also had two folks attend the Tech Con and they overheard one of HP's PR guys saying a few interesting things, but nothing that relates directly to this investigation.

With respect to Larry, Ann and I provided him with the draft report and spoke with him for a few minutes, but I haven't heard back from him. My guess is we'll have a more comprehensive meeting with him sometime next week.

Ann, have you heard anything from Larry?

So, with respect to today's call, I apologize for screwing it up. I can do it anytime between now and 2:00 or so, and then anytime after 4:30.. this afternoon. The dial-in is [redacted], or [redacted]79, with a[redacted]

I am actually going to be offline most of today, but if you can let me know via my cell phone [redacted] if there's another time that works for you, I will open the line at that time.

Again, I'm sorry for the mix-up.

Kevin

Kevin T. Hunsaker
Senior Counsel
HP Legal Department
Phone: 650 857-3079

Fax: 650 857-3710

-----Original Message-----
From: Pattie [mailto:pcdunn1@hotmail.com]
Sent: Friday, April 14, 2006 12:39 AM
To: Hunsaker, Kevin; Baskins, Ann
Subject: Friday call

Okay, this time I won't blow it. The double time change to and from daylight savings threw me and I was a hour off last week. I will call the 650 number Kevin provided tomorrow at 3 PM your time.

Regards,
Pattie

Sent via BlackBerry from Cingular Wireless
Be

HP 00469

TAB 80

From: Ron DeLia [rrd@security-outsourcing.com]
: Tuesday, April 18, 2006 1:53 PM
To: Hunsaker, Kevin; Gentilucci, Anthony R.; Nye, Vince; Adler, Frederick P.
Subject: Privileged Communication - HP CONFIDENTIAL
Attachments: Case 06-01-490 (GK Italy Residence) Photo 3 A.jpg; Case 06-01-490 (GK Italy Residence) Photo 1 A.jpg; Case 06-01-490 (GK Italy Residence) Photo 2 A.jpg

Team,

Attached are photo taken of GK's home in Italy. As you can see it is a very remote area.

I will send additional photo under separate emails.

Ron

Security Outsourcing Solutions, Inc.
Tel: (617) 426-3900 or (781) 444-9616

TAB 81

Jose Gurgel-Neto

From: Hunsaker, Kevin [kevin.hunsaker@hp.com]
Sent: Saturday, April 22, 2006 10:08 AM
To: Ron DeLia
Cc: Gentilucci, Anthony R.
Subject: RE: Privileged Communication - HP CONFIDENTIAL

We will need to have someone open it up to determine whether any of the data on the computer was accessed and compromised so we can assess whether HP-related data is now out in the public domain, so we'll need to determine who is best suited to do that. And, as part of that search, we'll have to determine whether it's appropriate to see if there's anything relevant to the KONA II investigation on the computer. So, we should probably have it returned to Fred in our Roseville office.

However, I'm open to suggestions if you have a better idea of how to handle the recovery and return.

Kevin

Kevin T. Hunsaker
Director of Ethics and SBC
Hewlett-Packard Company
Phone: 650 857-3079
Fax: 650 857-3710

From: Ron DeLia [mailto:rrd@security-outsourcing.com]
Sent: Saturday, April 22, 2006 7:40 AM
To: Hunsaker, Kevin
Cc: Gentilucci, Anthony R.
Subject: RE: Privileged Communication - HP CONFIDENTIAL

If we are likely and recover the laptop, how should returning it to GK be handled? We are fairly confident our LE contact that is assisting our investigator will turn the laptop over to him and our investigator will ship it to your office. Is this the way we should handle the recovery?

The content of this email transmission is intended only for the use of the individual or entity named above and may contain legally privileged or confidential information. If you are not the intended recipient, you are hereby notified that any disclosure, copying, dissemination, distribution, or use of this email transmission, or information contained herein, is strictly prohibited. If you have received this email transmission in error, please destroy all copies of this email and its attachments and notify the person whose name appears above.

Security Outsourcing Solutions, Inc.
Tel: (617) 426-3900 or (781) 444-9616

-----Original Message-----
From: Hunsaker, Kevin [mailto:kevin.hunsaker@hp.com]
Sent: Saturday, April 22, 2006 10:26 AM
To: Ron DeLia
Cc: Gentilucci, Anthony R.

Subject: RE: Privileged Communication - HP CONFIDENTIAL

I believe it belongs to GK, as each Board member is given something like $2000 a year to spend on HP products. So, while HP provided it directly to him, I do not believe it is tracked or considered to be an HP asset.

Kevin T. Hunsaker
Director of Ethics and SBC
Hewlett-Packard Company
Phone: 650[redacted]
Fax: 650[redacted]

From: Ron DeLia [mailto:rrd@security-outsourcing.com]
Sent: Saturday, April 22, 2006 5:41 AM
To: Hunsaker, Kevin
Cc: Gentilucci, Anthony R.
Subject: RE: Privileged Communication - HP CONFIDENTIAL

Kevin/Tony,

Is the laptop HP property? Did GK purchase or was the laptop provided to him by HP?

Ron

The content of this email transmission is intended only for the use of the individual or entity named above and may contain legally privileged or confidential information. If you are not the intended recipient, you are hereby notified that any disclosure, copying, dissemination, distribution, or use of this email transmission, or information contained herein, is strictly prohibited. If you have received this email transmission in error, please destroy all copies of this email and its attachments and notify the person whose name appears above.

Security Outsourcing Solutions, Inc.
Tel: (617) 426-3900 or (781) 444-9616

-----Original Message-----
From: Hunsaker, Kevin [mailto:kevin.hunsaker@hp.com]
Sent: Friday, April 21, 2006 3:30 PM
To: Ron DeLia
Cc: Gentilucci, Anthony R.
Subject: RE: Privileged Communication - HP CONFIDENTIAL

No problem. Now let's get those guys in Italy to find that laptop!!!! It could be the case breaker of all case breakers.

Kevin T. Hunsaker
Director of Ethics and SBC
Hewlett-Packard Company
Phone: 650[redacted]
Fax: 650[redacted]

From: Ron DeLia [mailto:rrd@security-outsourcing.com]
Sent: Friday, April 21, 2006 12:30 PM
To: Hunsaker, Kevin
Cc: Gentilucci, Anthony R.
Subject: RE: Privileged Communication - HP CONFIDENTIAL

Thanks

The content of this email transmission is intended only for the use of the individual or entity named above and may contain legally privileged or confidential information. If you are not the intended recipient, you are hereby notified that any disclosure, copying, dissemination, distribution, or use of this email transmission, or information contained herein, is strictly prohibited. If you have received this email transmission in error, please destroy all copies of this email and its attachments and notify the person whose name appears above.

Security Outsourcing Solutions, Inc.
Tel: (617) 426-3900 or (781) 444-9616

-----Original Message-----
From: Hunsaker, Kevin [mailto:kevin.hunsaker@hp.com]
Sent: Friday, April 21, 2006 11:19 AM
To: Ron DeLia
Cc: Gentilucci, Anthony R.
Subject: RE: Privileged Communication - HP CONFIDENTIAL

Here's the info on the laptop.

HP NC4200 laptop
- part number: EK740AW # ABA
- serial number: [redacted]

My mailing address has not changed, and probably won't for several months.

Kevin

Kevin T. Hunsaker
Director of Ethics and SBC
Hewlett-Packard Company
Phone: 650 [redacted]
Fax: 650 [redacted]

From: Ron DeLia [mailto:rrd@security-outsourcing.com]
Sent: Friday, April 21, 2006 8:21 AM
To: Hunsaker, Kevin
Cc: Gentilucci, Anthony R.
Subject: Privileged Communication - HP CONFIDENTIAL

Kevin,

I wanted to check in to see if we have obtained the serial number, make, and model of GK's laptop. Our local LE contact is scheduled to return from holiday on Saturday the 22nd.

Also, can you send me your new mailing address?

Thanks,

Ron

Security Outsourcing Solutions, Inc.
Tel: (617) 426-3900 or (781) 444-9616

TAB 82

DraftReport--Unauthorized Discl... Appendix1--1-23-06Article.pdf ... GKLinkAnalysis--DRAFT.pdf (10 ...

From: "Baskins, Ann" <ann.baskins@hp.com>
To: "Robert L. Ryan" [redacted]
CC: "Patricia Dunn-Jahnke" <[redacted]>
Subject: FW: KONA II Draft Report -- privileged communication
Date: Mon, 24 Apr 2006 14:01:40 -0500

PRIVILEGED AND CONFIDENTIAL; DO NOT FORWARD

Dear Bob,

At Pattie's request, I am forwarding the DRAFT Kona II report for your review. Kevin Hunsaker, who prepared and forwarded the draft, was until last week a member of HP's Legal Department with primary responsibility for advising on Standards of Business Conduct investigations. He is now the Director of the SBC compliance team, reporting to Diana Bell.

I will forward separately a collection of other CNET articles reviewed by the team during the inquiry.

Regards,
Ann

> -----Original Message-----
> From: Hunsaker, Kevin
> Sent: Monday, April 24, 2006 10:24 AM
> To: Baskins, Ann
> Subject: KONA II Draft Report -- privileged communication
>
> Ann,
>
> Per your request, attached please find three documents. The first > document is the Draft Report prepared by the Investigation Team based > upon the information gathered, reviewed and analyzed to date. The > second document is a complete copy of the January 23, 2006 CNET > article summarizing the issues discussed during the January 2006 Board > meeting. And, the third document is a draft link analysis chart put > together by the Investigation Team identifying a number of the > connections GK has to the individuals of interest in the > investigation. > > Please let me know if you have any questions or comments. > > Thanks. > > Kevin > > <<Draft Report --Unauthorized Disclosure 3-29-06.pdf>> <<Appendix 1 > -- 1-23-06 Article.pdf>> <<GK

PD 00045

TAB 83

From: Hunsaker, Kevin <kevin.hunsaker@hp.com>
Sent: Friday, April 28, 2006 10:48 AM
To: Gentilucci, Anthony R. <tony.gentilucci@hp.com>; Delia <rrd@security-outsourcing.com>
Subject: KONA II -- privileged communication

PREPARED AT THE DIRECTION OF COUNSEL.

Hi guys,

Per Ann Baskins' specific request, below is a draft email regarding how the Investigation Team obtained the phone records, and what we did to confirm the legality of do so. She wants to provide this information to Larry Sonsini and Bob Ryan before they interview GK. Please let me know if I have accurately captured everything. I am also interested in any suggestions you may have about the language, tone, etc.

Thanks.

As part of the KONA II investigation, the Investigation Team obtained phone record information (cell phone, home phone and home fax) with respect to several subjects of the investigation. To obtain the information, Ron Delia, through his company (Security Outsourcing Solutions), engaged the services of a company that has been in the business of performing this particular service for the past 20 years. The company, which is based in Florida, is licensed to conduct business in Florida and several other states, and only sells its services to licensed private investigators and law firms. They do not sell their services to the general public.

We provide Mr. Delia with the names and telephone numbers we are interested in, he passes the information to the third party company, and they then make pretext calls to the phone service providers. All information is obtained verbally from the phone service, and the phone service voluntarily provides the information. It should be noted that this is a common investigative tool that has been used by professional investigators and law firms for more than 20 years -- this fact was confirmed by discussing the issue with a number of experts in the field. It should also be noted that the only HP employee during the entire course of the KONA II investigation who had access to the phone records obtained was the attorney directing the investigation, Kevin Hunsaker. No other HP employee was given access to all of the phone records. The relevant records of specific phone calls were provided to the Investigation Team, but only Mr. Hunsaker had access to all the phone records.

During the course of the investigation, the Investigation Team took several steps to confirm the legality of obtaining the phone records information in the manner described above. Specifically, Mr. Hunsaker conducted some preliminary legal research and determined that the practice of pretexting phone companies to obtain information is not unlawful. In addition, Mr. Delia contacted the third party company conducting the research, who confirmed that they are very well aware of all potentially relevant state and federal laws, and that the manner in which they obtain the phone records information is not unlawful. And, finally, Tony Gentilucci (Global Security) contacted John Kiernan (from Bonner, Kiernan, Trebach and Crociata -- the firm primarily responsible for the ABB investigation), who confirmed that his firm had conducted extensive research on this issue, and that the practice of pretexting phone companies to obtain information is not unlawful.

As a result, the Investigation Team is confident that all phone records information obtained during the course of the investigation was obtained in a lawful manner.

Please let me know if you have any additional questions.

Thanks.

HP 00056

TAB 84

Subject: FW: Privileged Communication - HP CONFIDENTIAL
Attachments: Case 06-01-490 (KONA II Billing Detail) May 2, 06.xls

Importance: High

From: Ron DeLia [mailto:rrd@security-outsourcing.com]
Sent: Tuesday, May 02, 2006 1:22 PM
To: Gentilucci, Anthony R.
Subject: Privileged Communication - HP CONFIDENTIAL
Importance: High

Tony,

See attached Excel chart of KONA II cost breakdown. As I mentioned earlier, our sub contractors due not bill on a weekly or monthly bases, they bill on a per project bases. Therefore, we can not breakdown the cost by month.

Secondly, due to confidentiality concerns and the Attorney client privilege, I did not include the names of the interested parties, telephone numbers, investigative techniques and other confidential information in the chart.

Let me know if this will work or you need additional information.

Also, some of the costs have been estimated due to the final invoices have not been received. However, I do not anticipate any major changes to the cost projection.

Ron

The content of this email transmission is intended only for the use of the individual or entity

named above and may contain legally privileged or confidential information. If you are not the intended recipient, you are hereby notified that any disclosure, copying, dissemination, distribution, or use of this email transmission, or information contained herein, is strictly prohibited. If you have received this email transmission in error, please destroy all copies of this email and its attachments and notify the person whose name appears above.

Security Outsourcing Solutions, Inc.

PRIVILEGED COMMUNICATION
HP CONFIDENTIAL

KONA II BILLING DETAIL DECEMBER THROUGH APRIL 2006 (detailed billing of all hours abnd related investigation expenses are on file)	COST
SURVEILLANCE:	
Multiple Surv. And Sting Activity Palo Alto, Piedmont, SF, LA, CA & Denver, CO (Note: Includes surveillance & trash re-con of all areas)	$83,597.42
DUE DILIGENCE:	
Background investigations on multiple BoD members and their relatives, and reporters for the WSJ, CNET and other media outlets	$66,688.00
Background investigations on multiple HP employees Media Relatiions Dept.	$6,435.00
In depth review of KONA I Due Diligence investigation	$4,575.00
MEDIA ANALYSIS:	
Locate, review, analyze and catalog over 10,000 print and Internet media articles for parties of interest (reporters)	$37,535.00
Investigative Reporter Consultant	$7,312.50
TELEPHONE RESEARCH:	
Locate, identify, analyze, chart and catalog records of interested parties	$44,875.00
In depth analysis of KONA I and KONA II telephone research records	$6,425.75
GENERAL INVESTIGATIVE ACTIVITY:	
Laptop recovery activity in Italy (2 thefts - BoD members laptop)	$9,668.00
RRD daily case management, coordination and liaison (Jan-Apr - Daily meetings with legal)	$36,692.50
RRD daily case mtg's & surv., sting operation, Palo Alto and LA, CA	$21,837.48
* All RRD's hours are billed at discount rate of $65.00 per hour vs. normal rate of $125.00 per hour	
TOTAL COST OF KONA II INVESTIGATION	$325,641.65

ATTORNEY WORK PRODUCT
1

HP0007131

TAB 85

MINUTES OF A REGULAR MEETING OF THE BOARD OF DIRECTORS OF HEWLETT-PACKARD COMPANY

May 18, 2006

Pursuant to notice, a regular meeting of the Board of Directors of Hewlett-Packard Company, a Delaware corporation, was convened at the Company's principal offices located at 3000 Hanover Street, Palo Alto, California, at approximately 12:30 p.m. on May 18, 2006. The following directors were present:

- Lawrence T. Babbio
- Sari Baldauf
- Patricia C. Dunn
- Richard A. Hackborn
- John H. Hammergren
- Mark V. Hurd
- George A. Keyworth, II
- Thomas J. Perkins
- Robert L. Ryan
- Lucille S. Salhany

Director Robert P. Wayman joined the meeting in progress as noted herein. Also present was Company SVP, General Counsel and Secretary Ann Baskins, who recorded the minutes with assistance from Assistant Secretary Charles Charnas. There being a quorum present, the meeting was called to order by Chairman Dunn.

Special Investigation Report

Chairman Dunn reported that the findings of the investigation into a series of unauthorized disclosures of confidential information, about which the Board had been previously informed, had been summarized in a draft report, including conclusive findings regarding a press leak occurring after the Board's January strategy off-site meeting. She stated that the draft report had been provided to Audit Committee Chairman Ryan in accordance with the Board and Company's policies concerning Standards of Business Conduct, and that Mr. Ryan would summarize the report for the Board.

Mr. Ryan explained that his report would focus on the January 23, 2006 CNET article by Dawn Kawamoto that described certain confidential matters from the January Board meeting, including strategies, plans, acquisition intentions and other issues considered at that meeting. Mr. Ryan described the investigation team composition, summarized the investigative approach and process and reported that the investigative team had concluded that the source was an HP director. Mr. Ryan then informed the Board that the director identified by the investigative team met with Ryan that morning and readily acknowledged being the source for the CNET article. Mr. Ryan then distributed copies of the January 23, 2006 article.

The Board discussed procedural options for considering the matter. Mr. Perkins stated that while he had concurred with Chairman Dunn that an investigation should be conducted into the leak, he had advised against reviewing the findings in a full Board session. Instead, Perkins believed that the matter should have been handled confidentially by the Chairman and himself as Chairman of the Nominating & Governance Committee.

Following additional discussion regarding meeting procedures, Mr. Ryan informed the Board that Dr. Keyworth had confirmed that he was the source for the CNET article.

Dr. Keyworth then addressed the Board. He described the circumstances under which he became acquainted with Dawn Kawamoto, explaining that he initially established contact with Kawamoto at the request of former CEO Carly Fiorina, who asked Keyworth to speak with certain members of the media in support of the Compaq merger. He added that Kawamoto emerged as an influential reporter who reported favorably on HP. He said that his intent in describing the January Board meeting to Kawamoto was to help the Company and in particular to convey that HP and its CEO were addressing key growth opportunities and other important strategies rather than narrowly focused on cost-cutting efforts. Dr. Keyworth assured the Board that he had not been a source for other stories by different reporters, including articles written by Pui-Wing Tam of the Wall Street Journal. He indicated that he would not make unauthorized disclosures to the media in the future.

Keyworth then left the meeting.

The Board, absent Dr. Keyworth and Mr. Wayman, considered alternative measures that could be taken in response to Dr. Keyworth's actions. Matters reviewed and discussed included the Company's policy on unauthorized disclosure; prior Board discussions on the importance of preserving the confidentiality of Board deliberations; the explicit commitment to maintaining confidentiality made by all directors in February 2005; the significant contributions of Dr. Keyworth to HP; and the duties and obligations of directors, including the duties of care and loyalty. As part of the discussion, Chairman Dunn solicited each director for views and recommendations. Legal considerations were reviewed with the General Counsel and a range of options considered, and several courses of action considered.

Following this discussion, a motion was duly made and seconded that Dr. Keyworth be asked to resign from the Board. Additional deliberation ensued, following which it was proposed and agreed that a vote on the motion would be conducted by written ballot. The marked ballots were collected and tallied by Baskins, who reported that the motion carried by a six to three vote.

Mr. Perkins restated his strong objections to the process, specifically Chairman Dunn's decision to bring the matter to the full Board and the manner in which the meeting was conducted. Mr. Perkins then resigned from the Board and departed the meeting at approximately 2 p.m.

Additional discussion followed, during which directors expressed disagreement with Mr. Perkins' position and support for the process followed by Chairman Dunn.

Ms. Dunn and Mr. Ryan then left the meeting to discuss the Board's action with Dr. Keyworth, and the meeting went into recess.

Following the recess, the meeting was reconvened at approximately 2:20 p.m. with Directors Babbio, Baldauf, Dunn, Hackborn, Hammergren, Hurd, Ryan and Salhany present as well as Ms. Baskins. Ms. Dunn and Mr. Ryan reported that Dr. Keyworth had declined the Board's request that he resign and explained that Dr. Keyworth believed the Company would benefit from his continued service.

Upon a motion duly made and seconded the resignation of Thomas J. Perkins from the Board was unanimously accepted.

Director Wayman joined the meeting at approximately 2:25 p.m. Ms. Dunn and Ms. Baskins left the meeting and Assistant Secretary Charnas joined to record the minutes.

REDACTED

Perkins Resignation
Mr. Sonsini advised the Board that he had spoken to Mr. Perkins to help determine the appropriate disclosure of Perkins' resignation from the HP Board. Mr. Sonsini reported that Perkins confirmed that he had no disagreement with the Company or the Board and that his disagreement was with certain procedural decisions undertaken by Chairman Dunn.

Dr. Keyworth recused himself from the meeting at approximately 5:10 p.m.

Mr. Sonsini reported that he had reviewed the draft investigative report prior to its submission to Mr. Ryan and had provided advice with respect to the appropriate procedures for considering the report at the Board level. Mr. Sonsini then outlined Delaware law considerations and responded to director questions. It was noted that the report could now be finalized. After discussion, the Board asked Ms. Baskins and Mr. Sonsini to review the final report and to advise the Audit Committee as to any requirements or obligations imposed by Delaware law. It was also agreed that the Nominating and Governance Committee would consider the report in proposing the 2007 director slate.

Hurd, Dunn and Sonsini then left the meeting.

REDACTED

REDACTED

REDACTED

Other Matters
Ms. Dunn, Mr. Hurd and Mr. Sonsini rejoined the meeting and summarized a conversation with Dr. Keyworth, in which he confirmed his decision not to accede to the Board's request for his resignation.

Ms. Baskins advised the Board that in light of Director Perkins' resignation it was appropriate to amend the Bylaw provision regarding board size. Upon a motion duly made and seconded, Section 3.2 of the Company's By-laws was amended to read as attached hereto in Exhibit C.

Dr. Keyworth rejoined the meeting and spoke of his desire to continue as a director, his admiration for the company and his recognition that it had been a mistake to discuss Board matters with a reporter.

There being no further business to come before the meeting, it was adjourned at approximately 6:30 p.m.

Ann O. Baskins

Ann O. Baskins

REDACTED

REDACTED

REDACTED

REDACTED

REDACTED

REDACTED

TAB 86

From: Pattie [redacted]
Sent: Friday, May 19, 2006 4:11 PM
To: Ann Baskins; Sonsini, Larry
Subject: Fw: PR strategy

Meant to copy you.
------Original Message------
To: Lawrence T. Babbio
To: Sari Baldauf
To: Dick Hackborn
To: John Hammergren
To: Robert L. Ryan
To: Lucille Salhany
Cc: Mark Hurd
Sent: May 19, 2006 4:09 PM
Subject: PR strategy

Just wanted to give you a brief update on the results of discussions held today between a team of PR people, including an outside expert, Sonsini and Baskins. The upshot is that they concluded, with input from Mark and my concurrence, to do a straightforward announcement about Tom's resignation with a friendly quote from Mark. The strategy from here will depend on what kind of reaction occurs. Contingency plans to ramp up as needed are in place.

If you concur, we can schedule an update call early next week to talk through where we are at that point on Jay's situation and PR issues. To the best of my knowledge Jay has not indicated any change in his position since yesterday.

Best,
Pattie

Sent via BlackBerry from Cingular Wireless

WSGR-HP 1048

HP0018525

TAB 87

8-K 1 a06-12355_18k.htm CURRENT REPORT OF MATERIAL EVENTS OR CORPORATE CHANGES

SECURITIES AND EXCHANGE COMMISSION

WASHINGTON, D.C. 20549-1004

FORM 8-K

CURRENT REPORT
PURSUANT TO SECTION 13 OR 15(d) OF
THE SECURITIES EXCHANGE ACT OF 1934

May 18, 2006
Date of Report (Date of Earliest Event Reported)

HEWLETT-PACKARD COMPANY

(Exact name of registrant as specified in its charter)

DELAWARE	**1-4423**	[redacted]
(State or other jurisdiction of incorporation)	(Commission File Number)	(I.R.S. Employer Identification No.)

3000 HANOVER STREET, PALO ALTO, CA	**94304**
(Address of principal executive offices)	(Zip code)

(650) 857-1501
(Registrant's telephone number, including area code)

Check the appropriate box below if the Form 8-K filing is intended to simultaneously satisfy the filing obligation of the registrant under any of the following provisions:

☐ Written communications pursuant to Rule 425 under the Securities Act (17 CFR 230.425)

☐ Soliciting material pursuant to Rule 14a-12 under the Exchange Act (17 CFR 240.14a-12)

☐ Pre-commencement communications pursuant to Rule 14d-2(b) under the Exchange Act (17 CFR 240.14d-2(b))

☐ Pre-commencement communications pursuant to Rule 13e-4(c) under the Exchange Act (17 CFR 240.13e-4(c))

Item 5.02 **Departure of Directors or Principal Officers; Election of Directors; Appointment of Principal Officers**

(b) On May 18, 2006, Thomas J. Perkins announced his resignation as a director of Hewlett-Packard Company ("HP"), effective immediately. The text of HP's press release relating to Mr. Perkins' resignation is filed with this report as Exhibit 99.1.

Item 5.03 **Amendments to Articles of Incorporation or Bylaws; Change in Fiscal Year**

(a) In connection with, and immediately following, Mr. Perkins' resignation as a director, the Board of Directors of HP approved an amendment to Section 3.2 of Article III of HP's Bylaws decreasing the number of HP directors from eleven (11) to ten (10), effective immediately. The Amended and Restated Bylaws of HP reflecting such amendment are filed with this report as Exhibit 99.2.

Item 9.01 **Financial Statements and Exhibits**

Exhibit 99.1 Text of HP's press release relating to the resignation of Thomas J. Perkins as a director of HP, entitled "HP Announces Resignation of Director Tom Perkins" (filed herewith).

Exhibit 99.2 Amended and Restated Bylaws of Hewlett-Packard Company (filed herewith).

SIGNATURE

Pursuant to the requirements of the Securities Exchange Act of 1934, the registrant has caused this report to be signed on its behalf by the undersigned hereunto duly authorized.

HEWLETT-PACKARD COMPANY

DATE: May 19, 2006

By: /s/ Charles N. Charnas
Name: Charles N. Charnas
Title: Vice President, Deputy General Counsel and Assistant Secretary

EXHIBIT INDEX

Exhibit Number	Description
Exhibit 99.1	Text of press release of Hewlett-Packard Company, entitled "HP Announces Resignation of Director Tom Perkins" (filed herewith).
Exhibit 99.2	Amended and Restated Bylaws of Hewlett-Packard Company (filed herewith).

TAB 88

TalkingPoints06050
1.pdf (33 KB...

From: "Baskins, Ann" <ann.baskins@hp.com>
To: "Patricia Dunn-Jahnke" [redacted]
Subject: FW: PDF
Date: Mon, 22 May 2006 15:27:37 -0500

Pattie,

Here are Bob Ryan's talking points. Please let me know if you need me to do anything with them.

Ann

Discussion Topics

1. Background
2. Investigative Process
3. Report Findings
4. Evidence Supporting Report Findings
5. Next Steps

Background

- On January 20, 2006 CNet informed HP 's Public Relations Department that it was going to publish an article summarizing four issues discussed at the January 14, 2006 Board Meeting
- HPPR informed Mark Hurd, Pattie Dunn and HP Global Security Investigations of the call
- The article, written by Dawn Kawamoto, was published on January 23, 2006
  - "Contained a detailed, accurate summary of several issues discussed during the January Board Meeting"
  - Information attributed to a "Source within the Company"
  - "Information contained in the article was clearly non-public, confidential HP information that was discussed in detail during the Board Meeting"

Note: Material in quotation marks taken directly from the investigative report.

Investigative Process

- The HP Board Chair requested a formal investigation be conducted at the direction of the Legal Department *
- An HP attorney assembled a cross functional team – HP Legal, IT Security, Global Security, External Investigative Consultant
- Major actions taken by the team
  - Gathered, analyzed data on all individuals with access to the disclosed information
  - Analyzed thousand of internal documents
  - Interviewed individuals with access to disclosed information
  - Obtained, reviewed, analyzed phone records to identify calls to/from reporters**
  - Conducted e-mail and telephonic search between reporters and HP related individuals
  - Background searches and link analysis between possible leak sources and several reporters
  - Reviewed more then 1000 articles by Dawn Kawamoto to identify and analyze all references to HP
  - Etc.

* An HP attorney whose primary responsibility is conducting and advising on internal investigations led the project

** "It should be noted that, with respect to non-HP phone records, the investigation team utilized a lawful investigative methodology commonly utilized by entities such as law firms and licensed security firms in the United States to obtain such records"

5/22/2006 3

PD 00073

Draft Report Findings

- "... the overwhelming weight of evidence reviewed by the investigation team indicates the source of the leak is HP Board Member George Keyworth II. Evidence supporting this conclusion is extensive and multi-faceted"
- "The evidence also overwhelmingly indicates that Keyworth was the sources who leaked non-public, confidential information to Kawamoto in conjunction with at least six (6) other articles since March of 2002

Evidence Supporting Report Findings

- "Keyworth established a relationship with CNet reporter Kawamoto beginning in 2001 as part of a public relations campaign during the Compaq acquisition"
- Content of seven articles written by Kawamoto over the past four years citing an unidentified "source" contain confidential HP information that allowed the investigative team to "narrow the possible sources and ultimately point squarely at Keyworth"
- Phone records indicate telephonic contact between Kawamoto and Keyworth
  - After the January 2006 Board meeting and before publication of the January 23 article.
  - Again in February 2006

Evidence Supporting Report Findings

5/22/2006

PD 00076

Evidence Supporting Report Findings

- The team analyzed all articles written by Kawamoto since 2001 and further narrowed the source of the leaks
- "Since March of 2002, Kawamoto has written 10 substantive articles about HP... in which she cites a "source" who has provided non-public confidential information in the article"
- "The investigation team's detailed review of each of the 10 articles made three things clear"
  1. "that Kawamoto likely used the same sources in each of the 10 articles"
  2. "That the sources was most likely a pre-merger HP Director"
  3. "That Keyworth was most likely the source" *

* Based upon an analysis of each "source" statement, the individual(s) who had such knowledge, as process of elimination eliminated all but Keyworth

5/22/2006 7

PD 00077

Next Steps

1. Meet with Jay to
   - Review report findings, evidence
   - Obtain his response

2. Present findings, along with Jay's response, to the full Board

TAB 89

HP Confidential **For Named Individuals on the Distribution List Only**

SBC Investigation Report

Hewlett-Packard Company
Global SBC Compliance Team
3000 Hanover Street
Palo Alto, CA 94304

ATTORNEY-CLIENT PRIVILEGED; ATTORNEY WORK PRODUCT

Subject: Unauthorized Disclosure Investigation

From: Kevin T. Hunsaker, Director of Ethics and SBC

Date: May 24, 2006

To: Mark Hurd
Ann Baskins
HP Board of Directors

I. Background

On Friday afternoon, January 20, 2006, CNET reporter Tom Krazit contacted Bob Sherbin (HP Media Relations), advising him that CNET was going to publish an article summarizing at least four of the issues discussed during the HP Board meeting held two weeks earlier in Indian Wells, California. Sherbin promptly informed Mark Hurd and Pattie Dunn, as well as Jim Fairbaugh and Tony Gentilucci from Global Security Investigations. Gentilucci then immediately informed HP's Legal Department, and a preliminary investigation at the direction of the Legal Department was commenced over the weekend.

On Monday, January 23, 2006, CNET published the article as indicated by Krazit on the 20th. The article was written by Dawn Kawamoto[1], and it contained a detailed, accurate summary of several issues discussed during the January 2006 Board meeting. The article attributed all of the substantive information about the issues discussed during the January 2006 Board meeting to a "source with the company." Because the information contained in the article was clearly non-public, confidential HP information that was discussed in detail during the Board meeting, Pattie Dunn requested that a formal investigation into the information leak be conducted at the direction of the Legal Department. The Legal Department immediately assembled a cross-functional team of individuals with appropriate backgrounds and expertise to conduct a comprehensive, objective, and independent investigation of this matter.

II. Executive Summary

The Investigation Team began the investigation by gathering data and information with respect to any and all individuals who may have had access to the information disclosed in Kawamoto's January 23, 2006 article. During the course of the investigation, the Investigation

[1] It should be noted that Tom Krazit co-authored the article with Kawamoto, and Stephen Shankland "contributed" to the article. A copy of the article is attached hereto as Appendix 1.

Team (1) gathered, generated, reviewed and analyzed thousands of internal and external documents; (2) conducted interviews of individuals in possession of relevant information; (3) conducted extensive electronic searches of HP's systems and proxy servers for information pertaining in any way to the leaks; (4) conducted extensive telephone and email searches regarding dozens of individuals (including, to varying degrees, members of HP's Board[2], members of the Executive Council, as well as other HP employees, including several members of HP's Media Relations group); (5) conducted detailed background searches and link analyses with respect to several reporters and numerous potential sources of the information leak; and (6) engaged in a number of other investigative activities designed to obtain additional information potentially relevant to both the information leak and the source(s) thereof.

As a result of the foregoing investigative activities, the Investigation Team successfully narrowed the list of potential sources of the leak during the course of the investigation and, with the assistance of an interview conducted on May 18, 2006 by Robert Ryan (the Chair of the Audit Committee) the Investigation Team identified HP Board member George Keyworth II as the source of the leak. Evidence supporting this conclusion is extensive and multi-faceted. Among other things, (1) Keyworth established a relationship with CNET reporter Kawamoto beginning in 2001 as part of a public relations campaign during the Compaq acquisition; (2) the content of seven of the ten articles written about HP by Kawamoto in the past 4 years citing an unidentified "source" contain confidential HP information, descriptions of HP business dealings and points of view that narrow the possible sources and ultimately point squarely at Keyworth; (3) information obtained by the Investigation Team indicates telephonic contact between Kawamoto and Keyworth after the January 2006 Board Meeting and before publication of the January 23rd article, and again in February 2006 after the investigation of the leaks was under way; and (4) on May 18th, Keyworth admitted to both Ryan and the full Board that he was the source of the January 23rd article. As more specifically described below, all of the above, together with a number of other connections to the leaks established by the Investigation Team, clearly identify and establish Keyworth as the source of the leaks.

The remainder of this Report will set forth a comprehensive overview of the actions taken by the Investigation Team, the evidence and information supporting the Investigation Team's conclusion, and the recommendations for further action based on the conclusion reached by the Investigation Team.

III. Scope

The objective of the Investigation Team was as follows:

- **Determine the identity of the individual or individuals who leaked confidential, non-public HP information to CNET reporter Dawn Kawamoto in conjunction with the January 23, 2006 article summarizing the issues discussed during the January 2006 Board meeting.**

---

[2] It should be noted that the Investigation Team did not access or search the emails or email accounts of any non-employee Board members. The Investigation Team did receive and review approximately 30 email messages sent either to or from Pattie Dunn's personal email account that were voluntarily provided by Dunn in response to the Investigation Team's specific request.

IV. Approach

Investigation Team Members

Kevin Hunsaker (HP Legal), Fred Adler (IT Security), Tony Gentilucci and Vince Nye (Global Security Investigations), and Ron Delia (HP Investigative Consultant) were the lead investigators. Team members who also assisted in this investigation include Denis Lynch (Global Security), Tim O'Neill (IT Security), Jim Fairbaugh (Global Security) and Robert Ryan (Chair of the Audit Committee).

Procedures

As part of the investigation of this matter, the Investigation Team took the following actions:

- Obtained, reviewed and analyzed all presentations and other documentation utilized, generated, or relied upon in conjunction with the January 2006 Board of Directors meeting.
- Obtained, reviewed, and analyzed more than ten (10) thousand electronic and hard-copy articles pertaining to HP published by CNET, the Wall Street Journal and other periodicals during the past six years; obtained and analyzed all articles (on any topic) written or contributed to by Dawn Kawamoto, Tom Krazit, Stephen Shankland, Rachel Konrad and Pui-Wing Tam in the past 10 years; identified, reviewed in detail and indexed more than 1,000 electronic and hard-copy articles written by Kawamoto.
- Obtained, reviewed, and analyzed extensive internal HP documentation and information (both electronic and hard-copy), as well as external, publicly available documentation and information regarding all the members of the HP Board of Directors, HP Executive Council, HP Media Relations, and other HP employees who potentially had access to the presentations and issues discussed during the January 2006 Board meeting.
- Conducted extensive search and analysis of email and available telephone records of each member of the Executive Council, members of HP Media Relations and other HP employees who potentially had access to the presentations and issues discussed during the January 2006 Board meeting.
- Conducted extensive search and analysis of HP's email and internet servers to locate any traffic to and from any of the reporters or news agencies of interest in this matter.
- Conducted extensive background investigation, including obtaining, reviewing and analyzing publicly available documentation and information (both electronic and hard-copy) regarding relevant members of the media, including Kawamoto, Krazit, Shankland, Konrad and Tam.

- Obtained, reviewed and analyzed HP phone records and third party phone information to identify calls made to or from reporters or other individuals of interest during the relevant timeframes.[3]

- Collected and reviewed several thousand pages of documents (Word, PowerPoint, Excel, etc.) relating to the information discussed during the January 2006 Board meeting, the potential sources of the leak, the relationships of HP employees and Board members to members of the media, and other areas of inquiry relevant to the investigation.

- Engineered and executed a covert intelligence gathering operation pursuant to which an undercover investigator established email contact with Kawamoto using an untraceable hotmail account. The operation included placing a legally permissible software-based tracing device in an email attachment sent to Kawamoto. The objective of the operation was to track and determine whether the email was forwarded to the source or sources (internal or external to HP) by Kawamoto.

- Conducted surveillance activity and reviewed existing video surveillance footage in an effort to determine whether specific individuals were meeting with or speaking to certain members of the media.

- Conducted an in-depth review of all materials associated with the KONA I investigation, which was conducted in relation to information leaks that occurred during 2005 involving media sources such as the Wall Street Journal, Business Week and the New York Times.

Individuals Interviewed: The following individuals were interviewed in person by members of the Investigation Team:

- Ann Baskins (General Counsel);
- Pattie Dunn (Chairman of the Board);
- Bob Wayman (Chief Financial Officer);
- Mark Hurd (Chief Executive Officer);
- Charles Charnas (Legal);
- Alan Haggard (Legal);
- Bob Sherbin (Media Relations);
- Rosemarie Thomas (Board Liaison); and

[3] It should be noted that, with respect to non-HP phone information, the Investigation Team utilized a lawful investigative methodology commonly utilized by entities such as law firms, licensed security firms and law enforcement agencies in the United States to obtain such information.

- George Keyworth II (HP Board Member)[4].

V. Findings

Based upon the documents reviewed, information collected and interviews conducted during the course of the investigation, the Investigation Team finds as follows:

➢ **Did the Investigation Team determine the identity of the individual or individuals who leaked confidential, non-public HP information to CNET reporter Dawn Kawamoto in conjunction with the January 23, 2006 article summarizing the issues discussed during the January 2006 Board meeting?**

Yes. The documents and information reviewed and interviews conducted by the Investigation Team during the course of the investigation indicate that George Keyworth II is the source who leaked non-public, confidential information to Kawamoto with respect to the January 23rd CNET article.[5] During the course of the investigation, the Investigation Team narrowed the list of potential sources of the leak until it became clear that Keyworth was the source of the leak. The following is a summary of the evidence and information supporting the Investigation Team's findings.

(1) Kawamoto's January 23, 2006 Article.

Because the Investigation Team's primary objective was to identify the source of the confidential information leaked to Kawamoto with respect to the January 23rd CNET article, the Investigation Team commenced the investigation by conducting a detailed review and analysis of the article. The article attributes the following six comments and quotes to the source:

➢ Those in attendance worked from early morning to late evening, with few breaks given beyond meals. "By the time the lectures were done at 10 p.m., we were pooped and went to bed."

➢ HP is considering making more acquisitions in the infrastructure software arena. Those acquisitions would include security software companies, storage software makers and software companies that serve the blade server market.

➢ In IPG, the long-term plan to develop commercial printers is likely to continue. "We want to develop the next Heidelberg press."

➢ On the chip front, although HP and Intel have had a long relationship involving their collaboration on the Itanium chip, delays by Intel have created frustration in the HP camp. As a result, HP may use Intel's archrival AMD as a cattle prod of sorts to the chip giant. "We plan to use AMD's Opteron more and more."

---

[4] As previously noted, Keyworth was interviewed on May 18, 2006 by Robert Ryan.

[5] The evidence also overwhelmingly indicates that Keyworth was the source who leaked non-public, confidential information to Kawamoto in conjunction with at least 6 other articles since March of 2002.

- One area expected to get an internal technology revamp in the coming year and a half is direct sales. Though HP's direct sales technology is expected to undergo changes, one thing that's not likely to happen is a merging of the HP and Compaq PC brands. Because the Compaq brand is still recognized in the market, it offsets the additional costs associated with maintaining two brands.
- And, while HP has struggled with getting customers and the market to understanding its Adaptive Enterprise concept, the same mistake will not happen with HP's Next Generation Data Center. "Adaptive Enterprise. What is that? No one understood it. But the Next Generation Data Center is something that everyone can understand. The name is (cumbersome). Don't be surprised to see it changed."

Based upon (1) the detailed nature of the foregoing comments and quotes; (2) the Investigation Team's extensive review of each of the slide sets presented during the Board meeting and various committee meetings; (3) the Investigation Team's extensive email and internet proxy server search regarding all individuals who had access to the aforementioned slide sets; and (4) the interviews of witnesses who were present during the Board and committee meetings, it is clear that the source who leaked the information to Kawamoto was physically present during the presentations given during the Board meeting. The slide sets, which were not widely circulated (this was confirmed by electronic searches conducted by the Investigation Team), simply did not contain sufficient detail to enable someone – even someone with significant knowledge of HP's businesses and strategies – to make *all* of the foregoing comments and quotes based solely on reviewing the slides. The Investigation Team therefore determined that the source must have been physically present to hear the presentations given during the Board meeting, which means the source is either a member of the Board of Directors or a member of the Executive Council.

In addition, the Investigation Team concluded that the source was most likely present at the Technology Committee meeting held on January 11, 2006 (the day before the Board meeting commenced). According to witnesses present at the Technology Committee meeting, three of the topics from the January 23rd article (targeted acquisitions, Intel/AMD and Adaptive Enterprise) were discussed in significant detail (using many of the exact same terms) at the meeting and, according to witnesses interviewed during the investigation, those same topics likely were not covered in the Board meeting in sufficient detail to give the comments and quotes as they appear in the article. The individuals present during the Technology Committee meeting were: George Keyworth (Committee Chair), Robert (Bob) Ryan, Tom Perkins, Richard (Dick) Hackborn, John Hammergren, Pattie Dunn, Mark Hurd, Ann Livermore, Shane Robison and Alan Haggard.

The foregoing conclusions based upon the content of the January 23rd article enabled the Investigation Team to begin narrowing the list of possible sources. However, other aspects of the content and language used in the January 23rd article provided the Investigation Team with its first indications that the source may be Keyworth. Specifically, the Investigation Team made the following observations about the article:

- Adaptive Enterprise and the Next Generation Data Center. According to several witnesses, Keyworth has discussed these topics both frequently and passionately. Keyworth has also often commented that he believes the Next Generation Data

Center name should be changed – even suggesting a name himself (Neutron Data Center) during the January 2006 Board meeting.

➤ Intel/AMD. According to a number of witnesses, Keyworth is familiar with the HP/Intel relationship, the recent issues with Itanium, and HP's desire to use AMD's Opteron chip more frequently. In addition, according to one witness interviewed, Keyworth is the only Board member to bring up the Itanium subject during Board meetings. It is also worth noting that Kawamoto's "source" has previously discussed HP's relationship with Intel and our use of the Itanium chip in significant, technical detail.

➤ Acquisitions. A number of witnesses indicated that Keyworth has shown a keen, vocal interest in making targeted acquisitions to increase HP's breadth of products and services over the past 10 years. In addition, as the Chair of the Technology Committee and a member of the Acquisitions Committee, he would be well aware of HP's strategy with respect to acquisitions.

➤ Use of the term "lectures." This is an academic term, rarely used in the business environment. Keyworth is the only Board member with an academic background. Keyworth frequently gives and attends lectures on a variety of topics; this is a term he may use.

➤ "We were pooped." This is also an unusual term. A number of witnesses interviewed indicated that, contrary to a number of members of the Board, Keyworth often uses casual, colloquial terms in conversation, so this is a term he may use.

➤ Heidelberg Press. A number of witnesses interviewed indicated that this is a term many of the Board members likely would not be familiar enough with to comment on. Keyworth, however, would be.

➤ Scope of topics covered. Several witnesses interviewed indicated that Keyworth is likely the only Board member who could speak accurately and intelligently about each of the topics set forth in the article without extensive preparation. The breadth and detail of the various subjects covered requires a fairly comprehensive knowledge of several different HP business groups.

➤ Stephen Shankland "contributed to this report." This fact is significant because, as will be discussed in more detail below, there appears to be a fairly substantial connection between Keyworth and Shankland.

(2) Additional Articles Written by Kawamoto

After narrowing the potential sources of the leak to individuals physically present at the Board meeting, and likely also present at the Technology Committee meeting as set forth above, the Investigation Team reviewed and analyzed all articles written by Kawamoto regarding HP since 2001. The Investigation Team found that, since March of 2002, Kawamoto has written 10 substantive articles about HP (including the January 23rd article) in which she cites a "source" who has provided non-public, confidential information in the article. The Investigation Team's detailed review of each of the 10 articles made three things clear: (1) that Kawamoto likely used the same source in each of the 10 articles; (2) that the source was most likely a pre-merger HP director; and (3) that Keyworth was most likely the source.

Kawamoto most likely used the same source in all 10 articles. One of the first things the Investigation Team noted is that Kawamoto always cites just one "source," rather than citing "sources" or "people familiar with the situation" like other reporters who more frequently cover HP do, such as Pui-Wing Tam (WSJ), Peter Burrows (Business Week), Ben Elgin (Business Week), and John Markoff (NY Times). In addition, based upon the Investigation Team's research, Kawamoto does not appear to contact HP to confirm her stories, whereas other reporters such as Tam and Burrows essentially always contact HP's Media Relations group to confirm their stories and seek comment (which is an industry practice).[6] Moreover, despite the fact that Kawamoto cites only one source and never calls to confirm the stories, the information contained in the articles is highly confidential, detailed, and accurate. Finally, because Kawamoto has written just 10 substantive articles about HP in the past 4 years, it is highly unlikely that she has cultivated multiple sources from whom she can obtain the type of information that appears in her stories.

The foregoing facts indicate that Kawamoto's source is highly placed, has access to the specific information set forth in her articles, and that she trusts the source to provide accurate information. They also strongly support the conclusion that she has been using the same source since the first article citing an anonymous "source," which was written in March of 2002.

Kawamoto's source is most likely a pre-merger HP director. In 4 of the 10 articles, the "source" references specific events that occurred at HP before the merger, and in one of the articles, Kawamoto specifically identifies the source as an "HP director." For example, on March 19, 2002, Kawamoto quoted ***"one HP director who requested anonymity"*** as follows:

> "We had looked at consulting two years ago, when it was a growing business. But now, outsourcing is growing and consulting is not. I plan to recommend (to the board) we look at parts of Compaq's business that they might be interested in selling if the merger does not go through."

The only Board members in March of 2002 who were also Board members in 2000 were Pattie Dunn, Bob Wayman, Carly Fiorina, Sam Ginn, Dick Hackborn and George Keyworth.

On July 29, 2002, in a detailed article about the formation of the Technology Committee, Kawamoto quoted a "source close to the company" as follows:

> HP developed the idea behind Itanium before entering into a 1993 partnership under which Intel handles most of the work of designing and building it. HP's work has given the company a financial edge over competitors besides just the extra years of design experience – HP gets a deeper discount on Itanium processors than HP competitors. Because Intel doesn't pay HP Itanium royalties, that discount helps to offset some of the billions of research dollars that HP spent on Itanium.

The only Board members in July of 2002 that were even affiliated with HP in 1993 were Bob Wayman, Dick Hackborn and George Keyworth.

---

[6] The only exception uncovered to date was when Krazit called Bob Sherbin on Jan 20th to ask him for comment on the story published on January 23rd.

On March 29, 2005, in an article about HP hiring Mark Hurd, Kawamoto cites a "source close to the board" as follows:

> During the search, Hurd emerged as a clear frontrunner within the first month of the effort. And though the search ended quickly, Hurd was not well-known to HP prior to its CEO search. He was not among the candidates reviewed when HP selected Fiorina six years ago.

The only Board members in March of 2005 that were also on the Board when HP interviewed and hired Fiorina were Pattie Dunn, Bob Wayman, Dick Hackborn and George Keyworth.

And, finally, on January 23, 2006 (Kawamoto wrote 2 articles about HP on January 23rd), Kawamoto cites "an HP source" as follows:

> Five years ago, HP dropped its bid for the consulting arm of PWC . . . . The deal fell through as HP and the PWC partners wrangled over the pricing structure and the difficulty in dealing with a partnership.

The only Board members in January of 2006 that were also on the Board when PWC deal was contemplated were Carly Fiorina, Pattie Dunn, Bob Wayman, Dick Hackborn and George Keyworth.

In addition to the fact that the first article referenced above specifically attributes the quote to a pre-merger HP director, the Investigation Team was able to determine that, if the source was not an HP director before the merger, it is unlikely Kawamoto or any other reporter would accept and print the statements about events that clearly took place before the merger without confirming them with at least one additional source[7]. Since Kawamoto cites only the one source, the source most likely has personal knowledge of those items, thus eliminating any need for Kawamoto to confirm them with either HP or an additional source. The article with the information about the 1993 agreement with Intel is a good example – it seems highly unlikely that Kawamoto (or any reporter) would take the word of a pre-merger Compaq director, or of a new HP director, about the pricing HP gets or the royalty arrangements between HP and Intel based on a 1993 agreement. Consequently, the source must have had personal knowledge of the agreement, and the Investigation Team concluded that Kawamoto's source must be a pre-merger HP director.

The content of the Kawamoto articles indicates that Keyworth is most likely the source. As previously stated, since March of 2002, Kawamoto has written 10 substantive articles about HP citing a source and containing non-public, confidential information. Of those 10 articles, 7 of them contain information indicating Keyworth is most likely the source.[8] For example (and as set forth above), on March 19, 2002, Kawamoto quoted "***one HP director who requested anonymity***" as follows:

---

[7] The investigation Team further substantiated this conclusion by consulting with a media expert, who was a former investigative reporter for a large metropolitan news agency.

[8] It should be noted that the three articles the Investigation Team found to be unclear as to the source were written between July 11, 2005 and July 16, 2005 (a five day period) and covered the same topic as a July 14, 2005 article containing information indicating Keyworth was most likely the source. Thus, all 7 articles written by Kawamoto about different subjects contain information indicating Keyworth is most likely the source.

- "We had looked at consulting two years ago, when it was a growing business. But now, outsourcing is growing and consulting is not. I plan to recommend (to the board) we look at parts of Compaq's business that they might be interested in selling if the merger does not go through."

Because of the quote about looking at consulting two years before the date of the article, Keyworth and Dick Hackborn (Hackborn) are the only two feasible sources for this article. However, a number of individuals interviewed indicated that the language used in the article "I plan to recommend . . ." is the type of language often used by Keyworth when discussing his thoughts and ideas about HP; the same individuals felt quite strongly that Hackborn does not typically speak in this manner. In addition, because Keyworth has been a strong proponent of strategic acquisitions to enhance HP's product offering and was a vocal supporter of acquiring certain aspects of Compaq, Keyworth is more likely the source of this article.

On July 29, 2002, Kawamoto cited "a source close to the company" as follows:

- The Technology Committee will oversee some of HP's most pressing technology issues, which includes greater use of direct sales and ensuring its research work is firmly aligned with corporate strategy. "The technology committee will help the board look at the enablers for the merger." Tom Perkins suggested the creation of a technology committee and received strong support from Carly Fiorina.
- "The technology committee will receive input from the board as it reviews the complexity and evolution of moving HP to an Itanium architecture. Some of the issues include how fast should the transition move and some of the technological hurdles." It isn't known how long it will take for Itanium servers to outpace those with HP's PA-RISC and 32-bit Intel chips such as Xeon or Pentium.
- HP developed the idea behind Itanium before entering into a 1993 partnership under which Intel handles most of the work of designing and building it. HP's work has given the company a financial edge over competitors besides just the extra years of design experience – HP gets a deeper discount on Itanium processors than HP competitors. Because Intel doesn't pay HP Itanium royalties, that discount helps to offset some of the billions of research dollars that HP spent on Itanium.

Because of the quote about the 1993 agreement with Intel, Keyworth and Hackborn are the only two feasible sources for this article. In addition, because this article contains detailed, technical information, including detailed information about the 1993 agreement with Intel about Itanium, several individuals interviewed indicated that Keyworth is likely the only director who could have provided the content for this article without significant preparation. According to one witness, Itanium is an issue Keyworth has focused on for some time, and Keyworth is the only director who has ever mentioned Itanium in the board room setting. And, as will be more fully explained below, it is also significant that Stephen Shankland "contributed to this report."

On February 24, 2003, Kawamoto cited "a source familiar with the company's plans" as follows:

- HP sees licensing more of its intellectual property as a way to get a greater return on its substantial research and development budget. "HP is looking at licensing technology as a business. Currently, it has over $4 billion invested in research and development annually."

- "HP used to be a lot of disparate businesses, like the printer business, enterprise business and others loosely combined at the top . . . but over the past couple of years, Carly has made it more centralized. And now there is a better grip on the patent assets as a whole. Also, our growing portfolio of patents has been increased with the Compaq merger, which also includes technology from Compaq's DEC and Tandem mergers."
- "This has been a big area for [Carly]. She has been working with the labs and increasing the number of patent applications. There was a time in the economy where growth was valued over profit. But with the current market environment, profit is now valued over growth. And the licensing (revenue) will fall right to the bottom line since it all stems from the investments already made in R&D."

A number of individuals interviewed felt very strongly that the source for this article was Keyworth. According to the witnesses, Keyworth has often talked about the value add from the Technology Committee with respect to intellectual property generating revenue. Keyworth was very proud of this initiative, and the quote about licensing revenue falling right to the bottom line is an inaccurate statement that Keyworth has made on multiple occasions about the issue.

On March 29, 2005, Kawamoto cites "a source close to the board" as follows:

- Hewlett-Packard has selected Mark Hurd, NCR chief executive, as its next CEO. Hurd will serve as president and chief executive, with Patricia Dunn retaining the chairwoman title. "He has done as astonishing job at NCR and had inherited similar problems" to those at HP. "NCR sells into retail and enterprise markets, and has the same complexities."
- During the search, Hurd emerged as a clear frontrunner within the first month of the effort. And though the search ended quickly, Hurd was not well-known to HP prior to its CEO search. He was not among the candidates reviewed when HP selected Fiorina six years ago. "He's young, he has a fabulous record, he understands the industry, he's tough and recruits good people."

Because of the quote about Hurd not being on the list of candidates when Fiorina was hired, Keyworth and Hackborn are the only two feasible sources for this article. According to several witnesses, Keyworth is very proud of being involved in bringing Hurd on board at HP. One witness indicated Keyworth has said he "repaid Dave Packard by bringing Mark on board." A number of individuals interviewed also indicated that the specific language used during parts of the article ("fabulous", "astonishing") is language that Keyworth uses frequently.

It should also be noted that, during a presentation at a tech conference on March 20, 2005 with 750 attendees present, Keyworth informed the attendees that HP would likely announce a new CEO in the next two weeks. He was not authorized by the Board to make such a statement.

On July 14, 2005, Kawamoto cites a "source familiar with the company" as follows:

- HP executives are expected this weekend to put the final touches on a reorganization that could result in the loss of about 15,000 jobs. The job cuts would then be announced on Monday. Despite the prospect of massive layoffs, HP's workers are responding favorably to Hurd, who has been in the CEO post only a few months.

- "People feel he is a straight shooter and doesn't mince his words. People have responded to him positively; they like and respect him and view him as a leader. This response from the employees has happened in a much shorter time than was imagined."
- "What happened was, a year ago, Duane Zitzner wanted to retire by a specific date. He kept reminding Carly that the date was approaching, but she made little effort to fill his position. So when that date came and there was no replacement for Duane, it was put under VJ. But VJ already had his hands full and the PC business needed a lot of work, so, in the end, it was best to run them separately."
- At the same time, Hurd has found areas within HP where spending has been underinvested. The part of HP's sales force that helps large corporate customers integrate their computer systems is one area that needs further investment. Hurd is working closely with Ann Livermore, a longtime HP executive who oversees the company's server and storage group and its services and software.

A number of individuals interviewed felt the paragraph about Duane Zitzner is out of place in the article. It is essentially a derogatory remark about Fiorina that is completely unrelated to the rest of the content of the article. According to witnesses, both Keyworth and Hackborn were vocal about this particular issue, and it was a source of contention for both of them. However, according to at least one witness, the language used in the article sounds like what Keyworth would say, not Hackborn.

On January 23, 2006 (in the second article written by Kawamoto on the 23rd), Kawamoto cites "an HP source" as follows:

- Despite media reports that HP and Blackstone were in preliminary discussions to acquire CSC, such a deal never made it on the radar of HP executives and directors. Reports of the preliminary discussions took HP executives by surprise. "CSC has occasionally come up from time to time as a potential acquisition, but it's nothing that we ever seriously pursued and nothing we were in talks with recently.
- Five years ago, HP dropped its bid for the consulting arm of PWC . . . . The deal fell through as HP and the PWC partners wrangled over the pricing structure and the difficulty in dealing with a partnership.

This article directly contradicts itself in terms of insider information, which indicates it may be an intentional plant of false information. At least one individual interviewed thinks Keyworth would plant information such as this to further an acquisition he believed in. Keyworth has had a keen, vocal interest in making targeted acquisitions to increase HP's breadth of products and services over the past 10 years. This article was a very good thing for HP, as it would have a tendency to reduce CSC's stock price, which would enhance HP's ability to complete the acquisition. The source's apparent lack of inside knowledge about executives and directors being surprised by talk of a possible CSC deal is contradicted by the source's accurate details regarding why the PWC deal fell through. The "throw away line" about the PWC deal in this article is *definitely* inside information that was not made public when HP decided not to go forward with the PWC deal in 2001. It is unlikely that someone who knows the non-public details regarding the failure of the PWC deal would not know about CSC. And, because of the quote about the PWC deal (which was 5 years ago), Keyworth and Hackborn are the only two feasible sources for this article if the source was a member of the Board.

The likelihood that the information in this article was an intentional plant of false information is also enhanced by the fact that Kawamoto had not written a substantive article about HP since July of 2005 (more than 6 months). Given the lengthy break since her last substantive article about HP, it seems very unlikely that she would publish two completely different stories, based on confidential information from two completely different sources, on the exact same day. It seems more likely that the same source gave her information for both articles – and any source with detailed knowledge of what occurred during the Board meeting would know about the CSC negotiations. And, as more fully set forth in the section regarding the first January 23rd article above, the language and content of that article indicates that Keyworth is most likely the source Kawamoto used for that article, which (in combination with accurate knowledge regarding failure of the PWC deal) means Keyworth is also most likely the source she used for the second January 23rd article.

(3) Additional Information Connecting Keyworth to the Leaks.

Based on the foregoing overview of the Kawamoto articles, the Investigation Team found that Kawamoto likely used the same source in each of the 10 articles, that the source was a pre-merger HP director, and that, based on the content of the articles, Keyworth was most likely the source for at least 7 of the articles. As will be set forth in significant detail below, the additional information obtained, reviewed and analyzed by the Investigation Team, when combined with the foregoing summary of the Kawamoto articles, establishes Keyworth as the only feasible source of the information leaks to Kawamoto.

Keyworth has a number of direct connections to Kawamoto. According to several individuals interviewed, as well comments made by Keyworth himself during the course of the KONA I investigation, Keyworth was asked by Carly Fiorina to develop a relationship with Kawamoto and another reporter (Pui-Wing Tam) sometime in 2001. The purpose of developing the relationship was to promote the HP/Compaq merger. It appears clear that Keyworth did, in fact, develop a relationship with Kawamoto[9], as Kawamoto wrote an article on August 21, 2001 in which Keyworth was quoted as follows:

> "In the early summer of 1999, when we were interviewing Carly, we discussed it would take a minimum of three years to turn things around and there would be lots of ups and downs. We are absolutely behind her and know there will be challenges."

In addition to the foregoing direct connection to Kawamoto, the Investigation Team established that, ***at 5:25 pm PST on January 18, 2006*** (just two days before Krazit called Sherbin for comment on the article CNET intended to publish), ***a call was made from Kawamoto's cell***

---

[9] It is also clear that Keyworth developed a relationship with Pui-Wing Tam. On November 17, 2005, Keyworth contacted HP investigators in Palo Alto to report that Tam called his home phone in New Mexico on two occasions in January 2005. Keyworth indicated that Tam was attempting to ask him questions about a story she was writing, but that he did not return the calls. Keyworth stated that he had given Tam his home number during the HP/Compaq merger when the Board was encouraged to work with the press to promote the merger. He also stated that he now wanted to document Tam's calls before deleting them because of the previous issues with information being leaked out of HP to the press at that time. He also stated that he had not spoken with Tam in over two years. The messages were recorded and preserved.

phone to Keyworth's home in Piedmont, California. The call lasted approximately one minute. However, it should be noted that the phone is listed in Keyworth's wife's name [redacted]), and there is no documented 411 call from Kawamoto's cell phone prior to the call. This indicates that Kawamoto likely knew the home phone number, which is significant because it appears as though Keyworth moved permanently into his wife's home at or around the time they were married in August of 2005. This appears to indicate that Keyworth has stayed in touch with Kawamoto during the past several years.

Keyworth did not disclose the foregoing call to Bob Sherbin or Pattie Dunn, as is expected when Board members are contacted by members of the media. In addition, the Investigation Team identified no other calls to or from Kawamoto's cell or home phones by other directors prior to the January 23rd article.

In addition to the January 18th call from Kawamoto to Keyworth, the Investigation Team also established that, ***at 2:21 pm PST on February 3, 2006, a call was made from Keyworth's cell phone to Kawamoto's office*** (her direct line, not the switchboard number) at CNET. ***The call lasted approximately 10 minutes.*** No 411 call is documented prior to the 10-minute call either from Keyworth's cell phone or from his home phone at his New Mexico residence (which, based on phone information obtained by the Investigation Team, is where Keyworth was staying on February 3rd). This call is also significant because of the three calls documented below made from Keyworth's New Mexico residence to Tom Perkins on the same day.

Keyworth did not disclose this February 3rd call to Bob Sherbin or Pattie Dunn, as is expected when Board members have contact with members of the media. In addition, the Investigation Team identified no other calls to Kawamoto's office by other directors or persons of interest during this timeframe.

Finally, the existence of the foregoing calls is also potentially significant because, despite the fact that Keyworth was quoted in an article written by Pui Wing Tam on January 14, 2006 about Tom Perkins' new book, there does not appear to have been any phone calls to or from Pui Wing Tam to Keyworth at or around that timeframe. As such, it appears that Keyworth likely interacts with Pui Wing Tam (and Kawamoto) via email or Instant Messenger as well. It should be noted, however, that if Tam or Kawamoto called Keyworth's home phone from their respective offices, the Investigation Team would not be able to obtain any information regarding such calls.

Keyworth's Connections to Stephen Shankland. In 3 of the 10 substantive articles written about HP by Kawamoto since 2002 citing a "source," the article says "Stephen Shankland contributed to this report." Thomas Shankland [redacted] worked with Keyworth in the same Physics department at the Los Alamos Lab in New Mexico for approximately 6 years. Keyworth then left Los Alamos to join the Reagan administration. With the possible exception of when Keyworth was with the Reagan administration, Thomas Shankland and his family have lived close to Keyworth's New Mexico residence for many years. In fact, for approximately two years in the 1970s, Keyworth and Shankland lived less than two miles from each other, and Stephen and Keyworth's son, George, who are just two years apart, likely attended the same elementary school. Both Thomas Shankland and Keyworth are physicists, belonging to several of the same scientific societies.

Stephen Shankland also authored an article in August 2005 regarding the Progress for Freedom Foundation meeting held in Aspen, Colorado. Keyworth is the Chairman of the Progress for Freedom Foundation and was likely present during the meeting.

In addition, Stephen Shankland's wife, Rachel Konrad, a former CNET reporter and currently an AP journalist, authored a CNET article entitled "Failed HP-Compaq merger would be painful" on Nov. 12, 2001. In the article, which was written the week after Walter Hewlett announced he was going to vote against the merger, Konrad quotes "a source familiar with the board" as follows: "I don't think Walter has thought this through. [If the merger fails,] [n]one of the directors, except Walter, would stay, and I guarantee a lot of the senior management would leave too." Interestingly, Dawn Kawamoto and Stephen Shankland "contributed to this report."

The foregoing is important not just because Konrad is Shankland's wife, but also because Peter Burrows, on page 206 of his book, "Backfire," states that, following a Board meeting on November 16, 2001, Keyworth, Hackborn and Walter Hewlett walked into Hewlett's old office and one of them said, "Look, we are all friends, Walter, but have you thought this through all the way?" According to George Anders' book, "Perfect Enough," Hackborn then explained that, if the merger failed, directors would resign and executives would quit. Given the nearly identical nature of the two quotes, it seems likely that it was either Keyworth or Hackborn that gave the quote to Konrad and then the two of them later said the same thing to Hewlett. Unlike Keyworth, Hackborn has no known connections to Shankland or Konrad.

Information from the KONA I investigation. In mid-2005, an investigation team composed of a number of members from the Investigation Team in this matter conducted an investigation with respect to information leaks that occurred between January and July of 2005 involving media sources such as the Wall Street Journal, Business Week and the New York Times, and reporters such as Pui-Wing Tam, Peter Burrows, Ben Elgin and John Markoff. During the KONA I investigation, the investigation team identified a call from Keyworth's cell phone to John Markoff's NY Time's office on Feb 9, 2005. This call is significant because it occurred just two days after the Board meeting in Chicago, it was the same day HP terminated Fiorina and, the following day (February 10th), Markoff published two articles about HP's decision citing a source. One article purported to contain inside information about the top two internal candidates to replace Fiorina and cited "one company insider" as having provided said information. The other article discussed the Board's decision, and included a quote from "a person familiar with the board's decision" as saying "It's all about performance." Keyworth did not disclose this phone call to Media Relations, but he did disclose the call sometime after the fact to Pattie Dunn, indicating that he simply called Markoff back to tell him he could not comment.

The KONA I investigation also established that Keyworth has, or at least as of the time of the investigation had, an ongoing relationship with Peter Burrows of Business Week. Specifically, Keyworth was identified by Burrows in his book, Backfire, as the only HP Board member who would talk to him "on the record" after the merger. In addition, Burrows states in the book that Keyworth contributed "significant information" to him.

The investigation team in KONA I also established that Keyworth has a connection to George Anders, who is the San Francisco Bureau editor for the Wall Street Journal. For example, in his book, Perfect Enough, Anders cites Keyworth as a source of information, and Keyworth is one of only two HP Board members whose individual photos appear in the book. The book portrays HP and Fiorina in a favorable light. It should also be noted that, throughout 2005 and as recently as January 31, 2006, the Wall Street Journal (via reporter Pui-Wing Tam) has repeatedly published stories containing non-public, confidential HP information attributed to "sources" and "people familiar with the company."

Based upon the foregoing, the investigation team in KONA I determined that Keyworth was one of two Board members most likely leaking information to several different reporters in 2005. The other subject of interest during that investigation was Robert Knowling, who is no longer with the Board. It is also worth noting that the investigation team in KONA I believed there was more than one Board member leaking information to the various reporters in 2005.

Board member Tom Perkins softens and changes his position regarding the source(s) of the leaks. When the information leaks to the Wall Street Journal, Business Week and the New York Times occurred in 2005, Tom Perkins reacted very strongly to the leaks and felt strongly the source(s) of the leak should be removed from the Board, even telling Pattie Dunn in person and via email that he supported the use of Lie Detector Tests to identify the source(s). In addition, on January 23, 2006, after reading Kawamoto's article accurately summarizing the January 2006 Board meeting, Perkins contacted Ann Baskins and Pattie Dunn, stating that the leak could not have come from a Board member, and that it must have come from a member of the Executive Council. Perkins also sent Dunn an email indicating that he thought the leak came from an EC member reading straight from the slides presented during the Board meeting.

Then, during a recent discussion with Dunn during the week of February 6th-10th, Perkins abruptly and inexplicably changed his position with respect to the source of the leak(s). During his conversation with Dunn, Perkins said that, if the source of the leaks is identified, perhaps they should not automatically remove him or her from the Board. He further stated that, if the source "has been a major contributor to the Board," and promises not to leak any more information to the media, maybe the person should be allowed to remain a Board member.

The foregoing significant change in his position about the source of the leaks is significant for at least two reasons. First, immediately following the January 23rd article, Perkins insisted to Baskins and Dunn that the source could not possibly be a Board member, yet in his recent conversation with Dunn he seemed to believe it was a Board member. This tends to indicate that he now either has reason to believe the source is a Board member, or that he knows who the source is, and that the source is a Board member. Second, Perkins' drastic change of position is significant because it indicates that he either knows who it is, or strongly suspects he knows who it is, and that it is someone he both knows well and supports as a Board member. Keyworth fits both descriptions, as it is well known within the Board that Keyworth and Perkins have become good friends and are closely aligned as members of the Board. In addition, according to a number of individuals interviewed, Perkins and Keyworth have worked in a coordinated fashion in the past, working together to get Perkins back on the Board in early 2005 and in working to remove Fiorina as HP's CEO shortly thereafter.

Also supporting the significance of Perkins' discussion with Dunn during the week of February 6th is the fact that the Investigation Team has determined that Keyworth called Perkins at least six (6) times between January 30 and February 8, 2006, including at least three (3) times on February 3rd (the same day Keyworth called Kawamoto at her office). This is significant because of the timing of the calls with respect to Perkins communicating his change in position on the source of the leaks, and because of the high volume of calls during such a short timeframe. Indeed, Keyworth does not appear to have called Perkins more than six times during the six weeks preceding January 30th, then he called Perkins at least six times in an 8-day period.

Interestingly, since all the calls between Keyworth and Perkins in early February, Keyworth's call to Kawamoto on February 3rd, and Perkins call to Dunn during the week for February 6th, Kawamoto has not written a single article about HP in which she cites a "source," despite the fact that she has written *several* stories about HP since February 3rd.

It is also worth noting that, a few days before the March 2006 Board meeting, Perkins called Mark Hurd and asked him, among other things about the status of the investigation into the leaks. Hurd told Perkins that the Investigation Team had assembled a significant amount of circumstantial evidence, but that he was not sure where it would ultimately lead. In addition, during the March 2006 Board meeting, Perkins and Keyworth were seen arguing during two different breaks in the meeting. The arguments were mainly one sided, with Keyworth intently speaking and even pointing his finger at Perkins' chest several times. At the very end of the second argument/heated discussion, Keyworth was overheard saying: "they don't have enough to go there."

(4) Keyworth Admits Being the Source

On May 18, 2006, Robert Ryan (the Chair of HP's Audit Committee) interviewed Keyworth prior to the Board meeting scheduled later in the day. During their discussion about the January 23rd article, Keyworth admitted right away that he was the source who provided information to Kawamoto. Keyworth explained that, back in 2001, Fiorina had asked him to develop a relationship with Kawamoto in order to promote the HP/Compaq merger. Keyworth stated that he thought Kawamoto was a respected voice of the media in the technology sector, and that he had continued to interact with her over the years, including things such as having lunch with her on occasion.

With respect to the reason why he leaked the information in the January 23rd article, Keyworth indicated that he felt Hurd was being unfairly portrayed in the media as purely a cost cutter and that Keyworth felt it was important to make it known that Hurd was also making a number of significant, important strategy decisions that were having a very positive impact on HP's business and direction. Keyworth further stated he thought it was in the best interests of HP for the information in the January 23rd article to be made public – he acknowledged that it was wrong to leak the information, but made it clear that his intention was only to help both Hurd and HP.

During the full Board meeting later in the day on the 18th, Keyworth again admitted that he was the source of the January 23rd article, acknowledged that it was wrong, and explained that he was at all times acting in the best interests of HP.

VI. Summary Conclusion

As the foregoing summary clearly indicates, the Investigation Team successfully narrowed the list of potential sources of the leak during the course of the investigation and, given Keyworth's admission to Ryan and the full Board on May 18th, it is clear that Keyworth was the source of the January 23rd article written by Kawamoto.

VII. Impact to HP

The unauthorized disclosure of non-public, sensitive information at the Board level can cause significant and possibly irreparable harm to HP's reputation. The disclosure of information by Board members creates an environment of uneasiness and distrust within the Board, as such disclosures are clearly a breach of the fiduciary duty owed to HP by each and every Board member. Moreover, continued and repeated information leaks like those that have occurred since January of 2005 can significantly impair HP's ability to conduct its business in an appropriate fashion. If the leaks continue, HP's executives will likely be forced to limit the information provided to the Board in order to ensure that the company's plans and strategies do not appear the following day on CNET or in the Wall Street Journal. If the executives so limit the information provided to the Board, the Board members' ability to properly and efficiently carry out their duties and responsibilities on behalf of HP's shareholders will be dramatically and negatively impacted. This, of course, creates an untenable situation that will ultimately have a negative impact on HP, its employees and shareholders, and may even lead to potential governance and compliance issues with the SEC.

VIII. Recommendations

Based upon the information and conclusions set forth in this Report, the Investigation Team hereby recommends that the Executive Team (Hurd, Baskins and the HP Board of Directors) consider all of the information set forth herein and take action as they deem appropriate to (1) reduce the likelihood of similar leaks occurring in the future; and (2) ensure the HP Board members clearly understand that leaking information to the media is unacceptable and will not be tolerated.

With respect to item (1) above, the Investigation Team would be pleased to participate in any discussions regarding potential proactive measures designed to reduce the likelihood of similar incidents occurring in the future.

End of Report

TAB 90

From: Tom Perkins [redacted]
Sent: Wednesday, May 31, 2006 1:57 PM
To: Andrea Redmond-Chicago
Subject: FW: Hewlett Packard--Tom Perkins

Dear Andrea: Here is a confidential memo of explanation which I sent to NewsCorp directors. Keep it to yourself, please, but it sure isn't going to be easy to attract strong directors to the HP board. I struck out three times in getting a Silicon Valley entrepreneur, to try to keep the HP entrepreneurial tradition in place. Pattie wants only compliant "Wall St. window dressing types", and frankly, Mark will nor resist having a weak board (how many CEO's want any extra challenge?) Anyway, I feel very badly about the whole thing---but being me, couldn't do otherwise. My best regards, and hoping to work with you again. Tom

From: Tom Perkins
Sent: Monday, May 29, 2006 3:11 AM
To: andrew[redacted]; Dave Devoe [redacted]; Dot Wyndoe [redacted]; Lachlan Murdoch [redacted]; Lon Jacobs [redacted]; peter[redacted]Rod Eddington [redacted]; Rupert Murdoch; Stan Shuman [redacted]; Viet Dinh [redacted]
Subject: Hewlett Packard--Tom Perkins

Dear NewsCorp Director:

At the last HP board meeting I suddenly and unexpectedly resigned. The rumors have been flying (Perkins had a heart attack---there was a fist fight). I thought I should give you an explanation, which please keep confidential.

PD 00027

At the time of the CEO transition from Çarly Fiorina to Mark Hurd, there were numerous leaks from within the company, possibly including a few from the board, and the press had a field-day. When the dust settled, the board decided that there should be no more leaks. Period.

Last January there was a relatively benign leak, to CNet, with a very positive spin---designed to put the new CEO in a positive light---but it was un-authorized, and it almost certainly had to have come from some director. The chairman of the board, Pattie Dunn, became obsessed with finding the director or directors involved. A massive secret program, run by hired electronic security experts, was initiated. All telephone and e-mail connections for all directors for the past two years, from all their phones and computers, were examined. Apparently this is legal if the content is not transcribed.

About a month ago Pattie told me (I was chair of the Nominating and Governance committee), "I am getting close." I told her that I didn't really want to know the source, as the leaks had stopped, but if she did find out, the two of us should handle the matter off-line. We would obtain and apology, and a guarantee of non-repetition, and move on. Ibelieved that all the directors were too valuable to the company to be compromised with other members of the board. She agreed.

But that is not what happened. The board meeting opened with her review of the magnitude of her secret program (which shocked us all), and then she dumped the director's name on the table---a director from the pre-Compaq merger HP board. She asked the director to leave the room and a long discussion, a trial really, ensued. Finally, a motion was introduced to ask for the director's resignation. In this new era of Sarbanes-Oxley, it passed, the swing votes were from two very new directors. I resigned after the vote for two reasons: 1) I thought the secret spying (which involved a room-full of electronic gear) was a huge over-reaction, and 2) the chairman betrayed our agreement because, after all, this primarily was my responsibility as the N&G chair, and a very valuable director was being destroyed.

After the event, the director refused to resign, saying that the seat was voted by the shareholders, and should continue to be held until the shareholders spoke otherwise. So mine was the only resignation. I was very angry at the time, but now that over a week has passed, I think that I did the right thing, and to paraphrase the Revolutionary War hero, Nathan Hale ("I regret that I have but one life to give to my country"), I regret that I have but one HP board seat from which to resign.

Sorry to burden you with all this, but I wanted to spike the rumors.

Best, Tom

PD 00028

TAB 91

Subject: FW: HP Confidential

From: Sonsini, Larry [mailto:LSonsini[redacted]
Sent: Wednesday, June 28, 2006 4:05 PM
To: Tom Perkins
Subject: RE: HP Confidential

Tom,

I looked into the conduct of the investigation and got a report from counsel at HP who was responsible for the effort. I confirmed his input by talking to Ann Baskins. Here is what I learned:

1. There was no recording, review or monitoring of director e-mail.

2. There was no electronic surveillance to monitor director communications.

3. There was no phone recording or eavesdropping.

4. The investigating team did not attempt to obtain the phone records of non-employee directors

5. The investigating team did obtain information regarding phone calls made and received by the cell or home phones of directors. This was done through a third party that made pretext calls to phone service providers. Apparently a common investigatory method which was confirmed with experts. The legal team also checked with outside counsel as to the legality of this methodology.

6. There was no "secret spying" i.e. no electronic gear, listening devices, etc., were used.

It appears, therefore, that the process was well done and within legal limits. The concerns raised in your e-mail did not occur.

Let me know if you think I should proceed further.

Larry

From: Sonsini, Larry
Sent: Tuesday, June 20, 2006 10:30 AM
To: Tom Perkins
Subject: RE: HP Confidential

Tom, I will look into this.

From: Tom Perkins [mailto:TPerkins[redacted]

Sent: Tuesday, June 20, 2006 10:00 AM
To: Sonsini, Larry
Subject: RE: HP Confidential

Dear Larry:

Thanks for your prompt reply, and I value the reminder that my director's responsibilities continue after my resignation, which is why, in part, I make the following suggestion: I think you, or someone from your firm, should check into the sub-rosa investigation of the director's communications at HP. Larry, the investigation was a Pattie Dunn program, 100%---conceived and managed by her, and unknown to the board, except perhaps in the most vague and imprecise terms, with the possible exception of Mark, who she may have briefed.

In view of Viet's unqualified opinion that it was illegal, I think, the board needs to know the potential risks, if any. I resigned from the board and as chair of the N&G committee before I could look into this personally. If it was illegal, it occurred under my purview, and on my watch, so to speak, and I would like to know whether or not I share some responsibility.

Thanks, Tom

From: Sonsini, Larry [mailto:LSonsin[redacted]
Sent: Monday, June 19, 2006 2:29 PM
To: Tom Perkins
Subject: RE: HP Confidential

Tom,

I was not involved in the design or conduct of the investigation. The investigation was run by the HP legal department with outside experts. I reviewed the report after the investigation for the Board process. Pattie, was not involved in the design or conduct of the investigation either, to my knowledge. I am sure that Ann Baskin looked into the legality of every step of the inquiry and was satisfied that it was conducted properly.

Tom, be careful of your discussions about the inquiry and the HP Board process and deliberations in that all of that is confidential and, as you know, you have the obligation to continue to respect that confidentiality. You do not want to be in breach of your duties inherited while you were an HP director. Those duties of confidentiality continue. Also,remember, that you confirmed that you did not have any disagreement with HP or the Board as a whole (although you did have issues with the Chairman). I recognize that a duty of loyalty to the Newscorp Board may present some concerns for you, but in my opinion they do not , and should not. require you to disclose the details of the investigation or the HP Board deliberations. Also, Viet Dihn may be a lawyer but query whether your discussions are attorney-client privileged. If you want to talk about all of this please don't hesitate to call.

Larry

From: Tom Perkins [mailto:TPerkins[redacted]
Sent: Monday, June 19, 2006 1:18 PM
To: Sonsini, Larry
Subject: HP Confidential

Hi Larry:

Today I was at a NewsCorp board meeting in London, and I discussed the events of the most recent HP board meeting, on a confidential basis, with a fellow director, Viet Dihn. As you probably know, Viet is a Professor of Law at Georgetown, and his most popular course is "Corporate Governance."

Viet was shocked at the HP chairman's recording of board members telephone and computer inter-connections. I emphasized that no communications were actually transcribed. He said that even monitoring connections and/or e-mail addresses requires a subpoena (which as far as I know was never obtained) but, with or with e out a subpoena, such monitoring was simply "unconscionable."

Larry, was any of this cleared with you before the event?

Thanks in advance for your thoughts. Best, Tom

KP
CB
Kleiner Perkins Caufield & Byers

San Francisco Office
Four Embarcadero Center
Suite 3620
San Francisco, CA 94111
TEL • (415) 421-3110
FAX • (415) 421-3128

Partners
Frank J. Caufield
Thomas J. Perkins

Menlo Park Office
2750 Sand Hill Road
Menlo Park, CA 94025
TEL • (650) 233-2750
FAX • (650) 233-0300
www.kpcb.com

Partners
Brook H. Byers
Kevin R. Compton
L. John Doerr
William R. Hearst III
Thomas A. Jermoluk
Vinod Khosla
E. Floyd Kvamme
Joseph S. Lacob
Bernard J. Lacroute
James P. Lally
Raymond J. Lane
Douglas J. Mackenzie
Ted E. Schlein
Russell Siegelman

Recruiting Partner
Juliet Flint

Chief Financial Officer
Susan M. Biglieri

Chief Operating Officer
John A. Denniston

Recruiting Advisor
Norbert Gottenberg

TAB 92

To the Directors of the Hewlett-Packard Company:

As you know, I resigned in protest from the board of directors of the Hewlett-Packard Company, suddenly and unexpectedly, during a board meeting on May 18th of this year. The Nominating and Governance Committee of the board, which I chaired, had not been informed that the chair of the board had instigated a sub-rosa investigation to uncover the source of an alleged "leak" of information to the Internet news site CNET.com in January 2006. The chair's investigation used the fraudulent method of "pretexting" in order to obtain private telephone records of other board members.

We learned that the investigation did, indeed, uncover a contact between a director and this web news site—and it confirmed that I was not the source. I resigned solely to protest the questionable ethics and the dubious legality of the chairman's methods, as they were disclosed to the board for the first time during the meeting. I also questioned the wisdom and propriety of the chair's demand that the source of the "leak" resign from the Board. Apparently the board has come around to this view, as it has not initiated proceedings to dismiss for cause after the director rightly refused to resign.

In a subsequent press release and required Form 8-K filing with the SEC, the company announced my resignation, but made no reference to the cause or to the fraudulent activities involved. At no time has the Company provided me with a copy of the filing or advised me on my right to review and approve it, as mandated by Item 5.02 of Form 8-K. Concerned about the likely illegality of the chair's investigation, I asked outside counsel Larry Sonsini to look into the matter. On June 28, he confirmed in an e-mail that the investigating team "did obtain information regarding phone calls made and received by the cell or home phone of directors" and that it was "done through a third party that made pretext calls to phone service providers." In pretext calls, an impostor contacts a phone company posing as the company's customer (in this case the directors of Hewlett-Packard) and through false pretense and misrepresentation obtains the confidential records and information of that customer. The Federal Trade Commission and a number of state Attorneys General have brought enforcement actions against pretexting firms for violating federal and state laws relating to fraud, misrepresentation, and unfair competition. Indeed, director Larry Babbio's company, Verizon, has filed fraud suits against persons and companies engaged in pretexting.

I have direct proof of these untoward and illegal practices. My personal phone records were "hacked." Attached is a letter from AT&T confirming this unauthorized and fraudulent access of my personal phone records for January 2006, the month covered by the chair's investigation.

To be sure that the facts of my resignation were accurately recorded and reported, I wrote to the Company Secretary and Chief Legal Counsel on July 18th, requesting that the draft minutes of the May 18th meeting be corrected to reflect the reasons for my resignation and to remove the incorrect statement that as N&G chair I had been informed of the fraud and was thus by implication complicit in it. A copy of that memo is attached.

To date, I have received no response to my letter. My telephone messages to the Secretary and Chief Legal Counsel, also, have not been returned.

On July 28th I again wrote the Company with copies to the full board with detailed references to the illegality of pretexting. I also requested that the board appoint a special committee to investigate both the propriety and the legality of the chair's activities in this matter, and to take whatever disclosure and corrective action is required. This formal request has been ignored as well. A copy of that letter is also attached.

Having received no response to either communication, I am assuming that the Company has rejected my request to amend the minutes and to refer my concerns of illegal conduct to a special committee. Thus, it appears that my disagreement is not only with the chair, as I initially thought, but also with the Company. As my disagreement concerns probable unlawful conduct, improper board procedures, and breakdowns in corporate governance, it constitutes a disagreement "on any matter relating to the registrant's operations, policies or practices" requiring disclosure to the SEC under Item 5.02 of Form 8-K and section 409 of the Sarbanes-Oxley Act of 2002.

I am hereby providing the Company notice that I consider the Company's Form 8-K filed on May 22, 2006, relating to my resignation to be defective because it did not describe my objection to and disagreement with the Company's operations, policies and practices as they relate to the chair's improper and likely unlawful investigation. I therefore disagree with the Company statements concerning my resignation and ask that, pursuant to Item 5.02(a)(3)(iii), the Company file this letter and its attachments with the Securities and Exchange Commission.

As the Company failed to make a full and accurate report (as required by federal law) and having given the Company several opportunities to correct the record, I am now legally obliged to disclose publicly the reasons for my resignation. This is a very sad duty. My history with the Hewlett-Packard Company is long and I have been privileged to count both founders as close friends. I consider HP to be an icon of Silicon Valley, and one of the great companies of the world. It now needs, urgently, to correct its course.

Sincerely,

Thomas J. Perkins

[Signed originals sent to: Mr. Sonsini, Mr. Wayman and Ms. Baskins]

TAB 93

From: Baskins, Ann [mailto:ann.baskins@[redacted]
Sent: Monday, July 17, 2006 11:49 AM
To: Tom Perkins
Cc: Sonsini, Larry; Baskins, Ann; Hurd, Mark
Subject: Minutes

Dear Tom,

Attached are the confidential draft minutes of the May 18 meeting reflecting the portion of the meeting up through and including your resignation. If you have difficulty opening the file, please let me know and I will try to send a facsimile copy.

Regards,
Ann

From: Tom Perkins
Sent: Tuesday, July 18, 2006 3:22 AM
To: Baskins, Ann
Cc: Sonsini, Larry; Hurd, Mark
Subject: RE: Minutes

Dear Ann:

Thank you for sending the draft minutes of the May 18th meeting. I cannot accept the minutes as written.

Three essential matters of substance have been omitted:

1) An essential point, which I explicitly made, questioned the legality of the surveillance of director's communications by the chairman's outside experts. I specifically questioned this at the time of the meeting and I question it still. As written the minutes state that I concurred in the nature of the investigation—this is not true. I was under the impression that the investigation involved examining calendars, travel schedules, and such. I had no idea that personal communications were involved, and had I known that this was the case I would have brought the matter (of the intrusive nature of the investigation) to the board, for full examination, well in advance of this May 18th meeting;

2) I explicitly stated that the chairman and I (in my role as chair of the N&G committee) had discussed and agreed not to deal with the leak matter "on line," in an open board meeting. I said that I had been "betrayed" by the chairman—my use of the word betrayed was noted by other directors;

3) I specifically asked the board to delay any vote on the motion in regard to [REDACTED], to allow a "cooling off period"—this request was discussed and rejected by the board, as guided by the chairman.

Trusting that these essential elements will be included in the minutes, I will approve them, upon resubmission.

Best regards, Tom

From: Tom Perkins
Sent: Friday, July 28. 2006 1:52 PM.
Subject: Confidential: May 18th HP Board of Directors Meeting
Importance: High

Dear Ann and HP Board Members,

The twice requested final approved minutes of the May 18th minutes have not been forwarded to me. I assume that they do not differ significantly from the DRAFT version, and do not include the requests from my July 18th email to you, attached.

As previously stated, I cannot accept these minutes.

While a number of points were made in my earlier memo, the essential point to be acknowledged is that the sub-rosa surveillance of the HP Board member's personal communications was, and is, illegal.

I attach a memo from Larry Sonsini, in which he acknowledges that HP hired consultants who engaged in "pretexting," a practice using an illegal misrepresentation – the pretext – of identity to carrier companies in order to obtain confidential telecommunication records. This is a fraudulent practice.

Interestingly, HP has on its board an expert in the matter, namely Larry Babbio, whose company, Verizon, has testified before the F. C. C. on the illegality of the practice, and has filed suits against consultants who engage in "pretexting." I attach two pertinent documents pertaining to Verizon's activities in the area. Indeed, AT&T, my home telephone carrier, has confirmed that my confidential records have been compromised pursuant a fraudulent pretext, where the imposter pretending to be me opened an untraceable and inaccessible online account in order to steal the records. AT&T is investigating further.

That the illegal pretext was done by a consultant is no excuse or defense to HP, which authorized, induced and benefited from the illegal fraud.

As Chairman of HP's Nominating and Governance Committee, had I been informed of these illegal activities prior to the May 18th meeting, I would have stopped them, or, failing that, brought them to the attention of the full board. Now, I must insist that the HP board undertake a full investigation of the practices, via an independent committee of the board (not including the Chairman, who initiated the illegal behavior) and take whatever disclosure and/or corrective action is required.

This is an extremely serious matter, and I have engaged counsel for advice. I attach a copy of his CV from the Georgetown U. Law School, where he is a professor. I did not resign from the board for frivolous reasons, but because HP was standing into dangerous waters – waters hazardous with both illegal and unconscionable governance practices – and because my advice was being ignored. I have had a long history with the company; and I am appalled at the events, and at the disclosures of the May 18th meeting, which are so out of character for the corporation, formerly an icon of the Valley.

I trust that the board will undertake an investigation and take corrective action, without external pressure. I believer that my objections are material to the performance and prospects of the Company, and there may well be an obligation to ensure that proper and legally required disclosures are made. So, your urgent attention is required to confirm that full investigatory board action will, indeed, be taken – and taken promptly.

Sincerely,

Tom

TAB 94

From: Tom Perkins
Sent: Friday, July 28, 2006 1:52 PM
To: ann.baskins@hp.com; [redacted] [redacted] [redacted];
[redacted]; mark.hurd@hp.com; [redacted]
[redacted]; [redacted] [redacted]; [redacted]
Cc: [redacted]
Subject: Confidential: May 18th HP Board of Directors Meeting
Importance: High

Dear Ann and HP Board Members,

The twice requested final approved minutes of the May 18th minutes have not been forwarded to me. I assume that they do not differ significantly from the DRAFT version, and do not include the requests from my July 18th email to you, attached.

As previously stated, I cannot accept these minutes.

While a number of points were made in my earlier memo, the essential point to be acknowledged is that the sub-rosa surveillance of the HP Board member's personal communications was, and is, illegal.

I attach a memo from Larry Sonsini, in which he acknowledges that HP hired consultants who engaged in "pretexting," a practice using an illegal misrepresentation – the pretext – of identity to rrier companies in order to obtain confidential telecommunication records. This is a fraudulent practice.

Interestingly, HP has on its board an expert in the matter, namely Larry Babbio, whose company, Verizon, has testified before the F. C. C. on the illegality of the practice, and has filed suits against consultants who engage in "pretexting." I attach two pertinent documents pertaining to Verizon's activities in the area. Indeed, AT&T, my home telephone carrier, has confirmed that my confidential records have been compromised pursuant a fraudulent pretext, where the imposter pretending to be me opened an untraceable and inaccessible online account in order to steal the records. AT&T is investigating further.

That the illegal pretext was done by a consultant is no excuse or defense to HP, which authorized, induced and benefited from the illegal fraud.

As Chairman of HP's Nominating and Governance Committee, had I been informed of these illegal activities prior to the May 18th meeting, I would have stopped them, or, failing that, brought them to the attention of the full board. Now, I must insist that the HP board undertake a full investigation of the practices, via an independent committee of the board (not including the Chairman, who initiated the illegal behavior) and take whatever disclosure and/or corrective action is required.

is is an extremely serious matter, and I have engaged counsel for advice. I attach a copy of his CV from the Georgetown U. Law School, where he is a professor. I did not resign from the board for frivolous reasons, but because HP was standing into dangerous waters – waters hazardous with both illegal and unconscionable governance practices – and because my advice was being ignored. I have had a long history with the company; and I am appalled at the events, and at the disclosures of the May 18th meeting, which are so out of character for the corporation, formerly an icon of the Valley.

I trust that the board will undertake an investigation and take corrective action, without external pressure. I believer that my objections are material to the performance and prospects of the company, and there may well be an obligation to ensure that proper and legally required disclosures are made. So, your urgent attention is required to confirm that full investigatory board action will, indeed, be taken – and taken promptly.

Sincerely,

Tom

PD 00024

TAB 95

TJPMemo.doc (30 KB)

From: "Patricia Dunn-Jahnke" [redacted]
To: "Larry Babbio" [redacted]; "Sari Baldauf" [redacted]; "Dick Hackborn" [redacted]; "John Hammergren" [redacted]; "Bob Ryan" [redacted]
"Lucille Salhany", [redacted]
Subject: Confidential Memo
Date: Thu, 17 Aug 2006 20:22:01 -0700

I suggest you do away with this after reading it.

Regards,
Pattie

Date: August 17, 2006

To: Larry Babbio, Sari Baldauf, Dick Hackborn, John Hammergren, Bob Ryan, Lucie Salhany

From: Pattie Dunn

Re: Thoughts on the TJP Situation

Although mindful that lawyers will prefer minimal written communications related to the TJP situation, I thought it important to give you my reflections on what his motivations may be in pursuing the current matter to such a serious degree.

These thoughts are in no way meant to presuppose the outcome of the legal review (the "investigation of the investigation") that the Nominating & Governance Committee will hear next Wednesday. They are intended only to provide you broader context for what we are experiencing.

I did not share many details of my interactions with Tom during the year prior to his resignation, primarily because to have done so would have been the kind of personal complaint we have sought to avoid in rebuilding our board. Added to this was that Tom's behavior to me in our one-on-one interactions was often so over the top, and in contrast to his generally cordial behavior when in the company of other directors, that the simple facts would have seemed like exaggeration.

I won't indulge in a chronology of the intimidation, pressure, rudeness and criticism that Tom directed at me, but will simply say that I have never had remotely similar experiences with anyone. Having said that, I found it an interesting challenge to work with him, and tried hard to win his good opinion. Now that the proverbial sewage appears to be hitting the fan, that effort seems naïve and doomed from the start.

The question is why has Tom taken such an aggressive, take-no-prisoners stance that will, if pursued, redound negatively for everyone, not least himself, and hurting the company about which he professes to care so much?

I am convinced that the answer is founded upon temperament compounded by a fundamental difference in philosophy between me and Tom about the nature of the board and the conduct of its governance.

In the immediate wake of Carly's dismissal, the board asked me to serve as Chairman. I had no opportunity to test my ideas for how the Board should work with Tom or others to make sure we were aligned. I agreed to serve given the board's desire for immediacy and the clear need for someone to do so. I realize now that Tom would have never supported me (or proposed me, as he told me many times in anger when we disagreed, "But I made you Chairman!") for this role, had he not expected me to be compliant with his wishes.

What neither of us realized was that, coming as I do from a background steeped in fiduciary management, believing fundamentally that, when it comes to board decisions, "all of us are smarter than any of us," I could never agree to Tom's approach to governance. His approach reflects his background in venture capital. Jay, with Tom, used to say, when he and Tom wanted me to agree to something to which it was not clear the whole board would agree, that I was bending to "the tyranny of the minority." In Tom's governance world, the smartest make the important decisions offline and then "sell or tell" everyone else the answer. In my governance world, the best answers arise because the appropriate people deliberate, listen to others, influence and are influenced by others, ultimately—hopefully most of the time—agreeing or, if not, constructively dissenting. Tom's model of governance may be appropriate in the world of venture capital, but it is outmoded and inappropriate in the world of public company governance.

To those of you who have advised," Don't take this personally," deep down, I really don't. Tom's anger would be directed under similar circumstances to anyone who was in a position to act contrary to his wishes. I did happen to agree with Tom a good deal of the time, but this was clearly not sufficient.

My transgression was that I took the issue of what to do about our leaker to the full board. Tom was adamant that the matter of the leak be dealt with behind closed doors. I violated his wishes by seeking advice, bringing Bob Ryan, Larry Sonsini, Mark and Ann to debate the right way to handle the matter. Tom's close relationship with Jay made it difficult for him to view the matter dispassionately. It was determined that it had to go to the full board. To be clear, I never had an agreement with Tom to do it his way; rather, it was a source of his increasing anger that I didn't pre-commit to his particular way of handling the disposition of the matter.

The issue of the legality of the investigation is a question of fact that must be and is being dealt with. But as the linchpin of his issue with me and the Board, it is red herring that Tom has latched onto as a device for hitting back at the real infraction, which was that ultimately he didn't always get his way and in particular didn't do so in a matter that involved the unfortunate behavior of his friend and close colleague on the board.. In my view, the way we choose to deal with Tom will be a good proof point of the board's philosophy and approach to governance.

TAB 96

From: Nye, Vince
Sent: 08/23/2006 01:45:35 PM
To: Katalinic, Michael
Subject: RE: Standards of Business Conduct

Thanks...This investigation will be a defining case which will test the company's claim of having uncompromising integrity..

Vince

-----Original Message-----
From: Katalinic, Michael
Sent: Wednesday, August 23, 2006 12:59 PM
To: Nye, Vince
Subject: FW: Standards of Business Conduct

I am sure this was precipitated by your aggressive actions within the "hallowed halls" of building 20. He has to ensure there is not one person out there that can say "I didn't know........" Good job Mr. Nye.
m

-----Original Message-----
From: CEO, Mark Hurd@hp.com
Sent: Tuesday, August 22, 2006 2:04 PM
Subject: Standards of Business Conduct

To: All HP Employees
From: Mark Hurd
Re: Standards of Business Conduct

In the coming days, you will receive a hard copy of the revised Standards of Business Conduct (SBC). HP's business success requires each of us to understand and uphold the SBC. Therefore, we are making it a priority to get a hard copy of the SBC into the hands of every Hewlett-Packard employee so you can understand your role in conducting business with uncompromising integrity.

Each year the SBC is reviewed and updated to make the Standards clearer and easier to understand, and to align with current laws and regulations. Later in the year you will be asked to participate in our annual SBC training, which will highlight the recent changes to the SBC.

Please take the time to review this important document.

-- Mark

TAB 97

Jose Gurgel-Neto

From: Ron DeLia
Sent: Saturday, August 26, 2006 12:37 AM
To: 'Hunsaker, Kevin'
Subject: RE: Privileged Communication

It appears AT&T has filed lawsuits against online data broker companies for the same reason (providing customer call records) they have been sued for!

The content of this email transmission is intended only for the use of the individual or entity named above and may contain legally privileged or confidential information. If you are not the intended recipient, you are hereby notified that any disclosure, copying, dissemination, distribution, or use of this email transmission, or information contained herein, is strictly prohibited. If you have received this email transmission in error, please destroy all copies of this email and its attachments and notify the person whose name appears above.

Security Outsourcing Solutions, Inc.
Tel: (617) 426-3900 or (781) 444-9616

-----Original Message-----
From: Hunsaker, Kevin [mailto:kevin.hunsaker@hp.com]
Sent: Friday, August 25, 2006 3:04 PM
To: Ron DeLia
Subject: RE: Privileged Communication

I wasn't aware of this one. I did know that AT&T filed the lawsuit this week against the data brokers. Very interesting . . . .

Kevin T. Hunsaker
Director of Ethics and SBC
Hewlett-Packard Company
Phone: 650 857-3079
Fax: 650 857-3710

From: Ron DeLia [mailto:rrd@security-outsourcing.com]
Sent: Friday, August 25, 2006 12:04 PM
To: Hunsaker, Kevin
Subject: Privileged Communication

Kevin,

Were you aware of the following lawsuit filed against AT&T?

Ron

http://www.eff.org/news/archives/2006_01.php

The content of this email transmission is intended only for the use of the individual or entity named above and may contain legally privileged or confidential information. If you

TAB 98

To: Larry Babbio, Sari Baldauf, Dick Hackborn, John Hammergren, Mark Hurd, Bob Ryan, Lucie Salhany, Bob Wayman

From: Pattie Dunn Date: September 2, 2006

Re: Wrapping up on last board meeting

Because the last Friday's board meeting was running long, I did not have the chance to say everything I wanted concerning the outcome of the "investigation of the investigation." Without intending to belabor the issue, I think it is important to make sure that you have my views.

First, to re-iterate, I totally support the N&G Committee's findings and recommendations concerning the leak investigation. In particular, I accept their finding that "Kona I" was conducted with insufficient legal support or project infrastructure. In retrospect, I can explain why I chose not to utilize Wilson Sonsini in this matter, but I canot explain why I did not turn to alternative counsel. It was partly out of ignorance for how to proceed in such circumstances, which I offer as a reason but not as an excuse. I did learn from the experience of Kona I and applied this lesson in Kona II, but hope never to have another opportunity to use this experience in any setting.

Given the Committee's finding, I want to reassure the Board that I am neither comfortable nor prone to operating unilaterally. I firmly believe that "all of us are smarter than any of us," and I see the Keyworth matter at its base as an example of a director who disrupted the Board's functioning by believing otherwise—i.e., that the rules on confidentiality did not apply to him. I cannot today imagine the circumstances under which I would march off without Board support to undertake an important task.

I had planned, and indeed looked forward, to unburdening myself and sharing some insights about the investigation process with the Board, which was pre-empted by Tom Perkins' call for a full investigation. The work done by the N&G Committee was far more complete than it otherwise would have been, and as a result the Company's capabilities in this area will be substantially improved.

I want also to thank the N&G Committee for the extraordinary amount of time it spent on this matter. For those who think that Board service means showing up and colleting a fat stipend, this Committee serves as an example of the reality of board service today.

Regards,
Pattie

TAB 99

From: "Patricia Dunn-Jahnke" [redacted]>
To: "Sherbin, Robert" <robert.sherbin@hp.com>
Subject: RE: Q&A
Date: Tue, 5 Sep 2006 22:12:34 -0700

Bob, I was not aware of the details of the investigative techniques involving phone records to this extent. The word "pretexting" was never used with me (the first time I ever heard the word was in Larry Sonsini's email to Tom Perkins). I was informed that it was possible to legally obtain phone records simply by requesting them. I was not aware that disguised identities were involved. I gave this same input to the "investigation of the investigation" team at Wilson Sonsini.

PCD

> Subject: Q&A> Date: Tue, 5 Sep 2006 23:57:22 -0500> From: robert.sherbin@hp.com> To: [redacted]> > Pattie, > We are assembling a Q&A for use by the media team tomorrow in handling> the flurry of questions the K will trigger. These are being reviewed by> myself and Legal. There is one in particular that I want you to see and> amend the answer to as you see fit.> > At this point, it reads:> > > Q. Was HP's Board aware that pretexting was used by its outside agency?> A. HP's Chairman was aware of the investigative techniques used by the> outside agency, and that using disguised identities to obtain phone> record information was among the potential techniques that could be> utilized. > > > Any views?> B

TAB 100

From: O'Neill, Timothy (IT Security)
Sent: 09/06/2006 08:56:13 AM
To: Craparo, John; Ryan, Sherry
Subject: RE: media reports regarding BoD inv

Hi John,

I apologize for not being clear. I will try to provide some background and better context, something I should have done in the first place.

This investigation was led by Kevin Hunsaker, who at the time was the legal representative for the HP Stds of Business Conduct Compliance Team (SBCCT), and Tony Gentilucci, who is the manager for the REWs Global Security Investigations Team. Tony assigned his investigator, Vince Nye, to participate in the investigation. This was handled uniquely since it was outside the scope of the SBCCT since it dealt with the Board, not HP employees. As such, Kevin Hunsaker was dealing directly with Patty Dunn and Ann Baskins regarding the investigation. In this case, he was both the "Legal voice" for HP and he was the primary one directing the investigation and the one interacting with the executive sponsors.

Kevin and Tony solicited assistance from the IT Security Investigations team regarding the HP IT-related aspects of the case - I assigned Fred Adler to assist them. Fred was responsible for gathering HP IT-related data only. This included such things as HP email and HP's phone records. There was no pretext or deception involved in anything that Fred did. All of the records and data belonged to HP.

During the course of the investigation, Tony and Kevin decided to use one of Tony's 3rd-party contractors (a Private Investigator) to acquire the personal cell phone records and home phone records of the Board members. They wanted to determine who was interacting with reporters. Fred Adler and Vince Nye (who are both former law enforcement officers) believed this was a bad decision for a number of reasons and that it was potentially illegal.

Vince and Fred were so concerned about this that they came to me and asked me to intervene on their behalf because they felt their voices were not being heard. This was highly unusual. Though I had not been privy to the details of the investigation to this point, I inserted myself by contacting Tony and Kevin individually and then later met with them and their Private Investigator - I voiced my concerns, including the potential conflict with HP ethics/values, the legality of the pretexting tactic, and the potential for this to negatively impact HP. Each one of them assured me that what was being done was legal. Kevin and Tony further assured me the tactic was knowingly approved by the executives sponsors of the investigation.

Despite Tony and Kevin's assurances, I told them that I felt an obligation and responsibility to challenge this due to Fred and Vince's concerns, which I concurred with. Again, this was highly unusual for me to be challenging the legal decision of an HP atty and inserting myself into an investigation that was being led by Global Security. I felt both of them were professional and non-defensive and that my concerns were taken into consideration and that further due diligence would be occurring as a result of my actions - Namely, Kevin agreed to seek additional outside counsel opinion regarding the legal issues and agreed to bring this specific issue/concerns to the executive sponsors of this investigation before proceeding/using the data.

I met with Vince and Fred and told them what actions I had taken in response to them voice their concerns to me. Neither of them had any role in obtaining or using the cellular/home phone records of the board members. All of the actions that were taken associated with the phone records were done by Global Security's Private Investigator and in coordination between Tony Genitlucci and Kevin Hunsaker.

Please don't hesitate to contact me if you need further information.

Best Regards,

Tim

-----Original Message-----
From: Craparo, John
Sent: Wednesday, September 06, 2006 7:47 AM
To: O'Neill, Timothy (IT Security); Ryan, Sherry
Subject: RE: media reports regarding BoD inv

A little confused Tim. If there was no involvement, how was it that we commented and objected?
Thanks, John

-----Original Message-----
From: O'Neill, Timothy (IT Security)
Sent: Tuesday, September 05, 2006 10:13 PM
To: Craparo, John; Ryan, Sherry
Subject: media reports regarding BoD inv

Hi Sherry and John,

Media reports are surfacing detailing circumstances surrounding the investigation into leaks orginating from HP's Board. This includes allegations that 3rd parties obtained the cell/home phone call details obtained by "pretexting", a questionable and potentially illegal practice.

I will withhold any details since this is not an atty-client protected communication other than to assure you both that no one in IT Security was implicated, nor involved, in any of the suspected wrongdoing. The thrid-parties were not working at IT Security's direction. Rather, they were working strictly at the direction of HP Global Security and the SBCCT.

At the time of the investigation, IT Security raised questions regarding this issue to the SBCCT/Gloabl Security and was assured that full internal and external legal review had taken place and executive management sponsorship had occurred. Additionaly no one from IT Security came into contact or used any of the information - it was separate and apart from any assistance provided by IT Security to the SBCCT.

Here is the link to the detailed MSNBC article:
http://www.msnbc.msn.com/id/14687677/site/newsweek/

Best Regards,

Tim

TAB 101

From: Hunt, Peter (Corp Security)
Sent: 09/06/2006 10:30:04 AM
To: Gentilucci, Anthony R.
Subject: RE: Phone records scandal at HP

I don't believe half of what I read in the mags and rags...........neither does anybody else. This is no negative reflection on the investigative acts rather the senior mgmt that 'directed' it.

From: Gentilucci, Anthony R.
Sent: Wednesday, September 06, 2006 12:28 PM
To: Hunt, Peter (Corp Security)
Subject: RE: Phone records scandal at HP

Got it, not quite accurate, but we are being hung out to dry, the politics, smokes, mirrors are high, I have lost a lot of respect for a lot of people, amazing really. If I am still here next week, we can discuss over a beer in a week or two.

Tony

From: Hunt, Peter (Corp Security)
Sent: Wednesday, September 06, 2006 12:50 PM
To: Gentilucci, Anthony R.
Cc: Gentilucci, Anthony R.; Home, Christopher; Hunt, Peter (Corp Security); Huska, Kevin (Global Security); Reynolds, Denis (APJ Security); Smith, Frederick; Tillison, Michael; Winter, Stacey E; Fairbaugh, Jim (Global Security)
Subject: FW: Phone records scandal at HP

Tony,

Here is an article - you may already have it but just in case.

Peter

Intrigue in High Places

To catch a leaker, Hewlett-Packard's chairwoman spied on the home-phone records of its board of directors.

WEB EXCLUSIVE

By David A. Kaplan

Newsweek

Updated: 11:12 a.m. CT Sept 6, 2006

<< OLE Object: Picture (Metafile) >> The confrontation at Hewlett-Packard started innocently enough. Last January, the online technology site CNET published an article about the long-term strategy at HP, the company ranked No. 11 in the Fortune 500. While the piece was upbeat, it quoted an anonymous HP source and contained information that only could have come from a director. HP's chairwoman, Patricia Dunn, told another director she wanted to know who it was; she was fed up with ongoing leaks to the media going back to CEO Carly Fiorina's tumultuous tenure that ended in early 2005. According to an internal HP e-mail, Dunn then took the extraordinary step of authorizing a team of independent electronic-security experts to spy on the January 2006 communications of the other 10 directors—not the records of calls (or e-mails) from HP itself, but the records of phone calls made from personal accounts. That meant calls from the directors' home and their private

cell phones.

It was classic data-mining: Dunn's consultants weren't actually listening in on the calls—all they had to do was look for a pattern of contacts. Dunn acted without informing the rest of the board. Her actions were now about to unleash a round of boardroom fury at one of America's largest companies and a Silicon Valley icon. That corporate turmoil is now coming to light in documents obtained by NEWSWEEK that the Securities and Exchange Commission is currently deciding whether to make public. Dunn could not be reached for comment. An HP spokesman declined repeated requests for comment.

On May 18, at HP headquarters in Palo Alto, Calif., Dunn sprung her bombshell on the board: she had found the leaker. According to Tom Perkins, an HP director who was present, Dunn laid out the surveillance scheme and pointed out the offending director, who acknowledged being the CNET leaker. That director, whose identity has not yet been publicly disclosed, apologized. But the director then said to fellow directors, "I would have told you all about this. Why didn't you just ask?" That director was then asked to leave the boardroom, and did so, according to Perkins.

Close to 90 minutes of heated debate followed, but Perkins, the Silicon Valley venture capitalist, says he was the only director who rose to take Dunn on directly. Perkins says he was enraged at the surveillance, which he called illegal, unethical and a misplaced corporate priority on Dunn's part. In an interview with NEWSWEEK, Perkins says he was particularly annoyed since he chaired the HP board's Nominating and Governance Committee and had not been informed by Dunn of the surveillance, even though, he says, she had told him for months that she was attempting to discover the source of the leak.

After a divided board passed a motion asking the leaker to resign, Perkins closed his briefcase, announced his own resignation and walked out of the room. In media mentions the next day, Perkins's sudden resignation was noted, but without explanation and without any indication that his departure was a form of protest. (According to Perkins, the leaker-director himself refused to resign, saying it was up to shareholders to make such a decision; that director continues to serve on the board.) Thus began nearly four months of warfare between HP and Perkins about whether the surveillance would ever come to public light.

Any time a director resigns from a U.S. public corporation, federal law requires the company to disclose it to the SEC in what's called an 8-K filing. If the director resigned for reasons related to a "disagreement" with the company about "operations, policies or practices," that, too, is now required. HP reported Perkins's resignation to the SEC four days after it happened—back in May—but gave no reason for the resignation, instead including only a press release thanking Perkins for his years of service. Perkins has twice challenged that omission in e-mails to the HP board and, he says, he received no response from HP.

In early August, Perkins—represented by his own non-HP lawyer, Viet Dinh, a former Bush administration official—formally asked the SEC to force HP to publicly file his written explanation for resigning. According to a source who requested anonymity because of his closeness to HP, the company objected on the grounds that when Perkins resigned at the May board meeting he didn't indicate why. Perkins says his reasons for resigning were obvious and he stated them at the meeting. Now, sources say, the company could file such a document with the SEC as soon as Wednesday.

The entire episode—beyond its impact on the boardroom of a $100 billion company, Dunn's ability to continue as chairwoman and the possibility of civil lawsuits claiming privacy invasions and fraudulent misrepresentations—raises questions about corporate surveillance in a digital age. Audio and visual surveillance capabilities keep advancing, both in their ability to collect and analyze data. The Web helps distribute that data efficiently and effortlessly. But what happens when these advances outstrip the ability of companies (and, for that matter, governments) to reach consensus on ethical limits? How far will companies go to obtain information they seek for competitive gain or better management?

The HP case specifically also sheds another spotlight on the questionable tactics used by security consultants to obtain personal information. HP acknowledged in an internal e-mail sent from its outside counsel to Perkins that it got the paper trail it needed to link the director-leaker to CNET through a controversial practice called "pretexting"; NEWSWEEK obtained a copy of that e-mail. That practice, according to the Federal Trade Commission, involves using "false pretenses" to get another individual's personal nonpublic information: telephone records, bank and credit-card account numbers, Social Security number and the like. Pretexting is heavily marketed on the Web.

Typically—say in the case of a phone company—pretexters call up and falsely represent themselves as the customer; since companies rarely require passwords, a pretexter may need no more than a home address, account number and heartfelt plea to get the details of an account. According to the Federal Trade Commission's Web site, pretexters sell the information to individuals who can range from otherwise legitimate private investigators, financial lenders, potential litigants and suspicious spouses to those who might attempt to steal assets or fraudulently obtain credit. Pretexting, the FTC site states, "is against the law." The FTC and several state attorneys general have brought enforcement actions against pretexters for allegedly violating federal and state laws on fraud, misrepresentation and unfair competition. One of HP's directors is Larry Babbio, the president of Verizon, which has filed various actions against pretexters.

Legal experts vary in their views on the extent to which pretexting is a violation of criminal law. The Gramm-Leach-Billey Act of 1999 bars a range of fraudulent activity related to financial records, but its applicability to phone records is unclear. Experts agree that pretexting is often used to accomplish identity theft—to borrow money or buy merchandise—that clearly is criminal. But the pretexting itself may be harder to prosecute. Civil liability would seem to be much more a risk for pretexters, as they obviously engage in an invasion of privacy, achieved through misrepresentation.

Perkins himself was pretexted as part of Dunn's leaker probe. In the materials he sent to the SEC, Perkins includes an Aug. 11 letter from an attorney at AT&T spelling out to Perkins that he was a victim of pretexting in January 2006; Perkins had requested that AT&T examine whether he had been pretexted. The AT&T letter explains that the third-party pretexter who got details about Perkins's local home-telephone usage was able to provide the last four digits of Perkins's Social Security number and that was sufficient identification for AT&T. The impersonator then convinced an AT&T customer-service representative to send the details electronically to an e-mail account at yahoo.com that on its face had nothing to do with Perkins. Records for Perkins's home AT&T long-distance account in northern California were similarly obtained, except by someone using another yahoo.com e-mail account; both e-mail accounts are registered to the same Internet Protocol address, but for which AT&T says it does not know the identity of the user.

The materials before the SEC indicate that Dunn's consultants used pretexting for her investigation. In mid-June, according to a letter Perkins sent to the full HP board, Perkins contacted HP's outside counsel—Larry Sonsini, of Wilson Sonsini Goodrich & Rosati—and asked him to look into the Dunn investigation. In an e-mail to Perkins obtained by NEWSWEEK, Sonsini acknowledged that Dunn's security consultants "did obtain information regarding phone calls made and received by the cell or home numbers of directors" and that it was "done through a third party that made pretext calls to phone service providers." Sonsini's e-mail emphasized that the security consultants engaged in "no electronic surveillance," "no phone recording or eavesdropping" and "no recording, review or monitoring of director e-mail." His legal defense of the use of pretexting was that it is "apparently a common investigatory method" and that "there was no 'secret spying,' i.e., no electronic gear, listening devices, etc." Perkins quotes Sonsini's e-mail in the materials he sent to the SEC, Sonsini could not be reached for comment.

In the documents before the SEC, Perkins also protests that he was not allowed to review and approve the initial 8-K filing about his May resignation, which he says is required under SEC rules. And he requests that the HP board appoint a special committee to examine the legality and propriety of Dunn's investigation. In the documents before the SEC, after Perkins notes he was not the source of the CNET leak, he excoriates Dunn. "I resigned solely to protest the questionable ethics and the dubious legality of the chair's methods," Perkins writes. In his interview with NEWSWEEK, he added that he believed he was "legally obligated to do so" in his directorial capacity.

Perkins says he has asked other government agencies to investigate the sub rosa surveillance of the HP directors. Those agencies include the California attorney general's office, as well as the FTC, the Federal Communications Commission and the Justice Department.

Dunn, 52, has been on the HP board since 1998, and was elected non-executive chairwoman in February 2005. She was CEO of Barclays Global Investors from 1995 to 2002. Perkins, 74, is the cofounder of Kleiner Perkins Caufield & Byers, the venerable Silicon Valley firm that has bankrolled such venture-capital home runs as Genentech, Netscape, Amazon and Google. Perkins has an on-and-off history with HP that dates almost half a century. On graduating from Harvard Business School in 1957, he worked on a lathe in the company's machine shop. Then he helped launch its computer division in the 1960s, eventually becoming Bill Hewlett's staff assistant when Dave Packard went to Washington to work in the Pentagon as deputy secretary of Defense in the first Nixon administration. Perkins joined the HP board after HP merged with Compaq in 2001, then retired in 2004 and rejoined the board in 2005 when Fiorina was ousted. Perkins alludes to his HP heritage in his letter. "My history with the Hewlett-Packard Company is long and I have been privileged to count both founders as close friends," he writes. It "is a very sad duty," he says, to disclose "probable unlawful conduct, improper board procedures, and breakdowns in corporate governance." It remains to be seen if this final chapter in his relationship with HP changes the company's course.

Editor's Note: Kaplan is currently writing a book for HarperCollins on the superyacht that Tom Perkins recently built and launched in Europe.

<< OLE Object: Picture (Metafile) >> URL:
http://www.msnbc.msn.com/id/14687677/site/newsweek/

TAB 102

From: "Paul Taaffe" <Paul.Taaffe@hillandknowlton.com>
To: "Sherbin, Robert" <robert.sherbin@hp.com>
CC: <pcdunn1@hotmail.com>
Subject: HP Media Statement
Date: Thu, 7 Sep 2006 12:48:30 -0400

Attached is a draft of a possible Bob Ryan statement. We need to achieve two things: 1) show the board, including Pattie, was not aware of all of the specifics of the investigation (this needs to be true); 2) apologize and confirm that pretexting is not a tool or technique that HP supports or would knowingly use.

We need to act quickly to reclaim the high moral ground which we have lost. I am around.

Paul

When Pattie Dunn was asked to serve as Chairman of HP it was with the clear expectation that board governance practices would be upgraded. One of her top priorities was to restore the confidentiality to board meetings where leaks had become a major problem for the board and management.

An investigation was commissioned but the details remained unknown given that it involved all of the board members, including the chairman. The board was informed that the probe was ongoing and received assurances that it was legal.

Once completed, the Nominating and Governance Committee with the assistance of outside counsel, Wilson Sonsini, conducted a review of the investigation. While it was found to have complied with all aspects of the law, the Committee was troubled by the serious ethical questions raised by some of the techniques employed that emerged in the review of the probe and recommended to the board and HP that this type of investigation not be used in the future.

We want to be very clear. The board was not aware of the details of the investigation and the use of pretexting until after the probe was concluded. The board is troubled that such methods were used in its name and will not engage firms that employ them should the need arise again for outside inquiry.

PD 00008

The board's sole intention through the leak investigation was to ensure strict adherence to a code of conduct and accountability to operate as effectively as possible for the benefit of the company's stakeholders. Pretexting is not a practice that we endorse and we apologize for those affected outside of the board.

TAB 103

8-K 1 a06-19246_18k.htm CURRENT REPORT OF MATERIAL EVENTS OR CORPORATE CHANGES

UNITED STATES
SECURITIES AND EXCHANGE COMMISSION
WASHINGTON, D.C. 20549-1004

FORM 8-K

CURRENT REPORT

PURSUANT TO SECTION 13 OR 15(d) OF THE SECURITIES EXCHANGE ACT OF 1934

August 31, 2006
Date of Report (Date of Earliest Event Reported)

HEWLETT-PACKARD COMPANY
(Exact name of registrant as specified in its charter)

DELAWARE	**1-4423**	**94-1081436**
(State or other jurisdiction of incorporation)	(Commission File Number)	(I.R.S. Employer Identification No.)

3000 HANOVER STREET, PALO ALTO, CA	**94304**
(Address of principal executive offices)	(Zip code)

(650) 857-1501
(Registrant's telephone number, including area code)

Check the appropriate box below if the Form 8-K filing is intended to simultaneously satisfy the filing obligation of the registrant under any of the following provisions:

☐ Written communications pursuant to Rule 425 under the Securities Act (17 CFR 230.425)

☐ Soliciting material pursuant to Rule 14a-12 under the Exchange Act (17 CFR 240.14a-12)

☐ Pre-commencement communications pursuant to Rule 14d-2(b) under the Exchange Act (17 CFR 240.14d-2(b))

☐ Pre-commencement communications pursuant to Rule 13e-4(c) under the Exchange Act (17 CFR 240.13e-4(c))

m 8.01. Other Events.

On May 22, 2006, Hewlett-Packard Company ("HP") announced the resignation of Thomas J. Perkins from its Board of Directors. At the time of his resignation, Mr. Perkins did not provide any written communication to HP concerning the reasons for his resignation. Following his resignation, and after HP on May 22 had disclosed the fact of Mr. Perkins' resignation on Form 8-K in accordance with the applicable federal securities laws, Mr. Perkins notified HP that he had concerns with the HP Board's handling of investigations that had been conducted into leaks of confidential HP information from meetings of the HP Board of Directors. HP is filing this Form 8-K to report the following additional information about the circumstances relating to Mr. Perkins' resignation, to report the findings of its leak investigations, and to report other related events that have occurred subsequent to the completion of those investigations and Mr. Perkins' resignation.

HP has been the subject of multiple leaks of confidential HP information, including information concerning the internal deliberations of its Board of Directors. HP believes these leaks date back to at least 2005. In response to these leaks, outside legal counsel conducted interviews of directors in early 2005 in order to determine the source of the leaks and to obtain each director's reaffirmation of his or her duty of confidentiality. The interview process did not yield the source of the leaks. Notwithstanding these actions, the leaks continued. As a result, the Chairman of the Board, and ultimately an internal group within HP, working with a licensed outside firm specializing in investigations, conducted investigations into possible sources of the leaks of confidential information at HP. Those investigations resulted in a finding that Dr. George A. Keyworth II, one of HP's directors, did, in fact, disclose Board deliberations and other confidential information obtained during Board meetings to the media without authorization. At a Board meeting on May 18, 2006, after Dr. Keyworth acknowledged that he had leaked confidential information, the Board, after deliberation, asked Dr. Keyworth to resign his position as a director, which he declined to do. It is at that meeting that Mr. Perkins resigned from the Board after expressing personal frustration with the Chairman of the Board relating to the handling of the matter with the Board. He stated that he objected to the matter being brought before the full Board and that he believed the Chairman had agreed that he and she would handle the matter privately. The Chairman disputed Mr. Perkins' assertion, explaining that she was complying with advice from outside counsel on the appropriate handling of the matter. At the time, Mr. Perkins confirmed he did not have any disagreement with HP on any matter relating to HP's operations, policies or practices.

On June 19, following his resignation and after HP reported Mr. Perkins' resignation on Form 8-K, Mr. Perkins sought information from HP concerning the methods used to conduct HP's investigations into the leaks, asserted that phone and e-mail communications had been improperly recorded as part of the investigation, and informed HP that he had recently consulted with counsel regarding that assertion. In response to Mr. Perkins' request, HP informed Mr. Perkins that no recording or eavesdropping had occurred, but that some form of "pretexting" for phone record information, a technique used by investigators to obtain information by disguising their identity, had been used. Mr. Perkins, although no longer a director, then requested that HP conduct an inquiry into the propriety of the techniques used to conduct the investigation.

HP's Nominating and Governance Committee thereafter engaged the outside counsel to conduct an inquiry into the conduct and processes employed with respect to HP's investigation of leaks of confidential information (the outside counsel was not involved in the investigations of the leaks initiated by the Chairman or the internal HP group). The Committee was advised that HP had engaged an outside consulting firm with substantial experience in conducting internal investigations and that this firm had retained another party to obtain phone information concerning certain calls between HP directors and individuals outside of HP. The Committee was further advised that the Chairman and HP had instructed the outside consulting firm to conduct its investigation in accordance with applicable law and that the outside consulting firm and its counsel had confirmed to HP that its techniques were legal. After its review, the Committee determined that the third party retained by HP's outside consulting firm had in some cases employed pretexting. The Committee was then advised by the Committee's outside counsel that the use of pretexting at the time of the investigation was not generally unlawful (except with respect to financial institutions), but such counsel could not confirm that the techniques employed by the outside consulting firm and the party retained by that firm complied in all respects with applicable law.

Based upon its investigation, the Nominating and Governance Committee has recommended to HP's Board and Chief Executive Officer that controls relating to investigations be strengthened and that management should be in a position to assure that all aspects of HP's investigations comply with applicable laws and HP's code of ethics as applicable to HP's directors, officers and employees. HP's Board and Chief Executive Officer have accepted the conclusions and recommendations of the Committee.

HP recently has been informally contacted by the Attorney General of the State of California requesting information concerning the processes employed in the investigations into the leaks. HP intends to cooperate fully with that inquiry. HP also has received a comment letter from the staff of the Securities and Exchange Commission's Division of Corporation Finance with respect to its May 22 Form 8-K regarding Mr. Perkins' resignation. HP intends to respond to the SEC staff that it believes its disclosures in the May 22 Form 8-K with respect to Mr. Perkins' resignation were accurate and complete at the time of filing and were based upon Mr. Perkins' actions and representations prior to such time concerning the reasons for his resignation.

In addition, on August 31, 2006 the HP Board of Directors, upon the recommendation of the Nominating and Governance Committee, also determined that, based on his conduct, Dr. Keyworth should not be nominated for another term on the Board of Directors.

SIGNATURE

Pursuant to the requirements of the Securities Exchange Act of 1934, the registrant has caused this report to be signed on its behalf by the undersigned hereunto duly authorized.

HEWLETT-PACKARD COMPANY

DATE: September 6, 2006

By: /s/ Charles N. Charnas
Name: Charles N. Charnas
Title: Vice President, Deputy General Counsel and Assistant Secretary

TAB 104

From: Huska, Kevin (Global Security)
Sent: 09/07/2006 09:43:00 AM
To: Gentilucci, Anthony R.
Subject: RE: Daily News Report for Thursday, Sept. 7, 2006
Attachments: aprsLogo.gif; bwolLogo.gif; cnewsnLogo.gif; djiLogo.gif; djLogo.gif; factiva_flogostyle1.gif; fwstLogo.gif; jLogo.gif; latmLogo.gif; lbaLogo.gif; logoright.gif; nytfLogo.gif; pcwLogo.gif; sbeeLogo.gif; sfcLogo.gif; spacer.gif; wpLogo.gif

Hey Tony:

You will be around and it will be "something stronger".

Kevin

From: Gentilucci, Anthony R.
Sent: Thursday, September 07, 2006 11:27 AM
To: Huska, Kevin (Global Security)
Subject: RE: Daily News Report for Thursday, Sept. 7, 2006

Kevin,

Yea, behind the scenes he has been very supportive. This thing is taking on a life of its own, articles are in the tabloid stage, not sure I will survive after the steam roller runs me over, but totally out of my control now, can't say much more, but if I am around, maybe we can discuss over a cup of coffee or something stronger!!

Tony

From: Huska, Kevin (Global Security)
Sent: Thursday, September 07, 2006 12:23 PM
To: Gentilucci, Anthony R.
Subject: FW: Daily News Report for Thursday, Sept. 7, 2006

Hey Tony. You are right, people turning their heads (and backs) on this matter. I thought Jim's note was a bit "luke warm" in support of the investigative efforts.

WSJ - "H-P spokesman Mike Moeller said the company told the investigators conducting its internal probe that only legal means were to be used to obtain information. He added that H-P didn't know pretexting would be involved. "We have determined pretexting will not be used in any future investigation if we have to do another one of these," Mr. Moeller said."

Kevin

From: HP News.Dept
Sent: Thursday, September 07, 2006 10:19 AM
To: HP News.Dept
Subject: Daily News Report for Thursday, Sept. 7, 2006

The Daily News Report

HP Restricted. Brought to you by the HP News Dept <mailto:news.dept@hp.com>. See subscription and usage guidelines here.

Thursday, Sept. 7, 2006 | HPQ at 7:25 a.m. PT: 35.42 -0.42 (1.17%)

HP in the news:

HP board dispute:

H-P Faces Probe Over Its Inquiry Into Board Leaks
The Wall Street Journal, 9/7, Lawton, Searcey, Young

US and California probe HP leaks
FT.com, 9/6, Richard Waters

A Board in Need of an Emily Post
The New York Times, 9/7, Julie Creswell

With a Little Stealth, Just About Anyone Can Get Phone Records
The New York Times, 9/7, Matt Richtel

TAB 105

Minutes
Three sets of minutes were considered for approval. Upon a motion duly made and seconded, the minutes of the telephonic meetings of the Board held on June 16, 2006 and June 18, 2006 were approved as presented.

The minutes of the May 18 meeting of the Board were then considered. Ann Baskins distributed two sets of comments she had received regarding the draft minutes. The first, a message from former director Perkins, raised three issues with the draft minutes. The Board took the time to read the three points raised in Perkins memo. After discussion, the Board determined that one of Perkins claims, including that he questioned the legality of the investigative methods in the May 18 Board meeting, was rejected by the Board. The directors concluded that such concerns had not been articulated and accordingly could not be part of the record. With respect to other concerns regarding dialogue, the Board after review concluded that the minutes as drafted provided an accurate and adequate summary of the proceedings and that accordingly additional details were not required.

The Board then turned to a letter from Director Keyworth in which he asked that reasons for his decision not to resign from the Board at the Board's request were articulated. His comments were also reviewed and discussed by the Board. Again, the Board concluded that the specific reason had not been articulated in the course of the Board meeting and accordingly the minutes could not be altered to reflect such concerns. However, after discussion, it was determined that it would be appropriate to address the concerns addressed by Keyworth, specifically into the circumstances regarding the approval of a discretionary bonus in 2004, by assigning the matter to a special board committee. The Board then authorized the formation of a special committee to consist of directors Hammergren, Baldauf and Hurd. Specifically the Committee will examine whether any irregularities existed with respect to the consideration and approval of the bonus. Upon a motion duly made and seconded, the minutes of the May 18, 2006 meeting were then approved as presented.

The Board then adjourned to Executive Session and Hurd, Wayman and Baskins left the meeting. The meeting was subsequently adjourned at approximately 6:30 p.m. with no matters reported out of Executive Session.

Ann O. Baskins

TAB 106

From: "Patricia Dunn-Jahnke" [redacted]
To: robert.sherbin@hp.com, mark.hurd@hp.com
Subject: FW: BusinessWeek Online: Inaccuracies
Date: Mon, 18 Sep 2006 07:49:08 -0700

Two significant inaccuracies in this article:

1. The board was informed that a leak investigation had been initiated and was updated several times over the course of the year that it was underway that it was ongoing. This fact is in the public domain already, I believe. (Mark, my notes which I hope someone will ask for today corroborates this.)

2. I did not hire the investigators. They were brought in by HP's Security Department, for whom they had worked for several years.

Spitting in the wind, I know...but ya gotta keep trying!

Pattie

From: "HP News.Dept" <news.dept@hp.com>
To: "Archibald, Elizabeth (PR)" <elizabeth.archibald@hp.com>,"Bautista, Medalla" <medalla.bautista@hillandknowlton.com>,"Bergkamp, Brigida" <brigida.bergkamp@hp.com>,"Berman, David L" <dave.berman@hp.com>,"Bonney, Pamela" <pamela.bonney@hp.com>,"Burns, Duncan" <duncan.burns@hillandknowlton.com>,"Burton, Adam (Comptetive)" <adam.burton@hillandknowlton.com>,"Carasso, Claudia" <Claudia_Carasso@cohnwolfe.com>,"Cox, Melissa (Corporate PR)" <melissa.cox@hp.com>,"Davenport, Maureen (H&K)" <mdavenport@hillandknowlton.com>,"Devine, Kimberly" <kimberly_devine@sfo.cohnwolfe.com>,"Doherty, Katy Shea" <katy.doherty@hp.com>,"Donovan, Ryan J. (Corp Media Relations)" <ryan.j.donovan@hp.com>,"Fellows, Frank" <frank.fellows@hp.com>,"Fimbres, Caprice N." <caprice.fimbres@hp.com>,"Flynn, Gary" <gary.flynn@hp.com>,"Gentile, Don (Enterprise AR/PR)" <don.gentile@hp.com>,"Gillan, Elizabeth" <elizabeth.gillan@hp.com>,"Griffin, Alyson" <alyson.griffin@hp.com>,"Gunst, Jennifer" <jennifer.gunst@hillandknowlton.com>,"Guttman, Sabrina" <Sabrina.Guttman@bm.com>,"Haas, Marius" <marius.haas@hp.com>,"Hanes, Alexa C" <alexa.hanes@hp.com>,"Hayes, Danielle" <danielle.hayes@hillandknowlton.com>,"Heller, Mark"

<mark.heller@hp.com>,"Horn, Emily" <emily.horn@hp.com>,"HP Competitive Team" <hpcoteam@hillandknowlton.com>,"Humphries, Brian (Investor Relations)" <brian.humphries@hp.com>,"Hunt, Yvonne Cecelia" <yvonne.hunt@hp.com>,"Hutter, Lindsay" <lindsay.hutter@hillandknowlton.com>,"Jackson, James (Public Sector Mkting)" <jim.jackson2@hp.com>,"Jacobs, Les" <otilio.jacobs@hp.com>,"Johnson, Brittany" <brittany.johnson@hillandknowlton.com>,"Judge, Dana" <dana.judge@hp.com>,"LaRose, Brian (Investor Relations)" <larose@hp.com>,"Lewis, Mark (PDP-SPO)" <mark.lewis4@hp.com>,"Lusher, Carter" <carter.lusher@hp.com>,"Lyons, Cathy T" <cathy.lyons@hp.com>,"Martens, Claudia" <claudia.martens@hp.com>,"McMillian, Jane F." <jane.mcmillian@hp.com>,"Moeller, Michael" <michael.moeller@hp.com>,"Mullins, Julie" <julie.mullins@hillandknowlton.com>,"Neumann, Emily" <emily.neumann@hp.com>,"O'Keeffe, Tim" <tim.okeeffe@hillandknowlton.com>,"Olivero, Karen H" <karen.olivero@hp.com>,"Paluska, Joe" <jpaluska@hillandknowlton.com>,"Paperman, Jennifer (Corp Media Relations)" <jennifer.paperman@hp.com>,"Parrish, Diane" <diane.parrish@hp.com>,"Poulson, Lisa" <lisa.poulson@bm.com>,"Race, Lee" <lrace@hillandknowlton.com>,"Railton, Catherine L" <cathy.railton@hp.com>,"Rainville, Gary" <gary.rainville@hp.com>,"Read, Melanie" <melanie.read@hp.com>,"Sakuda, Kara R" <kara.sakuda@hp.com>,"Schneider, Christina" <christina.schneider@hp.com>,"Sherbin, Robert" <robert.sherbin@hp.com>,"Steven, Sarah K" <sarah.k.steven@hp.com>,"Svanstrom, Asa" <asa.svanstrom@hp.com>,"Taaffe, Paul" <paul.taaffe@hillandknowlton.com>,"Teigland, Dee (TSG Marcom)" <dteigland@hp.com>,"Temple, Jennifer" <Jennifer.Temple@HillandKnowlton.com>,"Topolski, Smita" <smita.topolski@hillandknowlton.com>,"Turner, Paul" <pturner@hillandknowlton.com>,"Vaughan, Douglas G" <doug.vaughan@hp.com>,"Wallace, Natalie B" <natalie.wallace@hp.com>,"Wandke, Laura" <laura.wandke@hillandknowlton.com>,"Wesselman, Tim R (Investor Relations)" <tim.wesselman@hp.com>,"Whitgrove, Patrick" <patrick.whitgrove@hp.com>,"Wischhusen, Emma" <emma.wischhusen@hp.com>,"Woodward, Ed" <ed.woodward@hp.com>,"Yanez, Vanessa (Enterprise PR)" <vanessa.yanez@hp.com>
Subject: BusinessWeek Online: What HP Should Have Done
Date: Mon, 18 Sep 2006 09:16:33 -0500

What HP Should Have Done
Past crises offer lessons for managing corporate tumult and resolving ethical dilemmas. Too bad Hewlett-Packard didn't pay better attention BusinessWeek Online, 9/18/06, Kirk O. Hanson

The debacle over Hewlett-Packard's handling of board leaks to the press was an eye-opener -- not just for junkies of boardroom drama, but to students of business ethics and crisis management. Even if HP (HPQ) Board Chairman Patricia Dunn deliberately set out to create a case study for debate in business school she couldn't have done any better.

Dunn will step down in January as HP board chair amid a furor over tactics used during an investigation into the source of boardroom leaks. Dunn will remain on the board. As part of the probe, contractors for HP's private investigator posed as journalists, directors, and HP employees to obtain telephone records -- all in the name of finding out which board member was feeding information to reporters. It's a tactic known as pretexting, and California Attorney General Bill Lockyer has said he has unearthed enough evidence of wrongdoing to issue indictments of people within and outside HP [see BusinessWeek.com, 9/12/06, "Charges on the Way at Hewlett-Packard?"].

ETHICAL DILEMMAS.

The whole episode, with its many twists, throws up an array of ethical dilemmas, many of which could be faced by other company directors. Here are just a handful:

Should the chair inform the board it is being investigated for leaks? Knowing that it was likely that only one board member was leaking to the press, Dunn either did or did not have an obligation to inform the board she was about to undertake an investigation and how it was to be conducted. I believe she did have such an obligation, out of respect for the innocent board members and their rights.

How do you pick an outside investigator and what kind of guidance do you give? Every company hopes its vendors, contract manufacturers, or business partners follow its standards and adhere to its values. Today, companies are increasingly being held accountable for what happens throughout the supply chain.

How explicit should HP be in giving direction to its outside investigators? I believe HP had an obligation to pick an investigator with a reputation for respecting the rights of those investigated, and the obligation to give explicit direction that the outside firm should follow HP values enshrined in the "HP Way."

Should ethics -- or legality -- be the standard for how an investigation is conducted? Investigative methods are evolving quickly. While companies have an increasing responsibility to investigate employee or even board misbehavior, they are also facing a legal landscape that is changing rapidly. It's clear the American public is deeply worried about the privacy of its financial, Web search, and, yes, telephone records.

Should HP be guided by what it and its lawyers believe is legal, or by the sometimes ambiguous standard of what is "ethical?" I believe HP has long been committed to acting"ethically," not just legally, and it would give up a major portion of its reputation by choosing mere legality as the standard.

FORCING THE BOARD'S HAND.

What should you do when a report to the board is based on private telephone records? We know only about director Tom Perkins' reaction when the board was presented with the report fingering George Keyworth as the leaker. Perkins slammed down the cover of his briefcase and immediately resigned. What should other board members have done?

I believe every member of the board should have been concerned that the report was based on private phone records, and recognized this was an ethical problem. That could have enabled the HP board to have moved quickly to clean up its own mess before Perkins forced its hand several months later through a flurry of letters and e-mails.

Do you apologize for what happened? Who should apologize and to whom? At what point in the emergence of a scandal is an apology warranted? How much "blame" does the company admit? I believe HP was a bit slow apologizing to board members and employees for the invasion of private phone records. To say one was "appalled" at the methods falls short of an apology. The board chair and management spokesperson should have apologized early and often.

Should anyone be punished? One of the fundamental ethical turning points is whether anyone is held accountable and whether the punishment fits the crime. You hope that any penalty communicates an unambiguous message about the values of the company and its commitment to accountability. I fear HP gave at best a mixed signal. Apparently the board concluded Dunn did something wrong but it was unclear what, and it's unclear why stepping down in January and then remaining on the board was the appropriate punishment.

OBVIOUS ANSWER.

Should HP explain to its employees and to the public exactly what steps have been taken to prevent a recurrence? I believe it must do this to quell the anxiety of employees who fear that their phone records could be examined next and to relieve the worry of HP customers that the data HP keeps on them might be used against them.

Should you also purloin the phone records of reporters? Sorry, the answer to this one is so obvious that you get no credit for saying: "No, they should not." This merely insured that negative media attention would follow.

Above all, I believe past episodes -- from the tragic poisonings of Tylenol buyers 25 years ago to the spate of corporate scandals that began with Enron in 2002 – have established a clear standard for the management of ethical scandals and other corporate crises. The four principles are a] tell everything you know as you learn it; b] apologize early and often; c] punish those who are guilty; and d] state clearly what the company has done to make another such incident unlikely. Unfortunately, the HP board stumbled on several of these.

Hanson is a university professor and executive director of the Markkula Center for Applied Ethics. He taught business ethics for 23 years at the Stanford Graduate School of Business before becoming head of the Markkula Center.

TAB 107

ar 07 05 11:35p rdelia 781-449-3211 p.1

99358119

ACTION ASSIGNMENT FORM

✓ NEW ASSIGNMENT CANCEL REQUEST

_____ REQUEST STATUS

ALL CANCELLATIONS MUST BE MADE IN WRITING VIA FAX. CONFIRMATION OF CANCELLATION WILL BE RETURNED TO YOU VIA FAX. WITHOUT PROOF OF CANCELLATION YOUR ACCOUNT WILL BE BILLED.

OFFICIAL USE ONLY

REC: _____

FAXED: _____

COMPLETED

BOOKED: _____

RECHECKED: _____

NO HIT: _____

REQUEST DATE: 3-7-05

COMPANY NAME: Security Outsourcing Solutions, Inc.

COMPANY ACCOUNT NO.: [redacted]

CONTACT NAME: Ron Delia Ext. _____

RRD@security-outsourcing.com

CONTACT FAX #: 781 449 3211 PHONE #: 781-[redacted]

REDACTED

REFERENCE NAME: 05-01-396 ACCT. NO. _____

SERVICE REQUEST

900 A & M REQUEST INFO Subscriber name and address

REQUIRED INFORMATION VERIFIED THRU DIRECTORY ASSISTANCE ____ YES ____ NO

NAME _____

LAST KNOWN ADDRESS _____

LAST KNOWN PHONE NUMBER SEE ATTACHED LIST

SSN ____-____-____ D.O.B. __/__/__

SPECIAL INSTRUCTIONS/COMMENTS: Attached list of 34 Telephone numbers. Cell OK RRD

[redacted]

MAR-26-2001 04:01 PM THE MY T ONE

#'s REDACTED
↓

A 203-[redacted] RS
B 203-[redacted] RS
C 212-[redacted] RS
214-[redacted]
240-[redacted]
281-[redacted]
281-[redacted]
D 281-[redacted] RS
281-[redacted]
281-[redacted]
281-[redacted]
E 281-[redacted] RS
281-[redacted]
281-[redacted]
281-[redacted]
281-[redacted]
401-[redacted]
408-[redacted]
408-[redacted]
408-[redacted]
F 408-[redacted] RS
G 408-[redacted] RS
512-[redacted]
650-[redacted]
713-[redacted]
713-[redacted]
717-[redacted]
H 760-[redacted] RS
800-[redacted]
832-[redacted]
832-[redacted]
832-[redacted]
832-[redacted]
978-[redacted]

Get N/A
OR cell
Specials

To: MATT

From:

1200

03-08-05

240-[redacted]

ROCKVILLE MD 20852

#'s + ADDRESSES REDACTED

281-[redacted]

HOUSTON TX 77070

19 A $28

1 K $4

14 M $

475 ~~380~~ 40

45

630

$1150

Subj: 7968-C
Date: 3/10/2005 1:16:14 P.M. Eastern Standard Time
From: Pivalerie
To: Actionresearch1

03/10/05
THURSDAY

7968-C

212-[redacted] # REDACTED

HEWLETT - PACKARD
[redacted]
NEW YORK, NEW YORK 10121-0899

212-[redacted] # REDACTED

VERIZON

$10

VPI

Subj: 7968-E
Date: 3/10/2005 1:29:03 P.M. Eastern Standard Time
From: Pivalerie
To: Actionresearch1

03/10/05
THURSDAY
(E)
281-[redacted] (DESK OF [redacted])
REDACTED NAME REDACTED
[redacted] ADDRESS REDACTED
HOSTON, TEXAS 77064-4856

MAIN #: 281-[redacted]
REDACTED

$10

VPI

Subj: 7968-F
Date: 3/10/2005 2:57:53 P.M. Eastern Standard Time
From: Pivalerie
To: Actionresearch1

03/10/05
THURSDAY

7968-F

408-[redacted] (DESK OF [redacted])

#'s, NAME, + ADDRESS REDACTED

[redacted]
SAN JOSE, CA. 95131-1726

PAC BELL

MAIN # IS 408-[redacted]

HE IS IN BUILDING 3

$10

VPI

Subj: 7968-G
Date: 3/10/2005 1:12:36 P.M. Eastern Standard Time
From: Pivalerie
To: Actionresearch1

03/10/05
THURSDAY

7968-G

408-[redacted] (DESK OF [redacted])

#, NAME, + ADDRESS REDACTED

HEWLETT - PACKARD
[redacted]
CUPERTINO, CA. 95014-2557

MAIN #: 408-[redacted]

REDACTED

PAC BELL

$10

VAL

Subj: 7968-H OOPS
Date: 3/10/2005 3:50:18 P.M. Eastern Standard Time
From: Pivalerie
To: Actionresearch1

03/10/05
THURSDAY

7968-H

760-[redacted]
#, NAME, + ADDRESS REDACTED
[redacted] (HOME - OFFICE)
[redacted]
CARLSBAD, CA. 92008-6101

PAC BELL

$10

VAL

To: MATT

From:

0301

03-08-05

713-[redacted]

HOUSTON TX 77002

#'s, NAMES, + ADDRESS REDACTED

713-[redacted]

HOUSTON TX 77002

760-[redacted]

978-[redacted]

HEWLETT-PACKARD

[redacted]

ANDOVER MA 01810

To: MATT

From:

7013

03-08-05

408-[redacted]
RESELLER

H'S • ADDRESS
REDACTED

408-[redacted]
RESELLER

650-[redacted]
HEWLETT-PACKARD
[redacted]
PALO ALTO CA 94304

To: Heidi
From: Darre

Ref# MATT-1

Cancel- this is a Verizon Wireless Cell #

Thats fine

my BAD FORGOT

Ref# MATT-2

[redacted] NAME+ADDRESS REDACTED TO [redacted] TELL YA

#BK ✓

HOUSTON
~~Tomball~~ TX 77070 ~~77375~~

281-[redacted]-[redacted]
#REDACTED

Ref# MATT-3

800#

[redacted] N'S, ADDRESS REDACTED [redacted] St

Compton CA 90220

800-[redacted]

N. terminates to T1 trunk

To: MATT

From:

03-08-05

1584

281-[redacted]
RESELLER

#, NAMES, + ADDRESSES
REDACTED

281-[redacted]
HOUSTON TX 77064

281-[redacted]
HOUSTON TX 77070

To: MATT

From:

8088

03-08-05

212-[redacted]
RESELLER

#'s REDACTED

281-[redacted]
RESELLER

281-[redacted]
HOUSTON TX 77069

#, NAME, + ADDRESS REDACTED

To: Heidi
From: Dan

Ref# MATT-1

cell BK.

[redacted]

[redacted]

NAME, ADDRESS,
+ # REDACTED

West Haven CT 06516

203-[redacted]

#'S REDACTED

203-[redacted]
203-[redacted]
212-[redacted]
214-[redacted]
240-[redacted]
281-[redacted]
281-[redacted]
281-[redacted]
281-[redacted]
281-[redacted]
281-[redacted]
281-[redacted]
281-[redacted]
281-[redacted]
281-[redacted]
281-[redacted]
401-[redacted]
408-[redacted]
408-[redacted]
408-[redacted]
408-[redacted]
408-[redacted]
512-[redacted]
650-[redacted]
713-[redacted]
713-[redacted]
717-[redacted]
760-[redacted]
800-[redacted]
832-[redacted]
832-[redacted]
832-[redacted]
832-[redacted]
978-[redacted]

ACTION RESEARCH GROUP

Please visit us at: www.actionresearchgroup.com
Email assignments: actionresearch1@aol.com

DATE: 3-11-05 ASSIGNMENT NO. 99358119

SENDER: HEIDI S. 2/15/1

COMPANY NAME: SECURITY OUTSOURCING SOLUTIONS, INC.

CLIENT NO. 2010

CONTACT NAME: RON DELIA

SERVICE REQUEST: 900 A x 19, 900M x 14, 900K x 1 PRICE $ 1150.00

REFERENCE: 05-01-396

REQUESTED INFORMATION

CELL NUMBER: LIST OF 34 NUMBERS

INFORMATION FOUND

#'s, NAMES, + ADDRESSES REDACTED

240-[redacted]
ROCKVILLE, MD. 20852

281-[redacted]
HOUSTON, TX 77070

281-[redacted]
HOUSTON, TX 77070

212-[redacted]
HEWLETT PACKARD
[redacted]
NY, NY 10121

281-[redacted]
HOUSTON, TX 77064

408-[redacted]
SAN JOSE, CA 95131

#'s, NAMES, + ADDRESSES
REDACTED

408-[redacted]
HEWLETT PACKARD
[redacted]
CUPERTINO, CA 95014

713-[redacted]
[redacted]
HOUSTON, TX 77002

978-[redacted]
HEWLETT PACKARD
[redacted]
ANDOVER, MA 01810

408-[redacted]
[redacted]
SUNNYVALE, CA 94086

281-[redacted]
[redacted]
HOUSTON, TX 77064

281-[redacted]
[redacted]
HOUSTON, TX 77069

800-[redacted]
[redacted]
COMPTON, CA 90220
TERMINATES TO T1 TRUNK LINE

203-[redacted]
[redacted]
BRANFORD, CT 06405

760-[redacted]
[redacted]
CARLSBAD, CA 92008

713-[redacted]
[redacted]
HOUSTON, TX 77002

650-[redacted]
HEWLETT PACKARD
[redacted]
PALO ALTO, CA 94304

408-[redacted]
HEWLETT PACKARD
[redacted]
CUPERTINO, CA 95014

281-[redacted]
[redacted]
HOUSTON, TX 77070

408-[redacted]
HEWLETT PACKARD
[redacted]
CUPERTINO, CA 95014

203-[redacted] CELL
[redacted]
WEST HAVEN, CT 06516

717-[redacted] CELL
[redacted]
YORK, PA 17402

#'s, NAMES, + ADDRESSES REDACTED

281-[redacted] CELL
[redacted]
KATY, TX 77450

281-[redacted] CELL
[redacted]
HOUSTON, TX 77070

281-[redacted] CELL
[redacted]
SPRING, TX 77379

281-[redacted] CELL
[redacted]
HOUSTON, TX 77095

832-[redacted] CELL
[redacted]
DAMON, TX 77430

214-[redacted] CELL
[redacted]
KELLER, TX 76248

281-[redacted] CELL
[redacted]
SPRING, TX 77381

832-[redacted] CELL
[redacted]
MAGNOLIA, TX 77354

401-[redacted] CELL
[redacted]
WARREN, RI 02885

512-[redacted] CELL
[redacted]
SPRING, TX 77379

832-[redacted] CELL
[redacted]
MAGNOLIA, TX 77354

832-[redacted] CELL
[redacted]
HOUSTON, TX 77080

THANK YOU FOR USING OUR SERVICES!!

<u>NOTICE: ALL CANCELLATION REQUESTS MUST BE IN WRITING</u>

<u>Terms & Conditions:</u>

All information obtained by us, or our affiliates, is intended for legitimate and lawful use only: by proceeding forth with this information request, you (the client), agree to indemnify, hold harmless, protect and defend (in a court of law) Action Research Group and/or it's affiliates if the information is misused in anyway. While Action Research Group believes the information to be reliable, human or mechanical error remains a possibility. Therefore, Action Research Group makes no guarantee to its' accuracy. Neither Action Research Group nor any of our sources of the information requested shall be responsible for any error or omissions, or for the use or results obtained from the use of this information.

TAB 108

99360544

COMPLETED 4/22

S.O.S.

Attn: Ron

Acct # 2010

Email rrd@security-outsourcing.com

N2 # 250

~~N3 #375~~

all calls (Feb-Apr)

Cingular

900N3 $ 375

All calls

BEN ELGIN

[redacted] ADDRESS REDACTED

SF CA 94121

SS [redacted] 10/20/72

#'s REDACTED

I received assignment no. 99360511 and would like to pull "ALL" the calls from cell phone number 415-[redacted] for February, March and April 2005.

14

Action Research

Please visit us at: www.actionresearchgroup.com
Email assignments: actionresearch1@aol.com

DATE: 4-22-05 ASSIGNMENT NO: 99360544

SENDER: RYAN S:

COMPANY NAME: S.O.S. CLIENT# 2010

CONTACT NAME: RON

SERVICE REQUEST: 900 N2 PRICE: $250.00

REFERENCE:

REGARDING PHONE NO: 415-[redacted]

BEN ELGIN # + ADDRESS REDACTED
[redacted]
SAN FRANCISCO, CA 94121

INFORMATION REQUESTED:
WE WILL HOLD FOR THE 4-28 BILL AND SEND BACK RESULTS ASAP

BILL DATE: 2-28-05

DATES	PHONE NUMBERS CALLED #'S REDACTED	REPEATS
1-29	415-[redacted]	2x
2-8	415-[redacted]	2x
2-9	650-[redacted]	
	212-[redacted]	
	650-[redacted]	
2-10	650-[redacted]	
	415-[redacted]	
	415-[redacted]	2x
2-11	415-[redacted]	
	415-[redacted]	2x
2-14	650-[redacted]	
	415-[redacted]	
2-15	650-[redacted]	
	650-[redacted]	
2-16	650-[redacted]	2x
	816-[redacted]	
2-23	415-[redacted]	
2-26	650-[redacted]	
	ALL CALLS	

H's REDACTED

BILL DATE: 3-28-05

3-1	415-[redacted]	
	415-[redacted]	2X
3-2	650-[redacted]	
	415-[redacted]	
3-4	650-[redacted]	
	650-[redacted]	
	650-[redacted]	
	650-[redacted]	
3-8	650-[redacted]	
3-9	650-[redacted]	
	650-[redacted]	
	212-[redacted]	
	312-[redacted]	
3-10	650-[redacted]	
	650-[redacted]	2X
	415-[redacted]	
	650-[redacted]	
3-16	650-[redacted]	
	650-[redacted]	
3-19	650-[redacted]	
3-23	650-[redacted]	
3-24	650-[redacted]	5X
	650-[redacted]	
	650-[redacted]	
	415-[redacted]	2X
	650-[redacted]	
	858-[redacted]	
3-25	650-[redacted]	3X
3-27	650-[redacted]	
3-28	415-[redacted]	3X
	ALL CALLS	

THANK YOU FOR USING OUR SERVICES!!

NOTICE: ALL CANCELLATION REQUESTS MUST BE IN WRITING

Terms & Conditions:
All information obtained by us, or our affiliates, is intended for legitimate and lawful use only; by proceeding forth with this information request, you (the client), agree to indemnify, hold harmless, protect and defend (in a court of law) Action Research Group and/or it's affiliates if the information is misused in anyway. While Action Research Group believes the information to be reliable, human or mechanical error remains a possibility. Therefore, Action Research Group makes no guarantee to its' accuracy. Neither Action Research Group nor any of our sources of the information requested shall be responsible for any error or omissions, or for the use or results obtained from the use of this information.

TAB 109

ACTION RESEARCH GROUP

Please visit us at: www.actionresearchgroup.com
Email assignments: actionresearch1@aol.com

DATE: 07/06/05

ASSIGNMENT NO: 99364152

SENDER: BOBIEJO

S: 14

CLIENT NAME: S.O.S.

CLIENT NO: 2010

CONTACT NAME: RON

SERVICE REQUEST: 900N NH

PRICE: $0.00

REFERENCE:

REGARDING: (917) [redacted] REDACTED
ROBERT KNOWLING

INFORMATION REQUESTED: THIS ACCOUNT HAS BEEN ACTIVE SINCE 06/09/05 WITH VERIZON. THE BILL DATE IS THE 13TH. THERE'S ONLY 3 TO 4 DAYS OF CALLS ON 06/13 BILL. IF YOU WANT 07/13 BILL, IT WILL BE READY AROUND 07/20. PLEASE LET US KNOW.

NO HIT

THANK YOU FOR USING OUR SERVICES!!

NOTICE: ALL CANCELLATION REQUESTS MUST BE IN WRITING

Terms & Conditions:

All information obtained by us, or our affiliates, is intended for legitimate and lawful use only: by proceeding forth with this information request, you (the client), agree to indemnify, hold harmless, protect and defend (in a court of law) Action Research Group and/or it's affiliates if the information is misused in anyway. While Action Research Group believes the information to be reliable, human or mechanical error remains a possibility. Therefore, Action Research Group makes no guarantee to its' accuracy. Neither Action Research Group nor any of our sources of the information requested shall be responsible for any error or omissions, or for the use or results obtained from the use of this information.

REDACTED

Subj: Ref: 4152 Verculty 917-[redacted]$15.00
Date: 7/8/2005 2:24:34 P.M. Eastern Standard Time
From: eyeintheskyiny@yahoo.com
To: mdhh2000@[redacted]

#'s REDACTED

6/9
734-[redacted]
858-[redacted]x2
303-[redacted]x2
303-[redacted]

6/10
303-[redacted]
917-[redacted]
303-[redacted]
202-[redacted]

6/11
720-[redacted]
303-[redacted]

6/12
no calls

6/13
no calls

ACTION RESEARCH GROUP

Please visit us at: www.actionresearchgroup.com
Email assignments: actionresearch1@aol.com

DATE: 07/08/05

ASSIGNMENT NO: 99364152

SENDER: BOBIEJO

S: 14

CLIENT NAME: S.O.S.

CLIENT NO: 2010

CONTACT NAME: RON

SERVICE REQUEST: 900N

PRICE: $125.00

REFERENCE:

INFORMATION PROVIDED: (917) [redacted] REDACTED

INFORMATION REQUESTED:

BILL DATE: 06/13

DATES	PHONE NUMBERS CALLED #'s REDACTED	REPEATS
06/09	734-[redacted]	
	858-[redacted]	X2
	303-[redacted]	X2
	303-[redacted]	
06/10	303-[redacted]	
	917-[redacted]	
	303-[redacted]	
	202-[redacted]	
06/11	720-[redacted]	
	303-[redacted]	
06/12	No calls	
06/13	No calls	

END OF CALLS

THANK YOU FOR USING OUR SERVICES!!

NOTICE: ALL CANCELLATION REQUESTS MUST BE IN WRITING

Terms & Conditions:

All information obtained by us, or our affiliates, is intended for legitimate and lawful use only: by proceeding forth with this information request, you (the client), agree to indemnify, hold harmless, protect and defend (in a court of law) Action Research Group and/or it's affiliates if the information is misused in anyway. While Action Research Group believes the information to be reliable, human or mechanical error remains a possibility. Therefore, Action Research Group makes no guarantee to its' accuracy. Neither Action Research Group nor any of our sources of the information requested shall be responsible for any error or omissions, or for the use or results obtained from the use of this information.

Action Research

Please visit us at: www.actionresearchgroup.com
Email assignments: actionresearch1@aol.com

DATE: 7-22-05

ASSIGNMENT NO: 99364818

SENDER: IVORY

S: 14

CONTACT NAME: S.O.S.

CLIENT# 2010

COMPANY NAME: RON

SERVICE REQUEST: 900 N ALL CALLS

PRICE: $125.00

REFERENCE:

REGARDING PHONE NO: 917-[redacted]
C/O ROBERT KNOWLING
[redacted] # + ADDRESS
NEW YORK, NY 10036 REDACTED

INFORMATION REQUESTED:

BILL DATE: 7/13

DATES	PHONE NUMBERS CALLED #'s REDACTED	REPEATS
6/12	858-[redacted]	
6/13	303-[redacted]	
	858-[redacted]	
6/14	734-[redacted]	
6/15	720-[redacted]	
	303-[redacted]	
6/16	718-[redacted]	
	909-[redacted]	
6/17	720-[redacted]	
	408-[redacted]	
	212-[redacted]	
	203-[redacted]	
	551-[redacted]	
6/19	832-[redacted]	
	917-[redacted]	
	317-[redacted]	
	317-[redacted]	
6/20	832-[redacted]	
	917-[redacted]	
	917-[redacted]	
	832-[redacted]	

#'s REDACTED

	720-[redacted]
6/21	713-[redacted]
	212-[redacted]
6/22	720-[redacted]
6/23	303-[redacted]
	720-[redacted]
6/24	917-[redacted]
6/26	303-[redacted]
6/27	404-[redacted]
6/28	303-[redacted]
	404-[redacted]
6/29	949-[redacted]
	646-[redacted]
	203-[redacted]
	917-[redacted]
	303-[redacted]
	646-[redacted]
	303-[redacted]
6/30	303-[redacted]
	303-[redacted]
	404-[redacted]
	646-[redacted]
	203-[redacted]
	303-[redacted]
	303-[redacted]
	303-[redacted]
7/1	978-[redacted]
	678-[redacted]
	303-[redacted]
	303-[redacted]
	303-[redacted]
	908-[redacted]
	303-[redacted]
7/5	212-[redacted]
7/9	303-[redacted]
	303-[redacted]
	303-[redacted]
	912-[redacted]
7/11	303-[redacted]
	720-[redacted]
	303-[redacted]

(ALL CALLS)

THANK YOU FOR USING OUR SERVICES!!

NOTICE: ALL CANCELLATION REQUESTS MUST BE IN WRITING

Terms & Conditions:
All information obtained by us, or our affiliates, is intended for legitimate and lawful use only: by proceeding forth with this information request, you (the client), agree to indemnify, hold harmless, protect and defend (in a court of law) Action Research Group and/or it's affiliates if the information is misused in anyway. While Action Research Group

TAB 110

ACTION RESEARCH GROUP

Please visit us at: www.actionresearchgroup.com
Email assignments: actionresearch1@aol.com

DATE: 07/08/05 ASSIGNMENT NO: 99364899

SENDER: BOBIEJO S. 25

CLIENT NAME: S.O.S. CLIENT NO: 2010

CONTACT NAME: RON

SERVICE REQUEST: 900BX4 PRICE: $ 500.00

REFERENCE: ATTORNEY CLIENT PRIVILEGES

REGARDING PHONE NO: (650) [redacted]

#'s + ADDRESS REDACTED

INFORMATION REQUESTED: CARLETON (CARLY) FIORINA
[redacted]
LOS ALTOS HILLS, CA 94022
(650) [redacted]

THERE ARE NO CALLS ON THIS LINE...THE NEW NUMBER IS
(650) [redacted]
REDACTED

BILL DATE: 01/15 DATES	(local & long distance) PHONE NUMBERS CALLED	REPEATS
12/24	415-[redacted] (l.d.)	
01/12	650-[redacted]	X2
01/14	650-[redacted]	
	>>END OF CALLS<<	

#'s REDACTED

BILL DATE: 02/15	(local & long distance)	
01/16	415-[redacted] (l.d.)	
	415-[redacted] (l.d.)	
01/23	650-[redacted]	X5
02/04	415-[redacted] (l.d.)	
02/08	510-[redacted] (l.d.)	X2
	650-[redacted]	X2

#'s REDACTED

02/10	415-[redacted] (l.d.)
02/11	415-[redacted] (l.d.)
02/14	415-[redacted] (l.d.)
02/15	415-[redacted] (l.d.)
	>>END OF CALLS<<
BILL DATE: 03/15	(local & long distance)
03/09	415-[redacted] (l.d.)
	415-[redacted] (l.d.)
	650-[redacted]
03/13	831-[redacted] (l.d.)
03/14	415-[redacted] (l.d.)
03/15	510-[redacted] (l.d.)
03/16	415-[redacted] (l.d.)
	>>END OF CALLS<<

DISCO NO INFO

BILL DATE: 04/15	(local & long distance)
03/18	650-[redacted]
03/22	650-[redacted]
03/24	415-[redacted] (l.d.)
04/12	510-[redacted] (l.d.)
04/14	650-[redacted]
	>>END OF CALLS<<

>>>ALL (650) #'S ARE LOCAL CALLS

THANK YOU FOR USING OUR SERVICES!!

<u>NOTICE: ALL CANCELLATION REQUESTS MUST BE IN WRITING</u>

<u>Terms & Conditions:</u>

8993

07-11-05

#'s, NAMES, & ADDRESSES REDACTED

A
A - 415-[redacted] ✓
SAN FRANCISCO, CA 94109

A - 415-[redacted] ✓
SAN FRANCISCO CA 94123

415-[redacted] / [redacted]
SAUSALITO CA 94965 ✓

A - 415-[redacted] ✓
SAN FRANCISCO CA 94123

A - SOS-1 BK 415-[redacted] ✓
SAN FRANCISCO CA 94103

A - Text100 corp. SOS-3 BK 415-[redacted]
SAN FRANCISCO CA ✓

9707

07-11-05

#'s, NAMES, + ADDRESSES REDACTED

M 415-[redacted] CINGULAR
[redacted]
SAN RAFAEL CA 94903 ✓

M 650-[redacted] CINGULAR ✓
[redacted]
MENLO PARK CA 94025

M 415-[redacted] ATT
[redacted]
CORTE MADERA CA 94925 ✓

M 650-[redacted] VERIZON ✓
[redacted]
PALO ALTO CA 94304

M SOS-2 CELL BK510-[redacted]
[redacted]
~~BREKLEY~~ CA ✓
BERKELEY

#DISC SOS-4 831-[redacted]
DISCOED TO LONG TO PULL INFOR

ONLY NO HIT

ACTION RESEARCH GROUP

PLEASEVISIT US AT: WWW.ACTIONRESEARCHGROUP.COM
EMAIL ASSIGNMENTS: ACTIONRESEARCH1@AOL.COM

DATE: 7-13-05 ASSIGNMENT NO. 99365189

SENDER: RYAN S.

COMPANY NAME: SOS CLIENT NO. 2010

CONTACT NAME: RON

SERVICE REQUEST: 900AX6/MX5 PRICE $375.00

REFERENCE: ATTORNEY CLIENT PACKAGE

REQUESTED INFORMATION:

415-[redacted]- LANDLINE
[redacted]
SAN FRANCISCO, CA 94109

#'s, NAMES, + ADDRESSES REDACTED

415-[redacted]- LANDLINE
[redacted]
SAN FRANCISCO, CA 94123

415-[redacted] – LANDLINE
[redacted]
SAUSALITO, CA 94965

415-[redacted]- LANDLINE
[redacted]
SAN FRANCISCO, CA 94123

415-[redacted] – LANDLINE
[redacted]
SAN FRANCISCO, CA 94103

#'s, NAMES, + ADDRESSES REDACTED

415-[redacted] - LANDLINE
[redacted]
SAN FRANCISCO, CA 94108

415-[redacted] - CELL
[redacted]
SAN RAFAEL, CA 94903

650-[redacted]- CELL
[redacted]
MENLO PARK, CA 94025

415-[redacted]- CELL
[redacted]
CORTE MADERA, CA 94925

650-[redacted]- CELL
[redacted]
PALO ALTO, CA 94304

510-[redacted]- CELL
[redacted]
BERKELEY, CA 94701

NO HITS
831-[redacted]- # WAS DISCONNECTED

THANK YOU FOR USING OUR SERVICES!!

NOTICE: ALL CANCELLATION REQUESTS MUST BE IN WRITING

Terms & Conditions:
All information obtained by us, or our affiliates, is intended for legitimate and lawful use only: by proceeding forth with this information request, you (the client), agree to indemnity, hold harmless, protect and defend (in a court of law) Action Research Group and/or it's affiliates if the information is misused in anyway. While Action Research Group believes the information to be reliable, human or mechanical error remains a possibility. Therefore, Action Research Group makes no guarantee to its' accuracy. Neither Action Research Group nor any of our sources of the information requested shall be responsible for any error or omissions, or for the use or

4899
99V3L ~~4~~

S.O.S. le V39

2010

REF NAME: ATTORNEY CLIENT PRIVELEGES

rrd@security-outsourcing.com

9005V

COMPLETED

CARLETON (CARLY) FIORINA

~~BX3 1/4~~
BX4 $ 500

THANKS
RON

[redacted]

Los Altos Hills, CA 94022

SS# [redacted]

#'s + ADDRESS REDACTED

HOME: 650-[redacted]

~~Cell 650-~~[redacted]

NEEDS 1/10 - 1/25
2/1 - 2/15
3/1 - 3/30

25

Subj: ~~8458~~ 4899

Date: 7/8/2005 4:07:23 P.M. Eastern Standard Time

From: Bryanandkalese

To: MDHH2000

650-[redacted] - NO TOLLS ON THIS LINE

REDACTED

650-[redacted] new #

(650) is loacl #'s REDACTED

Other line

1/15 bill long and local 12/16-1/14

12/24 415-[redacted]

1/12 650-[redacted]

1/12 *

1/14 *

* ALL 650 A/C ARE LOCALS

2/15 long and lcoal

1/16 415-[redacted]

1/16 415-[redacted]

1/23 650-[redacted] #'s REDACTED

1/23 *

1/23 *

1/23 *

1/23 *

2/4 415-[redacted]

2/8 510-[redacted]

*

2/8 650-[redacted]

2/8 *

*

*

*

*

*

*

w/up Matt before emailing back

2/10 ~~415~~-[redacted]

2/11 ~~415~~-[redacted]

2/14 415-[redacted]

2/15 415-[redacted]

3/15 long and local

3/9 415-[redacted]

3/9 415-[redacted]

3/9 650-[redacted]

3/13 831-[redacted]

3/14 415-[redacted]

3/15 510-[redacted]

3/16 415-[redacted]

4/15 long and local

#'s REDACTED

3/18 650-[redacted]
*
3/22 *
3/24 415-[redacted]
4/12 '510-[redacted]
4/14 650-[redacted]

TAB 111

REDACTED

Subj: SOS-Dawn 510-[redacted] NAT ok if needed on both ALL JANUARY
Date: 1/30/2006 2:20:58 P.M. Eastern Standard Time
From: clk06190619@[redacted]
To: MDHH2000@[redacted]

SOS-Dawn 510-[redacted] NAT ok if needed on both ALL JANUARY
Dawn Yoshitake-Kawamoto
[redacted] #'s & ADDRESS REDACTED
Albany CA 94706
ss:[redacted]

#'s REDACTED

01/30 08:03 AM	[redacted] DT 1
01/29 04:58 PM	[redacted] NW 14
01/29 02:02 PM	[redacted] NW 1
01/29 01:27 PM	[redacted] NW 6
01/29 01:07 PM	510-[redacted] NW VM 1
01/29 01:06 PM	510-[redacted] NW VM 1
01/29 01:04 PM	[redacted] NW 1
01/29 01:02 PM	[redacted] NW 1
01/29 01:01 PM	510-[redacted] NW VM 3
01/29 12:56 PM	[redacted] NW 2
01/28 01:23 PM	[redacted] NW 6
01/28 01:13 PM	[redacted] NW 2
01/28 12:50 PM	[redacted] NW 2
01/28 12:15 PM	[redacted] NW 1
01/28 10:13 AM	[redacted] NW 2
01/27 05:13 PM	[redacted] DT M2MCNG 3
01/27 09:46 AM	[redacted] DT 9
01/27 08:31 AM	[redacted] DT 2
01/26 04:46 PM	[redacted] DT M2MCNG 2
01/26 04:30 PM	[redacted] DT M2MCNG 3
01/26 04:29 PM	[redacted] DT M2MCNG 1
01/26 04:20 PM	[redacted] DT M2MCNG 1
01/26 04:10 PM	[redacted] DT 1
01/24 10:28 AM	[redacted] DT M2MCNG 1
01/24 10:27 AM	[redacted] DT 1
01/24 10:17 AM	[redacted] DT M2MCNG 1
01/24 07:40 AM	[redacted] DT 1
01/23 08:58 PM	[redacted] DT 9
01/23 08:57 PM	510-[redacted] DT VM 1
01/23 07:04 PM	[redacted] DT 2
01/22 07:04 PM	[redacted] NW 1
01/22 03:50 PM	[redacted] NW 1
01/22 03:33 PM	[redacted] NW 1
01/22 11:38 AM	[redacted] NW 1
01/22 11:13 AM	[redacted] NW 1
01/22 09:21 AM	[redacted] NW 7
01/21 07:39 PM	510-[redacted] NW VM 1
01/21 02:57 PM	[redacted] NW 1
01/21 01:40 PM	[redacted] NW 11
01/21 01:24 PM	[redacted] NW 1
01/21 01:00 PM	[redacted] NW 1
01/21 11:00 AM	510-[redacted] NW VM 1
01/21 10:31 AM	[redacted] NW 1

REDACTED

01/21 09:21 AM	[redacted] NW 1
01/21 09:16 AM	[redacted] NW 4
01/20 08:21 AM	[redacted] DT 7
01/19 04:22 PM	[redacted] DT 1
01/19 04:21 PM	[redacted] DT 1
01/19 04:13 PM	[redacted] DT 1
01/19 02:06 PM	[redacted] DT 1
01/18 08:36 PM	[redacted] DT 4
01/18 08:36 PM	[redacted] DT M2MCNG 1
01/18 09:16 AM	[redacted] DT 9
01/17 09:08 PM	[redacted] NW 1
01/17 07:36 PM	[redacted] DT 1
01/17 02:38 PM	[redacted] DT 11
01/16 05:04 PM	[redacted] DT M2MCNG 1
01/16 09:18 AM	[redacted] DT M2MCNG 1
01/15 05:05 PM	[redacted] NW 1
01/15 05:04 PM	[redacted] NW 1
01/15 04:19 PM	[redacted] NW 1
01/15 03:51 PM	[redacted] NW 2
01/15 03:48 PM	510-[redacted] NW VM 2
01/15 03:47 PM	510-[redacted] NW VM 1
01/15 03:46 PM	510-[redacted] NW VM 1
01/14 10:35 AM	[redacted] NW 1
01/13 06:41 PM	[redacted] DT M2MCNG 1
01/12 07:29 PM	[redacted] DT M2MCNG 2
01/12 07:20 PM	[redacted] DT 4
01/12 07:19 PM	[redacted] DT 1
01/12 07:09 PM	[redacted] DT 10
01/12 07:05 PM	[redacted] DT 1
01/12 05:18 PM	[redacted] DT 1
01/12 04:34 PM	[redacted] DT 2
01/12 04:19 PM	[redacted] DT 1
01/12 04:18 PM	[redacted] DT M2MCNG 1
01/12 04:00 PM	[redacted] DT 1
01/12 01:52 PM	[redacted] DT 1
01/12 09:20 AM	[redacted] DT 2
01/12 09:18 AM	[redacted] DT 2
01/12 09:16 AM	[redacted] DT M2MCNG 2
01/12 09:14 AM	510-[redacted] DT VM 2
01/11 03:07 PM	[redacted] DT 7
01/11 03:06 PM	[redacted] DT 1
01/10 08:57 PM	[redacted] DT 29
01/10 07:02 PM	[redacted] DT 1
01/10 05:49 PM	510-[redacted] DT VM 1
01/10 05:48 PM	[redacted] DT M2MCNG 1
01/10 05:26 PM	[redacted] DT 1
01/10 01:20 PM	[redacted] DT M2MCNG 4
01/10 10:24 AM	[redacted] DT 3
01/09 08:58 PM	510-[redacted] DT VM 1
01/09 07:33 PM	[redacted] DT 4
01/09 06:27 PM	[redacted] DT M2MCNG 1
01/09 06:23 PM	[redacted] DT 2
01/09 06:22 PM	[redacted] DT 1
01/09 05:36 PM	[redacted] DT M2MCNG 1
01/09 12:53 PM	[redacted] DT M2MCNG 1
01/09 12:10 PM	[redacted] DT 2

EDACTED

01/09 12:07 PM (	[redacted] DT M2MCNG 2
01/09 11:55 AM (	[redacted] DT 1
01/09 10:52 AM !	[redacted] DT M2MCNG 1
01/09 10:51 AM !	[redacted] DT M2MCNG 2
01/09 10:39 AM ,	[redacted] DT 1
01/09 10:38 AM	[redacted] DT 1
01/09 10:36 AM	[redacted] DT 2
01/09 10:33 AM	[redacted] DT 2
01/09 10:29 AM	[redacted] DT 4
01/09 10:26 AM	[redacted] DT M2MCNG 4
01/09 10:22 AM	[redacted] DT 1
01/09 09:59 AM	[redacted] DT 1
01/08 01:51 PM	[redacted] NW 1
01/07 01:14 PM	[redacted] NW 1
01/07 12:06 PM	[redacted] NW 2
01/07 12:00 PM	[redacted] NW 1
01/07 11:29 AM	[redacted] NW 30
01/07 11:18 AM	[redacted] NW 11
01/06 09:04 PM	I 510-[redacted] NW VM 1
01/06 05:08 PM	[redacted] DT M2MCNG 1
01/06 01:52 PM	[redacted] DT 2
01/06 01:49 PM	[redacted] DT 2
01/06 12:48 PM	[redacted] DT 1
01/05 05:05 P	[redacted] DT M2MCNG 1
01/05 04:16 P	[redacted] DT 1
01/05 04:00 P	[redacted] DT 1
01/05 03:59 P	[redacted] DT 1
01/05 03:55 P	[redacted] DT 1
01/05 12:11 A	[redacted] NW 1
01/05 12:10 A	[redacted] NW 1
01/05 12:04 A	I 510-[redacted] NW VM 1

TAB 112

Marion Keyworth

510-[redacted]-[redacted]

REDACTED

Subj: **sosmk 2/1**
Date: 2/6/2006 12:57:56 P.M. Eastern Standard Time
From: Bryanandkalese
To: MDHH2000

H's REDACTED

locals 2/1

1-10	1-05	845A V	925 [redacted]	D	1	.07
1-11	1-15	909P	510 [redacted]	N	1	.03
1-12	1-17	153P	925 [redacted]	D	2	.08
1-13	1-18	257P	925 [redacted]	D	3	.10
1-14	1-18	301P	925 [redacted]	D	1	.07
1-15	1-18	303P	925 [redacted]	D	10	.20
1-16	1-18	352P	925 [redacted]	D	17	.31

longs

2-09	12-14	517P V	310 [redacted]	DZ	1:00	.07
2-10	12-14	518P	303 [redacted]	DZ	1:00	.07
2-11	12-14	758P	505 [redacted]	DZ	10:00	.70
2-12	12-14	939P	303 [redacted]	DZ	25:00	1.75
2-13	12-15	746A	303 [redacted]	DZ	6:00	.00
2-14	12-15	1100A	530 [redacted]	DZ	1:00	.00
2-15	12-15	1101A	530 [redacted]	DZ	1:00	.00
2-16	12-15	1102A	530 [redacted]	DZ	2:00	.00
2-17	12-15	1120A	520 [redacted]	DZ	1:00	.00
2-18	12-16	104A	505 [redacted]	DZ	2:00	.00
2-19	12-16	1256P	C 202 [redacted]	DZ	1:00	.00
2-20	12-16	1131P	505 [redacted]	DZ	1:00	.00
2-21	12-17	1023A	A 310 [redacted]	DZ	9:00	.00
2-22	12-17	1031A	303 [redacted]	DZ	1:00	.00
2-23	12-17	419P	303 [redacted]	DZ	1:00	.00
2-24	12-17	419P	303 [redacted]	DZ	1:00	.00
2-25	12-17	712P	303 [redacted]	DZ	1:00	.00
2-26	12-18	1115A	303 [redacted]	DZ	9:00	.00
2-27	12-18	1124A	A 310 [redacted]	DZ	1:00	.00
2-28	12-18	1157A	310 [redacted]	DZ	11:00	.00
2-29	12-19	600P	303 [redacted]	DZ	1:00	.00
2-30	12-20	538P	917 [redacted]	DZ	26:00	.00
2-31	12-21	1017A	805 [redacted]	DZ	1:00	.00
2-32	12-21	1125A	925 [redacted]	DZ	11:00	.00
2-33	12-21	757P	301 [redacted]	DZ	1:00	.00
2-34	12-22	330P	303 [redacted]	DZ	1:00	.00
2-35	12-22	628P	301 [redacted]	DZ	5:00	.00
2-36	12-22	659P	505 [redacted]	DZ	1:00	.00
2-37	12-22	810P	505 [redacted]	DZ	1:00	.00
3-01	12-22	829P	505 [redacted]	DZ	1:00	.00
3-02	12-23	1137A	720 [redacted]	DZ	8:00	.00
3-03	12-23	1145A	303 [redacted]	DZ	6:00	.00
3-04	12-23	216P	530 [redacted]	DZ	1:00	.00
3-05	12-27	848P	A 310 [redacted]	DZ	23:00	.00
3-06	12-28	907A	530 [redacted]	DZ	13:00	.00
3-07	12-28	1142A	303 [redacted]	DZ	1:00	.00
3-08	12-28	1144A	303 [redacted]	DZ	1:00	.00
3-09	12-28	1212P	310 [redacted]	DZ	2:00	.00
3-10	12-28	1224P	303 [redacted]	DZ	40:00	.00
3-11	12-28	110P	310 [redacted]	DZ	9:00	.00
3-12	12-28	121P	650 [redacted]	DZ	1:00	.00
3-13	12-28	122P	650 [redacted]	DZ	1:00	.00
3-14	12-28	649P	505 [redacted]	DZ	1:00	.00
3-15	12-28	651P	505 [redacted]	DZ	1:00	.00
3-16	12-28	659P	303 [redacted]	DZ	1:00	.00

REDACTED

3-17	12-28	700F	3[redacted]	DZ	12:00	.00
3-18	12-29	1159	30[redacted]	DZ	1:00	.00
3-19	12-29	1222	310[redacted]	DZ	1:00	.00
3-20	12-29	1225	310[redacted]	DZ	1:00	.00
3-21	12-29	250F	01[redacted]	DZ	1:00	.00
3-22	12-31	1212	310[redacted]	DZ	34:00	.00
3-23	12-31	110	505[redacted]	DZ	1:00	.00
3-24	12-31	316	3[redacted]	DZ	1:00	.00
3-25	12-31	317	310[redacted]	DZ	21:00	.00
3-26	12-31	340	530[redacted]	DZ	20:00	.00
3-27	12-31	737	03[redacted]	DZ	1:00	.00
3-28	12-31	738	03[redacted]	DZ	1:00	.00
3-29	12-31	738	03[redacted]	DZ	1:00	.00
3-30	12-31	739	301[redacted]	DZ	1:00	.00
3-31	1-01	1004	530[redacted]	DZ	10:00	.00
3-32	1-01	1256	973[redacted]	DZ	13:00	.00
3-33	1-01	557	530[redacted]	DZ	5:00	.00
3-34	1-01	713	3[redacted]	DZ	24:00	.00
3-35	1-02	425	505[redacted]	DZ	1:00	.00
3-36	1-02	444	505[redacted]	DZ	1:00	.00
3-37	1-03	112	650[redacted]	DZ	18:00	.00
3-38	1-03	41	50[redacted]	DZ	12:00	.00
3-39	1-03	80	303[redacted]	DZ	1:00	.00
3-40	1-03	105	505[redacted]	DZ	2:00	.00
3-41	1-04	91	650[redacted]	DZ	4:00	.00
3-42	1-04	112	202[redacted]	DZ	2:00	.00
3-43	1-04	10	505[redacted]	DZ	3:00	.00
3-44	1-05	20	650[redacted]	DZ	1:00	.00
3-45	1-05	21	650[redacted]	DZ	1:00	.00
3-46	1-05	55	303[redacted]	DZ	12:00	.00
3-47	1-05	81	03[redacted]	DZ	2:00	.00
3-48	1-07	62	03[redacted]	DZ	9:00	.00
3-49	1-08	1	505[redacted]	DZ	1:00	.00
3-50	1-09	6	505[redacted]	DZ	1:00	.00
3-51	1-09	7	650[redacted]	DZ	15:00	.00
3-52	1-09	7	303[redacted]	DZ	2:00	.00
3-53	1-09	7	310[redacted]	DZ	28:00	.00
3-54	1-10	1	707[redacted]	DZ	3:00	.00
3-55	1-10	1	530[redacted]	DZ	2:00	.00
3-56	1-10	1	650[redacted]	DZ	7:00	.00
3-57	1-10	2	310[redacted]	DZ	8:00	.49 BP
3-58	1-11	6	08[redacted]	DZ	2:00	.14
3-59	1-11	1	925[redacted]	DZ	26:00	1.30

Subj: keyworth home
Date: 2/28/2006 10:34
From: Bryanandkalese
To: MDHH2000

Time

'S REDACTED

Jan 20	07:00 P	0 [redacted]	N	5	0.45
Jan 20	07:05 P	0 [redacted]	N	4	0.36
Jan 20	11:50 P	03 [redacted]	N	1	0.09
Jan 27	10:25 P	03 [redacted]	N	6	0.54
Jan 29	09:47 A	03 [redacted]	N	4	0.36
Jan 29	12:42 P	03 [redacted]	N	1	0.09
Jan 29	01:06 P	103 [redacted]	N	9	0.81
Jan 29	01:35 P	303 [redacted]	N	1	0.09
Jan 29	07:03 F	301 [redacted]	N	11	0.99
Jan 29	10:51 F	510 [redacted]	N	12	1.08
Jan 30	09:03 A	415 [redacted]	D	4	0.36
Jan 30	09:07 A	617 [redacted]	D	1	0.09
Feb 01	07:00 F	505 [redacted]	N	8	1.28
Feb 01	08:45 F	505 [redacted]	N	13	2.08
Feb 02	08:14 F	510 [redacted]	N	1	0.09
Feb 02	10:38 F	510 [redacted]	N	28	2.52
Feb 03	09:29 /	510 [redacted]	D	1	0.09
Feb 03	09:38 /	510 [redacted]	D	20	1.80
Feb 03	12:16 I	415 [redacted]	D	2	0.18

REDACTED

Feb 03	12:18 P	[redacted]	D	7	0.63
Feb 03	12:24 P	5[redacted]			

REDACTED

Subj: keyworth fax 505-[redacted] 505 is local
Date: 2/28/2006 10:35:38 A.M. Eastern Standard Time
From: Bryanandkalese
To: MDHH2000

#'s REDACTED

Jan 10	02:46 P	2 [redacted]	D	1	0.09
Jan 12	04:23 P	5 [redacted]	D	10	1.60
Jan 13	08:47 A	2 [redacted]	D	2	0.18
Jan 13	04:50 P	5 [redacted]	D	2	0.32
Jan 17	06:20 P	10 [redacted]	D	4	0.36
Jan 18	06:21 P	10 [redacted]	D	8	0.72
Jan 25	04:47 P	05 [redacted]	D	2	0.32
Jan 25	10:11 P	10 [redacted]	N	1	0.09
Jan 26	03:24 P	03 [redacted]	D	2	0.18
Jan 26	04:37 P	30 [redacted]	D	25	2.25
Jan 26	05:04 P	30 [redacted]	D	2	0.18
Jan 26	05:06 P	30 [redacted]	D	14	1.26
Jan 26	06:27 P	510 [redacted]	D	2	0.18
Jan 26	10:02 P	303 [redacted]	N	5	0.45
Jan 26	10:19 P	925 [redacted]	N	2	0.18
Jan 27	09:44 A	510 [redacted]	D	3	0.27
Jan 27	01:31 P	510 [redacted]	D	2	0.18
Jan 27	02:10 P	505 [redacted]	D	1	0.16
Jan 27	05:48 P	505 [redacted]	D	6	0.96

#'s REDACTED

Feb 03	05:27 P	505 [redacted]	D	2	0.32
Feb 03	06:08 P	505 [redacted]	D	1	0.16
Feb 03	06:08 P	505 [redacted]	D	1	0.16
Feb 03	06:10 P	505 [redacted]	D	2	0.32
Feb 08	06:33 P	505 [redacted]	D	1	0.16
Feb 09	07:40 P	505 [redacted]	N		

TAB 113

415-[redacted] REDACTED
TOM PERKINS
[redacted]
TIBURON, CA 94920

NAMES & ADDRESSES REDACTED

#'s REDACTED

BILL DATE: 1-26-06 - LONG DISTANCE

4-Jan	212-[redacted]	[redacted], [redacted], NY NY 10010
	441273 [redacted] UK	UNITED KINGDOM UNABLE TO OBTAIN INFO
	917-[redacted]	[redacted]NY, NY 10021
5-Jan	212-[redacted]	[redacted], NY, NY 10022
	212-[redacted]	[redacted], NY, NY 10022
	207-[redacted]	[redacted]DEN, ME 04843
9-Jan	212[redacted]	[redacted], NY, NY 10022
17-Jan	212-[redacted]	[redacted], NY, NY 10022
	442[redacted] UK	UNITED KINGDOM UNABLE TO OBTAIN INFO
18-Jan	212-[redacted]	[redacted], NY, NY 10022
	905[redacted] [redacted]	TURKEY UNABLE TO OBTAIN INFO
19-Jan	917-[redacted]	[redacted], [redacted], NY, NY 10021
	212-[redacted]	[redacted], [redacted], NY, NY 10010
	212-[redacted]	[redacted], [redacted]NY, NY 10010
20-Jan	212-[redacted]	[redacted], [redacted], NY 10022
24-Jan	442[redacted] UK	UNITED KINGDOM UNABLE TO OBTAIN INFO
	905[redacted]	TURKEY UNABLE TO OBTAIN INFO
	ALL CALLS	

BILL DATE: 1-26-06 - LOCAL

4-Jan	415-[redacted]	[redacted], [redacted], NOVATO, CA 94945
5-Jan	415-[redacted]	[redacted], [redacted] NOVATO, CA 94945
6-Jan	415-[redacted]	[redacted], [redacted] NOVATO, CA 94945
	ALL CALLS	

415-[redacted]
TOM PERKINS
[redacted]
TIBURON, CA 94920

BILL DATE 1-26-06 - LONG DISTANCE

REDACTED NAME + ADDRESS REDACTED

5-Jan 949-[redacted] [redacted] NEWPORT BEACH, CA 92663
ONLY CALL

BILL DATE: 1-26-06 - LOCAL
NO LOCAL CALLS

** BOLD INDICATES CELLULAR

*** LIST COMPLETE

TAB 114

W&GR Wilson Sonsini Goodrich & Rosati
PROFESSIONAL CORPORATION

650 Page Mill Road
Palo Alto, CA 94304-1050
PHONE 650.493.9300
FAX 650.493.6811
www.wsgr.com

PRIVILEGED & CONFIDENTIAL
ATTORNEY WORK PRODUCT
REFLECTS ATTORNEY-CLIENT COMMUNICATION

MEMORANDUM

To:	*HP Securities Litigation* Team
From:	Bahram Seyedin-Noor and Trevor Lain
Date:	August 21, 2006
Re:	**Interview of Ann Baskins - -** ***DRAFT*** **- -**

On August 11, 2006 Steven M. Schatz and Bahram Seyedin-Noor interviewed Ann Baskins, General Counsel of Hewlett-Packard Company ("HP" or the "Company"), via teleconference. On August 16, 2006 Steven Schatz conducted a follow-up teleconference interview with Baskins, the contents of which he relayed to me a few minutes afterwards. On August 21, 2006 David Berger, Steven Schatz, and Bahram Seyedin-Noor again interviewed Baskins via teleconference. The purpose of the interviews was to ascertain the steps HP took in the Kona II Investigation, for which outside investigators used "pretexting" to obtain the telephone records of certain persons. This memorandum reflects Bahram Seyedin-Noor's thoughts and impressions from the calls.

I. January 2005 Inquiry by Larry Sonsini

1. Baskins recalls that the HP Board asked Sonsini to look into the leaks of confidential information in January 2005. The leaks occurred after the January 2005 offsite Board meeting in San Francisco. Fiorina was very upset about the leaks.

2. Fiorina initially asked the Nominating and Governance Committee to look into the leaks. At the time, Knowling was chair of the Nominating and Governance Committee. The Board the commissioned Larry Sonsini to investigate the leak. Sonsini did the actual interviews of the directors. Perkins actually acknowledged being a leak for one of those.

3. In the view of the Board and at least some of the directors, Sonsini's investigation was more than merely an investigation into the leak and turned into more of a Board evaluation and assessment. For example, the unhappiness with Fiorina came out in the interviews. The directors were frustrated that Fiorina seemed overly focused on the leaks and not enough on other important issues.

II. Change in CEO and Other Governance Issues

4. The Board was very careful in the 6 weeks after Fiorina's termination to conduct its search for a CEO without involving management. They did not want Baskins or other management (except acting CEO Wayman) involved. Baskins took the minutes at Board meetings where the search was discussed, but Baskins had to step out for these portions of the meetings. Pattie Dunn told them she would step down as Chair if they could not agree to select the CEO without involving the media.

5. Baskins believes Dunn clearly felt she had a mandate to uncover leaks. When Hurd joined, he agreed that the leaks were outrageous. Baskins did not interfere in the investigation.

6. In summer of 2005, Dunn engaged a consultant, and she and Perkins got into a tussle about it because he did not see a need for it. Dunn wanted a consultant to weigh in on governance documents to make sure HP had "best in class" board documents. She brought in Mercer Consulting. They concluded that the documents were not very consistent.

7. In the course of evaluating HP's board documents, David Nigren of Mercer interviewed all the directors for input on the governance documents, charters, Board policies, and Board practices. Baskins believed that in Nigren's interviews with directors, some directors brought up the issue of the leaks.

8. Baskins said Charles Charnas did 99% of the work of evaluating the board documents, but Mercer took 99% of the credit.

9. At each governance meeting, Perkins would "blow his top" on this issue—Perkins generally felt he could write a book on governance and did not need outside help. Perkins' view was that a public company should post on its Website only those Board policies that are required to be posted by the securities exchanges, and should not inscribe in the company's governance guidelines policies that not required by the exchanges. In contrast, HP's internal policies contain more details than are required, including Mercer's recommendations.

III. Kona I (2005 Investigation)

10. In 2005, HP conducted an investigation into leaks of information to the press concerning, among other things, then-CEO Carleton Fiorina's departure from HP, Mark Hurd's joining HP, and HP's work force reductions.

11. Baskins had very little involvement in the Kona I investigation. As a result, she was not very familiar with Kona I. During one call, Baskins said she was aware of it and remembers attending one or two meetings relating to the investigation in the summer and/or fall of 2005. In a later call, Baskins reported that her calendar does not show any meeting in mid July 2005, and that she recalls attending a meeting possibly in the fall of 2005 where the status of the investigation was summarized. She remembers that Ron DeLia was at the fall meeting.

12. Baskins does not believe the Kona I investigation was discussed with the entire Board.

13. In Kona I, Baskins does not recall putting Dunn in contact with DeLia. Baskins may have put Dunn in contact with Kevin Huska, but does not remember.

14. Dunn informed Baskins of Perkins' insistence to use polygraphs.

15. Baskins was not aware in 2005 that the investigative team would need to obtain records from third parties for non-HP telephones. Baskins was definitely aware of HP's internal ability to provide telephone call data for internal HP phones but not for third parties.

16. The Kona I investigation was inconclusive but narrowed the list of potential suspects in the leaks to three individuals.

IV. Kona II (2006 Investigation)

A. Initiation

17. The Kona II investigation sought to determine the source of a leak to CNET regarding issues discussed at a Board meeting in January 2006.

18. Baskins first learned of the leak from Kevin Hunsaker on the weekend of January 21 and 22, 2006. She was at an offsite meeting in Palm Springs when she received a call from Kevin Hunsaker describing the leak. That weekend, Baskins discussed the leak with Hunsaker.

19. Specifically, Baskins recalls receiving either a call or voice mail from Hunsaker about the leak and knowing that by protocol this matter would be handled by the SBC compliance team. Thus, Baskins was informed about this after the team was already in place.

20. Baskins did not believe the individuals who leaked the information could have learned the information from the Board package alone.

21. Baskins recommended that Hunsaker discuss the leaked information with Shane Robison (HP's CTO) and Alan Haggard (Legal), who took the minutes of the technology committee's minutes, to confirm that the information could not have simply been glimpsed from the "dumpster or shredder box."

22. Baskins provided Hunsaker with the names of all who attended the offsite Board meeting during which the leaked information was discussed.

23. Baskins said the investigation was formally initiated by Pattie Dunn or Mark Hurd.

24. Baskins had greater knowledge of Kona II than Kona I because Dunn called her to express her concern that their team may not be the "best in class" to really ferret out the leakers. As a consequence, Baskins called Bryan Jenkins on January 30.

B. Bryan Jenkins

25. At some point during the investigations, Baskins and Hunsaker acted on Dunn's concerns that perhaps the investigation was not being conducted optimally (she did not want another inconclusive report like in Kona I) and consulted with investigative expert Bryan Jenkins (formerly of Kroll Assoc.). Jenkins specifically recommended that they conduct pretexting to get information if they had not already done so.

26. Baskins recalls a Friday meeting (likely in early February) with Dunn and the Kona II Investigation Team. That same day, Jenkins met with Hunsaker and Baskins, and Hunsaker explained to Jenkins what the Team was doing. Baskins was considering possibly retaining Jenkins or someone like him for the Investigation. Jenkins is a consultant HP uses on crisis management issues like terrorism (in Israel, Russia, and elsewhere), and helps HP do scenario planning for eventualities like a bird flu epidemic, etc.; the planning involves having facts thrown at you and you respond. Jenkins writes those scenarios.

27. One of the first things Jenkins asked was whether HP was using certain techniques for accessing telephone records. Baskins does not recall specifically what technique he recommended but thinks it was pretexting [Hunsaker told us Jenkins recommended pretexting]. The recommendation focused on third party telephone information. Jenkins asked Hunsaker if he was doing a particular thing, which Baskins could not specifically recall, and Kevin said yes.

28. As a result, Baskins was able to go back to Dunn and inform her that Jenkins agreed with their techniques.

29. Dunn had also just met with the Team that day and came away with impression the team was taking the right steps.

C. Methodology

30. HP has a "playbook" for these investigations that is more or less "self-executing." Generally, an attorney at HP Legal works with one of the investigators in the Global Security department. Early on in these investigations, the Company decides whether an attorney needs to be involved to envelope the investigation in privilege.

31. During the investigation, the team—consisting of Hunsaker (HP Legal), Tony Gentilucci, Ron DeLia and others—would provide Dunn weekly telephonic updates, which were generally held on Fridays at 3:00 p.m. Baskins was not involved in the earlier calls and did not play

an active role in the beginning because she was a suspect (along with other officers and directors). She was careful not to "interfere with or try to shape the inquiry." Later, however, Baskins attended the weekly updates.

32. As to Dunn's understanding of pretexting, Baskins believes Dunn may not have known the specifics about pretexting techniques. However, there was one meeting which Baskins did not attend, in which Dunn met with the investigators.

33. Hunsaker was in charge of the Kona II investigation. Since he worked with Baskins on many investigations, he often dropped by her office to discuss issues such as methodology.

34. At one point, Baskins remembers Hunsaker asking if all members of the executive committee had HP-issued phones that would allow for ready access to their records for review.

D. Pretexting for Phone Records

35. Baskins said she did not personally provide Hunsaker with the phone numbers of the directors. She believes Rose Thomas (Board liaison) would have done that.

36. Baskins does not specifically recall the use of the word "pretexting," but she recalls discussing cell phone records of suspects in February 2006.

37. Baskins believes her first conversations with Hunsaker regarding the phone records were with respect to phone records for the reporters who reported the leaked information, particularly Dawn Kawamoto.

38. After the meeting with Jenkins, Baskins recalls a meeting with Hunsaker in which the issue of billing cycles for cell phones came up. The problem was that HP could not get call information for third party calls in a certain period until the billing cycle closed. At this meeting, Hunsaker related in general terms that DeLia had arranged for investigators in Florida to get the telephone call records. DeLia had told Hunsaker these investigators only worked with the government, law firms and PIs.

39. At the above meeting, Hunsaker described to Baskins how investigators could call a phone carrier and ask for information about calls made during a past billing cycle. Baskins remembers learning at some later point that the information was taken verbally. Hunsaker did not discuss the use of impersonation, ruse, or pretexting. Baskins asked if the method the investigators used was legal. Hunsaker said, yes.

40. During her first conversations with Hunsaker, Baskins remembers Hunsaker saying that the investigator would ***not*** pretend to be someone else when retrieving information regarding phone calls. A few weeks after the meeting above (in or around early March 2006), however, Hunsaker came back to Baskins and told her that he had learned that if the investigator was not

having success retrieving the information from the carrier, he might employ a ruse whereby he pretended to be someone else. (Baskins made the same assertion in two separate calls.)

41. Baskins specifically asked Hunsaker if pretexting was legal and Hunsaker assured her it was both common and legal.

42. As a result of this conversation, Hunsaker, through Tony Gentilucci and Ron DeLia, confirmed with John Kiernan of the law firm of Bonner Kiernan Trebach & Crociata LLP that the practice of using a ruse to obtain telephone information was lawful.

43. Baskins recalls discussing the legality of pretexting with Hunsaker a second time. During the second discussion, Baskins specifically asked Hunsaker to consult a legal expert on this issue. She did not want to rely on the legal understanding of the investigators themselves (*i.e.* Ron DeLia or his investigators in Florida), but rather wanted an outside expert's view.

44. In response to Baskin's request to confirm the legality of pretexting, Hunsaker and Tony Gentilucci consulted with John Kiernan. (Baskins received a call from Kiernan confirming that Tony had called him on March 15, 2006 to specifically ask about the legality of pretexting.) Kiernan was considered somewhat of an expert because of his role in the ABB investigation regarding violations of the Foreign Corrupt Practices Act. Hunsaker reported to Baskins that Kiernan believed pretexting was lawful.

45. Baskins said she and Pattie Dunn were very clear on multiple occasions that the investigation needed to be conducted legally.

46. Baskins did not know anything about the use of Social Security Numbers ("SSNs") in pretexting. She made sure HP itself did not provide SSNs to third parties. She is generally aware that SSNs are available on the Internet. Baskins stated that she had a "knee jerk" reaction to protection of SSNs. She made it clear HP was not to provide SSNs to third parties without authorization.

E. Kona II Findings

47. The Kona II investigation had concluded by early March that Keyworth was the source of the leak. The investigative team discussed their findings with Pattie Dunn, Mark Hurd and Baskins at a meeting in L.A.–where the Board was conducting the annual shareholder meeting.

V. Perkin's Allegation re AT&T Account

48. On July 28, 2006, former HP director Tom Perkins emailed HP's Board of Directors that "my home telephone carrier, has confirmed that my confidential records have been

compromised pursuant to a fraudulent pretext, where the imposter pretending to be me opened an untraceable and inaccessible online account in order to steal the records."

49. Baskins is unaware of anyone opening an untraceable and inaccessible online account to steal AT&T phone records in conjunction with the investigation. She confirmed with Hunsaker that no one had done this. Hunsaker, in turn, had confirmed with his Florida investigators that they did not engage in any such act.

WSGR Wilson Sonsini Goodrich & Rosati
PROFESSIONAL CORPORATION

650 Page Mill Road
Palo Alto, CA 94304-1050
PHONE 650.493.9300
FAX 650.493.6811
www.wsgr.com

PRIVILEGED & CONFIDENTIAL
ATTORNEY WORK PRODUCT
REFLECTS ATTORNEY-CLIENT COMMUNICATION

MEMORANDUM

To: *HP Securities Litigation* Team

From: Bahram Seyedin-Noor and Bryan Ketroser

Date: August 25, 2006

Re: **Interview of Ann Baskins - - *DRAFT* - -**

On August 25, 2006, Steven Schatz, David Berger and Bahram Seyedin-Noor interviewed Ann Baskins, General Counsel for Hewlett-Packard Company ("HP" or the "Company"), via teleconference. This memorandum reflects the thoughts and impressions of Bahram Seyedin-Noor from the interview.

I. Kona I

A. Ron DeLia

1. Baskins is aware Gentilucci had been using Ron DeLia for a long time, and that the two go "way back."

2. Baskins was not aware that Patricia Dunn ever used DeLia on HP matters before Kona II. In fact, Baskins was not aware that DeLia was involved in Kona I until our interview of her.

B. Meeting Attendance

3. Baskins did not remember a June 15 meeting regarding Kona I. Her calendar has an entry "Pattie" for that morning. However, Baskins had an eighth-grade graduation that week and a meeting with Mercer regarding governance issues, and said that "what was on her mind" at the time vis-à-vis Patricia Dunn was Mercer, not Kona I.

4. Baskins did not remember the Kona investigation update on July 22, 2005, which DeLia and Gentilucci specifically recall. However, her calendar shows a morning Board meeting, and Baskins stated that when there is a Friday Board meeting, she usually leaves her afternoon open for follow-up items (such as the investigative update).

5. Baskins did remember being in the executive counsel room and seeing PowerPoint slides with DeLia, but thought the meeting occurred later than July 2005. She stated she had a clear memory of being in a meeting with Dunn and DeLia, and that Hurd, Jim Fairbaugh and/or others may have been present as well.

6. Baskins' calendar shows an August 31, 2005 meeting with Dunn and Fairbaugh.[1]

C. HP's Legal Department and the Merger with Compaq

7. Kevin Hunsaker was in HP's Legal department during Kona I and Kona II, and worked during that time with HP's global investigative group. In 2005, Hunsaker's boss was Lyle Keating. Keating was the head of the practice, and also had all employment lawyers reporting to him.

8. Baskins said that after the merger, HP and Compaq had different approaches to corporate investigation and compliance that were blended together, but did not report to her. She said that the processes that were handled well at HP were consolidated and formalized into what is now called the SEC Compliance team. Ultimately, Hunsaker became the primary lawyer assigned to this team, but Lyle was also heavily involved in the team's early days. The SBC team is in the marketing organization; Security is in REWS. Gentilucci came to Fairbaugh's organization through the merger. Baskins noted that while she has been at HP for more than 24 years, she only met Gentilucci after the merger.

D. Pretexting

9. Steven Schatz asked who would have been responsible within HP to assess the lawfulness of pretexting, assuming it were used in Kona I. Baskins replied that, if it had been made clear to her that they were going to engage in a deceptive act, she would have called Keating. Thus, if she had a conversation with DeLia or Dunn in June 2005 and she had been asked to opine on the matter, she would have consulted him.

10. Baskins stated she had never heard the word "pretexting" used in the Kona investigations. Steven Schatz then explained to Baskins that DeLia had told us he believes he discussed using ruses to obtain phone records with Baskins, but she replied that this did not trigger any memories. However, Baskins did not recall whether pretexting was used prior to Kona I.

11. Baskins said she first learned of the practice of pretexting—though Hunsaker did not use that word—in February or March of 2006.

12. Baskins believes she reviewed the June 14, 2005 investigative report by DeLia (attached as Exh. A) for the first time in August 2005. She stated she now recalls that phone numbers were discussed in the report, but does not remember a discussion regarding the specific

[1] Gentilucci later informed us that the August 31 meeting was cancelled and never took place.

methodology for obtaining phone information. Her recollection is that the discussion focused on Keyworth versus Knowling, rather than pretexting.

13. Baskins was not asked for her opinion regarding pretexting in Kona I. She noted a clandestine atmosphere at the Company between February and September 2005.

II. Kona II

14. Baskins said she had a series of messages from Hunsaker that confirmed her view of how she learned of the leak. She read for us a January 20 email from Bob Sherbin to Fairbaugh and Gentilucci that states: "Jim the report that has the latest leak is Krazit . . . Mark believes the names worth looking at are Hackborn, Babbio, Salhany, Keyworth and Perkins. I'm always happy to talk with you."

15. Baskins stated that Hunsaker had the authority to retain outside counsel. Asked why Baskins did not retain outside counsel, she replied that if Hunsaker's answer as to the legality of pretexting had been at all equivocal, she probably would have retained outside counsel. However, Hunsaker had received confirmation from John Kiernan that pretexting was lawful. Since Kiernan was represented to be an outside lawyer with experience, she felt comfortable with his advice.

650 Page Mill Road
Palo Alto, CA 94304-1050

WSGR Wilson Sonsini Goodrich & Rosati
PROFESSIONAL CORPORATION

PHONE 650.493.9300
FAX 650.493.6811

www.wsgr.com

PRIVILEGED & CONFIDENTIAL
ATTORNEY WORK PRODUCT
REFLECTS ATTORNEY-CLIENT COMMUNICATION

MEMORANDUM

To: *HP Securities Litigation* Team

From: Bahram Seyedin-Noor and Bryan Ketroser

Date: August 28, 2006

Re: **Interview of Ann Baskins** -- ***DRAFT*** --

On August 26, 2006, Steven Schatz, David Berger and Bahram Seyedin-Noor interviewed Ann Baskins, General Counsel for Hewlett-Packard Company ("HP" or the "Company"), via teleconference. This memorandum reflects the thoughts and impressions of Bahram Seyedin-Noor from the interview.

I. Kona I

A. General Information

1. Baskins said that after Carleton Fiorina was fired, relations between management and the Board—especially Lucille Salhany and Thomas Perkins—were strained. The Board was careful about dealing with management, "maintained a wall," and their behavior was guarded. Baskins said the atmosphere was strained, and the sense was that "you answered what you are asked," and that is it. Baskins felt that the investigation was a Board issue, rather than a management issue.

2. Baskins recalled at some point discussing the polygraph issue, and only the polygraph issue, during a call with Patricia Dunn and Ron DeLia.

3. If Dunn had asked Baskins about whom to speak with in HP's global security group, Baskins would have given Dunn either Jim Fairbaugh or Kevin Huska's name.

4. Baskins was positive that there was a Board meeting on July 21-22, 2005, and thought it was a reasonable guess that she attended the July 22 meeting regarding the investigation, even though her calendar does not reflect this.

5. Baskins stated that Perkins gave a speech in April 2005 in which he described a confidential HP labs project, and subsequently, Baskins and Bob Sherbin had to answer employee inquiries as to why that was acceptable, whereas any employee would have been fired for such

behavior. Thus, when Baskins learned of the inquiry into the leaks, she thought it was strange that Perkins' name was not on the list, and there was no apparent interest in Perkins' April statements.

B. Pretexting

6. Baskins recalled receiving the June 14 DeLia report. She thought the report was "sophomoric" and amateurish, but it did not occur to her at the time that it was the fruit of investigative methods that may not have been legal. Nobody asked Baskins for her legal opinion on this issue. Baskins was not sure why she was brought into the meeting, although she had been the Board Secretary and was taking the minutes.

7. We asked Baskins what her response would be if asked why she did not commission meaningful research when she learned that phone records of directors and reporters were being looked at. Baskins stated that the investigation was mid-stream, and had been commissioned by the Board, which had brought in an experienced third party, and the presentation (which Baskins remembered as being in August) was made by the investigator in a way that nobody would question. Baskins said the presentation had a matter-of-fact, somewhat clinical nature—in contrast with how the polygraph issue was raised—and she did not feel that she was being asked to opine on the issue.

8. We asked Baskins whether she felt uncomfortable about the processes used in Kona I. Baskins replied that it felt a little "silly" because it was inconclusive. Baskins came in mid-stream, and it seemed to her that they were chasing after something that occurred back in time, and the odds of proving it seemed remote.

II. Kona II

9. Baskins remembered that when the Kona II process was explained, she inquired about its legality. A lawyer was then approached, and that lawyer was represented to Baskins as being very experienced in the area.

10. Kevin Hunsaker, a lawyer skilled in investigations, was the point person in Kona II. But if Baskins had to choose a person to research the issue of the legality of pretexting, she said she would have gone to Lyle Keating.

11. Baskins said that Hunsaker could have commissioned independent legal research regarding pretexting, but she assumed that he was satisfied from what he had learned from a well-known private investigator, and from being told by a purportedly-experienced lawyer, that the practice was lawful.

TAB 115

WSGR Wilson Sonsini Goodrich & Rosati
PROFESSIONAL CORPORATION

650 Page Mill Road
Palo Alto, CA 94304-1050
PHONE 650.493.9300
FAX 650.493.6811
www.wsgr.com

PRIVILEGED & CONFIDENTIAL
ATTORNEY WORK PRODUCT
REFLECTS ATTORNEY-CLIENT COMMUNICATION

MEMORANDUM

To: *HP Kona II Investigation File*

From: Bahram Seyedin-Noor

Date: August 21, 2006

Re: **Interviews of Ron DeLia - - *DRAFT* - -**

On August 10, 2006, Steven M. Schatz and I interviewed Ron DeLia, an outside consultant retained by Hewlett-Packard Company ("HP" or the "Company") and founder of Outsourcing Solutions, Inc., via teleconference. On August 14, 15, 16 and 22, 2006, I conducted follow-up interviews with DeLia, via teleconference, in which Steven M. Schatz did not participate. The purpose of the interviews was to ascertain the steps HP took in the Kona II Investigation, for which investigators used "pretexting" to obtain the telephone records of certain persons. This memorandum reflects my thoughts and impressions from the calls.

I. Background

1. DeLia has been doing investigations for 33 years and has been working with HP for 8 or 9 years.

II. Kona I (2005 Investigation)

2. In 2005, HP conducted an investigation into leaks of information to the press concerning, among other things, then-CEO Carleton Fiorina's departure from HP, Mark Hurd's joining HP, and HP's work force reductions.

3. Pattie Dunn directly recruited DeLia to take part in the investigation. After Dunn recruited Tony Gentilucci (HP Security) to the investigation, DeLia communicated mainly with Gentilucci rather than Dunn.

4. DeLia has no doubt that he discussed methodology of pretexting (*i.e.*, impersonation) with Dunn at some point during the 2005 Investigation.

5. DeLia asked Kiernan to check the law in 2005 on pretexting because of the sensitivity of the Kona I Investigation. He wanted to be absolutely sure that the method was legal.

6. DeLia believes that Baskins and/or Dunn sought assurances during the Kona I investigation regarding the legality of pretexting. He would have advised them at the time that it was legal.

7. DeLia does not know if he specifically discussed pretexting with Dunn or others as part of this investigation. However, he recalls discussing by phone the pulling of telephone records.

8. DeLia recalls a specific meeting in Palo Alto in July 2005 at which he met with Dunn, Ann Baskins, Mark Hurd, Jim Fairbaugh, Kevin Huska and Tony Gentilucci regarding the investigation. When DeLia arrived at the meeting, Baskins, Gentilucci, Fairbaugh, Huska were already in the meeting. When DeLia arrived, Hurd was not in the meeting (he appears to have stepped out temporarily), but he stepped back in a few minutes later. DeLia did not recall whether Hurd was present for any discussion of phone records. At the meeting, Gentilucci gave an update on the Kona II Investigation. Any results would have had to include the results of the telephone research. DeLia explained at the meeting that his investigators did not use online brokers or obtain written copies of anyone's phone bills. Their technique was to obtain information orally through multiple calls to a carrier soliciting information. The Kona I Investigation was a much broader investigation than Kona II because it involved looking at a series of leaks involving multiple media outlets. They had more suspects, and more reporters. They used pretexting selectively in the Kona I Investigation. Given the breadth of the Investigation, however, they were ultimately unable to isolate the source of the leaks.

III. Kona II (2006 Investigation)

A. Initiation

9. Tony Gentilucci contacted DeLia on Friday, January 20, to retain him for the Kona II investigation. Gentilucci told DeLia that the leaked information likely came from someone on HP's executive committee or Board.

B. Methodology

10. DeLia recalls creating the investigation plan with Kevin Hunsaker's investigative team, which included Tony Gentilucci, Fred Adler, and Vince Nye. The Team held daily conference calls to discuss progress. Ann Baskins was typically not on these calls. However, DeLia does recall discussing the Kona II investigation with Ann Baskins when he came to Palo Alto in February to update Baskins and Dunn on the investigation.

11. Hunsaker instructed DeLia to conduct extensive background investigations on the media reporters and members of the Board.

12. In an attempt to identify CNET reporter Dawn Kawamoto's contact at HP, HP IT Security provided an electronic file attachment, which was sent to Kawamoto by email. The investigation team expected Kawamoto to confirm the validity of the attachment with her contact on the Board. In that case, HP, using particular software embedded in the attachment, would discover the IP address to which Kawamoto forwarded the attachment by email. DeLia asserted that this method is legal. However, the method did not work: it appears that CNET's firewall blocked the email and attachment because Kawamoto never responded to it.

C. Pretexting for Phone Records

13. DeLia believes the investigative team discussed obtaining phone records on the initial phones calls planning the investigation.

1. Action Research Group

14. DeLia retained a company called Action Research Group ("ARG") to conduct pretexting in the Kona II investigation.

15. For the past eight to ten years, DeLia has used ARG for pretexting. DeLia has known the folks in ARG for over 20 years. ARG employs licensed investigators working out of Florida. DeLia thinks there are 6 to 10 individuals working at ARG.

16. To DeLia's knowledge, none of the employees at ARG are named Mike.

17. The phone number for ARG is 800[redacted].

18. ARG did not sell consumer information on the internet or to the general public. Rather, DeLia was referred to ARG by a contact in New York. ARG also appears at trade shows to advertise its services to law firms, investigators and the government.

19. ARG's method of pretexting involved using a false or pretextual identity to obtain information regarding a suspect's phone calls by calling a phone carrier operator and obtaining information verbally.

20. ARG would never obtain written information from a carrier, but insisted on verbal information. Ron's understanding was that pretexting for phone records may be unlawful if physical files were obtained from a phone carrier. ARG, however, would record the information they learned on paper.

21. ARG used pretexting to obtain the telephone records of certain reporters, including Dawn Kawamoto, Stephen Shankland, and Tom Krazit and Pui-Wing Tam from the *Wall Street Journal*. In the usual case, ARG would call the carriers and ask for telephone records for specified dates.

2. Legality of Pretexting

22. DeLia periodically does research regarding privacy issues to assure the legality of his investigative methods. His understanding is that pretexting to obtain information from financial institutions is specifically prohibited. He also said that he periodically has an "analyst" conduct research into the legality of pretexting.

23. DeLia said Hunsaker had a concern with pretexting "right up front." DeLia called John Kiernan in February or March (after the pretexting had already occurred) to discuss the legality of pretexting because Gentilucci and Hunsaker wanted to verify that no law specifically outlawed the practice. Kiernan told him that there was no specific law prohibiting pretexting for phone records and it was not a crime. However, Kiernan cautioned that there was risk of litigation. DeLia passed on Kiernan's findings to Hunsaker. DeLia did not pay Kiernan's bills.

24. The only communications DeLia recalls having with Dunn in connection with the Kona II investigation was a meeting in March 2006 in which the investigative team updated Pattie Dunn and Mark Hurd on the conclusions of investigation. DeLia does not recall any specific meetings with Ann Baskins regarding the Kona II investigation. [DeLia's memory is likely faulty on this point, since Ann Baskins was likely present at the March meeting in L.A.] DeLia does not recall whether they specifically discussed pretexting at the March meeting in L.A.

3. Use of Social Security Numbers

25. DeLia subscribes to proprietary databases that are only for private investigators, law enforcement etc., and that contain Social Security Numbers ("SSNs") and background information on people.

26. DeLia does not specifically recall whether he pulled SSNs for the Kona II Investigation, but if he had pulled them, he would also have forwarded them to ARG in Florida, because forwarding SSNs to ARG is a part of normal protocol for pretexting. He said simply, if they had that information, they would forward it.

27. DeLia does not know whether ARG used SSNs in presenting pretextual identities to obtain information on the suspects' phone calls. He said that they certainly would not have given operators the entire SSNs, since operators would only request the last four digits. He said, however, that it was possible that ARG gave operators the last four digits, but that it would be impossible to go back and confirm that now.

IV. AT&T Letter to Perkins

28. AT&T stated in its letter to Perkins that someone with an IP address beginning 68.99 had tried to hack into his on-line account. DeLia checked and confirmed that his own IP address does not begin with 68.99; rather, his IP address is: [redacted].

Ron DeLia
August 21, 2006
Page 5

29. Also, DeLia did not recognize the emails referenced in the AT&T Letter (*i.e.*, mike@[redacted] and redsox9855@[redacted].

30. DeLia and his company do not use Cox Communications, the service providers referenced in the AT&T letter.

V. Going Forward

31. There is currently pending federal legislation and state legislation in California and Florida that would prohibit pretexting. The federal legislation is apparently hung up in the Senate, but expected to pass in 2007. DeLia believes the current legislation was prompted by concern about online data brokers who are selling information to anyone with a credit card.

32. Given the pending federal legislation and new state statutes making pretexting a crime, DeLia decided in June of this year to no longer use pretexting as a tool.

VI. Keyworth

33. DeLia is aware that Keyworth admitted to being the source of the leak after being confronted with the findings of the investigation.

650 Page Mill Road
Palo Alto, CA 94304-1050
PHONE 650.493.9300
FAX 650.493.6811
www.wsgr.com

WSGR Wilson Sonsini Goodrich & Rosati
PROFESSIONAL CORPORATION

PRIVILEGED & CONFIDENTIAL
ATTORNEY WORK PRODUCT
REFLECTS ATTORNEY-CLIENT COMMUNICATION

MEMORANDUM

To: *HP Securities Litigation* Team

From: Bahram Seyedin-Noor and Bryan Ketroser

Date: August 25, 2006

Re: **Interview of Ron DeLia** ***- - DRAFT - -***

On August 25, 2006, Steven Schatz, David Berger and Bahram Seyedin-Noor interviewed Ron DeLia, an outside consultant retained by Hewlett-Packard Company ("HP" or the "Company") and founder of Outsourcing Solutions, Inc. ("OSI"), via teleconference. This memorandum reflects the thoughts and impressions of Bahram Seyedin-Noor from the interview.

I. Background

1. DeLia stated that the best way to reach him is on his cell phone, 78[redacted] or via email.

2. Before his current job, DeLia, aged 56, was in the military.

3. DeLia said he has a contract with HP, and historically, about half of his work has been for HP. DeLia does not have a written contract with Action Research Group ("ARG"), which is owned by "Joe," whose last name DeLia does not know. DeLia has worked with ARG for 8 years.

II. Kona I

A. Introduction to Investigation and General Information

4. DeLia first learned about Kona I in mid-April 2005. Patricia Dunn contacted him directly. DeLia said that he had done HP-related due diligence and background work for her before on several occasions, but did not feel comfortable telling us that without her permission.

5. Though he did not recall exactly what was said during this initial conversation, DeLia remembered that Dunn asked for his assistance, explaining that information from Board meetings had made their way into the press, and that the only individuals privy to such information were those in the room at the time of the discussions.

6. DeLia stated that during initial conversations with Dunn, she gave DeLia any information she thought was pertinent, including, in April, a document with directors' telephone numbers (but not Social Security Numbers). DeLia did not know where Dunn got the document.

7. Initially, DeLia reported directly to Dunn about once every week to 10 days. DeLia also spoke with Ann Baskins, who was brought in on the investigation some time in June. After June 15, 2005, Tony Gentilucci became involved in the investigation, at which point DeLia's contact was with Gentilucci, not Dunn or Baskins.

8. Jim Fairbaugh was added to the team some time between June 15 and July 22. DeLia did not recall any direct conversations with Fairbaugh regarding Kona II.

9. Dunn never told DeLia whether she had discussed the investigation with Mark Hurd or the Board.

B. Methods of Investigation

10. Dunn asked DeLia how he would go about investigating the leaks, and whether he had undertaken similar cases in the past. DeLia replied that he had undertaken a similar investigation involving leaks from a Big 5 accounting firm to a Wall Street Journal reporter. DeLia was successful in finding the source of the leaks in that case.

11. DeLia told Dunn that he had found the source of the leaks in the accounting firm case through research. He had conducted visual—not electronic—surveillance of the reporter at issue while on vacation, then had Skip Tracers call the hotel the reporter had been staying at to obtain his hotel call records via pretexting, which revealed a call to a senior executive with the company. Pretexting was also used to determine where the reporter was vacationing—somebody called the reporter's office, saying the reporter had requested certain information, and asking someone in the office for the hotel number.

12. Dunn asked DeLia to submit an outline to her on April 19, 2005. The outline stated that there are many options in investigations of this sort, including, *inter alia*, surveillance and extensive research linking the reporters to an interested party. DeLia thought he included information in the outline about obtaining third-party phone records. Dunn responded orally to the email, essentially telling DeLia to move forward.

13. In his investigations, DeLia uses proprietary databases which are accessible by law firms, law enforcement agencies, insurance company investigators, and licensed private investigators. DeLia thought there were regulations restricting the distribution of information contained in such databases to those who had a need for it. Demonstrating such a need entails contacting the database company, filling out an application, and providing documentation such as proof of insurance, an investigator's license, and incorporation information. Generally, DeLia's analysts access the databases, not DeLia.

14. In July or August 2005, DeLia's team conducted visual surveillance in hotels, coffee shops and other locations. His team had pictures of the reporters and looked for them in or around Board meetings.

15. DeLia noted that a majority of the individuals relevant to the investigation were not on the HP infrastructure, meaning that he did not have access to their emails. DeLia stated that he never used eavesdropping, phone tapping or like methods, and did not think it was worthwhile to use lie detectors, since they are not admissible in court and may provide ambiguous results depending on the quality of the examiner. DeLia recalled a conversation with Dunn, Baskins or Gentilucci in which he explained that it was not legal to eavesdrop on conversations.

C. Pretexting

16. DeLia thought "in all probability" that he used the word "pretexting" with Dunn and explained the term to her, but he did not have a specific recollection of using the word. DeLia said he knows that he would have described the processes with Dunn, though he did not tell Dunn that he was using a subcontractor.

17. DeLia instructed ARG to pull call records from a specific time frame for: Robert Knowling, George Keyworth, Tom Perkins and Carleton Fiorina of HP; Roger Crocket, Peter Burrow and Ben Elgin of Business Week; Pui-Wing Tam and George Anders of the Wall Street Journal; and John Markoff of the New York Times. DeLia did not recall whether he called or emailed ARG with the request. ARG would have obtained information regarding both mobile and landlines, and either faxed or emailed the information to DeLia. Generally, ARG would send an Excel spreadsheet with date and phone number information.

18. DeLia has had numerous conversations with ARG in 2005 and 2006 about how they obtain phone records. ARG pretexts the operators, and if one operator does not provide the information, then they call another operator. Each phone carrier is different. ARG would get information on a certain number of days from one operator, then move to another operator. The information was "subject to error" because it was being recorded from an oral conversation.

19. DeLia supplied ARG with Social Security Numbers for all subjects of pretexting. DeLia thought that ARG used the last four digits of the numbers as required. Other than pretexting for phone records, DeLia is not aware of ARG doing any other work for Kona I or Kona II.

20. DeLia told us that pretexting is a common tool used in investigations involving, for instance, organized crime, and his analysts therefore periodically monitor the relevant law.

21. DeLia stated that he would not have decided by himself whose phone records to pull; rather, that decision was collaborative and people in HP would have had ultimate authority as to what activity was conducted.

22. When asked why he had not simply asked the relevant individuals (e.g. HP directors) for their phone records, DeLia responded that this was not his decision to make. Dunn had instructed DeLia not to discuss the investigation with anyone except her, so he felt it would not have been appropriate for him to speak with the Board.

D. Discussions with Baskins and Dunn

1. June Calls

23. DeLia's firm created a June 14 "Preliminary Draft Findings" document, sent to Dunn and Baskins, which refers to "intelligence gathered through telephone subscriber records." *See* Exh. A. DeLia noted that this comment refers to pretexting. The report mentions calls made by Keyworth, and footnote five references two "pretext calls" made to reporters. DeLia said that these calls were probably done by his firm, and that the "Dunn" mentioned in the document is not Patricia Dunn. DeLia said he also drafted an updated report on July 19, 2006 which he will email to us.

24. On June 15, DeLia, Dunn and Baskins conducted a conference call in which DeLia went over the results of the investigation to date, including third party phone records. During the call, DeLia explained pretexting, telling Dunn and Baskins that it involved investigators requesting information from operators orally, over the phone, "pretending" to be someone else if necessary. DeLia informed Dunn and Baskins that pretexting had been used in connection with reporters. DeLia thought most of the pretexting was done by June 15.

25. DeLia recalled that Baskins was curious about pretexting and concerned about its legality, and had asked DeLia whether it was lawful. DeLia replied that he was aware of no laws that made pretexting illegal, and was aware of no criminal prosecutions for such activities. DeLia thought he would have mentioned that he had done some research on the issue. DeLia also recalled talking to John Kiernan about the legality of pretexting some time before the June 15 call.

26. During the June 15 call, DeLia requested access to someone at HP Global Security in order to access the HP "infrastructure." This led to Gentilucci being added to the investigatory team.

2. July 22 Meeting (*see* Exh. B)

27. DeLia recalled attending two meetings on July 22. In the first meeting, DeLia, Huska, Fairbaugh, and Gentilucci went over PowerPoint slides ("Slides," attached as Exh. B) that Gentilucci had created.

28. After they had reviewed the slides, Huska, Fairbaugh and Gentilucci attended another meeting which DeLia did not join until about a half hour later. Slide 2 refers to this half-hour period between 1:30 p.m. and 2:00 p.m. as "Session One." DeLia was brought in for "Session Two," which began on Slide 3, at which point DeLia saw Huska, Fairbaugh, Gentilucci, Dunn and Baskins in the room. Hurd joined the meeting shortly after DeLia, but had to leave early. Gentilucci led Session Two, which lasted about an hour.

29. DeLia did not recall whether pretexting came up, but noted that the meeting covered a lot of material, and that it might have. He did not takes notes during the meeting.

30. DeLia said that the term "E-mail" on Slide 2 refers to internal HP email. He thought "Other parties privileged to information" probably referred to parties that had access to information that was leaked. "Insight from Bob" refers to Bob Sherbin, who was not present at the meeting.

31. DeLia was not sure what "Other intelligence gathering efforts," mentioned on Slide 5, referred to.

32. DeLia said that "Board Member 1," referred to on Slide 8, is Robert Knowling. DeLia recalled that he was on the phone with Dunn one evening when, during their call, Dunn received a call from Knowling, who told Dunn that he had just been called by a reporter with a warning that Business Week was going to run a story.

33. Regarding the comment on Slide 10 that "Intelligence revealed that BoD Member 2 appears to have contacted the NY Times," DeLia did not recall whether anybody specifically asked how this information was obtained.

34. Regarding Slide 12, DeLia noted that he would have had input in selecting investigative options. DeLia stated that he did not agree with the suggestions for using a polygraph or a covert undercover operation. DeLia was not sure what "Misinformation initiative" referred to.

35. DeLia stated that "30 days out – Executive Update Briefing" on Slide 13 probably just refers to a meeting with Gentilucci. DeLia did not recall being a part of a meeting in August, nor does his calendar show any travel to California that month. "Conduct in depth background investigation of BS" was done by DeLia, and involved media searches, inquiries into litigation, and other actions, but did not involve obtaining phone records for Sherbin.

III. Kona II

36. DeLia stated that during Kona II, pretexting was used to obtain phone information for Dunn, Keyworth, Perkins, Richard Hackborn, and Lucille Salhany.

37. DeLia agreed that Lawrence Babbio's status as a senior Verizon officer may have played a role in the decision to not use pretexting to obtain his records.

38. Kevin Hunsaker requested that DeLia do the pretexting For Kona II.

TAB 116

WSGR Wilson Sonsini Goodrich & Rosati
PROFESSIONAL CORPORATION

650 Page Mill Road
Palo Alto, CA 94304-1050
PHONE 650.493.9300
FAX 650.493.6811
www.wsgr.com

PRIVILEGED & CONFIDENTIAL
ATTORNEY WORK PRODUCT
REFLECTS ATTORNEY-CLIENT COMMUNICATION

MEMORANDUM

To: *HP Securities Litigation* Team

From: Bahram Seyedin-Noor

Date: August 21, 2006

Re: **Interview of Patricia Dunn** -- *DRAFT* --

On August 15, 2006 and again on August 21, 2006, Steven M. Schatz, David Berger and Bahram Seyedin-Noor interviewed Patricia Dunn, Chairperson of the Board of Directors of Hewlett-Packard Company ("HP" or the "Company"), via teleconference. The purpose of the interview was to ascertain the steps HP took in the Kona II Investigation, for which investigators used "pretexting" to obtain the telephone records of certain persons. This memorandum reflects my thoughts and impressions of the calls.

I. Background

1. At the outset of the August 15 call, Dunn indicated that she had just left a teleconference call with other members of the Board in which they discussed former HP director Thomas Perkins' concerns about the Kona II Investigation.

II. January 2005 Inquiry by Larry Sonsini

2. Dunn was out of the country for three weeks following the January 2005 HP Board offsite meeting. Dunn remembers she left from the restaurant at the end of the Board offsite in San Francisco to go to the airport for a flight to Bangkok. Then she saw a January 17 newspaper story revealing information from the January 14-16 meeting.

3. After the 2005 Board offsite meeting, the *Wall Street Journal* published two articles containing information from the offsite meeting. Then-CEO Fiorina was "extremely" upset about this. Through the end of January, the HP directors engaged in a great deal of discussion about the "unconscionability" of leaks.

4. Dunn was aware that Larry Sonsini had (at Fiorina's request) done an informal inquiry interviewing each director individually and asked them a set of questions to uncover leaks of information from HP's January 14-16 Board offsite in San Francisco. Sonsini interviewed Dunn too

as part of this inquiry. Sonsini went through a series of questions that dredged up various interpersonal problems directors had with each other. Sonsini's inquiry did not lead to any conclusions. No director admitted being the leaker. Dunn never saw any written materials from Larry's inquiry but Larry did give Dunn a high-level summary.

5. Dunn thought Sonsini's inquiry was very professional, and non-invasive—the kind of approach you would use with a Board you expected to get "honest answers from". Thus, Kona I was the second investigation into leaks.

III. Kona I (2005 Investigation)

A. Board Involvement

6. At about the time of the January 2005 Board offsite, the Board members were actively discussing Fiorina's "tenure." Dunn did not expect to be asked to serve as Chairman, but after former CEO Carleton Fiorina's dismissal, the HP Board asked Dunn to become Chairman.

7. Dunn had zero warning or heads up about her new role as Chair; this came in the immediate wake of Fiorina dismissal. At the meeting that Board decided to terminate Fiorina's tenancy as CEO, the Board asked Dunn to deliver the message of termination to Fiorina because Dunn was talking to both "camps" concerning Fiorina's termination. A few minutes after Dunn explained to Fiorina her termination, the Board reconvened and asked Dunn to serve as Chairman. Dunn was surprised – she did not expect to be asked to serve as Chairman. Dunn was the first non-executive (or outside) Chairman at HP.

8. After Dunn became Chairman, it was clear to her that someone needed to begin work on getting a search underway for a new CEO and give confidence to the market, etc. Dunn was not sure what the job entailed, and so in the first week or two of her Chairmanship she talked with many Board members one on one. In May 2005, Dunn visited each director personally in their home towns and talked to them about what they saw as the Board's priorities and roles of the Chairman. As a first priority, they wanted to get a search under way for CEO. As a second priority they wanted to find out the source of the leaks. Some on the Board believed that the leaks had unfairly undermined Fiorina. Dunn agreed that such disclosures of confidential information were inappropriate. Dunn "got the message" from Directors Robert Knowling, Bob Ryan, Lawrence Babbio and Tom Perkins that HP had to gain control of the leaks. (Perkins opined that the source of the leaks was someone in management.) The Directors made it clear that she should "go figure it out." Therefore Dunn's first step was to find out how HP deals with a leak. There was no formal Board resolution about this.

9. Kona I thus began as a result of a series of conversations between the directors. The conversations occurred within a week or two after Dunn became Chair.

10. Dunn asked management, principally HP General Counsel Ann Baskins, how to determine the source of the leaking. HP management said the Company had a team whose job was

to investigate information breaches of security and that she did not need to look to an outside entity to do the investigation. Dunn considered this suggestion and decided that there was no disabling conflict between the investigative team and the Board because their interests were aligned. Dunn told them to start the investigation with the HP team and see how it went.

11. Dunn reported on the Kona I Investigation to the Board in executive session at almost every Board meeting while the leak investigation was ongoing. In addition, individual directors asked her for progress reports. Dunn explained that the team had advised her that disclosure of the techniques to the persons being investigated would compromise the techniques. Accordingly, Dunn had to take it on herself to determine whether the Board would think it was a reasonable investigation. Dunn did not want information asymmetry among the directors – she did not want to tell more to some directors than to others. At times, directors would offer specific information relevant to the investigation. Ryan, for example, offered his phone records. [Dunn implied she did not accept Ryan's offer.]

12. Dunn recalls a Board meeting in March 2005 in Chicago at which she updated the Board on the Kona I Investigation. She described to them in executive session that a leak investigation was underway. Dunn did not disclose to the Board any specifics about what was being looked into. She wanted the Board to understand that there were things underway that could uncover the leaks. She also wanted to deter people from leaking by creating a fear that they would be discovered, but she did not disclose the methods.

13. Perkins was the only director who advocated lie detectors. Dunn did not know if this was good or bad. She therefore called an outside expert to determine whether it was appropriate. Dunn gave Perkins the report but did *not* tell the rest of the board that this method was considered and rejected.

14. Dunn tried to give the Board assurance that the investigation they had requested was underway and that the investigation team was taking appropriate steps. At no time did any director ask whether the investigation was being done legally – she thinks the Board presumed that.

15. Dunn did report to the Board that the investigation was being conducted within the scope of what was acceptable both legally and ethically. She thinks she repeated this assurance in each of her conversations with the Board. She raised the same subject in every conversation with Baskins.

16. At the time Kona I began, there was no pushback from any directors. The inconclusive results of Kona I were discussed with the Board, and at no time did anyone tell her the investigation was obtrusive. Dunn took their lack of questioning as acknowledgment that they knew this kind of work required confidentiality. Dunn discussed the fact that the investigation was ongoing at virtually every Board meeting, and she kept notes of what she brought up at executive session.

B. Investigation Method and Chronology

17. The Investigation involved heightened monitoring of selected persons as well as relationship mapping. Dunn said it seemed like a "gumshoe" operation and that the team expended a "moderate" level of activity on it.

18. Dunn first discussed the in-house investigative capacity with Baskins; Dunn thinks she learned about HP attorney Kevin Huska from Baskins. (Baskins was not actively involved in the investigation.)

19. Dunn spoke with Huska about how HP would do the investigation. Dunn asked him to describe the methodology. He and his team explained that they engaged the services of an outside organization that worked almost exclusively with HP and that complied with HP policy. Dunn accepted Huska's recommendations on how to do the investigation.

20. Dunn had three or four conversations with outside investigative consultant Ron DeLia. She wanted to gauge the extent to which this kind of investigation was common and the experience level of his group in doing such investigations. She also wanted to ascertain their level of commitment to conducting the investigation legally.

21. At the time it appeared that many reporters had high level sources at HP and were writing about Board business. DeLia told her that the investigation would involve "relationship mapping" to determine connections and see who may be natural conduits of inside information to the reporters. DeLia said that his group would determine the relationships by doing internet searches, looking at college alumni records, and the like. DeLia's group did most of the work for the 2005 Investigation.

22. DeLia reported to Huska, but Huska was not intensely involved in the 2005 Investigation – he focused on HP global security generally. Partly as a result of that, in the first few weeks of the 2005 Investigation DeLia updated Dunn directly through email reports.

23. Dunn emphasized that she did not independently retain anyone to assist with the 2005 Investigation. She did not use anyone that was not part of the normal HP procedures for investigating security breaches. Huska essentially told Dunn to consider DeLia to be an insider at HP.

24. As the Kona I Investigation started to "peter out," the Board learned of more leaks to the press.

C. Pretexting

25. Dunn reported that she was not familiar with the word "pretexting" prior to reading it in Larry Sonsini's email to Perkins a few weeks ago. Dunn did not know whether the Kona I

Investigation involved any pretexting. In response to her query on the most effective way to find out who talked to the reporters, DeLia said they could try to match up calls from directors to reporters, or *vice versa*. Dunn said that DeLia told her such information was basically "publicly available." DeLia said that one can call the phone company and get the information. Dunn did not ask how exactly he obtained these records.

26. Schatz explained that DeLia believes he shared with Dunn the concept of impersonation to get records. Dunn said she is not willing to contradict DeLia on this. She felt that he was using whatever the approved and lawful methods were that were standard in HP investigations of similar issues. She remembers him saying (in either Kona I or II) that sometimes one could obtain the records freely without pretending to be someone else. Dunn thinks it is probable that she was told that in some circumstances they may need to use false pretenses but that she was always assured the methods used were lawful and consistent with HP practices. Dunn does not recall ever asking DeLia to check with a lawyer as to the lawfulness of the 2005 Investigation.

27. Dunn said that there was never a conversation with anyone on this team where she did not "check that box" – meaning, in each conversation on the 2005 Investigation, Dunn asked DeLia and others to confirm to her that everything was lawful and within HP policy.

28. Dunn recalled having a meeting in mid July 2005 at HP in Palo Alto (it was the only physical meeting she attended). The purpose of the meeting was more or less to obtain a status report on the investigation. Dunn asked at the meeting that management confirm that the steps taken were legal and in compliance with HP policy. Baskins said, yes, and mentioned that the team had received a third-party legal sign off on the methods.

29. Dunn said she was never told that social security numbers or portions of social security numbers might have been used in the investigation.

30. Dunn was not aware that one method for retrieving phone records entails the callers pretending they are someone else. Dunn thought that the investigators were able to get the information just because of the administrative sloppiness of the phone carriers.

31. Dunn believed that the investigation was conducted lawfully and in compliance with HP policy based on her direct conversations with DeLia, Gentilucci and Huska.

32. Dunn only had one or two conversations with Gentilucci during the Kona I Investigation. She said, if she had had any inkling of doubt that the Kona I Investigation was not being conducted with integrity, she would have taken action.

D. Kona I Findings

33. The Kona I Investigation did not reach any conclusion on the source of the leaks.

IV. Kona II (2006 Investigation)

A. Initiation

34. Asked who ordered whom to initiate Kona II, Dunn replied that nobody authorized the Kona II investigation. From her standpoint, the leak investigation was ongoing from March 2005 and that the terms "Kona I" and "Kona II" are misleading. It was one ongoing investigation. Dunn thought her authorization came from the start when this investigation began.

35. Dunn saw a CNET headline on her "Google Alert" that referenced information from an HP Board meeting. Shortly after the January 2006 leak, Dunn sent an email to the Board indicating that a serious leak had occurred and said we will do what we can to find the source.

36. Mark Hurd was also aware of the headline. Everyone at HP who saw it was outraged about the story. This was one of a series of stories. Hurd was outraged. He told Dunn if she would not pursue this leak then he would begin the investigation because such publication of inside information indicated a management problem and he could not run a company this way. . Hurd and Dunn agreed that they would "tag team" on the investigation.

37. Dunn told Baskins the work to date had not yielded any result and asked her whether the investigation should still be done by HP. Baskins said we could "crank it up" and that HP had a very good team of people under her generally authority. Baskins introduced Dunn to Hunsaker. Hunsaker said his group would supervise the outside investigation firm.

38. Dunn recalled revalidating the legality of any investigation methods in the initial discussion. Dunn and Baskins both made the request to revalidate legality.

39. In a March executive session, Dunn informed the Board that the leak investigation was still underway but not complete.

40. Dunn recalled that the investigative team wanted to find out if the Directors' phone records included calls to or from certain reporters. Hunsaker explained to Dunn the techniques they could use to obtain this information. Relationship mapping was being done again and this time showed some fruit in that it unearthed a relationship between CNET and Keyworth. Another approach involved doing a "stake out" (surveillance) to see if Keyworth had coffee or other contact with the reporter. Hunsaker said this method would be expensive. Dunn does not recall saying yes or no to the approach. Dunn wanted to know what would be successful, as well as legal and ethical.

B. Pretexting

41. Hunsaker told Dunn that phone records were generally but not always accessible. It took time to compile them—"pick and shovel work."

42. Dunn never heard the word pretexting or got any sense that there was "fraudulent behavior" as Perkins alleges. Dunn was not aware that anyone would call up the phone company and pretend to be Keyworth or someone else. (She reiterated this statement at least one more time in the course of the interview.) She said she had no idea that the investigators might pretend to be someone they were not. Likewise, she had no idea that they might try to use Social Security Numbers or portions of them to further the pretense. If she had known about the use of Social Security Numbers, she would have sought the same assurance.

43. Dunn did not recall knowing that investigators were looking into the reporters' phone calls.

44. Dunn was aware of the plan to trace an email sent to the CNET reporter. As with other proposed techniques, she asked HP management if this technique was legal and in compliance with HP policy. Dunn did not know whether the investigation team ever tried this technique, but she recalled discussing it.

45. [With respect to the February 2, 2006 slides] Dunn generally recalled DeLia and Tony Gentilucci flying out for a meeting and slide presentation on the lawfulness of the Kona II Investigation.

46. Dunn recalls periodic reports on the Kona II Investigation. She received telephone updates on Fridays over the course of a few weeks.

47. Dunn thinks that at every meeting, she said for the record that everything being done was legal and in compliance with HP policy. Dunn repeated several times that the appropriateness and legality of the investigation permeated every discussion. She recalled discussing the appropriateness of the investigation with Hurd, but she did not mention any specific discussions with Hurd on the legality of investigation

48. Dunn recalled hearing – possibly at the February 2, 2006 meeting with the slide presentation or at the March meeting of the board – that Hunsaker consulted an outside lawyer on the legality of the methods used. Dunn recalled the March 2006 meeting in Los Angeles where phone records were discussed. At the March meeting, they discussed the preliminary findings of the investigation.

49. Dunn did not recognize Bryan Jenkins' name.

50. Dunn did not update the Board on the Kona II Investigation during the course of the investigation. Dunn believed Hurd was pushing the team to get the work done.

51. Now that she has learned of it, Dunn is concerned about the investigators using false identity to obtain information. She said she would go back to Hunsaker to ask him if he understood that the investigators were doing so.

IV. Going Forward

52. To recap the her points, Dunn emphasized that overarching concern throughout the Kona I and II Investigations was that the investigations be lawful and ethical. Given changing circumstances (and law), if the investigation were undertaken today, she would of course not authorize the use of pretexting. Dunn was aware that the investigators obtained phone records, but she did not know the technique involved the investigator's pretending to be someone else. If she had known that it involved pretending, it would have "piqued [her] curiosity" and she would have wanted to know if it was lawful and/or common. However, Dunn would not necessarily have said that this was improper if she were assured that it was legal.

53. Dunn emphasized that Kona II was a difficult leak to find, and "once that trust has been broken by the person who perpetrates the leak, one of the negative consequences is that the Board is forced to take action that under normal circumstances would have been very unappealing."

54. Dunn was under tremendous pressure from Perkins to find the leaker. (She felt pressure for not having gotten an answer in Kona I.) Perkins wanted to use lie detectors. Dunn commissioned an outside report on lie detectors that concluded it was inappropriate to use lie detectors in this context, and in light of the report Perkins backed off on this. Dunn thinks that Perkins was most aggressive when he thought the leak was by management. Dunn said she does not make a lot of unilateral decisions; her *modus operandi* is inclusiveness. So, if she had known about pretexting, she would have wanted Mark or another director to be aware of it.

55. Dunn said that the Board is very anxious to hear whether Tom's claims are valid. Dunn hopes they get some clarification about whether Tom's claims are valid.

56. Dunn said people should feel free to call her on cell: 415 [redacted]

W&R Wilson Sonsini Goodrich & Rosati
PROFESSIONAL CORPORATION

650 Page Mill Road
Palo Alto, CA 94304-1050
PHONE 650.493.9300
FAX 650.493.6811
www.wsgr.com

PRIVILEGED & CONFIDENTIAL
ATTORNEY WORK PRODUCT
REFLECTS ATTORNEY-CLIENT COMMUNICATION

MEMORANDUM

To: *HP Securities Litigation* Team

From: Bahram Seyedin-Noor and Bryan Ketroser

Date: August 28, 2006

Re: **Interview of Patricia Dunn** -- ***DRAFT*** --

On August 26, 2006, Steven Schatz, David Berger and Bahram Seyedin-Noor interviewed Patricia Dunn, Chairman of the Board of Hewlett-Packard Company ("HP" or the "Company"), via teleconference. This memorandum reflects the thoughts and impressions of Bahram Seyedin-Noor from the interview.

I. Kona I

A. Initiation of Investigation

1. Dunn stated that the following facts were not inconsistent with her recollection, but that she did not recall them specifically: she retained DeLia on April 19; the investigation initially consisted of just Dunn and DeLia; Baskins referred Dunn to Huska; and Huska referred Dunn to DeLia. Dunn said she did think that Baskins referred her to speak with Huska, indicating that Baskins was aware that some process was underway to dig into the source of the leaks.

2. Dunn said that she had worked with DeLia on a number of other matters prior to Kona I. She recalled one matter in connection with the CEO search. A standard item in looking at candidates is a full background check, including credit history. HP's Human Resources department referred Dunn to DeLia, and since Dunn was leading the search, she retained DeLia directly to do background searches on three candidates.

3. Dunn said Baskins was "fairly hands off," and not involved in the Kona I investigation in the first few weeks. Baskins thought the investigation was a confidential board matter.

4. Dunn did not believe she was undertaking the investigation "without HP help." Rather, she thought she was undertaking it in accordance with the recommendations she received from HP—specifically, Huska. Dunn was given a sensitive assignment by the Board, and did not

want to throw it into somebody else's lap. Dunn wanted to learn how an investigation like this occurred and what steps were taken. Dunn said she felt that the investigation was at all times "tethered to HP processes."

B. Apprising Management and the Board

5. Dunn said Mark Hurd first learned of the investigation soon after he joined HP on April 1, 2005. She said that she would have discussed the investigation with Hurd some time between April 1 and the May 18-20 Board meeting.

6. Dunn recalled advising the Board of an investigation during the executive session of the May 18-20 Board meeting. Hurd was not present during this session. Dunn said she would have made a high-level statement that the leak investigation was underway and continuing, and that she would let them know if she found out additional information. She told us that she never mentioned the term "Project Kona" to the Board; that was a term used by the team internally.

7. Dunn vaguely recalled the July 22 meeting at which Gentilucci and DeLia recalled giving a status report on the investigation, but did not remember whether Baskins attended. She said it makes sense that this meeting took place at the time of a Board meeting. Dunn said that there is usually a Board meeting in July on the third Thursday and Friday of the month, and that immediately after Dunn became the Chairman, they instituted a practice of having an executive session at every Board meeting. Dunn said she mentioned the investigation at every executive session.

C. Pretexting

8. Dunn did not specifically recall DeLia's June 14 report that speaks of tracing calls. Nor did Dunn recall having a June 14 conference call with DeLia and Baskins, though she stated it was entirely possible that such a call occurred, and that the participants may have discussed phone pretexting. Dunn said she generally recalled having a "touch base" every so often. She recalled talking to Baskins about the investigation in approximately the Summer of 2005, and said it was probably fair to say that Baskins was involved at the end of the process.

9. Dunn was aware that reporters' cell phones were being looked at, and thought this was standard. Her understanding was that since HP had tried and failed to uncover the source of the leaks the "gentlemanly way" by having Sonsini speak to the Directors, more aggressive measures were required, so long as they were undertaken in compliance with the law.

10. Dunn did not consider using outside counsel for the issue of pretexting. She thought DeLia was using processes that had been approved by HP and were used by HP in the normal course of business. She stated that for her to have gone outside for advice would have been to question HP's internal processes. Dunn also stated that she received repeated assurances from DeLia, whom the Company had used for many years, as to the propriety of the investigation.

11. Dunn said she would be surprised to learn that HP had used pretexting only a couple of times prior to Kona I. In other words, she was surprised to learn that DeLia may have been using techniques that were not part of HP's ordinary investigative protocol.

TAB 117

WSGR Wilson Sonsini Goodrich & Rosati
PROFESSIONAL CORPORATION

650 Page Mill Road
Palo Alto, CA 94304-1050
PHONE 650.493.9300
FAX 650.493.6811
www.wsgr.com

PRIVILEGED & CONFIDENTIAL
ATTORNEY WORK PRODUCT
REFLECTS ATTORNEY-CLIENT COMMUNICATION

MEMORANDUM

To: *HP Securities Litigation* Team

From: Bahram Seyedin-Noor and Bryan Ketroser

Date: August 25, 2006

Re: **Interview of Jim Fairbaugh** *- - DRAFT - -*

On August 25, 2006, Steven Schatz, David Berger and Bahram Seyedin-Noor interviewed Jim Fairbaugh, Director of Global Security for Hewlett-Packard Company ("HP" or the "Company"), via teleconference. This memorandum reflects the thoughts and impressions of Bahram Seyedin-Noor from the interview.

I. Background

1. Fairbaugh's email address is jim.fairbaugh@hp.com; his landline and cell phone numbers are 650-[redacted]nd 650[redacted]respectively.

2. Fairbaugh has been with HP for 22 years, and has been responsible for the Company's global security for more than five years. His division includes between 80 and 90 people, and uses third-party investigators as well. The bulk of the group's work is physical security, encompassing such elements as access control, fraud, and supply chain theft, and he also has a team that does security work for the federal government.

3. Tony Gentilucci (Manager of Global Security) oversees the day-to-day investigative processes at HP.

4. Early in the conversation, Fairbaugh asked who we represent. Steven Schatz replied that we represent HP, not any individuals involved in the Kona investigations.

II. Kona I

A. Introduction to Investigation and General Information

5. Fairbaugh remembered hearing about a leak to the press around January 2005. He thought the investigation began some time between when Carleton Fiorina left and Mark Hurd was

hired. He heard about the Kona I investigation in May, after Hurd was hired. Fairbaugh was certain that he did not hear about the investigation from Ron DeLia or Patricia Dunn.

6. Fairbaugh had a vague recollection that he was aware DeLia was leading an investigation alone for six weeks before Gentilucci became involved. Fairbaugh recalled that DeLia was engaged by either Dunn or Ann Baskins, who was also involved in Kona I. Fairbaugh thought Hurd would not have had any knowledge of DeLia, who Fairbaugh thought had done work for HP for at least five years.

7. Fairbaugh said that his team was involved in the investigation because it was one of his group's "core competencies." Gentilucci managed the investigation for the Global Security Team; Fairbaugh's role in Kona I was limited oversight.

8. Fairbaugh received periodic updates on the investigation in July and August from Gentilucci. These updates were typically relayed via telephone conversations, though Fairbaugh has two emails—from DeLia to Gentilucci—from August that he will forward to us.

B. July 22 Meeting

9. Fairbaugh was present at the July 22 meeting, and remembered the PowerPoint slides ("Slides," attached as Exh. A). He thought this was the first time that the executive team was engaged on the matter. Fairbaugh introduced DeLia and Gentilucci to the executive team.

10. Before the main meeting, Fairbaugh participated in a pre-meeting with his team members and DeLia. The main meeting was attended by his team and Baskins, Dunn and Hurd of the executive team, though Hurd was only present for part of the time.

11. Fairbaugh said that pretexting "certainly" came up during the pre-meeting, but he did not recall whether it was discussed with executives during the meeting. He recalled with certainty asking DeLia and Gentilucci during the pre-meeting whether pretexting was legal.

12. Fairbaugh stated that Slide 5, which indicated that Global Security was engaged on July 4, was consistent with his memory. *See* Exh. A, Slide 5.

C. Pretexting

13. Fairbaugh said HP was familiar with the technique of pretexting before Kona I, but did not believe HP ever employed the technique itself. Rather, he thought pretexting probably had been used by HP previously through someone like DeLia. Pretexting would be used predominantly in cases involving unauthorized disclosures to determine the identity of suspects.

14. Fairbaugh never commissioned research on pretexting or discussed it with anyone in the HP legal department. At the time of Kona I, Kevin Hunsaker was the lawyer assigned to SBC Investigations, and was therefore the in-house attorney who would have given the group advice on legal aspects of the investigation, including pretexting.

15. Fairbaugh defined pretexting as calling and having discussions with people to elicit information from them. No one ever told him what sort of information would be provided to get the target information. In particular he was not aware that pretexting would involve the use of Social Security Numbers. Fairbaugh stated, in fact, that he would be surprised if Social Security Numbers were used.

III. Kona II

16. In January 2006, after Fairbaugh received a call from Bob Sherbin saying there had been another leak, Fairbaugh turned the investigation over to Gentilucci.

17. On January 22, 2006, Gentilucci emailed Fairbaugh to tell him that Hunsaker had been engaged on the legal side.

18. Fairbaugh said that he would forward us the above email. He also said that he has an email folder with relevant emails, which he will also forward to us.

TAB 118

W&S&G&R Wilson Sonsini Goodrich & Rosati
PROFESSIONAL CORPORATION

650 Page Mill Road
Palo Alto, CA 94304-1050
PHONE 650.493.9300
FAX 650.493.6811
www.wsgr.com

PRIVILEGED & CONFIDENTIAL
ATTORNEY WORK PRODUCT
REFLECTS ATTORNEY-CLIENT COMMUNICATION

MEMORANDUM

To: *HP Securities Litigation Team*

From: Bahram Seyedin-Noor and Trevor Lain

Date: August 21, 2006

Re: **Interviews of Kevin Hunsaker** *- - DRAFT - -*

On August 9, 2006, Steven M. Schatz and Bahram Seyedin-Noor interviewed Kevin Hunsaker of Hewlett-Packard Company ("HP" or the "Company") over the course of two teleconference calls. The first call occurred at 3:00 PM and also present during that call were John Kiernan, a partner with the law firm Bonner Kiernan Trebach & Crociata LLP , and Ann Baskins, HP's General Counsel. Bahram Seyedin-Noor conducted follow-up teleconference interviews with Hunsaker on August 9, 14, 15, 16 and 18, 2006. The purpose of the interviews was to ascertain the steps HP took in the Kona II leak investigation, for which an outside investigator used "pretexting" to obtain the telephone records of certain persons. This memorandum reflects the thoughts and impressions of Seyedin-Noor from the interviews.

I. Background

1. Kevin Hunsaker is a Senior Counsel in the HP Legal Department. Hunsaker assumed his relatively new role in or around mid April. (That was after the most active phase of the Kona II Investigation.) Hunsaker's contact information is as follows: kevin.hunsaker@hp.com; (w) 650[redacted]; (c) 650[redacted]

2. Hunsaker said he has done "hundreds" of investigations, but the Kona II investigation was the first one he directed that involved the use of "pretexting."

3. Hunsaker said that he directed the investigation into the leak at the instruction of HP Chairperson Patricia Dunn. Ann Baskins was also aware of investigation.

4. Hunsaker provided the following list of individuals who participated in or are otherwise connected with the Kona II Investigation:

Name	Title	Solid Line Report
Fred Adler	Information Security Investigator, IT Security Investigations	
Jim Fairbaugh	Global Security Director—REWS: real estate and workplace services	Oversees Gentilucci and Huska
Tony Gentilucci	HP's manager of global security investigations, located in Boston	Reports to Fairbaugh
Kevin Huska	Manager, (GEPP) Global Employee Protection Program – *Not an attorney*	Reports to Fairbaugh; he is a peer with Gentilucci
Denis Lynch	HP Global Security	Reports to Huska in GEPP, has relocated to East Coast
Vince Nye	Senior Investigator, HP Global Security Investigations	Reports to Gentilucci
Tim O'Neill	Director of IT Security Incident Management, HP IT Security	
Bob Sherbin	HP's head of Public Relations ("PR")	

II. Kona II: First Steps

A. Investigation Team

5. Hunsaker found out on the Friday before Monday, January 23, 2006 that an article would be published with information about HP's latest Board meeting. According to Hunsaker, CNET reporter Tom Krazit contacted Sherbin and informed him that CNET was about to publish an article about five issues discussed at last HP Board meeting, including the issue of leaks relating to Carleton Fiorina's departure, the WFR announcement, and the hiring of Mark Hurd. After the call from Krazit, Sherbin emailed Bob Fairbaugh and Tony Gentilucci.

6. Within an hour of learning of the potential leak, Hunsaker informed Ann Baskins.

7. Gentilucci then contacted Hunsaker since he is the attorney on the global "SBC" team, which oversees investigations of violations of standards of business conduct. Gentilucci informed Hunsaker about the leak and they discussed undertaking a preliminary investigation.

8. Hunsaker forwarded Gentilucci's email to Baskins and asked whether she wanted him to direct the investigation, and stated that the investigation needed to be privileged. Baskins responded to Hunsaker and said she had talked with HP Board Chairperson Patricia Dunn and Mark Hurd and indicated that that is how they wanted it handled. Hunsaker talked with Baskin first thing Monday morning.

9. Hunsaker retained as a consultant an outside investigator named Ron DeLia, who is based in Massachusetts. DeLia is a licensed investigator who has access to certain databases of information.

10. Hunsaker assembled an investigation team ("Team") first thing Monday morning. In addition to himself, Gentilucci and DeLia, Hunsaker also selected for the Team: Vince Nye, of HP's Global Security Investigations, who reports to Gentilucci, and Fred Adler, of HP's IT Security, who assisted by imaging hard drives, pulling emails and pulling HP phone records.

B. The Preliminary Investigation

11. Hunsaker's team also pulled documents from the Board meeting immediately preceding the leak, and began interviewing relevant people.

12. The Team started by pulling the information and pulling PowerPoint presentations used at the prior Board meeting. Hunsaker received the PowerPoint presentations from Rosemary Thomas, who serves as HP's liaison to the Board, and one of whose tasks is posting materials to the Board Website before Board meetings. Charles Charnas provided one PowerPoint presentation Thomas did not have.

13. In conducting the preliminary investigation, the Team obtained details on the hotel information for Board meetings, including room charges. They also researched certain reporters on the Internet, in order to determine how frequently they wrote about HP, what they wrote, etc., and obtained their contact information from the HP Public Relations group and the Internet.

14. The Team discovered that one of the persons in HP's PR department, Brigida Bergkamp, had been looking at CNET and researching its articles. However, the Team ultimately determined that PR was not the source of the leak, but did find that the PR group had a lax policy on communicating with the press.

15. The Team also pulled every article that the CNET reporter Dawn Kawamoto had ever written and concluded that leaks to Dawn were all by the same director.

16. Hunsaker quickly concluded that the leak came from either the Executive Council or the Board of Directors. Thus, during the first few days of the preliminary investigation, Hunsaker interviewed Dunn, Baskins, Wayman, and Charnas. Based on information Hunsaker received from these interviews, he started pulling phone records on certain Board members that were identified

early on as potential "leakers," including Dr. George Keyworth, Richard Hackborn, Thomas Perkins, Dunn, and Lucille Salhany. Hunsaker said that Salhany quickly fell out as a potential suspect.

17. Hunsaker gave instructions to DeLia to find telephone numbers for the various reporters in whom the Team was interested. Hunsaker determined the phone numbers for some of the reporters from the HP Public Relations ("PR") group and from online sources. These numbers were checked against phone records for every member of the Executive Council. Then he pulled emails and phone records of the Executive Counsel and members of the Board of Directors and checked for emails or calls to or from those reporters. He also had the hard drives of every member of the Executive Council imaged. He added that individuals were not told that their computers were being monitored. (HP's standards of business conduct and business policies make clear that any information on HP computers and servers belongs to the Company and is viewable by the Company at its discretion.)

18. Hunsaker said that within the first 10 – 14 days of the investigation, he reviewed all of the PowerPoint slides and concluded that of the six items leaked, only two could be garnered from the slides, and therefore the leaker had to have been physically present at the Board meeting.

19. Hunsaker briefed Baskins and Dunn on the status of the investigation, the former every two days and the latter weekly.

20. The Team initiated several attempts to determine the identity of the leaker. One involved sending an attachment to the CNET reporter with an attachment purportedly containing internal HP information. The Team hoped the reporter would verify the contents of the attachment with her internal source. When she did this, software embedded in the attachment would transmit the web address of the source back to the Team. The Team sent the email but never received any response. Fred Adler (HP IT Security) suspects that the email did not make it past the CNET firewall.

III. Pretexting to Obtain Information on Phone Calls

A. Method

21. The Team decided to obtain the telephone records for select reporters and certain persons present at the Board meeting. Among the reporters whose records were checked were Tom Kravitz, Pui-Wing Tam, Dawn Kawamoto.

22. To get the records, DeLia retained a Florida company, Action Research Group ("ARG") that he has used for the last 18 years. DeLia contacted the company and gave them the telephone numbers and names of the persons whose records he sought, and indicated that he wanted the telephone records for the individuals. Hunsaker never spoke directly with ARG's investigators. Rather, he relied on DeLia's communications with them.

30. If simply asking the operator does not work, and the operator asked for the last four digits of the customer's social security number ("SSN"), then the pretexter would provide the operator with the SSN. Hunsaker said that he did not give DeLia any person's SSN, but added that DeLia as a licensed investigator has access to such information. (On August 14, 2006, Hunsaker said that neither he nor any other HP employee provide social security numbers to Ron or his investigators. During that call he added that, in fact, he was not aware if anyone used SSNs in obtaining phone records.

31. Hunsaker said he believes that the investigators may provide the last four digits of the customer's SSN when asked by the phone carrier. DeLia told him that there is a "hierarchy" of information the investigators would pass on to the phone operator.

32. No one specifically asked Kiernan to look at the issue of using SSNs to obtain phone records. In addition, no one researched that issue. Hunsaker asked DeLia how the investigators would know the customer's SSN. DeLia said they obtained the SSN from a proprietary database to which private investigators have access. Hunsaker never discussed with DeLia specific instances where SSNs were used.

C. May 24, 2006 Investigation Report

33. Hunsaker explained that "covert intelligence" (5/24/06 Investigative Report at 4): refers to the operation of sending Kawamoto the email with attachment and related emails.

34. "Surveillance activity" (5/24/06 Investigative Report at 4) refers to the following actions:

- In the first ten days of the investigation HP surveilled Keyworth at the University of Colorado, where he was present for a speaking engagement. Specifically, an agent attended the presentation and later asked a camera person recording the talk for a copy of the tape. The idea was to see who Keyworth interacted with, etc. The Team thought it was possible Kawamoto might attend the talk.

- HP also surveilled Keyworth at his home on the day that the email attachment was sent to Kawamoto. Two former FBI agents that DeLia and Gentilucci knew surveilled his home by sitting in a car outside the house and watching. They did not use listening devises, and they made no audio or video recording. They simply watched him and followed his actions.

- The Investigation Team may also have surveilled Perkins at a presentation; Hunsaker would have to check their records to be certain.

- Finally, the Investigation Team also reviewed video from HP cameras. HP phone records showed the placing of a number of calls from executive conference rooms to Kawamoto or Tam during the relevant time frame. Therefore the Team pulled tapes monitoring those conference rooms (during the period of the calls) to see who had placed the calls. One call was made by Hurd and Sherbin; another by Livermore and another PR person; and a third by Shane Robison. The Team later concluded these were prescheduled calls on specific topics with the reporters—and not leaks.

IV. Inquiries into the Legality of Pretexting

35. Hunsaker clearly understood that undertaking a lawful investigation was a priority.

36. Hunsaker remembers an initial interview of and discussion with Dunn on Thursday, February 2 at which he made a slide presentation. One of the thrusts of his slide presentation was that the Team would do everything to determine the identity of the leaker so long as it was lawful. At some point in the investigation, and possibly during the same slide presentation, he also discussed with Dunn the actual tactic of pretexting. (Hunsaker later said he did not remember whether he discussed the pretense aspect of pretexting with Dunn.)

37. With respect to Baskins, Hunsaker did not recall discussing the use of pretexting with her until later – that is, after he had confirmed with DeLia the legality of using pretexting and some pretexting had already been done.

38. During the Team's first discussion of pretexting, two members, Nye and Adler, had not done an investigation of this nature and questioned the method's legality. At the time, Hunsaker himself did not know whether the method was legal because he had not done any research on the issue. DeLia then said that his company used the method quite a lot and had spoken to attorneys and determined that it was lawful.

39. Hunsaker researched the legality of pretexting in the first few weeks of the investigation after Nye and Adler expressed concern about the legality of pretexting. Hunsaker also asked DeLia at that time to confirm the method's legality with the Florida investigators.

40. As to why Hunsaker himself looked into the question of whether pretexting was legal, Hunsaker said that it was not because of any prompting by Dunn but because he himself wanted to make sure that the investigation was lawful. He said that the Team had also considered (and rejected) methods that were not lawful (such as monitoring public discussions by the relevant individuals). HP has its own code of ethical conduct concerning surreptitious surveillance, which is available online at www.HP.com (type: "standards business conduct").

41. Asked about the scope of his research, Hunsaker indicated that he did about an hour's worth of online research on the legality of pretexting. In the course of that research, he came across the Verizon lawsuit and checked if they had cited any statutes. According to Hunsaker, Verizon had filed a civil violation of privacy lawsuit against an online company that offered private individuals' cell phone information for sale. He also reviewed commentary on the issue—including from a New York Senator who had commented that it was unlawful for financial information but not for telephone information.

42. One month into the investigation, the issue of pretexting came up again when Dunn and Baskins asked him to confirm the legality of the investigative method during a Friday phone call before the March Board meeting in Los Angeles. Dunn and Baskins wanted him to confirm the method's legality in case Hurd had any concerns during the presentation in Los Angeles. Hunsaker said yes, based on his previous discussions with DeLia and on his own preliminary research. But, he said, he would look further into it.

43. Pursuant to the conversation with Dunn and Baskins, Hunsaker made a March 15 call to Kiernan. Hunsaker does not believe HP paid Kiernan for legal advice. Both Gentilucci and DeLia have longstanding relationships with Kiernan on personal and professional bases. Hunsaker did not know who paid Kiernan's bill.

44. Hunsaker instructed Gentilucci to contact attorney John Kiernan concerning the legality of pretexting as an investigative method. Kiernan was known as one of the main attorneys who oversaw the investigation into whether a company named ABB violated the Foreign Corrupt Practices Act. Gentilucci duly talked with Kiernan but Hunsaker was not on the call. According to Hunsaker, Kiernan told Gentilucci that pretexting was lawful and that his firm had researched the issue just in the last year (2005), and added he would have someone in his office confirm the method's legality. Then, after someone in his office did the research, Kiernan called Gentilucci back and confirmed the legality.

45. Hunsaker reported back to Dunn and Baskins that he had reconfirmed the legality of the method. Hunsaker said that he thinks he had emailed Dunn and Baskins about this as well. [Later, Hunsaker forwarded Bahram Seyedin-Noor an email, dated May 1, 2006 (attached as Exh. A), that he had sent to Baskins on this issue, but not Dunn.]

46. Hunsaker said that he also received an email from DeLia that included DeLia's analysis on the legality of pretexting.

V. Perkin's Allegations re AT&T Account

47. Hunsaker was aware of an email from Perkins complaining that someone had broken into his AT&T online cell phone account. Hunsaker insisted that it was <u>not</u> DeLia's group, because, he said, all they do is pick up a phone and call the carrier. Hunsaker added that DeLia's group did not set up an account or anything similar.

48. According to Hunsaker, DeLia talked directly to the people who did the actual calls to confirm that all the pretexter did was call the operator by phone and gather information that way, and NOT by breaking into any online account as Perkins stated.

VI. End of Kona II Investigation and the HP Team's Conclusion

49. The Kona II Investigation technically ended with the interview of Keyworth at the May 2006 Board meeting, because that was the last investigative act. But from early April through

May, that interview was basically all that remained. After the March 11 report, Hunsaker's team checked into a couple of minor issues, but the Kona II Investigation was already fundamentally complete.

50. Based on Kawamoto's articles and the interviews done as part of the investigation, the Team concluded that the leaker was Keyworth. The records the Team obtained showed phone calls made from Kawamoto's cell phone to Keyworth's home phone just before the article was published in January and another call a few weeks later from Keyworth's cell to Kawamoto's direct office number. DeLia then had his source at the pretexting company find out the length of these calls. The first call was one minute, the second was ten minutes.

51. Hunsaker did not personally interview Keyworth. Hunsaker and Gentilucci flew down to the annual shareholder and Board meeting in Los Angeles in March 2006, and briefed Dunn and the others on the results of the investigation. At that meeting, the they discussed interviewing Keyworth. Ultimately, Bob Ryan interviewed of Keyworth right before the May 2006 Board meeting.

650 Page Mill Road
Palo Alto, CA 94304-1050
PHONE 650.493.9300
FAX 650.493.6811
www.wsgr.com

W&R Wilson Sonsini Goodrich & Rosati
PROFESSIONAL CORPORATION

PRIVILEGED & CONFIDENTIAL
ATTORNEY WORK PRODUCT
REFLECTS ATTORNEY-CLIENT COMMUNICATION

MEMORANDUM

To: *HP Securities Litigation Team*

From: Bahram Seyedin-Noor

Date: August 22, 2006

Re: **Interview of Kevin Hunsaker** *--DRAFT--*

On August 22, 2006, David Berger and I interviewed Kevin Hunsaker of Hewlett-Packard Company ("HP" or the "Company") regarding a recent phone call from the California Attorney General's (the "AG") office to Ann Baskins, General Counsel of HP, regarding Mr. Perkins' allegations that someone tried to hack his AT&T phone records.[1] This memorandum reflects my thoughts and impressions from the interview.

I. Document Preservation

1. David instructed Hunsaker to make certain he preserves all documents that could potentially relate to the Kona investigations or pretexting done in those investigations. Hunsaker confirmed he would put these aside and assure their safe-keeping.

II. Perkins' Allegations

A. HP not involved

2. Hunsaker said he has "done everything in [his] power" to research HP's potential involvement in the hacking described in the AT&T letter to Perkins and found no evidence of involvement whatsoever. Hunsaker's efforts included talking directly to Ron DeLia, the outside consultant that coordinated the pretexting in the Kona investigations.

B. Documents

---

[1] AT&T has sent Perkins a letter describing attempts by third parties to access his phone records online. It appears that Perkins may have contacted the California Attorney General and informed them that this hacking was the work of HP or its investigators as part of the Kona II investigation.

3. To the extent the AG's office may seek documents from the Kona investigation, Hunsaker said the documents in his possession are likely privileged because they were either created by him or at his discretion.

4. Hunsaker said he has some documents relating to the legality of pretexting, including emails or a memo he may have sent to Baskins.

5. Hunsaker also has two spreadsheets prepared by DeLia regarding phone calls from Perkins' home phone number (not his cell).

WSGR Wilson Sonsini Goodrich & Rosati
PROFESSIONAL CORPORATION

650 Page Mill Road
Palo Alto, CA 94304-1050
PHONE 650.493.9300
FAX 650.493.6811
www.wsgr.com

PRIVILEGED & CONFIDENTIAL
ATTORNEY WORK PRODUCT
REFLECTS ATTORNEY-CLIENT COMMUNICATION

MEMORANDUM

To: *HP Securities Litigation* Team

From: Bahram Seyedin-Noor and Bryan Ketroser

Date: August 25, 2006

Re: **Interview of Kevin Hunsaker** *- - DRAFT - -*

On August 25, 2006, Steven Schatz, David Berger and Bahram Seyedin-Noor interviewed Kevin Hunsaker, Senior Counsel for Hewlett-Packard Company ("HP" or the "Company"), via teleconference. This memorandum reflects the thoughts and impressions of Bahram Seyedin-Noor from the interview.

I. Kona I

1. Hunsaker did not even know about the Kona I investigation until Kona II.

II. Pretexting

2. Hunsaker first learned that HP had used pretexting to obtain phone records in July 2005 in connection with an unrelated HP investigation. One of the subjects of that investigation was going through a messy divorce, and his attorney contacted Hunsaker, claiming that HP had attempted to change his PIN in order to access his voicemail. Hunsaker's team told him they had not altered the subject's PIN or voicemail, but had used pretexting to obtain phone information about the subject.

3. Hunsaker did not do any research regarding pretexting until the first week or two of the Kona II investigation.

4. Hunsaker had been supporting the Global Standards of Business Conduct team since 2003, and therefore, if there had been a question about pretexting during a past investigation, they should have contacted Hunsaker. Hunsaker said that his old boss was Lyle Keating.

TAB 119

WSGR Wilson Sonsini Goodrich & Rosati
PROFESSIONAL CORPORATION

650 Page Mill Road
Palo Alto, CA 94304-1050
PHONE 650.493.9300
FAX 650.493.6811
www.wsgr.com

PRIVILEGED & CONFIDENTIAL
ATTORNEY WORK PRODUCT
REFLECTS ATTORNEY-CLIENT COMMUNICATION

MEMORANDUM

To: *HP Securities Litigation* Team

From: Bahram Seyedin-Noor and Trevor Lain

Date: August 14, 2006

Re: **Interview of Tony Gentilucci** -- ***DRAFT*** --

On August 10, 2006, Steven M. Schatz and Bahram Seyedin-Noor interviewed Tony Gentilucci, Manager, Global Security Investigations of Hewlett-Packard Company ("HP" or the "Company"), via teleconference. This memorandum reflects the thoughts and impressions of Bahram Seyedin-Noor from the call.

I. Background

1. Gentilucci is Manager of HP's Global Security Investigations. He said he has been with HP since March 1999. Prior to that date he was with Compaq and Digital Equip Corp.

2. Gentilucci provided his contact information, including his email address (tony.gentilucci@hp.com) and his cell phone number [redacted]

II. Pretexting

3. Gentilucci indicated that he has conducted probably thousands of investigations. He said that pretexting is done primarily through outside agents. He added that pretexting is a common investigative methodology. As an example, he said that recently he retained the services of a third-party individual to use pretexting to quickly obtain information about someone, though, he added, it was not necessarily to get phone records.

4. Aside from phone records, Gentilucci said he does not recall ever asking HP Legal for guidance on pretexting. Gentilucci said he has his own investigation guidelines, and pretexting is not covered.

III. Kona I (2005 Investigation)

A. Background

Tony Gentilucci
August 14, 2006
Page 2

5. On April 19, 2005 Patricia Dunn retained Ron DeLia, an outside investigator and consultant, because of the sensitivity of the investigation; the leaks appeared to be coming out of the top levels of HP. DeLia started the work and realized that he needed HP investigative assistance to properly investigate it. Thus a decision was made in early July 2005 to use Global Security Investigations to assist DeLia in his investigation.

6. The 2005 Investigation involved leaks concerning Carleton Fiorina's termination as well as Mark Hurd's joining HP and layoffs. The bulk of leaks occurred early in the year and continued into July 2005. DeLia gave Gentilucci a full briefing in Gentilucci's office in Cambridge in early July 2005. Gentilucci knew at that time that DeLia was using pretexting to get phone records.

B. Pretexting

7. During that investigation Gentilucci asked DeLia to ensure legality of the process. Gentilucci said that DeLia did extensive research. He added that DeLia touched base with attorney John Kiernan, and that according to DeLia's and Kiernan's assessment, the use of pretexting was legal. Gentilucci said he wanted this assurance before meeting with Ann Baskins and Mark Hurd in mid July 2005.

8. Gentilucci cannot recall any specific communications before mid July 2005 with Dunn, Baskins or Hurd about the use of pretexting. He thinks DeLia told him that he discussed pretexting with Dunn before July 2005.

9. With respect to the mid July 2005 meeting, Gentilucci recalls showing Baskins, Jim Fairbaugh (HP Global Security), Bob Sherbin (HP's Head of Public Relations), Hurd, Dunn, and DeLia slides about the methodology and facts gathered. He added that Sherbin may not have been privy to all of this. He said that the issue of obtaining phone records came up at this meeting. But, Gentilucci does not think details of pretexting were discussed. Gentilucci does not recall whether the slides referenced lawfulness or whether anyone at the meeting specifically asked about the lawfulness of the techniques he discussed.

10. Gentilucci recalled that in the July 2005 meeting other options for fact gathering were also discussed, including lie-detectors, which Gentilucci said he did not recommend. Gentilucci recalled that there were "challenges to the investigation" because information was difficult to obtain, and it would take time because his group had to adhere to HP procedures. He recalled a slide stating "Challenges," and remembered specifically discussing compliance with the law and adherence to HP policies. Gentilucci wanted to emphasize that point because people were anxious to get the investigation done and Gentilucci wanted them to know they were doing it the right way.

C. Kona I Findings

11. The 2005 Investigation concluded that the leakers were probably Keyworth and someone else.

12. Prior to the 2005 Investigation Gentilucci had been aware of using pretexting as an investigative practice and as an available tool but said that he never discussed the technique with anyone in HP Legal.

IV. Kona II (2006 Investigation)

A. Initiation

13. On January 20, 2006 the Company received word of leak to CNET. During that weekend Kevin Hunsaker pulled together a team to do an investigation.

14. Gentilucci and Hunsaker met attorney John Kiernan in Boston in December 2005, where Hunsaker was a speaker and Kiernan was a guest speaker on Sarbanes-Oxley.

B. Pretexting

15. Gentilucci recalled bringing Hunsaker up to speed on the 2005 Investigation and the methodology of pretexting. Hunsaker asked Gentilucci and DeLia about the legality of pretexting. DeLia walked through the law in detail and explained the track record of the investigative agency he used. He recalled DeLia saying that this agency had not been sued for that practice. DeLia mentioned Kiernan's prior research, and Gentilucci believed DeLia also mentioned discussing pretexting with Baskins during the 2005 Investigation. Gentilucci said he has received emails from DeLia about pretexting.

16. After this meeting Hunsaker asked Gentilucci to touch base with Kiernan to make sure that pretexting was still legal. (Gentilucci recalled also receiving emails from DeLia on this topic.) Gentilucci said he called Kiernan while the latter was skiing and Kiernan said he would have someone research the issue. Gentilucci recalled being at Logan airport in Boston with DeLia and getting a call from Kiernan's paralegal, who gave an update in which she said she could not find additional lawsuits or criminal charges to indicate that pretexting was (had become) illegal. Gentilucci recalled talking to Hunsaker either from the airport or after coming to Palo Alto about what he learned from Kiernan's paralegal.

17. Gentilucci said he and DeLia were at the [SFO] airport in late January or early February to meet with Dunn about the 2006 Investigation. Gentilucci said he had not spoken with Baskins or Dunn before flying out [from Massachusetts].

18. Gentilucci said that once he arrived in Palo Alto, DeLia, Hunsaker, Fred Adler (HP IT Security), Vince Nye (HP Global Security Investigations) and he met with Dunn to give her an update on the 2006 Investigation. Gentilucci presented slides to Dunn, which he said probably mentioned phone records. He did not recall any discussion of pretexting at this meeting – although it is possible that it was discussed.

19. There was a lot of pressure to get the 2006 Investigation done. Gentilucci recalled that during the week of his visit to Palo Alto, Baskins did a "process check" and wanted to review the investigating team's recommendations, and the investigative process, etc., with Bryan Jenkins, who, Gentilucci said, is a security consultant to HP and others. Gentilucci welcomed that "process check," though, he added, some people may have been taken aback by it.

20. Bryan Jenkins was with Kroll Associates in the past. Hunsaker met with Jenkins and reviewed the investigation and the methodology used. Gentilucci thought he recalled that Hunsaker and Jenkins discussed the pretext methodology and that Baskins was present. Hunsaker came back after the meeting and said everything was on target. Gentilucci added that Jenkins is a retained security consultant for the crisis management team.

21. Gentilucci then discussed an HP Board meeting in Los Angeles around March 15, 2006 where Gentilucci and his team presented their findings from the 2006 Investigation. He said that present at the meeting at the Century City Hyatt were Hurd, Baskins, Dunn, Hunsaker, and DeLia. Hunsaker was presenting and DeLia and Gentilucci were there to support the presentation. The conclusion from the 2006 Investigation was that Keyworth was the source of the leak. Gentilucci did not recall topic of legality ever being raised at the meeting. He said the meeting lasted about an hour and ten minutes, but that pretexting not discussed at that meeting. He said he believed that next step was to discuss the results with Larry Sonsini.

22. Gentilucci said that during the next Board meeting, he and Hunsaker were in Switzerland. Gentilucci said he was not sure what happened at that meeting, other than that Thomas Perkins resigned. Sometime after that Board meeting, the legality of pretexting came up. He said after that there was more follow up research with DeLia on the issue of pretexting and the same conclusion was reached, although, he said, the law is changing.

23. In sum, Gentilucci said, he has had conversations about pretexting in 2006 with Kiernan, DeLia, Hunsaker, and Kiernan's paralegal. He said he has had no conversations on the legality of pretexting with Baskins, Dunn or Hurd. He reiterated that the specific discussion with Dunn, Hurd and Baskins in mid July 2005 was about conducting the 2005 Investigation legally.

IV. Going Forward

24. Gentilucci would not use pretexting now because he understands from DeLia's research that some States have now banned pretexting as a means to access telephone records.

650 Page Mill Road
Palo Alto, CA 94304-1050
PHONE 650.493.9300
FAX 650.493.6811
www.wsgr.com

WSGR Wilson Sonsini Goodrich & Rosati
PROFESSIONAL CORPORATION

PRIVILEGED & CONFIDENTIAL
ATTORNEY WORK PRODUCT
REFLECTS ATTORNEY-CLIENT COMMUNICATION

MEMORANDUM

To: *HP Securities Litigation* Team

From: Bahram Seyedin-Noor and Bryan Ketroser

Date: August 30, 2006

Re: **Interview of Tony Gentilucci** *- - DRAFT - -*

On August 26, 2006, Steven Schatz, David Berger and Bahram Seyedin-Noor interviewed Tony Gentilucci, Manager, Global Security Investigations for Hewlett-Packard Company ("HP" or the "Company"), via teleconference. On August 29, Gentilucci sent the participants an email memorandum (the "Memo") discussing some of the issues raised during the interview, as well as seven email attachments.[1] This memorandum reflects the thoughts and impressions of Bahram Seyedin-Noor from the interview, as well as the contents of Gentilucci's email memo and its attachments.

I. Background

1. Gentilucci has been working with HP for seven-and-a-half years. Prior to the HP-Compaq merger, he was Manager of Corporate Investigations for Compaq. Before that, he was Manager of Global Investigations for Digital Equipment Corporation.

2. Gentilucci approves the bills submitted by Ron DeLia, of Security Outsourcing Solutions (SOS). He thought DeLia charged between $100K and $150K for Kona I. Gentilucci said that Action Research Group (ARG) billed DeLia directly, and that he never saw their bills. He said he would send us the billing records for DeLia and/or work orders.

3. Gentilucci's cell phone number is: [redacted]

II. Kona I

A. Introduction to Investigation and General Information

4. Around March 2005, Gentilucci's manager, Jim Fairbaugh, and/or DeLia informed Gentilucci that DeLia was doing investigative work for Patricia Dunn. *See* Exh. A. The work—due

---

[1] Gentilucci's Memo and attachments are attached to this memo as Exhibits A-H.

diligence investigations on candidates for senior executive positions after Mark Hurd's arrival—was very time sensitive, and Gentilucci needed to know that DeLia was going to be billing his group, Global Security Investigations. In his Memo, Gentilucci added that he thought he did not know the details of the backgrounds at the time, as they were deemed by Dunn to be extremely confidential. He also added that Fairbaugh concurred that his department would pick up the costs of the investigation. *See* Exh. H.

5. Gentilucci thought that his group had recommended DeLia's company to Dunn, and had done so because of its high quality work product, competitive rates, and excellent track record with a number of the Global Security teams.

6. Gentilucci's Memo stated that he thought he first became aware of a separate "sensitive investigation" being conducted by DeLia on behalf of Dunn on or about May 5, 2005. Gentilucci referenced an email, which he understood as indicating that DeLia spoke to Fairbaugh about several special projects, including both the background work mentioned above and "another sensitive investigation that was ongoing." Exh. B. Gentilucci thought Fairbaugh did not know the nature of the Kona investigation, and was instead briefed that DeLia was working on a sensitive special project for Dunn. Gentilucci said this approach was unique, but that "we" concurred it was the right thing to do for HP.

7. In late June, DeLia told Gentilucci he needed to have corporate security involved in the investigation he was doing for Dunn and Ann Baskins in order to access HP infrastructure documents. Gentilucci's understanding was that Dunn was managing the project, but Baskins was part of the investigation's management team.

8. Gentilucci was formally added to the Kona I team on or about July 7, 2005. DeLia informed him that the investigation was based on a suspicion that someone on the Board was leaking information to the media. According to the slides presented during a July 22, 2005 meeting, Global Security was engaged during the week of July 4. At the time Gentilucci was brought on, Kevin Huska, Manager of the Global Employee Protection Program was also part of the investigative team, and Jim Fairbaugh had "some knowledge" of the investigation, as indicated by an email Gentilucci received from Fairbaugh. Exh. C.

9. Gentilucci forwarded us a July 7, 2005 email string containing a draft report on the investigation from DeLia. Exh. D. Over the course of the string, the report was distributed to Dunn, Baskins, Fairbaugh, Huska and Gentilucci. Gentilucci received another draft investigative report—this time directly from DeLia—on July 15, 2005. Exh. E.

10. During the interview, Gentilucci recalled discussion of the steps that had been taken in the investigation, which included intelligence gathering (analysis of news articles and relationship mapping), media analysis, and review of phone records. Gentilucci said he was "playing catch up" until the July 22 meeting. He did not remember any other meetings with Dunn or Baskins regarding Kona I besides the July 22 meeting.

11. Although another investigation update had been scheduled for August 31, 2005, it was cancelled because, by that time, the leaks had subsided, and Gentilucci had been put on another investigation, called "On Design." Gentilucci forwarded us a draft update report he prepared and sent to Dunn, Baskins and Fairbaugh on August 8, 2005. Exh. F.

B. Pretexting

12. Gentilucci explained that pretexting is used on a daily basis for investigations, and could be something as simple as finding out if the subject of an investigation is at home.

13. Gentilucci said he understood that SOS had used pretexting in the past. He said that most of the investigations HP performs are internal, meaning that HP has access to the relevant phone records. Gentilucci thought that in some external investigations—*e.g.*, cargo fraud or electronics fraud—they may have used pretexting. He did not recall whether pretexting had been used at Compaq.

14. Gentilucci stated DeLia told him some time during the week of July 4 that pretexting was fully discussed with Dunn and Baskins in Kona I. In his Memo, Gentilucci reiterated that he recalled DeLia telling him that Dunn and Baskins approved of DeLia's recommendations regarding the overall investigation plan.[2] However, Gentilucci did not recall any direct conversations with Dunn or Baskins regarding pretexting in Kona I. In his Memo, Gentilucci said he recalled DeLia doing "extensive research" on the issue. He added that during this period, they were mostly preparing for the July 22 meeting, but were also looking at "proactive solutions" to prevent the problem from recurring in the future. *See* Exh. H (Memo).

15. Gentilucci said he was not aware of any lawyer looking into the legality of pretexting for phone records prior to Kona I. DeLia told Gentilucci that he had spoken to John Kiernan some time before April 2005 to check on pretexting's legality. Gentilucci thought that Kiernan was not DeLia's lawyer. In his Memo, Gentilucci said he recalled reviewing a memo prepared by Kiernan's law firm documenting that the process was legal.

16. Gentilucci thought he spoke with Kiernan a number of times in July 2005. For example, he recalled that around this time, he invited Kiernan to speak to his team during the team's annual "face to face" meeting in December. Kiernan has done a substantial amount of corporate governance work, and Gentilucci wanted him to speak regarding corporate governance. Kiernan did in fact present to Gentilucci's team in December 2005.

---

[2] Note that in his Memo, Gentilucci stated that the draft report he received from DeLia on June 7 was dated June 14, and that he spoke with DeLia "between this date and the 22nd." Exh. H. It is thus unclear whether Gentilucci now remembers his conversation with DeLia regarding the legality of pretexting as having taken place during the week of July 4, or some time thereafter.

17. We asked Gentilucci why HP attorneys were not consulted regarding the legality of pretexting. Gentilucci responded that the project was very time-sensitive, being driven by Dunn and Baskins (the "customers"), and that all of the work had been done and the leaks had subsided. Gentilucci said he was just double-checking pretexting's lawfulness to make sure "we were on solid ground."

18. Gentilucci did not recall pretexting being discussed at the July 22 meeting, which he said was attended by Hurd, Dunn, Baskins, DeLia, Kevin Huska, and, for a period of time, Bob Sherbin. Gentilucci did not have any direct conversations with Baskins regarding Kona I prior to July 22.

19. Gentilucci did not recall whether HP provided DeLia with anyone's Social Security numbers. He stated that HP would not have access to Board members' numbers, but would have them for employees, and stated that HP may have provided background information on HP employees to DeLia, including, possibly, media employees. Gentilucci did not know whether Social Security numbers were used during the investigation. He added that he understood investigators would use oral pretexting.

III. Kona II

A. Introduction to Investigation and General Information

20. Gentilucci recalled an initial meeting with Dunn and Kevin Hunsaker on February 2, 2006. The participants reviewed the investigation's methodologies and limitations. Dunn wanted to ensure that the investigation was done right, and that no laws or HP policies were violated.

21. Gentilucci stated that the Kona II investigation was different from the Kona I investigation because Hunsaker was driving it.

22. Gentilucci did not recall any direct discussions with Baskins during Kona II.

B. Pretexting

23. Gentilucci remembered a March 2006 meeting in Beverly Hills with Dunn, Baskins and Hurd. The participants discussed the investigation, including phone calls made by suspects, but did not discuss pretexting.

24. Gentilucci also recalled a meeting with DeLia and Hunsaker during Kona II in which the participants reviewed the findings and procedures of Kona I. Hunsaker asked if the investigation was legal and "above board." Gentilucci said there were multiple conversations on this topic, and that pursuant to Hunsaker's request, Gentilucci had Kiernan do additional research. In his Memo, Gentilucci added that Hunsaker did some of his own research as well, and emphasized that the topic

was revisited "several times on our daily case updates (telephone discussions)," but that the conclusion was that it raised no legal issues.

25. Gentilucci said he thought he gained the understanding during Kona II that Social Security Numbers were used during pretexting. However, he did not recall whether DeLia explained during the first meeting involving Gentilucci, DeLia and Hunsaker that the last four digits of a person's number were used. Generally speaking, with respect to HP employees, Gentilucci said he himself would probably pull information on such employees—possibly including Social Security Numbers—for use in an investigation.

26. Gentilucci said he asked DeLia about ARG, the Florida firm. DeLia stated that he had specifically used the firm for this kind of investigative work for an extensive period of time, and that ARG had not been sued for pretexting.

27. Gentilucci forwarded us a February 7, 2006 email he received from DeLia, in which DeLia stated that he had emailed ARG and asked whether there were any state laws prohibiting pretexting, and the company replied that: "As of right now there are no laws against pretexting. We are on top of everything going on regarding this issue and if any law were to pass we will be the first to let you know." Exh. G. Gentilucci stated the email was in response to a "process check" meant to ensure the Company was on "solid footing" regarding the legality of pretexting.

TAB 120

WSGR Wilson Sonsini Goodrich & Rosati
PROFESSIONAL CORPORATION

650 Page Mill Road
Palo Alto, CA 94304-1050
PHONE 650.493.9300
FAX 650.493.6811
www.wsgr.com

PRIVILEGED & CONFIDENTIAL
ATTORNEY WORK PRODUCT
REFLECTS ATTORNEY-CLIENT COMMUNICATION

MEMORANDUM

To: *HP Securities Litigation* Team

From: Bahram Seyedin-Noor and Bryan Ketroser

Date: August 25, 2006

Re: **Interview of Mark Hurd** *- - DRAFT - -*

On August 25, 2006, Steven Schatz, David Berger and Bahram Seyedin-Noor interviewed Mark Hurd, CEO of Hewlett-Packard Company ("HP" or the "Company"), via teleconference. This memorandum reflects the thoughts and impressions of Bahram Seyedin-Noor from the interview.

I. Background

1. Hurd began working at HP as CEO on April 1, 2006—the same day it was announced that he had been hired.

II. Kona I

A. General Information

2. Hurd knew there were leaks because the Thursday night before he was announced as HP's new CEO, Peter Burrow of Business Week called him at his home and told him that he had heard Hurd would become CEO of HP. The leaks stopped after a couple of weeks and did not resume until January 2006. In the interim, although Patricia Dunn was focused on the issue, Hurd was not.

3. Hurd had read about the leaks prior to joining HP, but did not have any conversations with anyone about them until later.

4. Hurd did not recall any discussions regarding the techniques being used in the investigation, or any specific questions by directors about investigatory methods. Nor did he recall anybody objecting to the investigation that was occurring.

5. Hurd supported Dunn, and around May 2005 he communicated to the Company that anyone leaking information would be terminated. He stated that Perkins in particular had suggested

that the leak was coming from management. Hurd told his the HP Executive Committee that anyone who leaked information would be fired.

B. July 22 Meeting

6. Hurd recalled attending a July 22 meeting that went from 2:00 p.m. to 3:00 p.m., but said he had to leave at 2:45 p.m. to catch a flight to Ohio. He said that Dunn was in the meeting as well as "external people," and that this was clearly the end of the process, not the beginning. Hurd remembered a summary of where the process was. Hurd said that Dunn was very clear that the leaks were unacceptable, and that she told the directors that there was an ongoing investigation to find the source of the leaks. Hurd was excluded from the executive session.

7. Hurd recalled there was a theory that Knowling had talked to a Business Week reporter and that Keyworth had talked to somebody else.

8. Hurd did not remember what investigative techniques were used. He said he probably knew that they were trying to get information about the reporters, but he did not remember the details, such as the particular information about the reporters to be obtained. Hurd said he did not remember any discussion regarding phone carriers at the meeting.

9. Hurd recalled thinking at one point that the people at the meeting did not know what they were talking about—that they had theories with "nothing behind them." He recalled a comment on Slide 10 of the PowerPoint presentation about what "intelligence revealed" about "BoD Member 2," as well as a chart reference "BoD Member 1" and "BoD Member 2." Hurd said that what stuck out in his mind was that these were describing the same story, and he recalled being underwhelmed by the details. To him, this "tail" to the investigation did not really reveal anything.

III. Kona II

10. The January 2006 leak included information not only about a Board meeting, but also HP's market position regarding Intel versus AMD. The leak also disclosed a false rumor about a takeover bid. These items affected the Company's stock and had securities law implications, and Hurd felt the issue was extremely serious. The leak was "as bad as it gets," in that it had lots of details and was wrong. Hurd was so upset over the issue that he thought he talked to every Board member about it, as well as Baskins.

11. Hurd remembered having a discussion with Dunn and Baskins in his office about the investigation. Dunn inquired about using HP resources to find the source of the leak. Hurd thought it was a good idea, because the Board is just as accountable as employees are with respect to policies set forth in the Standards of Business Conduct. Hurd asked Baskins whether it was legal to use HP resources thusly, and she replied that it was. Hurd said he and Dunn were in agreement that she would use HP resources and follow HP policies.

12. Hurd stated that he let "[Dunn] run with the ball" in carrying out the investigation. Hurd did not know the specific methodologies to be used.

13. Hurd did not believe the source of the leaks was a member of management. He thought he had discussions with Bob Sherbin about who the source was, and that Sherbin had strong opinions on the issue. Hurd did not recall telling anyone who he thought the source might be among the directors.

14. Hurd recalled that Pui-Wing Tam of the Wall Street Journal called at one point to validate a story. Tam told Sherbin that her source was the same as Burrow's source, which fact made Hurd very confident that the leak was coming from the Board.

IV. Pretexting

15. Hurd had never heard the term "pretexting" until recently.

16. Hurd recalled that during one meeting—probably the July 22, 2005 meeting—somebody mentioned obtaining phone record information off of the web. Hurd remembered thinking that there must be a website with such information.

17. During the March 2006 shareholder meeting at the Century Park Plaza hotel in Beverly Hills, Hurd met with Hunsaker, Dunn and others. Hunsaker was very focused on Keyworth during the meeting, and went into great detail. Hunsaker said he could not prove the source of the leaks was Keyworth, but he was close. Hunsaker explained that they had information regarding phone calls. Because Hurd had previously told Baskins that the investigation must be legal, he did not feel the need to question Hunsaker on this point.

18. Hunsaker did not mention Social Security Numbers during the March 2006 meeting, and Hurd said he would have been uncomfortable if he had known they were being used, even if it was by a third-party investigator. Hurd found out about their use only recently, from HP director Lawrence Babbio.

19. The night of the meeting with Hunsaker, Hurd had drinks with Keyworth and told him they were working very hard on discovering the source of the leaks. Although Hurd gave Keyworth an opportunity to confess, Keyworth was silent.

20. Hurd said that in his view, Dunn did precisely what one would have wanted her to in a situation like this.

TAB 121

Wilson Sonsini Goodrich & Rosati
PROFESSIONAL CORPORATION

650 Page Mill Road
Palo Alto, CA 94304-1050
PHONE 650.493.9300
FAX 650.493.6811
www.wsgr.com

PRIVILEGED & CONFIDENTIAL
ATTORNEY WORK PRODUCT
REFLECTS ATTORNEY-CLIENT COMMUNICATION

MEMORANDUM

To: *HP Securities Litigation* Team

From: Bahram Seyedin-Noor and Bryan Ketroser

Date: August 25, 2006

Re: **Interview of Kevin Huska** -- ***DRAFT*** --

On August 25, 2006, Steven Schatz, David Berger and Bahram Seyedin-Noor interviewed Kevin Huska, Global Security for Hewlett-Packard Company ("HP" or the "Company"), via teleconference. This memorandum reflects the thoughts and impressions of Bahram Seyedin-Noor from the interview.

I. Background

1. Huska, of HP Global Security, can be reached via email at kevin.huska@hp.com, or via his Madison, Wisconsin office phone at 608[redacted]

2. Huska manages the Global Employee Protection Program, which encompasses: crisis management; emergency preparedness and response; travel and special event security, and executive protection. He has six people reporting to him. One of the people to whom Huska reports is Jim Fairbaugh.

3. Huska has been with HP since 2000, prior to which time he worked at the U.S. Department of State as a special agent, analyzing terrorism. Huska is not an attorney.

II. Sonsini Investigation

4. Huska thought he first heard of the investigation into leaks by Larry Sonsini just after Spring 2005. He initially knew there was a leak following the publishing of the Wall Street Journal article by Pui-Wing Tam. Huska was not aware of the investigation in January 2005.

5. Huska recalled his team supplying the security for an off-site Board of Directors meeting that took place in San Francisco. When it was learned there was a leak relating to that meeting, there was a concern that security may have been breached. Huska noted that no press or others were present at off-site Board meeting from which information was leaked.

Kevin Huska
August 25, 2006
Page 2

III. Kona I

A. General Knowledge of the Investigation

6. In June or July 2005, Huska learned from either Fairbaugh or Tony Gentilucci that there had been a request to investigate certain leaks, and that Ron DeLia, an outside consultant, had been put on the investigation. Huska said it was not unusual to use an outside investigator. Gentilucci was in charge of Kona I, and met with Patricia Dunn and Ann Baskins. Gentilucci, who also reports to Fairbaugh, is Huska's peer.

7. Huska stated that his involvement in the Kona I investigation was primarily "keeping informed" of the investigation rather than active participation. Huska recalled discussions with Gentilucci regarding the circumstances of the Board meeting and whether Huska had any insights, and Huska remembered being asked about appropriate investigative techniques. However, Huska's team was not asked to performance surveillance or other investigative work.

8. Huska recalled attending, in an advisory capacity, a July 2005 meeting in the Executive Conference Room, which was also attended by Baskins, Gentilucci, DeLia, Dunn, and—for part of the meeting—Mark Hurd. Huska remembered a timeline chart that Dunn and Baskins presented, as well as slides. Gentilucci had told Huska that he had DeLia helping him construct the timeline.

B. Phone Records

9. Huska thought the concept of obtaining phone records was discussed at the July 2005 meeting, but did not know whether pretexting was discussed, and he believed that wire tapping was not discussed.

10. Prior to the start of the July 2005 meeting and before the Board members had arrived, Huska spoke with Gentilucci, Fairbaugh and DeLia. One topic they discussed was call records of, *inter alia*, the marketing team. Huska thought he told Fairbaugh that, as a former federal agent, he believed a subpoena would be required to obtain such records.

11. Huska did not recall any discussion regarding obtaining the phone records of officers or directors. He stated, however, that he may have been aware that there were going to be attempts to obtain phone records of individuals. Huska noted that it would not be unusual to look at records regarding HP phone lines, and to do so would have been acceptable protocol. Huska noted that while he does not have a "crisp" recollection of these events, he believes he discussed third party information with Fairbaugh.

12. Huska did not know whether pretexting was employed during Kona I, or what specific investigative techniques were used. In fact, Huska was not aware of pretexting ever being used at HP.

IV. Kona II

13. Huska thought Kevin Hunsaker had asked him to be part of the Kona II investigative team. Hunsaker asked him to sign a non-disclosure agreement after either he or one of his managers were identified as a resource for the investigation. Huska noted that he was not part of the team's daily meetings, nor was he asked for advice on how to conduct the investigation.

14. Huska thought Gentilucci had told him there had been a leak in January 2006 and had asked whether Huska knew of a Board meeting that month, to which Huska replied that there had been a meeting in Palm Springs. Huska thought his team may have been asked who attended the meeting.

15. Huska said he never received information regarding the investigative techniques that were being used, and was not aware that third party phone information was being retrieved from phone carriers via pretexting. He was not, however, surprised to learn that this information had been obtained.

16. Huska was never asked to do surveillance for the Kona II investigation.

TAB 122

WSGR Wilson Sonsini Goodrich & Rosati
PROFESSIONAL CORPORATION

650 Page Mill Road
Palo Alto, CA 94304-1050
PHONE 650.493.9300
FAX 650.493.6811
www.wsgr.com

PRIVILEGED & CONFIDENTIAL
ATTORNEY WORK PRODUCT
REFLECTS ATTORNEY-CLIENT COMMUNICATION

MEMORANDUM

To: *HP Securities Litigation* Team

From: Bahram Seyedin-Noor

Date: August 21, 2006

Re: **Interview of John Kiernan - -** ***DRAFT*** **- -**

On August 9, 2006, Steven M. Schatz and I interviewed John Kiernan, a partner at the Boston law firm Bonner Kiernan Trebach & Crociata LLP, via teleconference. Also participating on the call were Ann Baskins, General Counsel of Hewlett-Packard Company ("HP" or the "Company"), and Kevin Hunsaker, a Senior Counsel in the HP Legal Department. I conducted a follow-up interview with Kiernan on August 16, 2006, via teleconference. This memorandum reflects my thoughts and impressions from the calls.

I. Background

1. A partner at the law firm of Bonner Kiernan Trebach & Crociata LLP, Kiernan can be reached at (617)[redacted]

2. Kiernan has known Tony Gentilucci (Manager, HP Global Security Investigations) since 1980, when Gentilucci worked for First Security, one of Kiernan's clients. Tony Gentilucci later joined DEC (Digital Equipment Corp.), which also became a Kiernan client. Kiernan had done several investigations with Gentilucci before the Kona II Investigation. Kiernan forewarned that in trying to recall his conversations with Gentilucci he may "telescope" time.

3. Kiernan has also known Ron DeLia since about 1975.

II. Kona I

4. Kiernan remembers discussing pretexting with Ron DeLia in Spring 2005, but he could not recall what investigation the discussion related to.

5. Kiernan recalled subsequent conversations with DeLia concerning the parameters and legality of pretexting but he did not repeat the "legislative survey" he had done in 2005.

III. Kona II

6. Kiernan did not recall any specific discussion about the Kona II investigation – he said that, in any event, DeLia would not have revealed to him that his work was related to an investigation for HP.

7. However, Kiernan seemed to remember a call with Gentilucci and DeLia about a "leak." He said that Gentilucci asked him to talk with Ann Baskins about the Investigation, and Baskins gave him a description of the inquiry.

8. Kiernan does not believe anything improper occurred in HP's 2006 Investigation.

9. Kiernan did not bill either DeLia or Gentilucci for his legal advice on pretexting in 2005 or 2006. The request for legal advice in March 2006 came from Gentilucci (presumably on behalf of HP).

IV. Legality of Pretexting

10. In 2005, Valery Clecker, who was a law student and law clerk at Kiernan's firm at the time, did a research memo for Kiernan on the legality of pretexting. Kiernan is not sure whether he sent that report to Gentilucci or DeLia.

11. In March 2006, some time prior to March 13, Gentilucci and Kiernan discussed research into pretexting. On March 13, 2006, Kiernan's time entries show he spoke with Gentilucci again while on vacation skiing. Kiernan and Gentilucci talked again on March 15 (Kiernan was still skiing) on the topic of pretexting. Kiernan told Gentilucci he would have someone do further research.

12. Between March 15 and 24, Valery Clecker (who was by this time an attorney) did further research into pretexting and talked to Gentilucci on at least one occasion. Kiernan believes Clecker forwarded at least one case to Gentilucci on the issue of pretexting.

13. The first legislative proposals on pretexting for telephone records were made in the spring of 2005. In 2005, pretexting with financial institutions was already specifically prohibited, but no law existed banning pretexting for the purpose of obtaining telephone records.

14. There is a Massachusetts statute on privacy, but it does not prohibit specific conduct.

15. In July 2006, the state of Florida enacted laws prohibiting pretexting for telephone records. He added that Georgia and California are also changing their laws on pretexting. Finally, federal legislation on pretexting for telephone records is currently pending.

16. Kiernan believes pretexting for phone records occurs, but corporations typically "insulate" themselves by using investigators and simply asking them not to do anything "illegal" – without discussing specific techniques.

17. Kiernan is not aware of pretexting resulting in any lawsuits but has read articles on such lawsuits.

18. On the use of Social Security Numbers ("SSNs") in pretexting, Kiernan said his understanding of pretexting is very general: someone calls a telephone company pretending to be someone else and offers basic identifying information, such as an address, phone number, and name, if asked. Kiernan did not know that pretexting would involve the use of SSNs. Had he known this, he would have researched the legality of using SSNs as well.

TAB 123

W&GR Wilson Sonsini Goodrich & Rosati
PROFESSIONAL CORPORATION

650 Page Mill Road
Palo Alto, CA 94304-1050
PHONE 650.493.9300
FAX 650.493.6811
www.wsgr.com

PRIVILEGED & CONFIDENTIAL
ATTORNEY WORK PRODUCT
REFLECTS ATTORNEY-CLIENT COMMUNICATION

MEMORANDUM

To: *HP Securities Litigation* Team

From: Trevor Lain

Date: August 21, 2006

Re: **Conversation with Bob Ryan** *- - DRAFT - -*

On August 17, 2006, Steven M. Schatz received a telephone call from Bob Ryan, chair of the Audit Committee at Hewlett-Packard Company ("HP" or the "Company"). The subject of the ensuing telephone conversation was the Kona II Investigation, for which investigators used "pretexting" to obtain the telephone records of certain persons. This memorandum reflects Steven Schatz's thoughts and impressions from the call.

1. Ryan called Schatz after speaking to Patty Dunn, chair of the HP Board. Ryan informed Schatz that he wanted to give his recollection of the accounts in question. In sum, Ryan's view is that once they had determined the source of the leak he was hopeful that George ("Jay") Keyworth could stay on the Board, and that would be largely dependent on Keyworth's reaction to the finding.

2. In fact, Keyworth did admit to Ryan that he was the source of the leak and indicated that he may have had lunch with the reporter. After the [March Board?] meeting, the atmosphere was initially relatively amicable until the Board had a session where Keyworth was asked to resign from the Board. At that point a director, possibly John Hammergren, asked Mark Hurd what would happen to an employee who leaked this information. Mark said point blank that the employee would be fired. At this point the discussion turned sour.

3. Prior to that time there was much discussion about the investigation and the recognition that everything was lawful, but that phone records were being obtained. When the discussion began to turn toward the possibility of dismissal of Keyworth, Perkins became extraordinarily angry, directed it at Patty, and finally said he quit.

4. Ryan confirmed that in essence Perkins became ostensibly choleric only once he realized that Keyworth might be asked to leave the Board.

TAB 124

Project Kona 6/15/05

o obtaining phone #s is a time consuming process
call carriers (Nextel/sprint) + use pretext to extract info
ie I didn't make the call

o No match w/ Bd members' phone #s
→ [illegible]

o numbers for Burrows, Elgin, Crockett provided for study

Connections: Knowling + Crockett (deputy mgr in Chicago)
Motivation to leak? Who has relationship?
PCD →

o Crockett uses phone extensively

Crockett Elgin call each other

[illegible] Ron → Concerned re timing of Board's decision
PCD
– o Attn Hans?
– o Where to go from here? How to speed up? Ramp up? New tactics?
– o Bring SEC inquiry leak into discussion.
– o Bills

PCD : Wild idea
Susan Holm
Maintains relationship w/ Crocky ....

out of line
Not setting direction

TAB 125

From: Hunsaker, Kevin <kevin.hunsaker@hp.com>
Sent: Saturday, January 28, 2006 4:13 PM
To: Baskins, Ann <ann.baskins@hp.com>
Subject: RE: EC cell phones -- privileged communication

Question: on the cell phone stuff, do I ask Jane Ector or Olive Warren?

Kevin T. Hunsaker
Senior Counsel
HP Legal Department
650 857-3079 (phone)
650 857-3710 (fax)
1220 8573079 (voicemail network number)

-----Original Message-----
From: Baskins, Ann
Sent: Friday, January 27, 2006 10:20 PM
To: Hunsaker, Kevin
Subject: Re: EC cell phones -- privileged communication

I don't know, and I suspect that it's a mixture. Mine is an HP phone--tel [redacted] We can check with Mark's admin-she should have all of our numbers.

Charles has his own phone--it's 415 number--and I am not sure about Alan. Ann

----
Sent from my BlackBerry Wireless Handheld

-----Original Message-----
From: Hunsaker, Kevin <kevin.hunsaker@hp.com>
To: Baskins, Ann <ann.baskins@hp.com>
Sent: Fri Jan 27 23:43:40 2006
Subject: EC cell phones -- privileged communication

Hi Ann,

I apologize for peppering you with 1000 questions, but we're trying to be as thorough as we possibly can on this. Do you know whether the EC members' cell phones are in their own names, or are they under an HP account? As you know, I do not believe an EC member is the source, and having access to the cell phone bills will help corroborate my belief.

What about Charles and Alan? I KNOW they aren't the source, but I don't want to give any impression that I am playing favorites in the event the investigation is questioned at some point.

Thanks.

Kevin

Kevin T. Hunsaker
Senior Counsel
HP Legal Department
650 857-3079 (phone)
650 857-3710 (fax)
1220 8573079 (voicemail network number)

TAB 126

From: Ron DeLia [rrd@security-outsourcing.com]
:: Monday, February 06, 2006 8:08 PM
To: Hunsaker, Kevin; Gentilucci, Anthony R.; Nye, Vince; Adler, Frederick P.
Subject: RE: Privileged Communication - HP CONFIDENTIAL

I agree!

Security Outsourcing Solutions, Inc.
Tel: (617) 426-3900 or (781) 444-9616

-----Original Message-----
From: Hunsaker, Kevin [mailto:kevin.hunsaker@hp.com]
Sent: Monday, February 06, 2006 10:42 PM
To: Ron DeLia; Gentilucci, Anthony R.; Nye, Vince; Adler, Frederick P.
Subject: RE: Privileged Communication - HP CONFIDENTIAL

Is the number publicly listed? I just looked them up on Yahoo People Finder and neither Keyworth nor Schwartz came up with the number. It did come up under Howard Schwartz when I did a Google search. Sure seems odd to me that Kawamoto would know to call that number.

Kevin T. Hunsaker
Senior Counsel
HP Legal Department
650 857-3079 (phone)
650 857-3710 (fax)
1220 8573079 (voicemail network number)

-----Original Message-----
From: Ron DeLia [mailto:rrd@security-outsourcing.com]
Sent: Monday, February 06, 2006 7:52 PM
To: Hunsaker, Kevin; Gentilucci, Anthony R.; Nye, Vince; Adler, Frederick P.
Subject: RE: Privileged Communication - HP CONFIDENTIAL

The number is registered to Marion Schwartz prior to Keyworth moving to Piedmont. Keyworth placed a lot of calls to the number during and around BoD meetings in 2005.

Security Outsourcing Solutions, Inc.
Tel: (617) 426-3900 or (781) 444-9616

-----Original Message-----
From: Hunsaker, Kevin [mailto:kevin.hunsaker@hp.com]
Sent: Monday, February 06, 2006 10:24 PM
To: Ron DeLia; Gentilucci, Anthony R.; Nye, Vince; Adler, Frederick P.
Subject: RE: Privileged Communication - HP CONFIDENTIAL

Is Keyworth's Piedmont # in the phone book? If not, how the hell did Kawamoto know the number? Keyworth's only lived there for a couple months, right? Which means he must have given it to her recently . . . .

Kevin T. Hunsaker
Senior Counsel
HP Legal Department
650 857-3079 (phone)
650 857-3710 (fax)
1220 8573079 (voicemail network number)

-----Original Message-----
From: Ron DeLia [mailto:rrd@security-outsourcing.com]
Sent: Monday, February 06, 2006 7:22 PM
To: Hunsaker, Kevin; Gentilucci, Anthony R.; Nye, Vince; Adler, Frederick P.
Subject: RE: Privileged Communication - HP CONFIDENTIAL

Kevin,

Checking on that know,

Ron

The content of this email transmission is intended only for the use of the individual or entity named above and may contain legally privileged or confidential information. If you are not the intended recipient, you are hereby notified that any disclosure, copying, dissemination, distribution, or use of this email transmission, or information contained herein, is strictly prohibited. If you have received this email transmission in error, please destroy all copies of this email and its attachments and notify the person whose name appears above.

Security Outsourcing Solutions, Inc.
Tel: (617) 426-3900 or (781) 444-9616

-----Original Message-----
From: Hunsaker, Kevin [mailto:kevin.hunsaker@hp.com]
Sent: Monday, February 06, 2006 9:36 PM
To: Ron DeLia; Gentilucci, Anthony R.; Nye, Vince; Adler, Frederick P.
Subject: RE: Privileged Communication - HP CONFIDENTIAL

Ron,

Do we have the outbound calls from Keyworth's home from that date, so we can confirm that he and/or his wife made calls from the house that day (indicating that they were at home)? Any other way anyone can think of that we can verify that Keyworth was at home that day? It was a

Wednesday – timing's right, 2 days before Sherbin got the call from Kawamoto about the story.

Do you know what time of day the call went from Kawamoto to the Keyworth residence?

I'll find out if Keyworth reported any attempted contact by Kawamoto or any other members of the media in the past several weeks.

I'm starting to get excited . . . .

Kevin

Kevin T. Hunsaker
Senior Counsel
HP Legal Department
650 857-3079 (phone)
650 857-3710 (fax)
1220 8573079 (voicemail network number)

-----Original Message-----
From: Hunsaker, Kevin
Sent: Monday, February 06, 2006 6:18 PM
To: 'Ron DeLia'; Gentilucci, Anthony R.; Nye, Vince; Adler, Frederick P.
Subject: RE: Privileged Communication - HP CONFIDENTIAL

Thanks.

This is definitely great news, though. May be the direct connection we've been looking for!

Kevin T. Hunsaker
Senior Counsel
HP Legal Department
650 857-3079 (phone)
650 857-3710 (fax)
1220 8573079 (voicemail network number)

-----Original Message-----
From: Ron DeLia [mailto:rrd@security-outsourcing.com]
Sent: Monday, February 06, 2006 6:35 PM
To: Hunsaker, Kevin; Gentilucci, Anthony R.; Nye, Vince; Adler, Frederick P.
Subject: RE: Privileged Communication - HP CONFIDENTIAL

I don't believe we can determine this, however, I will ask....

and its attachments and notify the person whose name appears above.

Security Outsourcing Solutions, Inc.
Tel: (617) 426-3900 or (781) 444-9616

-----Original Message-----
From: Hunsaker, Kevin [mailto:kevin.hunsaker@hp.com]
Sent: Monday, February 06, 2006 9:09 PM
To: Ron DeLia; Gentilucci, Anthony R.; Nye, Vince; Adler, Frederick P.
Subject: RE: Privileged Communication - HP CONFIDENTIAL

How long was the call?

Kevin T. Hunsaker
Senior Counsel
HP Legal Department
650 857-3079 (phone)
650 857-3710 (fax)
1220 8573079 (voicemail network number)

-----Original Message-----
From: Ron DeLia [mailto:rrd@security-outsourcing.com]
Sent: Monday, February 06, 2006 6:25 PM
To: Hunsaker, Kevin; Gentilucci, Anthony R.; Nye, Vince; Adler, Frederick P.
Subject: Privileged Communication - HP CONFIDENTIAL
Importance: High

Team,

I received the following from our analyst this evening. I will personally review the call logs to verify the following information. It should be noted, the call was placed to Keyworth's residence from Kawamoto. Therefore, it is possible Kawamoto was attempting to solicit information from Keyworth. Do we know if Keyworth reported to the BoD or PD that a reporter (Kawamoto) attempted to contact him? It would appear out of contact if Keyworth did not, since he saved Pui-Wing Tam's attempts to contact him last year. We are also checking to determine if the following number has voice mail.

Ron

ATTORNEY CLIENT WORK PRODUCT - CONFIDENTIAL

We have prepared a chart of each spreadsheet you forward to date.

Kawamoto on 1-18 called [redacted] The aforementioned telephone number is registered to Marion Schwartz at her residence in Piedmont, CA.

During our telephone analyses last year, George KEYWORTH called the aforementioned number as follows in 2005:

	Date	phone number	
George Keyworth	1/10/2005	[redacted]	
George Keyworth	2/7/2005	[redacted]	X3
George Keyworth	2/19/2005	[redacted]	
George Keyworth	2/20/2005	[redacted]	X3
George Keyworth	2/21/2005	[redacted]	X3
George Keyworth	2/24/2005	[redacted]	
George Keyworth	2/25/2005	[redacted]	
George Keyworth	2/28/2005	[redacted]	X4
George Keyworth	3/1/2005	[redacted]	X5
George Keyworth	3/2/2005	[redacted]	
George Keyworth	3/6/2005	[redacted]	
George Keyworth	3/7/2005	[redacted]	
George Keyworth	3/9/2005	[redacted]	X2
George Keyworth	3/24/2005	[redacted]	

Security Outsourcing Solutions, Inc.
Tel: (617) 426-3900 or (781) 444-9616

TAB 127

From: Ron DeLia [rrd@security-outsourcing.com]
t: Wednesday, February 08, 2006 10:52 AM
To: Hunsaker, Kevin; Gentilucci, Anthony R.; Nye, Vince; Adler, Frederick P.
Subject: Privileged Communication - HP CONFIDENTIAL

Team,

The telephone analysis is continuing and following are some calls, which may be of an interest. Additional info regarding what phones were used to call the numbers will be forwarded at a later date.

- Bergkamp telephoned [redacted] which Tam, Peter Burrows and Ben Elgin called numerous times in 2005
- Bergkamp telephoned [redacted] which Tam called on 5-25-05.
- KAWAMOTO 1767 calls [redacted] Keyworth's residence.
- 1-17-05 and 3-6-05 Ben ELGIN calls Keyworth's home. (Ben Elgin is a reporter for BW and a key subject in the last investigation)
- 2-19, 2-25 & 3-2-05 KEYWORTH called HACKBORN
- Numerous dates TAM called MOELLER
- 1-13, 6-13-05 TAM called Moeller's office

  BURROWS called MOELLER
- MOELLER calls Robert SHERMAN at HP
- BURROWS calls Robert SHERMAN at HP (Burrows is a reporter for BW and a key subject in the last investigation0
- TAM calls Moeller's home

Security Outsourcing Solutions, Inc.
Tel: (617) 426-3900 or (781) 444-9616

TAB 128

From: Ron DeLia [rrd@security-outsourcing.com]
t: Thursday, February 16, 2006 7:30 AM
To: Hunsaker, Kevin; Gentilucci, Anthony R.; Nye, Vince; Adler, Frederick P.
Subject: Privileged Communication - HP CONFIDENTIAL
Importance: High

Team,

Were alive and kicking, following is the response we received from DK. Also, we can confirm from DK's telephone cell calls she is going to Disneyland. She has made numerous calls to a hotel in Disneyland.

Ron

Hi Jacob,

Sounds good. Fyi, I'll be on vacation starting tomorrow and through next week. I can be reached by cell: [redacted] Or will look for you e-mail when I return.

Take care, Dawn

-----Original Message-----
From: jacob goldfarb [mailto:ambitioustech@hotmail.com]
Sent: Wednesday, February 15, 2006 12:01 PM
To: Dawn Kawamoto
S' 'ct: Hi

Dawn,

I saw the piece by Tom Krazit on the handheld news.
I should have something more in a week or so.

Jacob

TAB 129

From: Ron DeLia [rrd@security-outsourcing.com]
Sent: Sunday, March 05, 2006 8:45 AM
To: Gentilucci, Anthony R.; Hunsaker, Kevin; Nye, Vince; Adler, Frederick P.
Subject: RE: Privileged Communication - HP CONFIDENTIAL

We are working on duration and time of calls of interest between Jan. 31st and Feb. 10th.

Ron

Security Outsourcing Solutions, Inc.
Tel: (617) 426-3900 or (781) 444-9616

-----Original Message-----
From: Gentilucci, Anthony R. [mailto:tony.gentilucci@hp.com]
Sent: Sunday, March 05, 2006 10:44 AM
To: Ron DeLia; Hunsaker, Kevin; Nye, Vince; Adler, Frederick P.
Subject: RE: Privileged Communication - HP CONFIDENTIAL

Ron,

Nice hit, any way to determine the time of the call?

Thanks,

Tony

From: Ron DeLia [mailto:rrd@security-outsourcing.com]
Sent: Saturday, March 04, 2006 4:37 PM
To: Hunsaker, Kevin; Gentilucci, Anthony R.; Nye, Vince; Adler, Frederick P.
Subject: Privileged Communication - HP CONFIDENTIAL

Kevin,

Attached are the media articles authored by DK, SS, TK an PWT from January 31, to February 10, 2006.

Note: We have a call from GK's cell [redacted]) to DK's office [redacted] on February 3, 2006. We are attempting to determine the duration of the call. We also have calls from GK's cell to Lucy Salhany, Tom Perkins, Pattie Dunn and one incoming call from Shane Robison between Jan. 30th and Feb. 10th.

Ron

Security Outsourcing Solutions, Inc.
Tel: (617) 426-3900 or (781) 444-9616

TAB 130

From: Hunsaker, Kevin <kevin.hunsaker@hp.com>
Sent: Sunday, March 5, 2006 8:49 PM
To: Gentilucci, Anthony R. <tony.gentilucci@hp.com>
Subject: RE: GK cell calls -- privileged communication

I think the call to DK was simply him calling her to say he is no longer able to be her source. I would bet that Perkins insisted that he promise not to leak any more info -- that way, even if we are able to show that GK was the source for DK's previous articles, Perkins would argue that GK should not be kicked off because he is a valuable contributor and has promised never to leak info again.

In any event, I think the call to DK from his cell phone is a HUGE piece fo the puzzle for us -- it clearly shows that he reached out for her, which is much, much bigger than a one minute call from her to him. I think we're pretty damned close to having everything we need. . . .

It was a great weekend in Sonoma, by the way. Bought 3 cases of awesome wine.

Kevin T. Hunsaker
Senior Counsel
HP Legal Department
Phone: 650 857-3079
Fax: 650 857-3710

From: Gentilucci, Anthony R.
Sent: Sunday, March 05, 2006 8:34 PM
To: Hunsaker, Kevin
Subject: RE: GK cell calls -- privileged communication

Makes sense Kevin, I think we are onto something, only thing that throws me off is the call to DK, but I am certain he doesn't suspect that we are that sophisticated....interesting....

Tony

From: Hunsaker, Kevin
Sent: Sunday, March 05, 2006 11:10 PM
To: Gentilucci, Anthony R.
Subject: RE: GK cell calls -- privileged communication

I think that's probably right. And, since there was no article that came out shortly after GK called DK, I suspect that he was calling her to tell her he couldn't be her source any longer (most likely at Perkins' insistence). That also fits with what Perkins told Dunn -- that we shouldn't kick the person off the board if they were a major contributor AND promised not to do it anymore. Considering Perkins and Keyworth spoke as many as three times on the day Keyworth called DK, I think Perkins essentially insisted that Keyworth stop leaking info, after which Perkins had his discussion with Dunn.

Kevin T. Hunsaker
Senior Counsel
HP Legal Department
Phone: 650 857-3079
Fax: 650 857-3710

From: Gentilucci, Anthony R.
Sent: Sunday, March 05, 2006 8:05 PM
To: Hunsaker, Kevin
Subject: RE: GK cell calls -- privileged communication

Kevin,

If I had to venture a guess, seems word may have gotten out in regards to our inquiry. Timing of the calls and Perkins change in behavior seem to coincide. Hope you got to relax a bit in wine country. Talk tomorrow.

Tony

From: Hunsaker, Kevin
Sent: Sunday, March 05, 2006 8:54 PM
To: Nye, Vince; Adler, Frederick P.; Gentilucci, Anthony R.; Ron DeLia
Subject: GK cell calls – privileged communication

Hi guys,

Below please find the list of HP-related calls made from Keyworth's cell between Jan 17 and Feb 10 -- I identified the HP folks on the HP numbers he called. Fred will have to tell us who the HP folks are that called him. Fred, can you check to see who at HP called [redacted] on the dates below indicating Keyworth had an incoming call from HP?

Keyworth sure was calling around like crazy on the 30th of January (Robison, Thomas, Salhany, Dunn, Hurd, Perkins). To put some context around that date, the 31st is the date Tam wrote the Wayman article and our meeting with Pattie Dunn was on February 2nd.

I should also point out that on the day Keyworth called Kawamoto, he also called Perkins at his office once and at his home twice (both calls were made by Keyworth from his NM home number).

17-Jan	[redacted]		HEWLETT PACKARD, 3000 HANOVER ST, PALO ALTO, CA 94304 – Rosemarie Thomas
27-Jan	[redacted]	INCOMING	HEWLETT PACKARD, 3000 HANOVER ST, PALO ALTO, CA 94304 – Can't tell which extension this comes from (this is a main HP number for outbound calls
	[redacted]	INCOMING	HEWLETT PACKARD, 3000 HANOVER ST, PALO ALTO, CA 94304 – same as above
	[redacted]	INCOMING	HEWLETT PACKARD, 3000 HANOVER ST, PALO ALTO, CA 94304 – same as above
30-Jan			
	[redacted]	2X	HEWLETT PACKARD, 1501 PAGE MILL RD, PALO ALTO, CA 94304 – [redacted]n
	[redacted]	2X	HEWLETT PACKARD, 3000 HANOVER ST, PALO ALTO, CA 94304 -- [redacted]
	[redacted]	2X	[redacted]
	[redacted]	7X	[redacted]
	[redacted]	4X	GEORGE KEYWORTH, [redacted]
	[redacted]		PATRICIA DUNN-JAHNKE, [redacted]
	[redacted]		HEWLETT PACKARD, 3000 HANOVER ST, PALO ALTO, CA 94304 [redacted]
	[redacted]		THOMAS PERKINS, [redacted]
3-Feb	[redacted]		HEWLETT PACKARD, 3000 HANOVER ST, PALO ALTO, CA 94304 -- [redacted]
	[redacted]		C-NET - [redacted] - Dawn Kawamcto's Ext.
7-Feb	[redacted]	2X	QWEST MESSAGING CENTER, 1372 CENTRAL AVE, LOS ALAMOS, NM 87544

	[redacted]	INCOMING 2X	2X	HEWLETT PACKARD, 3000 HANOVER ST, PALO ALTO, CA 94304 – same as above, can't determine HP caller
8-Feb	[redacted]			THOMAS PERKINS, [redacted]
	[redacted]	INCOMING		HEWLETT PACKARD, 3000 HANOVER ST, PALO ALTO, CA 94304 – same as above
	[redacted]			HEWLETT PACKARD, 3000 HANOVER ST, PALO ALTO, CA 94304 – [redacted]
9-Feb	[redacted]			HEWLETT PACKARD, 3000 HANOVER ST, PALO ALTO, CA 94304 – [redacted]
	[redacted]	INCOMING		HEWLETT PACKARD, 3000 HANOVER ST, PALO ALTO, CA 94304
10-Feb	[redacted]			HEWLETT PACKARD - 1501 PAGE MILL RD, PALO ALTO, CA 94304 – [redacted] Admin
	[redacted]	INCOMING		[redacted]

Kevin T. Hunsaker
Senior Counsel
HP Legal Department
Phone: 650 857-3079
Fax: 650 857-3710

TAB 131

From: Ron DeLia [rrd@security-outsourcing.com]
Sent: Monday, March 06, 2006 2:42 PM
To: Hunsaker, Kevin; Gentilucci, Anthony R.; Nye, Vince; Adler, Frederick P.
Subject: Privileged Communication - HP CONFIDENTIAL
Importance: High

Kevin,

We hare re-confirmed through a second investigation, the call made from GK's cell on Feb. 3rd to DK's office did occur. The call was ten (10) minutes in duration.

Ron

Security Outsourcing Solutions, Inc.
Tel: (617) 426-3900 or (781) 444-9616

TAB 132

From: Ron DeLia [rrd@security-outsourcing.com]
Sent: Friday, March 10, 2006 8:03 AM
To: Hunsaker, Kevin
Cc: Gentilucci, Anthony R.
Subject: RE: Additional phone records -- privileged communication
Attachments: Case 05-04-423 (KONA Markoff chart) Jul 19, 05.xls

I have an analyst looking it up. Also see chart on Markoff from KONA 1.

Security Outsourcing Solutions, Inc.
Tel: (617) 426-3900 or (781) 444-9616

-----Original Message-----
From: Hunsaker, Kevin [mailto:kevin.hunsaker@hp.com]
Sent: Friday, March 10, 2006 10:48 AM
To: Ron DeLia
Cc: Gentilucci, Anthony R.
Subject: RE: Additional phone records -- privileged communication

Do you have easy access to the March 2005 Markoff article? I know you've sent it before, but if you have quick and easy access to it, can you send it to me again?

Kevin T. Hunsaker
Senior Counsel
HP Legal Department
Phone: 650 857-3079
Fax: 650 857-3710

From: Ron DeLia [mailto:rrd@security-outsourcing.com]
Sent: Friday, March 10, 2006 7:38 AM
To: Hunsaker, Kevin
Cc: Gentilucci, Anthony R.
Subject: RE: Additional phone records -- privileged communication

I suggest we determine the usage and if it is significant we can pull the records.

Security Outsourcing Solutions, Inc.
Tel: (617) 426-3900 or (781) 444-9616

-----Original Message-----
From: Hunsaker, Kevin [mailto:kevin.hunsaker@hp.com]
Sent: Friday, March 10, 2006 10:34 AM
To: Ron DeLia
Cc: Gentilucci, Anthony R.
Subject: RE: Additional phone records -- privileged communication

Agreed. Orinda home, SF home, and cell phone. Thoughts about "car phone"?

Kevin T. Hunsaker
Senior Counsel
HP Legal Department
Phone: 650 857-3079
Fax: 650 857-3710

From: Ron DeLia [mailto:rrd@security-outsourcing.com]
Sent: Friday, March 10, 2006 7:34 AM
To: Hunsaker, Kevin
Cc: Gentilucci, Anthony R.
Subject: RE: Additional phone records -- privileged communication

Kevin,

PD has 2 homes in CA and one in Hawaii. I recommend pulling the land lines in SF and Orinda home (office number) and her cell. What are your thoughts? See attached list.

Ron

Patricia Dunn, Director
(415) [redacted]

(808)[redacted]home
(415)[redacted]mobile
(415)[redacted]car phone

The content of this email transmission is intended only for the use of the individual or entity named above and may contain legally privileged or confidential information. If you are not the intended recipient, you are hereby notified that any disclosure, copying, dissemination, distribution, or use of this email transmission, or information contained herein, is strictly prohibited. If you have received this email transmission in error, please destroy all copies of this email and its attachments and notify the person whose name appears above.

Security Outsourcing Solutions, Inc.
Tel: (617) 426-3900 or (781) 444-9616

-----Original Message-----
From: Hunsaker, Kevin [mailto:kevin.hunsaker@hp.com]
Sent: Friday, March 10, 2006 10:15 AM
To: Ron DeLia
Cc: Gentilucci, Anthony R.
Subject: Additional phone records -- privileged communication

Hi Ron,

Having looked through the Report, I believe we need to pull the phone records for Pattie Dunn and Shane Robison. I am also going to have Fred send me the Bob Wayman cell phone records. The reason for this is not because I believe any of them are the source, but because their names do come up at various points as possible sources -- as such, to maintain the integrity and completeness of the investigation, we need to treat them the same as the other individuals whose names came up as possible sources and get those numbers.

Thanks.

Kevin

Kevin T. Hunsaker
Senior Counsel
HP Legal Department
Phone: 650 857-3079
Fax: 650 857-3710

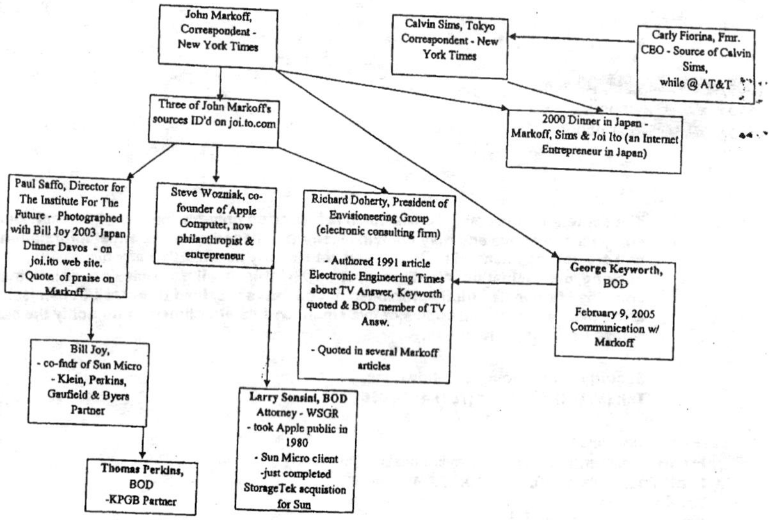
John Markoff, Correspondent - New York Times
Calvin Sims, Tokyo Correspondent - New York Times
Carly Fiorina, Fmr. CEO - Source of Calvin Sims, while @ AT&T
Three of John Markoff's sources ID'd on joi.to.com
2000 Dinner in Japan - Markoff, Sims & Joi Ito (an Internet Entrepreneur in Japan)
Paul Saffo, Director for The Institute For The Future - Photographed with Bill Joy 2003 Japan Dinner Davos - on joi.ito web site. - Quote of praise on Markoff
Steve Wozniak, co-founder of Apple Computer, now philanthropist & entrepreneur
Richard Doherty, President of Envisioneering Group (electronic consulting firm)
- Authored 1991 article Electronic Engineering Times about TV Answer, Keyworth quoted & BOD member of TV Answ.
- Quoted in several Markoff articles
George Keyworth, BOD
February 9, 2005 Communication w/ Markoff
Bill Joy, - co-fndr of Sun Micro - Klein, Perkins, Caufield & Byers Partner
Larry Sonsini, BOD Attorney - WSGR - took Apple public in 1980 - Sun Micro client -just completed StorageTek acquistion for Sun
Thomas Perkins, BOD -KPGB Partner

HP 00111

TAB 133

9:45 AM

04/20/06

PDJ / 1st Source Investigations
1099 Summary
January 2000 through December 2005

	Box 7: Nonemployee Compensation	TOTAL
CAS AGENCY	1,030,177.09	1,030,177.09
(no tax ID on file)		
CELLMAGIC	5,565.00	5,565.00
[redacted]		
CI OF IL	21,120.00	21,120.00
(no tax ID on file)		
CLAIMS RESEARCH & LOSS PREVENTION	112,757.97	112,757.97
(no tax ID on file)		
CONFIDENTIAL RESOURCES INC.	0.00	0.00
(no tax ID on file)		
DOUGLAS MOCKLES	7,405.00	7,405.00
(no tax ID on file)		
EXPRESS INFO	1,067.00	1,067.00
[redacted]		
INFODATA RESEARCH CORPORATION	2,375.00	2,375.00
(no tax ID on file)		
INFORMATION SPECIALISTS	47,835.00	47,835.00
[redacted]		
INFOSOURCE	176,630.50	176,630.50
[redacted]		
INVESTIGATIVE RESOURCES OF TEXAS (AP)	6,372.02	6,372.02
[redacted]		
JEFF SPRY	50,885.00	50,885.00
(no tax ID on file)		
JGJ & ASSOCIATES	199,565.00	199,565.00
[redacted]		
KARENE BRAVO	20,657.50	20,657.50
[redacted]		
LES COLLINS	60,588.00	60,588.00
[redacted]		
MATT CLOTH, PI	357,882.00	357,882.00
(no tax ID on file)		
MCCLURE & ASSOCIATES	0.00	0.00
(no tax ID on file)		
MINNEQUA FINANCIAL GROUP	2,567.00	2,567.00
[redacted]		
QUICK SOURCE	141,146.00	141,146.00
[redacted]		
QUICKSOURCE	4,002.00	4,002.00
[redacted]		
SAM PRICE	9,767.00	9,767.00
(no tax ID on file)		
SHELLEY HORNER	390,496.00	390,496.00
[redacted]		
Source Investigative Group	0.00	0.00
(no tax ID on file)		
SOUTHEASTERN INVESTIGATIVE SERVICES	10,445.00	10,445.00
[redacted]		
STEPHEN MOCKLES	1,400.00	1,400.00
(no tax ID on file)		
WILLIAMS & ASSOCIATES	8,205.00	8,205.00
(no tax ID on file)		
WORLD CENTER DATA	222,246.00	222,246.00
[redacted]		
WORLD WIDE	2,010.00	2,010.00
[redacted]		
TOTAL	2,893,166.98	2,893,166.98

WSGR

PRIVILEGED AND CONFIDENTIAL
ATTORNEY-CLIENT PRIVILEGE
ATTORNEY WORK PRODUCT

REPORT REGARDING KONA INVESTIGATIONS

August 30, 2006

WSGR-HP 1470

TOPICS

- Scope and Conclusions of Investigation
- Factual Findings
- Process Evaluation
- Conclusion
- Recommendations

SCOPE AND CONCLUSIONS OF INVESTIGATION

- **WSGR asked to review HP's investigations in 2005 and 2006 into leaks of confidential information (Kona Investigations):**
  - *Consider whether the processes used were adequate and conformed to best practices*
  - *Review the legality at the time of the investigations of an investigative technique called "pretexting" for obtaining third party phone information*
  - *Make recommendations as appropriate*

SCOPE AND CONCLUSIONS OF INVESTIGATION

- **WSGR's methodology:**
  - *Interviews of key witnesses (some on multiple occasions): Dunn, Hurd, Ryan, Baskins, Hunsaker, Delia, Gentilucci, Huska, Fairbaugh and Kiernan*
  - *Review of limited set of documents collected from HP*
  - *Legal research as necessary*
  - *Investigation did not include review of all documents relating to the Kona Investigations, or interviews with all persons with knowledge of the investigations*

SCOPE AND CONCLUSIONS OF INVESTIGATION

- **WSGR conclusions:**
  - *While all the persons involved in the Kona investigations acted in good faith and with best of intentions, certain errors in judgment were made*
  - *The use of pretexting at the time of the Kona investigations was not generally unlawful (except with respect to financial institutions)*
  - *HP subcontractors may have used social security numbers (not provided by HP) while pretexting, which more likely than not violates federal law*
  - *WSGR recommends HP immediately cease pretexting to obtain phone records, undertake a thorough evaluation of the legality of its investigative techniques, and closely monitor the activities of any third party contractors engaged in the course of investigations*

Privileged & Confidential
Attorney Work Product

Wilson Sonsini Goodrich & Rosati
PROFESSIONAL CORPORATION

WSGR-HP 1474

FACTUAL FINDINGS

- In 2005 HP victimized by a series of leaks concerning board deliberations and other material non-public information
- Larry Sonsini asked all directors about the leaks in early 2005, and none admitted to being the source
- Following consultation with numerous directors after becoming board chair in 2005, Ms. Dunn initiated an investigation ("Kona" or "Kona I") into the source of a series of leaks disclosing confidential Board deliberation
- Ms. Dunn contacted Kevin Huska (a senior officer in HP's security operations) who recommended Ron Della of Outsourcing Solutions, Inc. to assist Ms. Dunn in this investigation
- Mr. Della had substantial experience with HP and in conducting investigations and assured Ms. Dunn that all the methods he used were legal and common investigative techniques

FACTUAL FINDINGS

- Ms. Dunn did not involve HP legal in the investigation until June/July 2005
- Ms. Dunn did not disclose the specific investigative techniques to the directors based upon advice from investigative team
- Mr. Delia used many investigative techniques such as relationship mapping
- Mr. Delia, through subcontractors, also used "pretexting" to obtain phone record information of certain HP directors and reporters
- This investigation ultimately proved inconclusive

FACTUAL FINDINGS

- In January 2006 a CNET story detailing the internal deliberations of HP's Board led Ms. Dunn to call for another investigation (Kona II)
- HP directors were outraged by the on-going leaks
- Ms. Dunn consulted with Ms. Baskins in creating the investigative team in Kona II
- Kona II team led by Kevin Hunsaker (HP Legal, Director of Ethics and Standards of Business Conduct), Fred Adler and Tony Gentilucci
- Team again included Mr. Delia of Security Outsourcing Solutions, who again employed a third party to engage in pretexting for phone record information
- Mr. Delia repeatedly assured Mr. Hunsaker that pretexting was legal

FACTUAL FINDINGS

- Mr. Hunsaker, at Ms. Baskin's request, repeatedly asked Mr. Delia to confirm legality of pretexting
- Mr. Delia consulted with his outside counsel who advised pretexting was lawful
- Ms. Dunn and Ms. Baskins received repeated assurances that investigation techniques were legal and consistent with all HP policies
- Kona II investigation revealed source of leaks, who later admitted his role

PROCESS EVALUATION

- Board Chair Dunn acted with best of intentions
  - *Ms. Dunn continually and explicitly reminded investigation team of their duties to act lawfully and properly*
  - *Ms. Dunn retained Ron Delia because she was told that HP had used Mr. Delia in numerous investigations in the past*
  - *Ms. Dunn received assurances from Mr. Delia that pretexting was lawful*
- However, with respect to Kona I, it was an error in judgment not to involve either HP legal or outside counsel at the start of Kona I investigation
- In Kona II, Ms. Dunn reasonably relied on repeated assurances of legality by HP legal

PROCESS EVALUATION

- CEO Mark Hurd acted properly in all respects
- Mr. Hurd not involved in directing either Kona I or Kona II
- Mr. Hurd given assurances by investigative team that investigative methods were legal
- Reasonable for CEO to rely on these assurances, particularly since Mr. Hurd was not leading the investigation
  - *Kona I was confidential and lead by Ms. Dunn*
  - *Kona II had involvement of General Counsel*

PROCESS EVALUATION

- **Ms. Baskins not involved in Kona I until last stage, after pretexting already occurred**
- **Ms. Baskins relied on HP Senior Counsel Kevin Hunsaker in Kona II**
  - *Ms. Baskins repeatedly sought assurances that pretexting was lawful, and received assurances that it was*
  - *Ms. Baskins was told that HP had consulted an outside legal expert who advised pretexting was lawful*

- **Mr. Hunsaker acted with best of intentions and under pressure to achieve results in Kona II**
- **Mr. Hunsaker should have conducted or commissioned extensive research in determining legality of pretexting rather than relying on advice by experts or their counsel**
  - *Did not examine potential issues raised by use of SSN*

PROCESS EVALUATION

- Kevin Hunsaker (currently Director of Ethics and SBC) not involved in Kona I
- Mr. Hunsaker acted with best of intentions and under pressure to achieve results in Kona II
- Mr. Hunsaker should have conducted or commissioned extensive research in determining legality of pretexting rather than relying on advice by experts or their counsel
  - *Did not examine potential issues raised by use of SSN*

CONCLUSION

- The processes used in the Kona investigations contained certain flaws that, in retrospect, could have been avoided by Mr. Hunsaker (Kona II) and Ms. Dunn (Kona I)
- At the time of investigations, no laws specifically prohibiting pretexting for phone records (only with respect to financial institutions)
- To the extent that subcontractors used social security numbers while pretexting, such conduct would more likely than not constitute at least a technical violation of statute prohibiting the use of SSNs "for any purpose" even though applying statute to pretexting for phone information would be novel

RECOMMENDATIONS

- That HP cease the use of pretexting to obtain phone record information
- That HP conduct extensive analysis of investigative methods to broadly assure compliance with the law
- That HP adopt stricter controls over third party contractors used in internal investigations to ensure that these contractors act in a manner consistent with all laws and HP's policies
- That HP cooperate with all governmental or regulatory inquiries arising from the Kona investigations

Memorandum

Hewlett-Packard Company
Global SBC Compliance Team
3000 Hanover Street
Palo Alto, CA 94304

DRAFT

PREPARED AT THE DIRECTION OF COUNSEL

Subject:	Response to Claims of Former BoD Member Tom Perkins
From:	Kevin T. Hunsaker, Director of Ethics and SBC
Date:	June 21, 2006
To:	Ann Baskins Larry Sonsini

I. Background

On May 29, 2006, former HP Board member (and current NewsCorp Board member) Tom Perkins sent an email to his fellow NewsCorp directors[1] making a number of claims regarding the Unauthorized Disclosure investigation conducted at my direction[2] that identified George Keyworth as the source of the information leaks associated with the CNET article written by Dawn Kawamoto on January 23, 2006. Perkins' email message included the following claims regarding the investigation:

- It was a "massive secret program, run by hired electronic security experts";
- "All telephone and e-mail connections for all directors for the past two years, from all their phones and computers, were examined"; and
- It involved "secret spying (which involved a room-full of electronic gear)."

In addition to the foregoing email message, on June 19, 2006, Perkins sent an email message to Larry Sonsini on June 19, 2006 indicating that Perkins had discussed the events of the most recent HP Board meeting with Viet Dinh (a Georgetown Law professor and fellow Newscorp

[1] On May 31, 2006, Perkins forwarded the May 29th email to Andrea Redmond at Russell Reynolds Associates, who then forwarded the email to Pattie Dunn (Chairman of HP's Board) sometime between May 31 and June 7, 2006.

[2] At the time of the investigation, my title was Senior Counsel and I directed the investigation in my capacity as an attorney in the HP Legal Department. I have since taken the position of Director of Ethics and SBC and am no longer an attorney in the HP Legal Department. This Memo is being prepared at the specific request of Ann Baskins, HP's General Counsel.

Board member). The email stated that Dinh "was shocked at the HP chairman's recording of board members telephone and computer inter-connections." The email further indicated that Dinh said "monitoring connections and/or email addresses requires a subpoena" and, with or without a subpoena, "such monitoring was simply 'unconscionable'." In a follow-up email from Perkins to Sonsini on June 20th, Perkins indicated it was Dinh's "unqualified opinion that it was illegal."

This Memo will address each of the claims made in the two email messages written by Perkins.

II. Discussion of Specific Claims

➢ **It was a "massive secret program, run by hired electronic security experts."**

This claim is untrue. HP first learned of the information leak late in the afternoon of Friday, January 20, 2006 (three days *before* the article in question were published), and the investigation was commenced immediately thereafter with full knowledge and support of Pattie Dunn, Mark Hurd and Ann Baskins. It was conducted at my direction on behalf of the Legal Department in order ensure this very sensitive investigation was covered by the attorney-client privilege. In fact, at no time during the course of the investigation were there any hired electronic security experts involved in the investigation. The Investigation Team consisted of me, Tony Gentilucci and Vince Nye from Global Security, Fred Adler from IT Security, and and an outside security consultant, Ron Delia (managing director of Security Outsourcing Solutions[3]).

This was a comprehensive, thorough, time-consuming investigation directed by the Legal Department and conducted by a small team of experienced, dedicated, qualified investigators with full knowledge and support of HP's Chairman, CEO and General Counsel. Under no stretch of the imagination was it a "massive secret program, run by hired electronic security experts."

➢ **"All telephone and e-mail connections for all directors for the past two years, from all their phones and computers, were examined."**

This claim is also untrue. Since Perkins' email to Larry Sonsini on June 19th appears to include a very similar claim that the Investigation Team somehow recorded and monitored the board members' telephone and computer inter-connections and e-mail addresses, these claims will be addressed together in this sub-section.

Recording, examining or monitoring Board members' computer connections or email addresses. At no time did the Investigation Team attempt to record, examine or monitor any of the Board members' computer connections or email addresses. Nor did the Investigation

---

[3] HP often uses Delia and his company to obtain background information on entities and individuals, analysis of publicly available information and other important investigation-related services. While Delia and his company provide invaluable investigation support services, they are by no means "electronic security experts," and even if they were, they definitely were not hired to run or otherwise direct this investigation.

Team attempt to access or examine any non-employee Board member's[4] work or personal computer, email accounts, internet providers, internet proxy information, log-in records, or any other electronic data residing on or related to their computers. Obtaining such information would require a valid subpoena, so the Investigation Team did not attempt to obtain said information.

Recording, examining or monitoring Board members' telephone connections. Given Perkins' additional comment in his May 29th email that "[a]pparently this is legal if the content is not transcribed," it appears that Perkins claims the Investigation Team somehow recorded and monitored the Board members' telephone conversations or recorded or monitored their phone traffic on a real-time basis. This is untrue. The Investigation Team did not record or monitor any Board member's phone calls or phone traffic, nor did we obtain the phone records for any non-employee Board members. In fact, the Investigation Team never even considered doing these things, so I am unaware whether it is even technologically possible to do so.

Phone records and phone information of non-employee Board members. In the event Perkins' claims regarding telephone "connections" is intended to be a claim that the Investigation Team unlawfully obtained the phone records of non-employee Board members, it is important to point out that the Investigation Team did not seek, obtain or review any phone records of any non-employee Board members.[5] Obtaining such records would require a valid subpoena, so the Investigation Team did not attempt to obtain the phone records of any non HP-owned phones or phone numbers.

However, during the course of the investigation, the Investigation Team did legally obtain certain information regarding phone calls made and received by a number of non-employee Board members. The phone information was obtained regarding these individuals because, at the time the information was obtained, they could not be eliminated as possible sources of the information leaks to CNET. The Investigation Team limited its requests for phone information regarding these non-employee Board members to the time period from December of 2005 through March of 2006 – the period immediately preceding and following the January 23rd CNET articles.

To obtain the phone information, Delia's company retained a third party company who obtains the phone information by making pretext calls to the phone service providers, and the phone service providers voluntarily provide the information verbally to the third party. This information gathering technique is a common investigative tool that has been used by professional investigators and law firms for more than 20 years -- this fact was confirmed by discussing the

---

[4] Because Mark Hurd and Bob Wayman are HP employees whose computers belong to the company and whose Outlook email accounts reside on HP's systems, the Investigation Team did pull and review Hurd's and Wayman's HP email accounts in conjunction with the investigation. This is a common HP practice in SBC investigations and is expressly authorized by section 9.5 of the SBC.

[5] The Investigation Team also obtained the actual phone records for all HP-owned phones and phone numbers associated with Mark Hurd and Bob Wayman, both of whom are HP employees, for a period of one year. As these phones and phone numbers are owned by HP, there can be no doubt that obtaining and reviewing the phone records was not only perfectly lawful, but standard operating procedure in any investigation of this nature.

issue with a number of experts in the field, including Brian Jenkins (a world-renowned expert with whom HP consulted during the first two weeks of the investigation).

During the course of the investigation, the Investigation Team took several steps to confirm the legality of obtaining the phone information in the manner described above. For example, I conducted approximately 30 to 45 minutes of preliminary legal research and determined that the practice of pretexting phone companies to obtain information is not unlawful. The third party company conducting the research also confirmed in writing that they are very well aware of all potentially relevant state and federal laws, and that the manner in which they obtain the phone information is not unlawful. And, we contacted John Kiernan (an attorney with many years experience in these kinds of investigations, and a named partner at the law firm Bonner, Kiernan, Trebach and Crociata -- the firm primarily responsible for the ABB Foreign Corrupt Practices Act investigation), who confirmed that his firm had conducted extensive research on this issue, and that the practice of pretexting phone companies to obtain information is not unlawful.

As a result, I am confident that all phone information obtained during the course of the investigation was obtained in a lawful manner by using an information gathering technique that has been commonly used by investigators, law firms and law enforcement agencies for many years.

> **It involved "secret spying (which involved a room-full of electronic gear)."**

This allegation is also untrue. The Investigation Team did not use any electronic gear to secretly spy on anyone during the course of the investigation. At no time did the Investigation Team use listening devices or other means of electronic eavesdropping to listen in on anyone's conversations or phone calls. We did not use any secret (or overt) method of obtaining the Board members' computer traffic, and we did not have any room full of electronic gadgets or gizmos to develop information on the Board members or other individuals of interest in the investigation. The Investigation Team simply used its many years of experience, combined with good, old-fashioned diligence, dedication and hours and hours of hard work and meticulous attention to detail to successfully identify George Keyworth as the source of the leak.

III. Summary

As the foregoing discussion clearly indicates, the claims made by former Board member Tom Perkins regarding the investigation are completely untrue and off base. The Investigation Team did not do any of the things identified in the email messages drafted by Perkins, and we did not engage in any unlawful conduct at any stage of the investigation.

MR. WHITFIELD. You all are dismissed. Thank you very much for being with us, and at this time this is the final witness of the day, and that is Mr. Michael--Mark Hurd. Mr. Mark Hurd.

Mr. Hurd, we welcome you to the committee today, and I--

MR. HURD. Thank you. I can't see you.

MR. WHITFIELD. I can barely see you, but I know you are there.

MR. HURD. Thank you.

MR. WHITFIELD. And we do appreciate very much your being with us today to shed additional light on this important matter.

And as you know, an oversight investigation takes its testimony under oath, and I am assuming you have no objection to testifying under oath.

MR. HURD. Not at all.

MR. WHITFIELD. So if you wouldn't mind standing and raising your right hand, I will swear you in.

[Witness sworn.]

MR. WHITFIELD. You are now under oath, and under the rules of the committee and rules of the House, you are certainly entitled to legal counsel. And if you do have legal counsel with you today and would like to introduce them, that would be great.

MR. HURD. I have no personal legal counsel. I have some company counsel.

MR. WHITFIELD. Okay. Well, you are now sworn in, and we look forward to your testimony, and I recognize you for 5 minutes for your opening statement.

TESTIMONY OF MARK HURD, PRESIDENT, CHIEF EXECUTIVE OFFICER, AND CHAIRMAN OF THE BOARD, HEWLETT-PACKARD COMPANY

MR. HURD. Thank you, Mr. Chairman, members of the committee, thank you for the opportunity to appear before you today.

My name is Mark Hurd. I am with the Hewlett-Packard Company. I know that you have heard a lot of testimony. I know you have a lot of questions as a result. Before we do get to those, I would like to try and provide a larger context to you as to what you have heard.

And what is really hardest for me to explain is this: HP is a company that has consistently earned recognition for our adherence to standards of ethics, privacy and corporate responsibility, and yet these practices that we have taken such pride in have recently been violated by people inside the company and by people outside the company whom we hired.

This committee rightfully wonders what happened. What began as a proper and serious inquiry of leaks to the press of sensitive company information became a rogue investigation that violated our own principles and values. There is no excuse for this aberration. It happened, and it will never happen again.

Before I do anything else, I want to apologize to those whose privacy was infringed upon. This includes nine journalists and their families, two current HP employees, seven former or current HP Board members and their families. In varying degrees these individuals were investigated through the use of pretexting, a technique used to obtain their telephone call information.

In addition to a heartfelt apology, I want those whose privacy was violated to know that we will soon provide to the victims the details regarding the information obtained about them, the means by which it was obtained, and when it was obtained.

I also want to apologize to the employees of Hewlett-Packard, who on a daily basis carry on their work with the highest integrity. They are the reasons HP has been recognized so often for their ethics. This current mess in no way reflects upon the vast amount of our employees, their work, or their reputation.

The question remains how did such abuse of privacy occur in a company renowned for its commitment to privacy? And it is an age-old story that the ends came to justify the means. The investigation team became so focused on finding the source of the leaks that they lost sight of the values of this company. They lost sight of the values this company has always represented.

This company was built on integrity. If Bill Hewlett and Dave Packard were alive today, they would be appalled. They would be embarrassed. That is the way the great majority of the people in our company feel.

Members of the committee, I want you to know that I am not putting myself above the breakdown that occurred. I wish I had asked more questions. There are signs which I wish I had caught. I am responsible for the company, which means I am responsible for fixing it and leading it forward through this hard time. Our culture, our core, which we call the HP way, remains strong and ethical, but clearly changes are in order.

Mistakes will happen, and these are very serious and unsettling ones that we have been discussing, but what matters ultimately is how a company addresses the mistakes. HP has taken specific actions and will take further actions in the days and weeks ahead.

We have accepted the resignation of our previous Chairman and our General Counsel. Other employees have left the company. We have appointed a new lead independent director. We have appointed Bart Schwartz, the former head of Criminal Division of the U.S. Attorney's Office of Rudy Giuliani, to do an assessment of current practices and develop future best practices so our processes will always be legal, ethical, appropriate and without peer. We are putting into place new measures to maintain the highest levels of information privacy.

In summary, the big picture of what happened is that we began an investigation of our Board for leaks and have ended up investigating our investigation.

I pledge three things to the committee, to our employees and to our shareholders, and to those whose privacy was violated. I pledge that I will dig harder and deeper, and I will get to the bottom of this. I pledge that HP will take whatever steps necessary to make sure nothing like this ever happens again. And I pledge that this company will regain not just its reputation as a model citizen with the highest ethical standards, but we will regain our pride.

Thank you for the privilege of speaking today, and, Mr. Chairman, I will be happy to answer questions of you and the committee.

MR. WHITFIELD. Thank you, Mr. Hurd, and we appreciate those comments.

[The prepared statement of Mark Hurd follows:]

PREPARED STATEMENT OF MARK HURD, PRESIDENT, CHIEF EXECUTIVE OFFICER, AND CHAIRMAN OF THE BOARD, HEWLETT-PACKARD COMPANY

Summary of Mark Hurd Testimony

What began as a proper and serious inquiry of leaks to the press of sensitive company information from within the HP board became a rogue investigation that violated HP's own principles and values. There is no excuse for this.

As head of the company, I apologize to those whose privacy was infringed. This includes nine journalists and their families, two current HP employees and seven former or current HP board members and their families. To varying degrees these individuals were investigated through pretexting, a technique used to obtain telephone call information.

I also apologize to the employees of HP who on a daily basis carry on their work with the highest integrity.

How did such an abuse of privacy occur in a company renowned for its commitment to privacy? The end came to justify the means. The investigation team become so focused on finding the source of the leaks that they lost sight of the privacy of reporters and others. They lost sight of the values that HP has always represented.

We are making the necessary changes so that this never occurs again. We have accepted the resignation of our previous chairman. Other employees have left the company. We have appointed a new lead independent director. We have appointed Bart Schwartz, the former head of the criminal division of the US Attorney's Office under Rudy Giuliani, to do an assessment of current practices and develop future best practices so that our processes will always be legal, ethical, appropriate and without peer. We are putting into place new measures to maintain the highest levels of information privacy.

In summary, the big picture of what happened is that we began an investigation of our board for leaks and have ended up investigating our investigation.

I pledge that I will dig harder and deeper and I will get to the bottom of this. I pledge that Hewlett-Packard will take whatever steps necessary to make sure nothing like this ever happens again. And I pledge that HP will regain not just its reputation as a model citizen with the highest ethical standards . . . we will regain our pride.

Mr. Chairman, members of the Committee, thank you for this opportunity to appear before you today.

My name is Mark Hurd. I am head of the Hewlett-Packard Company. Before joining HP, I spent 25 years at NCR Corp. I began my career at NCR as a field salesman in 1980. Over the next two decades, I held a variety of other management, operations, sales and marketing roles, culminating in a two-year tenure as Chief Executive Officer and President. In early 2005, I joined HP.

HP, with headquarters in Palo Alto, California, was founded in 1939 by two Stanford Engineering graduates who shared a belief that technology could make a contribution to people's lives. The company that Bill Hewlett and Dave Packard started in a one-car garage is now a leading global provider of computing and imaging solutions and services. We conduct business in over 170 countries around the world. With 151,000 employees globally and revenues of $90 billion, HP is a true American success story.

And we have been heralded as a success story not just because of our technology but because of our reputation, which brings me to the difficult subject of why I am here today. I know that you have heard a lot of testimony and have a lot of questions as a result. But before we get to those, I would like to provide a larger context for what you have heard.

What is hardest for me to explain is this: HP is a company that has consistently earned recognition for our adherence to standards of ethics, privacy and corporate responsibility. And yet these practices that we have taken such pride in have recently been violated by people inside the company and by people outside the company with whom we contracted. This committee rightfully wonders what happened.

What began as a proper and serious inquiry into leaks to the press of company information became a rogue investigation that violated our own principles and values. There is no excuse for this aberration. It happened; it will never happen again.

Before I do anything else, I want to apologize to those whose privacy was infringed upon. This includes nine journalists and their families, two current HP employees and seven former or current HP Board members and their families. To varying degrees, these individuals were investigated through the use of pretexting, a technique used to obtain their telephone call information.

In addition to a heartfelt apology, I want those whose privacy was violated to know that we will soon provide to the victims the details regarding the *information* obtained about them, *the means* by which it was obtained, *when* it was obtained and *who* obtained it.

I also want to apologize to the employees of HP who on a daily basis carry on their work with the highest integrity. They are the reasons HP has been recognized so often for its ethics. This current mess in no way reflects upon our employees, their work or their reputation.

The question remains: how did such an abuse of privacy occur in a company renowned for its commitment to privacy?

It's an age-old story. The ends came to justify the means. The investigation team became so focused on finding the source of the leaks that they lost sight of the values of this company. They lost sight of the values that this company has always represented.

This company was built on integrity. If Bill Hewlett and David Packard were still alive, they would be appalled. They would be embarrassed. And that is the way the people in our company feel.

Members of the committee, I am not putting myself above the breakdown that occurred. I wish I had asked more questions. There are signs I wish I had caught. I am responsible for the company, which means I am responsible for fixing it and leading it forward through this hard time.

Let me give you a sense of where things now stand.

On September 8th, HP retained the law firm of Morgan Lewis & Bockius (MLB) to assist HP with multiple government inquiries. In connection with that, MLB began reviewing the investigation. During the last two weeks, numerous MLB lawyers have spent thousands of hours interviewing witnesses and collecting and reviewing more than a million pages of documents from inside and outside HP. While MLB's work is not complete, I am confident that today we have a better understanding of what had transpired around the investigation.

To fully understand what happened, it is important to know the context in which the investigation began. There has been a long history of company information leaking from within the HP board. Information leaked out about negotiations with major suppliers, transactions that were being considered and strategic decisions as to the future of the company. Board members have a fiduciary responsibility not to disclose internal deliberations, which can affect trust, board dynamics and effectiveness, not to mention share price and market trading.

This conduct is clearly in violation of HP's Standards of Business Conduct, our ethics policy that applies to all employees and all board members. Thus, it has been the responsibility of the Chairman of the Board to pursue leaks from the Board of Directors and that responsibility has been taken very seriously.

The investigation that has garnered so much attention in recent weeks really began in early 2005. At the request of the Board of Directors, Larry Sonsini, a highly respected lawyer, was engaged to assist HP in determining the source of the information leaks. He interviewed each director to determine the source of certain leaks and to impress upon each director the importance of maintaining HP's confidences.

In the spring of 2005, the Board commenced a more rigorous investigation into the leaks of information spearheaded by HP's Chairman, Patricia Dunn. Ms. Dunn enlisted the professional services of Ron Delia, of Security Outsourcing Solutions (SOS), an external investigation firm that had been providing investigative services to HP for a number of years. Although the Board was informed that an investigation had started, they were not told of the operational details. Similarly, I was apprised of the existence of the investigation by Ms. Dunn, but I was not involved in the investigation itself.

I want to be clear that there were two phases to the investigation. The first phase of the investigation, which came to an end in approximately November 2005, yielded inconclusive results.

Beginning in late January 2006, the leak investigation was renewed and entered into a second phase. This was prompted by further Board leaks of information which was reported in a late January news story.

The second phase of the investigation was in full operation between late January and May 2006. The investigative team was composed of a Senior Counsel in HP's Legal Department, and other HP employees from HP's Global and IT Security Departments. SOS was also involved in this second phase.

In the second phase, while many of the right processes were in place, they unfortunately broke down and no-one in the management chain including me, caught it.

Now let me address my knowledge of the events. I understood shortly after coming to HP that there was an investigation into leaks from the board. And in July 2005, I attended a brief portion of a meeting at which the results of the first phase of the investigation were discussed.

In January 2006, the HP Chairman asked to use HP resources to investigate the leaks. In February 2006, I was informed by the investigation team that they intended to send an email to a reporter containing false information in an effort to identify the source of the leaks. I was asked to and did approve the content of that email. I do not recall seeing, nor do I recall approving, the use of tracer technology.

In March 2006, I attended a meeting at which a verbal summary of the second phase of the investigation was provided, specifically, that the investigative team had identified the source of the leaks. I understand there is also written report of the investigation addressed to me and others, but unfortunately I did not read it.

I could have, and I should have.

I participated in a discussion at the May 2006 board meeting at which the results of the investigation were discussed. As we have said from the start, the intent of the original investigation was absolutely proper and appropriate. The leaks were wrong and we had an obligation to our employees and shareholders to resolve the problem. However, two wrongs do not make a right. Many of the actions taken to identify the leaks from our Board were unacceptable and inconsistent with HP's values, past behavior, and our privacy principles. But the inappropriate investigative techniques that were applied in this instance do not reflect the values of HP. They have no place in the company.

While our culture, our core, which we call the HP Way, remains strong and ethical. Clearly, mistakes will happen—and these are very serious and unsettling ones that we've been discussing. But what matters ultimately is how a company addresses the mistakes. HP has taken specific actions and will take further actions in the days and weeks ahead.

We have accepted the resignation of our previous chairman. Other employees have left the company.

We have appointed Richard Hackborn – who began his association with HP in 1960 and has been on the Board for 14 years -- as new lead independent director.

We have appointed Bart Schwartz, the former head of the criminal division of the US Attorney's Office under Rudy Giuliani, to do an assessment of current practices and develop future best practices so that our processes will always be legal, ethical, appropriate and without peer.

We are putting into place new measures to maintain the highest levels of information privacy. Let me elaborate on those internal policies.

--We are immediately adding clarifying language into the scope of all HP privacy policies related to inappropriate practices in obtaining confidential records or personal information without authorization from the individual–as well as specifying privacy policy compliance by all of HP—our officers, employees and contracted parties working on behalf of HP.

--We are expanding the privacy documentation and processes related to inappropriate practices in obtaining confidential records or personal information without authorization.

--We are adding specific content in HP's Privacy Training curriculum related to inappropriate practices in obtaining confidential records or personal information without authorization. This training is delivered to all employees worldwide, and it will expand as required training for all officers.

--We are also formally incorporating our Chief Privacy Officer in review processes related to HP's accountability in the collection and use of sensitive information, including how such information is used in investigations.

In summary, the big picture of what happened is that we began an investigation of our Board for leaks and have ended up investigating our investigation.

I pledge three things to this committee, to our employees, to our shareholders, to those whose privacy was violated.

I pledge that I will dig harder and deeper and I will get to the bottom of this.

I pledge that HP will take whatever steps necessary to make sure nothing like this ever happens again.

And I pledge that this company will regain not just its reputation as a model citizen with the highest ethical standards . . . we will regain our pride.

Thank you for the privilege of speaking today and I will be happy to answer any of your questions.

MR. WHITFIELD. After listening to the testimony of Ms. Dunn all day today, I come away from her testimony with the thought that she is a particularly strong individual, that she is quite focused, and from information I read about her, she is pretty meticulous. And I am sure she was determined to get to the source of the leaks out of the Board and was successful in doing that.

But she also made it quite clear to us that despite all sorts of evidence to the contrary--there was all sorts of evidence that she knew about pretexting early on--and every time we raised that evidence with her, she said, well, I don't think that is accurate, or, I don't recall that, or, I have never seen that, or, it was not mentioned to me, or whatever, whatever. And she did consistently say, I turned it over to the investigative team.

Now, in your mind--and I guess today it seems like this investigative team was the only thing going on at Hewlett-Packard, but I am sure there were lots of things going on at Hewlett-Packard. And maybe this was not even a priority at that time, but from your perspective, who was the investigative team among employees at Hewlett-Packard that were responsible for this matter?

MR. HURD. I understand, Mr. Chairman. Let me do the best I can, and the context I would like to provide you is that I started with the company in April of '05, so there is some time here that predates my arrival to the company.

Sometime in December, January of '05 there were--I am sorry, December '04, January '05, there were some of these leaks, I have come to learn; that as I came to the company, this had created quite a bit of sensitivity around the Board.

So there was an effort started roughly in that timeframe--and I think Mr. Sonsini talked to some of that--to begin the process of trying to investigate those leaks. There's really, two phases as I have come to understand it now, of this investigation.

The first phase, which you have heard referred to as Kona 1, really was an investigation that emanated from a private investigator who had a relationship with the Board. Some of it actually emanated from the background check that the Board did on the CEO, meaning me. And that continued on into Kona 1. That really did not have a lot of HP resources in the investigation, as you might think about it.

In the second phase, which really started after the Palm Springs leak that occurred, that actually had a different team on it. So think of this as two separate teams.

At the conclusion of the Palm Springs meeting, Ms. Dunn asked me if she could use HP resources to pursue the leak, to which I said yes.

That is where the second team came in place, where the new names you hear now would be Kevin Hunsaker and the team below Kevin. I know this sounds complicated, but there actually are two different groups.

MR. WHITFIELD. But on Kona 2, the names that she gave are the four or five--four names that you would identify also.

MR. HURD. Yes, Mr. Chairman. Yes, sir.

MR. WHITFIELD. So you would be in agreement with her on that?

MR. HURD. Yes.

MR. WHITFIELD. Was it your understanding that they did report--did they report to you, or did they report to Ms. Dunn?

MR. HURD. Well, this gets to the complexity of the governance of this. This is just not as straightforward as--I know how much the committee would like to get at it this way. You have a Chairman, you have a CEO, and that is me. And the chairman clearly was appropriately pursuing these leaks. The first set of resources really did not have anything to do with the company. It was contractors doing the work.

In the second one, clearly you had a reporting relationship where Kevin, who you have heard--Kevin Hunsaker reported in to Ann, but clearly as you look at the documents, there was a lot of communication going directly to the Board.

MR. WHITFIELD. As we speak today, all of those people have resigned from the company, is that correct, Ann and Kevin and Mr. Gentilucci?

MR. HURD. Correct.

MR. WHITFIELD. So those three have resigned.

MS. DUNN. Correct.

MR. WHITFIELD. And then Ms. Dunn has resigned from the Board.

MR. HURD. Correct.

MR. WHITFIELD. That is a total of four, and that is where it stands right now is my understanding.

Now, there has been also a lot of discussion today about this e-mail sent by a character who did not exist named Jacob. And that was sent to a reporter for CNET. And you probably heard this, but Kevin had sent an e-mail to Ms. Dunn saying that we want to do this, and here is what it is, and Mark Hurd is going to be meeting with the Wall Street Journal, and if she gets this, then we think we can trace who is doing the leaking.

And she said, it is very clever on your part to come up with that idea. And we need to get somebody to run it by Mark Hurd before we do it.

And then Hunsaker wrote back an e-mail and said, well, I talked to him about it--and I think this is in Exhibit 52, if you want to look at it in particular, but he basically says, I have run it by Mark, and the content and concept is fine with him.

And I would just ask you, do you remember having discussion with him about that or--

MR. HURD. I can tell you what I remember and also what I have learned, so I will try to bring the two together.

I clearly remember the effort on the part of the team to try to get some sort of approval on the content of the e-mail. And I think their view was that if there was going to be information put out into the market for whatever reason, it needed to be agreed to.

To the best of my memory and to my knowledge, I remember nothing about spyware or any of the other terms that have been discussed as it related to the e-mail, but I do remember a discussion about the content, yes.

MR. WHITFIELD. But you are testifying today that as far as the details of the mechanics of the way these things work and their real purpose, you are not really familiar with it?

MR. HURD. To the best of my knowledge, best of my memory, I do not remember a discussion about that type of methodology.

MR. WHITFIELD. Now, I know that sometime in March, March 10th, I guess, Mr. Hunsaker prepared a report about this entire investigation, Tab 72, and in that report he did a pretty thorough job of everything that was going on in this investigation. And he sent it to Pattie Dunn, Mark Hurd and Ann Baskins, and in there he talks specifically about pretexting. And this is after it has already been--they have already utilized pretexting for their information. But it is my understanding that you really never read this report; is that correct?

MR. HURD. That's correct.

MR. WHITFIELD. Were you able to--

MR. HURD. Not my finest hour, Mr. Chairman.

MR. WHITFIELD. But was there any reason particularly that you didn't read it or other pressing matters?

MR. HURD. I want to make sure I am clear. I am accountable for everything that is sent to me, and I should be reading it. I pick my spots where I dive for details. This was not a place that was a priority for me. It was the day of our shareholder meeting. And, again, I want to make sure I am clear. There is no excuse for that. If I had read it, I might have picked it up.

MR. WHITFIELD. From your viewpoint, how significant were these Board leaks? As the CEO of the company, was it something that really did--did it really disturb you or--

MR. HURD. I would say--because I didn't have the history, Mr. Chairman, I did not have the history of the December, January time frames. And during my time as CEO, we were not encountering a significant number of leaks, so I was probably not as concerned as some.

MR. WHITFIELD. Okay. I am not here to defend you in any way, and I will say that as a Member of Congress representing 650,000 people, there are a significant number of reports and letters that I do not read for one reason or the other, and I am not defending you, because I do think that the way that this issue has come up was certainly much different than anyone intended at HP. I am quite confident of that. And it has tarnished the reputation of the company, and I think it certainly violated the standards of conduct of the company.

At this time I will recognize Ms. DeGette for 10 minutes.

MS. DEGETTE. Thank you, Mr. Chairman.

Mr. Hurd, did you have the opportunity to hear the testimony of the previous panel?

MR. HURD. I heard some.

MS. DEGETTE. Now, in early January, that was the first you heard about this investigation of Board members and the leaks, correct?

MR. HURD. Just clarity, early January of '06?

MS. DEGETTE. Yes.

MR. HURD. No. I would say that when I first came to the company, there was discussion about the leaks. I can't give you specifics in that April, May timeframe the first few weeks I was there. But in July, as I was leaving town, there was a meeting that was designed to plug the leaks.

MS. DEGETTE. But in January, that is when Ms. Dunn came to you and she said, we are continuing the investigation, can we use the internal resources, right?

MR. HURD. Yes.

MS. DEGETTE. And you said okay. After that, what did you know about the ongoing investigation? Did you know about the searches of the trash?

MR. HURD. No.

MS. DEGETTE. Did you know about the monitoring of HP employees and of--or, I am sorry, of Board members and their families?

MR. HURD. No.

MS. DEGETTE. Did you know about the monitoring of reporters?

MR. HURD. No.

MS. DEGETTE. No one ever told you about any of this?

MR. HURD. No.

MS. DEGETTE. Did you know about the pretexting that was going on?

MR. HURD. No.

MS. DEGETTE. You didn't know about the whole Jacob incident?

MR. HURD. No. Let me go back to my previous testimony as we go through these. To the best of my knowledge, I do not remember any of the first points that you brought up.

MS. DEGETTE. Okay.

MR. HURD. The issue about the e-mail, I definitely knew about the content of the e-mail that was going out. There was clearly a communication.

MS. DEGETTE. Did you know about the fake person, Jacob?

MR. HURD. Yes, I knew about the objective.

MS. DEGETTE. What was your view of that? Did that seem ethical for the investigators to be coming up with a fake individual to be e-mailing reporters?

MR. HURD. Let me try to tell you what was going through my head at the time. I certainly was trying to--this was a team that was--

MS. DEGETTE. I only have 10 minutes. I am really sorry, yes or no?

MR. HURD. At the time, I agreed with the content of the e-mail.

MS. DEGETTE. So you thought that was just fine?

MR. HURD. It was appropriate to find the leak.

MS. DEGETTE. To be having fake people e-mailing reporters. Do you think that today?

MR. HURD. With the benefit of hindsight, I wouldn't do it again.

MS. DEGETTE. Did you hear when I asked Mr. Sonsini if all of these techniques, some of them though they may be legal or ethical for a major corporation like you--

MR. HURD. I agree.

MS. DEGETTE. --you agree none of these are ethical?

MR. HURD. I believe there is a difference between legal and ethical.

MS. DEGETTE. Do you think that HP should have been using techniques--

MR. HURD. No.

MS. DEGETTE. --like that to investigate leaks? No?

MR. HURD. No.

MS. DEGETTE. Thank you.

You said that a lot of things broke down here, and that you are trying to fix that. So I kind of want to go through where the breakdown was. First thing is that we have heard that it is very unusual to have a Nonexecutive Board chair; is that correct?

MR. HURD. I wouldn't call it unusual, but it is not common practice.

MS. DEGETTE. Ms. Dunn says it is not done very often, and because she was not paid like a CEO, she had no real responsibility to oversee what was under her in terms of the investigation. Do you agree with that?

MR. HURD. I--I--

MS. DEGETTE. Do you think that because of the structure, that she was the Chairman without being--just being an independent Chairman?

MR. HURD. I believe it is not as simple a governance model as--

MS. DEGETTE. Don't you think that the Chairman of the Board should have the same ethical obligations whether or not she is an employee of the company?

MR. HURD. There is no question about that.

MS. DEGETTE. Okay. So that is not really--I mean--just that structural function, that is not why there was a breakdown, right?

MR. HURD. I agree that there is no difference in ethical behavior no matter whether you are a nonexec chair, a chair exec, COO, at any level of the company.

MS. DEGETTE. I suppose you would also agree that the Chairman of the Board would have an ethical obligation, if she saw unethical things happening in an investigation of her own Board members, she would mention it to someone like, say, the CEO, correct?

MR. HURD. Certainly.

MS. DEGETTE. Did she ever mention it to you?

MR. HURD. No.

MS. DEGETTE. Take a look at Tab 29. This is the initial briefing slide show we've been talking about with--

MR. HURD. Let me catch up to you.

MS. DEGETTE. Have you ever seen that document?

MR. HURD. I have now.

MS. DEGETTE. Had you seen it at the time?

MR. HURD. I had not. This is basically the draft--no, I'm sorry, let me back up. No, I had not seen this document.

MS. DEGETTE. Okay. This is the one that talks about pretrash inspection and so on. No one ever gave you that?

MR. HURD. To the best of my memory, I never saw this document.

MS. DEGETTE. That's the first red flag. Take a look at Tab 60. I'm getting ahead of myself. Tab 30.

This is the senior management briefing on Project Kona 2 that we were also talking about earlier. It's a very similar briefing, talks about some of the same techniques. Were you ever given that?

MR. HURD. No. To the best of my knowledge--

MS. DEGETTE. Even though it's a senior management briefing, you never saw that?

MR. HURD. No.

MS. DEGETTE. Now take a look at Tab number 60. This is the e-mail communications between Ann Baskins and various people about the Jacob situation. And you have to start from the second page and go on, where--and part of that was--did you hear me, did you hear me when I was talking to Ms. Dunn about how she had said that they had to have your approval of this?

MR. HURD. Yes.

MS. DEGETTE. And did anybody come to you for approval of this?

MR. HURD. This would have been the first I would have seen of it that said, "Hi Mark," the e-mail that says 2/22.

MS. DEGETTE. Did you see the whole e-mail exchange?

MR. HURD. No.

MS. DEGETTE. What I'm saying, on 2/22, when you saw the Hi Mark e-mail, the other e-mails that say Hi Ann and Pattie and the rest, you would have seen those because they would have been attached to the e-mail exchange, correct?

MR. HURD. Can I just read it for one second?

MS. DEGETTE. You betcha.

MR. HURD. I don't remember seeing this, but I agree that I possibly could have.

MS. DEGETTE. And at that time, you didn't see anything wrong, as you had testified earlier, with this whole Jacob situation?

MR. HURD. I definitely remember the content, Congresswoman. I do remember it; and I agreed with content.

MS. DEGETTE. Okay. Now, take a look at Tab 72. Are you there?

MR. HURD. Yes.

MS. DEGETTE. Now, I think this is the document that the Chairman was just talking to you about, the draft of the investigation report, which you said that you frankly didn't read because it was the day of your shareholders' meeting and it was a mistake, right?

MR. HURD. Correct.

MS. DEGETTE. Now, here's my question to you is, didn't you think that leaks at the Board level were a very serious problem for the company?

MR. HURD. You know, Congresswoman--

MS. DEGETTE. Because Ms. Dunn certainly did.

MR. HURD. I know that she did, and I appreciate that concern. And I am not a supporter of leaks in any way, shape or form. I will tell you though, in terms of the priorities of the Hewlett-Packard Corporation at the point in time, this was not the CEO's number one priority.

MS. DEGETTE. Okay. The reason I just showed you all these documents, and there are more, is because you had testified earlier that there were--that the rules broke down. I see all of these as red flags in the organization that were never caught by anybody at the CEO level on down. And I'm wondering if you can tell me how on earth we have such a huge breakdown. I mean, you've been in corporate America for a long time; have you ever--number one, have you ever seen an investigation of corporate board members that involved these kinds of tactics that were involved here?

MR. HURD. Congresswoman, I've seen a lot of stuff in my career.

MS. DEGETTE. So your answer would be yes?

MR. HURD. No, I don't think I've seen anything like this. And there is two ways processes break down; they break down because of bad processes that don't have checks and balances, and they break down because of poor execution. Those are the two ways. We broke down here in both.

MS. DEGETTE. Okay. My question, though, is you broke down in both, but there were regular flags aplenty. Why was it that nobody in senior management of Hewlett-Packard caught any of these red flags?

MR. HURD. I'll speak for myself, I didn't catch them.

MS. DEGETTE. Why?

MR. HURD. Some was it was attention to detail, as you described. There is another piece of it that I will tell you from a checks and balances perspective, and a company of our scale, we have 151,000 employees, we're kind of a small city almost and have all the issues that go on in that size of an institution. The CEO cannot be the backstop for every process in the company. The processes have to be pushed into the organization with clear checks and balances and clear accountability. We broke down in both.

MS. DEGETTE. Mr. Chairman, I would just ask unanimous consent if Mr. Hurd would be willing to supplement his answer once the internal audit is completed, to let us know what internal checks and balances had been in place, because frankly this was a breakdown not just at the CEO level, but at every level of the legal department and senior management.

MR. WHITFIELD. Thank you.

Mr. Walden.

MR. WALDEN. Thank you. Welcome, Mr. Hurd.

When Ms. DeGette showed you Exhibit 60, I think I heard you say that February 22nd was the first time you heard of the e-mail sting operation; isn't that right? That was at Tab 60. Your testimony a few minutes ago was that--

MR. HURD. It was the first that I remember.

MR. WALDEN. It was the 22nd of February. Could you turn to Tab 52? In an e-mail from Pattie Dunn to Ann Baskins and Kevin Hunsaker, with the subject line of Konas, on February 9th, she says, and I quote, "I spoke with Mark, and he is on board with the plan to use the info on new hand-held leader. He also agrees we should consider doing something with the adaptive enterprise branding issue, given there is some chance that D.K. will seek clarification on this from her CNET source. Regards, Pattie." Are you the Mark in that e-mail?

MR. HURD. Yes, I am.

MR. WALDEN. Does this refer to the Jacob e-mail?

MR. HURD. No. It may have been using the same name Jacob, but they were two separate content subjects; one was the Next Generation Data Center, the first was the handheld person in the organization who would be brought out.

MR. WALDEN. But does this relate to the e-mail that would go to the reporter with false information?

MR. HURD. Congressman, I want to make sure I'm clear with you. I can't give you the detail of how the delivery, what was combined and not combined and what the methodology was. I do remember this content, yes.

MR. WALDEN. So this was talking about what would go to D.K., who is the reporter--

MR. HURD. One of the two subjects that would go potentially to the reporter.

MR. WALDEN. Right. I guess the point is you told us February 22nd is the first time that you're aware of this e-mail, and actually this was a February 9th e-mail to you about a conversation--

MR. HURD. I was trying to divide the two subjects, but I accept your point.

MR. WALDEN. Okay. So you probably knew before February 22nd?

MR. HURD. February 9th was the discussion about the hand-held, yes.

MR. WALDEN. You've undoubtedly heard the testimony by Ms. Dunn, who took no blame for this. I mean, she was asked very clearly by my colleague, Mr. Stearns, do you accept any culpability, any blame, she said no, and basically pushed it off on Ann Baskins as legal counsel, or others in the management side.

If she had no blame, and it was Ann--do you think it was Ann Baskins' fault, was she in charge?

MR. HURD. Congressman, I want to make sure I'm clear with you, I'm in charge of the company.

MR. WALDEN. So it wasn't Ann Baskins--

MR. HURD. I'm responsible for HP, Pattie was the Chairman. Responsibility goes across the entire company, Congressman, including myself.

MR. WALDEN. So why did Ms. Dunn resign?

MR. HURD. After deliberations from the Board, and the Board decided to change the leadership of the Board.

MR. WALDEN. They asked for her resignation?

MR. HURD. Yes, sir.

MR. WALDEN. Why, if she wasn't to blame?

MR. HURD. Well, I'm back to Board deliberations, Congressman. And I think there was a combination of effects, some of which was the concern about the ability to lead the company going forward, lead the Board going forward, given what had transpired.

MR. WALDEN. All right. In the Sonsini interview with Ron DeLia on Kona 1, which is Tab--we'll get you the number here, sir--115, item number eight.

MR. HURD. I'm sorry, I've got to go to another book.

MR. WALDEN. I understand.

MR. HURD. I'm sorry for that.

MR. WALDEN. No, we appreciate the willingness of you all to make all these documents available.

On number eight it says, "DeLia recalls a specific meeting in Palo Alto in July 2005, in which he met with Dunn, Ann Baskins, Mark Hurd, Jim Fairbaugh, Kevin Huska, Tony Gentilucci regarding the investigation. When DeLia arrived for the meeting, Baskins, Gentilucci, Fairbaugh and Huska were already in the meeting. When DeLia arrived, Hurd was not in the meeting; he appeared to have stepped out temporarily, but he stepped back a few minutes later. DeLia did not recall whether Hurd was present for any discussion of phone records."

Do you recall if you were there for a discussion of those phone records?

MR. HURD. No. But I remember the meeting, it was the day of a Board meeting, the Board meeting was either still going on or ending. I was relocating--I know you have a limited amount of time, I was relocating back home. I was just going back home because I was still living in Ohio. And I had to leave early, got there late, and that's what happened.

MR. WALDEN. So you don't remember any discussion about methodology?

MR. HURD. I really don't. Clearly the focus in the meeting was that they had not figured out who the leak was.

MR. WALDEN. Okay. And that was on Kona 1.

MR. HURD. That was Kona 1.

MR. WALDEN. And then we go on to Kona 2. And again, you heard this, I mean, I'm trying to sort out--who made the decision that allowed this to go forward? Because we all sort of thought Ms. Dunn did, but I didn't get the impression that she thought she did, and then she sort of said you--

MR. HURD. Let me make sure I am very clear with you on my opinion. This was a leak at the Board level, Pattie took it very seriously. And by the way, let me add, appropriately. She came to me and asked to be able to use HP resources, which came into the legal department, which is where the name Ann Baskins comes in. Pattie then was the business owner, I would describe it, of all of that, using HP resources to go execute.

MR. WALDEN. And I guess what I was troubled about was we had a lot of e-mail traffic back and forth to the investigators from her on pretty specific levels, and yet when we ask her about her involvement, it seemed to be it was a 30,000 foot level, and yet she's naming the name of the investigation, she's providing phone numbers, there are other e-mails from people saying she wants very specific things in the report, techniques, resources, but she doesn't have any recollection of any of that. Do you see why we're troubled by what we're hearing?

MR. HURD. I can understand why you're troubled by the whole thing; I understand, Congressman.

MR. WALDEN. And did you ever think that there would be--what I asked about access to public--that she thought you could just get somebody's phone records through public means? Did you believe that was possible, that I could just somehow--

MR. HURD. I would be speculating. I'm not just an expert in this area. I've come to learn a lot, and I'm very--

MR. WALDEN. I mean, come on, did you ever think you could just pick up a phone somehow and get my phone records or I could get yours?

MR. HURD. Congressman, it wasn't something I thought about; and I'm sorry, I just can't give you a comment on that.

MR. WALDEN. I can't imagine that that would be legal or appropriate--would you think it's appropriate?

MR. WALDEN. I would not want somebody, without my permission, to have my cell phone bill.

MR. WALDEN. Or your cell phone records?

MR. HURD. The cell phone records or cell phone bill. I wasn't trying to be cute with my answer.

MR. WALDEN. If you could turn to Exhibit 77. This e-mail states that Tom Perkins called you before the March 2006 Board meeting and asked you about the status of the investigation. Do you recall that conversation with Mr. Perkins? And I'll let you get caught up there, sir.

MR. HURD. I have a different--I have something that says Kevin Hunsaker to Tony Gentilucci under 77.

MR. WALDEN. Right. And it says on the second paragraph, "It's also worth noting that a few days before the March 2006 Board meeting Perkins called Mark Hurd and asked him, among other things, about the status of the investigation of the leaks. Hurd told Perkins the investigation team had assembled a significant amount of circumstantial evidence but that he was not sure where it would ultimately lead." Do you recall that conversation--

MR. HURD. No.

MR. WALDEN. Is that accurate? Because according to this e-mail, you apparently knew enough to tell Mr. Perkins what evidence the investigation uncovered.

MR. HURD. Well, remember just in timing wise, this e-mail would be posted when I knew the answer. So it went back to the meeting in Los Angeles, where I received here is the answer. And that meeting really reflected on who is your leaker. At roughly this timeframe, it would be logical that I would have known where the leak was coming from.

MR. WALDEN. And would you have ever asked how they got that information?

MR. HURD. Again--

MR. WALDEN. It just wasn't--

MR. HURD. I want to make sure I'm clear, I should have, I should have.

MR. WALDEN. I guess the thing we're struggling with is the public policy issue about pretexting, you know that, but also about, in a corporate environment, we haven't been able to figure out who should have asked this question and didn't. And there are a lot of people who show up that knew about it and other--you know, Mr. Adler and Mr. Nye and a few of them said wait a minute, this isn't right.

MR. HURD. Congressman, first of all, I appreciate exactly what you're saying. We have got to push this accountability further down in the company, but I don't want to stop, I should have been able to catch it, I didn't.

MR. WALDEN. I understand. Thank you.

MR. WHITFIELD. The gentlemen's time is expired.

Mr. Inslee, you are recognized for 10 minutes.

MR. INSLEE. Thank you. You talked about when checks and balances break down things, really go awry. Working in the Federal government, I want to tell you I can empathize with that.

MR. HURD. Congressman, I'm glad of where I am most of the time, maybe not today.

MR. INSLEE. You know, there has been a lot of bright days for HP, and you've done some great work for our economy and people in general, and there is going to be a lot of bright days--this is not one of them, of course, not your finest day of this great organization. And when organizations go awry, like I think happened here, sometimes it makes sense to do a little penance and help the cause out to try to see to it that we reduce this from happening again in your community. Now the situation here in Congress is this committee, as you have heard, has passed a bill to give the Federal Government tools to prevent illicit pretexting that you have run afoul of, or the organization has run afoul of.

We can't get the Speaker of the House to schedule a vote on this bill. I think it might be helpful if you called the Speaker of the House this afternoon and suggested to him that he schedule this bill since you have learned that this is not a real positive thing for American corporations or the economy or privacy in general. What do you think of that idea?

MR. HURD. Do you think he would take my call?

MR. INSLEE. You bet he would take your call. And he should take your call because you're a leader of a major corporation that's a major technology leader. And I'm very serious about this, we need to send a message to the country that we're going to stop this from happening.

MR. HURD. Congressman, I don't want to be trite with my comment, we are out in support of making pretexting illegal, creating clarity. And I don't want to hide behind the lack of clarity either, because there is a difference between legality and ethical behavior, and we don't want to confuse the two. We have a standard of business conduct that this violated, regardless of any clarity around legal issues. But I understand your point, and we're going to take efforts to support the legislation.

MR. INSLEE. I really do believe that can be helpful.

MR. HURD. You have our support.

MR. INSLEE. And I appreciate that.

I wanted to ask you about the tracing technology and its use by HP and what your current corporate policy is.

Mr. Adler suggested that this had been used in other contexts--as I understand his testimony, that it's been used in this context of trying to track down a leak in Board members, but also had been used by HP targeting other non-HP personnel on occasion. Are you familiar with what other occasions that has been?

MR. HURD. I believe that what Mr. Adler was describing about the use of it in other projects. We are currently going through a process right now to go directly at any use of a technology like that. I'm not intimate with that technology, several others I am. I'm not sure as we go into the future, we will be comfortable with the use of technology like that. It's a process we're going to review. And one of the reasons I mentioned in my statement our hiring of Bart Schwartz is to go through the process to make sure in every investigation we are behaving properly and appropriately as we go forward. So we will put lots of energy into this, Congressman.

MR. INSLEE. Are you familiar whether or not HP has used this technology against other non-HP targets?

MR. HURD. This tracer technology? Congressman, I have no evidence of that, I have no knowledge of us using it against a competitor or in any improper way, I have no knowledge of that. But as I said earlier, we're going to dig in toward the bottom of everything.

MR. INSLEE. Speaking for the 600,000 people I represent, I think their expectations of privacy is that a corporation would not use tracer technology to try to follow where they send e-mail or where they send attachments to report back to that corporation without their specific approval. That's the expectation that my constituents have.

Do you believe that HP should follow--and major corporations or minor corporations--should follow that privacy examination?

MR. HURD. I think for us at HP, it is not important for us to follow but to lead. And it's important for us to be a leader. And we have been a leader in consumer privacy. We are a leader in consumer privacy. This is an aberration to us. We need to make sure we're checking every process, not just with our customers, but internally, whether it's an investigation, use on our people, in any way, shape, or form to making sure we're appropriately dealing with things, which we will do, Congressman.

MR. INSLEE. Well, I hope do you so. And I hope that includes helping Congress to move forward on privacy legislation.

I think this hearing is peeling back a layer of an onion that's very disturbing, and that we need to do more work on privacy here in Congress. And I hope that you will put your corporate resources behind efforts in that regard so that others do not fall victim to this. I don't believe this should be left just to the whims of the CEO of these particular corporations. We need total clarity of this situation so that no others have to depend on the good graces of whatever management we have. And I hope you would render your weight to that effort and become a leader on this.

MR. HURD. Congressman, we actually believe we have been a leader, and that's what is so disappointing about this. We actually believe we've been a leader to point out where consumer privacy should be and should go. We've got many people in the company that all they do is focus on privacy, around our products, our solutions; makes this even a bigger disappointment.

MR. INSLEE. I appreciate what you're saying, but I'm suggesting that--and that is a good statement--but HP's leading legislative efforts to try to solve this problem is a next step that I would encourage you to consider.

MR. HURD. I couldn't agree with you more. We want to be that leader, Congressman.

MR. INSLEE. Thank you.

MR. WHITFIELD. Dr. Burgess--no, Mrs. Blackburn of Tennessee is recognized for 10 minutes.

MRS. BLACKBURN. Thank you, Mr. Chairman. And I want to thank our witness for being here with us.

I will tell you, quite frankly, listening to all of this today and spending yesterday going back through all the evidence, looking at the chain of e-mails, looking at the memos, it certainly provides a basis to us to believe that there were some folks at HP that certainly knew that they were pushing the envelope and they were skirting the edges. So I've got a few simple questions, and then I'm going to yield my time back. But Mr. Hurd, I want to know if you can tell me when was the first time you ever heard the term pretexting.

MR. HURD. To the best of my memory, it was in a memo or e-mail that went from Larry Sonsini to Tom Perkins that was in the--I'm going to say in the summer--it's in your documents, it's got to be--

MRS. BLACKBURN. It's Number 91. We know these now. We're very familiar with this documentation.

So this is the June 28th, 2006 memo. And this was the first time you ever heard the term pretexting? Who did you turn to to define the action of pretexting for you?

MR. HURD. What transpired, if you want this background--

MRS. BLACKBURN. Yes, please.

MR. HURD. Is that this resulted in a series of e-mails back and forth that are in your documents, where eventually not only did we uncover the term pretexting, but what surfaced within the next 3 weeks or so was a letter from a phone company that not only described the term pretexting, but described actually what happened. That trigger was the first specific trigger I'd had that this was wrong.

MRS. BLACKBURN. So you were this far into the Kona project and the Jacob project, and you didn't realize what pretexting was. And you had never, through this entire process, turned to somebody and said, tell me what this word pretexting is? I did not have that in vocabulary when I was in fifth grade or at Baylor University when I was in freshman English.

MR. HURD. I don't remember it in freshman English--

MRS. BLACKBURN. You would have never have heard it. I'm trying to figure out who you would turn to and whose advice you would ask to define the term and the action to know what this really was. And Mr. Hurd, the reason I'm doing this is not to be flippant with you, because I think as we live in this world where e-commerce is very much a part of our day and technology very much a part of our day, being certain that the statutes and the rules under which business operates each and every day and being certain that the leaders in the field, all the stakeholders understand is tremendously important to us. So that is why I had that question.

Now, let me ask you this, also. There seems to be disagreement between Ms. Dunn and you as to who actually said, the buck stops with me, and I'm making the decision.

MR. HURD. I will speak for no one else, that in Hewlett-Packard operations and strategy and everything else that goes on in HP, eventually the buck stops with me.

MRS. BLACKBURN. So you're the one responsible for ordering the investigation and the spyware technology, the tracer, if you will?

MR. HURD. No, I didn't do that. But that said, in the end, I'm responsible for everything that goes on at HP.

MRS. BLACKBURN. All right. Great.

Who actually made the decision to put the tracer--

MR. HURD. Well, I'm sure--I'm going to tell you what I think. My belief is the investigative team had a set of processes that they used. They were trying their best to fulfill the objectives that the Chairman had set forward, and that's what they did, they went and executed around that.

MRS. BLACKBURN. Who is running HP's investigative team as of right now today?

MR. HURD. As of now, we have an open position.

MRS. BLACKBURN. An open position?

MR. HURD. We are looking for qualified candidates, Congresswoman.

MRS. BLACKBURN. Sir, I have no doubt you are.

Is HP investigating or using spyware on or pretexting anyone, either an employee, a competitor or a Board member today and at this time?

MR. HURD. I have set up very clear instructions that any activity that you have described on the specifics of pretexting is to be ceased, and if anyone is confused they can call my extension.

MRS. BLACKBURN. And does that apply to spyware technology also?

MR. HURD. The spyware technology--I only put the caveat on it, as Fred described, there are a couple of dimensions to the use of this technology. I'm going to go back directly and make sure I look specifically at every use of that kind of--I think as you called it, send-receive technology and make sure that we have absolute clarity.

MRS. BLACKBURN. So people that you were running pretexting work on or people that you were running tracers through their correspondence, you have ceased that at this point in time?

MR. HURD. There is no--could you put your question one more time, Congresswoman, to make sure I got it right?

MRS. BLACKBURN. Did you stop offending; did you stop the tracer technology, the spyware technology to pretexting?

MR. HURD. We are stopping anything that isn't appropriate or ethical in the company. What we're looking for right now is why; we have got an investigation going on through the company that is still not complete.

MRS. BLACKBURN. Okay, great. The Kona project briefing that has been referred to by my colleagues a couple of times, who actually prepared that?

MR. HURD. I'm sorry. Which Kona briefing? Kona 1, 2? There were a multiple of the briefings.

MRS. BLACKBURN. There is two, who prepared them?

MR. HURD. Would have been the investigative team. But the Kona 1 briefing, that was the one at the conclusion of it, I believe would have been prepared by an outside contractor.

MRS. BLACKBURN. By an outside contractor. Have you terminated all of those agreements with the outside contractors?

MR. HURD. Yes.

MRS. BLACKBURN. And like Action--the different companies, how long have you had these investigative agreements with Action and some of these that we have in our documents?

MR. HURD. There are two sets of contractors. There is a subcontractor, and then I think there are actually a series of subcontractors to that subcontractor that we actually would not have an agreement with. We would have an agreement with the original subcontractor that has been terminated. I believe that the subcontractor in question had been working with Hewlett-Packard for roughly 8 years.

MRS. BLACKBURN. For 8 years. All right.

Well, Mr. Chairman, I'm going to yield back. Thank you.

MR. WHITFIELD. Thank you, Ms. Blackburn.

At this time, I would recognize Ms. Eshoo for 10 minutes.

MS. ESHOO. Thank you, Mr. Chairman. And good afternoon.

MR. HURD. Hi.

MR. WHITFIELD. Ms. Eshoo, excuse me. Mr. Burgess has not asked his questions, he is a member of the subcommittee, so --

MS. ESHOO. Absolutely, I'll wait.

MR. BURGESS. I'll yield to my friend from California.

MR. WHITFIELD. He yields to you, so--he is such a polite fellow. So go ahead.

MS. ESHOO. Thank you. Well, it's been a long day, and I think that you have the advantage of being last because everyone is somewhat exhausted. But nonetheless, there are still, I think, some questions to be asked.

Let me just comment first that--and I've said this with each group that has come in. For me, this is a sad day, I think it is for you as well. I keep thinking of the thousands of employees who no doubt have tried to access this at some point during the day on C-SPAN, so many of them are my constituents. They have worked hard to not only help make the company successful, they have a real investment in it, a great sense of pride, and I share that with them, and I think that you do as well.

This really needs to be cleared up. I don't think there can be anything that's lingering at the end of this. And I hope that there isn't, because it's something that needs to be thorough. The sunshine is really a disinfectant, I believe. One of our members, the distinguished Ranking Member of the full committee, uses that phrase a great deal, and that's what this process is about.

You're one of the survivors of the key people in this. Very distinguished General Counsel is gone, distinguished Chairwoman of the Board, gone. Mr. Hunsaker, the ethics officer of the company, gone. Mr. Gentilucci--I cannot remember his exact title, you know what it is--gone. And so I think with the individuals that are here, even Ms. Dunn did testify during the longest stretch of today's hearing, there are gaps, there are still a lot of gaps.

Now I asked Mr. Adler, whom I don't know, either couldn't hear me or hasn't worked at HP long enough to have an institutional history of how HP is operated, so let me start with the questions that I asked him.

How long has HP had a contract or retainer or retained SOS, ARG and the other outfit, Eye in the Sky I think is the name of it?

MR. HURD. The contract relationship, as I mentioned, was roughly around 8 years.

MS. ESHOO. And was it mostly with SOS, or all three?

MR. HURD. That's my understanding.

MS. ESHOO. Do you still have a contract with them? Are they still on retainer?

MR. HURD. No.

MS. ESHOO. Are you going to have any contract with outside investigators? Your answer is probably going to be no, given this experience.

MR. HURD. I think what we're going to do is get the best in class processes, Congresswoman, to make sure we understand how investigations, if they need to be done, are done, so they meet the level of our ethical standard as well as our--

MS. ESHOO. What did they do for 8 years ?

MR. HURD. I don't know, Congresswoman, they did many investigations over that period of time.

MS. ESHOO. In reading the background and preparing for this hearing, one of the breakdowns was the use of Social Security numbers. That's a huge violation, I have to tell you, in my view, which really goes after someone's privacy. You have a Social Security number, first of all you're holding gold, you're holding gold. Someone filed a fraudulent tax return in my name, and it was because they somehow got my Social Security number. So Social Security numbers are really the golden key that can open the door so that people can get a lot.

Can you explain to us from your investigation of the investigation how many Social Security numbers were used from inside the company to access information?

MR. HURD. I do not yet have a complete report on how many. Clearly there have been an effort to gather at least a couple that I've seen, which we're still not to the end of the trail. So certainly there have been a couple. And as I pledged to you earlier, we will dig to the bottom of it.

MS. ESHOO. Mr. Chairman, is that going to be requested as part of the record for this hearing?

MR. WHITFIELD. Would you repeat that question?

MS. ESHOO. I was asking Mr. Hurd about the--no one brought this up today--but part of what I've read is that Social Security numbers were used internally in HP in order to obviously go out and secure information. So Mr. Hurd doesn't know from the investigation into the investigation what the answer to my question is, and I asked if that would be requested from the committee to be made part of the record. I think it is an important part of it.

MR. WHITFIELD. Absolutely. Without objection, yes.

MS. ESHOO. Let me ask you this; does the Chair of the Board have the authority to initiate activities and to commit company resources?

MR. HURD. That's one of those issues of governance. I mean, you get down to the fact that the Chairman of the Board certainly can commit company resources, depending on the interpretation of what resources are being committed.

MS. ESHOO. Did Pattie Dunn commit HP resources for this investigation?

MR. HURD. The best thing I can tell you, Congresswoman, is the second phase, being Kona 2, which is when I was in place. Pattie did not. Pattie asked me if she could now engage with HP resource, which she--

MS. ESHOO. So there isn't a firewall there. The description of the Chair of the Board as it applies to HP seems to be just a little different. There are other models that are the same, but I think there are others that are more common to one another than what was described today.

But when you said Pattie took it seriously, I have to tell you that that sounded to me as if there was one person that took it seriously and went out on their own to do this. And I have to tell you--this is just the way it struck me --

MR. HURD. Can I clarify that?

MS. ESHOO. Pattie took it seriously. It seems to me that there were several members of your Board that took it seriously.

MR. HURD. If I said it that way, I mischaracterized it. This was a very serious issue. Leaks coming out of the company about strategy, about operations --

MS. ESHOO. I think so.

MR. HURD. This is a very serious issue. And I want to make sure I'm clear to everyone, it's unacceptable, it's unacceptable at Hewlett-Packard. We can't have that and run a company successfully. So I want to say one more time, Pattie appropriately took it seriously. I was only trying to make a comment relative to the abrogation of priorities in the company relative to what's gone on across all of Hewlett-Packard. It wasn't my personal number one priority relative to other things, but don't take anything away to diminish the importance of it.

MS. ESHOO. To whom does the ethics officer report to?

MR. HURD. The ethics officer reports to our total customer experience group, which is in our marketing organization.

MS. ESHOO. Are you going to change that?

MR. HURD. We're going to look at the entire process, Congresswoman, that's what I pledge to you.

MS. ESHOO. You know what I'm stuck by? And we're all somewhat guilty of this, but I am certainly reminded of it over and over and over again today. It doesn't seem to me that human beings sit down and talk to each other anymore. People are messaging and texting and we don't remember meetings and we're buzzing and we're wired, and there is all of this information that's going out there. No one remembers it. It's not used for anything. And look what's happened. I always want to look ahead, that we learn from the mistakes that we make, we're all human, it's the mark of our humanity. And my mother used to say, little people make little mistakes, big people make big mistakes, and there are big mistakes in this.

But I think when you reshape all of this, that given the reputation that HP has had, enjoyed, earned, that an ethics officer report to the CEO is just a suggestion of mine.

Where did the progress reports of the investigation go to? Were they shared, did they just go to one person?

MR. HURD. Are you talking on a go-forward basis, Congresswoman?

MS. ESHOO. No, what you're here for today, the investigation. Where did the progress reports on this go to?

MR. HURD. Where did they go?

MS. ESHOO. Yes. There were the investigators, outside, inside, they weren't just given instructions about what to do and then come up with a report, they must have had progress reports. Where are those progress reports?

MR. HURD. I want to make sure I'm clear, you're talking about the actual investigation themselves?

MS. ESHOO. Kona 2.

MR. HURD. There were some updates that went through the investigative team, and I'm not aware of them escalating beyond that.

MS. ESHOO. So it stayed in the same circle?

MR. HURD. That is, to the best of my knowledge, what transpired.

MR. WHITFIELD. The gentlelady's time has expired.

Dr. Burgess is recognized for 11 minutes for being such a great--

MR. BURGESS. Mr. Chairman, just for the record, we have heard about our bill that has passed out of committee that has not been heard on the floor, but I do want to draw the committee's attention to the fact that we did pass on the House floor H.R. 4709, the Telephone Records and Privacy Protection Act, that was a bill of Lamar Smith's out of the Judiciary Committee. And since it was out of the Judiciary Committee, it probably wasn't as good a bill as ours was, but I did want to point out that the House has acted on this concept, trying to provide that context and that bright line that several people have asked for. Now I know the

Senate has not done so, and perhaps when the conference is held we can actually conference both bills with whatever the Senate produces for us.

Mr. Hurd, in your written testimony you say that you don't recall seeing or approving the use of tracer technology. I guess of all the stuff we've heard, the tracer software or spyware, whatever it's called, is really the thing that is most disturbing to me. And you state that you don't recall seeing or approving the use of the tracer technology. What was the purpose then, how did you think this elaborate structure around the e-mail of the fictitious Jacob, how is it all supposed to work?

MR. HURD. Sir, first, you're correct, that's the best of my knowledge. But certainly, the objective of it was get whoever it was that was leaking company information to call back into the company to validate that whatever information in that e-mail was accurate.

MR. BURGESS. Let's see. I think it is Tab 62 in the big book, we have an e-mail exchange. And of course, I have trouble with e-mail exchanges, you always have to start at the end and then work up. But basically, the e-mail exchange gives the fake e-mail or a draft of the fake e-mail that will be sent to Dawn, and it seems like rather innocuous information, but anyway, it goes right up the chain to you. Now, it's your testimony, then, that you didn't know that the tracer software was going to be attached to this e-mail, this--

MR. HURD. To the best of my memory, I don't remember that.

MR. BURGESS. And I, of course, don't run a large electronics corporation, so this information seems relatively innocuous, it's hard to see how the information itself would provide a traceable event for you, but that's your contention, that someone would call back in about the next generation data centers?

MR. HURD. Oh, sure, that once that information was to get in the hands of whoever it was that was interested in leaking information, they would have to validate that the information was correct and talk to somebody who would be responsible for that. I think that's what the team's objective was.

MR. BURGESS. Well, it seems like the team--everyone else on the team knew about the tracer aspect, but you did not?

MR. HURD. I just don't remember, Congressman.

MR. BURGESS. Okay. In a public statement last Friday you stated you attended a meeting in July 2005 where Kona 1 was discussed, where a verbal summary of the second phase of the investigation was provided, the second phase of the operation being the tracer software or the fake e-mail?

MR. HURD. Okay. I think let's go back to the two investigations. What you described are the two phases. The Kona 2 phase is where this e-mail actually occurs. Kona 1 was that first piece that actually didn't even use this investigative team, it was a separate team. And that meeting you're describing, I believe, was a report of their lack of a finding of any type, in that meeting where none of that was actually involved.

MR. BURGESS. In the July meeting, were you present for the discussion--any discussion of phone records?

MR. HURD. I don't remember a discussion about that, Congressman. I wasn't in that meeting all that long, as I commented earlier.

MR. BURGESS. Let me ask you this; you attended the May 18, 2006, Board meeting; Mr. Perkins resigned.

MR. HURD. Yes.

MR. BURGESS. Mr. Perkins has been outspoken that he resigned in protest over the tactics that were used in the leak investigation. Did the company insist--did you insist that the form 8K filed by Hewlett-Packard announcing his resignation fully disclose the reasons for his resignation?

MR. HURD. Congressman, we always to want file an 8K that was appropriate and accurate and complete; so that's my first response.

Secondly, I clearly remember Tom's reaction to what had transpired. He was bothered by the way the meeting occurred and the way the meeting was going on, and he clearly made that very clear in his discussion as he departed.

Subsequent to Tom's departure, physical departure from the Board meeting, he actually had a phone conversation with Mr. Sonsini, who you heard from earlier. I was not party to that phone conversation with Mr. Sonsini. So the 8K itself reflects both what occurred in the meeting and the conclusions of the phone conversation between Mr. Perkins and Mr. Sonsini.

MR. BURGESS. Do you think that is an adequate--does that cover the explanation or is that an adequate explanation for Exhibit 92 that Mr. Perkins wrote to the Board? It seems just from the tenor of his letter that he's disturbed that there is not a complete disclosure of the activities that led to his resignation.

MR. HURD. So clearly there is a debate, I accept your point. The 8K was filed based on the data that I described, the two pieces of data that I described, what actually occurred in the Boardroom and the follow-up conversation between the two. To the best of my knowledge, Congressman, our 8K reflects both what happened in the Boardroom--and for that one, Congressman, I was there. I was not at the conversation between Mr. Sonsini and Mr. Perkins. So the combination of the two are a submission of the 8K. I understand the debate that occurred, subsequent to the debate that you see here represented in the documents. Tom also asked that we look into this deeper, into the investigative methods. That debate was occurring, as you can see by the documents, into late July. We subsequently started the investigation upon some of the evidence that Tom was describing, which led to what has transpired. So that is really how the flow worked, Congressman.

MR. BURGESS. It's been a long day. Exhibit 96, in response to your company-wide e-mail on August 23rd concerning standards of business conduct, one of the Kona investigators, Vincent Nye, comments, and I quote, "This investigation will be a defining case which will test the company's claim of having uncompromising integrity." I think we will both agree it has certainly done that. Do you feel that going forward you can restore Hewlett-Packard's integrity?

MR. HURD. Congressman, I will.

MR. BURGESS. What have you done through this process to keep the employees of your company informed of what has happened, and that the progress of not just this hearing today, but your internal investigations at Hewlett-Packard and what legal liabilities there may be?

MR. HURD. Well, we've made an effort to communicate with them as often as possible. We've communicated with them about our changes in governance, the issues around the investigation. I've been communicating to them frequently. I'll also communicate to them as soon as I return.

Our employees are great people, Congressman. And I'm not here to give you a commercial on HP, but I believe this to my core. The people of Hewlett-Packard are some of the most hard working, highest level of integrity people around, and we're going to get this right.

MR. BURGESS. And I sincerely hope that you do because as I pointed out earlier, 57,000 American jobs, nearly 10,000 of my home State of Texas and almost 200 in the District that I represent in north Texas, so it is personally important to me as well, and I do sincerely hope you are correct.

Can you just answer me this in the 5 minutes or so that I have remaining; how do you feel that this affects the country's perception of corporate America? Have we harmed the corporate image in general?

MR. HURD. It's hard for me to imagine it's been helpful, but I can tell you this, that one of our founders, Dave Packard, said--who is quoted quite a bit around corporate America and certainly around our company--there will never be a time that we don't make mistakes. And I guarantee you, Congressman, we'll make more. The defining point will be what we do about them, how we handle them and refine ourselves as we go forward in the future. And I promise you we are committed to our core to redefine our company in a way that not only we can be proud of, but that all corporate America can be proud of.

MR. BURGESS. Well, on behalf of your employees, your stockholders and the country at large, I sincerely hope you are correct. Thank you very much for your attendance at this long hearing.

Mr. Chairman, I will yield back the balance of my time.

MR. WHITFIELD. Well, thank you.

You know, today's hearing has focused, correctly so, in my view, on significant shortcomings at Hewlett-Packard that did involve activity that violated private rights of individuals, that possibly violated the law, and certainly violated the ethics of Hewlett-Packard.

But in departing, there is one bright spot that I would like to just point out once again, and I'm sure you're familiar with this. Back as far away as last February of 2006, Mr. Vince Nye, whom I've never met, wrote an e-mail--sent an e-mail to Kevin Hunsaker, and he says, "Tony, I have serious reservations about what we're doing. As I understand the methodology in obtaining this phone record information, it leaves me with the opinion that it is unethical at the least, and probably illegal. If it is not totally illegal, then it is leaving Hewlett-Packard in a position that could damage our reputation, or worse, and I am requesting that we cease this phone number gathering immediately and discount any of its information. I think we need to refocus our strategy and proceed on the high ground." And I think that's an employee of Hewlett-Packard that needs some sort of recognition--maybe give him the day off or something.

But with that, thank you for being with us today. And I know it's been a long day, we appreciate your testimony very much. And we have the greatest confidence that you will continue to lead Hewlett-Packard back to its standing and succeed in every way. With that, the hearing is--and the record will remain open for 30 days. And with that, the hearing is adjourned.

[Whereupon, at 5:34 p.m., the subcommittee was adjourned.]

RESPONSE FOR THE RECORD OF MARK HURD, PRESIDENT, CHIEF EXECUTIVE OFFICER, AND CHAIRMAN OF THE BOARD, HEWLETT PACKARD COMPANY

manatt
manatt | phelps | phillips

Stephen M. Ryan
Manatt, Phelps & Phillips, LLP
Direct Dial: (202) 585-6550
E-mail: sryan@manatt.com

November 1, 2006

VIA MESSENGER AND EMAIL

The Honorable Ed Whitfield, Chairman
Subcommittee on Oversight and Investigations
Committee on Energy and Commerce
U.S. House of Representatives
2125 Rayburn House Office Building
Washington, D.C. 20515

Re: Your Letter Dated October 19, 2006, to Mr. Mark Hurd, Hewlett-Packard Company

Dear Chairman Whitfield:

In response to your letter noted above concerning Mr. Mark Hurd's testimony before your Subcommittee on September 28, 2006, please find attached Mr. Hurd's detailed responses to the additional questions included in your letter.

Please do not hesitate to contact me if you have any further questions. Thank you.

Sincerely,

Stephen M. Ryan (jl)

Stephen M. Ryan

Enclosure

cc: Mr. Tom Feddo
Mr. Mark Paoletta
Mr. Christopher Knauer
Ms. Sharon Davis

manatt
manatt | phelps | phillips

The Honorable Ed Whitfield, Chairman
November 1, 2006
Page 2

bcc: Mr. Mark Hurd

Hewlett-Packard Company
3000 Hanover Street
Palo Alto, CA 94304
www.hp.com

Mark Hurd
Chairman & Chief Executive Officer

November 1, 2006

Chairman Ed Whitfield
Subcommittee on Oversight and Investigations
Committee on Energy and Commerce
U.S. House of Representatives
2125 Rayburn House Office Building
Washington, D.C. 20515

Dear Chairman Whitfield:

Thank you again for the opportunity to address the Subcommittee on Oversight and Investigations at the September 28, 2006 hearing. It was important to Hewlett-Packard Company ("HP") to address the mistakes that were made and to explain to the Subcommittee and to the public the steps HP is taking to ensure that such lapses do not happen again. Our challenge is to restore the great confidence that government and the general public has shown in HP over the years and the opportunity to provide testimony at the hearing greatly aided us in meeting this challenge.

As for the questions posed in your October 17, 2006 letter, I have attempted to answer them to the best of my knowledge and trust you will find the attached responses satisfactory.

Sincerely,

Mark V. Hurd

RESPONSES OF MARK V. HURD TO QUESTIONS POSED BY CHAIRMAN ED WHITFIELD IN HIS OCTOBER 17, 2006 LETTER

1. **For exactly how long did you attend the 2:00 p.m. meeting on July 22, 2005 ("Kona I" Meeting), and who else was present at that meeting?**

Answer:

I do not know exactly how long I attended the July 22, 2005 meeting. What I do know is that I did not attend the entire meeting, but instead arrived after the meeting started, left before it concluded and was called out of the meeting room several times.

I remember that Patricia Dunn and others were at the meeting. I now understand that the documents show that Patricia Dunn, Ann Baskins, Kevin Huska, Jim Fairbaugh, Anthony Gentilucci, and Ron DeLia attended the July 22, 2005 meeting. I do not have any reason to believe that information is incorrect, but I don't have a memory of every person who was present.

2. **Were you the intended recipient of the briefing that was provided during the "Kona I" meeting? If not, describe the purpose of the "Kona I" Meeting?**

Answer:

I do not know if I was the intended recipient since the meeting started without me. However, since I was asked to attend the meeting I assume I was one of the intended recipients.

3. **During the "Kona I" Meeting, identify who mentioned the issue of "obtaining phone record information off of the web."**

Answer:

I cannot say who made the remark about obtaining phone record information off of the web or when that remark was made without speculating. What I recall is that at some meeting someone mentioned getting phone record information off of the web and thinking there must be some sort of website with this information.

I would like to make clear that I am not certain whether the attributed remark was made at the July 22, 2005 meeting or on some other occasion. The question presumes the remark was made at this meeting, but I do not specifically remember that being the case. My response to this question (and to the other similar questions below) is therefore based on my having heard the remark at some point in time, rather than accepting the presumption contained in the question that I heard the remark at the July 22, 2005 meeting.

4. **Did any person attending the "Kona I" Meeting in any way discuss or describe exactly what types of "phone record information" could be obtained "off of the web"? If so describe in detail the explanation that you were provided, and by whom.**

Answer:

Not that I recall.

5. **Did any person attending the "Kona I" Meeting say that phone record information that was obtained "off of the web" included detailed calling records? If so, identify who made that statement or representation.**

Answer:

Not that I recall.

6. **Did you ask any person attending the "Kona I" Meeting to explain exactly what types of phone record information could be obtained off of the web? If so, describe in detail the answer or explanation that you were provided, and by whom.**

Answer:

Not that I recall. In retrospect, I wish that I had been more focused on investigatory methodologies when the remark was made. Had I been, I might have questioned the remark or pressed for more details on the investigation. Unfortunately, I was not focused on the issue, so I did not dive into the details.

7. **Did any person attending the "Kona I" Meeting explicitly mention that there was a "website with such information." If yes, who made such a representation, and to what Web site were they referring? If no, describe in detail your basis for "thinking that there must be a website with such information."**

Answer:

What I recall is that someone at some time mentioned getting phone record information off of the web. I do not remember the exact words used and do not recall any discussion of a particular website. At the time I heard the remark, I remember thinking there must be some sort of website with publicly available information but simply did not give any further thought to the matter.

8. **Did any person attending the "Kona I" Meeting state that such information could be obtained directly from the respective Web sites of the actual phone companies? If so, identify who made that statement or representation.**

Answer:

Not that I recall.

9. **Did any person attending the "Kona I" Meeting discuss or describe the intended purpose for obtaining "phone record information off of the web?" If so, describe in detail the purpose that was explained to you.**

Answer:

Not that I recall.

10. **Explain *exactly* what you meant during your August 25, 2006 interview with Wilson Sonsini by the statement that someone in the July 22, 2005 meeting "mentioned obtaining phone record information off of the web."**

Answer:

I cannot provide any further explanation for the remark I made to the Wilson Sonsini attorneys about getting phone record information off of the web. I recall only the remark being made by someone at some time and thinking that there must be some website with the information.

Further:

a. **During the "Kona I" meeting, explain *exactly* what your understanding was regarding what type of "phone record information" you thought could be obtained "off of the web." Further, with respect to the phrase "off of the web," did you mean: (i) from a specific Internet Web site or sites that serve as clearinghouses for such phone record information; (ii) from various telephone carriers' Web sites that offer their customers Internet access to their phone records; or (iii) something else. If something else, please describe in detail what you understood "off of the web" to mean.**

Answer:

When the remark was made, I did not have any specific understanding of what type of "phone record information" could be obtained or what was meant by "off of the web." I simply thought there must be some website containing publicly available information about phone records. I did not give any further thought to the issue and do not recall any other discussions about it.

b. **Explain in detail your understanding, at the time or upon the conclusion of the "Kona I" Meeting, of exactly how "phone record information" was assisting the "Kona I" leak investigation.**

Answer:

I cannot say that as of the July 22, 2005 meeting I understood that "phone record information" was being obtained in connection with, or was assisting in the "Kona I" phase of the investigation. At some point, I did come to understand that telephone call information was being used as part of the leak investigation. However, I do not recall when I became aware of that information or who made me aware of it, and I did not think that anything improper might have been done until after Tom Perkins resigned and subsequently contacted the company about the letter he received from AT&T suggesting that someone had accessed his phone records through the use of an e-mail account.

c. **Did you understand "phone record information" to exclusively mean the subscriber's name and address? If so, describe in detail your understanding of exactly how such information was assisting the leak investigation.**

Answer:

I did not have an understanding one way or the other about what "phone record information" meant in the context of the remark.

d. **Did you understand "phone record information" to exclusively mean the subscriber's phone number? If so, describe in detail your understanding of exactly how such information was assisting the leak investigation.**

Answer:

See answer to subpart (c).

e. **Did anyone in the meeting explain whose "phone record information" had been obtained, or was going to be obtained, "off of the web?" If so, list the names of those individuals whose names were brought up in the context of obtaining "phone record information off of the web."**

Answer:

Not that I recall.

f. **Are you aware today of any Web site where detailed calling records may be obtained for any given subscriber? If so, list the name of any such Web site.**

Answer:

I am not aware of any website where a person can obtain phone record information for someone other than himself or herself.

11. **During the "Kona I" Meeting, who provided the PowerPoint briefing to you and the other attendees?**

Answer:

I cannot say without speculating who provided the briefing during the portion of the July 22, 2005 meeting I attended.

12. **Given your recollection of reviewing Slide 10 of the July 22, 2005, PowerPoint presentation, explain in detail your understanding of what specific types of "intelligence" that would "reveal" who a Board member had contacted, how many times the Board member had made such contacts, and the dates on which those contacts had been made?**

Answer:

I do not recall a discussion during the portion of the July 22, 2005 meeting I attended about what "intelligence" meant or what specific types of "intelligence" had been obtained. What I recall is that the story was not convincing and that the investigators had a lot of theories but no conclusion as to the source of the leak.

13. **Did the person who provided the PowerPoint presentation to you at the "Kona I" Meeting explain that the "intelligence" mentioned on Slide 10 was derived from the Board member's phone records? If yes, did you inquire in any way as to how such phone records had been obtained? If yes, describe in detail the explanation provided to you, and by whom.**

Answer:

Not that I recall.

14. During the "Kona I" Meeting, did you otherwise have an understanding that the "contacts" referred to on Slide 10 had been discerned from the Board member's phone records? If yes, explain in detail why you understood that the "intelligence" was derived from the Board member's phone records. If not, explain in detail your understanding, at the time of the "Kona I" Meeting, of how such intelligence about contacts had been obtained.

Answer:

No. I do not recall investigation methodologies being discussed.

15. Do you recall anyone else present at the "Kona I" Meeting inquiring about how the intelligence regarding "contacts" made by a Board member had been obtained or determined? If yes, who inquired, and what explanation was provided and by whom?

Answer:

No.

16. Were you aware that the Investigation Team had obtained the phone records for your HP-owned phones? If so, identify the exact date that you learned that the Investigation Team had been obtaining these phone records, and describe in detail how you learned that phone records associated with your HP-owned phones had been obtained.

Answer:

I learned only after the conclusion of the Kona Investigation that the Investigation Team had obtained the records for my HP-owned cell phone. I do not recall exactly when I learned that fact or how I learned it, but believe it was after Tom Perkins resigned and subsequently contacted the company about the letter he received from AT&T suggesting that someone had accessed his phone records through the use of an e-mail account.

Further:

(a) **When you learned that your phone records associated with your HP-owned phones had been obtained, did you inquire how those "actual phone records" were obtained? If so, describe in detail the explanation provided to you, and by whom.**

Answer:

I do not remember asking how phone records for my HP-owned phone were obtained.

(b) **When you learned that the phone records associated with your HP-owned phones had been obtained, did you inquire whether phone records associated with other individuals' HP-owned phones had been obtained? If so, describe in detail the explanation provided to you and by whom.**

Answer:

After Tom Perkins resigned and subsequently contacted the company about the letter he received from AT&T suggesting that someone had accessed his phone records through the use of an e-mail account, I began to inquire about the methodogies the Investigation Team used. Therefore, I believe I had already begun this inquiry by the time I learned that the Investigation Team had obtained the phone records for my HP-owned phone.

(c) **When you learned that your phone records associated with your HP-owned phones had been obtained, did you inquire whether "actual phone records" associated with your private phones, or within other individuals' private phones, had been obtained? If so, describe in detail the explanation provided to you, and by whom.**

Answer:

See answer to subpart (b).

HEWLETT-PACKARD COMPANY'S RESPONSES TO QUESTIONS POSED BY CONGRESSWOMAN DIANA DEGETTE PURSUANT TO CHAIRMAN WHITFIELD'S OCTOBER 19, 2006 LETTER

Question #1:

You testified that no one at Hewlett-Packard saw any of the warning signs that improper and possibly illegal conduct was underway to find out who was leaking information from the Hewlett-Packard Board of Directors both because the company had "bad processes," without "checks and balances," and because of "poor execution." As I understand it, then, according to you Hewlett-Packard did not have sufficient rules in place to stop this conduct and what procedures it did have were not sufficiently followed by people at the company. When the investigation into this incident requested by Hewlett-Packard by the law firm of Morgan Lewis & Bockius LLP is complete, please submit answers to the following questions:

a. **What specific internal company procedures were in place in Hewlett-Packard while the conduct at issue took place which were supposed to have stopped it? In other words, what systems did not operate as intended at Hewlett-Packard so as to allow the conduct at issue to begin and continue unabated? How and why did these rules or procedures fail to achieve their purpose?**

b. **How and in what ways was there a failure by the Hewlett-Packard Board of Directors, management, or staff to follow the procedures referenced in question (1)(a) above which allowed the conduct at issue to start and not be stopped? Who demonstrated this failure? Why did he or she fail to follow the Hewlett-Packard rules as intended?**

Response to Question #1 (parts a and b).

There were various policies and procedures in place within HP during 2005 and 2006 that indirectly touched upon the Kona investigation. However, the policies and procedures directly applicable to the Kona investigation were HP's Standards of Business Conduct ("SBC") and the SBC Guidance Manual ("Manual") related to investigations. The SBC is intended to prescribe a code of conduct for HP directors, officers and employees and the Manual is intended to provide structure and guidance to SBC investigations.

It is fair to say that certain acts violated the spirit of the SBC, if not a specific provision within it. In the Opening Remarks to the SBC, it states that "We must have the highest expectations for ourselves and for each other. Unethical or illegal business conduct on the part of HP is simply unacceptable and will not be tolerated." The act of pretexting to obtain telephone call information was wrong. Unfortunately, HP did not have a specific rule or policy prohibiting such pretexting at the time of the Kona investigation and the general prohibition on unethical conduct in the SBC was insufficient. For those reasons HP has issued a company directive stating that such pretexting is prohibited.

The missteps in the Kona investigation are also attributable, at least in part, to the unique nature of the investigation itself. Kona was an investigation into inappropriate leaks from HP's Board of Directors undertaken at the request of the Chairwoman of the Board. Because of the sensitive nature of the investigation, Kona I began in an ad hoc fashion without active involvement by HP's Global SBC Team. Kona I was not logged into the SBC investigations database and a typical investigation team was not assembled. Instead, the outside investigative firm performed its work without any direct oversight or supervision from an HP employee experienced and trained in corporate investigations. While a Global SBC Team member was eventually introduced into the investigation, that did not occur until after the plan of action had been formulated and acted upon. The late addition of a Global SBC Team member did not change the ad hoc nature of Kona I and the existence and progress of the investigation was not reported to either HP's Ethics Committee or the Audit Committee of the Board of Directors, contrary to the recommended structure for such an investigation as set forth in the Manual.

The SBC investigation protocol, set out in the Manual, intended for HP personnel to actively manage and supervise (if not perform) each investigation. The Manual specified three different levels of investigations for allocating resources and structuring investigation teams. Under the manual, Kona I would have been subject to the most active management by the Global SBC Team and the greatest amount of scrutiny within the Company. Due to the sensitive nature of the investigation and the ad hoc manner in which it was conducted, Kona I received far less management by the Global SBC Team and far less scrutiny within the Company than it deserved.

Unfortunately, the ad hoc nature and top-down direction in Kona I also resulted in the typical contracting process with outside investigative firms not being followed. Although a master contract existed between HP and the outside investigative firm, it contemplated that a separate scope of work would be prepared for each investigation. In the case of the Kona investigation, no such scope of work was prepared. HP also had no meaningful control over the outside investigative firm's use of subcontractors, which was contrary to the spirit of the Manual.

Another consequence of the ad hoc nature of the Kona I phase of the investigation was that HP did not have adequate control over the investigative techniques being used by the outside investigative firm and its subcontractors. HP also did not adequately confirm the legality of the investigative techniques being used or vet those techniques with HP's professional investigative personnel prior to those techniques being used.

While a more typical Global SBC Team was assembled for purposes of conducting the Kona II phase of the investigation, the team apparently relied heavily on the practices used in Kona I, and therefore did not fully reevaluate the investigative techniques being used. Because the Manual did not expressly prohibit the use of pretexting to obtain telephone call information, the investigative team lacked clear guidance about whether the technique was illegal or considered ethical by HP. The investigative team also continued the ad hoc contract arrangement with the outside investigative firm and failed to establish sufficient control over the use of subcontractors.

The Kona II team also suffered from a structural flaw that to some extent compounded the other problems existing with the investigation. The senior legal counsel on the Global SBC

Team was responsible for both the operational and the legal and ethical aspects of the investigation. Thus, the senior legal counsel faced potentially conflicting goals of finding the leaker and upholding HP's ethical standards, which could have meant prohibiting certain investigative practices that would lead to uncovering the leaker's identity. That conflict may have affected how the senior legal counsel handled the concern expressed by at least one Global SBC Team member that pretexting for telephone call information was inappropriate or possibly illegal. Neither the Manual nor the SBC envisioned a situation in which the senior legal counsel on the investigative team would be responsible for deciding the propriety of actions that he had prior knowledge of or actively participated in.

As a result of this failure in the SBC investigation system, HP is completely overhauling its ethics and compliance structure, including establishing the position of Chief Ethics and Compliance Officer ("CECO"). The newly hired CECO is now responsible for reviewing and overseeing HP's investigative practices, SBC and codes of conduct applicable to outside investigative firms. As part of those duties, the CECO is responsible for reporting violations of any applicable codes of conduct by an outside investigation firm or an HP employee to the head of the appropriate business segment or function, who, in consultation with the CECO, will take appropriate action. If the head of the appropriate business segment or function does not take appropriate action, the CECO is to report the violation to the CEO and HP's newly appointed independent director. The CECO also is to submit a semiannual written report to the newly established Compliance Council, identifying all actions taken, and the Compliance Council will review the appropriateness of each action taken, including a review for consistency across actions taken.

Although the SBC and Manual should have guided the conduct of the investigation in a way that would completely avoid any question of legality, HP Legal raised questions about the lawfulness of pretexting during the Kona II phase of the investigation. However, HP Legal did not obtain a formal written opinion from an independent law firm addressing the issue. Instead, it relied upon advice informally obtained from a law firm associated with the outside investigative firm. There was no specific policy or procedure in place that required the Global SBC Team or HP Legal to obtain a formal written opinion, but HP Legal did not use best practices in this matter.

HP believes that the persons involved in the Kona investigation acted with the best of intentions and with the sincerest desire to protect the Company. Unfortunately, the unique nature of the Kona investigation, the ad hoc manner in which it began, the absence of clarity in the SBC and Manual regarding pretexting, and the potential conflicts of interest existing within the investigation structure, created a set of circumstances in which the HP personnel made misjudgments that resulted in a crisis for HP. As described in the response to Question #2, HP is fully committed to avoiding such occurrences in the future and is therefore enacting significant corporate governance changes and implementing substantial reforms that will profoundly change HP's investigative practices and its ethics and compliance organization.

Question #2:

On pages eight and nine of your prepared testimony you briefly describe new rules and training implemented already at Hewlett-Packard designed to prevent the actions undertaken to stop the Hewlett-Packard Board of Directors' leak from being repeated. You also testified that Hewlett-Packard has hired Mr. Bart Schwartz to help analyze its procedures and develop "future best practices." When his analysis is complete and Hewlett-Packard has finished making changes in response to this issue, please submit answers to the following questions:

a. **What are all of the new internal systems, procedures, or rules that Hewlett-Packard has adopted since the leak investigation came to light designed to prevent such actions from being commissioned or being allowed to continue if they are discovered in the future? Please provide more detailed information on the changes summarized in your prepared testimony as well as information on any other new internal systems or policies. Explain how all of these are a change from past Hewlett-Packard practices as well as how they are intended to work.**

b. **Even with Hewlett-Packard's new internal procedures, what will happen if there is a failure to properly carry them out again by the Hewlett-Packard Board of Directors, management, or staff? What steps are being taken or new training being provided to make sure the new internal rules will be properly followed? Please provide more detailed information on the changes to Hewlett-Packard's "Privacy Training curriculum," mentioned on page nine of your prepared testimony, as well as on any other Hewlett-Packard efforts to improve the future implementation of company ethics rules or guidelines.**

Response to Question #2a.

HP has made, is in the process of making, or has agreed to make in the future, numerous corporate governance changes and revisions to its internal systems, procedures, and rules, all for the purpose of establishing "future best practices" for corporate investigations. Most of the changes and revisions are described in the Final Judgment and Permanent Injunction ("Agreement") between HP and the California Attorney General (a copy of which is attached at Tab A to the December 7, 2006 letter from Charles N. Charnas to Congressmen Barton, Dingell, Whitfield and Stupak, and Congresswoman DeGette). There are, however, changes and revisions HP has made or is in the process of making that are not described in that agreement. For the sake of convenience and completeness, we have described the current changes and revisions below.

1. HP issued a company directive in September 2006 prohibiting the use of pretexting to obtain telephone call information in investigations performed by or for HP. As part of the settlement with the California Attorney General, HP has agreed to not use pretexting to obtain confidential, privileged, or proprietary information, from a utility, and to not unlawfully obtain personal identifying information, including social security numbers.

2. HP has appointed a new independent director responsible for reviewing and reporting on HP's compliance with legal and ethical requirements related to the conduct of investigations to the Board. All the training programs identified in paragraph 7 below will be

1-PH/2544788.1

subject to the approval of the Independent Director. The new Independent Director is G. Kennedy Thompson, Chief Executive Officer of Wachovia Corporation.

3. HP has retained an expert in the field of investigative practices, a former United States Attorney for the Southern District of New York, the Honorable Bart Schwartz, to perform a comprehensive review of HP's compliance with applicable legal requirements and ethical standards, as they apply to HP's policies and practices regarding investigations. The comprehensive review, which is ongoing, will culminate in additional recommendations by Mr. Schwartz for improvements in HP's Standards of Business Conduct, applicable codes of conduct and other policies regarding investigations.

4. HP has established the position of Chief Ethics and Compliance Officer ("CECO"), and in October hired Jon Hoak, the former General Counsel of NCR, to fill that position. The CECO reports directly to the General Counsel and the Audit Committee and has responsibility for, among other things, reviewing and overseeing HP's investigative practices, Standards of Business Conduct and codes of conduct applicable to outside investigative firms. As part of these responsibilities, the CECO will be reviewing the findings and recommendations of Mr. Schwartz and make his own recommendations for improvements in HP's investigative practices to the CEO, the Independent Director, and the Board of Directors. The CECO is also required to provide annual reports, and additional reports as appropriate, to the CEO and Board of Directors regarding HP's compliance with the recommendations for improvements in SBC, applicable codes of conduct and other policies regarding business ethics and privacy protection.

5. HP has agreed to expand the duties and responsibilities of HP's Chief Privacy Officer. The expanded responsibilities will include review of HP's investigation protocols and ethics training programs identified in paragraph 7 below to ensure they appropriately address matters related to privacy and ethics.

6. HP has agreed to establish a Compliance Council consisting of the CECO (who will chair the Council), the Chief Privacy Officer, the Deputy General Counsel for compliance matters, the head of Internal Audit, and several ethics and compliance liaisons (chosen by the CECO from each business segment and function). The Compliance Council will develop, initiate, maintain and revise policies and procedures for the general operation of HP's ethics and compliance programs consistent with applicable laws and regulations. The Compliance Council will provide written semi-annual reports to each of the CEO, the Audit Committee and the Nominating and Governance Committee, and written annual reports to the Board. Additionally, the Council's liaisons shall report to the Compliance Council as needed with respect to the investigatory methods used in investigations within their area of responsibility, including those conducted by outside vendors.

7. HP has agreed to enhance its annual training program to ensure that the business ethics component plays a more prominent role and to establish additional ethics training for those HP employees who are engaged in the conduct of investigations. The training will specifically provide, among other things, that pretexting of public utilities to obtain confidential information is prohibited. HP is also reviewing and revising its written training materials and all applicable investigation manuals to address pretexting and other investigative procedures.

8. HP is preparing to provide all outside investigation firms with written standards of conduct that pertain specifically to privacy and business ethics concerns regarding investigatory methods used in the course of investigations. HP will require that these outside investigation firms certify that their employees who work on HP matters have reviewed, understand, and will comply with these written standards of conduct.

9. HP is rewriting its form contract with outside investigative firms to require compliance with all of HP's applicable codes of conduct. The rewritten contract will also tighten the controls over the use of subcontractors.

10. HP has agreed to maintain an anonymous toll-free complaint line relating to privacy and ethics, which will be overseen by the CECO.

11. HP is establishing an Integrated Investigator Procurement Program ("IIPP") that includes a pre-qualification program for outside investigative firms as well as an application and vetting process for use with each outside investigative firm seeking to provide services on a particular investigation.

The foregoing changes and reforms comprise an integrated system of controls over HP's investigative practices that is intended to create transparency and accountability and to clearly define responsibility for ethics and compliance. The CECO is charged with day-to-day responsibility for ethics and compliance in the context of investigative practices. Mr. Schwartz, a qualified expert in investigative practices, is to support the CECO in establishing best future practices for corporate investigations. The independent director has ethics and oversight responsibilities that that serve to both supplement the work of and verify the performance of the CECO. The Chief Privacy Officer, as the person responsibility for leading HP's efforts in maintaining personal privacy, represents another check or balance in the system. Finally, the Compliance Council represents the vehicle in which all of the various parts of the system are integrated for purposes of creating consistency and accountability.

The system described represents a substantial change from the corporate investigation system that existed at the time of the Kona investigation, which was decentralized and fragmented and lacked insufficient checks and balances. Furthermore, the prior system was subject to an unnecessary conflict since the person responsible for ethics and compliance could also have responsibility for the operational details of the investigation. The new system does not blur these lines and therefore eliminates this potential conflict.

Response to Question #2b.

All of the corporate governance changes and reforms HP is undertaking are intended to eliminate the possibility that any future investigation will violate HP's code of ethics or the law. Changes to HP's training programs and materials and its ethics codes and guidance manuals are obviously important to preventing future violations. For this reason, Mr. Schwartz is conducting a comprehensive review of these programs and materials for purposes of making specific recommendations to HP's CECO. Because that process is not yet complete, HP is unable to provide details at this time. However, in general, HP has committed to increase the focus on ethics and compliance in its annual employee training program and to provide additional training to employees involved in conducting investigations for HP. HP also intends to provide employee guidance on HP's prohibition of pretexting to obtain telephone call information and to revise its materials and manuals to specifically address the subject matter.

To the extent there is a violation of HP's SBC or other policies applicable to conducting investigations, the new controls adopted by HP are intended to discover and a stop it as soon as possible. First, each HP employee is obligated to report any violation of the SBC. Second, the CECO is obligated to report any material violation to the head of the appropriate business segment or function, who, in consultation with the CECO, will take appropriate action. Third, if the head of the appropriate business segment or function does not take appropriate action, the CECO must report the violation to the CEO and the Independent Director. Fourth, the CECO is to submit a semiannual written report to the newly established Compliance Council, identifying all actions taken, and the Compliance Council will review the appropriateness of each action taken, including a review for consistency across actions taken. Fifth, the independent director is to review copies of any reports created by the CECO and the Compliance Council relating to the conduct of investigations and is authorized to report to the full Board and the Audit Committee, as appropriate. If the independent director concludes that in connection with any investigation HP or any of its vendors is in violation of any applicable HP code of conduct or California law, he is to immediately report the conclusion to the General Counsel, the CECO, the CEO and the Board of Directors. Should the independent director conclude that any violation of California law has occurred in conducting an investigation, the independent director is to report the violation to the California Attorney General.

All of the foregoing measures are intended to ensure that violations are addressed quickly and appropriately and that there is accountability for those persons charged with enforcing HP's rules.

PH/2544788.1

O